Introduction to Gender

Introduction to Gender

Social Science Perspectives

Jennifer Marchbank
Gayle Letherby

PEARSON
Longman

Harlow, England • London • New York • Boston • San Francisco • Toronto • Sydney • Singapore • Hong Kong
Tokyo • Seoul • Taipei • New Delhi • Cape Town • Madrid • Mexico City • Amsterdam • Munich • Paris • Milan

Pearson Education Limited
Edinburgh Gate
Harlow
Essex CM20 2JE
England

and Associated Companies throughout the world

Visit us on the World Wide Web at:
www.pearsoned.co.uk

First published 2007

ISBN 978-1-4058-5844-1

British Library Cataloguing-in-Publication Data
A catalogue record for this book is available from the British Library

10 9 8 7 6 5 4 3 2
10 09 08 07

Typeset in 9.75/13pt Minion by 30
Printed by Ashford Colour Press Ltd, Gosport

Contents

Contents

Contents

Contributors

Professor Gill Valentine	School of Geography, University of Leeds
Dr Nichola Wood	School of Geography, University of Leeds
Dr Lorraine Nencel	Department of Social Research Methodology, VU University Amsterdam
Dr Katherine Johnson	School of Applied Social Science, University of Brighton

Acknowledgements

To Jen's partner, Sylvie Traphan, a true student of gender.

Many people have been involved in the genesis of this textbook. Firstly we wish to thank the professional reviewers for their useful and supportive comments on the chapters as they developed. They are Victoria Robinson, University of Sheffield; Rachel Alsop, University of Hull; and Clarissa Smith, University of Sunderland.

We also greatly benefited from the perspectives and comments of Tom and David Hunt who belong in our target audience of early college/university level studies. Thanks are also due to Cathy Hunt and Sylvie Traphan for their proof reading and input to various chapters, to Jane Marchbank and Dorothy Thornton for their support and Helen and Robert McVey for computer access when Jen was residing in deepest, rural Scotland.

Finally we wish to thanks Andrew Taylor, Sarah Busby and Elizabeth Rix at Pearson for their infinite patience.

The publishers are grateful to the following for permission to reproduce copyright material:

Figure 1.1 photo Brian Hendler/Getty Images Entertainment/Getty Images; Figure 1.2 Scotch Beef advertisement reproduced with permission from Quality Meat Scotland; Figure 1.3 photo Dave Benett/Getty Images Entertainment/Getty Images; Figure 3.1 photo © Hulton-Deutsch Collection/ Corbis; Figure 4.1 cartoon, Jackie Fleming; Figure 5.1 photo © Darren Staples/Reuters/Corbis; Figure 7.1 photo, Getty Science Library; Figure 7.2 photo Tom Stoddart Archive/Reportage/Getty Images; Figure 8.1 photo © James Leynse/Corbis; Figure 9.1 photo © Stefano Bianchetti/Corbis; Figure 9.2 cartoon © Mike Baldwin, reprinted by permission of CartoonStock, www.CartoonStock.com; Figure 10.1 poster Advertising Archives; Figures 11.2 and 12.1 images from *Women and Health* (WEA 1986) reproduced with thanks to Angela Martin; Figure 11.3 photo OutRage! © All rights reserved; Figure 11.4 redrawn from The Royal Family Tree by David Johnson, http://www.infoplease.com/spot/royal3.html, reprinted by permission of Infoplease; Figure 12.2 Marie Stopes International advertisement reprinted by permission of Marie Stopes International and McCanns Manchester; Figure 13.1 photos, Jennifer Marchbank; Figure 14.1 cartoon, Jackie Fleming; Figure 15.1 photo Hugh Sitton/Photographer's Choice/Getty Images; Figure 15.2 from 'Been there, seen it, I've got the T-shirt from *Feminist Review*, Vol. 67, Issue 2, reproduced by permission of Palgrave Macmillan (Rickard, W. 2001); Figure 16.1 poster, The Zero Tolerance Charitable Trust; Figure 16.2 photo from Canadian Forces Image Gallery, http://www.combatcamera.forces.gc.ca, Department of National Defence. Reproduced with the permission of the Minister of Public Works and Government Services Canada, 2007; Figure 17.1 photo Evening Standard/Hulton Archive/Getty Images; Figure 17.2 photo Mark Allen Johnson/Rexfeaturesphoto.com; Figure 18.1 image © Advertising Archive; Figure 18.2; image © Advertising Archive and photo Jack Picone, Copyright © Jack Picone 2005.

'CSC loses Appeal in Transexual Human Rights Case' by Janice Tibbetts, material reprinted with the express permission of: "CANWEST NEWS SERVICE", a CanWest Partnership; 'Schoolgirl Fictions', by Valerie Walkerdine, material reproduced with the permission of Verso; 'Fathers in protest on city bridge', material reproduced with the permission of Bristol Evening Post.

In some instances we have been unable to trace the owners of copyright material, and we would appreciate any information that would enable us to do so.

Part One

Introduction

This textbook is divided into three parts. In this first part we address some basic overarching issues. Chapter 1, Gendered Perspectives – Theoretical Issues, provides the context of the concepts used in this text and explains the gendered approach we have developed. Fundamental issues, such as the social construction of gender and the binary nature of our, western, thoughts on gender are introduced, explained and discussed. By reading Chapter 1 you will come to understand what social scientists agree and disagree on about what gender is. You will then follow the journey social science has taken through feminist and Women's Studies, celebratory and critical studies of masculinity and gender studies to our end point of our gendered approach. This is not a chapter offering new theory. Instead, it is a review of some of the most basic principles that students of gender need to understand. It is your starting point, your reminder and your revision tool.

The second chapter in Part One, Method, Methodology and Epistemology, also addresses fundamental issues in any study of gender: the issues of how knowledge is created and valued, and the gender implications and outcomes of this collection of knowledge. Social scientists are empiricists. We require information, we need data, on which to base our explanations of the social world, that is our theories. So, it is never too early in a social science education to learn how data can be and is collected. In the context of gender there is a rich vein of information on method, methodology and epistemology. Chapter 2 provides a comprehensive summary of gendered knowledge production, critiques of the traditional research process, the developments following critiques, such as standpoint theory, the subsequent problems with such stances and much more. Chapter 2 also provides real world examples of research projects to illustrate and explain the development of inclusive gendered research approaches. The issues and considerations outlined and explained in Chapter 2 serve as examples of 'best practice' in social science research. This does not mean that all social scientists incorporate all aspects and in some of the chapters in Part Two, Disciplines, you will see differences in research approaches.

Although it is perfectly possible to start reading this text by going directly to a specific chapter, we think you will find that you read the chapters in Parts Two and Three (Disciplines and Issues, respectively) with a different eye after reading Part One. We, therefore, recommend you start with Part One, then follow your specific interests.

Chapter 1

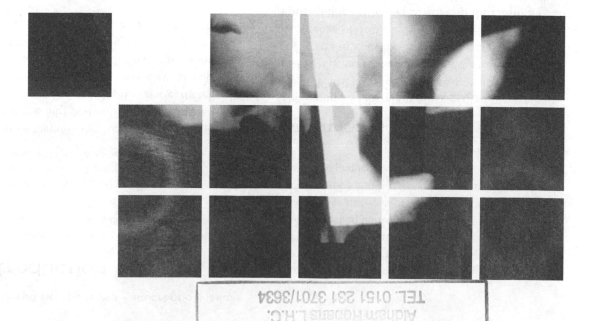

Gendered perspectives – theoretical issues

Key issues in this chapter:

► Gender is a social construct.
► The development of masculinity and femininity and arguments beyond such a binary divide.
► The development of the use of gender as an analytical approach to social sciences.
► The role of Women's Studies and Critical Studies of Masculinity in the development of gendered approaches to social sciences.

At the end of this chapter you should be able to:

► Understand the difference between biological sex and gender.
► Discuss the concepts of masculinity and femininity.
► Understand the limits of binary determinations of sex and gender.
► Recognise the fundamental contribution of feminism to the study of gender.
► Recognise both women and men as gendered.

Introduction

What are little boys made of?
Frogs and snails and puppy dogs tails
That's what little boys are made of.

What are little girls made of?
Sugar and spice and all that's nice
That's what little girls are made of.

Do you remember this from your childhood? Did you think it was fair? Not only does this rhyme allow little girls to poke fun at boys, it very clearly tells all children that there are two ways of existing, and only two. It also sends very specific messages about what is acceptable; boys can be a little distasteful but girls are always, and should always be, nice. These are messages about gender.

Understanding gender

In this textbook we aim to introduce you to the debates on gender within various social science areas and issues. Sometimes 'gender' is taken to be synonymous with 'women' as if men have no gender! In this text we argue that a true understanding of gender has to consider both masculinities and femininities, the range of ways in which these can be expressed and the interrelationship of these with other signifiers of social difference such as 'race', age, social class, sexuality, ability, amongst others. Prior to outlining the journey taken within social theory on gender issues in this chapter some key points are discussed, beginning with the difference between sex and gender, through surveys of explanations of gender differences and why it matters to consider gender in the social sciences.

So what is gender? We all have it yet most of us do not think about it much – for most (but not all) people being a woman or a man is not something consciously considered on a daily basis. Masculine and feminine behaviours are so routine, so usual that they become considered as normal and natural by the majority of society. So, does it matter? It matters both as members of our society and to the study of our societies. The first time we meet someone we 'read' their gender and our interaction with them is based on that reading, accurate or otherwise. In society and social

science gender matters greatly as the differences between the genders are the bases of inequalities: inequalities in power, inequalities in access to resources, inequalities in opportunities and therefore, inequalities in life experiences. As such, no study of society can be conducted without an understanding of the role of gender.

Studying society

The Women's Liberation Movement of the 1960s and 1970s created a sea change in the way society is studied, that change became embodied in the form of feminist challenges to knowledge and methods of seeking out knowledge [Hotlink → **Method, Methodology, Epistemology (Chapter 2)**], and in the creation of an interdisciplinary approach to investigating society, known as Women's Studies. Although women were involved in the creation of the social sciences and their methods (see McDonald, 1995) it became standard to study society from the position of only one dominant gender – that of the male. However, feminist work has challenged the 'conceptual straitjacket of understanding' (Stacey, 1981: 189) previously limiting our social science investigations, forcing social science to look beyond the male experience as the norm (and usually the heterosexual, white, western male experience at that). As Dale Spender explains:

Fundamental to feminism is the premise that women have been 'left out' of codified knowledge: where men have formulated explanations in relation to themselves, they have generally either rendered women invisible or classified them as deviant. (Spender, 1981: 2)

The past 40 years have seen an explosion of feminist work exploring and analysing such concepts and areas as femininity, media, work, leisure, health, sexuality, violence, family and so on, redressing the absences in history and the biases of political science (see Part Two). Although this has not been even across the social science disciplines it has been suggested that 'feminism was the single most powerful political discourse of the twentieth century' (Whitehead and Barrett, 2001: 3). Whereas feminism challenged social science not to see men as the norm and looked critically at women's experiences, a similar critical focus on men and masculinity has a much shorter history, or rather such studies by men, has a shorter history. Feminism, in pursuit of its goal of equality and social justice, has always placed the study of masculine power in the centre of analysis. However, by the last decade of the twentieth century there had been a proliferation of books, journals and other resources, authored by both men and women, providing feminist-informed work on men and masculinities.

No longer can gender be taken as synonymous for 'woman'. Due to feminist insights and their application by both women and men, men's gendered identity has been claimed within the social sciences. As such, it is time for the integration of feminist work on women and feminist-informed work on men to occur, for up until now much of this has taken place in separate domains leaving the reader to make comparisons and links. This chapter aims to introduce you to such an approach, the approach then employed throughout this text.

We will return to this history of theoretical debates later in the chapter, but first it is necessary to address some basic questions.

Stop and think 1.1

Think about the ways in which you have previously studied women and men. What was assumed as the 'norm'? Man or woman? What kind of man or woman? Was equal space given to each sex or was one tagged on at the end of the course as 'Men/Women and . . .'? If so, which one was the 'add on'? Has there been a difference in the way gender is studied in the different classes and courses you have taken?

Sex and gender – what's the difference?

Gender is usually seen as a socially determined difference based upon the biological differences between the sexes. Sex, the state of being either female or male, is determined by biological characteristics such as anatomical, reproductive and chromosomal attributes. Sex is deemed to be natural whereas gender is seen as the social expression of natural, biological differences

primarily based upon the appearance of genitals. This, in itself, is not unproblematic:

> When, in modern societies, a child is born with ambiguous genitalia, parents are asked to make a difficult decision: which of the two sexes will they choose for the sex of rearing? This decision is framed by medical expertise, made largely on the basis of the reproductive possibilities of the infant or its real genetic sex. In our highly medicalised modern societies, the resolution of ambiguous sex reveals how our bodies are rigorously policed into two sexes – male or female.
>
> (Cranny-Francis et al., 2003: 5)

This binary divide in biology is reproduced in society (though not in all; see World in Focus 1.1): sex is accepted as being one of two possibilities and we are required daily to define ourselves in such a manner; each time we go to the toilet in a public place (such as school or restaurant), each time we fill in a tax form or even each time we complete a shopping survey we are required to acknowledge our sex but only two categories are allowed. Thinking in terms of two distinct sexes has been criticised for a number of years; in the 1970s Ann Oakley (1972) suggested that it might be more appropriate to consider male and female simply being the opposite ends of a single continuum; and it has been proposed that the binary split between male and female may, itself, be a social construction. However, although sex may not just be male or female these two biological categories have concerned social scientists because sex differences have been proposed for the differences in the social roles women and men conduct, it is to the explanations of gender difference that we now turn.

Explanations of gender difference

Before we turn to look at gender difference it is necessary to note that just as Oakley (1972) commented on sex, gender too can be regarded as a continuum. This continuum has masculinity at one end and femininity at the other, with people all at different places along it. It is also important to note that masculinity is not only an aspect of male bodies and femininity of female

World in focus 1.1

Sex = Biology?

. . . gender is usually described as socially constructed, and sex as biological. The categorising of all human beings as 'male' or 'female' is left unquestioned. However, this does not always fit with local realities. For example, cultures of eunuchs in India, travestites in Brazil, ladyboys in Thailand, or transgender in the USA all suggest that there is more to sex than just male and female. Perhaps ideas of sex are socially constructed too?

Source: InBrief, 2002, BRIDGE, http://www.bridge.ids.ac.uk/dgb10.html

Figure 1.1 Dana International, winner of the Eurovision Song Contest. Dana is a transexual woman.
Source: Brian Hendler/Getty Images Entertainment/Getty Images.

bodies. A recent political and academic shift has been in the challenge to see gender beyond a duality of male or female, resulting in

> . . . the development of new identities that departed from the medical constructions of transsexual and transvestite. . . People would define themselves as gender-benders, gender-blenders, bigenders or simply describe their identity more loosely using the umbrella concept of transgender.
>
> (Wickman, 2003: 41)

Both male and female bodies can express both masculinity and femininity for, as a social construct, not biological characteristics, gender is not restricted by genes. However, it is the case that most explanations of gender difference retain a focus on the gender duality and seek to explore why it is that the polar ends of this gender continuum make real differences in peoples lives.

Controversy 1.1

Touching all the bases

Kate Bornstein questions what defines men and women. The following extract details just some of the problems there are:

> Most folks would define a man by the presence of a penis or some form of a penis. Some would define a woman by the presence of a vagina or some form of vagina. It's not that simple, though. I know several women in San Francisco who have penises. Many wonderful men in my life have vaginas. And there are quite a few people whose genitals fall somewhere between penises and vaginas. What are *they*? (emphasis in original).
>
> Are you a man because you have an XY chromosome? A woman because you have XX? Unless you're an athlete who's been challenged in the area of gender representation, you probably haven't had a chromosome test to determine your gender. If you haven't had that test, then how do you know what gender you are. . . . There are, in addition to the XX and XY pairs, other commonly-occurring sets of gender chromosomes, including XXY, XXX, YYY, XYY, and XO. Does this mean there are more than two genders?

> Let's keep looking. What makes a man – testosterone? What makes a woman – estrogen? If so, you could buy your gender over the counter at any pharmacy.
>
> . . .
>
> Are you a woman because you can bear children? Because you bleed every month? Many women are born without this potential, and every woman ceases to possess that capacity after menopause – do these women cease being women? Does a necessary hysterectomy equal a gender change?
>
> Are you a man because you can father children? What if your sperm count is too low? What if you were exposed to nuclear radiation and were rendered sterile? Are you then a woman?
>
> Are you a woman because your birth certificate says female? A man because your birth certificate says male? If so, how did *that* happen? A doctor looked down at your crotch at birth. A doctor decided. Based on what was showing of your external genitals, that you would have one gender or another.
>
> . . .
>
> I've been searching all my life for a rock-bottom definition of woman, an unquestionable sense of what it is to be a man. I've found nothing except the fickle definitions of gender held up by groups and individuals for their own purposes.

Source: Kate Bornstein (1994: 56–7)

A great deal has been written, across many disciplines, about gender, to explain differences and the effects of those differences. In the main, however, most of this writing has held on to a dichotomous view of gender as being either/or male or female. These fall into four broad camps:

1. the biological arguments

2. the arguments of social learning theory

3. materialist arguments, in particular, feminist materialists

4. the discourse arguments.

Biological arguments ascribe the different social behaviours and roles of women and men to biology, basically to the sexual differences between men and women. In the 1950s, Functionalist sociology argued that men and women are particularly suited for certain roles and tasks in society due to natural differences: this became known as the sex role theory. Sex role theory assigns women, deemed to have a nurturing instinct, to 'expressive' roles within a nuclear family whereas men, deemed to be competitive and aggressive, are allocated to an 'instrumental' role, that being to provide for their family. As you can see, inherent within this theory, is an assumption that part of both the male and female gender role is a heterosexual identity and practice. Despite the fact that biological arguments have lost primacy within social science they remain culturally strong, in that they influence everyday perceptions.

Proponents of social learning theory critique biological approaches for neglecting to consider the ways in which behaviour is affected by social influences. As biological approaches assume a biological dichotomy they are unable, according to their critics, to explain diversity amongst women and amongst men. In addition, if we look at different cultures, be that across geography and/or across history, it is clear that what it means to be a woman or a man differs. In fact as Margaret Mead's (1962, originally 1949) work shows [**Hotlink → Anthropology (Chapter 6)**], gender roles are exceedingly changeable across societies with certain tasks being assigned to the female in one society but to the male in another (however, one constant is that adult males do little childcare whilst women's role is primarily associated with childcare). Social learning theories purport that women and men are products not of biology but of culture and society, that girls and boys learn gender-appropriate behaviour from birth as we are all surrounded by gender socialisation messages from our families, peers and the media. Gender is, therefore, viewed as a learned set of behaviours not something biologically innate. Yet, the socialisation messages which are learned to create gender are based on biology; some messages are strongly provided to females with a different set provided and encouraged in males. The main point here is that the messages will differ over time and place, so what is learned about masculinity and femininity can be diverse.

A further critique of biological determinism is made by Lindi Birke (1992) who argues that the actual differences between men and women have been exaggerated and that it is problematic to try and separate out biology and culture as they are factors which interact – for example, a person's physical strength can be modified by diet and exercise and, whereas it has been argued that testosterone increases aggression the converse is also known, that is aggression can increase testosterone. As such, Birke contends that societies interpret biological factors in a culturally specific manner and also, that biological characteristics can be shaped by social factors.

Social learning theory has been the basis of most sociological work on masculinity and femininity, mainly focused on determining how we learn, internalise and then recreate gender stereotypical roles. However, this still assumes a single set of characteristics that denote masculinity/femininity which, Sylvia Walby (1990) maintains, cannot adequately account for the range of ways in which femininity and masculinity exist, and how they adapt according to other social factors such as age, social class, ethnicity amongst others. In addition, this approach also does not account for the ways in which people may resist, or subvert, messages about gender appropriate characteristics and behaviour.

So how then to move forward? Robert Connell argues that 'two significant alternatives can be found in recent debates: post-structuralist and materialist' (Connell, 2000: 19). Post-structuralism argues that the gender dichotomy is hegemonic but that, following Michel Foucault, the use of language, discourse, can create other ways to create masculinity and femininity, resulting in a plurality of masculinities and femininities (see A Closer Look 1.1). This is necessary for we 'cannot study masculinity [or femininity] in the singular, as if the stuff of man were a homogenous and unchanging thing' (Brod and Kaufman, 1994: 4). Likewise, Connell (1987) discussing western societies, contends that there is no single manner of being masculine or feminine but that there are certainly dominant – or hegemonic – forms of gendered existence (see A Closer Look 1.2).

A closer look 1.1

Discourses of gender

Under the influence of Foucault, a school of gender researchers has studied how discourses ranging from medicine to fashion have classified, represented and helped to control human bodies, emphasising how systems of knowledge function as part of an apparatus of power. . . . Foucault had no gender theory at all, though others have built gender analyses using some of his ideas.

Source: Connell (2000: 19–20)

A closer look 1.2

Hegemony versus plurality

Hegemony is a term originally devised by Gramsci (1998, written between 1929 and 1935) to explain and describe how one social group can use political power and ideology, rather than force, to achieve dominance over other groups (in Gramsci's case an elite social class). Hegemonic femininity and masculinity mean the ideology of the 'ideal' forms. Plurality simply means the existence of a number, a plural, of ways of expressing a concept – here gender roles.

Stop and think 1.2

Reflect upon your own identity. Do you perceive yourself as feminine or masculine or having traits of both? Which of your characteristics would you associate with which label and why? Can you identify if you are following an hegemonic gender script or a revised/adapted one?

Post-structuralism observed these different ways of being masculine and feminine and determined, like Mead decades previously, that gender is fluid and is both historically and culturally constructed. In a similar vein Judith Butler (1990) rejects the binary model of masculinity and femininity and describes gender as 'performative', that is we act out our gender roles. For some of us those roles follow a traditional script whereas others may reject, revise or adapt gender messages in the creation of an alternative, different way of performing femininity or masculinity. It is those refusing to conform to the hegemonic performances that can create what Butler refers to as 'gender trouble'.

A critique of Butler's performance theory is that it is 'strikingly unable to account for work, child care, institutional life, violence, resistance (except as individual choice), and material inequality. These are not trivial aspects of gender' (Connell, 2000: 20). As such,

material interests have begun to be examined by students of masculinity, though it has to be noted that feminist material analyses predate these by over two decades. Feminists, in particular those in Britain, extended the critique of class developed by Karl Marx and Friedrich Engels into a history and explanation of the economic and material subordination of women. The main question for Socialist and Marxist feminists was to identify the ways in which the institution of the family and women's domestic labour are structured by, reinforce and reproduce, the sexual division of labour found in workplaces and institutions external to the family. For example, see the early works of Juliet Mitchell (1984), Sheila Rowbotham (1973a) and Michèle Barrett (1980) and, from the USA, Heidi Hartmann (1983, originally 1979). Central to this analysis is the primacy of both class relations and patriarchy in protecting the gendered interests of men at the expense of women's unpaid and underpaid labour. Jeff Hearn (1996), amongst others, has taken this up in the examination of masculinities raising questions about the material interests of men in maintaining gender relations and existing gender practice, asking the politically difficult question as to what it is that binds men together as a group, in particular the material practice of men's violence targeted at women (Hearn, 1998).

For some materialist theorists femininity and masculinity are not polar opposites but rather gender itself has developed as an

. . . expression of the whole relationship between the spheres of production and reproduction. Industrial capitalism itself 'engendered' its opposite, the world of domesticity as against the world of wage work, and women as the other of men. . . In this view, gender articulates a basic class relationship, inherent in the wage labour relationship itself. The 'one' of wage labour is work, and the one doing it is a he. The 'other' is free time . . . posited by the first, relative to work. And the one making this free time possible, once more, is positioned very specifically as against the first. (Øystein Holter, 1995 cited in Connell, 2000: 21–2).

This view sees gender not developing from biological differences amongst human bodies but as features of social organisation based in a history of economic development – as men are associated with waged employment women were associated with the domestic sphere.

Stop and think 1.3

Think back about what you have just read about gender. Make a list comprising of the strengths and weaknesses you see in each approach.

Gender – why does it matter?

The term gender refers to the economic, social and cultural attributes and opportunities associated with being male or female. In most societies, being a man or a woman is not simply a matter of different biological and physical characteristics. Men and women face different expectations about how they should dress, behave or work. Relations between men and women, whether in the family, the workplace or the public sphere, also reflect understandings of the talents, characteristics and behaviour appropriate to women and to men. Gender thus differs from sex in that it is social and cultural in nature rather than biological. Gender attributes and characteristics, encompassing, *inter alia*, the roles that men and women play and the expectations placed upon them, vary widely among societies and change over time. But the fact that gender attributes are socially constructed means that they are also amenable to change in ways that can make a society more just and equitable.

(UNFPA, 1994).

. . . one cannot overlook how masculine hegemony becomes a successful strategy for subordinating women.

(Barrett, 2002: 96)

Gender matters because it denotes a hierarchy, one in which men usually dominate over women, and often also over younger men. As Harry Brod and Michael Kaufman argue, it has been a fundamental feminist insight that 'gender is a system of power and not just a set of stereotypes or observable differences between women and men' (1994: 4). This hierarchical system is usually referred to as patriarchy, a term which encapsulates the notion that social relations involve overarching structures and power differentials, an overarching system of male dominance according to theorists such as Kate Millet (1971). As a useful term 'patriarchy' has had its opponents – see A Critical Look 1.1 for critiques of such an all-encompassing employment of the term.

Understandings of patriarchy today are much broader and complex, for example, Sylvia Walby provides a more extensive definition of the 'system of social structures, and practices in which men dominate, oppress and exploit women' (Walby, 1990: 214). However, she recognises that the term can imply essentialist notions (as itemised by Rowbotham, A Critical Look 1.1) and subdivides patriarchy into six component parts:

1. the exploitation of women's labour by their husbands;

2. gender relations within paid labour;

3. the role of male violence;

4. patriarchal relations in the state;

5. patriarchal relations in sexuality; and

6. patriarchal relations in culture and cultural institutions.

She argues that the way in which each of these six combine with one or more of the others provides patriarchy, as a term, with the flexibility it requires to remain meaningful and not simply essentialise and universalise the experiences of all women and men.

In summary then, patriarchy is still a key term in gender relations as it involves such diverse institutions as state bureaucracies to child-rearing practices; economic systems; the media; culture; sexual practice and political leadership; family form. It is easy to see then why both feminists and students of critical masculinity continue to find the term patriarchy useful to describe the power relationships within societies.

A critical look 1.1

Patriarchy – a troubled term

The word 'patriarchy' presents problems of its own. It implies a universal and historical form of oppression which returns us to biology – and thus it obscures the need to recognise not only biological difference, but also the multiplicity of ways in which societies have defined gender. By focusing upon the bearing and rearing of children ('patriarchy' = the power of the father) it suggests there is a single determining cause of women's subordination. . . . The word leaves us with two separate systems in which a new male/female split is implied. We have patriarchy oppressing women and capitalism oppressing male workers. We have biological reproduction on the one hand and work on the other. . . .

'Patriarchy' implies a structure which is fixed, rather than the kaleidoscope of forms within which women and men have encountered one another. It does not carry any notion of how women might act to transform their situation as a sex. . . . 'Patriarchy' suggests a fatalistic submission which allows no space for the complexities of women's defiance.

. . .

If we could develop an historical concept of sex–gender relationships, this would encompass changing patterns of male control and its congruence or incongruence with various aspects of women's power.

(Rowbotham, 1983: 209–11; originally 1979)

The above extract comes from an article Sheila Rowbotham published in the *New Statesman* (December 1979), in which her aim was to challenge feminists to think more deeply about the concept, as she herself writes:

In criticising the term 'patriarchy' in the women's movement I was trying to warm up a few theoretical jellies that had got stuck in the fridge before the lumps melted properly. Since then socialist feminists internationally have become more wary of the word and cautious about its implications as a concept.

(Rowbotham, 1983: 207)

Likewise, as postmodernism argues that gender is not static but fluid this system of power must also include an ongoing negotiation within social structures with other structures of power, such as class:

Although gender ideals exist in the form of hegemonic masculinities and femininities and although gender power is a social reality, when we live in heterogenous societies, we each grapple with often conflicting pressures, demands, and possibilities.

(Kaufmann, 1994: 147)

A Critical Look 1.2 provides an example of how we have come to view the adaptations of patriarchy across historical eras.

A critical look 1.2

Adaptable patriarchy

Patriarchy is not a historical constant, for, as the first wave of Western feminism gained some victories, patriarchy adapted to keep women in a subordinate position in society. In Victorian times the condition of women was very much dominated by individual men having the legal right to dictate to individual women. In contrast to some of the liberties enjoyed by certain women prior to that era, for example the right to vote for women achieving the property qualification, the restrictions on Victorian womanhood were intense. The shift towards public patriarchy resulted from the successes of the first wave of feminism in the beginning of this [twentieth] century in conjunction with the increasing needs of a market economy. The increased access of women to a wider range of paid employment which occurred after the Second World War and the later second wave of feminism's achievements, manifest in equality legislation, further aided the transference from public to private patriarchy.

(Marchbank, 2000: 27)

As such, we are able to explain variations in gender power relations: for example, in certain situations a man of working class status may experience less power than a rich woman; likewise indigenous men have often been subservient to women of colonising ethnicities and young men, in school, college and even, at times, in the workplace are situated on a lower rung of the hierarchy than their teachers and supervisors. However, as noted above (A Critical Look 1.1) some feminists have stopped using the term patriarchy, seeing in its variations a lack of specificity and an excess of diversity. Others have recognised the fluidity of the term, over time, space and personal relationships and continue to find patriarchy: the integrated system of male dominance; a key concept in understanding social relations. In the context of a gendered approach to social sciences it is integral. In fact, even when alternative approaches to conceptualising the structure of gender relations are proposed, patriarchy remains a foundational aspect (see A Critical Look 1.3).

A critical look 1.3

Connell's four-fold model

Building upon his own earlier work (Connell, 1987) and Walby's (1990) six structures of patriarchy (see above), Connell has developed an alternative model of the structure of gender relations, yet patriarchy still finds its place within this new interpretative approach. Each of the four elements are summarised here based on Connell (2000):

1. *Power relations* – the main axis of power in western societies remains the domination of men and the subordination of women, what women's liberation referred to as patriarchy. This persists despite many challenges and resistances.

2. *Production relations (division of labour)* – a familiar concept is the gender division of labour. Equal attention needs to be paid to the economic consequences of this division, both in terms of the benefits men specifically accrue – called the *patriarchal dividend* (i.e. men's unequal share of the products of social labour) and to the gendered nature of capital. It is no accident that men and not women control the major corporations of the world; rather it is a part of the social construction of masculinity.

3. *Cathexis (emotional relations)* – in recent years emotion and desire have become increasingly important topics for social theory. The practices that shape, create and act out desire are an aspect of the gender order that is true for homosexual and heterosexual desire. As such, political questions regarding desire are raised, such as whether relationships are consensual or coercive. Feminist analyses have raised pertinent questions about the relationship of heterosexuality to men's dominant social positions.

4. *Symbolism* – a vital element of social processes is communication, including grammatical and other rules of language, both verbal and visual. These are important sites of gender practice. Gender subordination may be reproduced through subtle and overt linguistic actions, for example the practice of referring to women by titles which denote their relationship or not to men through marriage. Many other symbolic presentations of gender also exist, such as the presentation of the gendered self through dress [**Hotlink → History and national dress (Chapter 3)**], make up, voice tone amongst others.

Source: Adapted from Connell (2000).

Stop and think 1.4

In A Critical Look 1.3 the symbolic presentation of gender through dress is mentioned. In most western societies the wearing of 'skirt-type' garments is a signifier of femininity. Look at Figures 1.2 and 1.3. In Figure 1.2 the Scottish meat industry is using the image of a man in a kilt to promote meat eating. In Figure 1.3, the actor and comedian Eddie Izzard appears to be wearing both a skirt and make up. Which image is a challenge to hegemonic masculinity and which is promoting a hegemonic vision of men? Think about how cultural context, in this case involving men from neighbouring countries, influences how the symbols of masculinity/femininity are read. [**Hotlink → History (Chapter 3) → World in Focus 3.3**]

Figure 1.2

Source: Reproduced with permission from Quality Meat Scotland

Figure 1.3

Source: Dave Bennett/Getty Images Entertainment/Getty Images

The journey to a gendered approach

So, how did we get to such understandings of sex, gender and patriarchy? In this section we shall briefly outline the journey that social science has undergone to now. This journey begins with feminist challenges to what was, could and can be known [**Hotlink → Method, Methodology, Epistemology (Chapter 2)**]. As noted above feminism began a challenge to established ideas of knowledge which then led to the development of Men's Studies and to Gender Studies. This journey can be viewed as a series of stages:

1. feminism and Women's Studies

2. responses to feminism – celebrating masculinity

3. critical approaches to masculinity

4. our gendered approach.

We defend our use of such a linear progression as a reflection of how it has been. That is not to say that before one stage began the predecessor had to be complete – rather there is a degree of co-existence. However, as will be shown, the progressive elements of investigations into men and masculinity are based upon, and acknowledge their debt to, feminism. Similarly, the gendered approach used here is not a supplantation of feminism but a development which could not have occurred without it.

Feminism and Women's Studies

Women's Studies developed out of a social movement, that of feminism. Women's Studies not only challenged ways of knowing but methods of teaching and research [**Hotlink → Pedagogy (Chapter 9)**]. Early work of second wave feminism (from the 1960s) began to explain gender and gender difference building upon the work of, for example, Mead (1962, originally 1949) – who showed how gender roles are malleable across different societies; Simone de Beauvoir (1972, originally 1949) – who argued that motherhood explained women's lesser social position as it prevented women from achieving full humanity in the way that men could and Virginia Woolf (1929, 1938) – on women's exclusion from education and knowledge creation. Some of the classic texts of this time include Michelle Rosaldo and Louise Lamphere's (1974) edited collection exploring culture and society; Shulamith Firestone's (1971, originally 1970) polemic on sex differences, biology and the potential to solve gender differences through cybernetic reproductive techniques; Stephanie Coontz and Peta Henderson's (1986) exploration of the linkages between gender and class; Nancy Chodorow's (1978) psychoanalytical work on the role of human nurturing; Kate Millet's (1971) analysis of the politics of sex and sex differences and many, many more exploring, explaining and debating gender difference and the differential power held by women and men.

Such works aimed to deconstruct and challenge the ways in which human society and behaviours were explained, offering alternative insights, showing, for example:

➤ how the binary divide in biology (male and female) was transposed upon social and cultural organisation to create the 'separate spheres' of public and private (Rosaldo, 1974);

➤ how descriptions of human development were open to reinterpretation (Leibowitz, 1986), see A Closer Look 1.3;

➤ how history misrepresented the experiences of women (Hostettler, Davin and Alexander, 1979), and

➤ how women have been made marginal (Spender, 1981).

A closer look 1.3

Leibowitz on evolution

Lila Leibowitz (1986) explains the sexual division of labour, not based on 'man the hunter' but on 'woman the mother'. Her argument is that the development of projectile weapons by primitive societies increased the availability and amount of animal produce, resulting in an increased demand for hearth skills such as preparing hides, cooking meat and making cooking utensils. As these skills were new and complex children needed to be trained and to practise to develop proficiency, and children were tutored in the skills they would use as adults. Given that females would spend more time at the hearth than males in adulthood, due to the physical restrictions both of pregnancy and child-rearing, instruction in these new skills was directed at female children rather than at boys. As such, Leibowitz contends that females became more skilled in these areas and boys were taught other skills to compensate, generally those requiring physical strength rather than dexterity.

A major aim of feminist political and academic work and of Women's Studies was to 'alter fundamentally the nature of all knowledge by shifting the focus

from androcentricity to a frame of reference in which women's different and differing ideas, experiences, needs and interests are valid in their own right' (Bowles and Klein, 1983: 3). Now, in the early years of the twenty-first century, it is possible to conclude that in many aspects of social science this has been achieved. The varying extent of this in each discipline area, and the major features in each area, are delineated in Part Two of this book.

Women's Studies has also sought to challenge the divisions between discipline areas arguing that work which learns from, and develops across, a range of discipline areas results in the ability to examine issues from a variety of theoretical paradigms, utilising the most appropriate for the matter under study. Another major strand of Women's Studies has been in the approach to teaching, in challenging the very curriculum in terms of both content and practice, integrating the principles of feminist work into teaching methods – for example, the fundamental recognition of personal experience, the valuing of difference and the development of co-operation rather than competition (see Rich, 1980; Humm, 1995; Lubelska, 1991). This has not been without its limitations within traditional educational organisations (see Letherby and Marchbank, 1999), imposed both by educational establishments and student reluctance to the use of such pedagogies [Hotlink → Pedagogy (Chapter 9)], [Hotlink → Education (Chapter 13)]. Despite these restrictions many Women's Studies students have described the life enhancing experience of such study (Coate-Bignell, 1996; Letherby and Marchbank, 2001; Marchbank and Letherby, 2006; Stake, 2006).

Feminism and Women's Studies have generated a number of responses:

> On the one hand, there are specific, often feminist-inspired critiques of dominant masculinity, male violence and patriarchal power; on the other, there are men's responses, from outright hostility to sympathetic stances in the form of men's anti-sexist groups and other activities.
>
> (Hearn, 1987: 2)

For example, see the openly and strongly anti-feminist men's movements (see the UK Men's Movement, **www.ukmm.org.uk**) and mythopoetic movements celebrating the positive aspects of masculine experience to feminist informed and pro-feminist studies of men. Cutting across the latter category in particular are further layers which examine the gendered male experience alongside issues of ethnicity and sexuality.

Celebrating masculinity

By the 1990s popular media had begun to ask questions about men; this in itself indicated a development away from the assumption that all humanity could be subsumed under the heading 'men' towards recognition of men as different from women. The danger in this has been that some of these studies have utilised essentialist notions of masculinity and femininity to argue against equality of the sexes, offering, in Connell's opinion 'a highly simplified view of the problems of men' (Connell, 2000: 5), manifesting itself in a therapeutic movement to tackle the perceived psychological wounds being suffered by modern man, through re-establishing bonds amongst men, often following practices such as rituals and retreats.

Books such as Robert Bly's (1990) best seller *Iron John: a book about men*, have been critiqued for presenting differences between women and men as unchanging, timeless and biological whilst attempting to portray the authors as associated with a progressive 'men's movement' (Coltrane, 1994). A further aspect of such writings has been on the celebration of masculinity, including a focus on men's pain and suffering and the creation of homosocial spaces to permit such explorations (see Annandale and Clark, 1996). The value of such spaces for men to explore gender must not be underestimated, yet a common but major absence in such approaches is the lack of recognition of men's privilege in and across societies. Associated with some of these works are social organisations, collectively known as Men's Movements, which seek to promote men's interests and are frequently anti-feminist – either deliberately or consequentially. Given the inherent biological determinism of such mythopoetic men's movements and writings they have not contributed to the development of either critical studies on men (CMS) and masculinity nor on the creation of a gendered approach to social science. However, their social impact and political presence should not be underestimated [**Hotlink → Political Science (Chapter 8)**].

Stop and think 1.5

What disadvantages do you think affect men? What disadvantages affect women? How might these be related to the ways in which your society constructs notions of femininity and masculinity?

Critical approaches to masculinity

Stephen Whitehead and Frank Barrett (2001) note that the 1980s and 1990s were a period of great growth in the areas of research into men and masculinities, particularly in sociology. Between 50 to 100 programmes in masculinity were on offer across US educational institutions from the late 1980s onwards (Hearn, 1987; Whitehead and Barrett, 2001), a situation which has not been replicated across the UK, Australia or Europe. Nonetheless, all these regions have witnessed a massive increase on studying men, not that studying men is 'new or necessarily radical' (Hearn, 2004: 49), what was new was the study of men as gendered beings. Either labelled New Men's Studies (NMS) or Critical Studies of Masculinity (CMS), these developments, in response to feminist social science and feminist politics, take into account the role of social power in constructing both what it is to be male and how masculinity is practised. A further difference from the mythopoetic writings mentioned above has been the way that NMS/CSM (from here CSM) has presented itself alongside Women's Studies, rather than in a different circle:

> By placing gender at the center of their analyses, they attempt to overcome past tendencies to view men as generically human. By linking the ways that men create and sustain gendered selves with the ways that gender influences power relations and perpetuates inequality, feminist men's studies support and complement the critical perspectives of women's studies.
>
> (Coltrane, 1994: 44)

Initially this complementary analogy with Women's Studies was flagged as potentially dangerous, for if money for research, curriculum and teaching developments, writing, and so on, is available the 'study of men may attract the attentions of general (male) social science researchers with no particular commitment to critique, or worse, still committed to some form of anti-feminism' (Hearn, 1987: 9). A further concern was that the establishment of Men's Studies, before Women's Studies became secured, would 'put the focus back on men' (Robinson, 1993: 23). Yet this does not appear to have occurred, rather 'the exponential increase in research into men and masculinities' (Whitehead and Barrett, 2001: 2) has resulted in studies, primarily historical and sociological, which examine the nature of the public and private lives of men; men's behaviour and the construction of masculinity in a variety of contexts and societies. In fact, a recognition of the problems of denoting such studies as Men's Studies, or New Men's Studies has been the reformulation, by the most critical of exponents of this area, of the study of men as Critical Studies of Masculinity (CSM), that meaning not a celebration of masculinity but a full and open critique and examination of masculinity in all its manifestations.

A major contribution in the area of masculinity studies is the notion of hegemonic masculinity – that is, the concept that there exists in each society a specific way in which to do, and be, masculine. Conversely, alongside this is the argument that masculinity cannot, and must not, be viewed as singular (see Brod and Kaufmann, 1994). Hegemonic masculinity is now a well-used and recognised term and it has been useful in identifying the ways in which men dominate women and other men – in fact, some have preferred this term to patriarchy (see A Closer Look 1.2). However, it has not itself been free from problems just as patriarchy has also had its critics. Some, such as Whitehead have argued that the idea of hegemonic masculinity does not do much to reveal 'the complex patterns of inculcation and resistance' (1999: 58). In other words, the concept of hegemonic patriarchy is too broad to explain to most people just how it is that people, boys and men primarily, acquire and absorb the messages about masculinity and the ways in which some, if not many, boys and men resist these majority messages in the negotiation of their own ways of being male in their society.

It has been argued that theories of patriarchy need to acknowledge fluidity (see A Critical Look 1.1).

Likewise, the notion of hegemonic masculinities has been subjected to the same consideration. What is viewed as hegemonic cannot be static: across societies, across geography and across time what is viewed as the hegemonic construction of masculinity has to adapt to changing cultural and social factors. Yet, these changes need to continue to acknowledge differences between, and amongst, women and men which are both discursive and material – that is, not just how we talk about them but how they are also experienced and lived.

A gendered approach

Following the development of Women's Studies has been, not only Men's Studies but, Gender Studies. In some instances the generation of Gender Studies was a political move to have studies which considered gender as an important variable included in the mainstream, in others it was a deliberate attempt to dilute feminist Women's Studies by forcing the focus off women and back onto men and changing the paradigm from one of feminist critique to gender difference. So, Gender Studies can be, and has been, both a danger to, and an ally of, those seeking to examine gender relations from a progressive and critical standpoint.

In recent years some departments of Women's Studies in universities have either been transformed into, or added on, Gender Studies. The reasons for this have been attributed to a number of factors. Firstly, it has been seen as a response to perceived changes in market forces, offering gender rather than women as the focus of study. Secondly, and related to the first point, some see the move to gender as an act of academic survival, permitting feminist work to exist in a political atmosphere hostile to gender or as maintaining a focus on gender within the curriculum. A third push towards Gender Studies has been the aforementioned post-structuralist questioning of the usefulness of such concepts as woman/women and man/men [**Hotlink → History – Riley and Scott (Chapter 3)**]. It is probably true to conclude that all of these factors played their part, as did the rise in CMS.

So how is Gender Studies defined? Well, Gender Studies focuses on gender identity and the representations of gender as the central foci for analysis across a

World in focus 1.2

Studying Men around the World

The form that academic debates around men have taken varies from place to place depending on:

➤ the impacts of the form of feminism and 'men's politics'

➤ the location of these studies on men, including their relationship with feminism, women's studies and gender research

➤ the naming of these studies.

According to Jeff Hearn (2001) these can be broadly seen as follows.
The US: the largest and most diverse

➤ A large amount of literature, some from pro-feminist positions, others from mythopoetic men's movement to men's rights groups.

➤ Roots lie in response to feminism but also influenced by civil rights, gay and black movements.

➤ Questions around heterosexuality, whiteness and men increasingly addressed.

➤ The US academic context reproduced in this work – in that it is mostly based in positivistic, psychological and social psychological understandings of men and masculinity.

➤ Reflecting general US ideology of valuing the individual and the market there is little attention paid to structural analysis either economic or political.

➤ US is where the term 'men's studies' is most frequently used, often in relation to anti-feminist approaches.

The UK: power and structural analysis

➤ Developed in the context of left politics, with a mainly positive relationship to feminism, though also reflecting tensions within both feminism and the left regarding the role of the state.

➤ Reflects the integration of gay politics and gay studies.

➤ Changes in European social science, especially the critique of positivism, have been very important.

➤ Power and structural analyses have been central focus in regards to masculinity and men.

➤ Many examples of detailed ethnographies of different groups of men.

➤ Little demand to create separate discipline of 'men's studies'.

Australia: theoretical and empirical considerations

➤ A critical edge, sharing similarities of left politics with the UK.

➤ Mix of aboriginal struggles, white British, other European and increasing multiculturalism raised complex questions of gender and ethnicity.

➤ Relatively greater visibility of gay studies.

➤ As in the UK, relatively little demand to create separate discipline of 'men's studies'.

Nordic research: positive aspects of men

➤ Set within the context of a relatively homogeneous society ethnically which holds onto a faith in welfare and positive relations between the individual and the state.

➤ Feminism in Nordic countries less autonomous and more related to the state.

➤ Context of a myth of gender equality and of the genderless citizen exists which is reflected in studies of men.

➤ Active networking exists between women and men resulting in detailed surveys, directed at the positive aspects of men, on changing men, fatherhood and other social roles of men.

➤ Less emphasis on gay studies and on analysis of social structures, the latter meaning that there is a danger of downplaying men's structural power.

➤ Only really in Sweden is ethnicity in the analysis.

Source: Derived from Jeff Hearn (2001)

---

wide range of academic disciplines, as such it is interdisciplinary, as Women's Studies is and was before. Much of Gender Studies is inspired by feminist thought and writings and it also includes the use of other theoretical approaches to study the categories of gender. Gender Studies claims to include Critical Men's Studies, Gay and Lesbian Studies and Women's Studies – though there are those in Women's Studies who argue that the parent of an approach cannot subsequently become just one subset amongst many! Further, as in some formulations Gender Studies can constitute examinations of gender that see women and men as equally oppressed and positioned, this can only be viewed as a retrograde step by advocates not just of Women's Studies but also of Critical Men's Studies. However, this is not, in the main the approach to gender in most academic departments nor is it the gendered perspective that we employ in this textbook.

Rather, we seek to investigate gender, and the investigation of gender across disciplines and issues, from a position which integrates feminist work on gender with the concepts, ideas and notions developed by CMS and other critical perspectives. Whereas in the 1970s and 1980s feminists focused their lenses upon men and masculinity, CMS has appeared wary of reversing that lens. That is to say, whereas, from the late 1980s, CMS has been able to employ feminist paradigms (models) in their investigations into masculinity, and feminist studies have been challenging the mainstream since the late 1960s (at least in terms of the second wave of feminism), and a degree of mutual support has existed there does not seem to exist a synthesis of feminist work which integrates the basic paradigms of feminism with the basic paradigms of CMS. We aim to create such a paradigm. It includes the following principles:

➤ Gender is a social construct.

➤ There exist in each and every society hegemonic notions of gender roles, yet each of these is adaptable and open to adaptation.

➤ Our society, in the main, limits gender to one of two categories – feminine and masculine – yet many more possibilities exist, transgender being one.

➤ Women in the main have lesser power than men, and some men have less power than others therefore, analyses based around materiality and patriarchy remain useful.

➤ Gender is not expressed, experienced or performed separately from other social identities such as ethnicity, nationality, sexuality amongst others.

➤ As such, our gendered approach does not diminish but support the contribution of feminist theorising to the social sciences.

Conclusion

The aim of this text is not to develop and present a whole new theory of gender. Rather it is a much simpler aim, to introduce students to the debates around gender, be they from Critical Men's Studies, Gender Studies, Women's Studies or elsewhere both across academic discipline areas and interdisciplinary issues and concerns within the Social Sciences. As such, nor is this a book an introduction to Gender Studies, rather it is an introduction to *gender* as present in the issues and disciplines included in this text – a presence that would not exist without earlier feminist analysis. We hope you find this useful.

Further reading

Stevi Jackson and Sue Scott (eds) (2002), *Gender: A Sociological Reader*, London, Routledge. Extracts from: R.W. Connell 'Hegemonic Masculinity'; Heidi Mizra 'Redefining Black Womanhood' and Susanne J. Kessler, 'Defining and Producing Genitals'. This Reader provides a vast array of accessible and well selected articles on a diverse range of issues relevant to gender.

Robert Connell (2000), *The Men and the Boys*, Cambridge, Polity. This book surveys recent research and findings on masculinity providing a clear understanding of the growing range of work in this area.

Kate Bornstein (1994) *Gender Outlaw, On men, women and the rest of us*, Routledge, New York. In this book Kate discusses her own autobiography, issues of transgender and challenges the notion of only two genders existing.

Websites

Intute, **http://www.intute.ac.uk**. A portal to a wide range of social science issues and resources, accompanied by Experts' Choices, including many resources on gender issues.

Jeff Hearn (1987), 'Changing Men's Studies', *achilles HEEL*, Issue 8, April 1987, **http://www.achillesheel. freeuk.com/article08_11.html**. An article which critiques Men's Studies and presents thoughts for ways of moving forwards, as it is 20 years' old it provides some ideas of the historical development of the debates in CMS.

Jed Bland (2001), 'Preface', *About Gender*, **http://www. gender.org.uk/about/00_prefc.htm**. A site discussing what gender is and how it has been studied.

The Guardian. **Http://www.guardian.co.uk/life/feature/story/ 0,,937913,00.html**. An article entitled 'They just can't help it' in which Simon Baron-Cohen presents his argument that male and female brains are different.

New Internationalist, **http://www.newint.org**, from site select Back Issues and the number 373.

'Women's Rights: the facts', in NI 373, November 2004. An article, with useful graphics outlining the gender differences between women and men from political power to economic assets across the world.

End of chapter activity

Activity 1

Go to some of the following places and observe what people are doing:

➤ A busy high street/shopping mall

➤ Riding on public transport such as a bus, underground train

➤ A children's playground

➤ A social space such as your students' union bar, college cafeteria

1. Can you tell who is male and who is female? What 'clues' to gender are you reading? Do you think your reading is accurate? What ideas that you hold about gender are affecting your readings of others?

2. Do people behave differently? Are you noticing things you have not noticed before?

3. Is gender the only identity signified by people's appearance? If not, how do these identities interact and become expressed?

4. What do you feel when you can't determine someone's gender from their appearance? Why do you feel this?

Activity 2

Before you read this chapter what did you understand 'patriarchy' to mean? What do you understand about it now? Make a list of the ways in which patriarchy as a concept can be useful in understanding gender and social practices, make a second list of its limitations.

Method, methodology and epistemology

Well quite honestly, I said I hope this research is worth it. I said to my mum, I've got this lady coming to see me this morning. She said 'What about?' I said, I hope it's not a load of old rubbish. Because there's been so much research on such rubbishy things I feel money's been wasted. So she said 'Oh it probably is . . .' Well, it's a bit indulgent isn't it, really, just talking about yourself all the time?

(Oakley, 1979 cited by Roberts, 1992: 176)

Stop and think 2.1

This quote tells us interesting things about the perception of social research by the lay public, about the differential status given to quantitative and qualitative data collection methods and about women's feelings about their involvement in research. Although both the respondent and the researcher in this example are women this quote is also relevant to an understanding of men's research activity and experience. As you read this chapter reflect on why this quote is so important when considering the gendered aspects of method, methodology and epistemology.

Introduction

The production of methods literature is big publishing business and there are currently lots of books concerned with issues of *method* (the tools for data gathering, e.g. questionnaires, interviews, conversational analysis), *methodology* (the analysis of the methods used) and *epistemology* (the theory of knowledge). It is easy then to find books concerned both with 'doing research' and the philosophy of research practice. A significant and increasing amount of this published material is devoted to the gendered aspects of data collection and analysis. For some people this attention to research practice and the debate between researchers about these issues is at the expense of more important concerns. For example:

Despite the high profile now given to discussing feminist research . . . much of the material

published, with a few exceptions, tends to focus on the principles involved in a rather abstract way. This can sometimes be at the expense of exploring the dynamics of actually doing research in the field.

(Maynard and Purvis, 1994: 1)

Academia is a service occupation. What we should get serious about is not what we say to each other, but the extent to which our work resonates with the experiences and needs of people outside the academic world.

(Oakley 2004: 191)

However, we believe that the relationship between the *product of research* (the findings, and the theoretical pronouncements) and the *process of research* are intimately related. In other words, we need to recognise that the knowing/doing relationship is extremely important and intimately connected because what we do during the research process affects the product that we get (Letherby, 2003a, 2004a, 2004b).

In this chapter we focus on the gendered aspects of the knowing/doing relationship. The remainder of this chapter is divided into four sections. In 'Masculine knowledge production and the feminist critique' we outline the feminist critique of the historical production of 'masculinised' knowledge – that is knowledge grounded in men's experience. In 'Gendered research approaches and interests' we move on to contemporary research practice and critique the view that some methods are inevitably masculine and others feminine and reflect on the practice of male and female researchers and the experience of female and male respondents. Following our consideration of the gendered aspects of the philosophies and practice of social research our final main section focuses on the 'Gendered analysis and re/presentation of research'. To end the chapter we make some brief conclusions. Throughout the chapter attention will be given to other examples of difference and diversity and their relationship to a gendered approach to research. We also draw on research examples to demonstrate debates and concerns.

Masculine knowledge production and the feminist critique

Traditional and critical approaches

Traditionally the academy was a male space and it was not until the second half of the twentieth century that women began to enter higher education in any great numbers [Hotlink → Education (Chapter 13)]. Perhaps not surprisingly then, historically the focus of academic endeavour was men and male experience. Yet, in the past, and some would suggest even today, not all men were represented and therefore in the physical and social sciences, the arts and humanities:

> the perspectives, concerns, and interests of only one sex and one class are represented as general. Only one sex, and class are directly and actively involved in producing, debating and developing its ideas, creating its art, in forming its medical and psychological conceptions, in framing its laws, its political principles, its educational values and objectives.
>
> (Smith, 1988: 19–20)

However, historically, the problem was not only that men were the primary focus of research but that the so-called 'scientific' method was unquestioned as the best way to study both the natural and the social world [Hotlink → Anthropology (Chapter 6), Psychology (Chapter 7)]. From this perspective the view is that the 'neutral knower' (the researcher) can be separated from what is known; that different researchers exposed to the same data can replicate results and that it is possible to generalise from research to wider social and natural populations. In other words the scientific method allows for the objective collection of facts by a value-neutral researcher: reality (the truth) is out there and the researcher can investigate and discover the 'truth' independent of observer effects (Stanley and Wise, 1993; Letherby, 2003a). In addition those that aim for 'scientific' social science argue that the research process is linear and orderly – 'hygenic' in fact (Stanley and Wise, 1993; Kelly et al., 1994). This approach is generally known as positivism and associ-ated with quantitative methods (but it is important to remember that not all quantitative researchers are aiming for positivism/a 'scientific' approach; see Oakley (1999) for further discussion).

Early critics of the 'scientific' approach were them-selves male and although they were critical of the claims to objectivity, value-freedom and the search for the 'truth' their research still tended to focus on male experience and the sexist aspects of the approach were not challenged:

> An oft-quoted example of an early critique is the influential study of (male) youth culture by Paul Willis (1977, 1978). In the study, class was a focus and Willis gave a voice to an underprivileged section of society, yet women were absent except as portrayed through the sexist attitudes of the male respondents (Morley, 1996; Millen, 1997). Willis himself described young women as unforthcoming and unwilling to talk. He wrote that they retreated in giggles when asked questions and Morley (1996: 13) argues that Willis saw this as a symptom of the young women's social inadequacies rather than a result of his presence as a male researcher.
>
> (Letherby, 2003a: 66)

Willis' work is also relevant to a consideration of the differential gendered experience of researchers and respondents – an issue we return to later.

Stop and think 2.2

Next time you visit the library look through some of the journals of your discipline(s) and find some examples of research accounts. Is gender always a consideration both in terms of data collected and the methods used? If not, why not?

So it seems that historically both those who took a 'scientific' approach and those that criticised this phi-losophy ignored the issue of gender. In the 1970s feminist researchers began to criticise both male-dom-inated knowledge production and the methodological claims made by researchers who argued that their work was objective and value free:

Masculine ideologies are the creation of masculine subjectivity; they are neither objective nor value free nor inclusively 'human'. Feminism implies that we recognise fully the inadequacy for us, the distortion, of male-centred ideologies and that we proceed to think and act out of that recognition.

(Rich, 1986: 207, cited by Stanley and Wise, 1993: 59)

By way of challenge to an objective, value-free approach feminists argued that all research involves some element of the researcher's personhood – in terms of values, opinions, interests and approaches and the researched are themselves people who influence the research process as well as providing data for the final research product (e.g. Stanley and Wise, 1993; Cotterill and Letherby, 1994; Wilkinson and Kitzinger, 1996). Thus, in all research the product cannot be separated from the conditions of its production (Olsen, 1980). What is distinctive about feminist research, says Louise Morley (1997) is that it admits this. From this approach, as Renate Duelli Klein (cited by Wilkinson, 1986: 14) notes, 'conscious subjectivity' replaces the 'value-free objective' of traditional research. She suggests that this is not only more honest but helps to break down the power relationship between researcher and researched. A Closer Look 2.1 summarises the feminist critique of the traditional 'masculine' research model:

A closer look 2.1

Feminist criticism of the traditional research process

The feminist critique of the historical male-centred approach to research can be summarised as follows:

➤ the selection of sexist and élitist research topics

➤ biased research including the use of male-only respondents

➤ exploitative relationships between researcher and researched and within research teams

➤ claims to false objectivity (by those who seek the scientific)

➤ inaccurate interpretation and overgeneralisation of findings – including the application of theory to women from research on men.

(See Jayaratne and Stewart, 1991 for further discussion)

So what do feminist researchers think needs to be done differently? Judith Cook and Mary Fonow (1990) focus on the need for research to mean something, to lead to change in women's lives and insist on:

the search for techniques which analyze and record the historical process of change and ultimately the transfer of such methodological tools to the subjects [sic] of research so they might confront their oppression and formulate their own plan of action. Thus, 'the truth of a theory is not dependent on the application of certain methodological principles and rules but on its potential to orient the processes of praxis toward progressive emancipation and humanization' (Mies, 1983: 124). Feminist research is, thus, not research about women but research for women to be used in transforming their sexist society.

(Cook and Fonow, 1990: 80)

Others add to this and insist that the research process should be clear and accountable. For example:

social scientists have a responsibility to ensure that when they speak about other people, they do so on the basis of warrantable knowledge. The audit trail through research question, methods, data collection, analysis and interpretation needs to be clear, systematic and explicit.

(Oakley, 2004: 191)

Attention to the literature suggests further that feminist researchers (and others who aim for anti-sexist research approaches) should:

➤ Give continuous and reflexive attention to the significance of gender as an aspect of all social life and within research, and consider further the significance of other differences between women and (some argue) the relevance of men's lives to a feminist understanding of the world.

➤ Provide a challenge to the norm of 'objectivity' and assume knowledge can be collected in a pure, uncontaminated way.

➤ Value the personal and the private as worthy of study.

➤ Develop non-exploitative relationships within research.

➤ Value reflexivity and emotion as a source of insight as well as an essential part of the research process.

Diane Millen pulls together this critique thus:

> any research may be considered 'feminist' which incorporates two main aims; a sensitivity to the role of gender within society and the differential experiences of males and females and a critical approach to the tools of research on society, the structures of methodology and epistemology within which 'knowledge' is placed within the public domain.
>
> (1997: 6.3)

This challenge is now an established part of the epistemological and methodological debate in the social sciences. In A Closer Look 2.2 we look at some of the responses to an early challenge to the traditional approach.

A closer look 2.2

Great Sexist Pleasure

One of the earliest books focusing on both the feminist critique of research and on possible alternative approaches was *Doing Feminist Research* (1981) edited by Helen Roberts. A review of the first edition was written by Colin Bell (joint editor with Howard Newby of *Doing Sociological Research* (1977)). He wrote 'it gives me great sexist pleasure to report that it is far less gossipy than other similar collections – that will, I suspect, particularly disappoint male readers' (Bell cited by Roberts, 1990: xv).

However, Margaret Stacey, another reviewer of *Doing Feminist Research* (1981) wrote that the articles in the book demonstrated that there was still a long way to go before 'we achieve . . . a methodology, which can see beyond the confines of the society in which it is embedded' (Stacey, 1981, cited by Roberts, 1990: xix).

Stop and think 2.3

How relevant do you think Stacey's comments are today? Is there still a long way to go? In your experience, is gender now taken into account within research as a matter of course?

Gendered and other standpoints

One specific feminist philosophical critique of the traditional male-centred 'scientific' epistemology is feminist empiricism. This approach leaves intact much of the traditional 'scientific' understandings of the principles of adequate inquiry. Thus, feminist empiricists seek to use 'traditional' methods and approaches more appropriately, challenging the way that methods are used rather than challenging the methods themselves. Magrit Eichler (1988) produced a guideline for non-sexist research insisting on the elimination of sexism in titles, sexism in language, sexist concepts, sexism in research designs, sexism in methods and sexism in policy evaluation. This approach then challenges the 'value freedom' of traditional approaches but does not challenge the goals of such an approach (Letherby, 2003a; Stanley and Wise, 1993; Abbott *et al.*, 2005).

Like feminist empiricism, feminist standpoint epistemology begins from the view that 'masculine' science was bad science because it excluded women's experience and suggests the importance of developing a 'successor science' to existing dominant social science paradigms. Thus, feminist standpoint epistemology advocates that the 'personal is political'. Some suggest that this perspective draws on Marxist ideas about the role of the proletariat and that women are an oppressed class and, as such, have the ability not only to understand their own experiences of oppression but to see their oppressors' viewpoint. The view here is that research based on women's experience provides a more valid basis for knowledge because 'it gives access to a wider conception of truth via the insight into the oppressor' (Millen, 1997: 7.2). It is not just that the oppressed see more – their own experience and that of the privileged – but also that their knowledge emerges through the struggle against oppression: in this instance the struggle against men. Supporters of this approach suggest that objectivity *is* possible but that the critical scrutiny of all aspects of the research process is necessary to achieve objectivity. This presents a challenge to traditional notions of objectivity which Sandra Harding (1993) argues are weak because the researchers' own values, assumptions and so on are hidden.

Gendered research approaches and interests

Bringing women and men back in

As Harding (1987: 8) notes, studying women is not new, yet studying them from the perspective of their own experiences so that women can understand themselves and their social world has 'virtually no history at all'. The first step, then, is to make women's lives visible. In addition as David Morgan (1981, 1992) argues, 'taking gender seriously' means bringing men back in. He stresses that if we accept that man is not the norm and woman the deviation and if we want to fully understand the life experience and chances of all men and women we need to consider the social construction of both femininity and masculinity and focus our research on women and men's experience. Similarly, Sophie Laws suggests 'feminist research must go beyond the study of women to work out ways of studying for women if it is not to remain essentially a liberal rather than a radical liberatory force' (1990: 13). Arguably working in this way is more difficult for male researchers as 'taking gender into account' is a particular problem for male researchers given that the 'massive weight of the taken-for-granted . . . conspires with the researcher's own gender to render silent what should be spoken' (Morgan, 1981: 96).

If it is our aim to take gender seriously in research it is important, as Ellen Annandale and Judith Clark (1996: 33) note, we should remain 'congnisant of the possibility that "patriarchal discourse need not be seen as homogeneous and uniformly oppressive" . . . for women or uniformly liberating and unproblematic for men, and that women do not need to be portrayed as inevitable victims and men as victors'. Thus, men can be victims, women can be powerful, men and women often share experiences of powerlessness and an understanding of the differences between women in terms of power and privilege is a vital part of the feminist project (see below for further detail).

There are of course many examples of areas where more research on women's experience is needed but there are also areas where there is less research focusing on male experience. For example Frances

Stop and think 2.5

Think of some examples of where the gender order appears to work against women, against men and cases where other differences influence an individual's life experiences and life chances. See if you can find some examples of research focusing on the examples you have identified.

Goldscheider and Gayle Kaufman (1996) suggest that our understanding of men's fertility and involvement in family life resembles our understanding of women and work in the 1960s. They write: 'In the "separate spheres" of social research in the 1960s work and public life meant men, and for most of the time since then, family has meant women. It is clearly time to move on' (1994: 94). Similarly in his review of research on the relationship between infertility and psychological distress Arthur Greil (1997) argues that we need more research which considers differences between male and female infertility [**Hotlink → Family (Chapter 11), Health and Illness (Chpater 12)**].

Gendered paradigms

The methods that social scientists used can broadly be classified into quantitative approaches (those that involve the collection and analysis of numbers) and qualitative approaches (involving collection, observation and analysis of words and actions). In a paper focusing on historical and current gendered research philosophies and practices Oakley (1998: 708) argues that the 'critique of the quantitative' overlapped with the 'critique of mainstream/malestream' and thus 'To be a feminist social scientist one must have a certain allegiance to the qualitative paradigm'. This has resulted, she adds in a 'paradigm war' with male researchers being associated with quantitative methods of data collection and women researchers with qualitative methods (especially the in-depth interview).

However, we would suggest that it is a misconception that in-depth qualitative interviewing is the only 'feminist method'. Although historically feminists have been particularly critical of the survey method it was/is its epistemological appropriation by those who attempted a 'scientific', 'value-free' approach and the tendency of researchers to concentrate on male concerns that was/is the issue here (Oakley, 1981; Graham, 1984; Stanley and Wise, 1993). Indeed, as noted earlier, much of the work that challenged traditional philosophical approaches was equally gender blinkered.

So where has this misconception come from? Many feminists *have* argued that the in-depth interview that takes a life-history approach is a good way of achieving an 'equal' relationship between interviewer and interviewee. By letting individuals tell 'their story', this method allows the researched an active part in the research process and product as well as making the researcher more vulnerable and therefore diluting the power imbalance in favour of the researcher (Oakley, 1981; Graham, 1984; Stanley and Wise, 1993). So, the argument goes, this enables the production of research for women rather than research about or of women (Oakley, 1981, Bowles and Klein, 1983). However, there are potential problems with this approach, not least because as Caroline Ramazanoglu (1989) points out, women are divided by other variables – such as, race, class, sexuality and so on and this is likely to affect the research process and that research matching is impossible to achieve. Further, as Janet Finch (1984) argues the very fact that women are 'happy to talk' may be an indication of their powerlessness and researchers need to be very careful that information freely given cannot be used against those who gave it. Many others agree with this and add that some objectification of the researched is inevitable as the researcher has the ultimate control over the material (e.g. Ramazanoglu, 1989; Ribbens, 1989; Stacey, 1991; Cotterill, 1992).

So, it is important not to see face-to-face interviewing as the only feminist method. Liz Kelly and colleagues (1994) argue that appropriate methods should be chosen to suit research programmes rather than research programmes being chosen to 'fit' favourite techniques. It is not the methods 'but the framework within which they are located, and the particular ways in which they are deployed' that makes research feminist (Kelly *et al.*, 1994: 46) – namely, it is not what you do but the way that you do it that matters. In addition Oakley (2004: 191) suggests 'The

most important criteria for choosing a particular research method is not its relationship to academic arguments about methods, but its fit with the question being asked in the research'. Kelly and colleagues (1994) argue that by using only small-scale studies the researcher can be misled into believing that s/he has some knowledge that has not actually been collected. They use the example of work on sexual abuse and domestic violence arguing that most work on these areas have drawn on the experiences, interviews and discussion with women who have, somehow, made their lives public. For example most research on domestic violence is focused on women in refuges and this does not tell us if what is found here applies to those women suffering abuse who have not voiced their experiences. Kelly and colleagues add:

> Rather than assert the primary of any method, we are not working with a flexible position: our choice of method(s) depends on the topic and scale of the study in question. Whenever possible we would combine and compare methods, in order to discover the limitations and possibilities of each.
>
> (1994: 35–6)

As Kelly and colleagues (1994) argue, if feminist research is to be about women's experiences we must use our power as researchers to ensure that we have accessed all these experiences. Similarly, Toby Jayaratne (1983: 158–9) argues that it is important to have quantitative evidence which will counter the 'pervasive and influential quantitative sexist research which has and continues to be generated in the social sciences'. World in Focus 2.2 provides an example of a quantitative project which led to a positive change for women.

Several years ago we – Jen Marchbank and Gayle Letherby – undertook a piece of research focusing on perceptions and experiences of Women's Studies – 'Why do Women's Studies?' – using a mixture of qualitative (focus group interviews) and quantitative (a questionnaire, with some qualitative questions) methods. The focus group interviews enabled the generation of a series of statements that Women's Studies students themselves felt were relevant to Women's Studies and these were reproduced on a questionnaire asking respondents if they had heard the getting the job done. The first type were a problem while the second type were the best students. This was a lovely piece of data and I had no wish as a researcher to stop him. I listened, giving feedback in terms of head nods and indistinguishable 'umms'. However, as a feminist who did not share his assumptions about sexuality and power, I wanted to challenge him. When I left the office I was exhausted and unhappy about the interview. I had some good data but I had colluded with a powerful man in recreating understandings about women, sexuality and power.

(Ramsay 1996: 138)

Those who work for an emancipatory model of social research argue that in order to be ethically sound and non-exploitative research should be 'for' rather than 'of' those that are studied. Oakley (2000) gives an example of a research project that could be described as 'research of women' rather than 'research for women'. She cites a large research project on the social origins of depression and notes that the study resulted in a convincing explanation of the relationship between women's depression and their oppression. But there was no concern with whether or how women defined themselves as depressed, but only with how the state of women's mental health could be exposed and fitted into a system of classification developed by a profession of 'experts' on mental health (psychiatrists). Also, the researchers did not begin with a desire to study the situation of women or set out to give women a chance to understand their experience as determined by the social structure of the society in which they lived. The primary aim of the data was to study depression and women were selected as respondents because they are easier (and therefore cheaper) to interview, being more likely than men to be at home and therefore available during the day.

The response of some researchers to this is to argue that researchers should not aim to represent the 'other' – people that are not like them – in order to limit the possibilities of exploitation. However, there are problems here, not least because academia is not representative of all groups; in relation to gender, ethnicity, age, dis/ability and so on, which could mean that the experience of some groups remains unconsidered (Letherby, 2003a).

Issues of power are complex within research. And although there is an assumption that the researcher is always in control of the research situation and is the one who holds the balance of power it is often more complicated than this in reality. Therefore, we would suggest that it is important not to over-passify research respondents not least by assuming that they are always vulnerable within research. Some respondents do not feel disempowered by either their life experience or by the research relationship and it may be patronizing of the researcher to assume that the respondent needs to be empowered by the process. Also, as noted earlier, research relationships are fluid and jointly constructed and at times during the research process it is the researcher that might feel vulnerable and/or at a disadvantage. This may be the case when researching individuals who are older, more experienced, more knowledgeable and/or when undertaking research with people with sexist, racist, homophobic (and so on) views and attitudes (e.g. Cotterill, 1992; Collins, 1998). In addition to the emotional danger suggested here it is important to also acknowledge that research can be physically dangerous for researchers (Lee-Treweek and Linkogle, 2000).

Gendered analysis and re/presentation of research

Despite the fact that the balance of power is subject to re/negotiation during data collection and that this re/negotiation is affected by researchers' and respondents' (gendered, classed, racial and so on) identity, it is the researcher who is more often than not responsible for the final analysis and presentation of the data. Thus, researchers 'take away the words' of respondents and have the power of editorship.

In addition to the traditional 'scientific' approach being criticised for its sexist approach to subject and data collection it was also criticised because of the focus on theory-testing. Instead, those who challenge this approach argue, research should be ethnographic and describe 'life as it is' from which theories should be developed. One response was the development of 'Grounded Theory'. Grounded theory then is developed from data and aims to be faithful to the reality of situations (Strauss and Corbin, 1990). From this perspective the researcher does not begin with a theory and then prove it but allows the relevant theory to emerge from the data. Due to the concern to locate theory in respondents' worlds and the desire to reject abstract theory, grounded theory was once seen as highly compatible with a feminist approach (Morley, 1996). But many feminist theorists who initially rejected deductivism now reject grounded theory on the basis that no study (feminist or otherwise) can be completely inductive or solely based on grounded theory, as no work is free of politics and all work is theoretically grounded (Maynard, 1994b; Morley, 1996). Thus, as Liz Stanley and Sue Wise (1990: 22) argue 'researchers cannot have "empty heads" in the way that inductivism proposes' so one must acknowledge the gendered, classes, racial and so on intellectual and physical presence of the researcher.

Conclusion

As this chapter has shown, taking a gendered approach is relevant to issues of method, methodology and epistemology. Taking gender seriously not only leads us to challenge traditional research processes and products but to be continually vigilant of our own practice. Thinking critically about what we do and the relationship between this and what we get necessitates sensitivity to issues of gender and to other aspects of difference and diversity. Feminists have been instrumental in highlighting the importance of power and politics within research and

have foregrounded gender and other aspects of identity in their discussions of the relationship between the process and the product of research, and contemporary debate of method, methodology and epistemology within the social sciences and humanities is much more likely to be gender sensitive than in the past.

Further reading

Sandra Harding (1987), *Feminism and Methodology*, Milton Keynes, Open University Press and

Dorothy Smith (1988), *The Everyday World as Problematic: a feminist sociology*, Milton Keynes, Open University Press. Two classic texts that (amongst others) set the context for gender sensitive debates concerning method, methodology and epistemology over the past 30 years.

Gayle Letherby (2003), *Feminist Research in Theory and Practice*, Buckingham, Open University Press. A comprehensive text focusing on the epistemological, political and practical issues involved in doing feminist research. Overall, the book focuses on the relationship between knowing and doing.

Beverley Skeggs (ed.) (1995), *Feminist Cultural Theory: Process and Production*, Manchester, Manchester University Press. An edited book focusing on feminist examples of analysis of culture and cultural artefacts. Examples include 1950s female film representation; video-recorder use.

Liz Stanley (ed.) (1990), *Feminist Praxis: research, theory and epistemology in feminist sociology*, London, Routledge. Another edited text which focuses on a variety of methods and research topics.

In addition, a large number of articles on issues of method, methodology and epistemology can be found in the following journals: *Sociological Research Online* **www.socresonline.org.uk**; *Feminist Studies*; *Journal of Gender Studies*; *Signs*; *Women's Studies International Forum*. See if you can find others.

End of chapter activity

Focusing on any issue that interests you write a short (two-page) research proposal. Make sure that you pay attention to gender and other aspects of difference issues in relation to:

➤ the topic of research

➤ the respondent group

➤ access

➤ fieldwork

➤ analysis

Remember that your identity as well as those of your respondents is significant.

Part Two

Disciplines

In Part Two you will find discussion of a number of the main social science disciplines. Each chapter charts the history of the use of gender as an analytical category within one discipline. This history varies across disciplines:

➤ Some disciplines have moved towards quite comprehensive uses of gender as an analytical framework and had gender accepted within the mainstream of the discipline – see for example, Sociology (Chapter 4).
➤ Some have developed quite complex methods of analysis using gendered frameworks yet these remain on the margins of what remains accepted as the mainstream in that discipline – this can be seen to be the case in History (Chapter 3) where some aspects of the discipline resist.
➤ Some have developed strong gendered analyses and are beginning to examine what that means for masculinity as well as for feminine roles – see for example, Social Policy (Chapter 5).
➤ Some have developed gender as an analytical method but focused on women only – see for example, aspects of Psychology (Chapter 7).
➤ Some have utilised gender, or even sex, simply as descriptive tools, relating differences rather than analysing through a gendered lens – see, for example, Political Science (Chapter 8).
➤ Most, where a gendered analysis has been developed, have relied upon feminist work to do this task, often even when masculinity is under study – see for example, Anthropology (Chapter 6) and Pedagogy (Chapter 9).
➤ Some have developed methods of analysis that explore the complex and dynamic nature of gender – see, for example, Geography (Chapter 10) which investigates the ways in which the lived experience, significance and meaning of gender varies over space and time.

The fundamental point to remember is not that some disciplines have developed better or more sophisticated analyses than others. Rather it is the case that for some, acceptance of gender as an appropriate and 'proper' focus of investigation is closer to achievement than in others.

The discipline areas included here are not comprehensive – there are other areas of social science that could also have been included. The ones selected here have been chosen as they are indicative of the range of uses of gender within disciplines and the differing responses such developments have received in different areas.

If you read all the chapters in Part Two you will realise that gender is also employed differently in different disciplines, or within the same discipline at different times. If you have not already read Chapter 1, Gendered Perspectives – Theoretical Issues, you are advised to do so before beginning on any of the discipline chapters. This will help you see the different meanings of gender that are displayed. Basically gender can be seen to be employed in four broad ways:

1. Gender as a 'stand in' for women, that is gender is only mentioned where women and/or femininity is under investigation and discussion.
2. Gender as a binary, that is gender is utilised dichotomously. This view understands gender only as one of two poles: masculinity and femininity. Occasionally, this binary is simply a replacement for discussing two sexes, male and female and not gender at all.
3. Gender as fluid and consisting of a continuum rather than two opposing poles.
4. Gender as a category of useful analysis.

Introduction

In 1989 the journal *Gender and History* was launched with these words:

> *Gender and History* brings to the study of history the centrality of gender relations and to the study of gender a sense of history. As its editors, we seek to examine all historical social relations from a feminist perspective, to construct a comprehensive analysis of all institutions that take their gender-specific characters into account. In addressing men and masculinity as well as women and femininity, the journal will illuminate the ways in which societies have been shaped by the relations of power between women and men.
>
> (Davidoff, McClelland and Varikas, 1989: 1)

The next decade was a period of growth for gender and history, an examination of the articles published within this journal alone shows that work was being produced and published on ancient subjects to contemporary history, examining both masculinities and femininities. Topics include political movements and state bodies to the private domestic world of family and sexuality. It is not just this journal that has developed – so too has the whole field of Gender History, to a point where Pamela Cox (1999: 164) observed, 'Women's history, feminist history and gender history are becoming wonderfully unwieldly'. In this chapter we will review that development to provide a history of gender in history.

The study of gender within history has caused a considerable degree of controversy and debate in recent years. As a method of historical analysis gender aims to deconstruct essentialist notions of masculine and feminine, pointing out that 'the relations between the sexes are a primary aspect of social organisation; that the terms male and female identities are in large part culturally determined; and that differences between the sexes constitute and are constituted by hierarchical social structure' (Scott, 1988: 25). Many woman historians embraced this particular methodology finding that it allowed them to explore women's place in history in new and exciting ways. However, many others have found gender history difficult to accept because it challenges some of the assumptions which historians have held about the nature of history, knowledge, and historical truth. We will review the journey towards Gender History and how it is trying to deepen our understanding of history and how history is made.

'Traditional' history

Women have historically been subordinated in history. That is, not seen as historically significant. This is due to a number of factors: firstly, 'traditional' history favours male oriented elite studies; secondly, women have been excluded from the documentary evidence; and thirdly, women's spheres of influence, such as the home, have been ignored. Why the quote marks around traditional? Well, History is full of subdivisions, here are but a few: Contemporary History; National History; Prehistory; various regional histories; Ancient History; Medieval History; Social; Economic; Political and Military. We are not concerned here with these divisions but with the issue of gender. As such the quotes here indicate not that a particular subdiscipline is the topic but rather the whole gamut of history and how it has traditionally been presented, analysed and taught.

Given that histories were originally written by the literate and, usually, about the powerful, it is not surprising that the history of women and most men is absent from the canon. Also, many historical sources, such as estate account books, government records, trade receipts, archives of political office and military documents in many eras record only the lives and actions of the elite. Even standard sources such as census returns have been shown to provide an inaccurate picture (see A Closer Look 3.1). In addition, there are certain values attached to what is viewed as significant historically. June Hannam lists those viewed as the most significant: 'foreign policy questions, the development of formal political institutions and the growth of industry and commerce' (Hannam, 1993: 304). Clearly, those without a high profile in such areas were not documented, nor deemed worthy of documenting. On the whole, this has meant the exclusion of women from historical accounts generally and the reporting of only certain aspects of male experience, such as war, commerce and politics rather than men's role in the domestic sphere (Tosh, 1999: 2).

A closer look 3.1

Counting women out

A census is a periodic survey of a population and as such they are very useful for historians. However, they do have certain limitations. Discussing the 1861 census of England and Wales, Deirdre Beddoe states that:

> Census records are a useful source of information on [women's work] . . . but we should note that much of the work done by married women was invisible, i.e. untaxed and unregistered. Taking in washing, going out cleaning and babyminding at home were all largely invisible occupations.
>
> (Beddoe, 1983: 112)

Not only are there certain values as to what is viewed as historically significant, there are also certain assumptions. One such assumption is the idea that in prehistory the male hunter was the provider, this is deeply influenced by much later norms about male breadwinners.

> When anthropologists and archaeologists explain the origins of human societies, 'man the hunter' is the dominant figure. The meat he lugs to the family fire sustains his dependant wife and children. The powerful image of his protective brawn pervades Western culture from cartoons to serious science. A weak, subordinate woman is his implied mate: someone whose dull, repetitive chores need not be discussed because she contributed nothing to culture, history or civilization. The assumption that the representative human being is male is rooted in nineteenth-century speculation about the beginnings of human cultures. In the past twenty-five years some scholars have worked from different assumptions. What if 'woman the gatherer' returned to camp with most of the family food? What if women's choices were fundamental to human evolution? What if the first great human technological revolution – the discovery of agriculture – was carried out by women?
>
> (Shaver Hughes and Hughes, 1995: 10)

This is not to say that women have been totally absent from history – the recording of women can be categorised in two ways:

1. *Study of great women* – Women have been visible in (western) histories if they were deemed to be a 'great woman', for example Florence Nightingale, and despite the great achievements of such women, their representation reflects the influence of gender role norms of the historian, or more usually biographer. For example, most depictions of Nightingale are of the caring, 'lady of the lamp', not of the woman who had to endure extreme hardship, lack of provisions and sheer horror. What we know of Nightingale is deeply shaped by Victorian notions of appropriate femininity, which may also explain why Mary Seacole, a Caribbean women of African descent, who also nursed in the Crimean War is less well known.

2. *Study of women in men's world* – Women also begin to appear when they move into areas deemed to be important by historians. This includes women's role in national emergencies such as war when women entered munitions and other factories. Likewise when women became militantly involved in politics in the claim for suffrage.

However, as June Hannam (1993: 304) notes with reference to the representation of the 'Great Women' of the British Victorian era, such as Elizabeth Fry, 'It has been all too easy for historians, products themselves of a particular social context, to accept the Victorian model of women's essential passivity and domesticity and to minimize their contribution to historical developments'. Likewise, Joan Scott has argued that even

Stop and think 3.1

Think about historical topics you have studied, such as the Iron Age, Roman civilisation, the development of the European Union, the American Civil War and colonialism in Africa and South America. What do the topics tell you about what is valued in that curriculum? How are men and women present in that history? What did they do – were they leaders, soldiers, farmers, hunters, rulers, carers, inventors, parents, lovers, workers, teachers, reformers? Reflect on which words apply to the women and men you have studied – is there a balance?

radical historians, in this case E.P. Thompson (*The Making of the English Working Class*), reduce the role of women in radical labour politics due to their association of women with domesticity (Scott, 1988: 73). The point to understand here is that the views historians and other documenters hold of appropriate masculinity and femininity shapes the way the history is presented.

History of history

This history, like all histories, is partial. The history of gender in history begins with the history of women, with the adding in of women to the accepted historical narrative and the later, but parallel, development of adding in men where they too have been absent, such as men's role within households and as fathers. Feminist historians were the first practitioners of gender history, but now others have taken up the history of masculinity as well. This history of history begins with the reclaiming of women's past and moves on to consider the development of a history of masculinity. We then examine the critiques of such approaches and end with a discussion of the view that what is needed is an analysis of the construction of difference, be it gender, class, sexuality, ethnicity in historical studies. We shall begin with the project to uncover the history of women, sometimes referred to by feminist historians, as the development of a *herstory*.

The birth of women's history

The development of women's history really began in the early 1970s, a time when other areas of history were also becoming radicalised and previously marginalised experiences, such as those of the industrial classes, were being more closely examined, a new 'history from below' (Hobsbawm, 1971). From this time feminist historians began to meet the challenge of redressing the absence of women from historical texts and over the next twenty years a great deal of scholarship was produced in Britain and elsewhere. Subject matter was not the only thing to change – a concomitant development was in historical approach and methods.

One of the first jobs faced by feminist historians was to try to identify experiences in historical contexts and women's agency in creating historical change. A landmark text was Sheila Rowbotham's (1973b) book *Hidden from History*, which has been viewed as pioneering, opening up the way for a whole series of books and studies on women's lives, women's organisations, work experiences, leisure, family life and sexuality. The historical time of these works is significant: feminism and women's history were movements that fuelled each other. Women's history developed at a time when there was a burgeoning and active women's liberation movement (WLM) across the western world and when feminists believed that a knowledge of women's past would assist this movement. Feminist historians began with uncovering the role of women in the public worlds of politics and work. This has been described as 'contribution history', that is an historical project with the aim of illustrating to society that women have always contributed to its, society's, development and advancement. One critique of this approach is that it was seeking to find a place for women within the parameters of what was already accepted as history by men (Lerner, 1981) – that is in the areas of society valued by men rather than trying to show women's contribution outside of these parameters. In other words, 'contribution history' successfully indicated where women had achieved in a 'man's world' rather than questioned why history valued these areas over others.

Feminists, from the WLM and before, turned to history to provide evidence regarding women's abilities, as such this 'contribution history' had a strong political aim, that of legitimising women's demands, be they for education for girls or votes for women. As Joan Scott explains:

> If women's subordination – past and present – was secured at least in part by their invisibility, then emancipation might be advanced by making them visible in narratives of social struggle and political achievement . . . By recovering stories of women's activism, feminists provided not just new information about women's behaviour, but new knowledge – another way of understanding, of seeing, women, and another way of seeing and understanding what counted as history.
>
> (1996: 2–3)

Scott (1996) also points out that as the 'making women visible' project had to uncover new information, new facts, it raised another question – that being, why was it that these facts had been previously ignored? This project also encouraged the examination of new issues, such as domestic arrangements within households; sexual relations; culture and community. New questions were being asked and new facts being uncovered; this required new methods and new approaches (see World in Focus 3.1).

Sources and methods

Men controlled most historical records so women were often excluded (along with non-elite men) and where they were included it was frequently a narrow section: mostly, urban women from the elite social and ethnic classes. We have already noted gaps in documentary evidence regarding women's lives and even when records do exist they remain partial, as shown below in a statement on sources pre 1500:

Unfortunately, most surviving documents tell about the lives of elite women in civilizations and are seldom adequate to reflect the variations in women's experiences. Within literate societies the least information remains about rural women, working urban women, and slaves. Women's own spaces and cultures are poorly documented either because men were more often literate (except in Southeast Asia) or because men preserved records they perceived as significant. Glimpses of women's

World in focus 3.1

Differing foci of women's history

USA

Manuela Thurner argues that early Women's History in the USA focused on three areas: research into historical notions of femininity; biographies of the great and good and studies of women's organisations and collective actions, in particular suffrage. However, feminist historians soon realised that they were not challenging patriarchal history, rather they were imitating it. There was a move towards developing new methodologies and conceptual models, in particular concentrating on the development of a separate women's culture, family history and all-women institutions:

> this idea of a woman's sphere and a women's culture grounded in this sphere arguably became the major subject of US women's history. Not the least of its attractions was the fact that it opened up a vast space for research, discovery, and

interpretation, a space, moreover, in which women wielded power and enjoyed their lives.
> (Thurner, 2003: 3)

UK

Much early British work focused on the interplay of social class and gender, following a predominantly Socialist genre within social and economic history. The strong influence of Marxian thought in the 'history from below' approach did not assist women's history but actually marginalised the experiences and actions of women behind a main focus upon male workers organised against capital and for social change. British feminist historians have written on the sexual division of labour, women's labour movements, family and household structure, and the treatment of women as workers. The concept of patriarchy [Hotlink → Critical Looks, 1.1, 1.2 and 1.3, (Chapter 1)] was employed in many analyses as class struggle alone was found inadequate to explain the interrelationships of class, 'race' and gender.

Latin America

It has been argued that Latin American scholars were slow to develop Women's Studies and that what was developed early was not in the area of history. Now, however, according to Sueann Caulfield (2001) it is difficult to review the field due to the quantity and variety of work. She delineates three periods: firstly, from the mid 1970s–1980s when feminist historians were trying to 'carve out a space for historical perspectives within the burgeoning field of Latin American women's studies' (Caulfield, 2001: 452). Secondly, a renewed interest in colonial history which raised issues of morality, sexuality and everyday experience – this was especially strong in Brazil and Mexico. Related to this second category is a fusion of three traditions – family history, social history shaped by European micro-historical studies and, following Foucault, a cultural history. The third phase, as in other parts of the globe, was a shift from woman to gender.

romantic love for one another indicate that within the silences of gender-segregated cultures were many possibilities unknown to history. Women in nonliterate societies are least known to historians. The pasts of some can never be retrieved, though more may be recovered as scholars in many fields become sensitive to gender in origin myths, art and architecture, written texts, and oral histories.

(Shaver Hughes and Hughes, 1995: 5).

Trying to uncover information about the lives of previously ignored groups led to the development of a range of techniques, both by feminists and others, especially social historians. Scholars of women's history had to look to different approaches, such as social and cultural history, and to different sources such as diaries, to overcome this fragmented and partial view of the history of women. However, a great deal was also discovered by the application of established techniques to different materials, for example, document analysis not of parliamentary papers and minute books but of diaries, correspondence, hospital records, newspaper accounts of court cases, amongst others. All of these have revealed information on diet, household organisation, experiences of married women, servants and much more. Records of plantations, census data, and even missionaries have provided access to the lives of Black women in history. Another standard technique is the oral history interview, but what was non-standard was interviewing ordinary people rather than leading politicians and theologians. This method has proven to be particularly valuable where there are no written records. For those for whom keeping records in the past would have been personally dangerous, for example, lesbians and gay men (see A Closer Look 3.2), oral interviewing allows histories to be recorded, such as the oral history interviews in the Hall Carpenter Archives/Lesbian History Group (1989) study of British lesbians. Oral evidence may also raise new issues to the fore, not previously considered by the researcher.

Perhaps the greatest difference between feminist and 'traditional' historians is not in how they do history but in what they view as worth exploring historically. Feminist historians believe that the personal, emotional and family relationships of people

A closer look 3.2

Problems of sources in lesbian history

The Lesbian History Group was established in London in 1984. Here they comment on the difficulty of accessing the histories of such a marginalised group as lesbians.

Writing the history of women is difficult because in a patriarchal society . . . fewer sources concerning women exist and those that do have often been ignored as 'unimportant', or have been altered. The task of the feminist historian is first to rescue women from oblivion, and then to interpret women's experience within the context of the society of the time.

This is also true for the lesbian historian. In her case, however, the problem of sources is magnified a thousandfold. First, there is relatively little explicit information about lesbian lives in the past, though probably much more than we know about at the moment. Second, much important material has been suppressed as irrelevant, or its significance overlooked by scholars pursuing a different theory. Material may have been omitted as 'private' or likely to embarrass family or alienate the reader. Much of the evidence we do have has been distorted by historians who wilfully or through ignorance have turned lesbian lives into 'normal' heterosexual ones. Women can be ignored, but lesbians must be expunged.

Lesbians do not usually leave records of their lives. Those who do may not include any details which would identify them unmistakably as lesbians.

. . .

Even where the documents exist, their suppression may begin immediately after the author's death. Family members and literary executors withhold access to incriminating papers and sanction safe biographies . . . Scholars select material for publication to fit their preconceptions, often overlooking vital references because they are simply not equipped to see their significance. Publishers too will pander to market prejudice and omit controversial documents which may have legal repercussions.

Source: Lesbian History Group (1989: 3–4).

have as much historical significance as other relations such as between employer and employee. They also make the case that the power relationship between men and women has to be understood to understand history. This approach has allowed feminist historians to revisit existing historical materials and derive new, previously unearthed, analyses. Strikingly, it is not all that infrequent to find that established sources, especially modern ones, do document aspects of women's lives or even that respected historians have gathered data which is rich in women's experiences, it is just that this material has remained unpublicised or most often, unanalysed (Hunt, 2004).

Stop and think 3.2

Consider how you might conduct research into one of more of the following:

1. Slave life on the tobacco farms of Virginia, USA.

2. First Nations people in Canada.

3. Role of children as mine workers in seventeenth-century England.

4. Fatherhood in Ireland in the 1960s.

What methods could you use to collect data? What adaptations to standard methods would be required? What problems would you face? What analytical approach would be best?

History and masculinity

As feminists were raising new issues to historical awareness others began to realise that although history has been accused of being about men, it was perhaps only about some men and only about some aspects of men's lives. Women's history analysed the relationships between women, work and the domestic sphere and yet less was known about the relationship of men to the domestic sphere. The social construction of femininity, cults of domesticity, controls on women's sexuality, restrictions on women's religious activities were all becoming known and understood. Likewise, some began to turn the feminist lens onto men's experiences in such areas. This is the history of men as gendered persons, an historicisation of men's sex

roles. It began in the USA in the late 1970s, and again this time is of note – it is just after the beginnings of Women's History. However, although such work established a place for masculinity on the historical map, it remained specialised space. By the early 1990s John Tosh (1991) was putting forward a case for moving a history of masculinity out of specifically masculine contextualisations of areas such as work, men's organisations, men's clubs and family. Examples of such developments are the consideration of the very traditionally 'male' history topics of politics and war from a new perspective. As stated in a recent collection, the aim of this approach is to:

> address the masculinity of politics and war in modern history . . . to bring to the surface and unravel masculinity's relations with politics and war, relations that often took on a quality of such self-evidence that masculinity needed not even to be mentioned.
>
> (Dudink and Hagerman, 2004: 3–4)

[Hotlink → Violence and Resistance (Chapter 16)]

Analysing mainstream histories of national politics, of the state and of war using the lens of masculinity can and is providing new understandings, not just of masculinity but in the ways we can know about politics, the state and war. To do so means both uncovering political events and conflict situations that express masculinity directly and also 'relating . . . "unspoken assumptions" (e.g. male codes of honour) to the apparently unrelated exercise of power, and to political causality' (Thorne, 2000: 2). Not all historians agree that this is a worthwhile endeavour and some fail to see that investigations of masculinity are relevant to studies of, for example, nation building. In his critique of a leading feminist and gender history of Australian national development (*Creating a Nation*, Grimshaw *et al.*, 1994), John Hirst (1995) argues that gender is not of significance in national histories as nations were predominately created by the actions of men. In making this argument he seems not to consider that gender is an issue, in that the specific masculinities of these male nation creators shaped the nature of the Australian state that they developed.

As the activities of politics and war have been the domain of men more than women it is obvious that these provide historical moments that are ripe for analyses of masculinity, in particular hegemonic masculinity (Tosh, 2004) (**Hotlink → Gendered Perspectives – Theoretical Issues (Chapter 1)**. World in Focus 3.2 indicates a whole range of masculinities across Europe and how malleable these are.

Some political historians have used the concept of masculinity as a method of historical analysis, in particular showing how political arguments and campaigns employ idealised forms of maleness. These idealised forms present a particular 'racialised' view of masculinity. In the examples in World in Focus 3.2

nationality is very much part of the hegemonic masculinity. Such work as George Mosse's (1996) *The Image of Man* examine this intersection of 'race' and gender, showing how 'race', class, gender and religion all intersected across Europe building a model of manhood imbued with meanings of power and oppression. Such archetypes of masculinity required the construction of an 'Other', lesser man – often the men of lands colonised by Europeans or 'others' from within, such as European Jews.

One critique of the examination of masculinity in relation to political history is that despite the serious

World in focus 3.2

Masculinity and the politics of nation

Late-eighteenth-century Europe was a place of nation building. Creating a nation-state required a national identity, which would give the state legitimacy. In such times space is opened up to claims for inclusion by different groups, including women. John Thorne (2004) argues that at this time in Europe the idea of nation abounded with a prolific number of male roles and new forms of masculinity which aids understanding of the history of politics and the development of national political cultures. Here his work is extracted.

Not surprisingly, given the traditional prominence of warfare for masculine prestige, an updated and idealised version of the soldier provided one form of masculine claim on the nation, and vice versa. The volunteer ready to die in defence of the fatherland was the most obvious expression of this idea. The Prussian and German version . . . derived from the 'war of liberation' in 1813 against the Napoleonic occupation of Prussia, proved particularly

resilient. It resurfaced as the country faced catastrophe in the total wars of the twentieth century with calls in both 1918–19 and 1944–45 for male volunteers to sacrifice themselves in a last ditch defence of Germany . . . The equivalent myth deriving from the French Revolution was that of the volunteer of 1792 rising up to repel the Prussians at the battle of Valmy. This remained a powerful image of masculine Resistance used by the Communist Party during the Second World War. In like manner, Garibaldi and his followers in the 1860s incarnated a myth of national self-liberation by the volunteer soldier that remained potent down to the period of Fascism and the anti-fascist Resistance.

The keynote of these and other male myths of nation building was heroism.

. . .

The positive attributes of national masculine ideals were matched by the negative figures of the . . . Enemy – who might be pictured as either female or as a

derided or feared type of masculinity . . . English satire typically portrayed the half-starved and tyrannical *sans-culotte* as a man who could not afford to eat roast beef – a hallmark of John Bull's independent manhood.

. . .

Many registers of masculinity could be used to construct the image of the nation . . . [shown by an examination of] a domestic and deliberately anti-heroic British maleness during the Second World War. This had its roots in the self-image cultivated during the First World War of the 'Tommy' who met the horrors of the western front with irony and a cheerful indulgence in sport and in the music hall. Deployed in conscious opposition to the ultra-militarised masculinity of Nazi Germany, it also stood in marked contrast to the images of imperial manhood prevalent in the press and popular literature at the turn of the century . . . 'National' images of masculinity thus changed with historical circumstances.

Source: Thorne (2004: 27–30)

Stop and think 3.3

Look at the image in Figure 3.1. What can you tell about nation and masculinity from this image? What aspects of masculinity are celebrated here? What can this image tell us about the society to which this young man belonged?

Figure 3.1
Source: © Hultan-Deutsch Collection/Corbis

intent of the approach and the knowledge created, it is a study of masculinity and is only loosely associated with an examination of relations between and within genders. Social historians, however, have been more successful in showing how hegemonic masculinity has structured and defined social relationships, not just in terms of gender but also ethnicity and social class (see A Critical Look 3.1).

A critical look 3.1

Men in the domestic arena

Perhaps the most marked impact of the history of masculinity is in the arena of the family and domestic life. Until the 1980s the family was the domain of the demographic historian alone, that is those interested in mapping population changes and patterns. Feminists began the challenge to this monopoly when they brought the power dynamics within families into study, and then more recently the role of men began to be considered:

> The history of men in families simply did not exist until quite recently. The successes achieved in this field have not only made it possible to understand the family as an interactive group, instead of as a zone cordoned off for women and children; they have also begun to break down the gulf which historians traditionally observed between men's public lives and their emotional and domestic selves.
>
> (Tosh, 2005: 5)

As masculinity was studied within history it became evident that certain aspects resembled early feminist work on recovering the place of women, and aspects of 'contribution history'. John Tosh (2005) shows how a greater maturity developed in the historical analysis of masculinity:

> At first glance, the history of masculinity might appear to be another example of 'identity' history, in which the distinctive or exclusive experience of a specific social grouping stakes its claim for attention. Early work in the field sought to identify aspects of male experience which could be classified as 'gendered', by concentrating on activities which were self-evidently for men only: for example, single sex schools and youth organizations. But it soon became clear that to treat the history of masculinity in this way was a category error. The history of masculinity does not deal with a neglected group, nor can it be placed under the banner of 'history from the margins'. Rather, it is a new perspective which potentially modifies our view of every field of history in which men are the principal subject-matter – which is to say the overwhelming majority of written history.
>
> (Tosh, 2005:2)

Nonetheless, although both feminist histories and histories of masculinity have considered the role of gender as central, frequently studies of the gendered experience of history have focused on one alone. However, we are now moving on to the debates around the history of the relationship between femininity and masculinity.

Gender and history

Gender history has developed quite quickly, though this development has not been wholly comprehensive with most of the research focusing on the period since the late eighteenth century. Nor has this development been geographically even; existing as a healthy minority area in mostly, though not exclusively, western societies. Areas of strength include Britain, North America, India and Australia. Across Europe development has been uneven: in France many cultural and institutional barriers exist whereas in Eastern Europe and Russia gender history is only just at the beginning of development (Davidoff *et al.*, 1999).

A major influence on Gender History has been the work of Joan Scott (sometimes Joan Wallach Scott) (1988, 1996). Joan Scott has pointed out that the history of women and men as 'contribution history' does nothing to deconstruct the established notions of sexual norms of traditional history. She is not alone in this – Gerda Lerner (1981) has also made similar arguments and, as Manuela Thurner (2003) outlines, North American feminist historians have made a similar realisation. However, not all have enthusiastically moved in such a direction as Caulfield (2001) notes, many Latin American historians remain wary of postmodern approaches, frequently referred to as the 'cultural turn' (see Controversy 3.1). Having noted that some have reservations it is time to outline these debates.

Gender and historical analysis

Scott (1988) noted that feminist historians, like other historians, have traditionally been trained in the search for empirical information, for evidence. She also notes that feminists have sought out useful theoretical models to use to analyse gender in historical contexts. However, despite the quality of feminist work, she notes that 'For the most part, the attempts of historians to theorise about gender have remained within traditional social scientific frameworks' (Scott, 1988: 31). Scott recognised that the response of most non-feminist historians to Women's History in the 1980s was to argue that women had a history separate from men and that it was, therefore, of no concern to mainstream historians working on political or economic histories. This is a political dispute; those anti-feminists who were happy to accept the existence of Women's History are accepting that there is data to be collected, just that such data is not of interest to most other historians.

Scott argues that history needs to move beyond the collection and description of facts towards a focus upon different questions, questions that examine the connections between history and how history is currently created. Her main questions are summarised here:

1. How does gender work in human relationships?

2. How does gender give meaning to the organisation and perception of historical knowledge?

3. How have social meanings been constructed through language?

As such Scott critiques what she sees as the descriptive and reductive nature of historical practice, namely that history only describes rather than analyses historical events and by doing so merely reduces them to partial accounts, rather than offering explanations based on gender constructions of the period and in relation to the time of the creation of the historical reporting. She also argues that how gender is defined is vital to such analysis and an understanding of historical creation (see A Closer Look 3.3).

Scott (1988) also points to what she sees as limitations in the theories of patriarchy and social class, primarily as they are not able to explain, in her view, differences between women and between men. Scott's main points are that Gender History requires an investigation of how gender relationships are constructed and that gender is a 'primary way of signifying relationships of power' (Scott, 1988: 169). In addition, her critique of patriarchy and materialist (that is class based) explanations are that they have an essentialist notion that 'women' and 'men' exist as separate and

A closer look 3.3

Scott's definition of gender

In her groundbreaking essay on gender as an analytical category Scott (1988) notes that in its simplest usage 'gender' is used as a synonym for women, sometimes to indicate that the work is scholarly and objective by dissociating the work from the politics of feminism: 'In this usage, "gender" does not carry with it a necessary statement about inequality or power nor does it name the aggrieved (and hitherto invisible) party' (1988: 31). She goes on to discuss instances of 'gender' being used to investigate social relations between men and women and how this is limiting as issues such as war and politics have not explicitly been about such social relationships. She refers to these endeavours as inherently descriptive, and although this usage highlights the social aspect of the relationships between the sexes, rather than biological, it 'says nothing about why these relationships are constructed as they are, how they work, or how they change' (1988: 32–3). As such she advocated an alternative usage of gender, summarised below.

Gender-definition consists of two parts and several subparts. The core of this approach rests on the interrelationship of two tenets: (1) gender is a major component of social relationships based on perceived differences between the sexes, and (2) gender is a main way in which power relationships are signified. Following Michel Foucault (1980) she does not see social power as something coherent and unified but as a contested issue providing space for human agency.

To examine the first part, the social relationship between the sexes, requires exploring four subparts:

(a) The symbols available within a culture e.g. representations of women as Eve and the Virgin Mary. The questions for historians being what symbolic representations are raised, how are they raised and in what contexts?

(b) What are the normative concepts that limit the interpretations of symbols? These are derived from religion, science, politics etc. and frequently view men and women in opposition. These are the concepts that limit the presentation of women and men in history, making it unthinkable for Victorian writers to have considered Florence Nightingale as other than within accepted feminine norms of the times of the writer.

(c) A recognition that gender is broader than household and family relationships – including the labour market, politics and education amongst others as these are all places, as well as within the family, that gender is constructed.

(d) The fourth aspect is subjective identity. By this is meant an understanding of the ways in which gendered identities are built and how they relate to a range of activities and cultural representations of specific times.

Scott is keen to point out this model, what she refers to as a sketch of the process of constructing gender relationships, could also be used on any social process such as to discuss 'race', ethnicity, social class. In fact, she argues that in the nineteenth century in France, social class was expressed in heavily gendered ways: workers were encoded as weak and exploited by middle-class reformers but as producers and protectors by socialist and labour leaders. In doing so, she illustrates the interconnectedness of differing social relations.

distinct categories. Scott adopts an approach from postmodernism, seeing that

> . . . 'man' and 'woman' are at once empty and overflowing categories. Empty because they have no ultimate, transcendent meaning. Overflowing because even when they appear to be fixed they still contain within them alternative, denied, or suppressed definitions.
>
> (Scott, 1988:174)

Not all working in this area accept that these categories are 'empty and overflowing'; however, the field has always retained a consciousness of difference, not just gender difference but also other forms. The philosophy of the journal *Gender and History* illustrates this well:

In our commitment to publishing work which is exploratory of gender relations is a necessary implication that we believe that relations of gender are threaded through other forms of social relations – notably those of class, of race and of ethnicity. However, this does not entail an a priori assumption that gender is always of primary importance in describing or analysing particular historical moments . . . the analysis of gender requires examining the mutual determinations of, say, class and gender, or of race and gender or, most difficult of all, the inter-relation of all these dimensions.

(Davidoff *et al.*, 1999: 417).

Likewise, practitioners of Gender History also challenge the idea that there is any homogeneity (that is absolute sameness) in any of the categories of difference, usually gender, class, 'race' and ethnicity, or that these differences always operate in the same way across time and space (though it would also be remiss to say they are the only ones to hold such a position). Further, as Gender History examines the relationships among the genders and the changes within these, this cannot be achieved without a consideration and understanding of the way in which categories of difference interact (for example, Victorian notions of domesticity had different views of mothering for middle-class women than the role expected, and allowed, of African women enslaved on plantations in the Caribbean).

So, what differentiates Gender History from Women's History and the History of Masculinity are both the subjects of enquiry and approaches. In Women's History the subject is, of course, women, likewise histories of men have taken the main subject to be masculinity. In the case of Gender History the subject is not women and men, but power and the way that power is created through discourse and culture. This means that there are methodological differences too. We have already noted that feminist historians, as well as other historians of non-élite groups, developed new applications of traditional methods of historical investigation. Gender History differs from this, in that Women's and Men's Histories, especially the 'contribution' versions, remain rooted in empiricism whilst Gender History focuses more on interpretation. Whereas the story of early Women's Histories were of the things that women experienced and their reactions to events, the story of Gender History is about the subjective meanings attributed to sexual difference and how power operates via a gendering process. The objects of study then are phenomena, such as industrialisation, the economy, families, social movements, slavery and political ideas as well as gender, 'race' and

Controversy 3.1

Dealing with difference

Gender History, informed by a postmodern focus on discourse and the relationships between language and meaning, is sometimes referred to as a turn to culture. This linguistic or cultural turn offers a way of thinking about how society and individuals create meaning and also how meaning is affected by difference and diversity as well as all the potential for changes in meaning. These theories have been viewed as potentially very rich but also with great caution.

One critique of the postmodern approach is that too much attention to the construction of categories of difference detracts from the investigation of real activities, especially those of women. Others, such as Brazilian historian Maria Clementina Pereira Cunha, are concerned that a postmodern concern with power both hides differences between women, rather than dealing with them, and also obscures women's agency. This explains, according to Cunha, how some reports of Brazilian women's history look remarkably similar to those of Scandinavian women (Cunha, 1998, cited in Caulfield, 2001).

Yet, many attempts to include difference have resulted in the creation of a range of histories of difference, that is of Jewish Men, African Women, American Lesbians, amongst others, and this has been critiqued as simply using standard historiography applied to difference and thereby simply fixes and essentialises these categories without questioning where and how such identities arose.

class. Gender History seeks to explain how gender hierarchies are created, perpetuated and made acceptable and legitimate. As such it challenges the notion that there is anything natural or fixed about gender relationships, rather these relationships themselves become part of the meaning of power. To understand this more clearly it is useful to look at particular examples of changes to gender and power, one to create a new gender relationship and one reinforcing old gender relationships (see A Closer Look 3.4).

So, social change affects gender relationships [**Hotlink → Violence and Resistance → Uganda Case Study (Chapter 16)**]. Scott (1988) argues that alongside these changes come new kinds of cultural symbols, which permit us to reinterpret historical

A closer look 3.4

Change and constructions of gender and power

Social changes can result in renegotiations of gender relationships and the organisation of gender. Such changes then seek to become legitimated. Frequently the reorganisation of gender relationships can be contradictory.

War and Demography – after the First World War there was an imbalance in the numbers of women and men across Europe. In addition, many younger women had experienced relative freedoms of work in munitions and other factories. Such changes led to a questioning of the normative understandings of marriage in certain countries in the 1920s – a renegotiation to create new gender relationships – yet at the same time another response was the promotion by governments of pronatalist (promotion of birth and motherhood) policies (Riley, 1983) – a reaffirming of very traditional roles for women, that is as at-home mothers.

events and processes, some of which create new gender relationships and others that reinforce (supposedly) traditional relationships. Which one is successful is a political process, in that both sides are struggling for power and control.

We will end this section with an extended extract from Ida Blom (2004) which illustrates how gender and social class were employed to negotiate and renegotiate gender relationships with the state (see World in Focus 3.3).

World in focus 3.3

Clothing and nationalism

One signifier of gender is clothing [**Hotlink → Figure 1.2 (Chapter 1)**]. Ida Blom (2004) has shown how the duties and rights individuals hold within their nation are linked to the cultural formation of gendered national symbols, in this case national dress. Such national costumes are symbols that articulate the nature of a nation. Her analysis of national dress developments and practices in Norway and Iceland indicate the ways in which understandings of both gender and class are manifest in national symbols. Her observations are summarised here:

In its search for national identity the romantic nationalism of the 1800s in a number of European nations pointed to the peasant farmer population as carrier of

old traditions . . . The revival of national history meant an upgrading of folklore in the form of folk tales, folk dances, old recipes and not least folk costumes. To use 'folk costumes' – often clothes created on the basis of farmers' festive wear – signalled in many nations an understanding of national character. By analysing such processes . . . we can illustrate the changing significance of gender and class for national symbolism.

Similarities in these processes . . . can indicate more general traits. The folk costumes were *constructed* phenomena that were not identical with any of the clothing fashions that still existed, or had ever existed, in the peasant population. They were also used by the urban population and

signalled a sense of belonging to the national movement. To wear a national costume in Norway also indicated a critical attitude toward the new urban culture and a dislike of international fashion and manufactured clothing. The folk costumes were made by hand, and material made in Norway was preferred. In the beginning folk costumes were used by both men and women, but they gradually became mainly women's garments. While women continued to symbolise tradition, national masculinity changed. The peasant farmer as symbol of the democratic Norway was gradually replaced by a new, urban elitist nationalism.

. . .

In Iceland the folk costumes played a similar role. But here gender had a much more explicit

World in focus continued

significance. Only women used the Icelandic national costume, and attempts to create a male national costume was never any success [*sic*]. Furthermore, the Icelandic women's national costume was designed by a man. . . . It was also men, not women as in Norway, who tried to spread the custom of women using national costumes . . . meant to be a symbol of the nation as mother. The tightly fitted corset lifted the breasts which thereby also symbolised Iceland's

mountain landscape, while the skirt, which could be enlarged during pregnancy, indicated Iceland's 'fertile plains' – and the motherly bosom . . . the apron, which also belonged to the costume, pointed toward women's domestic duties.

. . .

   The symbolism of the Norwegian and Icelandic national costumes can be understood in two ways. That the national costumes in Iceland were used

exclusively by women, and in Norway more often by women than men seems to accentuate the polarisation of national femininity and masculinity. Yet at the same time the national costumes made women visible as members of the nation, and could thereby support arguments for women, as mothers and free individuals, to have full civic rights in the nation state.

(http://kilden.forskiningsradet.no/c18372/ artikkel/vis.html?tid=17561)

Conclusion

The Whig interpretation of history is one which views society as improving and advancing from one era to the next. A similar view could be taken with the histories described here, beginning with Women's History, via histories of masculinity and ending up with the new, 'improved' product of Gender History. However, this progress is not quite as linear or unidirectional as this. It is true that Women's History, undertaken by feminists in many countries, did create the momentum for the other two, but so did other academic activities, such as the development of sociological studies of masculinity and postmodernism's relativisation of power relationships. In addition, not all would accept some of the critiques laid at the door of older, feminist histories with their focus on patriarchy rather than on gender relationships. In particular, the accusation of essentialising the category woman (Riley, in Scott, 1988) can be viewed as overly harsh as considerations of differences have been included in Women's History (see Liddington and Norris, 2000).

   It is still the case that gender as a category of historical investigation is not universally accepted within the broader discipline. Work continues in all three areas covered here: at the level of uncovering women's hidden histories in countries where even the most fundamental aspects of women's lives remain undocumented through

to challenging the exclusions that remain within supposedly advanced nations (such as the assumption that histories of government policies have no need to include women).

Further reading

Sarah Shaver Hughes and Brady Hughes, (1995), *Women in World History*, New York, ME Sharpe. This two-volume collection provides extracts and readings from prehistory to modern times. Each section has an introduction situating the historical knowledge in the field which is followed by selected readings.

Joan W. Scott (1988), *Gender and the Politics of History*, New York, Columbia University Press. This is a collection of essays by the author covering topics from a review of Women's History and a reprint of her groundbreaking article 'Gender: A Useful Category of Historical Analysis'. It also includes two very interesting chapters, one addressing language and labour history and the other a discussion of the place of women in E.P. Thomson's *The Making of the English Working Class*.

Stefan Dudink, Karen Hagemann and John Tosh (eds) (2004), *Masculinities in Politics and War – Gendering Modern History*, Manchester, Manchester University Press. This is an exploration of masculinity in the 'age of democratic revolutions'. The geographical and political range is western covering the American Revolution, the Dutch Patriot movement of the 1780s, French and Prussian histories and hegemonic masculinity in times of war.

Gender and History – British-based journal publishing work from around the world.

Websites

The Victorian Web –
www.victorianweb.org/gender/genderov.html
This website is a project funded by the University Scholars Program at the National University of Singapore though it does seem to have a British focus. It covers literature, history and culture of the age and the representation of women in the arts. One caveat though – it does conflate gender with women – men are absent.

Institute of Historical Research –
http://www.history.ac.uk/ihr/Focus/Gender/index.html
The content of this site is Issue 8 (Spring 2005) of IHR's online publication, this one focusing on gender. It includes articles, other websites, book reviews, bibliographies and other resources.

End of chapter activity

Think about your last visit to a local history resource, such as a small museum; better still, go soon. Take note of the exhibits and how men, women and gender are represented. Does this change with the historical period? From the way men and women are presented in certain exhibits what can you derive is known about gender relations of these periods? What does it tell you about the construction of this history?

Chapter 4

Sociology

Key issues in this chapter:

➤ An historical critique of Sociology as gender blinkered.

➤ The influence of feminism on Sociology and Sociology on feminism in the development of a gendered Sociology.

➤ The sociological relationship between gender and other forms of stratification.

➤ Sociology, gender and politics and practice.

At the end of this chapter you should be able to:

➤ Critique mainstream Sociology from a gendered perspective.

➤ Show how feminism has influenced Sociology and been influenced by Sociology.

➤ Identify the relationship between gender and other forms of stratification such as class, age, 'race' and ethnicity.

➤ Reflect on whether Sociology is or should be a (gendered) political discipline.

In 1993 Stanley and Wise suggested that Sociology remained a male-dominated discipline, and this had implications for its theories, methods, research and teaching. Despite thirty years' criticism of the discipline for its male orientation and bias, little has changed. But in 2003 they argued:

> with regard to some sub-areas of sociological work . . . feminist thinking has in fact become central, and some feminist theorists have achieved canonical status in some aspects of social theory.
>
> (Wise and Stanley, 2003: 27)

Stop and think 4.1

Sociology as a discipline is often thought to be forward-thinking in terms of its receptiveness to feminist ideas and its sensitivity to gender. Liz Stanley and Sue Wise seem to be suggesting a particular shift in the last decade. Look through past copies of the journal *Sociology* (or other Sociology journals), which in 2007 celebrates its 40th year of publication, and try to identify any differences over time with respect to the consideration or not of gender.

Introduction

Sociology is the study of individuals and groups within society. It involves thinking beyond what is thought to be 'obvious' and/or 'just common sense'; it involves looking at the world in which we live our lives in a different way and moving beyond individual experiences for social explanations (Mills, 1959; Berger, 1967; Bauman, 1990). In explaining their work sociologists aim to use 'responsible' speech (which includes supporting arguments with appropriate evidence, acknowledging other relevant evidence and making transparent the research and presentation process) (see for example Bauman, 1990); similar to what Liz Stanley and Sue Wise (1993) call 'accountable knowledge'. So Sociology involves us in:

➤ thinking a bit differently about things;

➤ challenging beliefs that we have always taken for granted;

➤ being accountable for the knowledge we produce.

In doing this Sociologists can:

➤ widen the boundaries of knowledge by showing why individuals and groups act as they do, and;

➤ help us to understand the social structure in which we exist – i.e. in relation to social norms and patterns (what is expected of us) and the role of key institutions (such as the family, the education system, government, the criminal justice system and so on).

In addition some would also argue that Sociology is also useful for people who have a strong concern about social issues and social problems. Thus, Sociology can provide us with evidence to challenge existing norms and structures and argue for new ones.

Historically Sociology was a sexist discipline. It began at a time when there was a separation of industry from home and sociological attention was on the factory, the marketplace, the state – the public domain – the 'sphere where history is made' (Stacey, 1981: 6). Thus, as Ann Oakley (1974) argues, the theories and methods of Sociology were built upon, and from, men's view of and relationship to the social world. This she argues was because of the sexist interests and personalities of the 'founding fathers', the dominance of men in academic life and the unquestioning adoption of western societies' stereotypical views regarding gender roles. However, there have been many changes to the discipline since its conception in the nineteenth century and feminist sociologists have been particularly influential in challenging the male bias and in the development of a gender sensitive Sociology.

In this chapter we consider further – both historically and to date – the male bias within the concerns and practices of the discipline and the relationship between feminism and Sociology in the development of a gendered Sociology. The remainder of this chapter is divided into three sections. First, we consider 'The sexist history' of the discipline before going on to consider various aspects that have been relevant to 'Developing a gendered sociological imagination'. Having focused on the problem of sexism in Sociology and on the gender debate within the discipline we then go on to consider issues of 'Politics and practice' within Sociology with a particular emphasis on the significance of a taking a gendered approach.

The sexist history

In the beginning

In 1981 Margaret Stacey argued that because traditionally Sociology was focused – both in terms of empirical research and theoretical deliberation – on the public domain (the place where men dominated) this led to a 'conceptual straitjacket of understanding within which attempts to understand the total society are severely constrained' (Stacey, 1981: 189). The quotation in A Critical Look 4.1 shows us why.

So, focus on the public sphere led to Sociology being mainly concerned with areas and issues of concern to men and mainly concerned with research on

men and thus with theories of men. Even worse the research findings based on all-male samples were often generalised to the whole of the population resulting in women's experience being ignored or distorted and their subordination and exploitation justified (Abbott *et al.*, 2005). In summary then, Sociology has been seen as at best gender-blinkered, at worst sexist, leading some feminist sociologists to write and talk about malestream (rather than mainstream) Sociology. See for example, Abbott and colleagues (2005) who, alongside the large number of introduction to Sociology type texts, have produced one of the only texts which provides an overall feminist critique of the discipline at an introductory level (*An Introduction to Sociology: Feminist Perspectives*).

When writing about the history of Sociology most authors – both male and female – refer to the 'founding fathers' – or the 'Grand Old Men' (Delamont, 2003: 99) or the 'good ol' boys' (Wise and Stanley, 2003) of the discipline. Karl Marx (who was born in Germany in 1818 and died in London 1883), Max Weber (who lived in Germany and was born in 1864 and died in 1920) and Emile Durkheim (who was born in France in 1858 and died, also in France in 1917) are generally referred to as the founders of Sociology. Other key (male) figures in the development of the discipline as we know it today include Friedrich Engels, Talcott Parsons, Robert Merton, Sigmund Freud, Michel Foucault, Pierre Bourdieu, Erving Goffman, Georg Simmel, and Charles Wright Mills (although of course there are others).

However, there has always been a feminist challenge to 'malestream' Sociology as the origins of feminism date back to the same era as the origins of Sociology (Delamont, 2003). Furthermore, as Sara Delamont (2003) notes, just as we speak of 'founding fathers' it is possible to speak of 'founding mothers' such as, for example, Mary Wollstonecraft (1757–1797), Beatrice Webb (1858–1943) and Harriet Martineau (1802–1876). Yet, the work of these, and other women, is often hidden from the history of the discipline and the orthodox histories of Sociology give a partial account (as A Closer Look 4.1 demonstrates), focusing on what has been called 'The Grand Narrative'; the concern with the public (male) sphere.

A critical look 4.1

Concerns of early sociologists

As Pamela Abbott, Claire Wallace and Melissa Tyler (2005) note:

Sociology as a discipline developed in the nineteenth century, and early or 'classical' sociologists were primarily concerned with understanding political and economic changes relating to the development of industrial capitalism. These changes included the growth of factory production, new class divisions and relationships, the growth of a politically conscious (male) working class and the extension of political participation of the adult (male) population. A central aspect of this process [the development of industrial capitalism] was the increased separation of home from work, the separation of production from consumption and reproduction, and the development of an ideology that 'a woman's place is in the home'. Women became increasingly associated with the domestic (private) sphere of the home and with domestic relationships, and men with the public sphere of politics and the marketplace.

(Abbott *et al.*, 2005: 10)

A closer look 4.1

Re-reading the founding fathers

Sara Delamont (2003) suggests that whilst it is unreasonable and unscholarly to expect eighteenth- and nineteenth-century people to have a twenty-first-century position on gender it is reasonable and scholarly to expect contemporary texts about founding fathers to alert us to historically relevant sex-roles. This she says does not often happen. In addition Delamont notes that a re-reading of classic work and of less well-known work by the founding fathers indicates that they did think, write and theorise about issues of gender (although often in a stereotypical way) but this has been ignored in all of the well-known modern accounts (written by men) of their work.

One consequence of the lack of attention to gender within Sociology has been the identification of social class as the most fundamental form of stratification (hierarchically defined difference). Thus, class has been and is seen by many sociologists as the indicator and predictor of a wide range of individual and group social attitudes and attributes as well as an indicator and predictor of lifestyles and life-chances. Interestingly though until the feminist challenge from the 1970s onwards, social class was assumed to be defined for *all* members of a household by the occupation of the male who was defined as 'head-of-household' (Glass, 1954; Parkin, 1972; Goldthorpe *et al.*, 1980; cited by Jackson and Scott, 2002).

Further examples of sexist sociology

One early consideration of gender differences by a sociologist was the work of the American sociologist Talcott Parsons [**Hotlink → Gendered Perspectives – Theoretical Issues (Chapter 1)**]. Writing in the 1950s Parsons was concerned with age and sex in the social structure of the USA and he argued that there were natural differences between women and men which mean they are suited for particular roles in society (Parsons and Bales, 1956, Delamont, 2003). This sex-role theory, particularly dominant in the years from the Second World War until the (re)emergence of feminism in the 1970s, asserted that women have an instinct to nurture

which suits them for an 'expressive' (caring) role in the family; whereas male biology, which leads men to be more aggressive and competitive, means that men are suited to an 'instrumental' role in the family; providing economic support and links with the outside world. As such, biological differences were seen to constitute a practical and 'natural' basis for the sexual division of labour. Biological theories also often present heterosexuality as the 'normal' and 'natural' expression of human sexuality, and identify women and men as having different sexual needs and desires [**Hotlink → Gendered Perspectives – Theoretical Perspectives (Chapter 1; Hotlink → Family (Chapter 11); Hotlink → Sex and Sexuality (Chapter 15)**].

From this perspective then sex-roles were both associated with a certain status within society – in that men's roles where seen as more significant and important – and simultaneously provided a text, a script, for that role. Girls and boys, learn their script and their 'appropriate' roles through the process of socialisation. Girls and boys experience gender socialisation in different ways, learning appropriate behaviours, personalities and gender roles and developing their own gender identitification (own feelings and consciousness) [**Hotlink → Psychology (Chapter 7)**]. More recently the ways girls and boys learn gender roles have been subject to much critique as highlighted in A Critical Look 4.2.

Figure 4.1
Source: © Jackie Fleming

A critical look 4.2

Gender development

Sociological (and psychological) research has paid attention to various components and stages of gender development. In the 1970s and early 1980s especially there was a considerable amount of research which examined the differential learning processes of boys and girls. This included studies of such things as pre- and post-natal care, schooling, books, magazines and other media, clothing and toys. Many researchers have reported that there are different practices or expectations in relation to girls and boys which encouraged or reinforced 'feminine' behaviour in girls and 'masculine' behaviour in boys. A whole range of social processes have been identified as sites where gendered categories of femininity and masculinity are constructed. Sociologists have explored the diverse meanings attached to femininity and masculinity (see for example Oakley, 1981; Connell, 1987; Hearn, 1987; Seidler, 1989; Skeggs, 1997), so much so that there has been a shift towards talking about femininities and masculinities. Much of the sociological work on femininity and masculinity has adopted a socialisation perspective, in which the main concern has been how people learned gender stereotypes and internalised them. Although many sociologists accept that gender is learned and that socialisation plays a key role, an increasing number have pointed to the problems with taking a straightforward learning approach. Sylvia Walby (1990) argues that this approach still implies a static and unitary conception of gender differences: femininity is one set of characteristics that girls and women learn and masculinity another set that boys and men learn. She argues that this takes insufficient account of the different forms that femininity and masculinity can take and hence it does not account for diversity among women and men. This approach implies that each person is equally conforming to gender ideology and does not explore how masculinity and femininity vary according to a whole range of social factors such as class, age, 'race' and ethnicity. It treats people as relatively passive in their acquisition of gender identity. The emphasis on the passive learning of dominant ideology does not adequately recognise that people may resist, reject or subvert dominant meanings about gender (adapted from Chapter 7, Gender, in Marsh and Keating 2005).

Stop and think 4.2

Read the following and then consider the questions below:

John and Elizabeth Newson's (1978) UK based longitudinal study of the upbringing of children found that:

> The mothers in the . . . survey expressed a great deal of concern with traditional gender-role stereotypes. They were self-conscious or defensive about any deviation from the characterization of boys as rough, outdoor types, often grubby and careless of their physical appearance, interested in building, carpentry or mechanical model-making or in pursing technological hobbies. And of girls as: Following indoor pursuits, interested in making and exchanging gifts, writing stories and letters, buying or making clothes, keen on acting, dancing and so on.
>
> (from Newson et al., 1978, cited by Oakley 1981: 104–5)

The Newson's work was carried out nearly 30 years ago. Think about your own socialisation – was it gendered in the same way as children in the 1970s; if not what gender socialisation was there? What different types of femininities and masculinities can you think of?

In addition to a critique of traditional sex-role theory, as noted above, sociological work has been challenged both for its mis/representation of girls and women and for its treatment of boys and men as the norm and as essentially without 'gender'. Thus, work in the areas of education, work and leisure, deviance and criminal behaviour and so on have all been criticised for being gender blinkered. Just a couple of examples follow. From Delamont (2003: 132):

Sociology of education was almost devoid of research on gender, and of feminist perspectives, before 1980. Acker 1981 demonstrated the absence of gender as a topic and an analytic device by coding all the 184 articles published on education in the three generic Sociology journals [in Britain] (*Sociological Review, British Journal of Sociology, Sociology*) between 1960 and 1979. She concluded that a Martian arriving in Britain: 'would conclude that numerous boys but few girls go to secondary modern schools . . . that most students in higher education study science and engineering; that women rarely make the ritual transition called "from school to work" and never go into further education colleges. Although some women go to university, most probably enter directly into motherhood . . . and except for a small number of teachers, social workers and nurses, there are almost no adult women workers in the labour market.'

(Acker 1994: 30–31). [**Hotlink → Education (Chapter 13)**]

From Abbott *et al.* (2005: 231):

Most of the classical sociological studies of paid work were of men – of coal miners, affluent assembly line workers, male clerks, or salesmen for instance – and, until relatively recently, the findings of these studies formed the empirical data on which sociological theories about all workers' attitudes and experiences were based. Even when women were included in samples, it was (and sometimes still is) assumed that their attitudes and behaviours differed little from men's or married women were seen as working for 'pin money': paid employment being seen as relatively secondary to their domestic roles.

[**Hotlink → Work and Leisure (Chapter 14)**]

Even in areas more recently defined as being of sociological importance (often not least from the influence of feminism – see below for further explanation), such as the body and emotion, there is evidence of a one-dimensional view of gender. As David Morgan (1993: 70) notes:

where issues of men and their bodies do come under sociological examination, the consequences are often limited and disappointing. Thus accounts with strong sociobiological overtones of body language or bodily abuse in discussion of young men and agro, for example (March 1978), tend to present a relatively unproblematic and depoliticised equation of masculinity and violence. These kinds of emphasis are, or were, sometimes to be found in writing associated with men's studies or more critical accounts of men and masculinity. Here, a somewhat one-dimensional picture of men and their bodies

emerges, one over-concerned with hardness, aggression and heterosexual performance, a kind of 'over-phallusised picture of man'.

Historically, and sometimes to date, then, Sociology paid less attention to women and girls and their experiences and presented boys and men's experience as unproblematic. Thus, it failed to consider both girls and women's subordination and oppression – both outside of the discipline and inside of it – and when the gender order worked for and against boys and men. It also focused on areas of social life (the public sphere) to the detriment of others (the home and the private lives and experiences of individuals). [**Hotlink → History → History and Masculinity (Chapter 3)**]

Before we go on to consider in more detail some of the challenges to this sexist/ungendered approach and reflect on the development of a gendered Sociology it is interesting to reflect on the work of Charles Wright Mills (1959) who argued that the sociologist must be able to look at the familiar in social life and see it afresh. To do this (he argues) it is necessary to develop a sociological imagination which must include:

➤ a sense of biography

➤ an awareness of history

➤ an awareness of the social structure.

Thus, for Mills (1970[1959]: 12):

The sociological imagination enables us to grasp history and biography and the relations between the two within society. That is its task and its promise. To recognise this task and this promise is the mark of the classic social analyst . . . No social study that does not come back to the problem of biography, of history, and of the intersections within a society, has completed its intellectual journey

So, the sociological imagination is a tool that enables those who use it to understand individual experience with reference to time and place. It also enables us to understand and explain the relationship between 'the personal troubles of milieu' and 'the public issues of social structure'. In other words, it enables us to question whether those problems and experience that are sometimes defined as private and thus the responsibility of the individual are really the result of wider issues relating to society and societal norms and values. Despite the sexist terminology (Mills uses the generic 'he' and terms such as 'intellectual craftsmanship' and 'his' for 'his own low level of awareness' of the male-dominated nature of Sociology at that time; (Oakley, 1974: 24) feminist sociologists, and others who take a political approach to the discipline have been influenced by his work as will become evident in the remainder of this chapter.

Developing a gendered sociological imagination

In a recent debate in the journal *Sociological Research Online* concerned with the 'Future of Sociology' John Scott, reflecting on recent influences and changes within Sociology, wrote that: 'The most striking transformation of professional Sociology has been in its relation with cultural studies' (Scott, 2005: 5.1). To this Liz Stanley responded: 'A better case can surely be made for the more fundamentally transformative impact of a combination of feminism, gender and women's studies, in a world-wide context and also in the UK, on the domain ideas and working practices of Sociology and most other disciplines' (Stanley, 2005: 4.1). In this section we show how we support Stanley's pronouncement through a case-study consideration of the professional organisation of Sociology and sociologists and a brief overview of key developments in the discipline over the last 30 years or so, including the attention paid to the relationship between gender and other forms of stratification.

The British Sociological Association tackles gender

When I started in Sociology as a career [in the early 1950s] there was an awful lot of hostility to women, really a lot. [A male colleague] took me to one side and said 'You'll be much happier if you give up the idea of a career and stay at home and have a family' ... it was accepted that women just had to fit in, and must not raise gender issues.

(interview in Platt, 2003: 89)

A Closer Look 2 begins to show how things have changed in British Sociology since the 1950s.

A closer look 4.2

British Sociological Association – Golden Jubilee

In 2001, the British Sociological Association (BSA) celebrated its Golden Jubilee. In *Network* – the professional newsletter of the organisation – several past presidents of the association wrote about their views of the highlights and lowpoints in British Society over the previous 50 years. Here are some examples:

Sheila Allen, BSA President, 1975–77

A major breakthrough of the mid-1970s was made by those who took seriously the need to develop a Sociology which included both women and men as integral to a more adequate conceptualisation of society and so enabled many who followed to address more fully the realities of social life.

Margaret Stacey, BSA President, 1981–83

As a sociologist qualified in 1943, my first highlight was a meeting, half a century ago, which led to the foundation of the BSA. I recall a largely male gathering, made up of people from diverse backgrounds but with a common interest in the social. Living then as a 'College wife' in Swansea, I was academically isolated and without (paid) work, so it was great to meet with others in that action mode.

Looking back on the following years, the brightest light shines on the revolt of the women at the 1974 Aberdeen conference: a most exhilarating experience. The outburst undoubtedly shocked the men (and possibly some of the women). The BSA has never been the same since: for the first time serious attention was paid to the institutional masculinist bias and the empirical and theoretical neglect of gender. We still have some way to go.

David Morgan, BSA President, 1997–99

I did not attend the 1974 Aberdeen Conference which took as its theme 'Sexual Divisions and Society'. However, subsequent accounts suggest that this was a significant watershed in the development of British Sociology. Here, it seemed,

> we were dealing with something of a paradigm shift rather than simply the raising of a set of equal-opportunities issues. A critical gendered perspective within Sociology went well beyond well-established, if limited, discussions of 'the changing roles of men and women' to consider all areas of sociological enquiry including the higher reaches of theorizing, methodology and epistemology.
>
> Source: Network: Newsletter of the British Sociological Association (2001: 80: 1–4).

The 1974 conference mentioned in A Closer Look 4.2 is a significant landmark in the development of a gendered Sociology in Britain. As Jennifer Platt (2003), in her authorised history of the BSA notes, it seems possible that the conference topic, and the resultant political activity, was accidental rather than a planned political event. Originally the conference topic was to be 'Europe' but the BSA could not afford the expenses of the speakers from Europe that it was felt the topic required. The Association's Executive Committee's (EC) discussion of alternative themes resulted in the choice of 'Family', a topic on which there had not been any previous conference, and somewhere along the line this became 'Sexual Divisions and Society', a title reflecting ideas becoming current in the women's liberation movement.

At the conference a Women's Caucus was founded and Platt (2003) suggests that this appears to have been a spontaneous response amongst women attending the conference although a similar Caucus had been operating in the American Sociological Association (ASA) since 1969 and some women members of the BSA had spoken with American women at the International Sociological Association (ISA) World Congress of Sociology in Bulgaria in 1970. The formation of the Caucus was announced formally to the BSA after the conference and a related BSA study group on Sexual Divisions and Society was also formed.

Following the conference two volumes of papers were published: *Sexual Divisions: Process and Change* (Barker and Allen, 1976a) and *Dependence and Exploitation in Work and Marriage* (Barker and Allen, 1976b). As Miriam David (2003: 65) notes these high-lighted feminist concerns with traditional Sociology and attempted to open up debate on gender relations:

The papers in this volume thus deal with aspects of social relationships consistently neglected by sociologists, and ridiculed or denigrated by some. But in so far as sexism constitutes unproblematic, commonsense behaviour in contemporary British culture, it should not surprise us that it appears in Sociology.

(Barker and Allen, 1976a: 2)

At the Annual General Meeting of the BSA at the annual conference in 1975 the newly established Working Party of the Position of Women in the Profession put forward recommendations which were referred to the EC for 'urgent consideration'. The recommendations were that:

(i) The BSA should ask sociologists to eliminate all enquiries, both overt and covert, relating to the applicant's personal life, particularly marital status and child care, when interviewing potential students or staff.

(ii) Sociology department heads should be asked to review their staffing position and if they find a sex imbalance, they should consider how this came about. Particularly, they are asked to review their appointing and promotion polities.

(iii) The BSA should encourage systematic research into the position of women in general and in the profession in particular.

(iv) The EC (Executive Committee) should seek appropriate machinery to ensure that close attention continues to be paid to research, and action taken to eliminate the present inequalities between men and women sociologists.

(Platt, 2003: 92)

Further work by this group and the associated Working Party on Social Relations Associated with Sex and Gender in Sociology and Social Policy courses in Higher Education led to the formation of a subcommittee of the EC. The mandate of the Equality of the Sexes Subcommittee was:

to investigate and advise the BSA on policies which contribute towards the equality of access to, and equal treatment of, women sociologists within the profession, to advise the BSA on making recommendations for non-sexist teaching and research in Sociology and which contribute positively towards the position of women in society; to investigate, in conjunction with the Professional Ethics Committee complaints alleging discrimination against women and allied matters . . . [and] also deal with cases of discrimination against individual men, should it ever become a problem.

(Platt, 2003: 93)

This raised the question of the role (if any) for men in developing a gendered Sociology. Tensions emerged at the 1975 BSA conference when some men wanted to attend Caucus. The response to this was:

as ours is in essence a political struggle, we think it important that members of this disadvantaged minority should work together, without outsiders, however sympathetic, be they men or non-sociologists, to share common experiences, define our objectives, forge our policies and consolidate our achievements.

(*Network 1976*, cited by Platt, 2003: 101)

However, despite the support that many women have received from Caucus (it met at, and outside of, the conference until the late 1990s), its help in the promotion of a more egalitarian community of sociologists, we acknowledge that there are problems with this type of separatism:

I had difficulty with certain aspects, maybe because I didn't understand well enough. There seemed to be a thread running through the debate in the BSA which said we must have private meetings and debates, and I think I, with one or two other men, felt that was all very well but why didn't they engage back with us? For those women we the men were the problem, so tell us about it, let's have it out, what were the issues.

(Interview with pro-feminist man in Platt, 2003: 101)

In practice the epithet 'feminist' has been hijacked for a subjectivist position within Sociology that some of us rejected back in the 70s . . . As an academic strategy . . . it requires no change from men . . . it simply sets up an alternative channel of work for women, and principally about women.

(Barrett, 1986: 20, in Platt, 2003: 101)

Yet, it is important not to negate the very positive influence of feminism and the women's movement on the BSA and on professional Sociology in Britain. As Platt (2003: 102) notes, outcomes include:

➤ *Sociology* (one of the official journals of the BSA) is now normally edited jointly by a man and a woman, and women have become the majority among authors of its articles.

➤ Two annual conferences since the 1974 have had a gender theme, and those which did not have almost invariably had a gender stream, whatever the theme topic.

➤ Female plenary speakers have become much more frequent at conferences, and the proportion of women non-plenary speakers has risen (with variations by conference topic) until at half of the conferences from 1991 to 2000 they were in the majority.

➤ Several study groups have been founded which deal with gender and women's issues.

➤ Women have become the majority of executive members, and the sexes have, while not alternating mechanically, been very evenly represented among the officers (Chair, Vice-Chair and Treasurer).

A gendered sociology for women and men

So what of the changes in the writings and teaching of Sociology? Referring to two specific areas – the Sociology of the family and of sexuality – in 1976 Diane Barker and Sheila Allen wrote:

It might be expected that work on gender relationships would be most advanced and the theory the most critical. However, it suffers from a marked lack of status in British Sociology, deriving from its lack of 'theory' – except for Parsonian functionalism, its concern with the so-called non-work/non-market area of social activity, and its attention to women and children . . .

There is an even more marked lack of sociological interest in sexuality (human sexual conduct).

(Barker and Allen, 1976a: 2)

With these types of omission in mind, Abbott and colleagues (2005) note that the feminist challenge to mainstream/malestream Sociology is one that requires more than an 'add on' approach but a radical rethink of the content and methodology of the whole discipline. Thus, it is important not to just see society from the position of women as well as from the standpoint of men, but to see the world as fundamentally gendered. This they say has had implications for not only the areas that sociologists study but the theories they develop.

In addition to the changes in the BSA and other professional Sociological Associations the 1970s was a decade of importance in relation to the publishing of feminist Sociology. For example, Ann Oakley published three texts in the 1970s that were challenging and controversial in gender terms. The first – *Sex, Gender and Society* (1972) – offered a critique of traditional sociological concepts and set out new approaches to considering differences between men and women. As David (2003) notes, a number of feminist writers have hailed this as innovative in introducing the term 'gender' into social sciences. Oakley followed *Sex, Gender and Society* with *Sociology of Housework* (1974) and *Housewife* (1976) which drew on her material from her doctoral studies on the lives of mothers with pre-school children – not concerned with motherhood but with women's household work:

> The two studies and their particular focus were, interestingly, very much products of their time and the key conceptual notions about women's lives in families in the 1960s and early 1970s. They may also have been influenced by American approaches, in particular that of Betty Friedan's (1963) notion of the 'problem without a name' addressed about the concerns of American middle class housewives. They focused . . . on women's lives as wives, and drew on the traditional or then conventional sociological views about work and how to understand and analyse work as an economic activity.
>
> (David, 2003: 77)

Oakley's work challenged the myths and stereotypes surrounding gendered behaviour in general and housework in particular. In A Closer Look 3 we provide a little more detail on Oakley's groundbreaking work and its relationship to more recent work in the social sciences:

A closer look 4.3

Oakley (1974) undertook empirical work with 40 London housewives. She found that on average women spent 77 hours a week doing housework and that working-class women liked the housewife role but disliked the tasks whereas middle-class women disliked the label 'housewife' but did not mind the tasks. Not surprisingly the middle-class respondents had better working conditions and more resources (everything from running hot water to freezers and fitted carpets).

Since the 1970s there has been much more research on the gendered experience of housework and both men and women have been studied. In addition attention has been paid to other aspects of difference such as families with children and not; families where there are two wage earners, families from different cultural and ethnic groups and so on (Delamont, 2003). The research in this area has also broadened beyond looking at who does what and how. For example the work of Judy Wajcman (1991) who reflects on whether developments in domestic technology are liberating or oppressive and Sarah Pink (2004) who considers the relationship between how homes are defined by smells, sounds, textures and objects and what this tells us about gender roles and relationships.

Oakley later went on to consider several other issues including childbirth, miscarriage and motherhood, all issues previously taken for granted and considered not necessary of sociological attention. Overall her work demonstrated in her own words the 'sociological unimagination' (Oakley, 1980: Ch. 3) of mainstream sociologists for ignoring these issues. In 1980 Oakley wrote: 'The trouble with Sociology (as with many other academic subjects) is that it is not merely sexist on the surface, but deeply and pervasively so' (Oakley, 1980: 2). A cursory look through any Sociology book catalogue or in any library will demonstrate a significant amount of work challenging traditional sociological perspectives on work, education, the family and so on, work which demonstrates how gender shapes the experiences of women and men differently in many areas of social life and remains a source of inequality in society. It is not only women sociologists who are interested in these topics and Jeff Hearn (and colleagues), who along with other male sociologists such as David Morgan and Robert Connell, has always focused on gender in his work, reminds us that there is still more to do:

> Further exploration of the complex dynamics surrounding negotiations between women and men in relationships . . . would be welcome. It would be interesting to see how and when, if ever, women and men form coalitions through a politics of reconciliation, and how gender constellations at 'work' and in the private 'sphere' influence each other.
>
> (Hearn, 2002: 399)

In addition to the gendering of traditional sociology, under pro/feminist influence new topics, new intellectual spaces and new definitions of 'knowledge' have arisen. Pro/feminist sociologists have highlighted, amongst other things, the importance of turning our (gendered) sociological imagination to the study of ethics, caring, bodies, emotions, science and technology, violence against women and children including domestic violence, food and drink and travel [**Hotlink → ISSUES – Interdisciplinary Perspectives (Part 3)**]. Some of these issues are the subject of whole chapters in the third part of this book; for now we provide a few further examples of thinking sociologically about gender, gender roles and gender relations in A Closer Look 4.4.

Private parts and secret places . . .

How hard one 'looks' at genitals and what one 'sees' is not constrained by the optic nerve but by ideology. Given gender socialization, boys probably look at each others' genitals more than girls do. This is not because boys' genitals are objectively more obvious than girls' but because 'male' genitals have a different sociological import.

(Kessler originally 1998 in Jackson and Scott, 2002: 452)

Caring . . .

There is a clear relationship between gender and caring. While elderly and disabled married women may get care from husbands . . . the vast majority of carers are female, and bear the double burden of the physical labour and the guilt. The caring that starts with motherhood extends far into the future, while the duties of being a daughter loom on the horizon.

(Delamont, 2003: 45) [(**Hotlink → Social Policy (Chapter 5)**)]

Friends . . .

. . . girls and boys . . . sometimes use different rhetorics to describe their same-gender relationships: boys talk about 'buddies', 'teams', and 'being tough', whereas girls more often use a language of 'best friends' and 'being nice'.

(Thorne originally 1993 in Jackson and Scott, 2002: 292)

A closer look 4.4

Gender is everywhere

Talk . . .

. . . the uses women make of the telephone are not taken very seriously. Jokes about women gossiping on the telephone are familiar to everyone . . . Women's talk has no high social prestige: it is mostly described in rather negative terms such as 'chatting', 'visiting' or 'gossiping', and is often considered to be idle and a waste of time . . . All these familiar negative connotations related to women's talk and women's sphere are also recognisable in discourses surrounding women's uses of the telephone.

(Frissen, 1995: 80 and 87)

Stop and think 4.3

Take one of the following topics – emotion, technology, body, sport, food and food preparation. How might a gender sensitive Sociology challenge stereotypical views of your chosen area?

Such work has led to both a challenge to the traditional sociological curriculum and a challenge to what should count as knowledge, what is worthy of study [**Hotlink → Psychology (Chapter 7)**]. Feminists insist that not only is the 'personal is political' but 'the personal is also theoretical'. Recognition of this includes valuing reflexivity and emotion as a source of insight as well as an essential part of research (Okley, 1992).

Sociology then, is no longer gender-blinkered and includes the critical study of women's and men's lives – see Chapters 1 and 2 for discussions on why and how a gender sensitive approach includes a focus on female and male experience. However, the debt that Sociology owes to feminism in terms of these intellectual achievements is not always acknowledged/ recognised, as A Critical Look 4.3 demonstrates.

In addition, it is possible to argue that the influences and challenges of feminism and of a gender sensitive Sociology remain ghettoised and marginalised. Abbott *et al.* (2005) suggest that this is particularly relevant in terms of sociological theory which remains heavily dominated by male thinkers and writers. Furthermore, in the 1990s we experienced a backlash to feminist ideas, both in the academy and outside of it (Coppock *et al.*, 1995; Delamont, 2003). All of this leaves some feminist sociologists concerned to continue to challenge the mainstream/the malestream. Others though are keen to shake off the label of lesser, of secondary. For example:

A critical look 4.3

The Reith Lectures*

In 1967, Professor Sir Edmund Leach, a social anthropologist was invited to present an analysis of family change and family life in the post-Second World War period. This was the subject of his Reith Lectures. Thirty-two years later Professor Anthony Giddens (now Lord Giddens), a sociologist, also spoke about the family in his Reith Lectures. In the period between the two presentations sociological analysis of the family had developed considerably [**Hotlink →Family (Chapter 11)**] not least because of the influence of feminist concepts and theories and the associated recognition of recognising the relationship between the personal and the political. Thus, although he did not focus on feminist contributions, Giddens considered questions of the family and the 'personal' in ways that many social scientists had chosen not to before, foregrounding an agenda set by feminists.

Source: Adapted from David, 2003: 40–1.

* Reith Lectures are an annual series on radio given by leading figures of the day. Broadcast by the BBC they began in 1948 in honour of the first Director-General of the BBC, John Reith.

National sociologies are frequently very different from each other and it is difficult to generalise across (using examples we are familiar with) ex-Soviet now Russian Sociology, Finnish Sociology, South African Sociology, US Sociology, and UK Sociology. Moreover, these differences multiply depending on where people are positioned in the hierarchies of any national Sociology, as well as concerning the particular sub-areas or specialisms they are involved with . . . Given the proliferation of sub-areas, specialisms and national differences, the idea that there is 'a mainstream' becomes difficult to sustain, for it is more a matter of centres and peripheries in each of these areas of activity, with their own key texts, dominant ideas, gurus, preferred ways of working, journals, book series and so forth. Consequently any claim that feminist Sociology is 'other' makes little sense to us – it all depends on which national Sociology, the specific feminist Sociology or sociologist, where people are organisationally located, and what sub-area of specialism is being referred to.

Here for instance (and again with regard to UK Sociology in particular), ideas about the work/leisure relationship and domestic divisions of labour, or concerning reflexivity and the grounded nature of sociological modes of inquiry, have gained wide currency but are not seen as particularly feminist in character. However, those of us with 30 year involvement in the discipline can note that the emphasis given them in feminist teaching, debate and publications have played an important role in ensuring their wider sociological currency.

(Wise and Stanley, 2003: 25–6)

Putting a different twist on the argument, rather than insisting that Sociology needs feminism, Stevi Jackson (1999: 2.4) argues that feminism *also* needs Sociology. Jackson is concerned that the turn away from issues of structure and material in/equality to issues of culture in the social sciences is detrimental to the critical study of gender. Thus:

That non-sociological accounts of feminist theory are so pervasive is a result of shifting disciplinary hierarchies and changing intellectual fashions. It has been argued that the 'cultural turn' of the 1980s led feminists to shift their focus from 'things' such as housework, inequalities in the labour market or male violence – to 'words', to an emphasis on language, representations and subjectivity (Barrett 1992) . . . While there have been theoretical gains as a result of these shifts, much has been left out, in particular the older emphasis on the material underpinnings of gender inequality. Neither sociologists nor feminists can afford to lose sight of the materiality of social relations but this does not mean ignoring issues of language, culture and representation.

(Jackson, 1999: 24)

Gender and other differences

The opening up of new areas of study within Sociology has been accompanied by the challenge of difference and diversity. Thus, just as feminist influence has led to the consideration of new topics so the recognition of the importance of gender as a marker of difference between people has led to similar considerations in terms of other differences. Differences such as, for example, 'race' and ethnicity, sexuality, age, (dis)ability and differences related to places i.e. local, national and global location. As noted above, Sociologists label the social and cultural differences between people and the associated differences in terms of power (or lack of it) and opportunity (or lack of it) stratification. Stratification is a feature of all societies but varies between and within societies and a lower place on the hierarchy leads to social exclusion, exploitation and powerlessness (Macionis and Plummer, 2002; Abbott *et al.*, 2005). Consider the relationship between gender, age and community in World in Focus 4.1.

Traditionally sociologists have tended to argue that in capitalist societies class is the primary form of stratification but if we consider women's experience worldwide we can see the importance of recognising gender as a form of stratification (for example, see World in Focus 4.1 and 4.2).

As noted elsewhere in this book, although feminists were the first to 'take gender seriously' they have been criticised for lack of attention to other differences. bell hooks (in Marsh 1988, originally 1984) encourages us to reflect on the disadvantages of focusing on one form of difference (measure of stratification) to the exclusion of others:

As a black woman interested in the feminist movement, I am often asked whether being black is more important than being a woman; whether feminist struggle to end sexist oppression is more important than the struggle to end racism and vice-versa. All such questions are rooted in competitive either/or thinking, the belief that the self is formed in opposition rather than compatibility. Rather than see anti-racist work as totally compatible with working to end sexist oppression, they are often seen as two movements competing for first place . . . Given the fear of being misunderstood, it has been difficult for black women and women in exploited and oppressed ethnic groups to give expression to their interest in feminist concerns.

World in focus 4.1

Boys and girls and exclusion

Research by Russian sociologists has highlighted that 'street children' have begun to be recognised as a prominent social problem in post-communist Russia . . . children aged under 13 comprise about 50–60 per cent of the total number of street children . . . most working street children in Russia are boys; the same is true of children involved in criminal activities. Girls on the other hand are over-represented in underage prostitution and some 1,000,000 girls and young women in Russia are thought to be working as street prostitutes, as call girls, or as prostitutes in parlours or bars or clubs. (p. 119)

. . .

Source: From Abbott *et al.*, (2005).

World in focus 4.2

Gender and stratification

We know that the material conditions of women's lives worldwide are worse than those of men. Worldwide, women are poorly represented in ranks of power, policy and decision making. Women work more and their labour is of less value and care work and emotion work are also gendered

with women more likely to bear multiple burdens both at home and at work. . . . heterosexual relationships and the patriarchal family are supported by all social institutions . . . violence against women is often not taken seriously by the criminal justice system and often sanctioned, even promoted by the media, by culture and/or religion as in foot-binding and female genital

mutilation and some would argue internalized by women themselves in attempting to meet the so-called ideal. Thus, as C.F. Blake (1994: 678) argues: 'Gender differences are not only biologically determined, culturally constructed, or politically imposed, but also ways of living in a body and thus of being in the world.'

Source: Adapted from Letherby 2003a: 55

Thus, a focus on class or gender, or indeed any other form of difference/stratification, to the exclusion of others leads to narrow definitions and overgeneralisations (Maynard, 1994a). The feminist critique of class analysis within Sociology demonstrates this and 30 years of debate surrounding the ways in which class is categorised in terms of the household as the unit of assessment and in terms of occupational status and the value of treating women as having their own occupationally based class identity has led to a much more sophisticated analysis of the relevance of class to everyone's life-experience and life-chances (see for example Roberts, 1993; Abbott *et al.*, 2005). And of course the sociological study of class and gender focuses on much more than occupational boundaries and opportunities as Bev Skeggs' work on working-class women demonstrates:

> The media turn to the unhealthy eating habits of the nation [the UK] places specific emphasis on fat people, for example Health of the Nation (BBC2) and You Are What you Eat (Channel 4). These 'fat' programmes predominantly expose working-class families, especially mothers, as incapable of knowing how to look after themselves and others, as irresponsible . . . . [also] it is women's 'binge' drinking that has been highlighted as a significant threat, not only to the state of the nation, but also to herself. To smoke, drink, be fat and publicly fight and/or participate in loud hen parties is a national sin.

(Skeggs, 2005: 967)

Hotlink → Culture and Mass Media

Stop and think 4.4

Make a list of the forms of stratification that are most relevant to your own life-experience and life-changes. Do you think this list is different than it would have been 10 years ago? Do you think it might be different in 10 years' time? Why?

Politics and practice
Making a difference?

In addition to the challenge to the gender-blinkered theories and empirical focus within mainstream/malestream Sociology, feminists and pro/feminist men have also challenged the traditional use of methods and methodological approaches within the discipline [**Hotlink → Methods, Methodology and Epistemology (Chapter 2)**]. For many feminists, feminist research is feminist theory in action: the aim being to understand the world and change it. Thus, feminist research and ultimately feminist theory has political aims in that it celebrates and is grounded in the daily experiences of women (and men), and by focusing on experience it is able to challenge mainstream/malestream knowledge. Analysis is grounded in the experience of respondents and research informed by feminist principles has the 'desire' and the 'goal to 'create useful knowledge which can be used by ourselves and others to make a difference' [**Hotlink → Methods, Methodology and**

Epistemology (Chapter 2)]. With reference to this particular challenge the work of Ann Oakley, Liz Stanley and Sue Wise, and Helen Roberts (amongst others) has been influential in Britain, and in North America. Sandra Harding, Shulamit Reinharz and Judith Stacey and others have also contributed much to the debate.

However, it is not just feminists who are interested in politics and practice. Think back to the call for a 'sociological imagination' (Mills 1959 [1970]) mentioned earlier. Following on from Mills the work of Alvin Gouldner and Howard Becker in the 1960s and 1970s led to reflection on the political potential or not of Sociology. This debate has continued more recently amongst sociologists in America, Canada and Britain who have been particularly concerned with the presentation of academic work beyond the academy. Michael Burawoy, in his 2004 Presidential Address to the American Sociological Association, argued for 'public Sociology' thus:

> The bulk of public Sociology is indeed of an organic kind – sociologists working with a labor movement, neighbourhood associations, communities of faith, immigrant rights groups, human rights organisations. Between the organic public sociologist and a public is a dialogue, a process of mutual education. The recognition of public Sociology must extend to the organic kind which often remains invisible, private and is often considered to be apart from our professional lives. The project of such public sociologies is to make visible the invisible, to make the private public, to validate these organic connections as part of our sociological life.
>
> (Burawoy, 2005: 8–9)

Burawoy, and others in America and Britain, argue for a special place for Sociology and sociologists within the social sciences as 'public intellectuals'. For example, in Britain John Scott (2005: 7.2), drawing on Mill's ideas, argues:

> The core concerns of the sociological imagination have to be sustained within the Sociology curriculum. There is a general framework of ideas about social relations that may be the *common*

concern of the social sciences but is the *particular* concern of Sociology. Professional Sociology is the specific guardian of these intellectual concerns . . . This intellectual task centres on the idea of what it is to talk about human 'society' in all its complexity. (See also other articles in the 'Future Trends' debate in *Sociological Research Online* 2005 Vol. 10.)

Whilst in Canada, Caelie Frampton and colleagues (2006) in their edited collection of essays on political activist ethnography, credit their approach to the feminist sociologist Dorothy Smith:

> As an approach to producing a reliable knowledge of the social in order to facilitate transformative aims, political activist ethnography finds its roots in the work of Dorothy E. Smith. Contrary to the premises of official Sociology, which aims to explain people using categorical abstractions like 'socialisation', 'social roles and norms' or 'dysfunctionality', D. Smith developed what she called institutional ethnography as a Sociology for women, for the oppressed and – ultimately – for people (D. Smith 1987, 1999, 2005) . . . institutional ethnography show how the practices of ethnography can be turned against the ruling institutions in our own society.
>
> (Frampton *et al.*, 2006: 6)

This debate then, and the wider concern of Sociology making a difference, is closely linked to broader feminist concerns of praxis (an active connection between theory and research and real-world experience).

Facing the challenge

Researching and writing in a different and challenging way can of course attract criticism. Taking gender seriously and exploring the associated new topics, new methods and new approaches to writing and presentation has been criticised within Sociology as within other academic disciplines. Take for example the work of Eric Mykhalovskiy (1996) whose auto/biographical sociological writing has been described as 'self-indulgent' by an academic orthodoxy which stands by its view that there is one correct way to write academically (Mykhalovskiy, 1996; Temple, 1997). As

Mykhalovskiy himself notes, auto/biographical Sociology gives offence to the masculine academic discourse of Sociology:

> the criteria of sociological orthodoxy as expressed by a masculine academic discourse or voice, itself propped up by forms of thinking, writing, doing research and so on. As sociologists, this is a voice with which many of us are familiar; which we listen to and often reproduce as part of our apprenticeship. Authoritative, at times arrogant, it is a voice that speaks unitarily with confidence . . .
>
> Autobiographical Sociology gives offence to this voice. As Sociology, it comes to 'not' speak in that it does not rely on standard ways of being sociologically meaningful to readers.
>
> (1996: 139)

So although academic pro/feminism can both articulate and challenge dominant ideologies there is always the threat of dismissal and the labelling of this type of work as lesser, as maverick (Morley, 1995). Liz Stanley and Sue Wise admonish that: 'all feminists [and like-minded others] who are involved in writing and research should be more adventurous, more daring, and less concerned with being respectable and publishable' (1993: 137).

We agree that it is morally and politically, as well as academically, important to keep working in this way but would also suggest that it is not always easy for academics who want to have their work published. Yet, supporting Audre Lorde's (1984) view that you cannot 'dismantle the master's house using the master's tools' pro/feminist sociologists continue to challenge the jargon and overcomplication of some of the sociological mainstream.

Conclusion

Although feminism has had more of an impact in Sociology than in some other disciplines and although sociologists on the whole 'take gender seriously' there are some areas of sociological thought where a gendered analysis is still ignored or marginalised. New

challenges, approaches and topics are still at times treated with suspicion and, probably even worse, there are times when the approaches and methods of feminist academics are adopted by mainstream writers with no acknowledgement of the debt to feminism.

Further reading

Pamela Abbott, Claire Wallace and Melissa Tyler (2005), *An Introduction to Sociology: Feminist Perspectives*, London, Routledge (third edition). A comprehensive introduction to feminist Sociology that considers theory and method and covers a broad range of topics and areas: stratification and inequality, education, the life course, the family and household, health, illness and caring, sexuality, work and organisation, crime, violence and criminal justice, politics, mass media and popular culture. (The first edition (1990) and the second edition (1997) were written by Abbott and Wallace.)

Sara Delamont, (2003), *Feminist Sociology*, London, Sage. A detailed, historical consideration of the relationship between feminism and Sociology. Delamont highlights the contribution of feminist to thinking sociologically.

Stevi Jackson and Sue Scott (eds) (2002), *Gender: A Sociological Reader*, London, Routledge. A book containing 50 short readings that clearly demonstrate the 'gendering of Sociology'.

John Macionis and Ken Plummer, (2002) *Sociology: A Global Introduction*, London, Prentice Hall (second edition). A mainstream Sociology text that takes a global perspective incorporating a consideration of feminism and gender throughout.

Websites

www.britsoc.org.uk/specialisms – links to various BSA Study Groups including: Family, Race and Ethnicity, lesbian, Sexual Divisions Study Groups.

A Sociological Tour Through Cyberspace – **http://www.trinity.edu/~mkearl/gender.html**

A beautifully illustrated site based at Trinity University in Texas. It covers a wide range of relevant topics such as work, family, education, media, militarisation, globalisation, men's studies with links to other sites.

Understanding Men: Gender Sociology and the New International Research on Masculinities – an overview essay covering recent sociological work on men and masculinities – by R.W. Connell at **http://toolkit.endabuse.org/Resources/ UnderstandingMen**.

End of chapter activity

Read the first chapter of C. Wright Mills (1959) *The Sociological Imagination*, Harmondsworth, Penguin. There have been several reprints since 1959 so it will be easy to find a copy of the book. Once you have read the chapter answer the following questions:

1. According to C. Wright Mills what is the task and promise of the sociological imagination?

2. Using the example of unemployment Mills demonstrates the relationship between the 'personal troubles of milieu' and 'public issues of social structure'. Taking a gendered and cross-national perspective consider interpersonal violence, cigarette production and smoking or debt and do the same.

3. Reflect on your own educational and career choices with references to issues of history and structure and biography. How relevant is gender to your consideration.

4. You will be aware that at times Mills uses the generic he to refer to both men and women. For the last 30 years or so sociologists have been more aware of the negative consequences of excluding women and other minority groups through language. Look at the website of the British Sociological Association **www.britsoc.org.uk** for guidelines on a more inclusive approach to language.

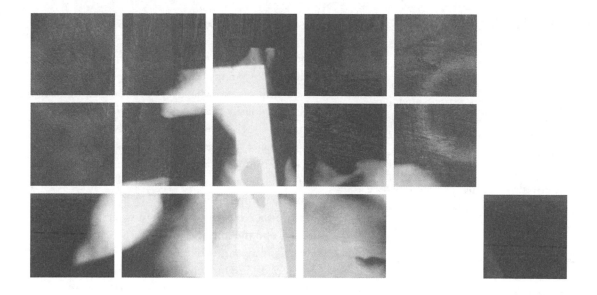

Chapter 5

Social policy

Key issues in this chapter:

➤ Social policy and social welfare systems reflect and reinforce the gender norms of the society which created them historically and presently.

➤ The same gender assumptions which shaped social policy affected the study of social policy until recently.

➤ The concepts of citizenship and family are vital to an understanding of the gendered nature of social policy.

➤ Social policies alone do not create welfare states, policies on tax, employment, immigration amongst others and the structure of the labour market are also involved.

At the end of this chapter you should be able to:

➤ Critique social policies from a gendered perspective

➤ Understand different types of models of social policy

➤ Discuss care as a gendered concept and as a cause of concern to feminists and other critical social policists

➤ Show how social (and other) policies prescribe particular family forms

Introduction

Fathers in protest on city bridge

Protesting fathers caused traffic mayhem this morning when their demonstration led to the closure of the Clifton Suspension Bridge.

Four campaigners from Fathers 4 Justice, dressed as Superman, Spiderman, Batman and Robin, climbed the tower . . . just after 6.30am. The four, . . ., unveiled a banner proclaiming they were 'Superheroes fighting for their children's rights' . . . Mr Skinner, aged 37, said: . . . 'This is a campaign to raise awareness that there are thousands of dads who do not have access to their children because of an outdated family law system which we want abolished as soon as possible. We apologise for the inconvenience to motorists who have been denied access to the bridge but imagine how they would feel if they had been denied access to their children as we have been'.

(*Bristol Evening Post*, 2 February 2004)

Figure 5.1
Source: © Darren Staples/Reuters/Corbis

What is social policy?

Before we can review the impact of gender upon social policy and upon the study of social policy it is useful to quickly review what is understood to be social policy. Primarily social policy is both an area of government legislation and of academic study. Traditionally social policy was seen as including areas such as health, education, housing and social security – in fact, the areas associated with social welfare. A strong trend in this mainstream tradition in academia has been a concern with analysing the processes of welfare and the implementation of policies, for example the ways in which housing policies can be developed, designed and delivered most efficiently. This element of social policy is known as Social Administration. Whilst critical approaches have examined the implementation of social policies the most fundamental challenge to traditional social policy has been that of feminism which broadened the definition of social policy to also include personal violence, childcare, care of elders and reproduction, amongst other areas. This has involved critical examinations of the structures of welfare systems; of the relationship between caring and employment; of the notion of citizenship and on the dichotomy of public and private (see A Critical Look 5.1). As such, feminism contributes strongly to 'critical social policy' which takes as its starting point a view of social policy as being underpinned by social inequalities such as ethnicity, social class and gender, sexuality and other social differences. As such Gillian Pascall's prediction that the result of feminist analyses of social welfare would be 'a new understanding, not only of the way the Welfare State deals with women, but also of social policy itself' (Pascall, 1986: 1) has come true. Our gendered approach to social policy builds upon this rich tradition to discuss social welfare systems and social policies from the differential positions of women and men and from the differential positions individual men and women hold: based on factors such as age, ability, citizenship status, sexuality, amongst others.

A critical look 5.1

'Health warning' on public/private

Social Scientists refer to the public and the private not because they think the world is so neatly and rigidly divided but due to the power of these concepts to frame discussions around inclusion and exclusion, around what has been deemed as appropriate for study and what has not. The fluidity between these two categories must be kept in mind. As Marchbank states:

'although, . . ., I dispute the actual existence of these two separate spheres I do find them useful shorthand for the way in which patriarchy views society. Nonetheless, the public/private spheres vary in definition over cultures and historical periods and do not always equal male/female divide; that is, even if women are excluded from the public sphere men have never been excluded from the private sphere, the family sphere.' (2000: 26).

A gendered approach to social policy

Social policies have a two-way relationship with gender roles: the first is that social policies inherently reflect the gender assumptions of the time of their creation and the other is that social policies can also be used to attempt to recognise changing trends in gender roles or to encourage changes in gender roles. We shall begin by reviewing these points in order, starting with the way in which social policies reflect gender roles. In doing so it is necessary to acknowledge the developments in the study of social policy which have occurred, primarily a move from social administration to feminist critiques of welfare. One gap has been the examination of social policy in the lives of men, in fact the majority of critique on welfare and men has been through the lens of social class (see Esping-Andersen, 1990) (one exception being Pringle, 1995) and that has most frequently been focused on class oppression not on examining where men as a group, irrespective of social class, are privileged in society. However, feminist attempts to build new models of social policy have pulled masculinity and men into a gendered analysis. In addition, some activists, such as Fathers 4 Justice (F4J) and politicians have been active in critiquing social welfare arguing that men are disadvantaged by welfare states. Our gendered approach to social policy encompasses an examination of all of these areas and of all the differential positions of women and men.

Gendered assumptions in social welfare

It is not possible to understand the underlying principles, structure and effects of our social welfare systems and policies without understanding their relation to gender roles and gender ideology.

(Sapiro, 1990: 37)

What does Virginia Sapiro mean by this? Well, she is stating that each society has established gender roles, and an ideology of gender which creates and sustains these roles and that these are not restricted to the private domain. In fact, these roles and ideologies are the very keystones to understanding social welfare systems. In this example, Sapiro is discussing the United States system, as was Nancy Fraser (1989: 149–51) when she observed that the social security system is 'officially gender-neutral' but 'gets its structure from gender norms and assumptions'; however, it is possible to apply both these observations to any state welfare system.

These assumptions are not always accurate but are frequently *prescriptive*, that is, they are concerned with the views of how men and women should live, an example of such prescription is a social security system that assumes that when two adults of the opposite sex live together as a couple then they should be financially dependent upon each other; in fact, this assumption exists even for such adults living together *not* as a couple who have to prove they are not a couple. The prescription here is that couples are required to be financially, as well as romantically, entwined – that is, it is as if by living together the government tells you that you must share finances too. It is only recently in Britain that such assumptions have begun to be considered for same-sex couples also. As such, yet another layer of prescription exists – one of 'telling' people that heterosexuality is preferred as the state, the government, seems not to have recognised same-sex relationships in this policy area in many countries.

In addition, at the time of the creation of most welfare systems in the twentieth century the gender ideology not only prescribed the shape of social policies (see A Closer Look 5.1) but also created, via social policies, implicit ideologies of the family. Whilst Marxist theorists have argued that the welfare state exists to provide capitalists with healthy and educated workers, Marxist feminists have argued that a further role of the welfare state has been to manage women in terms of family and motherhood balanced against the needs of certain industries for cheap female labour (Wilson, 1977) and, as such, created familial ideologies as well as gender ideologies. Yet, these familial ideologies are as prescriptive as the gender ideologies – that is, social policies operate in such ways as to support certain family forms over others. The creation of part-time work opportunities has been viewed by Elizabeth Wilson (1977) as a solution to the needs of industry for cheap workers without reducing women's abilities to fulfil their reproductive and family responsibilities (see A Critical Look 5.2).

A closer look 5.1

Beveridge and the construction of dependent womanhood in the British welfare state

William Beveridge's 1942 Report is recognised as the document which created the modern British welfare state. In it Beveridge had seen a particular role for women, reflecting the gender ideology of his time. This led to a welfare state design predicated on full *male* employment with married women receiving their protection through marriage. People were divided into different categories and were to receive their social security benefits and to make their contributions based on the rules for those categories – these included employed, self-employed, too old to work, etc. Married women were constructed as a wholly distinct and separate class of contributors whose access to benefits in their own right were severely curtailed. That is, upon marriage, working women were to move from the employed category to that of wife. Whether they continued to work or not, and even if they had built up a long record of contributions in their own right:

> Every woman on marriage will become a new person, acquiring new rights, and not carrying on into marriage claims to unemployment or disability benefit in respect of contributions made before marriage.
> (Beveridge Report, 1942: para. 339)

The basis of this was a gender ideology that saw it as the husband's responsibility to provide for his wife and the wife's responsibility to be providing in the private sphere and not working in the public sphere. As such, women's rights to pensions and benefits were wholly reliant, after marriage, on her husband's contribution record. Despite recent changes this still affects both men and women.

A critical look 5.2

Women's part-time work in Britain

The ability to work part time was not universal. Carby (1982) argues that the part-time work of White women was only made possible by the full-time work of Black immigrants, especially Caribbean women. Black women were not considered in the same context of familialism as indigenous women for their family responsibilities were not considered and often their children were unable to live with them due to restrictions of immigration or availability of childcare.

Stop and think 5.1

Many welfare systems in the past, and some in the present, provided tax breaks for being married, i.e. a reduction in the family tax bill. Consider what social messages such policies send about what kind of family form the state prefers.

Citizenship, qualification and family

Another area of gendered assumptions has been in the definition of citizenship. Historically the basic qualification for citizenship has been independence and this has been based on masculine criteria. T.H. Marshall's (1950) famous work outlining the various aspects of citizenship (political, social and civil) has been shown to be based on the experiences and rights of men (Hernes, 1984; Pateman, 1988a, Gordon, 1990):

... citizenship, originally resting on the capacity to provide military service, was eventually extended to most men while women's relationship to their states remained defined through men (husbands or fathers). Women were ascribed the status of 'the protected' and located within the private/domestic sphere, even when lived realities were starkly different.

(Jacobs *et al.*, 2000: 7)

In modern times the criteria for citizenship has shifted from military service to worker, yet in the formation of welfare systems, women remained defined through men, that is as the dependants of male workers rather than as workers in their own rights. This is relevant to social policy as one's rights to social welfare are related to one's citizenship status, which is achieved through contributions made in the public sphere (Marshall, 1950) as workers. Worker was defined as a man with a dependant family, a *breadwinner*, and this definition has been built into notions of welfare across the western world (Pateman, 1988a). As such, women were and still can be required to gain their subsistence via their husbands' contributory record and not their own.

Why does it matter if women gain their social rights via men? It matters as it makes a significant difference to entitlement (as shown by the details of the Beveridge system given in A Closer Look 5.1) and responsibility. Welfare states require that working-age adults contribute to the state and many have training schemes which unemployed workers are required to attend as a condition of receiving state aid. Defining a worker as male has meant that women have not been obliged to actively seek work or training, unlike men. For example, it was only in 1998 that the wives and female partners of unemployed men in Britain were required to also seek work. In his 1998 Budget, Chancellor Gordon Brown, announced that the New Deal for Workers would be extended to such women, to assist them in achieving their role as workers. Such an action shifted these women's status in the eyes of the government from one of dependants of men, sustained through payments made to men, to one of workers with equal rights to the same services but also with equal responsibilities to the state. As such, it was a subtle but major change towards gender equity in the British welfare system (see A Closer Look 5.2).

A closer look 5.2

Budgeting for equality

Chancellor Gordon Brown used his 1998 Budget to make two changes to British social policy, balancing gender rights and responsibilities for both men and women.

1. Tax allowances which had previously only been available to men with children and an incapacitated wife now to be applied to women with an incapacitated husband.

2. Women included in the New Deal for Workers – extended the requirements of unemployed men to their female partners, that is, these women now have to participate in training and actively seek work, just like the men.

Jonathan Scourfield and Mark Drakeford (2002) argue that New Labour in Britain have broken new ground as they have also made policies around masculinity: 'it is only in the last few years that a government has made quite such explicit references to men some areas of policy. The most high-profile initiatives have been in relation to fathering and the education of boys' (Scourfield and Drakeford, 2002: 619) [**Hotlink → Education (Chapter 13)**]. In fact they argue that New Labour have made policies to support men in the home and women in the workplace. The policy direction on men includes a certain pessimism regarding men outside the home, especially in relation to criminal justice policies which view men as a 'problem'; they conclude that:

New Labour can be seen as optimistic about men inside the home and pessimistic about men ourside, whereas, in contrast, there is policy pessimism about women inside the home and policy optimism about women outside ... Although political rhetoric is often negative about men, some actual policies could be seen as representing the retrenchment of traditional masculinities predicated on social advantage.

(Scourfield and Drakeford, 2002: 634)

[**Hotlink → Political Science (Chapter 8)**].

Gendered assumptions in the study of social policy

Not only have there been gendered assumptions in social policies reflecting and reinforcing traditional gender roles but also reflecting and adapting attitudes towards these. Further, it is also clear that approaches to studying social welfare, or welfare states, have also taken a similar journey. Using the British welfare state as an example, we will now follow the footsteps of these studies towards our goal of a gendered approach.

Collectivism

The British welfare state developed from a Collectivist tradition, sometimes referred to as Fabian, an approach identifiable by its three central values of solidarity, equality and freedom and by its methods. These methods can be described as rationalist and empiricist and they derived from a desire to use social policy to relieve social problems. Britain had a long history of men and women working in these ways documenting and studying social problems so that they might be ameliorated, for example Charles Booth, Joseph Rowntree (see A Closer Look 5.3), Women's Co-operative Guild, amongst others. This was an approach that focused on determining what worked or what did not, rather than asking fundamental questions regarding the distribution of social and economic resources, and on how best to administer social welfare.

The gender problem in social administration is twofold: firstly, a social administrative approach never questions the division of social and economic resources based on gender nor the structure of the 'normal' family; secondly, the language and analysis of social policy hides gender differences. Pascall (1896) shows how most work actually about women in social administration has been disguised within other categories, such as 'elderly' or 'single parent families' (both of which are gender neutral categories dominated by women).

The opposite position from Collectivism is that of Individualism, a belief that it is not the state's responsibility to provide for the welfare of its people but the

A closer look 5.3

Booth, Rowntree and poverty measures

Between 1886 and 1903 Charles Booth mapped poverty in London in his *Survey of Life and Labour*. His maps show the social condition of every street in London, classifying people in a colour code of class and income. These can be accessed online at http://booth.lse.ac.uk/

A few years later Joseph Rowntree, of the famous chocolate family of York, developed notions of poverty to include a 'basic level', the first time a poverty line was determined. Although Rowntree argued for social costs, such as newspapers and social interactions, to be included in his minimum needs, not just food and shelter, these are not universally accepted to this day as necessities of life.

responsibility of individuals and that people can do this by earning money in a market, a market kept free by the state. This approach accepts that inequalities exist between different members of society and does not see this as a social wrong, as they are inequalities created by the market. Individualism views attempts to reduce or hide inequalities as restrictive and as a preventive force upon individuals taking risks on which wealth and progress depend. The classic work here is Frederick Hayek's (1944) *Road to Serfdom* within which the individual in the marketplace is the primary focus of his analysis. This individual is masculine, though as can be seen in the A Closer Look 5.4, forty plus years on, individual women were recognised by Margaret Thatcher. However, their (Hayek's and Thatcher's) opinions regarding families reflect similar positions, that is families are adjuncts to the individual worker – be that male or female – and that these families are constructed in very traditional ways, that is traditional in Judeo-Christian western terms. This means that families are self-supporting and, in individualistic terms, women carry the costs of individualism in terms of caring for dependent children and adults – we will return to the importance of care below.

A closer look 5.4

Individualism

In an interview with the magazine *Woman's Own*, Margaret Thatcher, then Prime Minister of the United Kingdom, expressed her view of society:

> I think we have gone through a period when too many children and people have been given to understand 'I have a problem, it is the Government's job to cope with it!' or 'I have a problem, I will go and get a grant to cope with it!', 'I am homeless, the Government must house me!' and so they are casting their problems on society and who is society? There is no such thing! There are individual men and women and there are families and no government can do anything except through people and people look to themselves first. It is our duty to look after ourselves and then also to help look after our neighbour and life is a reciprocal business and people have got the entitlements too much in mind without the obligations, because there is no such thing as an entitlement unless someone has first met an obligation.

Source: Woman's Own, 31st October 1987.

Stop and think 5.2

Attempt these tasks; re-read the section above if necessary.

1. List the three central values of the Collectivist tradition.

2. How do Individualists view inequality?

Marxist approaches

Whilst Individualism represents the philosophy of the political right many writers on the welfare state from the 1960s took a left-of-centre stance, one also involving analysis from a political economy perspective. From the late 1960s Marxist critiques of the role of welfare states were developed which pointed out the ways in which the welfare state acts as a form of social control which, rather than meeting the needs of the people creates a dependency upon the state, whilst denying those in receipt of welfare any control over the nature of the service. Marxist theory critiques liberal welfare states (for example, the UK, USA, Canada, New Zealand, Australia) for being products of, and founded within, capitalist relations of production. Marxist writers argue that liberal welfare states are the product of two opposing forces, that of working-class struggle and the needs of capitalism and that they are engaged in two distinct activities. The activities are firstly, to ensure the reproduction of the labour force, for capitalism requires healthy workers and, secondly to preserve the state through maintaining social order – this is achieved by the provisions of certain services and benefits to ameliorate the worst excesses of capitalism.

Marxism seems to have provided some space for a feminist analysis of state welfare in that it opens up questions as to the ways and means of reproducing workers. Whereas Marxism pointed towards the role of state welfare in reproducing workers, Marxist feminists pointed out that most social, as well as biological, reproduction was actually done by women. In addition, Marxist analysis of labour also showed how women have been used by capital as a 'reserve army' of labour. These approaches provide two ways in which women are located within Marxist interpretations and understandings of state welfare but the purely economistic focus on the reproduction of the worker rather than the reproduction of people did not provide all the answers. For instance, it offers no explanation as to why it is that women, not men, do the majority of work within the home and family and it also makes the public world of work and state the prime focus, ignoring the ways in which the public and private spheres are inextricably linked. Yet, long before the Second Wave of feminism, work on social policy existed which did address the experiences of the private aspects of life (Pember Reeves, 1913).

Regime types

An influential approach on the studying of welfare systems has been the numerous comparative studies. One such approach has been to look at the ways countries cluster along certain factors, perhaps the best known of these being Gösta Esping-Andersen's (1990, 1996) work on the three worlds of welfare capitalism. Esping-Andersen's analysis results in three different versions of social welfare: social democratic, liberal and conservative (see Table 5.1).

Of course, none of this work stands alone, and Marshall's notions of citizenship, and the class focus of Marxism has been combined with these regime types (Esping-Andersen, 1990; Korpi and Palme, 1998) to reveal linkages between politics and social rights. Marxism has pointed out that many of the gains of state welfare have resulted from workers' movements demanding social rights. Esping-Andersen (1990) argues that to understand the ways in which welfare systems affect the relationships between social classes it is necessary to measure the level of social rights. The ultimate social right being complete *decommodification* of labour. Decommodification means the ability to maintain one's lifestyle without recourse to selling one's labour in the employment market. In such a situation workers are protected somewhat from the demands of capitalism by being protected from the pressures of capitalism to certain degrees.

Feminist approaches

Feminists have focused on the dynamics between public and private spheres, the shifting boundary between the two and the interdependence between them. As such, decommodification has been critiqued as being inherently male – being focused on a measure of social rights derived from, and related to, the degree of participation in the labour market. It has been suggested that to use decommodification as a true measure of social rights requires some modification. Basically, the addition of the consideration of (1) access to paid work and (2) the ability to create and maintain independent households (Orloff, 1993). This is important for both men and women but particularly for women as the ability to live outside of marriage or cohabitation is necessary for women. Without freedom from economic dependency women are not free, in a gendered labour market, to make real choices about entering into partnerships.

Of course, as Jan Pahl (1989), Christine Delphy and Diana Leonard (1992) and others have shown, financial

Table 5.1 Features of Esping-Andersen's Regime Types

Regime Type and Examples	Features
Liberal: USA, Canada, Australia, UK	➤ Differentiate between people based on whether they are able to self support through the market or need state support. ➤ Services provided by the market as well as state. ➤ Few alternatives to participating in the labour market as welfare is at low levels/limited.
Social Democratic: Sweden, Norway, the Netherlands	➤ All citizens covered by state provision. ➤ Universal, egalitarian and significant public services. ➤ Decommodification of labour – that is, alternatives to labour market participation exist and provide a sufficient standard of living.
Conservative: Austria, Germany, France, Italy	➤ All citizens covered by state provision. ➤ Retain class differences, inegalitarian with few public services. ➤ Rights to benefits based on employment.

resources are not always equally available to all family members, sometimes based on sex and sometimes on other factors such as age. Ruth Lister (1994) uses the term *defamilialisation* to act as the measure of social rights. Unlike decommodification, defamilialisation is 'the degree to which individual adults can uphold a socially acceptable standard of living, independently of family relationships, either through paid work or social security' (Lister, 1994: 32).

Stop and think 5.3

Think about decommodification and defamilialisation. Without looking back briefly outline each. Now check your answers.

Feminist social policy has a long history, which indicates that mainstream social policy analysis has had this information available, just not made use of it. The political and social work of women such as Maud Pember Reeves (1913), Margery Spring Rice, Eleanor Rathbone and of organisations such as the Women's Cooperative Guild in the first half of the twentieth century in Britain provides this evidence.

Although there are many feminist theoretical positions it is possible to summarise feminist views of social welfare. In summary, feminist critiques of state welfare take account of social welfare relationships in both the private and public spheres, acknowledging the linkages between the two spheres and that actions in one sphere have implications in the other. In other words, feminist analyses reject the dualism characterising classical approaches in which economic and social policy, the private and the public, are deemed to operate independently of each other. Treating these worlds as unconnected enables other non-feminist theorists to ignore the contribution the domestic economy makes to sustaining and reproducing accepted public welfare relationships. In addition, it also ignores the role of the reproduction, not just of workers – that is their social reproduction – but the actual biological reproduction of people.

Not only can it be seen that welfare states reflect and reinforce gender and family assumed norms, but it has also been shown that social policies can be used to reproduce other social relations such as between social classes and between people of different ethnic origins. Fiona Williams (1989) has clearly shown that there have been two dominant themes in British social policy: themes of nation and of the family. She notes the ways in which reforms of social welfare were introduced in Britain to preserve existing power relations rather than to change them, these being the power relations of imperialism, capitalism and patriarchy. In this light, Williams argues that the welfare systems of western industrialised states have not only institutionalised gender relations (which she describes as patriarchal) but also institutionalised racism. This racism has operated through denying certain people access to services and benefits through differential provisions and treatment and the maintenance of immigration controls. However, in some countries indigenous people were also not included or treated differently – see World in Focus 5.1 for examples of such cases.

World in focus 5.1

Racism and social policy

Some of the earliest examples of welfare provisions from the state include services to mothers to ensure infant health and well-being. However, the well-being of some babies was deemed more important than that of others. As O'Connor, Orloff and Shaver (1999: 37) note: 'In the United States, Australia and Canada, maternalist programs – mothers' pensions, maternal health programs, and the like – were not consistently accessible to African-Americans, other women of colour and indigenous women.'

In addition, even where non-white women could receive benefits implementation practices resulted in lack of support. In the USA in the 1950s illegitimacy and welfare reduction had become a national cause with many believing that Aid to Dependent Children (ADC) went to

World in focus 5.1 continued

the undeserving, associating illegitimacy with African-American mothers. As such many:

states made concerted efforts to purge black families from welfare rolls, especially through laws withdrawing support from illegitimate children. Louisiana's 1960 law stated: 'In no instance shall assistance be granted to any person who is living with his or her mother if the mother has had an illegitimate child after a check has been received from the

Welfare Department unless and until proof satisfactory to the Parish Board of Public Welfare has been presented showing that the mother has ceased illicit relationship and is maintaining suitable home.' A Gallup Poll taken soon after the passage of this legislation reported that a majority found it acceptable to withhold federal support or food money from illegitimate black babies. But facts and social perceptions often fail to match.

In 1959, 30 per cent of unwed white mothers who kept their children received ADC grants – nearly twice as many as black unwed mothers. Nonetheless, ADC became stigmatized as a black program because of the growing numbers of black recipients. Meanwhile, immigrant women, especially the increased numbers who entered the country illegally, could not even apply for such assistance.

(Boris, 1995: 172)

Model making

In order to understand welfare systems and variations several attempts have been made to devise ideal type models. These have been found to be weak in their predictions of how welfare systems treat women and men (Sainsbury, 1996), the first problem being that most of the models developed have made assumptions that gender is not an issue and that welfare systems treat women and men the same. Ironically too, it is clear that there have been times where welfare policies have been specifically designed to benefit one gender rather than another. For example, early welfare reforms in the USA included protective measures for women and children at work, pensions for mothers and public health care for children but did not include social insurance schemes for working men akin to those being introduced in western Europe at the same time (Skocpol, 1992). In more recent times it has been shown that advances in welfare provision have had a beneficial, even emancipatory, effect for women (O'Connor 1993; Orloff, 1993) leading some to discuss states in terms of the potential for 'woman-friendliness' (Hernes, 1987).

Only a few years ago, mainstream comparative research and gender-sensitive work on welfare states were almost mutually exclusive sets. The result of which was that there was little systematically comparative work on gender and welfare states (O'Connor *et*

al., 1999: 10); see A Closer Look 5.5 for a feminist critique of mainstream modelling.

The advantage of model building is that it allows analysts to look beyond the features and idiosyncrasies of any one state and to see if particular variations in type result in specific outcomes. In contrast to the

A closer look 5.5

Making gender visible

Sainsbury (1996) summarises the achievements of feminist critiques of mainstream models:

1. brought gender into focus by making women visible in analyses which focus on individuals, households, occupations and/or social classes;

2. displayed how social programmes, policies and rights have been gendered;

3. shown how mainstream concepts and assumptions are gendered;

4. emphasised the interrelationships amongst family, state and market;

5. re-examined the analyses of welfare which focus upon the ways in which social programmes and policies redistribute income and services amongst sectors of the population, usually by class, generation or other social group, to include the distribution between sexes.

mainstream comparative approaches which have used measures of state provision, extent of state spending on welfare, whether (and to what extent) coverage is based on citizenship or occupational status or the relationship between the state and the market as the basis for devising typologies, feminist comparative research has included analyses of *unpaid* work. [**Hotlink** → **Work and Leisure (Chapter 14)**]

Modelling the ideology of male breadwinner

We have already looked at the ways in which the British welfare state reflected gender role norms of the time of its creation, with men being constructed as workers and women as dependant wives. The result of such constructions is that when in need of social assistance that assistance was to be offered in ways which reflected the man's 'job' to provide financial security for the family. In terms of employment this was expressed in pay policies which paid men a 'family wage' and justified paying women less, for they had, supposedly, no equivalent family responsibilities. In terms of social welfare it permitted differential rates of social security to be paid to men and women, youths and adults. Feminist work has shown how women's social entitlements have been as wives and the implications for social provision in many states and comparative work has been able to reveal variations in the breadwinner model across states (Lewis, 1992; Sainsbury, 1996).

For the Breadwinner Model to exist certain characteristics must be in place, which are:

1. A familial ideology supporting and celebrating marriage.

2. Traditional sexual division of labour within the marriage; husband being responsible for providing for the family through his employment, this making him the 'Head of the household'.

3. The role and responsibility of the wife is to ensure the social reproduction of the husband and to care for non-independent others within the family, most likely children. This role is unpaid.

4. The state recognises the family as the unit not the individual and benefits are paid to support this unit

and taxes collected which recognise this unit, not the individuals within it. Benefits are paid to the 'Head of the household' and embody notions of the family wage. Taxes are calculated based on the income of the household with deductions permitted for dependants.

Not only are social policies imbued with the Breadwinner ideology, so too are fiscal policies in the structuring of the tax system and also employment policies in the sense that men, given their responsibilities, have to be given priority in the workplace over women and their earnings have to be sufficient to cover the costs of keeping a family.

The Breadwinner Model has been employed primarily for two purposes amongst social policists. Firstly, to provide a focus for analysing the extent of gender inequity within and across states – though disagreement exists as to the categorization of certain states (see Controversy 5.1). Secondly, to act as the starting point to the development of other models of social welfare which, if enacted, would lead to more gender equitable social welfare. A major influence in this area has been Individual models, such as that of Sainsbury (1996).

Individual model

The Individual Model is the polar opposite of the Breadwinner Model as it makes no assumptions about family form, providing no social welfare benefits to support or encourage marriage or any other family form. Within this model household labour is shared between partners as is paid work. As both parents are earners and both are carers both have the same entitlements to benefits – not through their relationship to anyone else but due to their membership of society, their citizenship. Correspondingly, they are treated as individuals in terms of contributions and qualifications and the 'unit' which makes contributions and receives benefits is the individual not the household. Likewise, the tax system does not provide allowances for spouses and both are taxed as individuals sharing whatever tax relief exists for their dependent children. A further difference from the Breadwinner Model is in the area of social care and reproduction; in the

Controversy 5.1

Classifying the breadwinner states

Lewis (1992) argues that the male breadwinner model has been the basis of all modern welfare states, but that it has been adapted in different ways in different societies. Her study examines Britain, Ireland, France and Sweden. She examines the way women have been treated as wives and mothers in terms of social security, services for working mothers and women's position in the labour market generally. On this basis she describes Britain and Ireland as *strong breadwinner* states, classifies France as a *modified breadwinner* state and Sweden as a *weakened breadwinner* state.

Sainsbury (1996) uses a different approach and reaches some differences in her conclusions. Using both the male breadwinner model and its opposing ideal type – an *individual* model – also on four countries, in her case: Britain, USA, the Netherlands and Sweden. She concludes that Sweden has *never* been a male breadwinner state. Rather, she argues that Swedish social policies were historically grounded in a strong emphasis upon citizenship (male and female) as the basis to entitlements. So, rather than representing, as Lewis argues, a male breadwinner state weakened by women's entry into the labour force, Sweden, from the beginning of social welfare, created policies which weakened the influence of the breadwinner male. Sainsbury cites as examples policies from the 1930s which provided comprehensive benefits for mothers, e.g. maternity grants, child benefit, collective care.

Individual Model this not only has an element of pay but also has a strong state involvement which is absent in the Breadwinner scenario.

The Individual Model opens up other ways of analysing welfare regimes in terms of gender. Further, welfare systems which contain all, or some, aspects of the Individual Model are more positive towards women's independence from men. Likewise, the Individual Model provides a place for recognising the role of men in caregiving. Nonetheless, it too remains rather prescriptive in that amongst its characteristics is an ideology which supports shared roles for husband and wife (or their unwed equivalents). As such, it implicitly reinforces the hegemony of a household and family structure of dual-earning heterosexuals. Not all families fit this, for example migrant women with their children in another country, lesbian couples, single parents, extended families, amongst others. In fact, the presence of migrant women workers can be seen as making it possible for a dual-earning household to operate, through the provision of paid care (Williams, 1989).

New world, new model?

Earlier it was noted that welfare states are a product of industrial capitalist states and that their structure encoded the 'norms' of industrial capitalism into welfare systems, for example with the family wage. Yet, this is not the world as it is today; in many societies the labour market does not pay a family wage and many families need two adults to be earning to survive. In addition, as commented upon above, the 'family' in post-industrial society can no longer be assumed to be any one thing [Hotlink → Family (Chapter 11)]. So, it has been argued that a new world of less stable employment and more diverse family forms needs a new form of welfare state (Fraser, 1997). Fraser's argument is that such a welfare state must support a new gender order, that of gender equity. She examines two feminist models – the first where women also become breadwinners – a universal *breadwinner* – a second whereby both sexes share the care work – *caregiver parity*. Elements of both of these models are visible in modern social welfare systems. The United States is perhaps the furthest along in terms of achieving Universal Breadwinner by increasing the number of women in employment. Aspects of Caregiver Parity are visible in the practice of most western European states, with the Dutch 'Combination Model' being a good example – [Hotlink → Work and Leisure (Chapter 14), World in Focus 14.3] By supporting informal care work, through caregiver allowances such as the British Home Responsibilities Pension, gender equality can be increased. A major criticism of these alternative models to male breadwinner is that they do little to change the role of men. Gender equality can be increased in the Universal Breadwinner by making women more like men in terms of employment patterns; gender equality in terms of entitlements to pensions and benefits can be increased by recognising caregiving as a contribution to the welfare state. Again, however, nothing changes for men, this time it is the state that changes. Fraser (1997) flips all of this on its head and suggests that it's not that women need to have work patterns like men but that men need to have work and care patterns like women – a *universal caregiver* model. The elements of this model need to include:

1. All jobs designed in such a way as to allow for the combination of paid work and informal unpaid work; there would be leave for both men and women to support their parenting role.

2. Care would be performed within the household, which need not be either heterosexual nor nuclear.

3. The state would provide finance and services to support care done in the household.

Stop and think 5.4

What reasons might there be to explain why in many western societies aspects of the Universal Breadwinner model seem to be more common than the Universal Caregiver?

Key debates in gender and social policy

All areas of social policy have been subjected to a gendered analysis, from health care to education. As these topics have their own chapters here we will focus on the fundamental debates around the issues of care work and family. This overlaps with the relationship of both these areas and paid employment and you should read this section in conjunction with the chapters on Work and Leisure (Chapter 14) and Family (Chapter 11). A further key issue, citizenship, has already been discussed.

Care

Hernes (1984) points out that many tasks previously conducted within the private sphere, the family, are now in the public domain. They may be provided by the state (as in formal education), regulated by the state (as in childminding) or supported by the state (such as universal child benefits). What this means is that with the advent of state welfare there has been a shift in family–state relationships. In what follows we will trace the provision of care in Britain, or rather the debates and discourses on care in Britain, to show how gender norms have shaped, reshaped and been shaped by social policy.

Care as cause of women's dependency

The fact that the majority of care work, be it for dependent children, dependent elders and other dependent adults, is still performed by women is shown across nations (see Table 5.2), affects women's lives in ways that it does not affect men's. Should care not be the starting point for social policy rather than services, and debates, on the periphery (Graham, 1988)?

In some cases, care of small children is only possible through either the parent/s combining paid work with care (for example Britain, the Netherlands) [**Hotlink → Work and Leisure (Chapter 14)**] or concentrating on care alone or work alone (e.g. the USA, though only a few have the luxury of choice). In a few places the support offered to parents allows a real

---

Table 5.2 Gender of carers across the European Community

	Denmark	Spain	France	Ireland	Austria	Sweden	UK	UK
Year	2002	1999	1999	2000	2000	2000	1989	1995
Men	20	26	36	33	20	27	35	42
Women	80	74	64	67	80	72	65	58

Source: Derived from Table 23 Distribution of informal carers by sex in %, Grammenos (July 2003).

choice to be made regarding care and paid work (Sweden). In all of these cases, however, it appears that the majority responsibility for raising children remains in the female gender role (Marchbank, 2000).

Not surprising then that care work has been seen as a cause of women's dependency, either on the state or on individual men, and examined as such. Marxist feminists, seeking a way to improve women's lives, asked whether they should campaign to increase the services and benefits women received from the state or increase women's independence from both men and the state by increasing women's paid work. Seeking independence meant for some, such as Mary McIntosh (1981), the latter position was preferred. But what room then for women who are not free to enter the labour market? The answer lay in the public provision, not of benefits and pensions for caring but of caring work. There are two problems with this: firstly, even with increasing the state's role in care, the care work which remains within the community, remains as women's responsibility (Finch and Groves, 1980; Finch, 1984), with three times as many women as men caring for dependent adults in Britain in 1980 (EOC, 1980) though in recent years this has become more balanced. Secondly, this approach ignores the emotional element involved in providing social care for family members; as Hilary Graham (1988) makes clear, care is about labour *and* about love.

Ignoring the emotional role underplays the identity of many carers, that is, it minimises and undervalues their role. In addition, describing care in the terms of industrial economics and labour market participation access limits the debate to women's access to paid employment, not women's access to care. As such, as British social policy moved away from institutional care towards community care to replace state care from the 1950s to the 1980s, this was viewed as a threat to equality between the sexes for, 'community care equals care by the family, and in practice care by the family equals care by women' (Finch and Groves, 1980: 494). As such, some feminists argued against increasing community care and for new forms of residential care (Dalley, 1988). Unfortunately, this was done without considering that many of those in need of care and are women, especially elder and disabled women, were in support of care in the community (Morris, 1991).

State support for caring work has disadvantaged both women and men due to the gender norms inherent within the welfare system. It was not until 1998 that the allowance paid to husbands to support them caring for invalid wives was made available to married women in Britain as it was assumed that caring for a husband was a wifely duty. Likewise, the assumption that men need more help than women in caring is visible in findings that show that male carers received more help and received it earlier than female carers due to their supposed other responsibilities (EOC, 1984: 31). Even when social policies recognise men's caring role, such as the European Union's granting of

World in focus 5.2

Gender of carers

Men's role as carers has been increasingly recognised as has their contribution. In 1980 in Britain, three times as many women as men were carers but by 1995, 42 per cent of carers were men. Yet women still perform the majority of care work. As Eurostat explains:

> Data in Great Britain indicates that women were more likely to

be carers than men were but the difference was not marked, 14% compared to 11%. However, since there are more women than men in the total adult population of Great Britain, it is true that the number of women caring is considerably greater than that of men, 3.3 million compared with 2.4 million. This gives 42% men and 58% women.

> Grammenos (2003: 87)

In Spain . . . there is a significant difference concerning the origin of help between elderly men and women with disabilities. About 45% of men receive assistance from a partner and 21% from a daughter. In comparison, the rates for women are 15% and 37% respectively. This might be partly due to the longer life expectancy of women.

> Grammenos (2003: 89)

Source: Grammenos (2003).

the right to all fathers to receive parental leave to care for their children, they often are not as generous as those for women. For example, paternity leave is a legal right for British fathers as is maternity leave for mothers, but only mothers receive payments from both employers (forced to by the state) and the government. This might be assumed to explain why many men do not take such leave from work, and why even in countries where such leave is paid, such as Norway, the majority of fathers still prefer to go to work. Many men are simply not aware of this right – over a quarter of men surveyed across the European Union claimed to be unaware of their right to parental leave (European Opinion Research Group, 2004), with the least informed Europeans being Irish and Portuguese men (only 57 per cent of both knew about parental leave). See Figures 5.2, 5.3 and 5.4 which show the rates of uptake, reasons for these rates and opinions of men on how to increase uptake.

Where men have been disadvantaged is in the same assumption that women are naturally more caring. Look back to what the F4Jsuperheroes are protesting about. They are protesting that they have no access to their children, no rights to determine which schools,

what activities their children attend. Women tend to win 'custody' of children, that is, unless they are lesbians (Charles, 2000: 181). So although British family law states that access decisions are to be made based on the best interests of the child, organisations such as Fathers 4 Justice claim that the courts are biased towards children remaining with their mothers. It is not just in the UK that such a movement exists; in the USA since the 1990s a men's movement [**Hotlink → Political Science (Chapter 8)**] the Fatherhood Responsibility Movement mobilises around the issue of the need for fathers to be present in families (see World in Focus 5.3). Time now to turn to the area of family policy, but first stop and think.

Stop and think 5.5

Think about the care you have experienced, this could be the care you received as a child as well as the care and support you both receive and provide now. Who provided care for you? For whom do you provide care? Make a list of all the care roles in your life and one of another person, one who differs from you in generation. Are there gendered elements in these roles?

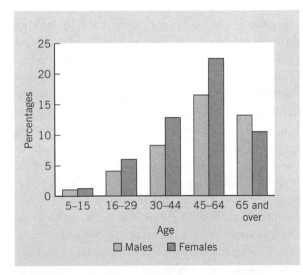

Figure 5.2 Gender of carers by age and sex, England and Wales, 2001

Source: National Statistics Office http://www.statistics.gov.uk/cci/nugget.asp?id=925

World in focus 5.3

Fatherhood Responsibility Movement

Since the mid-1990s, the self-proclaimed FRM has managed to establish fatherhood at the center of U.S. national politics. This movement claims that fathers have become marginalised in the family, with catastrophic societal consequences. Increasing numbers of female-headed households as well as shifting conditions for work, family formation, and care have allegedly contributed to the redefinition of the family into 'mother and child'. According to the FRM, fathers are thus marginalised and the family has become feminized.

(Gavanas, 2004: 248)

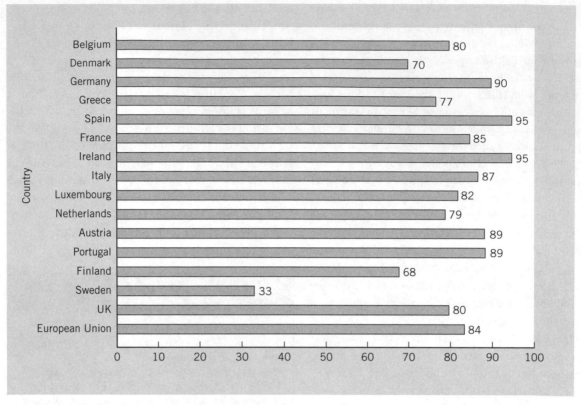

Figure 5.3 Parental leave: Rate of Non Uptake by Fathers, Europe
Source: European Opinion Research Group, 2004

The gendered family

Stop and think 5.6

Which of these would you list under family policy?
Family Allowances, Child Support Agency, Working
Families Tax Credit, Marriage Laws, Immigration
rules, Income Tax?

No doubt you found it easier to place some of these
under Family Policy more easily than others.
However, the way a 'family' is viewed shapes policy
more widely, from marriage laws to who is permitted
to reside in the country and who can receive state support. [**Hotlink → Family (Chapter 11)**].

We have already pointed out that the British welfare state, and all others, is based upon assumptions

regarding gender and family form. Look back to the
different models. It has been shown that for welfare
systems to treat men and women equitably in terms
of the division of labour and finances requires that
the relationship needs to be between the state and the
individual not the family. Yet, as can be seen, Britain
is defined as a breadwinner state, as such even the
system of social security – that is, income maintenance – becomes family policy. How does it do this?
Well, in a welfare system that considers the access an
applicant for income maintenance has to other
resources, such as the earnings of a partner, an
implicit family policy is automatic. What's more is
that the implementation of policies such as cohabitation rules (whereby males and females are assumed to
be economically intertwined if they live in the same
place) reinforces not just heterosexuality but also a
nuclear family form.

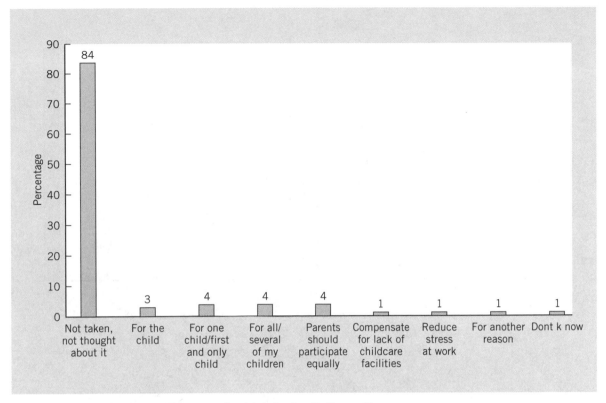

Figure 5.4 Parental leave: Reasons for Uptake by Fathers, Europe
Source: European Opinion Research Group, 2004

Social policies can be used to shape family forms, this can be/is done via a system of rewards and penalties. For example, many welfare systems provide tax allowances and benefits/pensions for dependant spouses and for children. In some cases these can act to discourage family breakdown or even women's participation in the workforce. An example of this was the Dutch dependants' allowance which was payable to the father and included not just an allowance for a wife and juvenile children, but also for daughters who stayed at home to assist in the household to the age of 26 (Sainsbury, 1996).

When considering penalties the first areas to come to mind are those policies which operate to make the breakdown of the family costly, for example spousal support and child support, not to mention the legal costs. However, these are the penalties that affect the 'normal' family – that is, the family that fits with social norms, rather than the average family. Penalties can operate to encourage the 'normal' family to remain that way but operate differently with other family forms. Likewise, what are rewards for the 'normal' family are, by their absence, penalties to other families. For example, in a system where marriage is supported by tax allowances, unmarried couples, heterosexual or homosexual, are financially treated as individuals and have a greater tax bill. Where the heterosexual couple has a choice, in the majority of welfare systems, the homosexual couple does not (as civil partnerships and gay marriage still only exist in a minority of countries [**Hotlink → Family (Chapter 11)**]. The privileging of heterosexuality is a gender issue, for it reinforces gender messages about appropriate masculinity and femininity [**Hotlink → Sex and Sexuality (Chapter 15)**], **Hotlink → Gendered Perspectives → Theoretical Issues (Chapter 1)**]

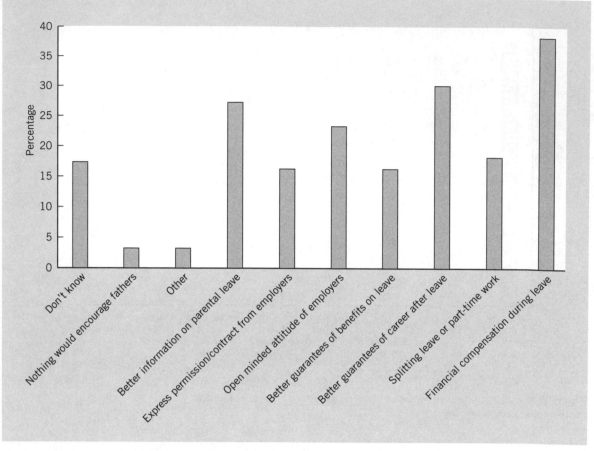

Figure 5.5 Parental leave: Ways to Increase Uptake by Fathers, Europe
Source: European Opinion Research Group, 2004

A critical look 5.3

Being careful about gender

It is widely accepted amongst academics and other commentators that the British welfare state has had a strong gender order reflected both in policy and practice. However, policy makers have been careful to ensure that assumptions about men and women are not blatantly accepted into the text of policy. A shift is visible away from assumed masculine and feminine roles as seen in the Beveridge Report to more gender neutral terms. This is clear from the Child Support Agency. Set up in the early 1990s the Agency was careful not to refer to 'mothers' and 'fathers' but to two new categories: 'parent with care' and 'parent without care'. This blurred the fact that in the vast majority of cases the former category consisted of women and the latter of men.

By the twenty-first century the use of gender neutral language has become less coy. Government sponsored TV adverts to encourage people to apply for Children's Tax Credit described how the tax credit worked. That is, working parents pay tax and an allowance is paid back to the 'parent with majority responsibility for care, we realise that in most cases this will be the mother'.

Conclusion

In this chapter we have covered a number of areas: social policy has been defined and the gendered assumptions in both the practice and study of social welfare have been explained. We have presented summaries of different, traditional, approaches to social policy and shown where these have 'missed the gender point'. Feminist work really opened up social policy to examine the 'norms' of systems and those who study them. By providing summaries of alternative models of social welfare and of the debates on two key issues it has been shown that social policy cannot be studied or practised without a deep understanding of the gender order and its variations across generation and place.

Further reading

Diane Sainsbury (ed.) (1999), *Gender and Welfare State Regimes*, Oxford, Oxford University Press. A collection of work by leading researchers in this field which examines, explains and analyses the construction of gender in various government welfare schemes across a number of countries.

Julia O'Connor, Ann S. Orloff, Ann and Sheila Shaver (1999), *States, Markets, Families: Gender, Liberalism and Social Policy in Australia, Canada, Great Britain and the United States*, Cambridge, Cambridge University Press. Although this is quite an advanced text it is full of detail and clearly shows the linkages between the market, family form and government policies in a thematic and comparative way.

Jennifer Marchbank (2000), *Women, Power and Policy: Comparative Studies of Childcare*, London, Routledge.

Chapters 3 and 4 of this book detail the politics of care around the issue of public daycare in Britain historically and across the European Union and beyond contemporarily. Attention is paid to the ways in which the priorities of different states and discourses shape childcare policies.

Critical Social Policy: A Journal of Theory and Practice in Social Welfare, Sage. This journal is always useful for discussions of race, class and gender. Especially useful issues are: No. 87, May 2006 which is themed around issues of children, families, gender and has lots on masculinity; No. 22, February 2002 which contains articles on work, life, care policies from, amongst other countries, the Netherlands, Australia, the USA and Britain.

Websites

Intute, **http://www.intute.ac.uk**
A wonderful gateway to many sources of information on all aspects of social policy.

UK National Statistics, **http://www.statistics.gov.uk**
This excellent site not only provides details of statistical returns of Government surveys but also links to useful publications, such as *Labour Market Trends*.

Robert Gordon University – An Introduction to Social Policy, **http://www2.rgu.ac.uk/publicpolicy/introduction/wstate.htm**
An award winning website which does exactly what it says – it provides an introduction, brief but accurate, to the main areas of social policy required in early undergraduate study.

EUROPA – European Commission for Employment and Social Affairs, **http://europa.eu.int**
An excellent source of information about the member states of the EU.

End of chapter activity

Multiple choice questions

1. Decommodification means:
   (a) not able to live without having to perform paid work
   (b) able to live without having to perform paid work
   (c) not having many possessions
   (d) living on one's partner's earnings

2. In a male breadwinner system the husband:
   (a) is viewed as the sole/main earner
   (b) is viewed as the sole/main carer
   (c) shares care and work roles
   (d) is a baker

End of chapter activity continued

3. Defamialialisation means being able to maintain a socially acceptable standard of living independent of:
   (a) family relationships
   (b) state assistance
   (c) paid work
   (d) a lottery win

4. The term social policy means:
   (a) legislation on social welfare matters
   (b) the academic study of social welfare
   (c) both
   (d) neither

5. Feminists have made gender visible in social policy by:
   (a) showing how social policy programmes are gendered
   (b) emphasising the interconnections amongst family, state and market
   (c) bringing gender into focus
   (d) all the above

6. What percentage of men surveyed knew about parental leave rights in the European Community?
   (a) 10%
   (b) 25%
   (c) 50%
   (d) 75%

7. What does 'normal' family mean in social policy?
   (a) average
   (b) married
   (c) conforming to social norms
   (d) headed by Norman and Norma

8. Which Superhero is your favourite?
   (a) Batman
   (b) Robin
   (c) Superman
   (d) Spiderman

Answers

Stop and think 5.4: High cost to the state, and therefore the tax payer, of servicing Universal Caregiver. Plus Universal Breadwinner can be presented as a gender equal system, i.e. all have to have 'male' work role. As such, the latter is usually less politically difficult.

Multiple choice questions:

1. (b)

2. (a)

3. (a)

4. (c)

5. (d)

6. (d)

7. (c)

8. Wonder Woman!

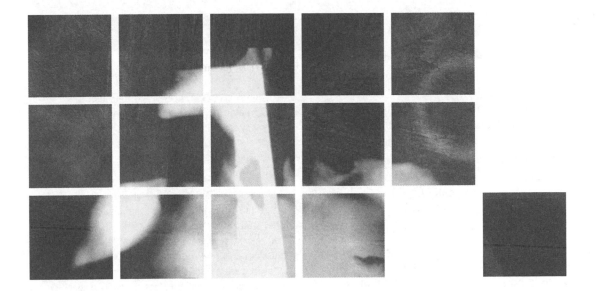

Anthropology

Lorraine Nencel

Key issues in this chapter:

➤ Key characteristics of anthropology and their relationship to feminist anthropology.
➤ The historical development of gender in anthropology.
➤ The development of masculinity studies in anthropology.
➤ The importance of the concept of power and how it has been developed and challenged.
➤ Examples of gender at work in cross-cultural contexts.
➤ Dilemmas involved in feminist anthropological fieldwork.

At the end of this chapter you should be able to:

➤ Distinguish what makes a study feminist and anthropological.
➤ Identify the period in which feminist anthropological study emerged.
➤ Make links between feminist anthropological studies and gender studies.
➤ Understand why gender is defined in relation to difference and given the attributes of fluid and unfixed.

Chapter 6

Introduction

Anthropology is a study taught differently throughout the world. If you are a student living in North America then most likely anthropology is considered a four-tier discipline, consisting of physical anthropology, archaeology, cultural anthropology and linguistic anthropology. According to the North American tradition, anthropology is the science of human behaviour and therefore it is not only contemporary behaviour that is of interest but also historical, ancient and prehistorical. If you are a student in a European university, then anthropology will be taught from either a cultural or social perspective. North American anthropology was developed in relation to the concept of culture, studying subjects like rituals, symbols and religion. While social anthropology traces its roots to Europe and more specifically Britain, here the emphasis was placed on the study of things like social structures, stratification and livelihoods. Today, although you will still hear some anthropologists talk about social or cultural anthropology, for many this differentiation has become obsolete. There is a general consensus that one cannot, for example, understand a symbol or ritual without understanding the structure in which it is embedded. Likewise, one's comprehension of structure is not complete if it does not include an understanding of the cultural symbols and meanings on which they are grounded. In this chapter we discuss the developments following the European tradition and include cultural and social anthropological studies conducted by both North American and European anthropologists.

Anthropology is concerned with understanding different (contemporary) cultures: their dynamics, their patterns, their institutions and how people adapt, think, perceive, behave and define themselves and their cultures. Anthropologists try to answer questions concerning how culture makes people and how people make culture. It is a comparative science explaining how different groups of people live and give meaning to their lives in different environments. Anthropology is considered a holistic science because it is not concerned with only one particular aspect of culture, society or the groups that live there, but it concerns everything (see A Closer Look 6.1).

A closer look 6.1

Holism and anthropology

Holistic/holism: The physical proposition that the whole is greater than the sum of its parts. In anthropology, an approach that focuses on the elements of culture, the relationships among these elements, and the relationship of culture to biology and environment.

> Anthropologists use a holistic approach. They are interested in the total range of human activity . . . They study the ways in which mothers hold their babies or sons address their fathers. They want to know not only how a group gets its food but also the rules for eating it. Anthropologists are interested in how human societies think about time and space and how they see colors and name them. They are interested in health and illness and the significance of physical variation. Anthropologists are interested in sex and are interested in folklore and fairy tales, political speeches, and everyday conversation. For the anthropologist, great ceremonies and the ordinary rituals of greeting a friend are all worth investigating. When presented out of context, some of the behaviors anthropologists study seem strange or silly, but every aspect of human behavior can help us to understand human life and society.
>
> (Nanca and Warms, 2002: 2)

Nowadays given that the world both locally and globally has become extremely complex, anthropologists generally focus on one area of interest but needless to say they approach the subject of study holistically. For example, in a study conducted about sex workers in Lima, Peru (Nencel, 2001), one of the objectives was to debunk ugly stereotypes concerning women who prostitute by letting them speak for themselves and at the same time researching the cultural context in which they live. The following steps were taken to reach this goal:

➤ Collection of secondary and primary sources on the history of the laws concerning prostitution.

➤ An analysis of newspaper articles that appeared on the subject which were collected during the fieldwork period and a database.

➤ Interviews were conducted with men, not necessarily clients, to understand how using or not using prostitutes' services fit into their ideas of sexuality.

➤ The stories of the women were collected through interviews and participant observation – a method of research that is frequently used in anthropological studies and will be discussed further on.

In its entirety these different steps helped to present a holistic picture of their situations as sex workers and their daily-lived experiences as women.

A final attribute giving anthropology its unique character is that nothing is ever taken for granted. Continuing on the previous example, although prostitution appears to be universally the same, in an anthropological study it cannot be assumed that what it means to be a prostitute in Peru is the same as being a prostitute in the Netherlands, and Thailand. Legislation, local gender ideologies, institutions such as religion all inform how prostitution is experienced by a man or woman in a specific cultural context. This 'do not take anything for granted' stance concerns everything in daily life. It means that one always asks questions and does not assume, for example, what the meaning of snow is in an Inuit society or another example, as in the case of one of the American pioneer anthropologists Margaret Mead, what it means to be a child in a given society.

Margaret Mead was not only one of the first female anthropologists she has also been considered one of the foremothers of feminist/gender anthropology. Her studies such as *The Coming of Age in Samoa* (1928), *Growing up in New Guinea* (1930) or *Sex and Temperament in Three Primitive Societies* (1935) (see A Closer Look 6.2) are all examples of an anthropological tradition that does not take anything for granted and at the same time uses the material collected in far away places to come to a better understanding of her own society. For the feminist anthropologists of the 1970s, Mead's work was considered an excellent illustration that proved that male and female 'sex' roles and activities were not universally the same. The exploration of cultural difference and for that matter cultural similarity showed, on the one hand, what it meant to be a woman and man was lived differently worldwide. On the other hand cultural comparison also revealed many similarities between women's position worldwide. This supported the feminist anthropologists of the 1970s to search for universal answers to women's universal subordinate, oppressed or subjugated position. The following sections map out the different debates that developed from the 1970s onwards.

A closer look 6.2

Studying different cultures

This excerpt from *Sex and Temperament* shows, in a nutshell, the central characteristics of Margaret Mead's approach to studying societies both her own and what contemporaneously was called 'simpler' or 'primitive' societies. It highlights the importance of cultural relativism – the study of different cultures in their own right and the anthropologist's ability to accept, respect and be emphatic to cultural difference encountered – for the advancement of our knowledge of differences between men and women. Mead states clearly, that difference is not just biological but culturally made. Mead strategically distances herself from contemporaneous feminist struggles – keeping the division between politics and objective [Hotlink → **Method, Methodology and Epistemology (Chapter 2)**] science intact. Her studies, such as the excerpt presented here, are concerned with issues important in the struggles of second-wave feminist academics.

This study is not concerned with whether there are or not actual universal differences between the sexes, either quantitative or qualitative . . . It is not a treatise on the rights of women, nor an inquiry into the basis of feminism. It is, very simply, an account of how three primitive societies have grouped their social attitudes towards temperament about the very obvious facts of sex difference. I studied this problem in simple societies because here we have the drama of civilization writ small, a social microcosm alike in kind, but different in size and magnitude, from the complex social structures of peoples who, like our own, depend upon a written tradition and upon the integration of a great number of conflicting historical traditions. Among the gentle mountain-dwelling Arapesh, the fierce cannibalistic Mundugumor, and the graceful headhunters of Tchambuli, I studied this question. Each of these tribes had, as has every human society, the point of sex-difference to use as one theme in the plot of social life, and each of these three peoples has developed that theme differently. In comparing the way in which they have dramatised sex-difference, it is possible to gain a greater insight into what elements are social constructs, originally irrelevant to the biological facts of sex-gender.

Our own society makes great use of this plot. It assigns different roles to the two sexes, surrounds them both from birth with an expectation of different behavior; plays out the whole drama of courtship, marriage, and parenthood in terms of types of behavior believed to be innate and therefore appropriate for one sex or for the other . . .

All discussion of the position of women, of the character and temperament of women, the enslavement or the emancipation of women, obscures the basic issue – the recognition that the cultural plot behind human relations is the way in which the roles of the two sexes are conceived, and that the growing boy is shaped to a local and special emphasis as inexorably as is the growing girl.

(Mead, 1935: 219–24)

Stop and think 6.1

Think about the last vacation or new place you went to either in your own country or a foreign one. Can you see any cultural differences?

➤ What expectations did you have of the place and people?

➤ How did these compare with what you experienced?

➤ What are the first things you remember about the place? Are these things differences or similarities?

➤ What can this comparison tell us about your own country or place you live?

➤ What does the comparison with your own country and life tell you about the country or new place you visited?

A brief history of gender and anthropology: from woman, to women, to gender and difference

Making women visible

This book has its roots in the women's movement. To explain and describe equality and inequality between the sexes contemporary feminism has turned to anthropology with many questions in its search for a theory and body of information . . .

The subjugation of women is a fact of our daily existence, yet it neither began with modern capitalism nor automatically disappears in socialist societies. In looking at other cultures, we find that sexual inequality appears widespread and that the institutions in which it is embedded have a long and complex history. To truly understand the phenomenon we must find its roots and trace them in their many permutations and transformations. Our political critique must be based on this understanding of the origins and development of sexism.

(Rapp Reiter, 1975: 11)

Whereas, Margaret Mead clearly took distance from contemporaneous feminist initiatives, the anthropologists of the 1970s claimed the feminist political agenda as a starting point for their queries. The excerpt above is taken from the introduction of what is now considered one of the classics of what from then on would be called feminist anthropology – *Toward an Anthropology of Women*. It illustrates one of the objectives of feminist anthropology of the 1970s: to understand the origin and mechanisms of oppression in order to contribute to changing women's position in society. One of the guiding assumptions of this period was that 'sexual asymmetry is presently a universal fact of human social life' (Rosaldo and Lamphere, 1974: 3). Thus, women were universally oppressed and feminist anthropologists set out to research its varying manifestations. In another classic volume, edited by Michele Rosaldo and Louise Lamphere (1974), *Woman, Culture and Society*, the contributors set out to find answers to the original questions concerning women's oppression:

> Are there societies that, unlike our own, make women the equals or superior of men? If not are women ' naturally' men's inferiors? Why do women in our own society and elsewhere accept a subordinate standing? How, and in what kinds of situations, do women exercise power? How do women help to shape, create and change the private and public worlds in which they live?
>
> (Rosaldo and Lamphere, 1974: 3)

All of these studies concluded that women's position was universally inferior to men. Sherry Ortner (1974), wanted to understand why and searched for the answer to the question 'is female to male as nature is to culture?' She asks: 'What could there be in the generalised structure and conditions of existence, common to every culture that would lead every culture to place a lower value upon women?' (1974: 71). The generalised structure in culture which helps us to understand women's position as inferior is the universal relation between nature and culture. Nature is universally valued less than culture and in this article she shows how women are always associated with nature and men with culture.

During this period the concept gender became firmly rooted in the feminist anthropological discourse. Gayle Rubin (1975) developed a complicated but nonetheless influential theory based on Lévi-Strauss, Freud and Lacan concerning the sex/gender system and claims that to understand the causes of women's oppression it is necessary to study the relationship between sex and gender. She states, 'Gender is a socially imposed division of the sexes. It is a product of the social relations of sexuality' and transforms males and females into 'men' and 'women'. Men and women are socially constructed as two mutually exclusive categories (Rubin, 1975: 179). Thus, gender was the social enactment of biological sex and sexuality. In this period, sexuality or sex was not a separate analytical category from gender – [**Hotlink → World in Focus 1.1 (Chapter 1)**].

The proof that women's position was universally oppressed led to an epistemological claim that would influence feminist anthropological research for at least the next decade. Namely that despite all the diversity encountered in women's oppression, women's situation was universally the same and therefore feminist anthropological research began from the universal category of the woman. The category woman was a homogeneous category that recognised that women experienced oppression differently on a daily level, but nonetheless their communal experience of oppression erased all differences that could be discerned. In other words, women's situation worldwide was more similar to each other than different. Oppression erased the differences found between cultures, ethnicity, class, and so on. It was feminist anthropology's task to study the differences and the cultural specificities in order to get more insight into mechanisms of universal oppression and domination. This implied that the power relationship between men and women was universally the same: men were the oppressors and women were oppressed. Just like women, men were conceptualised as a homogeneous group. In this period of feminist anthropology, there were very few social scripts attributed to men and women. The discovery and analysis of women's oppression went hand in hand with a second objective, namely, making women visible. This objective will be discussed in the following section. First, however, look at World in Focus 6.1 for examples of how assumed biological characteristics have different results in different parts of the world.

Erasing male bias and making women visible

A second and intimately related objective of feminist anthropology of the 1970s was its aim to correct the androcentric bias. Male standpoints both in academia and in the cultures studied were the norm. Male anthropologists brought to the field their own gender beliefs of what was considered naturally male and female. Thus, for example, many western anthropologists began from the western notion of the male breadwinner – [**Hotlink → Social Policy (Chapter 5)**] based on the 'natural' division of labour between men

World in focus 6.1

Sex–gender relation: the nimble fingers myth and other stories

One of the few 'universal' assertions that can be made is that throughout the world what men and women do in a society is distinct – this was first called the sexual division of labour but contemporarily many academics call this the gender division of labour. Often this division is based on what is assumed to be biological characteristics that make it natural for women to do one type of work and men another. Thus, it was considered natural for men to carry heavy loads in western countries, because men were supposedly stronger than women, but if we look at, for example, African countries, women carry heavy burdens of water, firewood, and their children on their back daily and this is considered women's or even female children's responsibilities. Thus, 'natural qualities' are transformed into social activities and roles. This process, which was one of the dimensions of the sex–gender system is also found in more complex work organisations such as the Free Trade Zones in Central America and South East Asia. Women were and are still hired more frequently than men because of these supposed 'natural qualities' that made them into better workers. Feminist anthropologists

studied these and other phenomenon to reveal the social mechanisms employed that transformed biological sex into social roles (gender). They intended to debunk these myths and simultaneously, deepen our understanding of the relations of subordination and exploitation. But they did not question whether this was the only relationship possible between sex and gender. It would take some more time before the relationship between gender and sexuality would be questioned. [**Hotlink → Gendered Perspectives – Theoretical Issues (Chapter 1); Hotlink → Sex and Sexuality (Chapter 15)**]

Diane Elson and Ruth Pearson (1981) asked the question why are the overwhelming amount of factory workers in world market factories young women? They came to the following conclusions:

> [T]here is a widespread belief that it is a 'natural' differentiation, produced by innate capacities and personality traits of women and men, and by an objective differentiation of their income needs, in that men need an income to support a family, while women do not . . .
>
> Women are considered not only to have naturally nimble fingers, but also to be naturally more docile and willing to accept tough work discipline, and

naturally more suited to tedious, repetitive, monotonous work. Their lower wages are attributed to their secondary status in the labour market which is seen as a natural consequence of their capacity to bear children The fact that only young women work in world market factories is also rationalised as an effect of their capacity to bear children – this naturally means they will be either unwilling or unable to continue in employment much beyond their early twenties . . .

The famous 'nimble fingers' of young women are not an inheritance from their mothers, in the same way that they may inherit the colour of her skin or eyes. They are the result of the training they have received from their mothers and other female kin since early infancy in the tasks socially appropriate to women's roles. For instance, since industrial sewing of clothing closely resembles sewing with a domestic sewing machine, girls who have learnt such sewing at home already have the manual dexterity and capacity for spatial assessment required. Training in needlework and sewing also produces skills transferable to other assembly operations.
(Elson and Pearson, 1981:148–9)

and women. When going to new and far away countries, this assumption was not put to the test and they sought out the persons they thought were the 'male heads of households' to answer their questions or become their informants. However, in many societies the gender division of labour might be more complementary or influenced by other differentiating factors such as age, or kin relationship. This type of male bias was ethnocentric – the process of using one's own cul-

ture values and meanings as the norm to judge and understand distinct cultures. Hence, this made women invisible. Moreover, mainstream anthropological research all too often studied formal institutions such as formal politics, productive activities and the like where women's presence was underrepresented. Women's views were often received through male members of a given culture and put down to gossip. Rayna Rapp called this a '"double bias" that trivialised and misinterpreted female roles for so long' (Rapp, 1975: 16). This double bias made women invisible.

As in other disciplines feminist anthropologists worked to make women in society more visible. And they succeeded. They showed that women were not powerless but rather the power they exercised was not always formal and as visible as men's. Even gossip was seen to have a function in influencing and decision making; their daily activities contributed to the daily reproduction of the family and could no longer be brushed away as mere household chores. Theoretical concepts were developed such as the private–public binary, which divided society into two spheres: the private sphere associated more with women and the public with men. This enabled feminist anthropologists to study women's activities in the private sphere and how they related to the public. Women's activities were no longer conceptualised as isolated from the broader society [Hotlink → Sociology (Chapter 4)]. Although through the years, this theoretical binary has lost its analytical value, criticised because culture is not easily reduced into two spheres nor do the things people do solely belong to one or the other, it nonetheless served the objective of making women's lives and experiences visible and counteracting the trivialised images and roles produced in mainstream anthropology. Finally by making women's activities and presence visible, men's contribution to society was put back into proportion. For example, in hunting and gathering societies, classical anthropological studies accentuated men's contribution through hunting for the survival of the community. Exploring women's roles as gatherers revealed that it was women's gathering activities that sustain the daily diet [Hotlink → A Closer Look 1.3 (Chapter 1)].

European feminist anthropology – the fem-socs

European anthropologists were also preoccupied with the same issues. Yet the striking difference with the European (predominantly British) feminist anthropological traditions was the strong Marxist influence in their studies. British feminist anthropologists' queries originated from their dissatisfaction with the treat-

ment of women in Marxist theory. A classic volume that challenged orthodox Marxist thought was Kate Young, Carol Wolkowitz and Roslyn McCullagh (1981) *Of Marriage and the Market: Women's subordination in international perspective*. They were in search of better 'analytical and conceptual tools for the development of a theory of social relations which would encompass not only the so-called economic relations of society but also what been called the relations of every day life' (Young *et al.*, 1981: viii). Following the Marxist tradition they were not only concerned with relations of production, sexual division of labour and women's position within, but developed the Marxist concept of reproduction to a dynamic and multi-level concept (daily maintenance, biological reproduction, and reproduction of the workforce) that made women and their activities visible and embedded them within the broader societal context. Domains such as the household are no longer envisioned as natural nor neutral but studied as social domains where women are active, and as one of the sites where the gender relations of subordination were reproduced and contested. Thus, feminist socialist anthropologists defined society as consisting of two spheres: the productive and reproductive spheres. Like their North American colleagues, their concern for women's position in society developed from the feminist political agenda and their studies are aimed to contribute to social change by analysing the many manifestations of subordination in societies cross-culturally.

Challenges from within feminist anthropology

From the early 1980s onward, feminist anthropologists began to find suspect the universal object of sameness (Rosaldo, 1980). 'The common identity of women as subordinate to male dominance could not be upheld in the face of a proliferation of cultural, gender, class and race differences' (Pels and Nencel, 1991: 11). However the 'loss of universal "sameness"' (Moore, 1988: 10) would reach a crescendo with the entrance of critical voices of Third World feminist scholars in the debate. In one of the most influential articles of this period, Chandra Mohanty (1988) concisely spells out the critique from women of colour of western feminist thought. She analyses several western feminist studies on third world women and comes to the following conclusion:

> feminist writings I analyse here discursively colonise the material and historical heterogeneities of the lives of women in the third world, thereby producing/representing a composite, singular 'third-world woman' – an image which appears arbitrarily constructed but nevertheless carries with it the authorising signature of western humanist discourse.
> (Mohanty, 1988: 63)

Mohanty's critique (see A Closer Look 6.3) and that of other third world women and women of colour was taken very seriously. She not only criticised feminist academics for creating a one-dimensional identity of Third World women – imposing western norms of oppression and emancipation on women who lived in totally distinct cultures and embedded in distinct histories – she showed how feminist analysis began from a position that prioritised western ways of thinking about humanity and in turn how this related to their colonial heritage. This critique hit feminist anthropology particularly hard. In the first place it accused feminist anthropologists of being ahistorical and even worse ethnocentric. Secondly, the critique showed that despite the good intentions of feminist academics their work contributed to reproducing the colonial relationships that assigned authority and power to the west and left those from the Third World with virtually none.

At this time gender began to replace the category women [**Hotlink → History → Scott (Chapter 3)**]. Although it was defined as the social meaning and construction of masculinity and femininity, in the beginning gender was nearly always synonymous to women [**Hotlink → Gendered Perspectives – Theoretical Issues (Chapter 1)**]. Men's presence in feminist studies was usually confined to the hegemonic role as oppressor. As we will see below, it took some time before men and masculinity would be approached from the same dynamic framework used to study women's daily lives [**Hotlink → Gendered Perspectives – Theoretical Issues (Chapter 1)**].

Stop and think 6.2

At the completion of this exercise you should be able to grasp the critique that academics like Chandra Mohanty made in relation to western feminists constructing a homogeneous category of woman.

Imagine you are visiting a culture very different from your own, perhaps one that you have visited on vacation. You are walking along the open market and you see many different women/men with and without their children selling goods and food products to make a living. Since you have taken a tour of the island or city, you have seen where many people live and the living conditions of the poor. Many of the market vendors are economically struggling to survive. Now, try to make a comparison between one of the women or men on the market and yourself and your life. What are possible similarities and what are possible differences? Of course you will find some similarities, but there will also be an enormous amount of differences.

Taking this one step further – you are standing at a market stall waiting to buy some tropical fruit that looks absolutely delicious. The market vendor is helping a person who is the same sex as themselves: well dressed, children in name brand clothes and the newest model car parked a few steps behind him or her. Now try to make a comparison between the individual buying fruit and the market vendor. What are the similarities and what are the differences? This is a simple illustration of what it means to recognise difference. Although individuals from the same gender, culture and country share similarities, their situatedness in society can make them more different than similar.

A closer look 6.3

Under western eyes

Mohanty (1988) analyses three presuppositions, which are present in western feminist discourse:

> The first is the assumption of women as an already constituted and coherent group with identical interests and desires, regardless of class, ethnic or racial location, implies a notion of gender or sexual difference or even patriarchy which can be applied universally and cross-culturally . . . The

second analytical presupposition is evident on the methodological level; in the uncritical way 'proof' of universality and cross-cultural validity are provided. The third is more specifically political presupposition, underlying the methodologies and the analytic strategies, i.e., the model of power and struggle they imply and suggest. I argue . . . that a homogeneous notion of the oppression of women as a group is assumed, which, in turn, produces the image of an 'average third-world woman'. This average third-world woman leads an essentially truncated life based on her feminine gender (read: sexually constrained) and being 'third world' (read: ignorant, poor, uneducated, tradition-bound, religious, domesticated, family-oriented, victimised, etc.). This, I suggest is in contrast to the (implicit) self-representation of western women as educated, modern, as having control over their own bodies and sexualities and the 'freedom' to make their own decisions.

(Mohanty, 1988: 64–65).

Thus, Mohanty showed western feminism how their studies contributed to making women of the Third World the 'Other', and consequently converted western feminist norms and values into the only feminist legitimate doctrine. She objected to the predefined definitions of oppression and liberation which straitjacketed feminist research into supporting only one particular (western) feminist political agenda. For example, in western eyes motherhood was assumed to be a site of oppression, even though in many non-western societies motherhood is celebrated. Feminist assumptions on motherhood blinded them to other readings of its significance. Third World women were either seen as in need of consciousness raising or possessing a false consciousness. In either case, Third World women's experiences were used as proof to show universal subordination. Mohanty showed, that universal subordination was an ahistorical, acontextual concept that ignored Third-World women's experiences, perceptions and the context in which they lived.

Her critique shook feminist foundations in anthropology and caused feminist anthropologists to not only question their analytical concepts and theories, but also demanded that they critically look at their role as researchers in relation to their privileged western position, the power relations, as well as their relation to the colonial past. [**Hotlink** → **Method, Methodology and Epistemology (Chapter 2)**]

Enter postmodernism: challenge or ally?

Paralleled to this was the entrance of postmodern theory in anthropology. Referred to as the new ethnography or literary turn – which was the recognition that anthropologists were not only 'researchers and theorists, anthropologists are ethnographers, that is: writers' (Pels and Nencel, 1991: 13). Concepts such as 'polyvocality' (Clifford, 1986) – the representation of various voices in the text – were presented as the ethnographic ideal. Grand theories in both feminist and mainstream anthropology were criticised for their essentialising nature. Of course this parallels many of the developments that were taking place in other disciplines. As in other areas postmodernism was critiqued as in their publications, little or virtually no recognition was given to the previous work done by critical and feminist anthropologists that had been challenging research relations, the concept of power and representation for nearly a decade [**Hotlink** → **Method, Methodology and Epistemology (Chapter 2)**]. In fact feminist anthropologists were, to put it mildly, surprised to find out that their texts were not considered innovative (Behar and Gorden 1995: 9). It was claimed that the ideological and political nature of feminist anthropology impeded the creation of innovative texts. Secondly, feminist and critical anthropologists were worried about the effect that the postmodern turn would have in relation to the concepts such as power. Universal terms such as oppression and subordination were labelled as essentialist and privileged the researcher's voice above the research subject. Would it still be possible to do studies that would contribute to broader social change and address the issues on the feminist political agenda? Contemporarily, the tension that existed between postmodernism and feminist anthropology has to a large extent subsided. Postmodernist anthropology shares with critical and feminist anthropologists common grounds in relation to such issues involving the researcher's authority in the field and in the text, the conceptualisation of social constructs as fluid and unfixed and finally the multi-positioned notion of identity.

From women to difference

The work of scholars from other disciplines such as the historian Joan Scott and her multi-layered concept of gender [Hotlink → History (Chapter 3)], Sandra Harding's epistemological analysis of feminism and science [Hotlink → Method, Methodology and Epistemology (Chapter 2)], and Donna Haraway's (1991) concept 'situated knowledge' – knowledge being defined as partial and depending on the position and embeddedness of the subject – also contributed to the shift that did away with the homogeneous category of woman to be redefined as women – a heterogeneous category that recognises difference. [Hotlink → Method, Methodology and Epistemology (Chapter 2)]. It was through these developments that gender eventually became defined as situated, multi-positional, fluid. What does this mean for the study of gender, gender relations and gender identity? (see World Focus 6.2). In the first place, gender is not fixed. As in all anthropological queries, we cannot assume beforehand what it means to be a man or woman in a given society [Hotlink → Gendered Perspectives – Theoretical Issues (Chapter 1)]. But it means even more.

The conceptualisation of gender as such contains various ontological assumptions [Hotlink → Method, Methodology and Epistemology (Chapter 2)]. It means that there is not one unified definition of gender out there waiting to be discovered, applicable to every nook and cranny of a society. Rather there is a multitude of meanings that are constructed in relations and can change, shift or contradict depending on the context in which they are constructed. It is constructed through relations, be that between individuals, in institutions, or through identity. The acceptance that gender is unfixed implies the acceptance of another ontological assumption, namely that gender is not merely the definition of what it means to be man or a women in society, but that the construction of masculinity and femininity is constituted by the intersectionality of gender, sexuality, race/ethnicity, age, and class, and so on. Gender cannot be studied 'purely' as it will always be analysed in relation to other identity markers. Thus, gender has moved far beyond being a category which translated biological sex into a social construct. Contemporary analysis of gender implies the study of difference [Hotlink → (Chapter 1)].

Gender and difference

The world is far more complex than previously assumed. Yet the objective of feminist anthropology has not altered, still being concerned with trying to understand what Sylvia Yanagisako and Carol Delany (1995) call the 'naturalising power' of gender. Naturalising power makes the gender order seem 'natural, inevitable, and even god-like' (Yanagisako and Delany, 1995: 1), and it is the feminist anthropologist's task to find out how cultural meanings, structures and experiences contribute to creating an illusion of seamlessness. However, this task has become more complicated. With the shift from woman, to women to gender and difference a new conceptual framework was needed.

One of these frameworks was proposed by Sherry Ortner (1996), who called this 'practice theory'. She struggled to find a way to conceptualise women and men as active agents in charge of their destinies and at the same time recognise the structural constraints that exist which limit opportunities, possibilities for negotiation and choice. She presents what she calls a framework of practice and defines it as follows:

> there is an insistence, as in earlier structural-determinist models, that human action is constrained by the given social and cultural order (often condensed in the term 'structure'), but there is also an insistence that human action *makes* 'structure' – reproduces or transforms it or both.
>
> (Ortner, 1996: 2)

Her underlying argument to this perspective is that human action is made by 'structure' and at the same time makes it and unmakes it. The study of society and culture as a dynamic relationship between structure and agency supports a definition of gender that recognises difference as well as situatedness. Louise Lamphere, Helena Ragoné and Patricia Zavella (1997) define gender as follows:

> Gender is historically contingent and constructed simultaneously embedded in material relations, social institutions and cultural meanings. Finally

gender is intimately bound up with inequalities, not only in the often dominant relation of men to women but also to those of class and race.

(di Leonardo, 1991: 28–32, cited in Lamphere *et al.*, 1997: 3)

These authors recognise the importance of human agency and simultaneously define gender as a construct in which structural and institutional constraints are recognised, is constituted by class and 'race' among other markers of difference, and acknowledges gender as a relation of power which is more often than not unequal. This last component illustrates the shift that was made from defining power *a priori* as oppression and conceptualising power as a component essentially needed for understanding gender. Power has become a complex definition. Power is situated and as such implies that there are situations in which a person can have more power than in others. Power is not defined neutrally; it is still more often than not defined as a relation of inequality with adverse effects for women.

The centrality of the concept of power within gender analysis is the factor that makes feminist anthropological studies different from studies about women and men. Studies that begin from a gender perspective seek to understand the equalities and inequalities of power. It is one of the driving forces behind the political dimension of feminist anthropological studies today. By studying culture and society and revealing the contradictions, strengths, the moments of resistance, subordination and so on, feminist anthropology is still politically charged. However, change is no longer conceptualised as lineal or accumulative (i.e. from oppressed to emancipated) but conceptualised as unfixed and fluid (see World in Focus 6.2).

World in focus 6.2

Understanding difference in relation to gender and identity

Dorinne's Kondo's (1990) study on gender and identity in a Japanese sweet-making workplace is an example of doing an ethnographic study which starts with the notion of difference and tries to understand the process of identity construction as multipositioned, intersecting features of 'race', gender and age. In addition her queries are an illustration of how feminist anthropologists use what Ortner (1996) called practice theory. Finally, it also illustrates how the concept of power is prominently intertwined in contemporary feminist ethnography.

I assumed my goal as anthropologist to be a description of a 'concept of self' characteristic of all members of any particular culture. Collective identities like 'the Japanese' or 'Japanese concepts of self' no longer seem to me to be fixed essences, but rather strategic assertions, which inevitably suppress differences, tensions, and contradictions within. Given these moves toward practice, nonessentialism and radical cultural and historical specificity, I develop in the present inquiry themes of personhood, work, and family by asking a . . . question: How did the people I knew craft themselves and their lives within shifting fields of power and meaning, and how did they do so in particular situations and within a particular historical and cultural context? In framing a reply to this query, I detail the dynamically engaging, everyday contests over the meanings of company and family, the two most salient sites of symbolic struggle in the Satō factory, and the ways identities are asserted in those struggles. In turn, these terrains of contest cannot be understood without reference to the larger movements of what we would call history, politics, and the economy . . .

I attempt to build on feminist scholarship that expands our definitions of what counts as political. Power can create identities on the individual level, as it provides disciplines, punishments, and culturally available pathways for fulfillment; nowhere were these forces more evident to me than in my relationships with the Japanese people I knew. At stake in my narrative . . . are the constantly contested and shifting boundaries of my identity and the identities of my Japanese relatives, friends, and acquaintances. We participated in each others' lives and sought to make sense of one another. In that attempt to understand, power inevitably came into play as we tried to force each other into appropriately comprehensible categories. The sites of these struggles for understanding were located in what we might call silent features of 'identity' both in America and in Japan: race, gender and age.

(Kondo, 1990: 10–11)

The engendered man and masculinities

Anthropology has always involved men talking to men about men. Until recently, however, very few within the discipline of the 'study of man' had truly examined men as *men*. Although in the past two decades the study of gender comprises the most important new body of theoretical and empirical work in the discipline of anthropology overall, gender studies are still often equated with women's studies.

It is the new examinations of men as engendered and engendering subjects that comprise the anthropology of masculinity today.

(Gutmann, 1997a: 385)

As the above quote shows the problem with the study of men in anthropology is not that they were invisible, rather their position in society was assumed to be universally natural and therefore was not questioned. A classic example is found in the anthropological literature on Mediterranean societies in which the honour and shame complex was used to understand the working of these societies. In a feminist critique of its omnipresent use in Mediterranean studies, Victoria Goddard defines honour as 'a quality of groups, not only of individuals – rather a single person symbolises the group whose collective honour is upheld by its different individual members' (Goddard, 1987: 167). Both men and women must behave honourably, but it was men's responsibility to assure that no shame would come to the family, clan or community. Men must protect as well as control its members. One of the ways that this was accomplished was through controlling women's sexuality [**Hotlink → Sex and Sexuality (Chapter 15)**]. Studies on honour and shame emphasised the significance of men's roles in maintaining society. Women, on the other hand were conceptualised as passive with no autonomy.

With the rise of feminist anthropology, men's engendered position within society became visible, but was initially confined to one type of representation, namely as dominant. Men were attributed both as individuals and group the role of oppressor. As Andrea Cornwall and Nancy Lindisfarne point out 'It is ironic that the logic of feminism as a political posi-tion has often required the notion of "men" as a single, oppositional category'(Cornwall and Lindisfarne, 1997: 1). Thus, through the 1970s and 1980s, what we learnt about men, their behaviour, their activities was restricted to showing how their individual and group actions contributed to the collective reproduction of the mechanisms of subordination and oppression.

The recognition that masculinity needed to be defined as plural, situational and fluid came somewhat later than the call for the deconstruction of the unitary category of woman. It would be a misrepresentation to attribute this development purely to feminist anthropology. Masculinity studies and postmodernism also played a role in the questioning of the natural position of men in society whereas feminist anthropology contributed to a cross-cultural deconstruction of the concept of masculinity. Cornwall and Lindisfarne (1997) challenged the hegemonic category of masculinity, treating masculinity as plural and investigating the different configurations of power without preconceived assumptions. Following Carrigan and colleagues, they speak of hegemonic masculinity defining it as 'a question of how particular groups of men inhabit positions of power and wealth and how they legitimate and reproduce the social relationships that generate their dominance' (Carrigan *et al.*, 1985, cited in Cornwall and Lindisfarne, 1997: 19). Of further significance was the recognition of what they call subordinate masculinities which are never totally silenced by the hegemonic, interact with it and have their own dynamics. Anthropological studies on masculinity seek to 'dislocate' the hegemonic [**Hotlink → (Chapter 1)**] – notion of masculinity to reveal the different versions of masculinities that exist in a given context.

Engendering the concept of men and masculinity implies the study of masculinity in relation to the concept of power. This involves the study of how men's power has become naturalised in gender relations. Also, given that masculinity is a relational construct, it must be studied in the multi-various relations that exist between men and women, between men, and between women. Mathew Gutmann states that ethnographies of men should not be

. . . viewed, understood, or utilised primarily as a complement to women's studies. Rather, they must be developed and nurtured as integral to understanding the ambiguous relationship between multigendered differences and similarities, equalities and inequalities. As with the study of ethnicity: one can never study one gender without studying others.

(Gutmann, 1997a: 401–2)

See World Focus 6.3 for an example of how this works in practice.

Today, it is becoming more common that gender is studied as a relational concept. Although research might be focused on women as the research subject, their lives and experiences will also be discussed in relation to men as an engendered category, and visa versa. To sum up,

the entrance of masculinity into gender anthropology has brought the study of gender to a new dimension of holism in which the gender relations of power between men and women are studied in relation to each other within a specific cultural context.

Sexuality and gender in anthropology

The development of sexuality studies in anthropology can be traced to several developments in the broader anthropological academic field.

The contribution of Gay Studies, Third Gender Studies (Kulick, 1998; Prieur, 1998) as well as studies that originated out of concern for AIDS

World in focus 6.3

The meanings of macho: changing Mexican male identities
[Hotlink → History, World in Focus 2.2 (Chapter 3)]

Macho is a label for men that through the years has lost its Latin American origins and has become a definer of masculinity in other regions and continents. Men are not only designated machos in Latin America but in other parts of the world. Machismo has been defined as a cult of virility. Still machismo is a construct that is generally used to describe certain elements of the gender order in Latin America in general. Being a good macho entails having numerous relationships with different women, numerous children that were borne out of this relationship, being aggressive and not showing emotions. Approximately a decade ago, the hegemonic and homogeneous representation of machismo began to be questioned.

Mathew Gutmann set out to study what it means to be a macho in modern day Mexico and came to the conclusion that there is not one Mexican masculinity but one must talk of masculinities.

It is common to hear women and men in Col. Santo Domingo say that while there used to be a lot of macho men, they are not as prevalent today. Some people who make this comment are too young to know anything firsthand about the old days, but regardless, they are sure there was more machismo before. If some oldtimers like to divide the world of men into machos and *mandilones* (meaning female-dominated men), it is far more common for younger men in Col. Santo Domingo to define themselves as belonging to a third category, the 'nonmacho' group, '*ni macho, ni mandilón*', neither macho nor *mandilón*''. Though others may define a friend or relative as 'your typical Mexican

macho,' the same man will frequently reject the label for himself, describing all the things he does to help his wife around the home, pointing out that he does not beat his wife (one of the few generally agreed on attributes of machos) and so on. What is most significant is not simply how the terms macho and machismo are variously defined – there is little consensus on their meanings – but more, that today the terms are so routinely regarded by men of the working class in Col. Santo Domingo, Mexico City, as pejorative and not worthy of emulation. Further, while many men in Col. Santo Domingo have considered the relative merits of being macho, fewer have changed the way they refer to a group of men that, for them, is beyond the pale, that is the *maricones*, queers, homosexuals, who thus constitute an especially marginalised fourth category of Mexican masculinities.

(Gutmann, 1997a: 229)

prevention (Parker *et al.*, 1991, 2000) have firmly anchored the premise in social sciences that sexual and gender identities need not coincide, reflect or conform to each other: one's gender identity is not naturally one's sexual identity or vice versa; both are socially and culturally constructed within specific dynamics in historical contexts.

(Nencel, 2005: 132)

In essence, this implies that sexuality must be studied in its own right, however,

> . . . it is really not possible to analyse sexuality without reference to the economic, political and cultural matrix within which it is embedded. It would be more accurate to say, perhaps, that in modern society we have an *idea* of sexuality as a specific concept, but we cannot in actual fact understand it without contextualizing it.

(Caplan, 1987: 25)

So, for example on ethnographies on workfloor experiences, flirting is one relation that has received considerable attention. Kenneth Yelvington's studies (1995, 1996) on a factory in Trinidad shows how flirting is both an instrument of domination and a tactic by women to resist. Flirting not only sexually objectified women but women's active participation in flirting relations also objectified men [Hotlink → Sex and Sexuality, Controversy 15.2 (Chapter 15)]. Leslie Salzinger's work concerning a Mexican *maquiladora* (export-oriented, free trade zones industries) shows how 'productivity at Panoptimex is born out of the routinised sexual objectification of women workers by their male superiors' (Salzinger, 2000: 82) and flirtation is a 'social relation that defines and frames the interactions of supervisors and workers overall' (Salzinger, 2000: 86). One of the strengths of the anthropological approach is that it enables the researcher to study sexuality – its daily construction within the cultural context it is embedded.

Sexuality is a situated concept and although it has its own dynamics within a given context, like gender it is constructed through relations with other identity markers such as class, age, gender, ethnicity/'race'. In many Latin American countries the gender order of society has a sexual rationale. In other words gender and (hetero) sexuality are interrelated. Lorraine Nencel (1996) shows how middle-class heterosexual men con-

struct their notions of their sexual selves in part through creating labels which divide women into three different groups: the *chica de su casa* (the homebody), *pacharacas* and *rucas* (girls for consensual recreational sex) and prostitutes. Interesting to note is that the same girl in one context, for example in her community, will be considered a *chica de su casa*, while in another context, for example in a disco, she may be considered a *pacharaca*. This example shows how men's perceptions and sexual desires create gender categories of femininity, and is an example of the intimate relation between sexuality and gender in a Latin American context (see Stop and think 6.3 for a further example).

There is one other area in which anthropologists are concerned with sexuality, namely in fieldwork and fieldwork relations (Whitehead and Conaway, 1986; Kulick and Wilson, 1995). Although as early as 1914 one of the first social anthropologists, Bronislaw Malinowski, wrote in his diaries (published after his death in 1967) about the sexual desire he felt during fieldwork, it is in the last decade that anthropologists have begun to question how their sexual identity, their sexual preferences and experience influence the research process and research relation [Hotlink → Method, Methodology and Epistemology → The person in research (Chapter 2)]. This process of analysing the research relation – being reflexive – is part and parcel of anthropological methodological practice and feminist research practice in general.

Stop and think 6.3

Below you will find a drawing, which was found in a vocational manual written for secretaries in Lima, Peru (1986). This picture was used in focus groups with secretaries in research concerning their working identities. This research was conducted by Lorraine Nencel (2000–2003). Look at the picture carefully. It concerns the proper dress code for secretaries. The woman on the left is named Model Maria and the woman on the right is Calamity Dorothy.

1 Find the differences between the two images.
2 What do these differences concern?
3 What do you think these images project?
4 What does this tell us about the socially constructed identity of Peruvian secretaries?

5 What does this tell us about the relationship between sexuality and gender?

El vestido debe ser sobrio y discreto.
Recuerde a la Oficina se va a trabajar
y no a conquistar ni a impresionar al sexo opuesto.

Figure 6.1 Dress should be sober and discrete. Remember one goes to the office to work not to conquer or impress the opposite sex.
Source: Morales, 1987

Doing feminist anthropology: epistemology, fieldwork and reflexivity

Feminist anthropologists do anthropology like any anthropologist by doing ethnography. Although methodologically speaking, ethnography is not the sole possession of anthropology – there are other disciplines like sociology, education which claim it as an important methodological tool – it is nonetheless the identity-making feature of the anthropologist. According to Charlotte Aull Davis ethnography is:

a research process based on fieldwork using a variety of (mainly qualitative) research techniques but including engagement in the lives of those being studied over an extended period of time. The eventual written product – an ethnography – draws

its data primarily from this fieldwork experience and usually emphasises descriptive detail as a result.
(1999: 4–5)

Doing feminist anthropological research entails the use of a feminist research epistemology. It calls for a continual reflexive position during all phases of research: the writing of the proposal, the fieldwork, analysis and writing up [**Hotlink → Method, Methodology and Epistemology (Chapter 2)**]. Reflexivity is one of the ways that feminist anthropologists attempt to adhere to good feminist research practice:

Reflexivity, broadly defined, means a turning back on oneself, a process of self reference. In the context of social research, reflexivity at its most immediately obvious level refers to the ways in which the products of research are affected by the personal and process of doing research. These effects are to be found in all the phases of the research process from initial selection of topic to final reporting of results.
(Davis, 1999: 4)

Being reflexive implies a constant questioning whether the research and the researcher is living up to her ethical and epistemological principles and is used solely by feminist anthropologists. Critical anthropologists who question power regimes between themselves and the research subjects are also constantly being reflexive.

A closer look 6.4

Ethnographic fieldwork relations, reflexivity and cultural meaning

In anthropology the most important methodological tool is the researcher. She is constantly present in the field. Her position and identity are continuously being scrutinised by herself and the research subjects. This is not always an easy process but eventually the reflexive analysis can reveal even more than just how the researcher's identity influences the research. It will also give insight into the cultural meanings that are produced in the setting.
Research on Sex Workers in Lima (Nencel, 2001) showed that the identity of the researcher as a white,

foreign, non-prostituting woman influenced the kind of information she received.

It took some time but eventually it became clear that the women who prostituted had given the anthropologist an identity that could be defined as the 'good woman'. This was an ambiguous term containing both negative and positive elements. On the one hand, they saw Nencel as an ally, someone who respected them and supported them in their work. For example, she distributed condoms and did not lecture them about what they were doing. This sent out a message of respect. On the other hand, she was the 'good woman' reflecting the dominant gender imagery prevailing in many Latin American countries, where women are symbolically divided into two categories: the good (the mother) and bad (the whore). Labelling her as the good woman inadvertently labelled them as the bad woman. Although on another level, many of the women who had children, felt that prostitution enabled them to fulfil their role as mothers. Thus, talking to the researcher reminded them of a part of their self-image which they would rather not dwell upon. Reflexively analysing her identity in the field not only helped Nencel to understand the limitations of the fieldwork relationship but it also gave insight into cultural meanings that were significant in their world. It showed that the gender dichotomy of femininity was one that the women used to make sense in their daily lives. In addition it also suggested that women who prostituted lived and embodied their stigmatised position in society and that this subject of stigmatisation was one that had to be followed up during fieldwork.

Doing feminist ethnographic research and being reflexive implies that feminist epistemological principles are constantly being put to the test in practice. Unlike other disciplines in which feminist research may rely on secondary sources, data sets or the like, feminist anthropologists collect the bulk of their material in the field and through research relations. Being in the field, constructing relations and identities have made various feminist anthropologists critical of these epistemological principles. Diane Wolf has elaborated on the dilemmas that arise in fieldwork when starting from feminist standpoint theory [**Hotlink** → **Method, Methodology and Epistemology (Chapter 2)**]. She

points out that giving epistemic privilege to those who are marginalised produces a different process of essentialisation which ultimately reduces them to homogeneous groups (Wolf, 1996). Moreover, when feminist anthropologists assume a natural recognition between the researcher and research subject, this does not take into consideration for example how personality is involved in creating relations: 'Do we need to identify with all our subjects? What if we don't like them, or vice versa?' (Wolf, 1996: 17). Highly related are issues concerning intersubjectivity. Nencel (2001, 2005) shows in her study on women who prostitute in Lima that striving for an intersubjective relation is one of the ways feminist anthropologists attempt to correct the power dyad between the researcher and the research subject, the former being considered the more powerful and privileged and the latter as lacking power and authority. However, her fieldwork showed that this is an epistemological illusion. Not only does it embark from a homogeneous conceptualisation of power – either you have it or you do not – it also statically assumes that the research subject lacks power and in turn, does not acknowledge their power, which has many manifestations including the power as the knower, the power to be silent and as individuals who have defining power [**Hotlink** → **Method, Methodology and Epistemology (Chapter 2)**]. In the fieldwork setting Nencel (2001) was confronted with many different situations in which the research subjects determined, when, what and how things would be discussed.

To sum it up, through fieldwork practice feminist anthropologists have shown that the epistemological principles conceal ethnocentric and essentialist notions. What is considered an intersubjective research relationship cannot be defined beforehand – it is situated. There are some basic ethical and epistemological principles that must be respected but whether that is in a relationship as two equals or one that allocates authority or power to one of the parties is determined in fieldwork and is defined by the context and differences such as class, age, sex, gender, marital status, child status, and so on. Epistemological principles can serve as a guideline for good feminist research practice. Thus, we can strive to have egalitarian non-hierarchical relationships but it does not necessarily mean that we can obtain them. In the act of striving, however, a relationship is constructed which is generally based on mutual respect and a degree of trust. It is not always feasible or advisable to obtain the ideal, but the ideal helps the feminist anthropologist to do good research.

These methodological and epistemological issues are part and parcel of the feminist anthropological tradition. They cannot be resolved nor expected to disappear for ever; rather they must be evaluated and re-evaluated in every study the researcher undertakes. This held true for the feminist anthropological studies in the 1980s and 1990s and still holds true in the contemporary situation. The new directions of gender anthropology will be discussed below.

Stop and think 6.4

You are doing anthropological research on professional cheerleaders. As a teenager in high school you always felt excluded by the group of cheerleaders at your school. They made it clear that you were not wanted and that your type of femininity was not theirs. Now you have been asked to do research on cheerleading, femininity and conceptions of power and/or resistance.

➤ What type of reflexive steps must you take to assure that your past experiences will not influence the research negatively?

➤ What would be the ideal research relationship between yourself and the research group of cheerleaders?

Contemporary studies: new directions, new foci but the same principles

Since the developments of the notion of difference and theories such as practice theory, very little has changed in regard to the ground rules of feminist anthropological practice. Today feminist anthropology attempts to find answers to its queries by researching the issue in question holistically, studying how structural constraints and limitations influence individuals and groups and how they, groups and individuals, influence, challenge or maintain these same constraints. The notion of difference demands that the researcher explores signifiers such as gender, 'race'/ethnicity, class, sexuality in relation to each other and the context in which they are (re)produced and above all they are still conceptualised as fluid and unfixed. Nonetheless, things have definitely changed. The subjects under consideration have broadened to include domains such as modernity, globalisation and transnationalism. Dorothy Hodgson defines these three concepts as follows:

> Modernity [is studied] as the cultural dimension of transnationalism and globalization. Both are somewhat vague terms, but 'transnationalism' usually refers to people, processes, or products that cross national boundaries while the related term 'globalisation' is used in a broad sense to refer to processes such as capitalism and nationalism that have spread, however unevenly through the world.
>
> (2001: 5)

Feminist anthropologists study these new domains as gendered processes that have different influences on men and women because of their positions within society. Thus, migration is a process which has different consequences, motivations and objectives for men and women. Their motivations to leave their country are different; some women leave to be able to save for their or a sister's dowry, while others are attempting to escape an arranged or bad marriage. Men's motivations conform to the gender role of provider or breadwinner; they have nothing to be ashamed except if they fail to send remittances to the family left behind. Another example of gender anthropology, is found in the World in Focus 6.4, which describes a study of new forms of work made possible through new technology and globalisation.

In a recent edited volume on gender and globalisation the authors Tine Davids and Francien van Driel (2005) take on the challenge of elaborating an analytical perspective that enables a gendered analysis of the landscape of globalisation to simultaneously look at 'how globalisation shapes the lives of men and women in a local setting and by looking at men and women as actors in global processes' (Davids and van Driel, 2005: 3). The volume concerns a range of subjects such as safe sex and masculinity in Dakar (van Eerdewijk, 2005), single migrant mothers' experiences in the Netherlands (Ypeij, 2005), reproductive rights violations in the export-oriented industries in Mexico and Morocco (Reysoo, 2005), and meanings of community for Iranian women in exile (Ghorashi, 2005). What all the articles have in common is that they explore global processes and discourses in relation to local settings and not only attempt to show how they have influenced, been incorporated and transformed but also, the tension that exists between the two, and how individuals make sense of these processes within their lives.

As Hodgson asserts ethnography is an excellent method for researching issues on modernity/modernities, and we include globalisation and transnationalism. She states that ethnography has the power to

... elucidate the specificity and diversity of men's and women's lived experience of Modernity, their strategies for working and reworking Modernity, and the interplay of agency, structure, culture, history and power in the production of gendered modernities.

(Hodgson, 2001: 9)

She continues, ethnography moves beyond:

... language as dominant mode of signification, to examine other modes of cultural expression and production such as visual images, aesthetic styles, practices, performance, gestures and even smells. These are also key, prisms through which to access and analyse the often muted voices, experiences and agency of women.

(Hodgson, 2005: 9)

These new domains of enquiry bring new methods into being, for example what Marcus (1995) has called 'multi-sited ethnography'. An example of which is found in studies on migration. Contemporarily, migration studies are not only centred on the host-country but follow the migrants back to their home. It is through this methodological decision – to do multi-sited ethnography – that it is possible to get insight into how dreams and hopes are realised or fade away.

In sum, the new directions of feminist anthropological research have given the possibility to explore even further the complexities involved in the construction of gender, the gender order, institutions and identities.

World in focus 6.4

The case of the pink collar workers: high tech and high heels in the global economy

Globalisation and more particularly its new technologies has made new forms of labour and labour agreements possible. Carla Freeman (2000) did research on a relatively new type of 'feminine labour' – offshore data processors in Barbados. Women working in 'Third World countries' who are processing data for multinational and large enterprises from the west. Freeman calls these women 'pink collar workers'. Her study is one of the growing number of ethnographies which shows the directions that

gender anthropology is going. Without losing sight of notions concerning power, the relation between agency and structure, these studies explore new areas of interest and concern and illustrate how global processes influence the local and vice versa.

The concept 'pink collar' is central to my insistence that the dialectics of globalization/ localization, production/ consumption, and gender/class be analysed in a way that keeps them linked. 'Pink collar' denotes two major processes within informatics and its workers. The first is the feminization of work such that informatics is itself gendered, not only because it recruits women

workers almost exclusively, but also because the work process itself is imbued with notions of appropriate femininity, which includes a quiet, responsible demeanour along with meticulous attention to detail and a quick and accurate keyboard technique. The second process is the linking of work and clothing – production and consumption. The particular appearance of informatics workers – the bodily adorned skirt suits and polished high heels – and the physical space they inhabit as workers – the air-conditioned and officelike setting – are integral to women's experience of these jobs and ultimately to their emergent identities. . . .

Globally, the new pink-collar informatics worker represents

both a reconfiguration and a cheapening of white-collar service work. What was once considered skilled, 'mental' information-based computer work can now be performed 'offshore' without compromising the 'product' or the speed with which it is produced. Simultaneously, the informatics worker offshore also represents a growing Third World market for a wider and wider range of commodity goods, including fashions, housewares, electronics, music and videos, and the expansion of transnational networks of trade. Locally, in Barbados, the pink-collar informatics operator represents a new category of feminine worker, symbolically empowered by her professional appearance and the computer technology with which she works. Her air-conditioned office appears to be a far cry from the cane fields and kitchens in which her mother and grandmothers toiled, while the work she does represents a significant new emphasis of economic diversification by this sugar- and tourism-based island economy.

These processes have profound implications for our understanding of the gendering of class identity and consciousness. They help to explain, for example, why these particular global workers remain non-unionised in a nation known for its strong tradition of trade unionism. As such, they invite us to rethink the relationships between discipline, agency and pleasure. By taking seriously the dimensions of these jobs that give women pleasure even in the face of numerous stresses, speed-ups, and monotony, we see that women are agents in ways that simultaneously inscribe patriarchal notions of femininity and create a space of invention and autonomy.

(Freeman, 2000: 3–5)

Stop and think 6.5

Situation 1:

You are on a lunch break and it is a beautiful sunny day and decide to take a stroll in a nearby situated park. You pass a playground and are taken by surprise by the amount of women of colour who are taking care of undeniably white children. You stop and think about who these women might be:

➤ Are they distant relatives?

➤ Are they working their way through Europe by doing odd jobs like babysitting?

➤ Or have they left their country, children and family and been hired by an agency to take care of children of prosperous working parents in the west?

Situation 2

You are at a party and meet a young woman from an eastern European country who is married to a man who is from your own country. You hit it off well and she confides in you that she is recently married and met her husband through an online dating service that couples women from her country with men from western countries?
You stop and think:

➤ What do you think of this arrangement?

➤ Is there something that makes this different from internet dating which you and your friends have tried?

➤ What do you think of this woman after you hear her story?

Situation 3:

You pick up a newspaper and you read a story about arrests at an illegal brothel that is around the corner from where you live. The majority of the women were illegal migrants. The newspaper does not make any distinctions and assumes that all the women were trafficked. It paints a very sad picture of victims of trafficking.

➤ Are all women working in the sex industry who are illegal migrants trafficked?

Conclusion

Doing anthropology from a gender perspective, adhering to a feminist epistemology implies holding on to certain basic premises, some of these are shared with mainstream anthropology, and/or the different types of critical anthropologies which exist today, but they nonetheless make feminist anthropology what it is today. Below you will find a list of the premises and characteristics of gendered anthropology elaborated in this chapter, it is not exhaustive and it provides an excellent example of the issues discussed in Chapter 2, Method, Methodology and Epistemology

➤ Feminist anthropology shares basic characteristics with all types of anthropology. It does not take anything for granted and is interested in cross-cultural comparison and the use of ethnography as the main type of method.

➤ Feminist anthropological studies on gender are reflexive, continually questioning the choices made throughout the research process, the positionality of the researcher within the research process and the research relations during fieldwork, as are feminist studies in other disciplines.

➤ Research done on gender from a feminist perspective implies that the research has a political dimension. In some ways, it is the researcher's intention that their research can inspire, influence or contribute to social change whether that be material, relational or ideational.

➤ Doing research on gender implies that the research concerns the complexities of the construct power. This is one of the central characteristics which differentiates gender feminist research from studies on men and women.

➤ Power and accompanying concepts such as dominance and subordination appear to be natural; it is the objective of gender anthropology to deconstruct this illusion of naturalness to show how it is socially constructed.

➤ Attuned with the holistic approach of anthropology, gender studies in anthropology approach their subject holistically, never in isolation, embedded in a socio, economic and historical context.

➤ Studying gender implies the acceptance of plurality. This stands as a symbol for the acceptance of difference and situated knowledge.

➤ What it means to be a man or woman cannot be defined beforehand. Likewise the relationship between identity markers such as gender and sexuality, gender and ethnicity or gender and class cannot be assumed but must be researched. Thus labels such as macho, gay, lesbian; the meaning of motherhood, sex worker or factory worker must be investigated.

In this chapter the term feminist anthropology has been used interchangeably with other terms such as research on gender, gender perspective or gender and anthropology. It has more often than not referred to gender anthropology as feminist anthropology. Perhaps this can be a generational difference. College students today might want to avoid using the term feminist, finding it a remnant of the women's liberation of the 1960s. Although it can be said that calling yourself a feminist anthropologist or labelling your research as feminist anthropological is a political choice, it is not obligatory for doing research that complies with the premises and characteristics listed above. You can call it anthropology from a gendered perspective, gender anthropology or feminist anthropology, as long as the research's point of departure is from the construct of gender: the study of masculinity and femininity as fluid, situational and unfixed from a cross-cultural perspective, which not only assumes that gender is a relational construct but also one of the most pervasive relations of power that orders contemporary societies.

Further reading

Ravina Aggarwal (2000) 'Traversing lines of Control: Feminist Anthropology today' *The Annals of the American Academy of Political and Social Science*, Vol. 571, no. 1, 14–29. A state of the art article on contemporary issues and dilemmas in feminist anthropology departing from a feminist anthropological of difference. This article explores how theoretical interventions made by third-wave feminists on subject such as fieldwork, culture and writing.

Ruth Behar and Deborah A. Gorden (eds) (1996) *Women Righting Culture*. Berkeley: University of California Press. This a volume which poses critical and epistemological questions concerning the practices involved in women writing about women. There are pieces that reinvestigate the work of pioneer female anthropologists and others that are searching for new ways of writing feminist ethnography.

Ellen Lewin (ed.) (2006) *Feminist Anthropology*. Oxford: Blackwell Anthologies in Social and Cultural Anthropology. This recent anthology is a compilation of classic and contemporary articles on feminist anthropology. It gives insight into the theoretical development as well as deals with contemporary feminist anthropological issues cross-culturally.

Irma McClaurin (ed.) (2001) *Black Feminist Anthropology. Theory, Politics, Praxis and Poetics*. New Jersey: Rutgers University Press. This is a collection by black feminist anthropologists that not only pays tribute to writers about the black feminist anthropological past as well as explores new perspectives they bring to the field.

Henrietta Moore (1988) *Feminism and Anthropology*. Cambridge: Polity Press. This book is the closest that comes to resemble a textbook. It gives a historically developed theoretical overview of feminist anthropology by discussing different relevant themes such as gender and status, women and the state, women's work and kinship. It is a definite must for those who want to quickly become initiated in feminist anthropology.

Diane L. Wolf (ed.) (1996) *Feminist Dilemmas in Fieldwork*. Boulder Colorado: Westview Press. This volume compiles articles concerning the dilemmas that arrive doing feminist fieldwork in the field. It has an excellent introduction which critically deals with and gives an overview of the dilemmas encountered while doing feminist (anthropological) fieldwork. The articles that follow are case studies which illustrate methodological or epistemological dilemmas encountered in different research locations.

As mentioned feminist anthropology does not have one particular journal to call its own. Articles of feminist anthropologists are found in both mainstream anthropological journals such as *American Ethnologist*, regional journals such as *Journal of Latin American Anthropology*, as well as Women Studies journals such as *Signs, European Journal of Women Studies*.

Websites

Association for Feminist Anthropology (AFA) section of the American Anthropological Association **http://sscl.berkeley.edu/%7Eafaweb/links.html**. This is the only on-line website for feminist anthropologists in English. It is an open member site for feminist anthropologists of the American Anthropological Association. It not only includes member news, calls for papers, vacancies but also has some articles posted, book reviews and the publication of their sporadic online journal.

End of chapter activity

Surprisingly, feminist anthropologists do not have their own professional journals. Their articles appear in general anthropology journals, women's studies journals, area journals, etc. Therefore, to get an idea as to what types of articles are published, you are asked to do the following:

1. Choose a friend–colleague and go to the (on-line) library of your university.

2. Revise 5 anthropology journals and 5 women's studies/gender journals for the last three years.

3. Read and analyse the abstracts of feminist anthropological articles.

4. Compare your findings:

   a. What are the feminist anthropological subjects dealt with in the two types of journals?

   b. Are there differences or similarities?

   c. Do you have an idea what these differences or similarities can be based on?

   d. How many articles did you find? What can the amount of articles tell us about feminist anthropology (if there are no articles, explain the possible reason for the lack of articles)

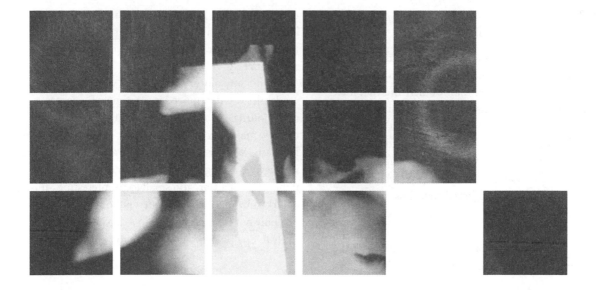

Chapter 7

Psychology

Katherine Johnson

Key issues in this chapter:

➤ Researching 'sex' and 'gender' in psychology.
➤ Gender differences in cognitive abilities.
➤ Theories of gender identity development.
➤ Androgyny and intersexuality.
➤ Feminist challenges to psychological research on gender.

At the end of this chapter you should be able to:

➤ Highlight methodological issues for conducting non-sexist research in psychology
➤ Understand a range of psychological theories in gender development, including biological, evolutionary, psychoanalytic, social learning theory and social constructionist approaches.
➤ Evaluate key topics such as gender differences in behaviour and cognitive abilities, and the development of gender identity.
➤ Understand feminist challenges to understandings of gender within mainstream psychology.

BATTLE OF THE SEXES:
Who has the bigger brain?

It was one of the summer's top stories. In August [2005], two British academics announced that men are significantly cleverer than women and that male university students outstrip females by almost five IQ points. 'Girls need manpower' and 'IQ tests: women just don't get it' claimed the headlines.

The announcement was the latest round in a battle that has come to dominate psychology in recent years and has triggered countless workplace arguments and marital rows over the years. In this case, the formidable nature of the statistics used by the study's authors – Dr Paul Irwing and Professor Richard Lynn – seemed to land a hefty blow for the men-are-cleverer camp. 'It confirms what we've long suspected' said a (male) writer in the *Sun*. 'The male of the species is cleverer than the female. It's a no-brainer'.

But not any more. Last week the work of the two academics was denounced in startlingly fierce terms in the journal *Nature*... 'Their study – which claims to show major sex differences in IQ – is simply, utter hogwash,' said Dr Steve Blinkhorn, an expert on intelligence testing... 'Sex differences in average IQ, if they exist at all, are too small to be interesting'. It is a stark, unequivocal statement – although it will certainly not be the last word in a debate that seems likely to dog psychology for years to come.

McKie, 2005: 210

Figure 7.1 Battle of the Sexes
Source: © Getty Science Library

Stop and think 7.1

Do you think men are more intelligent than women? What evidence is there to support your answer?

Introduction

These types of 'scientific' declarations that women are intellectually inferior to men are not so recent. Accounts such as this can be found throughout nineteenth- and twentieth-century medical and psychological literature where women have been conceptualised in relation to their biology whilst intellect is firmly seen as the possession of men. These sentiments can be found in the work of Charles Darwin (1896) and Henry Maudsley (1874) both of whom argued against the growth in numbers of women entering higher education in Britain and America during the late 1880s. Feminist psychologist, Jane Ussher suggests that women in Victorian England were caught in a double bind whereby they were discouraged from studying or working because it was thought their physical health and reproductive abilities would be damaged, but at the same time their lack of prominence in education or work was interpreted as evidence of men's greater mental ability. As she states:

> None of the scholars of the day, who insisted on keeping women in the home to protect them from the evils of the world, saw any connection between their absence from education and the workforce and the limited opportunities open to them. The absence of women proved their inability to compete with men, rather than men's failure to grant them the opportunity.

> (Ussher, 1989: 3)

The rapid increase in the number of women attending university since the 1970s and the current higher performance of girls than boys throughout school age education (Deptartment for Education and Skills, 2004) shows that significant inroads have been made in challenging the status of women as intellectually second-rate to men. A similar picture can be found in other western countries such as the USA and Australia, suggesting that the improvement in girls' academic abil-

ity is due to cultural changes that have allowed them access to continuing education – [**Hotlink → Education → Failing boys discourse (Chapter 13)**].

Stop and think 7.2

If girls are currently outperforming boys at all ages in education why is so much media attention given to research that claims that boys are more intelligent? [**Hotlink → Education → A Closer Look 13.4 (Chapter 13)**].

However, psychology stands accused to this day of constructing 'differences' between men and women as 'inferiorities' except when the difference is something that aids women in their 'natural' roles as mothers or wives (Wilkinson, 1997). Thus, while mainstream psychology attends to finding and explaining gender differences or understanding gender identity development, primarily in biological or cognitive terms, the focus within feminist psychology has been predominantly on making the experience of women visible and challenging psychological findings that act as a form of oppression or social control.

Researching gender in psychology

Psychology defines itself as the science of mind and behaviour and relies heavily on experimental methods of research that are more commonly found in the physical sciences. Thus, for psychologists, research is often based on quantifiable measurements of difference between groups that can be analysed statistically and interpreted in terms of a general law of behaviour that is applied to all people. For example, psychologists might administer an intelligence test to a group of women and a group of men. They would then calculate the mean score for the women (by adding all the scores together and dividing by the total number in the group) and compare this with the mean score for the group of men. If a significant difference between the scores were found across several comparative groups the researchers then generalise their findings to the wider population by making claims such as found in the above newspaper article that 'men are significantly cleverer than women'.

One of the key justifications for using experimental methods is that they provide objectivity [**Hotlink →** **Methods, Methodology and Epistemology (for a critique of objectivity) (Chapter 2)**]. They can tell us the truth about ourselves and the world by controlling and comparing certain variables such as 'gender', 'age' and 'intelligence'. Yet, as US based feminist psychologists Rhonda Unger and Mary Crawford (1992: 9) state:

> Scientific research is often represented as a purely objective process in which a neutral, disinterested scientist investigates and reveals the secrets of nature. However, as some of the pioneering women psychologists realized, psychology has sometimes been anything but neutral when it came to understanding and explaining the behavior of women.

Thus, feminist psychologists argue that differences found between men and women are often the result of how a particular phenomenon has been researched. Historically, participants in research experiments were usually male yet research findings would be generalised to the whole population. This approach to research can be criticised for being androcentric or male-centred (see A Closer Look 7.1). As Naomi Weisstein famously declared in an early critique 'Psychology has nothing to say about what women are really like, what they need and what they want . . .

because psychology does not know' (Weisstein, 1968/1993: 197).

One commonly cited example of androcentric research is Lawrence Kohlberg's (1958) stage theory of moral development (see A Closer Look 7.2). Kohlberg used moral dilemmas to access children's moral reasoning. Based on answers he found to stories that required children to distinguish between concepts of right and wrong, he constructed a three-level model of cognitive development that entailed preconventional, conventional and principled levels.

Each level consisted of two stages and Kohlberg proposed that development was sequential, where children could potentially progress through each stage as they matured. Thus, in order to reach the final and most superior sixth stage children must first pass

Figure 7.2 Nelson Mandela
Source: © Tom Stoddart Archive/Reportage/Getty Images

A closer look 7.1

Androcentrism

Research that fails to recognise the viewpoint of women is seen as androcentric. This takes place when research findings that are taken from a male research population are generalised to all humans. Another form of androcentrism is the tendency to see topics that are especially relevant to men, such as the relation between television violence and aggression, as key areas of research whilst topics that are more relevant to women, such as motherhood, appear less frequently in psychological literature and rarely outside of a focus on the psychology of women.

A closer look 7.2

Kohlberg's (1958) stage theory of moral development

Levels and stages	Orientation of moral reasoning	
Preconventional level		
Stage 1	Punishment and obedience	Wrong things are those that are punished and you obey rules to avoid punishment.
Stage 2	Hedonism	Good and bad are to do with satisfying your own needs. You do what is best for you.
Conventional level		
Stage 3	Interpersonal concordance	Being good is about being loyal and looking after the interests of those you care about, who show empathy and affection towards you.
Stage 4	Law and order	Being good is about obeying the law and following the rules, which may be statutory or religious.
Principled level		
Stage 5	Social contract	Being good is about fostering the welfare and well-being of others.
Stage 6	Universal ethical principles	Being good is defined by your own conscience, in accordance with self-determined ethical principles.

Source: Stainton-Rogers and Stainton-Rogers (2001: 78).

through stages 1–5. However, Kohlberg argued that only a few people moved beyond conventional morality to the highest stages of moral development and these select few included people who might break conventional laws because they believed them to be unfair and operate in the process of oppression. Examples here would include people like Nelson Mandela who spent 30 years in prison for challenging the rules and laws of South Africa during apartheid. At the time the state could construct Mandela as a 'terrorist' but according to Kohlberg's model his actions showed higher standards of justice as the existing laws served to marginalise and oppress black South Africans.

While not everyone would reach the principled level of stage 6, Kohlberg claimed that boys and men tend to achieve at least stage 4. In contrast, he argued that girls and women were more likely to stop developing at stage 3, seemingly suggesting that women have an underdeveloped and less mature sense of morality.

Kohlberg's theory has received much criticism from feminist psychologists over the years. The better

known of these critiques comes from Carol Gilligan (1982) who demonstrates the androcentrism of the research by highlighting a number of methodological flaws. Firstly, Kohlberg constructed his theory from data that he collected via a longitudinal study where he repeatedly tested *boys* in moral reasoning tasks as they matured from early childhood into adulthood. In addition, all of the test characters described in the moral dilemmas were also male. Thus, the entire model of moral development was based on a male-centred view of rules, values and moral obligations. Gilligan suggests that it is not surprising that when women are asked to respond to similar dilemmas they respond in different ways. The problem is when this is interpreted as performing less well or as being morally inferior. As such, she suggests that the model itself is conceptually flawed as it promotes principles of law and order above principles of human relationships and that this model arose because men tend to prioritise justice over care. Gilligan proceeded to develop her own theory of women's development through interviewing pregnant women who were considering having an abortion. She concluded that men and women have different approaches to moral questions neither of which is inferior to the other. She suggested that women are more commonly concerned with an ethics of responsibility while men are more commonly concerned with an ethics of rights; however, in order to achieve the highest level of development, both men and women should strive to integrate the two approaches.

A critical look 7.1

Gilligan's theory of a 'different voice'

When controlling for other factors, such as level of education, or conducting direct comparative studies, other research findings contest the notion that there is any difference in men and women's moral reasoning (e.g Ford and Lowery, 1986; Crandall *et al.*, 1999). Unger and Crawford suggest that Gilligan may have identified a 'different voice' in moral reasoning but 'whether the different voice is a woman's voice is still being actively debated' (Unger and Crawford, 1992: 50).

Whilst Gilligan's account has its own methodological limitations (Unger and Crawford, 1992) it was instrumental in the development of a body of knowledge that counters psychological theories that posit women as inferior to men. It did this by highlighting the biases in the research design of the original study that predisposed women to perform badly. Feminist psychologists have done much to promote the principles of non-sexist

research and outline how gender biases can enter into the research process at any stage. This can happen in the initial stages of research through the very act of deciding what should be researched without acknowledging whose interests this serves. Thus, 'unexamined personal biases and androcentric theories often lead to biased research questions' (Unger and Crawford, 1992: 11). Furthermore, gender biases and stereotypes can enter into the research design, the meaning and significance attributed to statistical findings and the way in which research is written up and published. Hence, feminist psychologists promote psychological knowledge that can be used to create social change that will benefit women, rather than maintaining the *status quo* (e.g. Hare-Mustin and Marecek, 1990; Unger and Crawford, 1992; Burman *et al.*, 1996; Gergen and Davis, 1997).

In recent years qualitative research methods have begun to grow in popularity and acceptance within academic Psychology. These have permitted psychologists in a range of subdisciplines such as social, development and clinical psychology to better capture the experiences of women and men and tackle androcentric assumptions that underpin some experimental approaches. From her analysis of two leading journals, *Psychology of Women Quarterly* (USA) and *Feminism & Psychology* (UK), Sue Wilkinson (1999) claims that within qualitative research interviewing is the most popular method of data collection. However, despite the potential that qualitative research affords for the collection of diverse experience, overall, quantitative research still makes up the majority of research published on gender issues in psychology (Brannon, 2005).

World in focus 7.1

The psychology of women

Since the 1970s subsections of national psychological associations, including America, Australia, Canada and the UK, have established special interest groups that promote the psychology of women. This offers a support network for women who work

in psychology as well as a focus for research about women. However, in order to be seen as legitimate academic groups they have been cautioned against being labelled as 'a quasi-political pressure group concerned with feminist causes' (Wilkinson, 1997: 248–9). Despite feminism not being directly mentioned within the subsection's

name, many members do adhere to a feminist agenda by attempting to highlight inequalities within the discipline and tackle social and political inequalities that impact on women in a range of settings. For example, a recent article in *The Psychologist*, the monthly publication for members of The British Psychological Society, addresses issues of institutionalised sexism within Psychology, and makes a series of recommendations for promoting equality. This includes monitoring the content of articles for androcentric assumptions, recognising the diversity of research within psychology to include social theory and qualitative research, as well as challenging the gender pay gap (Riley *et al.*, 2006). This is seen as particularly important as the majority of psychology undergraduates are female, yet women are underrepresented in senior positions of authority. For those who do make a career within academic psychology they tend to have higher teaching responsibilities which leaves less time for research activities (APA, 2000), which are seen as crucial for promotion. Thus, there is some way to go before women achieve equality within the discipline of psychology.

'Sex' differences or 'gender' differences?

As an academic discipline, psychology is far more reliant on biological explanations for human behaviour than other social sciences. This is why in traditional, mainstream psychology differences between men and women are usually referred to as 'sex differences', rather than 'gender differences' (see A Closer Look 7.3). However, many social psychologists and feminist psychologists reject the use of the term sex differences and refer to these in terms of gender. They do this in order to highlight that differences found in the behaviour of men and women are not simply the result of innate biological, hormonal or genetic factors that might determine things such as the size of the brain. Instead, they suggest that differences arise because of environmental influences that socialise boys and girls into different gender roles and behaviour. [**Hotlink → Gendered Perspectives – Theoretical Issues (Chapter 1)**].

in some instances, such as on application forms, 'gender' has simply replaced the term 'sex'. In order to unpick these concepts in a little more detail it is useful to outline a number of ways in which gender can be thought of:

Sex – biological terms
Sexuality – incorporating sexual practices and erotic behaviour
Sexual identity – the naming of self and others as heterosexual, gay, lesbian, bisexual, asexual
Gender identity – a psychological sense of oneself as a man or woman
Gender role – a set of cultural scripts for the appropriate behaviour in order to be a man or woman
Gender role identity – the extent to which a person feels comfortable and participates in the behaviours considered appropriate to cultural expectations of his or her gender.

(Adapted from Hawkesworth, 1997)

All of these usages can be found in psychological literature as researchers attempt to explore the complex relationship between gendered behaviour and biological difference.
[**Hotlink → Chapter 1 → Sex and gender, what's the difference?**]

A closer look 7.3

Differentiating between the use of terms 'sex' and 'gender' in psychology

The terms 'sex' and 'gender' have multiple usages. Whilst 'sex' in everyday use might refer to an act or something people 'have' with themselves or others, in psychological research it is generally used to relate to anatomical differences in male and female bodies. In contrast, 'gender' has a more recent conception and has been commonly used by feminist and social psychologists since the 1970s to distinguish social aspects of behaviour from biological differences. However, the terms can be used interchangeably and

Do men and women have different cognitive abilities?

In a now classic literature review of an enormous body of sex difference research, Eleanor Maccoby and Carol Nagy Jacklin (1974) state that the similarities between men and women by far outweigh the differences. However, they claim there is enough evidence to support the argument that men and women differ in cognitive ability in three key ways:

➤ *Verbal ability* – girls do better on tests of verbal fluency, comprehension, creative writing and spelling.

➤ *Visual–spatial ability* – boys do better on visual–spatial tasks such as the ability to rotate a three-dimensional figure or the Rod-and-frame test.

➤ *Mathematical ability* – post age 12 boys typically show better performance in maths skills

See A Closer Look 7.4

A critical look 7.2

Language and definitions of difference

Unger and Crawford (1992) point out that it is important to pay attention to the way that differences are labelled as they often carry value judgements about what characteristics are deemed more positive. To illustrate this they use the example of research by Denmark *et al.* (1988) which proposes differences between men's and women's cognitive styles. Here, the 'male style' is labelled *field independence* and the 'female style' *field dependence*. Unger and Crawford argue that these labels reinforce gender stereotypes and suggest that the findings would seem quite different if they had been labelled *field insensitivity/sensitivity*.

One of the problems with these types of conclusions is that it can lead us to assume that all boys are better than all girls at maths and that all girls have more developed verbal abilities than all boys. In more recent years new statistical methods for aggregating research findings have been developed. This includes techniques for conducting meta-analysis. These provide a more robust method of comparing and summarising findings from a vast array of experimental studies. Meta-analysis of studies on gender differences have allowed for more sensitive accounts of the way in which gender impacts on particular variables, and crucially, it provides insight into the size of the effect. It also allows us to see the influence of other variables, such as individual differences and situational factors that might have greater likelihood of accounting for the difference in the findings than gender

(Hyde and Linn, 1986). For example, one the first meta-analyses of Maccoby and Jacklin's literature review concluded that only 1 per cent of difference in verbal abilities related to gender, meaning that 99 per cent of difference was related to other factors (Hyde, 1981). Thus, there is far more place for the impact of a range of individual differences on cognitive abilities and we frequently find cases that counteract these generalised assumptions.

Stop and think 7.3

Can you think of girls or women you know who are good at maths? Can you think of boys or men you know who are good at verbal tasks such as anagrams or reading aloud?

General assumptions about differences in cognitive ability are also complicated by closer analysis of the type of tasks people are asked to complete. Janet Hyde and Marcia Linn's (1988) meta-analysis revealed that women are only better than men at some verbal tasks rather than all verbal tasks. Recent studies on visual–spatial ability also provide evidence against a straightforward conclusion that here men are better than women. For example, women tend to do better on tasks where people must rapidly match items or remember the placement of objects (Brannon, 2005).

Research conducted in the US also complicates the assumption that boys have a greater mathematical ability than girls (Willingham and Cole, 1997). However, other studies continue to support the claim that boys have a higher level of maths skills (e.g. Beller and Gafni, 2000). What is important to note is that this gender gap has narrowed considerably in recent years and in the UK in 2001, at A level, women outperformed men in terms of the percentage receiving grades A–C (DfES, 2002). While those that took A level maths seem to be fairing well in comparison to boys, there are still significant differences in the number of women opting out of maths or science-based subjects. Several reasons have been put forward to account for why this might be. It has been argued that prior to age 12 there are no gender differences in mathematic abilities (Hyde *et al.*, 1990). Yet, from age

12 girls show signs of reduced confidence in their ability to study maths (Eccles, 1989). As they get older the gender difference in confidence increases and this trend continues into adulthood. Linda Bannon (2005) suggests that despite evidence that real gender differences in maths ability are relatively low, gender-role stereotypes that promote maths as a 'male domain' are likely to impact on girls' confidence in tackling maths courses. Thus, these social influences could be the key determining factor rather than other explanations that point to innate cognitive differences between men and women [**Hotlink → Education, Tables 13.3 and 13.4 (Chapter 13)**].

Theories of gender identity development

Even though evidence suggests that gender differences are less stable than we might initially suppose there are a number of theoretical approaches within psychology that attempt to explain why men and women differ in their propensity for certain cognitive abilities, forms of social behaviour and personality characteristics. In this section we consider these in relation to three perspectives: biological, psychoanalytic and socio-cultural.

Biological approaches

The biological perspective incorporates biological and evolutionary explanations and has become increasingly popular in recent years for explaining gender difference. It includes the influence of a range of factors including chromosomes, hormones and brain studies, as well as drawing on research from sociobiology and evolutionary psychology. Physical differentiation between men and women begins at conception when chromosomal sex is determined as either XX (female) or XY (male). Despite different chromosomal differences sex hormones play a key role in the differentiation of sex organs. This is because, at this stage, all embryos have both a Wolffian (male) and Müllerian (female) system that provide the capacity to develop the internal reproductive organs of both males and females. Thus, until six weeks there are no differences that signify that the embryo will develop as

male or female. After seven weeks the foetus' sex organs begin to differentiate depending on the level of surrounding hormones. The presence of androgens, which is determined by information on the Y chromosome, stimulates the development of the Wolffian system. This masculinises the foetus and leads to the growth of the male reproductive system. This process is also reliant on the secretion of a second hormone that causes the Müllerian system to degenerate. In contrast, in a foetus with an XX chromosomal pattern no surge of hormones is required to develop the Müllerian system as this system develops and the Wolffian system degenerates due to a lack of pre-natal hormones. Thus, it is often claimed that, in biological terms, 'femaleness is the default state – an embryo develops a female reproductive system unless it is masculinized by hormonal action' (Stainton-Rogers and Stainton-Rogers, 2001: 15). However there are a number of variations in this developmental pattern that can result in the birth of 'intersexed' children who have anomalies in either their chromosomal sex or reproductive organs. Anne Fausto-Sterling (2000) suggests that 1.7 per cent of births are classed as intersexed, although this rate is not uniform across the world. Sometimes intersexuality is not immediately noticeable as 'sex' is predominantly identified on the basis of a newly born baby's genitals. The most common sex-chromosome anomaly is Klinefelter syndrome where a male child has the chromosomal configuration XXY. Here, individuals have male genitalia but their testes are small and they are unable to produce sperm resulting in infertility (Brannon, 2005). Sometimes this form of intersexuality is not identified until the boy reaches puberty when, unlikely other boys, they do not experience further masculinisation from the effects of testosterone. A more unusual form of intersexuality results from androgen insensitivity syndrome. In this case the child is born with XY chromosomal characteristics, but without masculinised genitals, and they will be identified on the basis of their genitals as female. This is because their androgen receptors were not activated by the release of pre-natal hormones so they developed the external genitalia of a baby girl. Internally, however, the Müllerian system responded to the second hormonal signal and began to degenerate leaving the child with testes that remain in the place of ovaries. A final example of intersexuality is the very rare hermaphroditism where an individual is born with both testicular and ovarian tissue [**Hotlink → Chapter 1 → Controversy 1.1**)].

Some debate exists over the status of 'intersexuality' and whether it is a biological mistake that should be treated, or rectified by medical science, or whether it indicates that the binary sex system limits our understanding of biological variation. Suzanne Kessler (1998) points to the complexity of trying to identify 'sex' as it depends on what markers we use in order to do this: these markers might include chromosomes, hormones, genitals, overall body structure, or gonads and will depend on how we prioritise them. Thus, definitions of 'sex' are influenced by culture as well as biology.

Controversy 7.1

How many 'sexes' are there? [Hotlink → (Chapter 1)]

Feminist biologist Anne Fausto-Sterling (1993) suggests that biological variations in the case of intersexuality do not have to be interpreted as 'abnormality'. In contrast, she proposes that there may be more than just two sexes – male and female. She suggests that if we include 'herms' (true hermaphrodites), 'merms' (male pseudo-herms) and 'ferms' (female pseudo-herms), alongside 'male' and 'female', there would be five sexes.

To many this idea is very challenging. As one critic responded 'It is maddening to listen to discussions of "five sexes" when every sane person knows there are but two sexes, both of which are rooted in nature' (cited in Fausto-Sterling, 2000: 78). But, if biology is aligned with 'nature' then perhaps we need to acknowledge that there is greater biological variation than the current male/female model implies.

Here we have seen how hormones and chromosomes interact in the early stages of gender development. However, hormones do not only play a role in sex differentiation of male and female bodies. They are also seen to explain differences in gender related behaviour.

Stop and think 7.4

Can you identify examples of men and women's behaviour being explained in terms of their hormones? Before you read on consider what behaviours are deemed to be due to male hormones and what to female ones? Do you believe these to be based in biology or can you think of some alternative explanations?

There are two key areas in which hormones are frequently cited as reasons for behaviour. For women this tends to be in relation to reproduction, either when they are pregnant, or through what is known as premenstrual syndrome (PMS). In contrast, for men, hormones are a common explanation for aggression and violence. Despite this the actual relationship between hormones and behaviour is not clear-cut. For example, women report a range of physical and emotional symptoms in the time preceding menstruation including backaches, abdominal bloating, breast tenderness, irritability, depression and tension and both men and women attribute these symptoms to hormone levels. However, there is little evidence to support any pattern between hormone levels and experience of PMS (Brannon, 2005). Equally, testosterone is a common explanation for elevated levels of aggression. This hormone is more frequently associated with men, but this relationship between testosterone and aggression has been supported by research including both males and females who have been involved in violent criminal activity. Yet claims for a single-direction, causal relationship between hormone levels and behaviour are not well supported as some evidence suggests that higher levels of testosterone might actually be the result of engaging in aggressive behaviour. For example, studies with athletes reveal that competitiveness can raise testosterone levels, rather than the other way round (Brannon, 2005). [**Hotlink → Chapter 1**].

Brain studies reveal that the only difference in brain structure that exists from birth is that the brains of men are larger than the brains of women (Breedlove, 1994). Other studies reveal small differences in brain structure that may relate to gender identity or sexual behaviour (e.g Swaab *et al.*, 1995),

A closer look 7.4

Socio-biology

Is a derivative of Darwin's theory of evolution and natural selection. Darwin was concerned with the evolution of species and reproduction is the key to evolutionary survival. Socio-biology uses this assumption to account for sex-differentiated behaviour such as reproduction strategies and violence. Accordingly men are seen as 'pre-programmed' to promiscuity as this offers the best opportunity to propagate their genes while women are 'pre-programmed' for mate selectivity and nurturing as these strategies are seen as the most effective to allow them to raise a child to maturity and therefore maintain the chain in their own genetic heritage.

however this process of differentiation takes place between ages 2 and 4 so it is not clear if this is caused by innate factors or environmental influences that impact on the way the brain develops (Brannon, 2005).

Evolutionary psychology draws on the principles of natural selection and socio-biology (see A Closer Look 7.4) in order to explain a range of differences in gender-related behaviours. These types of explanations are hugely popular and underpin a large amount of 'pop-psychology' publications including self-help books such as *Men are from Mars, Women are from Venus* (Gray, 1993); *Why men don't listen and women can't read maps* (Pease and Pease, 1999); and the monthly magazine, *Psychologies*, that has recently been released in the UK.

Warning: these publications should be treated with suspicion. It is not uncommon to find in them dubious explanations for gender differences such as this:

> The modern male driver sits behind the wheel, hands his wife a map and asks her to navigate. With limited spatial ability she becomes silent and starts turning the map around and feels incompetent. Most men don't understand that if you don't have a specific area in the brain for map rotation, you'll rotate it with your hands. It makes perfect sense to a woman to face a map in the direction she is travelling. For a man to avoid arguments he should avoid asking a woman to read maps.
>
> (Pease and Pease, 1999: 127)

Here we can see the authors are presenting a crude understanding of the claim that men are better at visual–spatial cognitive tasks than women and reducing this to 'women have limited spatial ability' which in turn means 'women can't read maps'. Here, the differences for spatial ability are generally explained in terms of how men's and women's brains are hard-wired in relation to their evolutionary heritage. For example, John Gray (1993) suggests that men are often unable to find objects in the fridge because their vision is adapted to scan wide-open spaces, in the model of the 'hunter'. In contrast, women are good at finding such objects because their cognitive abilities have developed in line with skills needed to survive as the 'gatherer'. Yet, perhaps other explanations could suffice – for example, women frequently do the grocery shopping and therefore are more likely to know where they put the butter when they unpacked it.

These types of publications pose as aids to foster better relationships between men and women through an understanding of their innate differences. Yet, they serve to fix both men and women in stereotypical forms of behaviour through largely unsubstantiated research claims drawn from evolutionary accounts that have a legacy of positioning women as inferior to men. These types of arguments can also be criticised as reductionist as they set out to explain complex social behaviour in terms of a single factor. Evolutionary psychologists also lack scientific validation for their theories as they are 'inherently untestable' (Stainton-Rogers and Stainton-Rogers, 2001: 35) and frequently it is possible to find evidence that contradicts their conclusions. For example, Martin Daly and Margo Wilson (1988) have highlighted a link between genetic-relatedness and homicide and/or male violence. They suggest that men are less likely to kill their biological children than their wives and step-children because as 'selfish gene' theory (Dawkins, 1976) predicts, there is a stronger urge for altruistic behaviour towards those who have a closer genetic resemblance. The problem with this explanation is that it does not explain why many people choose to 'unselfishly' invest time, love and energy in raising adopted children, or why evidence suggests that domestic violence often begins at the time a woman is pregnant with the man's baby (Segal, 1999). Finally, there has been rapid transformation in the reproduction of western couples in last 30 years with women having fewer children and their first child much later on average than women in their mother's generation. This is not to do with evolution, as the speed of change is far too quick, rather it is the result of greater equality for women in education and the workplace. Thus, as feminists argue, social and cultural factors are far more influential in determining gender-related behaviour than evolutionary psychologists acknowledge. For more detail of debates in this area see Controversy 7.2.

Controversy 7.2

Evolutionary psychology versus feminist critique

Research suggests that men and women express differences in their sexual practices and relationship expectations. Men rate themselves as more promiscuous than women, always on the look out for a young, attractive female date and women declare themselves looking for a hard-working, committed and financially stable partner. Evolutionary psychologist David Buss (1994) explains this difference in what he describes as human 'mating strategies' in terms of natural selection and propagation of genes – our goal is to find the best strategy to reproduce.

Feminist psychologist, Lynne Segal (1999: 89) suggests that these gender differences can be explained equally well by social scripts for masculinity and femininity. 'In male-dominated societies boys learn to see heterosexual activity as a confirmation of masculinity (and certainly know that boasting about their desire to perform it is the single easiest way of proclaiming their "virility": "whoooa!"); girls learn to value committed relationships above casual sex (or, at least, certainly discover that they ought to say so to escape being branded whatever the local vernacular for "slag" might be.' Thus it would appear that social factors offer a more plausible explanation for differences in sexual behaviour.

Furthermore, other research also suggests the accounts of men and women's 'mating strategies' do not compute: one study found that heterosexual men reported having three to four times more sexual partners than women, which begs the question 'who are they having sex with?' (Segal, 1999: 90).

[Hotlink → **Sex and Sexuality (Chapter 15)**]

Psychoanalytic approaches

Despite the influence of biological theories in explaining gender development, predominantly in terms of 'sex', it is generally accepted that gender is not fully stamped on identity at birth. Yet by age 3 most children have developed a strong sense of themselves as either a girl or a boy. Psychoanalytic explanations offer an approach to understanding how this gender identity development occurs by integrating the notion of biological drives with postnatal social interaction. Sigmund Freud (1905, 1925, 1931), founder of a school of psychoanalytic theorists who attempted to understand the complex processes of personality development, developed his theory during the late nineteenth and early twentieth centuries with a central focus on issues of gender and sexuality. Key to his understanding of personality was the role of the unconscious, an aspect of the mind that he saw as operating beyond our conscious awareness. Freud proposed that the unconscious consisted of a collection of instincts, or drives, that underpinned thought and action, and these drives were biologically determined. In relation to gender identity development Freud posited that infants are sexual beings and that a biologically determined, sexual instinct propels infants through a series of psychosexual stages of development.

He defined these as the oral stage, anal stage, phallic stage, latency stage and genital stage. The oral stage refers to the first year of life when the mouth is the site of sensuous pleasure for babies, indicated through their sucking and chewing on objects that they place in their mouth. By the end of the first year this site of pleasure is believed to have moved to the anus, where the child is theorised to gain pleasure from the sensation of excretory functions. The crucial developmental process at this stage is toilet training. Any unresolved issues are seen to reappear later in adult life in people who have overly intense concerns with tidiness, stubbornness and retaining possessions. In common, everyday parlance these traits are recognised through reference to 'anal personality'. Through these two stages, Freud hypothesises that personality development is the same for boys and girls; however, it diverges at the crucial phallic stage (Freud, 1933/1964). At this stage, reached by children in the third and fourth year of life, the site of pleasure moves to the genitals, and is provided through masturbation. Young children's engagement in their own sexual pleasure can be disturbing for parents and other adults. Yet, Freud believed two processes take place at this stage. Firstly, children notice their genital differentiation in that they either have or do not have a penis and, secondly, the focus on genital pleasure leads to sexual desire for the parent of the opposite sex. Yet, the way this stage is resolved is significantly different for boys and girls. For boys, the phallic stage is resolved through the Oedipus complex, which is instigated by their startling recognition that girls do not have a penis. This results in castration anxiety as they become concerned that their own penis could also be removed. The father, or father figure, is seen to be the source of threat and fear as it is he who appears to compete with the boy for the mother's affection. Thus, in order to overcome the anxiety boys must end the sexual competition with their fathers for their mother's affection. Giving up sexual desire for the mother and identifying with the father leads to the development of a masculine identity, but this is premised on the loss of his mother.

For girls, Freud proposed a slightly different developmental process that required the resolution of their own version of the castration complex. Here, anxiety is created by recognition that they do not have a penis and girls are seen to be envious and 'lacking' which leads them to feel inferior to boys. This results in a hostile reaction towards the mother because, as Freud theorised, the girl blames her mother for not giving her a penis when the possession of a penis is important to capture the mother's desire. Freud labelled this 'penis envy' and suggested that girls, like boys, also unconsciously reject 'femininity' as a desirable state and begin to identify with their fathers. However, when this 'unrealistic project fails, Freud argues that the girl abandons this temporary identification with the father and falls in love with him' (Alsop *et al.*, 2002: 45). Thus, girls finally develop a feminine identity through a secondary identification with the mother.

Boys and girls only reach the last two stages of development once they have resolved the Oedipus complex. During the latency stage there is little activity and sexual feelings remain under the surface. These re-

emerge in the genital stage which is reached after the physical effects of puberty. This is the final stage of development where males and females will desire genital relationships and the areas that were highlighted as sensual zones during infancy become a secondary and lesser focus for sexual pleasure.

Whilst Freud's work has received criticism on a number of levels (see A Critical Look 7.3), not least from feminists who describe his work as *phallocentric* because of the focus on castration anxiety and penis envy, it is still influential today in relation to understanding gender and sexuality. This is in part because it offers one of the most nuanced accounts of gender development. It rejects notions of pure masculinity and femininity and highlights the complexity that many men and women experience in living their gender and sexuality identities. It is able to do this because of the role it accords to unconscious processes in regulating these identities and behaviour, and because it acknowledges that men and women both unconsciously repress masculinity and femininity identifications. As Rachel Alsop, Annette Fitzsimons and Kathleen Lennon (2002: 47) summarise:

in Freud's theory, what culture calls 'masculinity' and 'femininity' emerge as forms of identity which refuse to be confined inside the boundaries of male and female bodies leaving men and women as inherently bisexual mixtures of gender.

A critical look 7.3

Psychoanalytic theory

Freud's approach has been criticised on a number of grounds. Modern day experimental psychology has little time for the hypothesis that our thought and actions are largely driven by the sexual instincts of the unconscious mind. This is because these claims are difficult to validate as Freud's theory relies on the method of introspection. This method is seen to lack empirical rigour as it relies on subjective accounts rather than objective knowledge collected with experimental methods.

A second criticism of Freud's work is that it positions women as psychoanalytically inferior to men and incapable of full, mature development. This was

▶

largely in line with the social and cultural mood of the era in which he was writing. However, whilst he saw women as failed men, because their identity was grounded in penis envy, he did not see them as intellectually inferior to men (Brannon, 2005), and he trained a generation of female psychoanalysts including Karen Horney and his daughter Anna Freud. Later, feminist psychoanalysts such as Juliet Mitchell (1974) reconceptualised his use of the term 'penis envy'. Rather than envy of the actual physical appendage the 'penis' it should be understood as representing the unconscious envy of what the penis signifies. Thus, it is envy of the power and social standing that is accorded to men.

A third critique of Freud's work cited by some feminists questions the way he theorised his female patients' accounts of seduction during childhood by their fathers or close family friends (Stainton-Rogers and Stainton-Rogers, 2001). Initially Freud saw this as a form of 'child sexual abuse' that interfered with normal development. Later, however, he revised his position under the pressure of medical colleagues who refused to believe this was true. Thus, Freud has been accused of silencing these accounts and failing to engage with the implications of child sexual abuse – a topic that did not really come into focus until the end of the twentieth century.

Socio-cultural approaches

In contrast to psychoanalytic claims of inherent drives that are mediated by parental interaction, socio-cultural approaches posit that the defining factors that promote gender difference come from the social world around us. In this paradigm the individual is seen as shaped and formed into a particular gender role through the process of socialisation. There are several perspectives within this approach in psychology including social learning theory [Hotlink → Chapter 1], gender schema theory and social constructionist accounts.

Studies suggest that from birth parents and other adults interact differently with infants depending on whether they are labelled 'boy' or 'girl' (Brannon, 2005). Social Learning Theorists such as Albert Bandura (1986) attempt to explain this process through emphasising the role of observational learning and reinforcement in the development of particular gender-related behaviours. This approach builds on the behaviourist assumptions embedded in the principles of operant conditioning: that we learn to do what is expected of us through a system of rewards and punishments. In relation to gender this would take place through reinforcing gender appropriate behaviour (such as a girl playing with a doll) with praise, and punishing gender inappropriate behaviour (such as a boy playing with a doll) by scolding. Social learning theory develops the principles of behaviourism to take account of the role of internal mental processes that aid in the process of learning. Higher-order cognitive processes such as imitation and modelling are seen as key to the learning of gender roles and emerge as a result of the child's observations of the world around them. Maccoby and Jacklin (1974) surmise that this is because the speed in which children acquire their appropriate gender role cannot be explained by reinforcement alone but must involve a complex internalisation process involved in imitation. Parents are seen as particularly important as they are the people children are more likely to model in the early stages of development. While modelling is a strong force in prompting the performance of gender-related behaviour, children do not simply copy the same-sex parent's behaviour patterns, mannerism or expressions. They also use cognitive skills to select role models they see as similar to themselves thus same-sex parents, peers, siblings, teachers and popular media representations of men and women all play a part in the development of gender.

Gender schema theory offers an alternative approach to understanding gender development with a greater emphasis on processes of cognitive development more generally. Here, researchers such as Sandra Bem (1981, 1985, 1993) have developed Kohlberg's cognitive developmental theory in an attempt to explain why children choose gender as a principle factor around which to organise information. Kohlberg (1966) suggested children, rather than continuously learning about gender through modelling and imitation, developed their sense of gendered self through a series of cognitive competencies in relation to gender. The first of these is gender labelling where children become able to accurately attribute the terms 'girl' and 'boy' to themselves and others. The second stage, gender knowledge, is when children accumulate knowledge about the characteristics of female and male gender. Finally, gender identity development ends in late childhood once children have established a sense of gender constancy, in that they recognise that gender is unchanging, which then leads them to develop gender stereotypes (see A Closer Look 7.5).

A closer look 7.5

Gender stereotyping and psychological health

Gender stereotypes are made up of a collection of factors including personality traits, social roles and behaviours as well as physical characteristics. Conventional thought holds that masculinity and femininity are oppositional poles on the same continuum and various psychometric tests have been used to measure these traits. However, these tests have been largely discredited because they do not measure actual differences in terms of masculinity and femininity, rather they measure stereotypical accounts of what masculinity and femininity are thought to be. One response to this has been the development of multidimensional scales that measure how men and women score on both masculinity and femininity scales. One of the most well known is Sandra Bem's gender role inventory. Bem theorised that men and women who scored highly in measurements of both masculinity and femininity traits could be classified, in terms of their gender-role identification, as psychologically androgynous. She argued (1974) that androgyny offers a 'psychologically healthier' gender-role identification than single dimension traits (masculinity or femininity), or an undifferentiated gender identification where people have low scores on both traits. Thus the androgynous person functions well as they can be independent and affectionate, assertive and understanding, and as Bem suggests, the androgynous person should define a more human standard of psychological health than the existing oppressive model of conforming to traditional gender roles. In recent years Bem's notion of androgyny has been criticised on methodological and conceptual grounds, but it has been crucial in creating alternative understandings of people who do not exhibit traditional traits of masculinity or femininity as psychologically healthy and adjusted, rather than abnormal

(Burr, 1998).

Bem (1985) highlighting the limitations of Kohlberg's approach, argued that he does not account for why gender, rather than 'race', height, hair colour or all number of other categories, is such a dominant category around which we understand our selves and others. She also suggests that not all children have the same cognitions about gender and that some individuals organise and respond to information in different ways. Thus, individuals may develop different gender schemata and cognitive structures that provide their own, individualised, internalised mental framework that helps them make sense of the world. This, she suggests, is because information is always gathered in relation to a specific social environment that defines maleness and femaleness. Furthermore, because experience is filtered through a social context we do not all hold the same schemata and these variations affect how we understand ourselves in terms of masculinity or femininity as well as how we process gender-related information (Brannon, 2005). Thus, Bem (1985, 1987) suggests that the development of typical gender roles and gender stereotyping are not inevitable. These can be avoided if parents take appropriate steps to raise 'gender-aschematic children'. As the world is dominated by information organised around gender, Bem suggested that parents should try to counter this by teaching their children alternatives to the images of gender stereotypes found in everyday interaction. For example, parents should focus on differences that are due to biology, such as anatomy and reproduction, rather than socially defined differences that dominate occupations, household chores, leisure activities, toys and colour preferences. They can do this through challenging stereotypical images found in the media and by eliminating gender-related differences from their own activities. Research from single-parent families and non-traditional families, such as those where parents question traditional attitudes to gender-related behaviours and those that include lesbian parents, have confirmed that it is possible to raise children with more flexible attitudes towards gender (Brannon, 2005). However, as Brannon (2005) points out 'no family attitudes or behavior can completely counteract the influence of society's pervasive gender associations' (2005: 152).

Stop and think 7.5

If you rated yourself on a masculinity scale and a femininity scale do you think you would score low or high on one or both traits? What would this mean in terms of your sense of self as masculine, feminine or androgynous?

Bem's account of gender schemas highlights the social nature of knowledge and that people engage with this to create similar but individualised cognitions. However, her work on androgyny in particular has been criticised by others for failing to engage theoretically with gender (Hollway, 1989) and for ignoring the power relationship between men and women (Eisenstein, 1984). In recent years, social constructionist theories have become increasingly influential in psychological research. These move away from notions of internalised mental states to highlight the socially constructed nature of the world. This approach draws on debates that have taken place in philosophy and other social sciences such as sociology and critical psychology in order to critique what they see as taken-for-granted knowledge assumptions and power differentials (Burr, 2001). Rather than seeing differences between men and women as set truths documented by biological and scientific research, social constructionist accounts focus on the role of language and interaction in creating meanings for the way in which we can experience ourselves (Burr, 1998).

Thus, gender stereotypes are not seen as fixed mental representations that help people make sense of people and the world around them. Instead, they are seen as discourses or dominant ways of speaking that perpetuate particular social relations and limit the way that both men and women can experience themselves in relation to each other. This is because there are particular expectations of masculinity or femininity embedded in these discourses which promote certain styles of interaction. For example, in terms of personality characteristics, masculinity is associated with 'rationality' and femininity with 'emotionality'. These cultural expectations can be limiting especially for men and women who transgress specific codes of gender-related behaviour.

One of the benefits for feminist psychologists of this approach is that it opens up the possibility of challenging dominant ideologies and theories that have traditionally positioned women as inferior to men. For example, social constructionist accounts show that our understandings of maleness and femaleness are not stable features. If we look at different historical periods or across cultural divisions we find a range of competing understandings of what it means to be male or female that are shaped by cultural and economic forces, rather than inherent biology [Hotlink → History (Chapter 3); Sociology (Chapter 4); Gendered Perspectives – Theoretical Issues (Chapter 1)]. For example, there have been rapid shifts in the role expectations for men and women in the last 50 years, particularly in relation to fatherhood where it is much more common to find closer and more emotionally involved models of fatherhood as a cultural ideal. While by no means the norm, in a move to greater gender equality, it is more acceptable that women may be the main earner within families and that some men will stay at home to care for children [Hotlink → Social Policy (Chapter 5)]. Thus, as Joseph Pleck (1987) claims, there has been a fragmentation in the previous link between specific roles and gender, so that now men and women might pick up different roles at different times, independent of gender. See World in Focus 7.2 for a discussion of gender identity. [Hotlink → Gendered Perspectives – Theoretical Issues (Chapter 1)].

There has been an explosion of publications by feminist psychologists in this area as they attempt to 'reconstruct the psychological subject' (Gergen, 2001) and social constructionist thinking can be found to underpin a whole range of psychological studies on the subjective experiences of women including PMS and mental illness (Ussher, 1989, 1991); exclusion (Burman *et al.*, 1996); 'race' and ethnicity (Bhavnani and Phoenix, 1994); rape (Gavey, 2005) and child sexual abuse (Reavey and Warner, 2003). The aim embedded in the phrase 'reconstructing the psychological subject' has always been to make women's experience a greater focus within an academic discipline that has frequently produced androcentric research. This has taken place in the UK through a range of publications such as *The Psychology of Women Section Review, Feminism & Psychology* and the *Women & Psychology* book series (Routledge) edited

World in focus 7.2

Cultural variations in gender identity

When people do not conform to societal ideals of male-masculine and female-feminine there are different cultural responses. In the UK, and other similar western cultures people are seen to have a 'gender identity disorder'. These are listed in the Diagnostic and Statistical Manual of Mental Disorders (DSM, 1994) and have been predominantly theorised through medical and scientific approaches which value biological and causal explanations. In this context the most familiar example of

a 'gender identity disorder' is 'transsexualism' where individuals transition from one gender to the other while undergoing hormonal and surgical procedures. This transition can only take place once sanctioned by a psychiatric diagnosis. Social constructionist challenges to this understanding (e.g. Billings and Urban, 1982; Kessler and McKenna, 1985; Johnson, 2006) suggest these medical interventions serve to legitimise and regulate a two-sex system, where there are only, and can only be, two sexes.

In other settings there is evidence of wider variation in gender

expectation. For example, in India, the Hijras are a recognised 'third sex' (Gerdt, 1993). Some hijras engage in the same processes as male-to-female transsexuals living in western countries as they also undergo castration and take on a female identity. However, this is not classified as a disorder rather, historically, hijras were seen as having special, shamanic powers. Yet the impact of western values during the colonial period in India has led to shifts in cultural perceptions so that hijras now have a less positive place in society [**Hotlink → Chapter 1, World in Focus 1.1**].

by Jane Ussher. Within these forums the scope of feminist and critical psychology has broadened from a focus on 'women' to include diverse concerns such as lesbian and gay lives, child development, relationships and heterosexuality, transsexual and transgender issues. As part of this trend there has also, since the 1990s, been a growing interest amongst feminists and social psychologists in subjectivity and identity issues faced by men. This is an expanding area in psychology and has produced a range of theoretical and empirical studies that have investigated masculinity and men's experience in relation to adolescence (Frosh *et al.*, 2003), unemployment (Willott and Griffin, 1997), masculinities (Segal, 1990), sexism (Gough, 1998) and identity and power (Edley and Wetherell, 1995). In 2005 Jeff Hearn presented a keynote address at the *Psychology of Women Annual Conference* in Huddersfield (Hearn, 2006) illustrating that masculinity and men are beginning to be seen as essential topics in the psychology of gender. However, those who are addressing issues of masculinity within psychology tend to be informed by sociological analyses. Furthermore, these recent moves towards socio-cultural explanations for gender differences are located in the margins of a discipline that overwhelmingly values biological and cognitive approaches above

socio-cultural understandings. Thus, the need for engagement and critique with a psychology discipline that maintains its androcentric core is a key requirement for those attempting to understand how gender is lived in everyday life.

Conclusion

In evaluating the evidence from these theories we can assume that there is a place for biological accounts in determining the sexed bodies men and women have. Yet the gender roles and behaviours that are related to a particular anatomical body are always filtered through social processes. Psychological theories vary in the emphasis they accord to social and environmental forces, from acknowledging social influence as a factor in the way we learn about gender to presenting gender as a fluid concept that is open to change and reinterpretation, across time and culture. Psychoanalytic theories are still drawn on by those attempting to theorise the complex internal life of gender and its relationship to self and identity (e.g. Hollway, 1989; Frosh, 1991; Segal, 1999). However, these perspectives are less central to mainstream psychological debates because they are seen to lack the empirical rigour that a scientific discipline requires. Unfortunately, explanations for gender identity development are left pivoted across what is commonly referred to as the '*nature versus nurture*' divide (see A Critical Look 7.4). The problem with this is that no one, single perspective is likely to provide the answer to how we develop our sense of gender identity. Furthermore, the differentiation between myriad perspectives focuses our attention on the grand narratives of gender theory, yet psychology is also interested in individual experience. Here, we encounter some profound limitations in understanding gender identities and the way we live them as it is almost impossible to predict, or document, the individual pathways we each experience in the development of our sense of self as male or female.

A critical look 7.4

Nature versus nurture

The nature–nurture debate attempts to distinguish which human characteristics are innate and which are learnt. Lipton (2005), in an overview of 'the case for nature' and 'the case for nurture' points out there is no more contentious area in the nature–nurture debate than the study of gender. This is because historically 'nature' based explanations have posited that women are physically, psychologically, intellectually and emotionally inferior to men and that these differences are seen as innate, fixed, unchangeable. In contrast, feminist critics have demonstrated how biological explanations often mask sexist ideologies and contest the notion that personality and behaviour is determined by genetics or hormones: biology is *not* destiny. On this side of the debate evidence is provided that we learn behaviour from our surroundings and this has the greatest impact on the type of people we become and the gendered behaviour we exhibit. For example, women learn that they are inferior to men and therefore behave in that way, while men learn that they are supposed to be more aggressive which influences their behaviour, rather than it being the result of innate testosterone levels. Yet, this polarised debate is rather simplistic. We are all biological creatures and there are anatomical, genetic and hormonal differences between men and women. Yet, biology does not exist in a vacuum –

environmental factors also impact on biology and cultural factors influence the way that biological differences are interpreted. Thus, it is unlikely there will ever be an answer to the nature–nurture debate that clarifies whether gender is determined by either innate or learnt characteristics. This leaves the question of 'nature or nurture' redundant as the answer is always both.

Further Reading

Linda Brannon (2005), *Gender: Psychological Perspectives*, 4th edition, Boston, Pearson Education Inc. A wonderful and comprehensive overview of the diverse psychological approaches to understanding gender from biology to cognition to social perspectives. A key text for any student studying the psychology of gender.

Vivien Burr (1998), *Gender and Social Psychology*, London, Routledge. Clearly written and accessible account of social psychological perspectives as applied to gender. Focuses well on issues of work and education as well as feminist interventions.

Nigel Edley and Margaret Wetherell (1995), *Men in Perspective: Practice, Power and Identity*, London, Prentice Hall. A key book in the emergence of masculinity studies within social psychology. Presents masculinity as both a social and psychological phenomenon and links to issues of history, culture and power.

Wendy Stainton-Rogers and Rex Stainton-Rogers (2001), *The Psychology of Gender and Sexuality*, Buckingham, Open University Press. Outlines in an accessible manner the theories and approaches in psychology that have been used to understand gender and sexuality. Highlights feminist and critical psychological critiques of biological and cognitive approaches.

The Psychology of Women Section Review – The official publication from the British Psychological Society Section, Psychology of Women. Presents a forum for discussion of issues relating to the psychology of women in research, teaching and professional practice. In recent years has broadened its focus to include papers on masculinity and sexualities.

Feminism & Psychology – A leading journal in the field of gender and sexuality studies both within and outside of psychology. It provides a forum for the application of feminist theory to issues of gender and sexuality within a range of contexts including work, relationships, sexual identity and professional practice.

The Psychology of Women Quarterly – The official publication on behalf of the American Psychological Association Society for the psychology of women. Publishes a range of quantitative and qualitative research papers on issues such as health, education, employment, sexuality, ethnicity and social and cognitive processes.

Websites

The British Psychological Society **www.bps.org.uk** – The BPS website is a useful starting point for information relating to practice and research within psychology, including publications, careers and courses.

The Psychologist **www.thepsychologist.org.uk** – Website for the monthly publication from the BPS. Can access articles from previous editions and these are written in an accessible style.

The America Psychological Association **www.apa.org/topics/** – The APA website that provides information on a range of topics and issues in psychology including women, men and sexual orientation.

End of chapter activity

Collect a recent catalogue from your local branch of the *Early Learning Centre* or alternative children's toyshop that has an educational focus. Look at the toys and the children depicted playing with them and discuss the following questions with others in your class.

➤ What toys do boys play with? What toys do girls play with? What toys are non-gender specific?

➤ How might the toys influence the type of cognitive and social skills children develop? What tasks will they be good at as adults? What gender roles do you imagine them playing in 20 years time?

➤ Do you think gender differences are inherent, learnt or socially constructed?

➤ Do you think it is possible to avoid traditional gender roles?

Chapter 8

Political science

Key issues in this chapter:

➤ Certain 'myths' were created by studies in the mid- to late-twentieth century which included gender uncritically in the research. These have been challenged and addressed by feminist Political Scientists.

➤ Gender differences in political behaviour and knowledge do exist, though in many cases these are minor.

➤ Feminist Political Science has challenged the very basis of Political Science both in its findings and in its approaches and methods.

➤ Gender is beginning to emerge as an issue in Political Science.

At the end of this chapter you should be able to:

➤ Explain the misrepresentation of women in early Behaviouralist research.

➤ Outline an overview of feminist Political Science's contribution to the discipline.

➤ Discuss the current position of gender within the discipline of Political Science.

➤ Interpret gender disaggregated data.

Introduction

'All for one, one for all'
the theme of the Million Man March

October 16, 1995
From Correspondent Bob Franken

WASHINGTON (CNN) – Hundreds of thousands of African-American men came to the Washington mall – some searching for meaning, some to make personal statements. There may have been as many messages as there were participants. Self-help and self-respect were constant themes but it was the man who conceived the march, Louis Farrakhan, whose words electrified the crowd. 'God called us here to this place at this time for a very specific reason and now I want to say my brothers, this is a very pregnant moment, pregnant with the promise of tremendous change in our status in America and in the world,' Farrakhan said to the marchers.

Earlier statements by Farrakhan calling some Jews and others 'financial bloodsuckers' attracted much negative publicity in the days prior to the march. But entertainer Stevie Wonder spoke Monday of the common suffering of Jews and blacks. 'We cannot act as if we don't hear nor see. Like in the holocaust of six million Jews, and 150 million blacks during slavery. All for one, one for all,' said Wonder to the massive crowd.

The rank and file of marchers explained why they felt the need to be in this place at this time. 'Minister Farrakhan has some very strong viewpoints on certain issues. We may not agree with everything, but we thought this was larger than just Minister Farrakhan,' said one marcher.

'This is not just for today, this is a beginning. Keep carrying on. All the genocides, drugs in our neighborhoods. This is powerful, black men together, and I love it,' said another man.

CNN at **http://www-cgi.cnn.com/US/9510/megamarch/march. html**

The Million Man Movement calls upon African-American men to express a collective commitment to restoring the moral responsibility of men to act and take leadership in families and communities in crisis or under stress.

Figure 8.1 Millian Man March
Source: © James Leynse/Corbis

Stop and think 8.1

Look at the image above (Figure 8.1), read the news report. What forms of masculinity are fostered by this movement? What crisis is perceived to be occurring to African-American men? What do you think is the role of gender in such an organisation?

Such a movement, that could organise hundreds of thousands to a rally in the US capital, is surely a powerful political organisation. Many other organisations and movements have also been able to mobilise around various issues, from anti-war to 'race' equality, from trade union powers to reproductive rights. Feminist movements have also mobilised large crowds of people for various issues. What makes such a men's movement different is that unlike the others the Million Man March was aimed not just at changing the policies of politicians, not just at shaping public opinion but at changing the behaviour of the participants too. It is also an example of organising at the intersections of identity; in this case 'race' and gender, and even rarer, 'race' and the masculine gender. In fact, in politics and Political Science rarely has the lens of analysis and study been turned upon the masculine gender and it is only relatively recently that either thought to consider gender at all, with the journal *Politics and Gender* only appearing in 2005. To explore this assertion it is necessary to explore the history of gender issues in Political

Science. We will return to discussions of men's movements later, but first we will trace some of the major developments in Political Science's treatment of men and women, finally turning to examples of how gender, rather than comparisons of women to men are beginning to emerge.

Political Science and gender

The history of gender as a factor for analysis and study in Political Science is very much tied up with the recent history of the discipline itself. As a discipline Political Science deals with the theory and practice of politics. It seeks to describe and analyse political systems, political behaviour and political policies. The study of politics is actually quite ancient, though Political Science as a modern academic discipline is really a product of the twentieth century. A major influence on this development was the rise of the modern university, in particular the growth of universities in the United States which brought about a gradual Americanisation of Political Science (Guy, 2001). The main feature of this Americanisation was a desire to use modern scientific approaches to study politics and separate out the study of political behaviour from the rest of social behaviour, referred to as a drive towards scientism. The discipline of Politics can be roughly divided: the Traditionalist School and the Behaviouralists, and from both, the Post Behaviouralists. The former view themselves as observers, observers of policy decisions and of political actions. This view sees the study of politics as an art, as analysis involves values, ethics and morals to be included in the development of explanations of the things observed. The Behaviouralists grew from the ranks of those who sought to find a degree of accuracy and measurement to explain political actions; this meant that their observations need to be value-free and they employ the skills of science and concepts from other social sciences. The latter seek to take the best from both approaches to develop theories for change for the better (see A Closer Look 8.1).

A closer look 8.1

Characteristics of different approaches

Traditionalist approaches to political analysis

The main approaches are those of description and explanation of observed acts, however they may be observed (from reading policy decisions to interviewing people about their political beliefs). The researcher applies their own knowledge and expertise to the issue to describe and analyse it, as such the analysis cannot be value-free. On the whole quantitative methods are not used as Traditionalists doubt the validity of measuring human behaviour. More often Traditionalists will employ methods of historical research, collecting archival sources and primary data to develop a story of 'what has happened' and to point to a conclusion of 'why'.

Behaviouralist approaches to Political Science

Behaviouralists focus on the scientific and systematic understanding of the world of politics and political behaviour through the use of rigorous scientific and statistical methods to achieve value-free results. This approach employs surveys and polling techniques to gather data regarding actual, observable behaviour of individuals and groups, rather than institutions, looking to find patterns that could become predictive and explanatory generalisations (e.g. young voters do X, retired voters do Y). Methodologically this approach is quantitative and utilises scientific methods of establishing an hypothesis and classifying variables used to test the hypothesis (also referred to as Positivism). Its aim is to generate a set of tested hypothesis from which theories of causality can be developed.

Post Behaviouralism

The main credo behind Post Behaviouralism is that Political Science needs to have a public purpose. This requires a scientific approach to understanding politics and political processes to address important political issues and problems. Research needs to inform policy makers about how to make things better and the approach is methodologically diverse in that it combines scientific method with value-based conclusions deduced from the analysis of data. This can involve the use of a range of methods, and requires not only technique but also values such as justice, ethics and morals.

Stop and think 8.2

Without referring back to the material above, think about the differences in the approaches of Traditionalists and Behaviourists. Can you list three ways in which they differ? If not, go back and re-read A Closer Look 8.1.

The rise of, a mostly US, Behaviouralist dominance in Political Science from the 1950s onwards has been seen as impeding the development of feminist scholarship (or any other radical scholarship) in this field. Joni Lovenduski (1981) has argued that the more philosophical approach to politics, inherent in the Traditional approach, permitted space for the exploration of what constitutes knowledge, and therefore space for radical critiques of that knowledge. She points out that Political Science cannot be seen as existing outside of those who perform it, in other words, it is 'a product of the interplay of its practitioners rather than a set of truths or laws discovered by them . . . a construct of Political Scientists. It is a convention' (Lovenduski, 1981: 86). Whereas the empirical and positivistic approach of Behaviouralism became less concerned with such epistemological debates and more with studying what politicians regard as political and, as such, the study of gender became limited. Within the greater philosophical openness of the Traditionalist approach feminism may have found a place to question the very nature of politics (see Controversy 8.1 and 8.2) and thereby Political Science. However, given that the empirical focus of Behaviouralism has been virtually exclusively upon the exercise of observable power, political elites and institutions of government, it could not 'fail to be sexist' (Lovenduski, 1981: 89).

Controversy 8.1

Feminist redefinitions of 'Politics' 1

Just as gender has been reconceptualized, 'politics,' too, has been expanded by feminists. In its narrowest definition, politics has to do with participation in government, party politics, and elective or appointed office. More broadly, however, politics has to do with power: getting people to do what you want them to do. This definition is still being challenged by academics, but feminists have refused to limit a political analysis to that of formal roles. Politics, feminists believe, includes relations in the world of work: for example, who is hired, who is fired, who is always boss, who is never boss. In *Sexual Politics*, Kate Millett's definition of sexual politics goes even further: Sexual politics, she writes, is the power relationship between men and women in formal groups and in the family.

Thus, sexual politics must include the politics of motherhood. Although from one perspective, contraception and abortion pertain only to a woman and her pregnancy, the question of whether a woman is legally obligated to carry her fetus to term is, in most countries today, determined by society. In some, it is never appropriate to end a pregnancy, even if it is medically possible. In others, it is the decision of the husband and father because the fetus is considered to be his property. In the United States since 1973, the decision may be made only by the person who is pregnant, in consultation with her medical adviser – not the father of the child and not the state. But these are political issues, not issues determined by nature.

To take another example based on this broader definition of politics, child care today is considered a political issue, but in a different society or at another time, it might have been considered a family or a private matter. Politics impinges on the right to work, marriage and divorce, participation in the military, pornography, and even advertising, which, as feminists see it, affects people's view of women and women's view of themselves.

Feminists did not always define politics this way. In the nineteenth century at the beginning of the women's rights movement, women activists concentrated on bringing balance to the civil and political (in the narrow sense) rights of men and women, and in time their work focused on a complex, protracted struggle for the right to vote. To win this battle, our foremothers had to form strong organizations that could work across the nation concurrently for a common goal.

Source: Extract from Tobias (1997).

This epistemological issue has, according to Lovenduski (1981), not only been sexist in the study of women but also in the treatment of women within the profession:

> Whilst any radical critic of a socially constructed discipline must contend with the cultural biases such a construction contains; the dominance of Political Science by scholars who had not developed the habit of systematically engaging even rudimentary theories of knowledge compounded the problem enormously. There is, of course, no doubt that Political Science has been sexist. Not only did it exclude women from its concerns, it also excluded them from membership in the profession.
> (Lovenduski, 1981: 88–89)

Thus, although women were included from the outset in studies of political participation, as gender (or more accurately, sex) was included as a variable, their absence from all other areas was not seen as an issue by the increasingly empirical discipline through the 1950s to 1970s. Nor has that meagre inclusion been seen as accurate.

Sex bias in Political Science research

The rise of the Behaviouralist approach meant the development of a large number of surveys in search of answers as to how people behave politically and why they behave in certain ways. From the outset these studies of political participation did include both men and women. As Karen Beckwith (2005: 128) notes, the early 'studies of women and politics relied on an "add women and stir" model'. In addition, although data on gender was gathered it was frequently not analysed and there was not a lot of it (Lovenduski, 1981: 90), or it was distorted. This distortion of data on women's political participation took several forms, as summarised by Susan Bourque and Jean Grossholtz in an important article in 1974, one which has been included in several feminist Political Science collections since (see A Closer Look 8.2).

Such distortions created certain 'sexist myths' (Lovenduski, 1981: 93) about female political

---

A closer look 8.2

Ways in which women's political participation was misrepresented/distorted

In 1974 Susan Bourque and Jean Grossholtz published an article which outlined what they saw as the misrepresentation of women's political behaviour. They based their argument on the analysis of text books that were both widely used and cited. They examined the way in which data on women's political acitivity was analysed and found that four trends emerged. They outlined these as:

1. fudging the footnotes

2. the assumption of male dominance

3. acceptance of masculinity as the ideal political behaviour

4. commitment to the eternal feminine.

Fudging the footnotes – this was applied when they found that texts were claiming certain aspects of female political behaviour that were not substantiated in the work being cited as the source of the finding. It was usually achieved by the inclusion of certain findings, e.g. *women vote less than men*, but not the careful, qualified language used to describe the findings in the original study, i.e. *but this is a small difference in comparison to the influence of occupation.*

Assumption of male dominance – they found a lack of questioning of why men dominate in politics, an approach that predisposed certain expectations of sex differences in politics.

Masculinity as ideal political behaviour – this explains the acceptance of certain traits deemed to be masculine as the norm for political activity, i.e. competition, aggression, pragmatism, which were left unexamined and used as a standard against which women were measured.

Commitment to the eternal feminine – explanations of female political behaviour derived from an unexamined stereotype regarding, and acceptance of, women's domestic role.

---

behaviour, based on 'often minute political differences between men and women' (Lovenduski, 1981: 94). An illustrative list of these myths is provided below:

➤ women are less politically aware than men;

➤ women are less politically active than men;

➤ women are more conservative than men;

➤ women have lower self efficacy than men in relation to politics, and

➤ women have less political knowledge than men.

This is summarised in one statement from a classic Political Science text; Gabriel Almond and Sidney Verba's *The Civic Culture: Political Attitudes and Democracy in Five Nations*:

> It would appear that women differ from men in their political behavior only in being somewhat more frequently apathetic, parochial, conservative, and sensitive to personality, emotional, and aesthetic aspects of political life and electoral campaigns.
>
> (Almond and Verba, 1963: 325)

(See A Critical Look 8.1 for details of sex differences in an early study.)

Stop and think 8.3

Read the above quote from Almond and Verba; they say women and men differ 'only somewhat'. Think how, if those two words are omitted, fudging of the footnotes can occur with this statement. Look too at the words used, do you find these to be gendered? How do the words used relate to Bourque and Grossholtz's notion of the assumption of masculinity in politics?

It would be wrong to argue that such assertions have no basis in truth as one careful, and under utilised, study shows that sex differences between men and women were apparent – the main point being though that the differences were not found to be significant (see A Closer Look 8.1).

As the study of political participation developed throughout the late 1950s and 1960s there was a limited amount of work on female political participation

A critical look 8.1

Maurice Duverger's *The Political Role of Women* (1955)

Duverger was commissioned by the International Political Science Association and UNESCO to conduct a comparative study of the political behaviour of women in Yugoslavia, West Germany, France and Norway. The research was conducted in 1952 and 1953. The focus of the research was to determine the role of women in relations to elections and political leadership. Obtaining the data itself was not easy as the political science and other organisations approached did not see the research as a priority. In addition, there were limits to funding and other resources. Duverger was aware of these limitations and the fact that this meant that some of the data was inadequate.

Analysis of the election data revealed certain findings; these were:

➤ Women were more likely than men not to vote.

➤ Women showed greater support than men for parties of the centre-right.

Likewise, the study of political leadership also made certain findings:

➤ Few women held office anywhere, their membership levels in political parties was small and few stood as candidates.

➤ Male dominance of office holding increased as the level of the political body increased, i.e. greater in national than in local legislatures.

➤ When in office women spoke less than men.

➤ Women positioned themselves outside of the political mainstream and were involved in issues of family, health, children's and women's rights.

Duverger was sensitive to sexism and was careful to note, in relation to the voting differences between men and women, that these were small and varied with occupation, region and age. In fact, he found that spouses tended to vote alike and that small overall sex differences that were found were found to be diminishing.

Source: Derived from Lovenduski (1981).

and what work that did exist tended to rely upon explanations such as women's lesser political knowledge or efficacy (see Almond and Verba, 1963; Milbrath, 1965). For most Political Scientists it seemed that women's underrepresentation in political life was not a great concern, in fact according to Murray Goot and Elizabeth Reid (1974), some seemed to overtly approve, whilst others either focused on men alone or were blatantly sexist (Lovenduski, 1981). Given this history it is not surprising that in the 1970s and 1980s feminist Political Scientists focused on exposing and debunking the sexist myths in a search for a more accurate understanding of the role of gender differences in political behaviour, for example:

➤ on women's participation in elite politics see Sharyne Merritt (1977); Elizabeth Vallance (1979),

➤ on voting behaviour see Sandra Baxter and Marjorie Lansing (1983); Kristi Andersen and Elizabeth Cook (1985); Pippa Norris (1986),

➤ on the marginalisation and integration of women see Marianne Githens and Jewel Prestage (1977); Virginia Sapiro (1984),

and many other areas. There is no space here to go through the thirty plus years of examination and re-examination; however, it is useful to look at a few key issues regarding gender, or rather, sex differences.

Some key issues

Here we explore the history of Political Science in relation to studies of voting behaviour and other political acitivites.

Voting behaviour

As previously noted sex, as a variable, has been included from the beginning in studies of voting behaviour, along with other variables such as social class, educational level, age and so on. One such study was the influential seven-nation comparison conducted by Sidney Verba, Norman Nie and Jae-On Kim (1978) which found that in all the countries for which they had appropriate data, men were more politically active than women (for a critique of what counts as politically active see Controversy 8.2), supporting the orthodoxy taught uncritically to many undergraduates.

Controversy 8.2

Feminist redefinitions of 'Politics' 2

In her book *Women and Politics*, Vicky Randall (1982) argued that a wider definition of political activity is required to fully understand women's role. Her discussion includes women's work 'within community-action movements, self-help groups and single-issue campaigns, often employing the tactics of pressure politics. Randall points out that women often play a preponderant role in campaigns on housing, government benefits and childcare' (Marchbank, 2000: 23). Likewise, Sheila Rowbotham (1995) and Amrita Basu (1995) provide details of a wide range of protests, collective and social actions, worldwide in which women were the instigators. The exclusion of such issues from the mainstream focus of Political Science has, it has been argued, underrepresented the political activities of women.

The challenge to this orthodoxy has come from later studies which found that traditional sex differences in voting rates has either reduced, or in some cases, reversed in many western democracies (Christy, 1987; Verba, Schlozman and Brady, 1995; Norris, 2001b). An examination of voting in USA Presidential elections shows that women's turnout, proportionally, has been greater than men's since 1980 and, as Table 8.1 shows, this even occurs in states viewed as crucial to an electoral outcome, known as 'battleground' states.

In fact, the gender gap in turnout reversal, as evidenced by various studies by CAWP (Center for American Women and Politics), has led them to develop a further usage of the term. Writing about the 2004 Presidential election CAWP (2004) defined the gender gap as 'the difference between the proportion of women and the proportion of men voting for the winning candidate'; a gap they measured at 7 per cent, i.e. women voted for Bush at 7 per cent less than did men (48 per cent for women, 55 per cent for men), a gender difference found to be true across different ethnic groups. Likewise, in the UK, Pippa Norris

Table 8.1 Gender differences in voter turnout, 2000 Presidential Election, USA, battleground states

State	Percentage of women eligible to vote who did	Percentage of men eligible to vote who did
Arizona	48.7	44.6
Arkansas	51.4	47.2
Florida	53.5	49.5
Iowa	66.3	62.0
Maine	70.5	67.7
Michigan	61.6	58.5
Missouri	66.6	64.0
Nevada	48.4	44.7
New Hampshire	65.2	61.3
New Mexico	53.9	48.3
Ohio	59.8	56.2
Oregon	63.0	58.4
Pennsylvania	56.1	55.4
Tennessee	53.4	51.2
Washington	58.9	58.3
West Virginia	52.0	52.2
Wisconsin	69.3	66.2

Source: Derived from Center for American Women in Politics, 2000.

(1999) found that the gender gap in turnout had reversed by 1979 (Norris, 1999). Further, her analysis of survey data on electoral participation across 19 countries (the Comparative Study of Electoral Systems) shows that any tendency for women in the past to display lesser electoral participation has, in established democracies, diminished and the only countries where it still remains significant are some post-communist states (Norris, 2001b).

In addition to examining gender differences in voter turnout work has also been done on the 'myth' that women are more conservative than men (as asserted by Almond and Verba, albeit qualified, and others). Throughout the 1980s work appeared which indicated that this pattern was changing and although it was still the case that women in western Europe were found to still be a little more right-wing than men when other factors such as controlling for participation in paid work and religious belief were introduced, this gender gap was reduced, and some even found that women in Europe are more left-wing than men (Jelen *et al.*, 1994). Ronald Inglehart and Pippa Norris (2000) analysed data from the World Values Survey to examine gender gaps in political ide-

World in focus 8.1

Electoral participation by gender

One means of measuring gender differences in electoral participation is to look at the differences in the numbers of men and women who report *not* voting. The Comparative Study of Electoral Systems collected this data from various countries in the 1990s. In the graph in Figure 8.2 a positive figure represents the difference between the number of women reporting *not* voting and the number of men reporting *not* voting. Therefore, a negative figure shows the countries where women voted at a greater rate than men. Overall, a gender gap of 1.8 per cent, i.e. more men than women voting, exists across the whole study.

Source: Derived from Comparative Study of Electoral Systems, detailed in Norris (2001b).

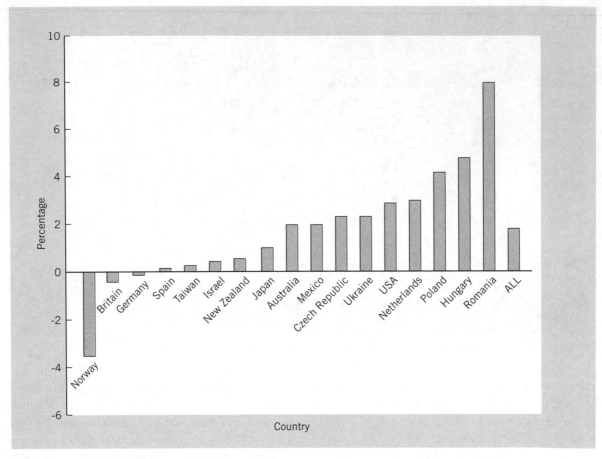

Figure 8.2 Gender Gap Difference in Reporting Non Voting
Source: Derived from Inglehart and Norris, 2000

ology and trends in those gaps. Figure 8.3 illustrates some of their analysis, where a negative figure means that women are more right-wing than men and a positive figure indicates women more left wing than men.

What Figure 8.3 shows is that during the 1980s, changes to the gender gap in ideology occurred. In only three countries did women increase their right-wing support compared with men; these being Canada, South Korea and, to a marginal respect, Belgium. At the same time in Denmark, although women remained more left-wing than men, this gap had closed somewhat. In all countries where, in 1981, women were more right-wing than men, all (bar Belgium) reduced the gender ideology gap, in some places reversing it by 1990.

Gender differences in other forms of political activity

Voting is not the only political activity – one may be a party member, be active in a particular campaign or provide financial support to either or both of such bodies. The diminishment of a gender gap in voter turnout in many states does not mean that gender gaps in other forms of political activity no longer exist (see A Closer Look 8.3) – separate investigation is required. M. Margaret Conway (2000) provides such a discussion in relation to the USA where she found that for 'two of the three types of electoral activities (contributing money and engaging in campaign activities) men were more active than women in 1996' (Conway, 2000: 77). She goes on to summarise and evaluate

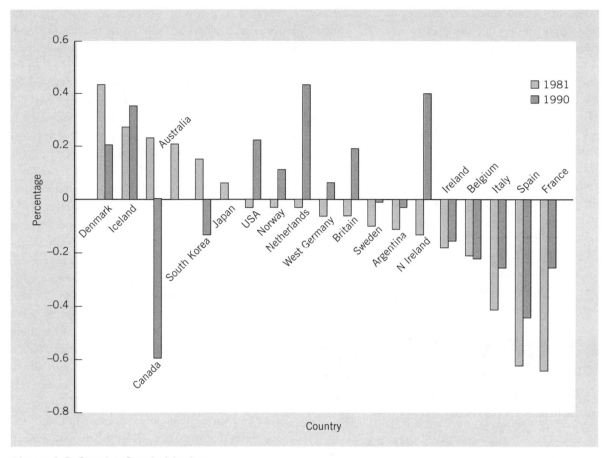

Figure 8.3 Gender Gap in Ideology

Note: no figure for Australia in 1990. Figure for Japan in 1990 is 0.0
Source: Derived from Inglehart and Norris, 2000

factors which might be responsible for inhibiting women's activity in relation to men's. Her list includes political socialisation and access to resources and she subdivides resources into the areas of education; income and occupation; social contexts of people's lives and generation. It is informative to review them here as they cover the standard explanations.

Socialisation: as M. Margaret Conway notes, research on girls in the 1960s 'suggests girls learned a passive orientation towards politics' (Conway, 2000: 77). Likewise for young women in the 1970s in the USA Virginia Sapiro found that most still accepted the traditional view of women's role as being in the private sphere (Sapiro, 1984: 6–7). Yet, in recent years women have increasingly taken up positions of elective office providing opportunities for resocialisation mes-

sages such as women's place is in politics. In fact, one finding of the British Electoral Commission's report (Norris *et al.*, 2004) was that 'women's elite participation appears to be a determinant of women's mass participation' (Childs, 2004: 423).

Access to resources: these include (a) education; (b) income and occupation; (c) social contexts; and (d) age (see also Norris, 1999, on generation and gender). M. Margaret Conway (2000) provides a succinct review of the established work on each of these issues pointing out that there is a strong relationship between higher educational levels and increased political activity, often as higher educational levels provide access to other networks involved with political activity. In terms of occupation and income it is clear that economic activity outside the home not only provides social interactions which can increase political awareness and opportunities but also greater access to financial means to contribute donations. Indeed, with 'unequal domestic and family responsibilities and suffering from the gender pay gap, women are more likely than men to be both time and money poor' (Childs, 2004: 423) [Hotlink → Work and Leisure (Chapter 14)].

It is likely too, argues M. Margaret Conway (2000), that the social contexts in which people live, their family, social organisations, religious practices amongst others, influence the time people have to participate and their attitudes towards issues. Age too affects political participation and 'generational differences existed . . . with the oldest and the youngest . . . being less likely to participate in even one campaign activity' (Conway, 2000: 80), and within each generation men were more likely to vote and to participate in at least one other category of political activity in her analysis.

A closer look 8.3

Gender differences in British political behaviour

A recent study undertaken for the Electoral Commission (Norris *et al.*, 2004) examines gender issues in participation. Sarah Childs (2004) has summarised the findings:

> There is a gender gap in participation, men are more active than women . . . men and women are similar in some political activities and women are more active in some . . .

➤ There is no gender gap in voter turnout at national, regional or local elections.

➤ Women are more likely than men to be involved in 'cause' orientated activities (such as signing petitions or boycotting products) but significantly less likely than men to participate in campaign orientated activities (contacting politicians; donating money to, or working for, or being a member of, a political party).

➤ Women are less likely than men to join voluntary organisations.

➤ In parliamentary constituencies with women MPs women are more politically active.

(Childs, 2004: 422)

Related to all these issues is access to political knowledge. Michael X. Delli Carpini and Scott Keeter point out that 'political knowledge . . . promotes participation and engagement in politics'(Delli Carpini and Keeter, 2000: 23) and explore this through analysis of two national surveys conducted in the USA (1989 and 1996). They conclude that in 'both surveys . . . about three fourths of women scored at or below the average for men' (Delli Carpini and Keeter, 2000: 24–6) and that only by the 1990s were there signs of a greater parity in knowledge between men and women. In addition, they found that gender differences in knowledge were much less when the subject matter related to women, such as on issues of health or reproductive rights and in local politics, where 'both structural and psychological barriers to women are less formidable' (Delli Carpini and Keeter, 2000: 45) there is no evidence of a gender gap. However, the evidence of such a gender gap in what is defined as the main political issues, i.e. those defined as by Political Science and politicians, provides, they contend, part of the explanation for women's lesser ability to actively pursue political pursuits.

One conclusion that can be drawn from all of the above is not that there are gender differences between the political activities and knowledge levels of women and men; but still, as Susan Bourque and Jean Grossholtz pointed out over thirty years ago, male actions and definitions are still taken as the norm, the yardstick, by which women are measured.

Perhaps other factors in explaining gender differences are the very debates and discourses surrounding the notion of what is political (see Controversy 8.1 and 8.2). Vicky Randall states that 'at one time convention tended to define women and politics as mutually exclusive' (Randall, 1982: 41) and in a similar vein Suvi Salmenniemi, in her exploration of gender differences in civic (i.e. societal) organisations and political institutions in Russia, argues that 'the political space, agency and citizen identities are gendered in such a way that civic activity is discursively constructed as feminine and institutional politics as masculine'. (Salmenniemi, 2005: 736). Such ideas have been one aspect of feminist contributions to Political Science, an area to which we now turn.

Feminist contribution to the discipline

Since its emergence in the 1970s, feminist scholarship has claimed to be corrective and transformative ... feminist scholars have sought to correct omissions and distortions that permeate political science. Through the use of gender as an analytical tool, they have illuminated social and political relations neglected by mainstream accounts, advanced alternative explanations of political phenomena, demonstrated the defects of competing hypotheses, and debunked opposing views. Despite such impressive accomplishments, feminist political science has not become a dominant paradigm within the discipline.

(Hawkesworth, 2005: 141).

It is true to say that feminism has challenged the very basis of Political Science as well as questioning and adapting the dominant paradigms and frameworks of mainstream Political Science (Phillips, 1998). Feminism has shown that gender relations are inherently political and argued that '[f]eminist political science must question why women's political actions and treatment by the polity should be gauged on our ability to succeed in, and affect, masculine structures' (Marchbank, 2000: 6). As such, feminist work has raised 'fundamental questions about the way that politics is conceptualised' (Randall, 2002: 129) and has interrogated the conventions and ways of studying politics. As shown above, feminist Political Scientists have challenged and corrected previous instances of masculine bias in research, and in particular, critiqued the Behaviouralist stereotypes of women's role as an 'add women and stir' approach rather than an integrated approach. In addition, Political Science has been challenged not to examine gender (where this is done) as a 'separated out' variable, rather that as people lead lives which intersect more than one identity, the 'actuality of layered experiences cannot be treated as separate or distinct parts' (Simien, 2004) and that there are problems with measuring, for example, African-American women's political attitudes using generic surveys adapted for measuring feminist attitudes. As Evelyn Simien points out surveys of feminist consciousness result in 'a measurement of support for white feminism among black women – not black feminist consciousness' (Simien, 2004: 86). In this section a brief overview and summary of the main areas of feminist Political Science is provided, including a discussion of the place of feminism in the Political Science curriculum.

Much early feminist work was directed at redressing the masculine bias in existing research (see above on voting and political behaviour). In addition, political theory has also been a focus, shown in the work of Susan Moller Oken (1979), Zillah Eisenstein (1981) and Carole Pateman (1988b), all of whom challenged the masculinist tradition of political theory. The 1980s witnessed a growth in work which outlined the exclusion of women by Political Science and in the public sphere (Evans, 1980; Lovenduski, 1981; Gelb and Palley, 1982; Dahlerup, 1984; Jones and Jonasdottir, 1988). This was followed by examinations of gender within political bureaucracies, with Kathy Ferguson's (1984) argument that as such institutions are inherently male, it is imperative that alternative organisations be created. Others took a more pragmatic approach preferring to find ways in which feminists could succeed within such places, resulting in the notion of a 'femocrat', a feminist within a bureaucracy, and their experiences and achievements (Eisenstein, 1990; Sawer, 1995; McBride Stetson and Mazur, 1995; Chappell, 2000). Other work examined the impact of policy upon women, providing critiques and evidence of gender bias in policy making and delivery (Sweibel, 1998; Bacchi, 2000; Marchbank, 2000) both in relation to women-specific issues and others not so immediately obviously gendered (see A Critical Look 8.2 for discussion of Women's Interest Issues). In addition, there continues 'an emphasis on electoral behavior and other measurable participation [for] such data are the stock in trade of mainstream political science, hence the terrain on which feminists must prove themselves – an instance of having to perform masculinity, perhaps?' (Lovenduski, 1998: 351). Such areas being: public policy, political representation and political institutions. Political representation:

represents the most identifiable area of concentrated work by feminist political scientists in

British politics . . . In part, it stems from the fact that feminist political science never abandoned its interest in the political, conventionally defined . . . [yet] . . . insisted that gender is also central to conventional political processes and institutions with far reaching implications for the analysis of public power and political life.

(MacKay, 2004: 100)

As more women have entered political elites at all levels the focus has turned to issues of critical mass (Dahlerup, 1988; Bochel and Briggs, 2000; Brown *et al.*, 2002), the effect upon established gender and power relations within these bodies and the attributes of these elite women (Childs, 2001a, 2001b). Critical mass theory (in social science terms) argues that as a group moves from being a minority (when its members need to adapt to existing conventions for survival) to a more substantive body it will start to assert itself and by doing so will begin to effect change upon the culture, practices and norms of the institution. It can only operate if women and men in political elites differ significantly. Recent work on the increased numbers of women in the British parliament found that

. . . there is no support for any claims that women leaders can be expected to be consistently more liberal or more conservative than men in issues like crime, censorship, or the redistribution of income. Nor are they more 'internationalist' in orientation. . . . Yet the results also show that on two scales, – both of which are directly related to women's interests – there is a strong and significant gender gap within all the major parties.

(Norris and Lovenduski, 2001: 5–6)

One area where gender does make a substantial difference in representation is that women tend to lead on feminist issues whilst men do not (Lovenduski, 1998). In addition, research into party candidate selection processes at local level has shown that these are gender biased (Chapman, 1993).

By the 1990s a substantial body of feminist examination of gender in organisations existed, including Cynthia Cockburn's (1991) groundbreaking study of the way that certain masculinities are both institutionalised and privileged within organisations. In this she

A critical look 8.2

Women's issues and interests

In Political Science it is assumed that there are certain issues of particular concern to women, often referred to as Women's Issues. However, Jen Marchbank (2000) argues that established definitions of Women's Issues are inadequate, preferring to group issues as Women's Interest Issues. She points out that there are two extant versions of Women's Issues: firstly, a category of political policies that are explicitly addressed to women; such as female enfranchisement. Secondly, there are newer feminist issues which seek to change society's structure and assumptions regarding gender roles; such as equal pay and equal opportunity. However, there are also issues which do not explicitly mention gender but affect men and women differently due to their differing societal positions, e.g. raising taxes by indirect rather than direct means (on goods and services rather than based on income). This policy would differentially affect women more than men due to women's lesser earnings [**Hotlink → Work and Leisure (Chapter 14)**]. This broad definition includes both the previous versions of Women's Issues as well as those issues which have a gendered effect and, as it encompasses all, Marchbank defined a new label, Women's Interest Issues.

shows how men's privileged positioning within such institutions as trade unions enabled resistance of government moves to increase gender equality, and to the non-prioritisation of issues, such as childcare and maternity leave. To counter such behaviour women began to create feminist networks at all levels to enhance the advancement of policies for women (Marchbank, 1996) with Catherine Hoskyns (1996) providing a detailed analysis of the influence of such networks within the European Commission.

Within the area of public policy a substantial amount of work has been produced examining the workings of welfare states, in particular the failure of such policies to recognise the importance of women's work, both paid and unpaid. This has led to the development of new approaches to studying and categorising welfare systems [**Hotlink → Social Policy (Chapter 5)**].

A further fertile area of investigation for feminist Political Scientists has been on the notion of the state asking basic questions such as do feminists need a theory of the state (Allen, 1990) and should feminists give up on such a gendered concept (Stewart, 1996)? Feminist writings on the state range from explaining how masculine power is embedded in both policies and apparatus to challenging theories that fail to consider gender as a dimension of state power (Watson, 1990; Randall and Waylen, 1998), whilst others have critiqued western typologies of the state (Rai and Lievesley, 1996) and examined the gendered nature of states in terms of conflict and resistance (Jacobs *et al.*, 2000). Feminist post-structuralist analysis sees the state not as a monolith but as a collection of institutions and power relations (Watson, 1990) each containing embedded gender practices whilst reconstituting the same (Pringle and Watson, 1992). Feminist Political Scientists, amongst others, also examine the concept of being a citizen within states developing a rich literature which attempts to regender citizenship away from established notions of 'citizen-soldier' – that being the idea that citizenship comes through the ability to provide military service [**Hotlink → Gendered Perspectives – Theoretical Issues (Chapter 1)**]. Feminists have shown how the relationship of women to the state has been one of being 'the protected', defined through women's relationships to men as fathers or husbands and located in the private domain 'even when lived realities were starkly different' (Jacobson *et al.*, 2000: 7) and have created alternative ways of examining and discussing the notion of citizenship (Walby, 1994; Lister, 1994, 1997).

Feminists have also explored gender in international politics with Cynthia Enloe's (1990) exposition of how trade and militarisation affects women being one example of the challenge to include an analysis of conditions women experience and endure in the world. Feminist perspectives on international relations have highlighted the extent to 'which masculinity has distorted conceptions of power and epistemology within the discipline' (Stone, 2002: unpaginated) and raised questions regarding the notion of a singular masculine experience (Pettman, 1996; Peterson and Sisson Runyan, 1999) as well as giving voice to the experience of women (Ehrenreich and Hochschild,

2002). In addition, by the late 1990s questions were raised regarding what it means to use gender as a category of analysis in Political Science (see *Politics and Gender*, 2005, volumes 1 and 2).

This overview is indicative rather than comprehensive but it does serve to illustrate the extent and range of feminist Political Science. How then, given all this material, is it that Vicky Randall can conclude that British Political Science 'remains a very "male" dominated profession' (Randall, 2002: 129) as does its core material whilst Marian Sawer (2004) comments that the impact of feminism remains additive rather than transformative? The answer seems to lie in what is accepted as necessary for the instruction of new Political Scientists in universities.

Gender in the Political Science curriculum

Pick up most introductory Political Science textbooks and you will find very little reference to gender. These wide ranging and valuable books will contain explanations of government structure, administration, political actors, political theory and ideology, elections and electoral systems, political parties and pressure groups, nations and states, perhaps even chapters on international relations and diplomacy. All of which, as we have seen, have received feminist analysis. Yet, that analysis is not included at this introductory level, nor even often in graduate studies. As Mary Hawkesworth (2005: 141–2) notes about the USA, '[f]ew doctoral programs allow students to develop areas of concentration in feminist approaches to political science . . . None requires familiarity with leading feminist scholarship as a criterion of professional competence'.

Stop and think 8.4

Reflect on your introductory education in Political Science and the textbooks you used. How has gender been included in your studies? Write down examples of inclusion and absence in relation to the topics you have studied and compare the lists. What have you found?

Marian Sawer investigated the status of gender in undergraduate Political Science curricula. She notes that despite the Australian Political Science Association (APSA) passing a resolution in 1981 to ensure the study of women in all politics courses (Sawer, 2004) repeated reviews of curricula in Australian Political Science departments, utilising an analysis of the contents of the introductory textbooks employed, display a continuing failure of the profession to integrate feminist scholarship (Thornton and Thornton, 1986; Grace *et al.*, 1991, both cited in Sawer, 2004). The last survey also included universities in New Zealand (Dudley and Palmieri, 1999, cited in Sawer, 2004) yet the result was the same: where women were included it tended to be managed by the inclusion of a separate chapter on feminism rather than for gender analysis to be integrated throughout the text as appropriate. In addition, men were rarely considered as gendered and gender was synonymous with women and, as such, not considered as an aspect of the overall construction of politics (Sawer, 2004). Marian Sawer then turns to consider the fate of feminist scholarship in textbooks beyond the Antipodes, citing work conducted in the USA by Nancy Harstock (CSWPS, 2001, cited in Sawer 2004) which concluded that notwithstanding decades of feminist study no significant changes to the methods or approaches to the discipline could be evidenced. Likewise, she also details the findings from Canada (Trimble, 2002, cited in Sawer, 2004) where Linda Trimble failed to find any textbook that integrated gender into all aspects of politics and that where gender was included it meant women and existed in a separate chapter (see World in Focus 8.2).

Marian Sawer also went on to examine what was being taught outside of introductory courses in Australia and found that a number of gender courses exist, yet all being taught by women, leading her to conclude that men in Political Science appear to be more reluctant than their peers in other disciplines, such as Sociology, to develop an interest in gender. This may be due to the fact that, as noted above, the terrain of Political Science seems to require adherence to particular areas to be accepted as appropriate work in the discipline, thereby acting as a discouragement to those men and women who might be interested in such areas.

Having now established the range of feminist contributions to the discipline and their reception it is now time to consider work which, following feminist challenges, has picked up the mantle of gender, rather than sex.

Gender and Political Science

As has already been shown mainstream Political Science has not fully integrated gender and, where gender has been included it has often been the comparison of women to men within established modes of thinking and research techniques without a fundamental revision and reshaping of the basic paradigms and theories of the discipline. In addition, we have seen how feminists have both followed the comparative path, uncovering the biases in earlier work and also moved towards a wider discussion of gender difference, which includes challenges both to what is known and how knowledge within Political Science is created. An example of this latter approach is the British government funded research series *Gender,*

World in focus 8.2

Gender and Canadian textbooks

Or rather, not! That is, there is not much mention of gender in the textbooks commonly used to introduce Political Science in Canadian universities. Our research for this chapter found only two Canadian Political Science textbooks that mention women, and only one mentions gender. In fact, in the first (Guy, 2001) gender is absent but feminism is included in political ideologies. Interestingly, the only one that mentions gender, and uses it in an integrated way throughout the text, was edited by a woman (Brodie, 2002).

Participation and Citizenship (Economic and Social Research Council) which aims to move research away from straightforward sex differences between women and men to considerations of masculinity and femininity and the neglected 'area of gender construction, reinforcement and perpetuation' (ESRC Seminar Series, 2005). This is still an area under development and it is still the case that when gender is referred to it all too often means women only. However, there are some notable exceptions to this, for example Mark E. Kann's (1999) investigation of the ways in which gender bias was built into the foundations of US political systems. He provides an examination of how the founders of the US political state understood, altered and affirmed women's political exclusion and the political subordination of most men, including how these positionings were challenged and defended. He also shows how some politicians have utilised various forms of masculinity for political purposes, for example, his analysis of Abraham Lincoln during the American Civil War (1860–65):

> First, he played the part of a stern but affectionate father figure – Father Abraham – who ruled the national family, resanctified it, called for filial sacrifice, sought the redemption of the South, and brought forth the rebirth of the nation . . . Second, Lincoln was a . . . man of action who, in the midst of crisis, showed little regard for legal restraints and procedural niceties. He declared martial law, suspended *habeas corpus*, centralized power, used soldiers to suppress dissent and allowed generals such as Sherman and Grant to ignore international law by waging total war against the South. Like many founders, Lincoln felt that great patriarchal leaders did whatever they thought necessary to resolve immediate crises and secure the nation's future.
>
> (Kann, 1999: 155–6)

However, gender is developing a focus within Political Science. At a conference of the American Political Science Association in 1997 gender, as an analytical category within the discipline, was up for discussion and debate. One result of which has been the recent creation of a new journal, *Politics and Gender* – see A Critical Look 8.3 for details of how gender is now being considered by some within Political Science.

Stop and think 8.5

In the above extract Mark E. Kann describes Lincoln presenting two masculinities: the tough but loving father and the man of action prepared to do all necessary to defend his country. Think about other leaders such as George W Bush, Nelson Mandela, Winston Churchill etc. What kinds of masculinity are presented by them? Now think about female leaders, for example, Indira Ghandi, Margaret Thatcher, Benazir Bhutto and consider how they performed gender.

A critical look 8.3

Politics and gender

In the following Karen Beckwith (2005: 133) summarises her view of how gender and politics interact.

> How does the political construct gender? Public practice shapes private behaviour and possibilities. For example, the state engages in the normalization, authorization, legalization, and otherwise privileging of heterosexual marriage, with division of marital powers according to gendered actors known as 'husband' and 'wife'. In these cases, distinctions of masculine and feminine, connected if loosely to sex distinctions, construct gendered relations of political dominance and subordination.
>
> Second, gender as process suggests not only that institutions and politics are gendered but also that they can be gendered; that is, that activist feminists, religious fundamentalists, social movements, and political parties can work to instate practices and rules that recast the gendered nature of the political.
>
> . . .
>
> Recent research has employed gender as process to demonstrate, for instance, female agency in regendering state processes and institutions . . . These studies do not depend on women as the exclusive actors but, rather, on the process of actively gendering institutions – which can shape masculinities and femininities that have political ramifications for actually identified women and men. This work explicitly asks questions about how gender constructs the state.

Despite this new focus on gender amongst some Political Scientists and the emerging area of investigation into masculinity it is still the case that, as a discipline, Political Science does not view gender as a mainstream analytical framework. In addition, despite the fact that there has also been a great deal of work done by those outside Political Science on the politics of masculinity it remains the case that masculinity within politics is an under-researched area. It is valuable though to detail a couple of examples of work in this area that have emerged.

Men's movements

The rise of men's movements, from pro/feminist organisations to the mythopoetic movements – [**Hotlink → Chapter 1**] has recently been placed under the academic lens. Most of this work has been undertaken by Sociologists and Social Policists (Kimmel, 1995; Messner, 1997; Gavanas, 2004) yet it provides lessons for students of politics. Michael A. Messner believes that many of these movements, though not all, share a distrust of women but also share a belief that it is necessary to re-establish bonds between men:

> many of the men's movements that have sprung up in the 1980s and 1990s share a commitment to rebuilding and revaluing bonds among men, to overcoming men's fears of each other, and to pushing men to be responsible and peaceful fathers and husbands . . . But many of these groups also share another troubling characteristic: They clearly believe that for men to overcome their fears of other men, they must separate themselves from women.
>
> (Messner, 1997: xiv)

Through an analysis of eight different men's movements Messner devised a diagrammatic representation of the terrain of the politics of masculinity within which each of the contemporary men's movements (in the USA) occupies a particular location based upon the position of each group in relation to three factors:

1. costs of masculinity, e.g. missing out on parenthood;

2. institutionalised privileges, and

3. differences/inequalities among men.

The position of each group being 'determined by which of these three factors . . . are emphasised and foregrounded, or alternatively rendered to the background or even ignored' (Messner, 1997: 12). This analysis permits him to determine the likelihood of each movement of engaging in progressive coalition building across differences amongst men and between men and women and to engage in 'a conscious politics of masculinities' (Messner, 1997: 11).

One of the movements he researched was the Million Man March which took place in Washington, DC in October 1995 (see beginning of this chapter) and involved hundreds of thousands of African-American men to express 'a collective commitment to restore men's sense of moral responsibility and leadership in crisis-torn families and communities' (Messner, 1997: 2). However, it was also an expression of the contradictions and tensions within racialised masculinity politics in the United States. On the one hand the aim of the march was expressed in the language of equal rights, though much dialogue in the months preceding the actual march revolved around the question '[w]hen we ask black men to "stand up" *as men*, are we asking them to stand up hand-in-hand with women, as equals, or are we asking them to stand up above the women and children as black patriarchs?' (Messner, 1997: 70). Whilst men were called upon to march, others were called upon to partake in a 'Day of Absence', to stay away from work, school and places of business, as such a gender division of labour was intentionally built into the march itself. Whereas many women such as Rosa Parks (a civil rights activist) supported the march, others such as Angela Davis (equality activist and author) opposed it stating that:

> No march, movement or agenda that defines manhood in the narrowest terms and seeks to make women lesser partners in this quest for equality can be considered a positive step.
>
> (Davis, quoted by CNN at **http://www-cgi.cnn.com/US/9510/megamarch/march.html**)

What this Sociological study of men's movements shows, as illustrated by the discussion of the Million Man March, is that masculinity is a politically contested concept, that gender differences remain politicised and that this is fertile ground for future work in Political Science.

New Labour and masculinity politics

In the Social Policy chapter it is pointed out that the New Labour government of the UK has taken steps to engender policy. This has not just been in the direction of women, but they have also made 'policy on masculinity' (Scourfield and Drakeford, 2002: 619) and for

> . . . the first time, a government is consciously addressing, in relation to specific social problems, the issue of how society deals with men, what it expects of men and how men should behave. This is not to suggest that particular strands on policy making did not previously identify men as a specific target. Criminal justice discourse, for example, has long concentrated upon the 'problem' of boys . . . [with] . . . a chain of gender-centred concern . . . The difference between these previous concerns and the approach of New Labour is the pervasive way in which gender considerations, and a concern with masculinity in particular, can be found across a far wider social policy canvass.
>
> (Scourfield and Drakeford, 2002: 620)

In their examination of New Labour policy Jonathan Scourfield and Mark Drakeford argue that although policy is always inevitably gendered (see A Critical Look 8.2), it is only recently, in the UK, that a government has made explicit references to masculinity and men in some areas of policy. They note that the most frequently addressed issues, and the ones given the greatest attention, are in relation to men's parenting and the education of boys [**Hotlink → Education (Chapter 13)**]. Their investigation of policies relating to gender lead them to conclude that New Labour is both pessimistic and optimistic in their treatment of men and women but that this is enacted in different arenas. That is, there is an expression of policy optimism about men in the home and pessimism about men in the public domain, whereas for women this situation is reversed. In terms of men as fathers they note that New Labour is, on the whole, positive about fathers and seeks to remove institutional barriers to men spending time with their families. Relating this to Michael A. Messner's terrain of the politics of masculinities they conclude that 'New Labour policies on fatherhood are . . . more focused on the costs of masculinity than on its privileges' (Scourfield and Drakeford, 2002: 623) and that there is an assumption that men in the UK want to spend more time with their children rather than in paid work. They conclude that:

> New Labour responds to the 'problem of men' in a variety of ways. There are policy areas where men/boys have been very overtly named, parenting and education being obvious examples. In relation to some other policy issues, such as employment, there has been a less explicit gender dimension in government documents.
>
> (Scourfield and Drakeford, 2002: 634)

What this example shows us is that masculinity is not only becoming addressed by policies and politicians, but it is also under academic scrutiny.

Conclusion

In this chapter we have charted the development of the study of gender within Political Science from the early days of exclusion of women to the addressing of biases and the development of an extensive amount of feminist work. It has also been shown that this has not fundamentally reshaped the discipline as the basic parameters, paradigms, theories and methods remain, on the whole, unchanged. Likewise, it has been shown that gender has not made it into either introductory texts or courses. It remains the case that gender is still often synonymous with women in Political Science and what examples of gendered studies of politics that do exist tend to be, on the whole, conducted by those in other areas.

Further reading

Politics and Gender – a journal published by Cambridge University Press which leads the way in debates on these issues.

Anne Phillips (ed.) (2001), *Feminism and Politics*, Oxford, Oxford University Press. A collection of 20 important articles dealing with various aspects of feminism and Political Science. Covers issues from the treatment of women in political studies to interests, representations, citizenship, political theory, the state and beyond. Includes the Bourque and Grossholtz article.

Ronald Inglehart and Pippa Norris (2000), 'The Developmental Theory of the Gender Gap: Women and Men's Voting Behavior in Global Perspective' in *International Political Science Review, Special Issue on Women and Representation*, 21 (4), pp. 441–62. A detailed analysis and discussion of gender gap political differences between women and men based on an analysis of the World Values Survey, a three-wave survey covering early 1980s to mid-1990s across sixty societies.

Michael A. Messner (1997), *Politics of Masculinities, Men in Movements*, London, Sage. This book provides an analysis and discussion of a range of recent men's movements, including Men's Liberation, essentialist, pro/feminist, and the racialised and sexualised gender politics of men.

Joni Lovenduski (1998), 'Gendering Research in Political Science', *Annual Review of Politics*, vol. 1, pp 333–56. This article provides an overview of feminist work in three areas of public policy, political representation and political institutions as well as discussing how the mainstream paradigms and methods of Political Science have been, and continue to need to be, adapted to fully integrate gender as a focus of investigation.

Jen Marchbank (2000), *Women, Power and Politics: Comparative Studies of Childcare*, London, Routledge. This book offers a feminist approach to understanding policy making utilising theories of unobserved power, in particular non-decision making, to explain why certain challenging issues do not achieve the political agenda.

Websites

www.electoralcommission.org.uk – online access to Pippa Norris, Joni Lovenduski and Rosie Campbell (2004), *Gender and Political Participation*, a survey of gender in British politics.

http://www.ipu.org/iss-e/women.htm – the IPU is the International Organization of Parliaments of sovereign states, established in 1889. The Union is the focal point for worldwide parliamentary dialogue and works for peace and co-operation among peoples and for the firm establishment of representative democracy. This site is full of empirical information about men and women in political systems.

http://www.cawp.rutgers.edu/index.html – the home site of the Center for American Women and Politics (CAWP). An incredible resource for information of women and political behaviour and activity in the USA.

http://www.sfu.ca/~aheard/elections/women.html – a site detailing data regarding women in Canadian politics, full of tables and data and clear explanations.

End of chapter activity

1. Look at Figure 8.1. Rank the following countries in the order of the greatest change in the ideology gender gap to the least: France, Northern Ireland, Britain, Canada, Netherlands.

2. Using any major search engine on the internet search the key terms 'political science gender' and browse the findings. Examine them closely; on the whole do they really refer to a study of gender *per se* or to comparisons of sex differences between women and men?

Answers

(Answer: N. Ireland = 0.53; France = 0.49; Netherlands = 0.46; Canada = –0.29; Britain = 0.25)

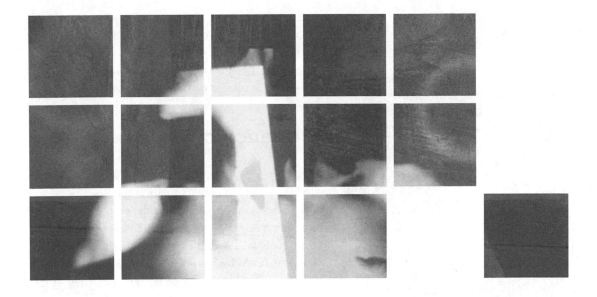

Chapter 9

Pedagogy

Key issues in this chapter:

➤ Progressive education has a very long history.
➤ The concept of a 'scientific' or 'natural' education embodies notions of gender, class and 'race'.
➤ Critical Pedagogies challenge traditional transmissive education.
➤ Critical Pedagogies do not include a focus on gender.
➤ Feminist Pedagogies begin with a focus on women but have developed to permit a wider focus upon other social cleavages.

At the end of this chapter you should be able to:

➤ Identify the roots of 'natural' and 'scientific' education.
➤ Realise the limitations of Critical Pedagogy in relation to gender.
➤ Outline and describe the basic common practices of Feminist Pedagogy.
➤ Describe the basis tenets of Feminist Pedagogy.
➤ Critique both Critical and Feminist Pedagogy.
➤ Problematise the notion of empowerment.

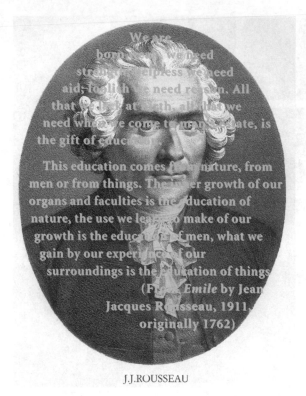

We are born weak, we need strength; helpless, we need aid; foolish, we need reason. All that we have not at our birth, all that we need when we come to man's estate, is the gift of education.

This education comes to us from nature, from men or from things. The inner growth of our organs and faculties is the education of nature, the use we learn to make of our growth is the education of men, what we gain by our experience of our surroundings is the education of things.

(From *Emile* by Jean Jacques Rousseau, 1911, originally 1762)

J.J.ROUSSEAU

Figure 9.1
Source: © Stefano Bianchetti/Corbis

Introduction

Pedagogy as a term describes both the methods and practices of instruction. It has been the subject of debate since the time of Plato. Many theories exist in regard to the best way to educate children and adults some of which challenge the 'traditional' model of authoritarian, knowing teacher who imparts knowledge to learners. In this chapter we will look at some of these in particular relation to gender.

We begin in the eighteenth century with Rousseau and Mary Wollstonecraft and the notion of 'natural' education. We then turn to the history of Progressive education, in particular in the early twentieth century in the USA, followed by feminist critiques of this approach in both the USA and the UK. A major issue in pedagogical considerations is power. We examine the debates from Critical Pedagogy and discuss the

politics of Pedagogies of the Oppressed. Our next focus is the feminist challenge which also has a long history. The final section details and discusses what constitutes feminist pedagogy and the role of Women's Studies in pedagogical change.

Pedagogic movements

The range of theory, the diversity of practice manuals and the variety of public policies on pedagogy is far too vast to be encapsulated in a singular chapter. Even when we restrict our focus to gender and pedagogy any introduction is selective. It is important to note from the outset that gender has not always been a consideration of forward thinking on pedagogy and when it has appeared it has frequently served to reinforce gender difference. Let us return to *Emile* and his creator Jean Jacques Rousseau, left, which shows just this.

Natural education

In his novels Rousseau presented an argument for education based on the needs of the child and influenced by the environment, in order to preserve the 'nature of the child'. Fundamental to Rousseau's argument is the notion that the drive for learning is provided within each person, not by an outside teacher; as such the role of the pedagogue, the educator is one of facilitator of learning opportunities. As such, some have pointed to *Emile* as the beginnings of the theories of child-centred educational practices. Rousseau argued that boys should be left without restriction to find their own knowledge and to experience no constraint other than those imposed by natural laws or self will to enable them to develop into rational beings, a concept referred to as 'negative education'. However, this concept was not extended to women, who were not seen as capable of rationality and whose destiny had already been determined by nature (as wives and mothers). As such Rousseau recommended an 'education' for girls consisting of little more than a minimal level of vocational training, personal presentation and fashion.

Despite admiring Rousseau's intentions regarding the education of Emile, a contemporary of his, Mary Wollstonecraft, was greatly disappointed in his ideas for the 'training' of Sophie (Emile's perfect wife) and was moved to write perhaps her best known work, *A Vindication of the Rights of Women* (1792). In this Wollstonecraft argued that boys and girls should be educated not in relation to each other, but together. She advocated allowing girls to develop physically and mentally so that they could support themselves independently. She was careful to point out that she was not presenting a case for the generation of independent women but for the development of capable women better to become the next generation of mothers, all of which would benefit society. Despite her ideas being bitterly attacked after her death (at a time when Britain saw all revolutionary ideas as dangerous) she remains a major influence on, especially British and American, feminism.

Both Rousseau and Wollstonecraft contributed to later developments in education such as teaching by the exploitation of natural curiosity and the requirement for practical applications of knowledge, a current example of which is the system devised by Maria Montessori. Perhaps the most radical contribution is Wollstonecraft's argument that women and men be educated together.

Progressive education

The term progressive is used in different manners in the literature of pedagogy, reflecting differences in geography and time. In the USA context it has come to signify the educational movement of the early twentieth century, as exemplified by such as John and Evelyn Dewey amongst others, and sometimes referred to, both then and earlier, as 'scientific pedagogy' (Walkerdine, 1990). In addition, it has also been employed to describe the challenge to teacher-centred pedagogies arising amongst other social movements of the late 1960s, relating mainly to higher education in western societies and adult basic education in Latin America. In these latter cases a fundamental issue has been that of power.

Progressive reform movement

Before we look at the Progressive education movement of the early twentieth century in the USA, it is necessary to note that there remained a constant representation of scientific education across Europe and north America from the eighteenth century onwards (see A Critical Look 9.1), with the aim of creating a new society of non-oppressed but self-regulating and productive individuals. The basis of this approach is that children who have not been oppressed by their educational experience, that is made to learn what others set out for them and to follow rules, will have no internalised oppression and therefore no aggression to express.

A critical look 9.1

Scientific pedagogy

In the following, Valerie Walkerdine provides an overview of the philosophy and development of 'scientific pedagogy' and points to several of the ironies contained therein.

In the nineteenth century science was used to calculate and produce a knowledge of the population on an unprecedented scale. The production of 'knowledges' became intimately bound up with the devising of new techniques of population management. The school was the arena for the development of one set of techniques for 'disciplining' the population . . . Schooling was seen as one way to ensure the development of 'good habits' . . . The original strategy was to engage children in ceaseless activity, with constant surveillance to ensure these habits. Subsequently, this strategy was abandoned in the face of children's ability in rote-learning . . . without actually assuming the rigid moral habits.

It was at this point that the kind of pedagogy which had been advocated in terms of overt authority began to be challenged. There were many examples of such challenges, from the work of Froebel and Pestalozzi, to Robert Owen and his school in the New Lanark Mills to Itard and Seguin in France (whom Maria Montessori followed). In their differing ways they began to advocate an education 'according to nature'.

. . .

A critical look continued

Education according to nature became the way of ensuring a natural path of development, the best kind of civilizing process. Theories of instincts and animality were thus connected to the regulation of the population, many of whom (particularly the urban proletariat) displayed all too obvious signs of animal passions. Degeneracy was seen as an aberration of nature. The part played by the environment was made clear by the mapping of the city – the spread of typhoid, its criminal quarters, and so forth. The environment too could be watched, monitored and transformed.

I am glossing over a great deal of political struggle, but my aim is to demonstrate that the advent of naturalism – that is, the ensuring of a correct passage from animal infant to civilized adult – became understood both as 'progressive' (according to scientific principles) and effective. It would prevent the threatened rebellion *precisely* because children who were not coerced would not need to rebel – the lessons would be learned, and this time properly. Docile bodies would become a self-disciplined workforce.

What was proposed was a process – a scientific process – whereby the schoolroom could become a laboratory where development could be watched, monitored and set along the right path. There was therefore no need for lessons, no discipline of the overt kind . . . The ultimate irony is that the child supposedly freed by this process to develop according to its nature was the most classified, catalogued, watched and monitored in history. Freed from coercion, the child was much more subtly regulated into normality.

Source: Extracted from Walkerdine (1990: 19–21)

According to Kathleen Weiler (2003) the Progressive educational reform movement of the first two decades of the twentieth century in the USA was clearly linked to movements for social reform also of this time in the USA. The founders of the early progressive schools were influenced by romantic ideas of the creativity of children and conceptualisations of teachers as guides not masters within the classroom – here we can see echoes of Rousseau's 'child of nature' and facilitator. Also, like Rousseau, this movement believed in the power of the environment in determin-

ing the success of educational encounters. The practice of these schools was to follow the natural growth of pupils and common features included a focus upon discovery, growth, and activity developing from the interests expressed by each child.

"I didn't feel answers were necessary. All the questions seemed rhetorical."

Figure 9.2
Source: © Mike Baldwin. www.CartoonStock.com.

John Dewey is often referred to as the 'father' of the Progressive movement in the USA. He researched and wrote about Progressive schools, both public and private, developing in the USA in the early twentieth century, sometimes in conjunction with his daughter Evelyn. He concluded that traditional schools, with rigid procedures, rules and compulsory curriculum, dulled the natural curiosity of children whilst the Progressive schools valued freedom, emphasised learning through play and treated children as individuals.

Truly scientific education can never develop so long as children are treated in the lump, merely as a class. Each child has a strong individuality, and any science must take stock of all the facts in its material. Every pupil must have the chance to show what he truly is, so that the teacher can find out what he needs to make him a complete human being.

(Dewey and Dewey, 1915, cited in Weiler, 2003)

However, the application of these Rousseauian ideals differed in the private and public schools: in the former they were employed for the development of the individual, whilst in the public schools for concerns of broader social reform through 'making up' for deficiencies in the home lives of children, providing them with healthy and useful activities and also to improve conditions in the neighbourhoods around the schools (Weiler, 2003). As Kathleen Weiler (2003) notes, in one such school in Indianapolis based in a poor African-American area, this meant industrial training in areas such as cooking and shoemaking. Although John Dewey argued against vocational training in his discussion of a middle-class school (the Laboratory School in Chicago) he accepted that for working-class children the aim of their education was to 'fit' them for their future roles in their community; boys received instruction in trades and girls in domestic skills, referred to as 'shop':

The aim of the work for the girl, just as it is for the boy, is to help her find her life work, to fit herself for it mentally and morally, and to give her an intelligent attitude toward her profession and her community, using the shop experience not as an end in itself but a means to these larger ends.

(Dewey and Dewey, 1915, cited in Weiler, 2003)

It is clear then that the Deweys accepted that differences in sex and class, and implicitly of 'race', were inevitable, and for this they have been criticised for viewing schools merely as a mechanism for reproducing social differences rather than challenging them. However, they did recognise that broader social change was required, were aware of social divisions in US society and warned against the danger of schooling becoming simply a training ground to benefit business interests. Weiler (2003) points out that contradictory discourses exist throughout John Dewey's writings:

Schools of To-morrow is a complicated text. It juxtaposes the freedom of privileged children to learn

through play with the mastery of manual skills for the working class children . . . It acknowledges the dangers of individualism and the abuses of industrial capitalism even while it is confident of reform, that a better, more just society is both possible and probable . . . John Dewey's commitment to democracy and his respect for the capabilities of children is unquestioned. But by envisioning children of different class, race, and gender locations through different lenses, his vision of educational change was compromised from the outset.

(Weiler, 2003: 7–9).

The failure of progressive educators and advocates to address structural issues such as 'race', class and gender oppression has led to a critique that they merely helped sustain an unequal system rather than undermined it. The fact that progressive curricula were followed in the schools within Japanese internment camps in the USA in the Second World War provides an example of the massive irony that can occur if wider social and political matters are not considered (Weiler, 2003). Indeed, Valerie Walkerdine (1990) argues that rather than Progressive education freeing children from authoritarianism it merely masks the results of oppression and hides powerlessness within a system where 'bourgeois culture is taken as nature' (Walkerdine, 1990: 25) and where the 'education of working-class and black children is something of a problem, since they rarely conform to the ideal child' (Walkerdine, 1990: 24). Nor do girls conform to the ideal of the naturalised child for within progressivism they are often seen as 'lacking: they demonstrate either deviant activity or a passivity which means they must be found lacking in reason and compensated for this lack' (Walkerdine, 1990: 24). Walkerdine then provides a critique of progressivism based on its assumption of 'nature' which only certain children are deemed to fit.

Writing of the Progressive education advocated in British teacher training colleges in the 1960s, Walkerdine (1990) also argues that this system is detrimental to both girls as pupils and women as teachers for this pedagogy validates a masculine sexuality. Walkerdine (1990) employs observations of pupil/teacher interactions in pre- and primary schools to make her argument. In one such exchange preschool boys continually employ sexualised language and discourses of masculine power, both towards the teacher and female pupils. As Progressive pedagogy requires that children not 'be oppressed' the teacher in this instance does not confront the boys with the unacceptability of this behaviour and so becomes disempowered herself, situated as the oppressed. In addition, the notion of nurturing children to become free individuals also acts as a trap for women:

> the liberation of children . . . did not mean the liberation of women. In some ways, it actually served to keep women firmly entrenched as vital carers. Women teachers became caught, trapped inside a concept of nurturance which held them responsible for the freeing of each little individual, and therefore for the management of an idealist dream, an impossible fiction.
>
> (Walkerdine, 1990: 19)

She also notes that many studies of education conclude that progressivism has never really existed in Britain and that most classrooms are not child-centred but retain instruction and rules for the children to follow and learn. As such teachers 'turn out to be more traditional than expected and feel guilty because the future and "freedom for our children for ever" is laid at their door' (Walkerdine, 1990: 25).

Stop and think 9.1

Valerie Walkerdine offers a number of critiques of Progressive Education. Without re-reading the above grab pen and paper and list what they are. Now, go back and re-read the relevant section above, and complete your list. Do you agree with her critiques? If so, why? If not, why not?

Power and Pedagogy

Unlike the Progressive movement of the first decades of the twentieth century the politics of educational reform from the 1960s focused on challenging the wider political and economic system. These grew with, and developed amongst, other social movements of the time, for example anti-war, anti-racist and feminist movements. Rather than being based on the philosophy of Rousseau, exponents of these movements for progressive education look more to critiques of capital and theories of power to develop arguments that educational institutions serve to reproduce knowledge within existing social divisions and to maintain these social divisions. One such development, commonly referred to as Critical Pedagogy, has little to say regarding gender, whilst the other, Feminist Pedagogy, concentrates on gender, but both share a focus on power relations. Both examine the ways in which power is employed by dominant groups to reinforce social divisions, a process described by Antonio Gramsci as hegemony [**Hotlink → Gendered Perspectives – Theoretical Issues (Chapter 1)**]. Likewise, both benefit from Michel Foucault's (1980) description of power as a process which is actively and constantly at work, rather than as a static entity. As such, power is seen to be at work in the ways we construct knowledge and meaning in the world, in what is accepted as knowledge and what knowledge is valued [**Hotlink → Method, Methodology and Epistemology (Chapter 2)**].

Although Critical Pedagogy says little in regard to gender it is worth including here as many of its concerns relate to the development of greater equality and, as such, are of concern to gender scholars. In addition, feminist educators have found commonality within its practices and adopted and adapted these for their own purposes. Here we focus on power in relation to Critical Pedagogy.

Critical Pedagogy

As with other Progressive movements Critical Pedagogy seeks to advance democratic ideals within education and recognises the contribution made by the earlier Progressive educators incorporating their principles – these are listed below:

➤ Education must engage with and enlarge the experience of the student.

➤ Thinking and reflection are central elements to the art of teaching.

➤ Students must interact freely with their environments in the practice and process of construction knowledge.

To these principles Critical Pedagogy adds a critique of capitalism emphasising the importance of the role of the school to the political economy:

> In the arena of schooling and the political economy, the work of such noted theorists as Samuel Bowles and Herbert Gintis, Martin Carnoy, and Michael Apple all contributed greatly to the forging of a critical pedagogical perspective that upheld the centrality of the economy to the configuration of power relations within schools and society. Through their persistent critique of capitalism, these theorists argued in a variety of ways that the problems associated with schooling were actually tied to the reproduction of a system of social relations that perpetuate the existing structures of domination and exploitation. Michael Apple, in particular, linked notions of cultural capital with the school's reproduction of official knowledge – knowledge that primarily functioned to sustain the inequality of class relations within schools and society.

(Darder *et al.*, 2003: 4–5)

The political challenge within Critical Pedagogy is clear; it is a view that education is a mechanism by which those with power maintain their dominance by regulating what is to be known (the curriculum), who can be taught what (for example, selection of pupils into different forms of education such as academic and vocational), and to inculcate all with the norms of the dominant society. Feminists have further developed this position adding in that one of the elements of domination is masculinity and 'masculine' knowledge and ways of knowing [**Hotlink → Method, Methodology and Epistemology (Chapter 2)**]. That these arguments are political can be seen in the biographies of two Brazilian men, Paolo Freire and Augusto Boal, both of whom were persecuted by the Brazilian military and exiled for their work with the 'dispossessed' in the early 1970s – see A Closer Look 9.1 for more detail on their work.

A closer look 9.1

Practical education for the 'oppressed'

Paolo Freire (1970) *The Pedagogy of the Oppressed*

In this book Freire grounded the politics of education within the wider social structure and made central to his educational practice questions related to social agency, voice and democratic participation. Through his work in Brazil and Chile he sought to increase peasants' literary skills whilst at the same time opening up their perceptions of social, political and economic conditions.

He characterised the traditional education process as an oppressive and hierarchical *banking system*, where knowledge is a commodity to be accumulated in order to gain access to positions of power and privilege. Instead he proposed an *Education for Liberation* where learners and teachers are engaged in a process in which abstract and concrete knowledge together with experience are integrated as praxis. Critical thinking and dialogue are fundamental features in this process which seeks to challenge conventional explanations of everyday life while considering the action necessary for the transformation of oppressive conditions. Through reflection and dialogue a *Process of Conscientisation*, is created.

His strategy is very practical, based around problem solving and dialogue to challenge dominant discourses and reveal the participants' rights to become social actors. It has been widely used and adapted by educators in adult education, development agencies and community education. It can be summarised as five stages:

1. What is the problem? – listening to people, beginning to identify the issues they face.

2. The problem is presented – as a role play, pieces of writing, images, anything which encapsulates the issues and can be 'unpicked' in a group to deepen people's understanding.

3. What do I know about this problem from my experience? – group discussion on the issue reflecting on it in relation to their experience.

4. What do I want to know more about? Where can I find out? – this process may have raised other issues for discussion, someone in the group may have answers or know where to find them.

▶

5. What can we do about this? – with a better understanding of the problem the participants are in a better position to decide what has to be done to change it.

Boal (1971) *The Theatre of the Oppressed*

Boal developed a form of theatre which rather than simply delivering a performance creates a dialogue between audience and those on stage. Performers act, then stop and ask the audience for suggestions and demonstrations, this collective participation then generates the next actions. He created various forms of theatre workshops and performances not just to develop acting skills but to provide a space for dialogue and reflection through which participants will come to realise the basis of a situation and their own ability to affect it. As such he provides a practical strategy for the exploration of issues, a stark contrast to other heavily theoretical works on Critical Pedagogy.

The contribution of Freire and Boal is that they have produced actual methods of enacting the theories of Critical Pedagogy, processes whereby individuals and communities can develop a critical awareness of the root causes of the problems they face which empowers them to seek solutions by taking direct action. As such, these processes aim not to adapt or reform existing social relations but to transform them. Perhaps the most frequent use of these practices occurs in the Popular Education movements in Latin America where it has been intimately linked to organised collective action for social change and where it has had a great impact over the past thirty years. For a summary of Popular Education see World in Focus 9.1.

Although none of the practices and theories developed by Critical Pedagogy address gender issues it is important to note that many of their concepts and particularly, their practical applications are reflected both within Feminist Pedagogy and its expression as the academic study of Women's Studies. As noted above, feminist educators have made use of these practical principles in the development of feminist teaching practice. However, feminists point to exclusions within Critical Pedagogy based on gender, 'race' and sexuality. Such critics argue that although Critical Pedagogy challenges societal structures it does not include the female experience, partly due to a continuing theoretical preference within Critical Pedagogy which privileges reason and rationality as the ultimate means of knowing. Like Freire, and like Popular Educationalist, feminists value experiential knowledge expressed in auto/biography and narratives. For some

World in focus 9.1

Popular Education in Latin America

There is no one definition that applies to all Popular Education in Latin America; however, it is true to say that it is usually associated with political movements and aimed at empowering those normally excluded from full participation in politics and political processes. It is aimed at 'ordinary' people for the purposes of enabling them to become politically aware and active. In practice it is based very much on Freirian principles of problem-identification and dialogue. The elements of Popular Education are:

➤ horizontal relationships between the facilitator and participants (i.e. the facilitator is not positioned as powerful and the only person with knowledge);

➤ responds to a need identified and expressed by the group, not the facilitator;

➤ group involvement in the planning of training and decision making on political action;

➤ recognition that knowledge exists within the community, that the participants have knowledge from their own experience;

➤ often initiated from the outside by a popular educator.

In other words, Popular Education operates collectively to produce knowledge and insight by building on the experiences of the participants and operates within the group according to democratic principles.

the close link between Critical Pedagogy and Marxist analysis of economics and society is viewed as bias towards European philosophical traditions and therefore Eurocentric, resulting in a failure to question the subordinate position of marginalised cultures and communities from the specific position of racialised and colonised populations themselves. In fact, in the USA, both feminist and 'race' critics have

> ... insisted that questions of race/gender/sexuality be given equal weight in any critical analysis of schooling ... in an effort to not only produce different readings of history but to reclaim power for those groups that had existed historically at the margins of mainstream life.
>
> (Darder *et al.*, 2003: 17)

The challenge from feminism

As we have already seen above, feminist challenges to educational theories have existed for a very long time and certainly before the Second Wave feminist movement of the late 1960s/early 1970s. In the 1920s and 1930s the author Virginia Woolf penned two short pieces: *A Room of One's Own* (1929) and *Three Guineas* (1938). In the first, Woolf details how women have been excluded from learning throughout history. Explaining the lack of great works by women on university library shelves, she concluded that with physical and psychological space as well as economic resources not usually available to women, this absence would be addressed. It is in *Three Guineas* however that she determines the nature of higher education as patriarchal (see A Closer Look 9.2).

Despite Woolf's arguments for an 'outsiders' college based on feminist philosophy it was not until the advent of the Second Wave feminist movement that Feminist Pedagogy and Women's Studies can be said to have been created. Nor were they created in a vacuum for it is true to say that many of the concerns of Critical Pedagogy are shared by Feminist Pedagogy, in particular the techniques of Popular Education, many of which were transferred to, and adapted for, the feminist classroom. However, feminist pedagogy places 'a much greater emphasis on actual classrooms

---

A closer look 9.2

Virginia Woolf – *Three Guineas*

In this text Woolf focuses on the relationship between male power and medicine, law, education and militarisation. She argued that militarism, fascism and legal injustices are all derived from patriarchal formations, early sex divisions and the antagonisms between women and men. *Three Guineas* is written in three parts as responses to three letters all asking for money; the first from a man hoping to establish a pacifist society, another for a woman seeking resources to establish a women's college and the last an appeal for money to aid women enter the professions. Woolf saw these three appeals as interconnected: that a major way of promoting pacifism would be to create a women's college, which would be anti-militaristic and which would have neither a system of hierarchy nor status. In addition, a women's college would facilitate more women entering the professions.

Not only did Woolf reject the frills of traditional higher education as personified by Oxford and Cambridge she critiqued them for a focus on status rather than on the creativity of students. She advocated an alternative curriculum, a curriculum of the arts that can be taught cheaply and practised by poor people, such as medicine, mathematics and so on, rather than the arts of war and domination. This would be a college for 'Outsiders'.

---

and classroom practices ... and seems less inclined toward grand theorizing' (Gore, 2003: 337–8) than does Critical Pedagogy. This does not mean that theory has been absent (see A Critical Look 9.2), rather that feminist pedagogues and practitioners have focused on praxis – that is on finding ways of integrating theory with practice in a reflexive manner. Louise Morley encapsulates the essence of Feminist Pedagogy:

> [Feminist Pedagogy is] ... process-oriented and ambitious, implying transformations, consciousness-raising, healing even. Feminist pedagogy for empowerment crystallizes around a common purpose to change gender relations in a society characterized by power inequalities. Changes start in the micropolitics of the classroom . .. Mechanisms for achieving feminist pedagogy's

aims are the validation and sharing of women's experiences, democratized organizational arrangements and use of the group for support and development. Underpinning these approaches is the desire to counter women's internalized oppression and the recognition that confidence and self-esteem are gendered attributes.

(Morley, 2001: 33)

Others have added that a feminist pedagogy must also recognise that internalised oppression and a lack of confidence and self-esteem affect both students and faculty and also interact with other issues of social difference such as 'race' (bell hooks, 1984; Johnson-Bailey, 2001; Bell and Golombisky, 2004) and social class (Zmroczek and Mahoney, 1997; Bell and Golombisky, 2004; Reay, 2004) amongst others.

A critical look 9.2

Adrienne Rich – *Towards a woman-centered university*

Adrienne Rich published an essay with the above title in 1973. In it her fundamental argument is that knowledge – its creation and content – and education, must focus on women. Like Woolf, Rich perceives a new form of educational institution without hierarchy, without competition but where faculty and staff work collectively. She aims to dissolve the border/boundaries between academia and the community.

Rich argues that the structure of universities is male, which reinforces women's oppression and marginalisation. She provides an illustration of a professor who is supported at home by his wife and au pair, at work by a secretary, teaching assistant, technical support and a student mistress. In this way she shows how men's work is reliant on the subjugation of women. Although this description of academia is very dated it remains true that academia remains a masculinised environment and profession.

Rich views universities as linked to external power structures that influence society and the development of societal values, which are not feminist ones. She discusses the nature of research arguing that research should not be driven by the needs of government but by the needs of the community, and focus on such areas as adult literacy, birth control, drug addiction,

the psychology of ageing and death and so on. A woman-centred university would, she foresaw, change the production of knowledge [**Hotlink → Method, Methodology, Epistemology (Chapter 2)**]. In such an institution teaching should focus on new, non-traditional learners, be feminist and empowering, not colonising and should empower through the recognition of experience. Fundamentally, education in her university would support and acknowledge women.

She rejects the notion that co-education is sex neutral, but she states that it is not equal, and as such she rejects the liberal feminist position of equal access to what men learn. She argues that the content of education in the male mode obscures and devalues women. However, her view is that Women's Studies courses, staffed by feminists can make a change and act as a focus for feminist work even within a patriarchal context – and that the resources accumulated by men can be used to create influence beyond the academy. So, she does not assume that simply increasing the numbers of women in university will lead to the construction of more woman-centred knowledge as access is not the only issue. For access merely permits a woman to enter and be treated as an honorary man – what matters is the content and context of education and the right for women to be recognised as originators of enquiry and knowledge not just the subjects of it.

(Rich, 1980)

Stop and think 9.2

Read the summary of Adrienne Rich's arguments in A Critical Look 9.2. Consider her arguments regarding the reproduction of a specific form of knowledge, the privileging of specific groups of people and the political direction of her views on research and teaching content. What commonalities are there in Rich's vision and interpretation with Critical Pedagogy? Make a list of them. It may help to read 'working class' where she writes 'women'.

So what exactly constitutes Feminist Pedagogy in practice? Well, as with Popular Education (see World in Focus 9.1) there is no one set of rules but there are certain common themes and principles. However, also, like other pedagogies these principles and themes are not static but adapt with time and place. Penny

Welch (2002) refers to her own practice, informed by both feminist and non-feminist sources, as feminist so as to:

> signal that it is part of the only body of educational writing in English that systematically deals with inequalities of gender, colour and sexual orientation in the . . . classroom and with the conflicts that arise out of difference.
>
> (Welch, 2002: 115)

In addition, feminist pedagogy is not just about what is taught or what is learned. Fundamental for Feminist Pedagogy is the questioning and deconstruction of what is deemed to be knowledge, as with critical pedagogues, feminist pedagogues ask questions about what is known, how things are known, what knowledge has been granted value and what biases are present in knowledge? A full discussion of these issues is provided in: [Hotlink → Method, Methodology and Epistemology (Chapter 2)]. From the beginning Women's Studies and feminist educational practice were political, questioning the very structure of educational institutions: both Woolf (1938) writing in the inter-war years, and Rich (1980, originally 1973), writing in the early days of the Women's Liberation Movement, argued for a new form of educational institution without hierarchy, without competition but where staff and faculty worked collectively and where the boundaries of academia and the world are dissolved. As shown in A Critical Look 9.2, Rich advocated teaching practice that focused on new, non-traditional learners, that was feminist and empowering and that valued the knowledge of experience. Feminist Pedagogy also includes the view that traditional transmission teaching leads to social powerlessness and passivity. In many ways, these principles share values with Paolo Freire's (1970) work on education. As a Critical Pedagogue Freire argued that the educational process transmits both objective knowledge and a hidden curriculum [Hotlink → Education (Chapter 13)] that supports the dominant culture and class, but that change can be made. As we have seen, Freire characterised the education process as a banking model and feminists, like Freirian educationalists, have employed processes and practices that value the knowledge of the student and that integrate abstract knowledge with experience.

The early days of Women's Studies – often reported as the 1970s as this was when the first courses began, although for many the same issues had to be addressed and challenged in the 1980s – can be characterised as a time when students and staff were engaged on the same project, a project to change both the structure of traditional learning and the knowledge tradition recognised. It was also about activism, both within and beyond the academy to create not just educational change but societal change (Michielsens, 2003: 17–18). With these values as the driving force feminist pedagogues developed approaches to teaching and learning that:

➤ recognise the value of experience;

➤ involve peer support;

➤ involve peer teaching;

➤ involve group work;

➤ contain flexibility of learning modes;

➤ are interdisciplinary in content and approach;

➤ aim for the empowerment of the individual student; and

➤ implied horizontal relations between staff and students.

Controversy 9.1

Fighting the good fight?

In the following extract Jen Marchbank and Gayle Letherby reflect on the need for feminist pedagogy to acknowledge the reality of the educational environment.

> Dever (1999) . . . argues that it is possible to counter what she observes as a move back away from liberatory methods of teaching towards the 'banking' system . . . She sees this retrograde drift as creating not only 'conservative notions of "knowledge transfer"', but also leading to student passivity, isolation and competition, perhaps another manner in which mass Higher Education negates collective approaches to student concerns and self responsibility (Dever, 1999: 221). Dever goes on to argue that it is possible to overcome this trend:

Controversy continued

This means working to recover, retain or reinforce that sense of the political and politicized context of learning that was once so central an element on our programmes, but which have been displaced or diluted in recent years . . .

Dever is not the first feminist to remind us that it is hard to be a feminist pedagogue, but what is needed is to keep trying to 'relinquish our ties to traditional ways of teaching that reinforce domination' (hooks, 1989: 52). [Yet] . . . maintaining 'the cherished stereotype of the feminist classroom as a scene of perpetual collaborative bliss' does not permit us any room for change nor solutions (Schlib, 1985: 256, cited by Coate-Bignell, 1996: 323). However, just as feminist theory and pedagogy have challenged the claims to be holding the 'truth', it is now time for us to question the nature of the role of feminist pedagogy in the increasingly bureaucratized and marketing driven world of Higher Education.

Source: Extracted from Marchbank and Letherby (2002: 149)

Stop and think 9.3

Refer back to World in Focus 9.1 on Popular Education in Latin America. Although Popular Education has no explicit gender agenda, certain elements are common to feminist teaching practice. Consider the historical context of the development of both – what might be shared?

Classroom and institutional relations are a main focus for Feminist Pedagogy, as it is the form and approach of knowledge. Many feminist teachers are also social activists and their educational interests and activism were and are often related; for example, teaching and researching on issues of interpersonal violence and working with support groups or using their expertise to shape policy on a range of issues from reproductive services to hospitals, as Rich (1980) advocates. In addition, many have found their activism to be in the very doing of feminist pedagogy, working to facilitiate the development of empowerment and self-actualisation with students.

Such an environment requires the creation and process of knowledge to focus on women. Thus, the catalyst of this liberating and empowering education is seen to be women's studies. This is more than a simple theoretical challenge. Although both the political climate and the structure of educational institutions have made the models of Rich and Woolf virtually impossible to create on the scale advocated, it is clear from the writings of women's studies practitioners that innovative work has been attempted, and has succeeded in this area.

(Marchbank *et al.*, 2003: 77)

Feminist pedagogues have all also had to face one particular political decision – that being whether to work within educational institutions recognised as patriarchal or to remain outside developing alternative modes. It is exactly this tension that academic Women's Studies has worked within since inception. As Women's Studies is a main area for feminist pedagogy, though not the only one – as much feminist teaching and research occurs in areas not labelled Women's Studies (see World in Focus 9.2) – it is necessary to look at it a little more closely.

World in focus 9.2

Where the feminists are?

In the UK there are a number of academic professional bodies, for feminists there is the Women's Studies Network (UK) Association. In 2003 the members voted to change the name as many feminist scholars no longer, or never did, work within departments of Women's Studies *per se* 'although they are certainly very involved with and committed to feminist teaching and research' (Jackson, 2004: 1). The organisation is now the Feminist and Women's Studies Association and covers both the UK and Ireland.

Women's Studies

Women's Studies initially developed in conjunction with the Second Wave feminist movement of the 1970s and as such began with a focus on sexism and issues specifically of concern to women. Modern Women's Studies has a much broader scope including the concerns of other marginalised groups and the interacting issues of various social cleavages such as 'race', ethnicity, age, sexuality, ability, social class amongst others. Women's Studies has always been a place of struggle. Struggle both to establish programmes and a struggle to maintain them. In some countries feminist work has become integrated into other disciplines reducing the need for separate departments whereas in others Women's Studies remains flourishing or is just beginning, in some places has become Gender Studies and in others a combination of the two (see World in Focus 9.3).

Fundamental to any Women's Studies class is the process of teaching, and a belief that non-feminist teaching practice will negate any feminist content of classes:

the methods which we employ in our teaching remain, by and large, traditional, mainstream and oddly incongruous with our goals. Innovative methodology, in its widest and most dynamic sense, should encompass the ways we teach and the environment in which we do this. The consequences of neglect are serious. How we teach is as, if not more, important than what we teach.

(Lubelska, 1991: 41)

Yet, it has to be recognised that there have always been restraints in achieving these goals, given that Women's Studies has primarily taken place not in the community but higher education institutions with their requirements for formal assessments, established learning outcomes and class scheduling. As such, in reality, in higher education feminist teaching approaches are:

limited within an academic framework by what is acceptable to university hierarchies. Attempts to follow good feminist practice by utilising small groups, fewer lectures, more workshops and project based activities and team staffing . . . from which the students benefit most are restricted by the demands of mass teaching

(Letherby and Marchbank, 1999: 173)

World in focus 9.3

Women's Studies in global context

Jayne Stake (2006) points out that the 'development of WGS [Women's and Gender Studies] has followed unique paths across cultures, shaped by established political and educational structures and prevailing values within societies'. She goes on to itemise by countries and regions:

'WGS has been well accepted at some U.S. universities where students are required to complete diversity courses such as WGS, and students can study WGS at the doctoral level . . . the first WGS programme in Australia was founded [in] . . . 1976 and by 1982 WGS courses were offered at most Australian universities . . . scholars in Eastern Europe were not allowed to offer WGS while under the domination of the Soviet Union. However, since democratization . . . almost all former communist states have established WGS programmes . . . In contrast to Western countries, WGS has been generally slower to develop in Eastern societies. The feminist movement, although worldwide, tends to be viewed as antithetical to Eastern cultures and irrelevant to the most central concerns of women in those societies. For example, WGS did not begin to be represented in the Indian academic curriculum until the mid 1980s . . . Conservative Muslim states have been particularly resistant to WGS, seeing it as a Westernized movement that challenges the very basis of the Islamic culture . . . Japan has shown tremendous growth in the number of WGS courses offered over the past 20 years . . . Japanese WGS faculty have been strongly influenced by Western scholars and have a strong academic focus, with little connection to the women's activist movements in their own country.

Source: Extracted from Stake (2006: 199–203).

Despite these limitations Feminist Pedagogy is alive and thriving, and increasingly accepted, though sometimes resisted (Letherby and Marchbank, 1999; Marchbank *et al.*, 2003), within education, especially higher education.

Final comments and concerns

From the above we can see that there are several strands to progressive educational approaches, many sharing the same fundamental goals of utilising education as a means of challenging political and academic hegemonies; of challenging who can be viewed as knowledgeable and of what is known. Another common feature is the notion that such progressive approaches can empower and it is to critiques of this latter view that we now turn in conclusion of this discussion.

Jennifer Gore (2003) argues that pedagogical discourses, including both Critical and Feminist, that claim to empower may themselves 'serve as instruments of domination' (Gore, 2003: 331). She is critical of any pedagogical approach that claims to give empowerment through teaching, as this automatically implies that the teacher has agency whilst students are passive receivers – the opposite of what both Popular and Feminist educationalists aim for. Not only does she view this as impossible as power is not a commodity to be transferred, but can only exist in action (Foucault, 1980), she questions whether critiques of dominant arguments and discourses are always liberationary. Further, she shows that notions of an empowered teacher imparting power to students implies that teachers are completely empowered and without restriction themselves, which others have shown to not be the case (Anderson and Williams, 2001; Letherby and Shiels, 2001; Marchbank *et al.*,

2003). In addition, others, particularly feminists, have raised difficult questions regarding the apparent continued oppression of students experiencing 'empowering' pedagogies (Coate-Bignell, 1996; Letherby and Marchbank, 1999; Marchbank *et al.*, 2003), though some of this has been explained by the view that 'such oppressions are not so much due to feminist practice but to the artificial constraints put upon students and staff by the structural limitations of the institutions in which we work' (Letherby and Marchbank, 1999: 181). This last statement is not to let progressive pedagogies 'off the hook' for it has to be recognised that critical pedagogies, including feminist ones 'can be disciplining as well as empowering, merely replacing one type of "authorised" approach with another' (Marchbank *et al.*, 2003).

Conclusion

At different times in the past century new emphases have been given to some very old ideas regarding the role, function and practices of education. Liberationary aspects to education are very political and, as such, have challenged the fundamental aspects of knowledge. Perhaps surprisingly the only versions to explicitly address gender have been feminist approaches though specific programmes for boys and masculinity have been developed (Clark and Millard, 1998; Quicke, 1998; Warren, 2003; Keddie, 2005) [**Hotlink → Education (Chapter 13)**]. In addition, issues of sexuality have also been raised (Epstein *et al.*, 2003) along with other social divisions. Nonetheless, it is fair to conclude that Critical Pedagogies with their focus on class divisions have continued the marginalisation of other social cleavages whilst Feminist Pedagogies have been developing towards a deeper understanding of the linkages amongst social divisions.

Further reading

Harry Daniels, Angela Creese, Valerie Hey, Diana Leonard and Marjorie Smith (2001), 'Gender and Learning: Equity, Equality and Pedagogy', *Learning Support*, 16(3). In this article the authors argue that boys experience a contradiction between the cultural messages and practices associated with masculinity (competition and individuality) and the teaching practices typical of successful primary schooling (collaboration and codependency). Considering the effect of this they ask if this accounts for boys' underachievement and question if girls and boys have different learning styles.

Gillian Howie and Ashley Tauchert (eds) (2002), *Gender, Teaching and Research in Higher Education*, London, Ashgate. A collection of chapters addressing a variety of issues in contemporary higher education from a range of feminist perspectives. Issues range from philosophical considerations to classroom practices to issues of management and student feedback.

Gayle Letherby and John Shiels (2001), '"Isn't He Good but Can We Take Her Seriously?" Gendered Expectations in Higher Education', in Pauline Anderson and Jenny Williams (eds), *Identity and Difference in Higher Education: 'Outsiders Within'*, Aldershot, Ashgate, pp. 121–32. In this chapter the authors relate the different experiences they have had of student and faculty treatment based on their differing gendered positions. They show how men who provide student support are viewed positively by students but that this is expected of women and can actually diminish the students' opinion of female faculty.

Gender and Education – an international journal covering multidisciplinary educational research and ideas that focus on gender as a category of analysis. It seeks to further feminist knowledge, theory, consciousness, action and debate. The journal takes a broad definition of education from formal to informal and at any level.

Pedagogy, Culture & Society – an international journal that provides a forum for pedagogy discussion and debate. Based on principles such as not restricting debate based on geography or to educationalists alone it covers culturally diverse issues in an interdisciplinary manner.

Websites

Critical Pedagogy on the Web – This site has a dual focus, providing both a general overview of critical pedagogy – its definitions, history, key concepts, and major theorists – and links to other critical pedagogy resources on the web: **http://mingo.info-Science.uiowa.edu/~stevens/critped/ index.htm**

Feminist Pedagogy – a site from the University of Texas which provides a very clear outline of the nature and roots of feminist pedagogy, including its links with Freire's work. It includes a list of common criticisms of feminist pedagogy and multiple links to other relevant sites: **http://www.edb.utexas.edu/wie/pmain.htm#_top**

End of chapter activity

All of us, whether educated within public or private schools, at home, or in universities have an educational biography. Reflect upon your own; you may also wish to interview others with differing educational biographies. Ask these questions:

1. Was my/your education progressive? If so, how?

2. Did/does my education ask questions regarding gender?

3. Do I see any hegemonic processes in practice in my education? If so, which ones?

4. As an educator what would I do?

5. Is gender really a worthwhile issue for consideration in pedagogy?

Chapter 10

Geography

Gill Valentine
Nicola Word

Key issues in this chapter:

➤ Gender relations and geographies are mutually constructed and transformed – spaces affect gender and gender affects spaces.

➤ Assumptions about gender have influenced the study of geography and the position of women in the discipline.

➤ Conceptions of the body are central to understanding gender and space relations.

➤ Gender influences the ways in which people understand, experience and use spaces like the home, the workplace and the street.

➤ Although geographic research on gender has 'traditionally' focused on the experiences and needs of women, geographers are increasingly interested in gaining a greater understanding of men and masculinities.

At the end of this chapter you should be able to:

➤ Critique works on people and their understandings, experience and use of space from a gendered perspective.

➤ Summarise how geography has engaged with gender and outline the liberal, socialist and post-structuralist approaches.

➤ Explain how the body is central to understandings of gender and space relations.

➤ Debate how the social construction of the home, the workplace and the street affects the ways in which people engage with and (inter)act in these spaces.

Introduction

Gender has become a key analytical category within contemporary human geography. Since the impact of feminist scholarship in the 1970s, geographers have, to varying degrees, begun to think about how people, knowledge and institutions are subject to and defined by unequal gender divisions and, where possible, to implement more equitable alternatives. Such engagements with gender have been most significantly developed and sustained by scholars working within feminist geographies; however, interests in gender extend to other areas of the discipline including social and cultural, historical, political and urban geographies.

Geographers have been interested in the ways in which genders and geographies are mutually constituted for over 35 years. In this chapter we will firstly outline some of the key developments in geographers' approaches to gender. Secondly, we will 'flesh out' some of these developments through an examination of some of the ways in which the body has become central in geographers' understandings of gender and space relations. Thirdly we will look at how gender and space relations are constituted within three different spatial contexts – the home, the workplace and the street – in order to illustrate how spaces affect gender and gender affects spaces and finally we will demonstrate how contemporary geographers have broadened their understandings of gender through the development of a body of research on men and masculinities.

Gender and Geography?

Geographers' engagements with gender have evolved over three overlapping phases, ranging from the initial inclusion of women in academic thinking to deeper and more sophisticated understandings of male and female gender identities. The first phase in the 1970s, drawing on liberal approaches and the broader feminist movement, showed how social and economic processes created and maintained inequalities between men and women. They examined the ways in which differently gendered groups with varying types and degrees of power used, controlled or operated space (Women and Geography Study Group [WGSG], 1997). Questions were also raised about the place of women within geography as a discipline and in geographical research. In the UK concerns over the role of women in geography led to the establishment of the Women and Geography Study Group (WGSG) within the British professional association, the Institute of British Geographers (now merged with the Royal Geographical Society). This group had the dual aim of promoting theoretical work on gender in geography and improving the position of women (and their opportunities for career progression) within academic institutions (WGSG, 1984; McDowell, 1999). Elsewhere, Janice Monk and Susan Hanson (1982) argued that sexist bias in the content, methods and purpose of geographical research meant that only 'half of the human' were being included in human geography. Indeed, geography research, it was argued, took and reflected white, able-bodied, male, middle-class values and issues as the norm. Challenges to this male bias resulted in a growth in research into women's lives particularly in the spaces of the home, the workplace and the street.

The second phase, from the 1980s onwards, moved from simply placing women in geography, to examining the mechanisms that created the wide range of socio-material inequalities between men and women, particularly in the context of the workplace and the home. These works tended to be influenced by more radical socialist/Marxist trends and were concerned, for example, with examining gendered 'divisions of labour' in society and men and women's differential access to and roles within the labour market (see, for example, Massey, 1984) [Hotlink →**Work and Leisure → Gendered Labour (Chapter 14)**]. Space, which had previously been viewed as fixed and 'neutral', became increasingly recognised as being socially produced and interpreted, a phenomenon which Edward Soja (1985) referred to as *spatiality* (WGSG, 1997). In other words, space came to be understood as the product of social forces that create expected patterns of behaviour in spaces like the home, the street and the workplace which, in turn, as we will illustrate shortly, affect how people experience, use or avoid these spaces.

Part of this reconceptualisation of space involved a recognition that spaces were gendered. Men and women perform their gender in different ways, thereby constructing and reflecting the discourses around what it means to be a man or a woman. However, these actions have, at least historically, favoured men, to the point that patriarchy (men dominating women) became the norm. What is more, it has been argued that patriarchy operates within a heterosexual context, so that heterosexual values, norms and behaviours have come to be accepted and expected. Therefore, space can be seen to promote and reflect gendered and heterosexual values and norms so that many spaces can be argued to be *hetero-patriarchal* spaces (Valentine, 1993). For example, in public spaces like the street, a man and a woman kissing is unlikely to be noticed by many, yet a same-sex couple kissing is more likely to be perceived as being 'out of place' and receive disdain from others (Valentine, 1996a). However, it is not only 'public' spaces that are dominated by heterosexual and patriarchal values; these have often been replicated in 'private' or domestic spaces, such as the home.

Stop and think 10.1

Next time you walk down a street think about the ways in which the people and the objects that surround you (including buildings, public art, window displays in shops, advertisement boards etc.) reflect, promote or challenge patriarchal and heterosexual norms, values and behaviours.

The third and current phase recognises that even when increasing numbers of women are achieving economic equality with men, broader social and cultural beliefs and practices still influence the opportunities and expectations of women. Drawing on socio-cultural geography and post-structural and post-colonial approaches, feminist geographers from the 1990s onwards have thought about the ways in which gender is constructed through *gender identities*, where men and women become associated with particular spaces, jobs, interests, appearances and behaviours (Panelli, 2004) (see A Closer Look 10.1). This shift in approach has been accompanied by a growing interest in the geographies of the body and research on masculinities. Works in this area have further developed geographers' understandings of gender so that in the contemporary era gender is understood

to be a contested and heterogeneous category, which varies over space and time. This means that geographers have begun to unsettle the binary construction 'male'/'female' and have become increasingly interested in the differences that exist amongst and between men and women [**Hotlink → Gendered Perspectives – Theoretical Issues (Chapter 1)**].

A closer look 10.1

Feminist approaches in Geography

Feminist geographies of gender have drawn on liberal, socialist and post-structuralist approaches to understand both how spaces become gendered and the spatiality of gender.

Liberal Feminist

Public and private spheres are regarded as different spaces; the space of the private is free from the intervention of the state. Their approach to gender is that there should be equality between men and women. However, liberal feminists have tended to add or increase women to existing situations without recognising the need for structural changes in society. In so doing, they also tend not to recognise the intersections with other identities which differentiate women e.g. class, age, sexuality or ethnicity. The liberal approach ties into the initial attempts by feminist geographers to include women in geography and geographical research.

Socialist Feminist

They believe that class and gender inequalities and the oppression of some social groups work to the advantage of others within the capitalist system. Links are made between the home as a site of reproduction and the workplace as a space of production, thereby linking patriarchy and capitalism.

Post-structural Feminism

This concentrates on the connections between power and the production of knowledge, the constitution and performativity of subjectivity, and the importance of difference. In short, it seeks to disrupt what is taken for granted. Feminist geographers have challenged binary constructions e.g. male/female and challenged essentialist ideas about gender. They explore differences among and between women and men and have considered the ways in which identities are embodied.

Source: Blunt and Wills (2000).

Having outlined the broad history of gender in geography, we will now 'flesh out' some of these developments in greater detail. More specifically, we consider the central role that the body has played in geographers' understandings of gender and space relations and then in turn, will examine how gender and space relations are constituted in three different spatial contexts, which have received considerable attention by feminist geographers: the home, the workplace and the street. This chapter will therefore examine how gender affects spaces and spaces affect gender. Much of the research in this area has reflected the experiences of women and has highlighted the assumption of heterosexual norms, values and behaviours. However, as we will demonstrate at the end of this chapter, in recent years geographers' understandings of gender have been broadened through the development of a body of research on men and masculinities.

Embodying Geography

The idea that there are only two sexes (men and women) and that gender (drawing on notions of masculinity and femininity) is based on the biological differences between these sexes does not fully account for the complex nature and experience of sex and gender [Hotlink → Chapter 1]. Human geographers have made significant contributions in critiquing the binary construction 'male'/'female'; see, for example Julia Cream's (1995) work, which identifies three bodies that disrupt traditionally accepted notions of sex and gender: transsexuals, intersexed babies and XXY females. However, whilst biology cannot explain the difference between the experiences of men and women it is connected to the ways in which genders are socially constructed. The effects of these social constructions are significant and affect men and women's everyday lives. This also helps to explain why some spaces or actions are regarded to be gendered so that there are men's spaces and jobs and women's spaces and jobs. In the past these gender associations have been taken for granted and viewed to be fixed, but they are in fact dynamic and can be challenged by both men and women breaking from their gender's mould. This is not to suggest that all the roles or iden-

tities constructed around gender have changed, indeed, many roles still remain: for example, women are still often the primary carers for children.

In this section we explore the central role of the body in gender and space relations by drawing on four approaches that attempt to explain (or unsettle) gender differences and men and women's differential access to and experience of particular spaces. The first two approaches focus on fixed and essentialised conceptions of gender, whilst the second two highlight the ways in which gender is understood to be (re)produced through learnt bodily actions and performances.

The natural and the social

Historically, women have been stereotypically defined in terms of their biology. The notion that women were closer to nature and the animal world than men because they menstruate and give birth gained important currency in the sixteenth and seventeenth centuries. Women's menstruation was read as signs of women's inherent lack of control over their bodies. Women leaked, while men were self-contained (although see Grosz's 1994 discussion of seminal fluid). Their role in reproduction was also understood to mean that they were 'naturally' more nurturing and therefore more closely linked to 'Mother Earth' than men. The other side of this association between women and nature was an assumption that just as nature was wild and potentially uncontrollable (except by rational male science) so women were less able to control their emotions and passions than men (Merchant, 1990). Indeed, women's unstable bodies were considered to be a threat to their minds (Jordanova, 1989). In the late nineteenth century when the suffragette movement with its campaigns for women's right to vote and to education began to gain momentum, opponents used scientific claims that women had naturally smaller brains than men and that education might damage their ovaries to justify excluding them from public life (Shilling, 1993). In other words, women's bodies were used to justify what was regarded as a 'natural inequality' between the sexes.

These notions that women's bodies are both different and inferior to men's persisted into the twentieth century. Chris Shilling (1993) notes that even in the

1960s, the argument that women's hormones meant that they were inherently intellectually and emotionally unstable, was used to prevent women from being allowed to train as pilots in Australia.

These claims about the 'natural' differences between men and women are what are known as essentialist arguments. They assume that sexual differences are determined by biology, that bodies are 'natural' or pre-discursive entities – in other words that bodies have particular stable, fixed properties or 'essences' (Fuss, 1990). Essentialist explanations have been challenged by social constructionists. They argue that there is no 'natural' body, rather that the body is always 'culturally mapped; it never exists in a pure or uncoded state' (Fuss, 1990: 6). So that what essentialists 'naturalise' or portray as 'essence' is actually socially constructed difference. These differences are produced through material and social practices, discourses and systems of representation rather than biology. Social constructionists demonstrate this by pointing to the fact that what is understood by 'man' and 'woman' varies historically and in different cultural contexts. What is perhaps most significant though is that gender – the social meanings which are ascribed to men and women – is socially constructed in a hierarchical way (WGSG, 1997; Laurie *et al.*, 1999).

The mind/body dualism

The seventeenth-century philosopher Descartes established a dualistic concept of mind and body. He argued that only the mind had the power of intelligence, spirituality, and therefore selfhood. The corporeal body was nothing but a machine (akin to a car or a clock) directed by the soul (Turner, 1996). The Cartesian division and subordination of the body to the mind and the emphasis placed on dualistic thinking and scientific rationalisation had a profound impact on western thought.

This distinction between the mind and the body has been gendered. Whereas the mind has been associated with positive terms such as rationality, consciousness, reason and masculinity; the body has been associated with negative terms such as emotionality, nature, irrationality and femininity. Although both men and women have bodies in western culture

white men transcend their embodiment (or at least have their bodily needs met by others) by regarding the body as merely the container of their consciousness (Longhurst, 1997). In contrast, women have been understood as being more closely tied to, and ruled by, their bodies because of natural cycles of menstruation, pregnancy and childbirth. Whereas, Man is assumed to be able to separate himself from his emotions, experiences and so on, Woman has been presumed to be 'a victim of the vagaries of her emotions, a creature who cannot think straight as a consequence' (Kirby, 1992: 12–13).

Feminist geographers such as Gillian Rose (1993) and Robyn Longhurst (2001) have argued that these dualisms are important because they have shaped geographers' understandings of society and space and the way geographical knowledge has been produced. As a result of this belief in the objectivity of masculinist rationality – that it is untainted by bodily identity and experience – Rose claims that it is assumed to be universal, the only form of knowledge available. In other words, she argues that white, bourgeois, heterosexual man tends to see other people who are not like himself only in relation to himself. She writes: 'He understands femininity, for example only in terms of its difference from masculinity. He sees other identities only in terms of his own self-perception; he sees them as what I shall term his Other' (Rose, 1993: 6).

Applying these arguments to geography, Rose (1993) shows how white, heterosexual men have tended to exclude or marginalise women as producers of geographical knowledge, and what are considered women's issues as topics to study [**Hotlink → Method, Methodology and Epistemology (Chapter 2)**]. The mind/body dualism has therefore played a key role in determining what counts as legitimate knowledge in geography with the consequence that topics such as embodiment, emotion and sexuality were, until the mid–late 1990s, regarded as inappropriate topics to teach and research. They have been 'othered' within the discipline (Longhurst, 1997; Bondi *et al.*, 2005).

Fortunately, these sorts of critiques have played an important part in stimulating geographers at the end of the twentieth and at the beginning of the twenty-first centuries to challenge the privileging of the mind over the body within the discipline. As a result, what Longhurst (1997: 494) terms 'dirty topics' are being put on the map and geographers are beginning to think about ways of writing (for example, using autobiographical material and personal testimonies) and methodological practices which recognise that all knowledges are embodied and situated and appreciate that emotions lie at the heart of all human (inter)actions (Rose, 1997; Bondi *et al.*, 2002; Davidson *et al.*, 2005). However, as Juanita Sundberg (2005) argues this shift in geographical practice has not occurred in every part of the world (see World in Focus 10.1).

Stop and think 10.2

Whose understandings of gender most strongly influence the discipline in which you study/work? Are there any examples of alternative voices, perspectives or approaches that shed a different light on hegemonic conceptions of gender?

Performing gender

Understandings of gender in geography have been fundamentally challenged and reworked by the philosopher Judith Butler (1990, 1993). She rejects the notion that biology is a bedrock which underlies the categories of gender and sex. Rather, she theorises gender as performative, arguing that 'gender is the repeated stylisation of the body, a set of repeated acts within a highly rigid regulatory framework that congeal over time to produce the appearance of substance, of a natural sort of being' (Butler, 1990: 33). In other words, gender is an *effect* of dominant discourses and matrices of power. There is no 'real' or original identity behind any gender performance. Butler (1993) suggests that social and political change within the performance of identity lies in the possible displacement of dominant discourses. In a reading of drag balls she argues that the parodic

World in focus 10.1

Why bodies and geographies matter in the doing of geography

Recent debates in feminist geography have sought to raise awareness of the fact that much of feminist geography (and human geography more generally), is dominated by works written in the English language, which have been produced in Anglo-American universities. For example, in a recent survey of articles published in *Gender, Place and Culture* (one of feminist geography's key publications) Maria Dolors Garcia Ramon and colleagues (2006) state that out of the 242 authors who have been published in the journal between its first issue in 1994 and June 2005 only 19 were not based in Anglo-American universities or research centres (7.3 per cent of the total). In addition, out of the 320 books reviewed, only seven were written in a language other than

English (2.19 per cent of the total) and looking at the bibliographies of the published articles only 5 per cent of the books and papers cited were written in non-English languages. Ramon and colleagues (2006) argue that the topics and theoretical elaborations that are featured in the journal may not represent the concerns and works of those geographers who are employed in non-Anglo-American institutions. In other words, there may be a whole range of feminist geographies that are not being represented in the journal.

This point is relevant for the ways in which gender has been conceptualised in geography. As Juanita Sundberg (2005) points out, many of the developments outlined above are at odds with the Latin Americanist geography within which she works. This is because prevailing notions of objectivity have (at least) two effects upon geographies in Latin America. The first is the

disappearance of the geographer as a corporeal being, due to an embedded belief in the mind/body dualism, and the associated idea that researchers can be 'rational', 'value neutral' subjects. The second involves the obliteration of geography as a constitutive factor in the social and institutional life of the geographer, whereby no attention is paid to the different subject positionings of Latin American geographers who have a different relationship to the legacies of European colonisation and contemporary practices of US imperialism than their Anglo-American counterparts. Ramon and colleagues (2006) and Sundberg (2005) are important reminders that understandings of and engagements with gender differ spatially between different social groups and that the developments within Anglo-American geography may not mirror those in other parts of the world.

repetition and mimicry of heterosexual identities at these events disrupts dominant sex and gender identities because the performers' supposed 'natural' identities (as male) do not correspond with the signs produced within the performance (e.g. feminine body language, dress etc.). And that 'by disrupting the assumed correspondence between a "real" interior and its surface markers (clothes, walk, hair etc.), drag balls make explicit the way in which all gender and sexual identifications are ritually performed in daily life' (Nelson, 1999: 339). In other words, they expose the fact that all identities are fragile and unstable fictions.

Butler's (1990) writing has become important within social and cultural geography. The notion of performativity has been used to frame geographic studies, and to talk, not only about bodily identities, but also about space (Bell *et al.*, 1994; McDowell and Court, 1994; Kirby, 1996; Lewis and Pile, 1996; Sharp, 1996; Valentine, 1996a; Rose, 1997; Delph-Januirek, 1999). Instead of thinking about space and place as pre-existing sites in which performances occur, some of these studies argue that bodily performances themselves constitute or (re)produce space and place. However, geographers have also been criticised for overlooking the problematic aspects of Butler's work (particularly in relation to her assumptions about subjectivity, agency and change) when employing her theorisation of performativity (Walker, 1995; Nelson, 1999) (see A Critical Look 10.1).

A critical look 10.1

Bodies (and spaces) *do* matter

Lise Nelson (1999) argues that most geographers need to read Judith Butler's work on performativity in a more critical manner. She argues that Butler (1990) 'provides no space for theorizing conscious reflexivity, negotiation or agency in the doing of identity' and that the subject of Butler's performance is 'abstracted from personal lived experience as well as from its historical and geographical embeddedness' (Nelson, 1999: 331). Nelson therefore argues that in order to properly understand how gender performances work, geographers need to recognise that the subjects of gender performances

are thinking/speaking subjects located in particular times and places. Whilst there may be no 'real' or original identity behind any gender performance, Nelson suggests that the subjects of those performances are capable of intentionally performing their gender in particular ways in response to, for example, past gender performances and the spatial and temporal context in which they are located.

Bodily comportment

In an essay titled 'Throwing like a girl' Iris Marion Young (1990) argues that women are alienated from their bodies and, as a result, occupy and use space in an inhibited way compared with men. She begins her analysis by drawing on the observations of the writer Erwin Strauss about the different way that boys and girls throw a ball. Whereas boys use their whole bodies to throw, leaning back, twisting and reaching forward, girls Strauss noted, tend to be relatively stiff and immobile, only using their arms to produce a throwing action. Young (1990) argues that women demonstrate similar restricted body movements and inhibited comportment in other physical activities too. For example, women tend to sit with their legs crossed and their arms across themselves, whereas men tend to sit with their legs open and using their hands in gestures. In other words, Young (1990) claims that, women do not make full use of their bodies' spatial potentialities. This is not because women are inherently weaker than men but rather it is to do with the different way that men and women approach tasks. Women think they are incapable of throwing, lifting, pushing and so on and so when they try these sorts of activities they are inhibited and do not put their whole bodies into the task with the same ease as men (for example only using their arms to throw). Young (1990: 148) describes this as 'inhibited intentionality'. It is a bodily comportment which is learned. A number of writers have argued for example that teenage girls give up sport and leisure activities in order to spend time with boys (Griffin, 1985) whereas schools promote physicality amongst boys through sport (Mac an Ghaill, 1996) [**Hotlink → Work and Leisure (Chapter 14)**].

Not only do women underestimate their physical abilities and lack self-confidence but they also fear getting hurt. Describing women as experiencing their bodies as a 'fragile encumbrance', Young writes that 'she often lives her body as a burden which must be dragged and prodded along and at the same time protected' (1990: 147). Women also experience their bodies as fragile in another sense too, in that their bodies are the object of the male gaze. Young (1990) suggests that it is acceptable for men to look at, comment on or touch women's bodies in public space and that as a result women are fearful that their body space may be invaded by men in the form of wolf whistles, minor sexual harassment or even rape. As part of a defence against this fear of invasion women experience their bodies as enclosed and disconnected from the outlaying spatial field. Young writes: 'For many women as they move . . . a space surrounds us in imagination that we are not free to move beyond; the space available to our movement is a constricted space' (1990: 146). It is important to note, however, that Young (1990) does point out that her observations apply to the way women typically move but not to all women or all of the time.

In contrast to women, men learn to experience a connectedness between their bodies and their surrounding spatial field and to view the world as constituted by their own intentions. Bob Connell (1983) for example, argues that whereas women are valued for appearance, men are expected to demonstrate bodily skill in terms of their competence to operate on space, or the objects in it, and to be a bodily force in terms of their ability to occupy space. This competence is developed through cults of physicality, sport (formal and informal), drinking, fighting, work and so on. For example, certain forms of manual labour like lifting, digging, carrying are closely linked to some sense of bodily force in masculinity. Although economic restructuring means the stress on pure labouring has declined the social meanings and relations of physical labour, and bodily capacity to masculinity have not (Connell, 1995). According to Young (1990) men live their bodies in an open way. They feel about to move out and master the world. Connell explains: 'To be an adult male is distinctly to occupy space, to have a physical presence in the world.

Walking down the street, I square my shoulders and covertly measure myself against other men. Walking past a group of punk youths late at night, I wonder if I look formidable enough' (1983: 19).

The difference in the meanings of men and women's physicality is evident in relation to naked bodies. Whereas a male stranger's naked body is seen as a sign of aggression and as frightening or threatening to women, a female stranger's body is not read in the same way by men. Men do not feel assaulted or threatened by seeing an unknown woman naked. It is assumed that men want to look at the nude bodies of women because they are an opportunity for pleasure. Consequently, in the eyes of the law women cannot commit the crime of 'flashing' because in contrast to men, their naked bodies are regarded as non-aggressive and not sexually threatening, being read instead as entertaining. The only time a woman can be arrested for indecent exposure is if her actions are understood to be an offence against public sensibilities (Kirby, 1995).

Stop and think 10.3

Collect a range of different women's and men's magazines. How are different bodies represented in these texts? What gender discourses can you identify? What are the similarities and differences in the ways that men and women perform their identities?

Gender and space relations in context

So far we have explored gender and space relations in relatively abstract ways highlighting some of the main theoretical approaches that geographers have drawn on to explain (or unsettle 'traditional') conceptualisations of gender. In this section we will think in more depth about how gender and space are mutually constituted by drawing on three spaces where gender and space relations take place: the home, the workplace and the street. Geographers' engagements with gender have not been confined to these spaces; however, they have been popular locations for thinking about how spaces affect gender and gender affects spaces.

Gendered geographies of domestic space

With the development of industrial capitalism there was a separation of activities with production increasingly taking place in large-scale factories; and reproduction being removed from the communal sphere of the village and relegated to the private sphere of the home. At the same time the meanings attached to family and home, and to men's and women's roles, also changed (McDowell, 1983). Families in pre-industrial societies were not very child-oriented, instead most acted like small businesses with all members, including children, working in order to contribute to the household economy (England, 1991). When production moved out of the home into the workplace so the house became a private place for the family – in other words a home. Whereas before, cooking, childcare, cleaning and so on had been done on a collective basis, this communal style of living broke down and families became emotionally and physically more enclosed or privatised. This definition of 'home' as a place separate from employment devalued the unpaid work done within it, precisely because it was not paid.

Women's roles also changed. In the sixteenth and seventeenth centuries women had participated in commercial life, but with the privatisation of the family and the separation of home and work a new ideology of gender difference emerged. A key element of this was the 'cult of true womanhood'. Women were attributed with the sort of emotional qualities necessary to nurture families and run the house (i.e. gentle, mild, passive) whereas men were seen as fiery, active, aggressive and so more suited to the public world of work. Soon the idea that a mother/wife was necessary for the healthy functioning of the family home became a taken for granted 'norm' (England, 1991). Women were regarded as responsible for the upkeep of the house, the emotional well-being of the family and reproducing the paid labour force (Bowlby et al., 1982).

By the end of the nineteenth and early twentieth century, this privatisation of family life and women was articulated in changes in the built environment. On a city scale residential areas developed along road and railway lines allowing men to travel into the city to the workplace, leaving women and children in residential suburbs in the urban fringe. In other words, the built environment became characterised by a divide between specialist areas of reproduction: the suburbs, and production in the centre of cities. During this time having a non-working wife at home became a hallmark of respectability in upper- and middle-class households. While many low-income, working-class and immigrant women have always been engaged in paid employment outside the home, such households also began to aspire to replicate upper- and middle-class gender ideology (England, 1991). The Second World War brought a breakdown in many class divisions and a collapse of divisions between middle and working women (e.g. with the decline in domestic servants middle-class women became responsible for the domestic tasks that had previously been carried out for them) leading to the emergence of the classless 'housewife' (Ravetz, 1989).

Assumptions about gender roles were articulated in the design and layout of houses built immediately after the Second World War (Roberts, 1991). One of the major ideals of wartime social policy had been to preserve and protect the sanctity of family life. After the war nuclear families became prioritised over all other household types. Planners in both the UK and the US took what was called a *pro-natalist* approach to housing design. They were concerned about falling birth rates and argued that improved family housing would persuade more women to have children and remove temptations for them to work outside the home.

With rising standards of housing after the war also came rising standards of housework. Consumer durables such as washing machines and vacuum cleaners became commonplace and, as Justine Lloyd and Lesley Johnson (2004) illustrate, women's magazines became increasingly preoccupied with cleaning technologies and products (see Figure 10.1). In particular, the development of open plan houses began to erode traditional divisions between formal and informal space so that women were expected to keep a much larger space clean and tidy for 'show' (Matrix, 1984). Domestic ideology was such that housework became understood not just as a set of chores but as a moral undertaking. A woman's moral status could be read from the way she managed her house and by implication her family too (Roberts, 1991). A dirty home was equated with slovenliness, while cleanliness was equated with goodness. This ideology placed a heavy burden on women, as this statement from Mackintosh illustrates: 'The house is inseparable from the housewife. If it becomes dilapidated it becomes the wheel on which the housewife is broken' (Mackintosh, 1952: 110, cited in Roberts, 1991: 93).

Figure 10.1
Source: © Advertising Archives

In the late twentieth and early twenty-first centuries the growth of women engaged in paid work outside the home, and the emergence of more female headed households, has led to a contradiction between the urban spatial form and contemporary gender roles and relations (England, 1991). Studies suggest that when women are in paid employment they continue to do the lion's share of domestic work and childcare. In trying to juggle these dual roles women confront spatial constraints in terms of a lack of affordable childcare in accessible locations and poor public transport which inhibit their employment opportunities outside the home (Tivers, 1985). As a result, feminist geographers have argued that the built environment with its dichotomous assumptions about home and work, has become dysfunctional for suburban women with multiple roles, and that indeed it never worked for those who were single, lone parents, elderly, or who wanted to live in other household arrangements (MacKenzie, 1984; England, 1991). It is a critique shared by the disabled who point to the ableist assumptions of the design professions and the consequent lack of affordable housing that is built to meet the needs of people with physical impairments (Imrie, 1996, 2004; Gathorne-Hardy, 1999).

The emphasis within housing design on the stereotype of the nuclear-family – which physically represents and reinforces the cultural norm of the reproductive, monogamous heterosexual unit – assumes and reproduces a privatised form of family life in which all tasks such as cooking, eating and childcare are contained within the home. There is a rich history, however, of academics speculating or theorising about alternative ways of living and of organising society that transcend the traditional divisions and limitations of home and workplace. For feminist planners and architects this has taken the form of considering what non-sexist housing and non-sexist cities might look like (see A Critical Look 10.2).

Despite these criticisms, this does not mean that geographers should abandon thinking about the relationship between gender, housing design and the spatial structure of the urban environment altogether. Because as Boys explains 'while architecture does not "reflect" society, and is only partially shaped by our

A critical look 10.2

Critiques of work on gender and housing

Studies of gender, housing design and the spatial structure of the city played an important part in the development of feminist geography in the 1980s. In particular, by highlighting the social construction of the public as male and the private as female, and by demonstrating how the home has been regarded as the primary space of women's identification and work as the primary space of men's identification, feminist work has shown how these binary categories have played a part in defining women as secondary and as other in relation to men. As such this feminist writing laid the groundwork for the challenging of dualistic (male/female, public/private, home/work) ways of thinking and the collapsing of these boundaries. However, these studies of gender, housing design and the spatial structure of the city have also been criticised for a number of reasons.

Much of this writing was based on the misconception that the built environment is a simple metaphor for the society that produced it. Jos Boys (1998) recognises this failing in her own early work and acknowledges that feminists in the early 1980s often failed to think closely enough about who has access to, and control over how meanings about gender and the built environment are made, and about the mechanisms of translation through which society is articulated in space.

The work generally assumed uniform approaches to housing design, ignoring the fact that architectural knowledges, and positions within and between architects and builders about 'appropriate' socio-spatial concepts, are contested (Boys 1998).

It often came close to being environmentally determinist in the way that it cast women as the passive victims of housing designs and urban spatial structures produced by architects, planners, property developers and the state (England, 1991). In doing so it oversimplified complex relationships between society and space, failing to recognise that material environments are physically realised in different ways by different residents or 'consumers' and that as such, confusions about designs, unintended uses, and transgressions often arise. It also underplayed the role of women in actively contesting and transforming housing and the spatial structure of the city. For example, women have developed alternative housing and ways of living (Ettorre, 1978; Holcomb, 1986; Crabtree, 2006).

In focusing on male/female and public/private dichotomies feminist work has also treated men and women as homogeneous groups, ignoring the ways that gender identities are cross cut by other social identities. Most notably the research tended to focus on traditional heterosexual, white nuclear family households and as such it overlooked the fact that other social groups (such as lesbians and gay men, women gentrifiers, low-income female headed households and so on) may have had different living arrangements, experiences of, and relationships with, their spatial settings (Bondi and Rose, 2003; Blunt and Varley, 2004).

continuing and contested struggles for identity, the buildings . . . we inhabit remain deeply implicated in shaping our everyday experiences' (1998: 217).

Gender and the workplace

In the 1980s feminists argued that 'Our whole world is gendered, from shampoo and tissues and watches to environments as local as the "ladies' toilet" and as large as a North Sea oil rig. Things are gendered materially (sized or coloured differently) and also ideologically' (Cockburn, 1985). This process, it was argued, was extended not only to work tools (e.g. the typewriter is feminine and the crowbar masculine) but also to occupations themselves. Such is the association made between gender and sexuality, some writers argued that the heterosexuality of a person perceived to be in the 'wrong' gendered job would automatically be questioned. For example, nursing is gendered as a female job and as a consequence male nurses are commonly assumed to be effeminate and therefore gay. This carry over of gender/sex based expectations in the workplace is what Veronica Nieva and Barbara Gutek (1981: 59) termed 'sex role spillover'. In other words, the gendered characteristics of workers and occupations are mutually constituted [**Hotlink → Work and Leisure (Chapter 14)**].

In a classic study of the printing industry Cynthia Cockburn (1985) shows how both *essentialist* and *moral* explanations were used to justify men's claims that women were unsuited to the skilled and relatively well-paid work of print composition, although the men showed no concern about women doing less remunerative jobs that involved similar skills but to which men had no claim. These essentialist justifications included assertions such as: women had weaker spines than men and so would not be able to stand up for long periods of time; that women were too soft and afraid of getting hurt to do what is a potentially dangerous job; that women were too irrational for an occupation that requires logical and problem solving abilities; that women had an innate aversion to machinery. The social and moral justifications rested on assumptions that it was logical and proper for the male head of the family to be the breadwinner and so well paid jobs should be the preserve of men; and that women would be coarsened by working alongside men because they would be subject to swearing and the general sexist abuse and so would lose their femininity.

Louise Johnson (1989) found evidence of similar arguments in her study of the Australian textile industry. Here skill was differentiated by sex and connected to sexed bodies. In the mending room speed and nimbleness combined with dexterity and a domestic skill produced a highly specialised and supposedly feminine task. Such a skill, although developed on the job was never seen as such, but was seen as an innate part of being a woman. In contrast men's skills were understood as acquired through conscious effort and training which enhanced their innate capacities such as technical competence, and mechanical affinity. Johnson (1989: 137) concluded that men's and women's bodies were characterised in different ways to the benefit of men over women and thus that 'an awareness of the sexed body in space, especially as it is lived and historically constituted is . . . a vital addition to any understanding of the workplace'.

There have been/are very different constructions of gender, each historically specific, and articulated in different ways within the societies in which they appear [**Hotlink → History (Chapter 3)**]. The post-industrial service economy which has emerged in the late twentieth and early twenty-first centuries has brought new ways of working. The recognition in the studies of traditional industries that gendered characteristics of workers and occupations are mutually constituted has been extended to the structure of employees' bodies (McDowell, 1997). Within contemporary western economies aesthetic and emotional components of labour now increasingly have more value than their technological capabilities (Lash and Urry, 1994). Indeed, in relation to interactive service work Robin Leidner argues that:

> Workers' identities are not incidental to the work but are an integral part of it. Interactive jobs make use of their workers' looks, personalities, and emotions, as well as their physical and intellectual capacities, sometimes forcing them to manipulate their identities more self consciously than do workers in other jobs. As a result it is increasingly difficult to make a distinction between subjects (workers) and objects (commodities and services).
> (1991: 155–6)

Bodily 'norms' and standards – in which being slim, attractive and able-bodied are seen as aesthetic ideals for both women and men and as the physical embodiment of productivity and success – are an aspect of many organisations' recruitment criteria (McDowell, 1995). Working in a merchant bank in the City of London involves the expectation of conforming to gendered and embodied performances. The working environment is male-dominated and aggressive and is underpinned by heterosexual expectations and homophobia. Women need to appropriate masculine styles of behaviour to be accepted in this space, yet they are constantly reminded of their sex by negative comments from male colleagues. Linda McDowell (1995, and McDowell and Court, 1994) found that both women and younger male employees spend time and money on 'body work' and that consequently they were remarkably uniform in their appearance. Although, the effort and resources which are devoted to maintaining a particular state of embodiment are not usually recognised as part of the labour process and so are not remunerated as 'waged labour' (Shilling, 1993).

Through employee dress codes, appraisals, performance reviews, counselling and stress management employees are also being encouraged, or forced, to be self-reflexive (Lash and Urry, 1994). The assumption is that workers must manipulate their bodily performances to 'embody' the organisations in order to become and remain employees of particular companies (McDowell, 1997).

In another example, Leidner (1993) illustrates how an American insurance company tries to mould its employees' lives by shaping their family life, political convictions, religious beliefs and even friends in a process which it terms 'duplicating'. The (hetero)sexuality of most organisations means that such institutional practices can exclude or alienate lesbian and gay employees (Hearn *et al.*, 1989; Valentine, 1993). In these ways institutions seek 'to gain a pervasive influence in every area of the employee's life' (Casey, 1995: 197). Surveillance – the open plan design of work spaces, electronically mediated panopticism such as the use of closed circuit television or electronic tills, and bodily screening through drug and alcohol testing – is used to enforce or encourage compliance. In this sense the body has become an important regulatory issue in the contemporary workplace (Casey, 1995).

Employees' bodies are not therefore merely reflections of wider social relations but are a product of organisational dynamics and the ability of these institutions to wield power and construct meanings. Though it is worth remembering, as Susan Halford and Mike Savage (1998) point out, that employees also take direct and covert forms of action to resist their employers.

Streets of fear

Street violence is regarded as an increasingly common problem in most North American and European cities. Although statistically it is young men who experience violence most in urban areas, it is women who are regarded as the group most at risk (Bondi and Rose, 2003) [**Hotlink → Violence and Resistance (Chapter 16)**]. The crimes women are most fearful of are sexual violence or assault by strangers. Statistically such incidents are relatively rare (especially in comparison with figures for domestic violence) although at some point in their lives most women encounter more minor forms of sexual harassment in public space such as verbal abuse, wolf whistling or flashing (Wise and Stanley, 1987). These 'everyday' incidents are linked on a continuum with extreme forms of violence and therefore are often regarded as a potential precursor to more serious forms of abuse. In other words, an 'everyday' awareness of the possibilities of harassment can contribute to some women's perceptions of insecurity on the street (Valentine, 1989) [**Hotlink → Work and Leisure (Chapter 14)**]. These anxieties are compounded for those who believe themselves to be unable to defend themselves against a male assailant. Some individuals consider themselves to be unable to do so, perhaps because they are elderly, ill or have a physical impairment which restricts their vision, mobility or strength. Others imagine that all women would be unable to defend themselves against a man because they regard all men as larger and stronger than all women (even though this is not the case and also overlooks the fact that self-defence techniques do not necessarily require bodily strength).

The media plays a part in exaggerating the extent of violent crimes such as rape and murder (Smith, 1984). Crime stories are easy to obtain, the human interest angle sells newspapers and they are also a useful editing device. The selective reporting of violent incidents also generates images about *where* and *when* women are at risk (Valentine, 1992). By disproportionately publicising attacks which occur in public space rather than domestic violence, the media contribute to creating a perception that the street is a dangerous place despite the fact that statistically women are more at risk from domestic violence (Warrington, 2001) [**Hotlink → Crime and Deviance (Chapter 17)**]. This maps onto the historical public–private dualism, in which women have been associated with the private space of the home and men with the public world of the street. This dualism has been used to draw a distinction between 'respectable' women and 'less deserving' women and between 'sensible' women and 'reckless' women. For example, in cases where women have been attacked in public space at night the police and the media have sometimes implied they are to a certain degree responsible for their own fate and have warned other women to avoid putting themselves in similar situations of vulnerability (Valentine, 1989) [**Hotlink → Sex and Sexuality → A Closer Look 15.5 (Chapter 15)**].

Women's perceptions of fear on the street are closely associated with their perceptions of who occupies and controls the space. Fear is closely associated with disorder. Graffiti (Ley and Cybriwsky, 1974; Cresswell, 1992), litter, groups of young people or the homeless on the street are often read as a sign that the space is not looked after or controlled, either formally by the police or private security forces, or informally by local residents, passers-by, store keepers and so on. This in turn erodes women's confidence that anyone would notice or intervene to help if they were attacked (Valentine, 1989). Some commentators argue neighbourhood community is in decline and that this is contributing to people's perceptions of vulnerability in public space. Consequently, initiatives such as Neighbourhood Watch are launched to try to generate this sort of informal social control artificially.

Fear of crime increases at night because the use of the street changes so that this space is produced in a different way. During the day-time the street is usually occupied by people from all walks of life going to school, work, shopping and so on. However, at night, not only does darkness reduce visibility and increase the perception that potential attackers might be able to strike unobserved but there are also less people on the streets and they are usually dominated by the group women are most fearful of: unknown men (Koskela and Pain, 2000).

As a result many women adopt precautionary strategies to keep themselves safe at night. These might be *time–space avoidance strategies* to distance themselves in space and time from perceived danger (for example, by avoiding going out at night after a particular time, or by using a car or taxis to avoid walking in public space after dark) or *environmental response strategies* adopted by women when they are in public space (such as walking confidently, carrying a rape alarm or knife etc.). While most women might use a combination of strategies to keep themselves safe not all women have the same ability to adopt particular precautions. For example, those who work shifts may be unable to avoid public space at night, those on a low income do not necessarily have the option to use private transport or taxis. As a result some women's fear structures their use of space more than others. Indeed, although women may be frightened by an awareness of potential violence on the street many regard it as important to control these emotions so as not to let these fears restrict their use of public space and to resist discourses which construct women's place as in the private sphere (Mehta and Bondi, 1999) (see A Closer Look 10.2).

A closer look 10.2

Bold walking

Hille Koskela (1997) argues that most studies agree that women's fear is partly a reflection of gendered power structures in the wider society. If women's fear of male violence is understood to be a reflection of gendered power structures, Koskela argues that it follows that in societies with a relatively high degree of gender equality – such as her native Finland – women should feel confident in using public space. Drawing on research with 43 women between the ages of 20 and 82, Koskela reveals that although not all women in Finland are fearless (which is perhaps an indicator that the gender equality in Finnish society is partly a myth), there is a tradition of 'boldness' and independence amongst its female population. Note that boldness is not equated with recklessness: women who 'walk boldly' decide to go somewhere despite the perceived risks, but remain alert in their environment so that they can either escape or defend themselves or others if necessary. The fact that some women are bold and confident shows that women do not always have to passively experience space, rather they can actively take part in producing it. Indeed, Koskela argues that women can reclaim space for themselves through everyday practices and routinised uses of space (such as walking in public space at night, not taking alternative routes to avoid spaces that are perceived to be 'fearful' etc.). Through these acts of resistance – and an increased presence of women in public space – Koskela argues that women can produce space that is more available for other women. Just as women can learn to restrict their mobility in order to avoid fear of danger, they can also learn (or re-learn) to be spatially confident. If women can challenge the often unfounded 'fearful' representations of space that are promoted by the media, public opinion and parents, then they could become bolder in public space and encourage other women to reclaim the streets rather than be intimidated by continued warnings and restrictions [**Hotlink → Violence and Resistance (Chapter 16)**].

Recent research suggests that it is not only women who are fearful of violence on the street. There are also growing concerns in North America and Europe about children's safety in public space (Valentine, 1996b) and about the impact of fear of crime on the elderly

(Pain, 1999). Well publicised cases of murders and violence assaults which have been motivated by racism and homophobia have also drawn attention to an escalation in 'hate crimes' (Herek and Berrill, 1992; Valentine, 1993). In 2004 the Federal Bureau of Investigation (FBI) recorded 7,649 hate crime offences in the US.

In addition, in a study of young people's leisure activities in a British town, given the pseudonym Thamestown, Paul Watt (1998; see also Watt and Stenson, 1998) found a strong degree of localism amongst Asian young men who spent much of their time in Streetville, the neighbourhood where they lived. In contrast to the white middle-class youth Watt (1998) attributed this difference not just to the fact that the Asian young people had a strong sense of loyalty and belonging to where they lived, but also to the fact that this was a place where they felt safe from the sort of racist aggression and harassment which they encountered in other parts of the town. Indeed, the research also found some evidence that the Thamestown white youths actively used violence to exclude other ethnic groups from their neighbourhood streets (Watt and Stenson, 1998), although it did not uncover quite the same degree of territorialism – termed by Colin Webster (1996: 26) 'ethnic apartheid' – that has been evident in studies of other English towns and cities (Keith, 1995; Webster, 1996).

Geographies of masculinities

As the above discussion on geographies of fear partially illustrates geographers have, in recent years, begun to broaden their understandings of and engagements with gender through the development of a body of research on men and masculinities. Geography is a discipline that has been viewed as being 'traditionally' androcentric and masculinist (van Hoven and Hörschelmann, 2005) and it has a history that details the activities of men (albeit under the guise that male views and experiences were objective and 'rational'). This fact, as we discussed earlier, has affected the production of geographic knowledge (Rose, 1993; Nelson and Seager, 2005). However, where gender has been the focus of research, this has been assumed to mean research on women. Since the early 1990s (and in particular the late 1990s), geographers have sought to redress this imbalance with increasing attention being paid to men and masculinities. Interestingly, work in this area has been developed across many of geography's subdisciplines including urban geography (Sommers, 1998), economic geography (Blomley, 1996) and post-colonial geographies (Phillips, 1997; Berg, 1998), but discussions of masculinities are still absent or at least limited in some areas of the discipline including physical geography, Geographic Information Systems (GIS) and population geography.

In a review of masculinities and geographies Lawrence Berg and Robyn Longhurst (2003) summarised this development from an initial focus on 'sex roles' to recognising the importance of the 'social relations that constitute the gender order' (Carrigan et al., 1987: 89). Whilst Bob Connell (1985, 1987) is an important figure in the development of geographies of masculinities (see also his work with Carrigan et al., 1987), it is perhaps Peter Jackson, who is largely responsible for the current growth of interest in this area. Jackson argues that gender relations are 'embedded in a matrix of social relations involving *both men and women*' (1989: 129, emphasis in the original) and that studies of gender need to examine the extent to which patriarchal gender relations 'lead to the oppression of some (gay and heterosexual) men as well as being inherently exploitative of women' (1991: 199). However, rather than advocating a situation where heterosexual men join forces with other groups that are attempting to challenge and resist patriarchal oppression (namely feminists, gay men and lesbians), Jackson (1991) argues that heterosexual men have their own political agenda to attend to where they should not only challenge theoretical connections, but certain ways of living and relating as men. Jackson himself has furthered geographers' understandings of men and masculinities through a number of studies including an extensive analysis of masculinities and men's magazines (Jackson et al., 1999, 2001).

Since Jackson's initial intervention there has been an explosion of work on men and masculinities, which has highlighted how ideas of masculinities differ over space and time and has sought to examine the ways in which masculinities intersect with a range of other identities. Indeed, as Berg and Longhurst (2003) demonstrate studies of the geographies of men and masculinities are as varied as the subjects that they explore. For example, masculinities have been explored within rural landscapes (Bell, 2000; Liepins 2000; Little, 2002) and urban environments (Krenske and McKay, 2000; Lysaght, 2002); in historical contexts (Tervo, 2001; Myers, 2002) and in connection with other identities such as 'race' and ethnicity (Nayak, 1999; Day, 2006) and class (Mee and Dowling, 2000; McDowell, 2002).

Conclusion

In this chapter we have outlined some of the key themes in geographers' understandings of and engagements with gender. It has:

➤ outlined how gender has influenced the production of geographical knowledge;

➤ demonstrated the centrality of the body in understandings of gender;

➤ explored some of the ways in which gender and space are mutually constituted (through an investigation of the home, the workplace and the street); and

➤ highlighted how geographic works in geography are increasingly including the experiences of men and studies of masculinity.

However, this chapter has also (hopefully) demonstrated the complex and heterogeneous nature of gender. Understandings and experiences of gender shift over space and time and gender differences occur both among and between women and men. In the future it seems likely that geographers will continue to deepen their understanding of gender through studying the ways in which gender intersects with a range of identities (including those based on 'race', ethnicity, sexuality, (dis)ability and age) and investigating how gendered identities are performed in (and constitute) a range of different spaces.

Further reading

Linda McDowell (1999), *Gender, Identity & Place: Understanding Feminist Geographies*, Cambridge, Polity Press. This is a clearly written book that explores the ways in which gender, space and place are interrelated at a range of scales from the body to the nation-state. It also demonstrates how spatial divisions have been crucial in the establishment, maintenance and reshaping of gendered differences since the time of the industrial revolution.

Bettina van Hoven and Kathrin Hörschelmann (eds), (2005), *Spaces of Masculinities*, London, Routledge. This is a comprehensive introduction to the diverse and innovative research on spaces of masculinity. Drawing on a range of geographical projects, this book highlights the significance of research on masculinity in social science studies of gender.

Women and Geography Study Group (1997) *Feminist Geographies: Explorations in Diversity and Difference*, London, Longman. This groundbreaking text charts the development of feminist geographies in the UK. It introduces the key analytical concepts, outlines the history of the subdiscipline, explores methodological issues and considers the various ways in which feminist geographers have examined some of geography's key concepts including space, place, landscape and environment.

Gender Place and Culture – contents listing available online at: **http://www.tandf.co.uk/journals/**. This journal, which is international in its focus, aims to provide a forum for debate in human geography and related disciplines on theoretically informed research concerned with gender issues. It also aims to highlight the significance of geographic research on gender for feminism and women's studies.

Websites

Geographical Perspectives on Women (GPOW) specialty group of the Association of American Geographers: **http://www.personal.psu.edu/users/a/k/akt122/gpow/index.htm**. This is the website of the main professional organisation for feminist geographers in the United States. It includes an online 'gender in geography' bibliography (established collaboratively with the WGSG) and web links to a range of websites that may be of interest to people studying/working in the field of gender and geography.

Women and Geography Study Group: **http://www.wgsg.org.uk/**. This is the website of the Women and Geography Study Group of the Royal Geographical Society with the Institute of British Geographers. It features a link to the online 'gender in geography' bibliography (established with GPOW) and information on a self-published CD-Rom 'Geography and Gender Reconsidered' which was produced to celebrate and reflect upon the 20 years since WGSG's (1984) groundbreaking work *Geography and Gender*.

End of chapter activity

Watch the first twenty minutes of the film *Disclosure* (1994). As you do so, consider whether the jobs in the firm were gendered and, if so, how? Think about the different ways in which the characters were dressed – what did their appearances say about their different roles in the workplace? How many examples of sexuality at work did you notice? How did these shape the production of different spaces? How are 'public' and 'private' spaces produced within this workplace?

Part Three

Issues – Interdisciplinary Perspectives

In this section of the book we explore various issues from interdisciplinary perspectives within the Social Sciences, of course, always with a focus on gender. In recent years there has been an increasing recognition of the value of interdisciplinary investigation. Such an interdisciplinary approach allows us to understand issues in a more holistic manner through employing data, analyses and theories from across disciplines. As Social Scientists seek to understand our social world, not just in isolation but also in conjunction with environmental, political, economic and health factors, interdisciplinarity seems most appropriate.

You may be a student of one or two single disciplines, for example, Psychology or History, or of subjects which are themselves interdisciplinary, such as Gender and Women's Studies, Criminology, Health professions, Labour Studies etc. In either case you will find the chapters here provide a comprehensive, accessible overview of pertinent issues. In addition, they provide a detailed introduction to many of the major social debates useful both to the beginner seeking an overview and more advanced students requiring quick reference on specific concerns.

Each chapter stands alone but also links to each other and to the chapters in Part 2 (the Disciplines). When reading we advise that you follow the Hotlinks to gain as full an understanding as you can. If you have not done so already we strongly advise that you read Chapter 1, Gendered Perspectives – Theoretical Issues, as this explains the gendered approach taken throughout this text. This approach may be different from approaches to gender with which you may already be familiar.

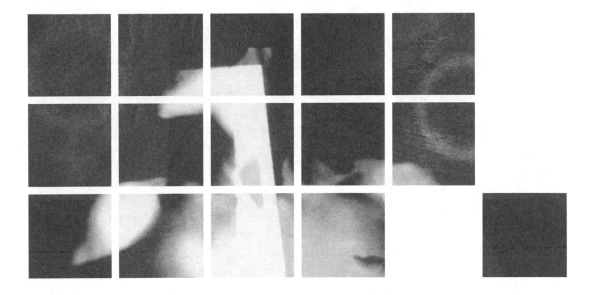

Chapter 11

Family

Key issues in this chapter:

➤ The concept of 'family'.
➤ Exploration of the difference between the 'family' and families.
➤ Theories of family life.
➤ The experience of living in gendered families.
➤ Motherhood and fatherhood.
➤ Families, gender and other aspects of difference and diversity.

At the end of this chapter you should be able to:

➤ Challenge common-sense definitions of the family.
➤ Challenge the view that the family is always a sanctuary from life outside of the home.
➤ Describe various historical and current theories of family life.
➤ Acknowledge – in relation to gender and other differences – both the diversity of family forms and the diversity of family life.

Figure 11.1 Happy Families
Source: © Advertising Archives

These images of family life were all used to advertise goods and services at various points in the twentieth century.

Stop and think 11.1

What messages do these publications give about the 'typical' family? How similar and different are these images from the advertisements depicting family life today?

Introduction

The family is a concept and an institution that we all take for granted. Most people regard themselves as members of one or more families which highlights our first problem: just how do we define family? All around us we see images of a particular type of family – what the anthropologist Edmund Leach (1967) has called 'the cereal-packet norm family' – consisting of husband as head of household with wife and children (often a boy and a slightly younger girl). Despite the consistent representation of this as the 'normal', 'natural' and 'inevitable' family form only a small percentage – about one in twenty – households in Britain at any one time consists of a father in paid employment, a dependent wife and two children. In addition although in western industrialised societies we are forever bombarded with glorified images of heterosexual marriage, thinking globally we know that marriage as a binding relationship between a man and a woman is not universal. It is estimated that only 10 per cent of all marriages in the world are actually monogamous and the ways which Europeans classify kin relationships is only one way of identifying familial relations (Jackson, 1997).

Yet, as Pamela Abbott and colleagues (2005) note the so-called ideal – the nuclear family – is enshrined in legal, social, religious and economic systems reflected in the fact that it is promoted in advertising, referred to by government and reflected in housing and social policy. This in turn reinforces the view of this type of family form as 'normal', 'natural' and 'inevitable' and leads to prejudice and discrimination towards those who are not part of families who meet this 'ideal'. Thus, assumptions are made concerning how people do and should live and that one particular type of family best serves the interest of its individual members and of society generally (Abbott *et al.*, 2005) [**Hotlink → Social Policy (Chapter 5)**]. Yet, there is some acknowledgement that traditional, simplistic definitions of family forms are inadequate. Consider for example the Canadian census presented in World in Focus 11.1.

In this chapter we problematise the idealised image of the family – both in terms of structure and practice

World in focus 11.1

Statistics in Canada 2001 – Census definition of the family

Two persons living in a same-sex common-law relationship, along with either partner's children, are now considered a census family.

Adults in a census family may now have been previously married, in previous censuses they had to be 'never-married'.

A grandchild living in a three-generation household where the parent has never married is now considered a child in the census family of his or her parent. In previous censuses, the census family consisted of the two older generations and the child was considered a non-census family person.

A grandchild of another household member, where the middle generation is not present, will now be considered a child in the census family of his or her grandparent. In previous censuses, the grandchild was considered a non-census family person.

Source: Statistics Canada 2003 cited by Mandell and Duffy (2005: 5).

– with particular reference to gender. The rest of the chapter is divided into five main sections. In 'The family and political rhetoric' we consider how our image of the 'ideal' family is supported by political pronouncements and policies in Britain and elsewhere and this is followed by a focus on 'Theories and experiences of family life'. This attention to the actual experience of living in families is further considered in 'Mothers and fathers' as are issues of rhetoric in relation to the experience of motherhood and fatherhood. Throughout the chapter we identify the ways that family forms and family life differ from the ideal and focus specifically on what is some times referred to as 'alternative' (as in alternative to the nuclear ideal) families in '"the family"' and families: difference and diversity'. Finally we end with a Conclusion.

The family and political rhetoric

Although we know that the nuclear family – the 'cereal-packet' family – is actually in the minority in the industrialised west this does not stop political parties on the right and the left holding up this 'ideal'. In Britain the Conservative government elected in 1979 and led by Margaret Thatcher presented itself as the 'party of the family'. In a reaction to the so-called permissiveness of 1960s Britain Conservatives argued for the return of the 'traditional' family, one in which the father sets and enforces standards of behaviour: the patriarchal family. Similarly in the United States of America the conservative moral majority proposed a series of laws in the late 1970s aimed at restoring the 'traditional family'. For example they wanted to give a $1,000 tax exemption on the birth or adoption of a child but only for married couples and provide tax incentives to discourage women's employment and promote wives' economic dependence on their husbands (Liazos, 2004).

However it is not just conservatives that think like this. For example Ramesh Mishra argues, that in relation to the family, there exists 'a bipartisan political consensus' (cited by Coppock, 1997: 61) and it appears that the political right and the left in the UK still hold the 'traditional' nuclear family as the ideal family form [**Hotlink → Social Policy (Chapter 5)**]. The Labour Government (elected in 1997) were the first government to produce a consultation paper on the family – *Supporting Families* in 1998 – and this is a positive initiative. However, it seems yet again that the nuclear family is reiterated as the most desirable type of family:

> Many lone parents and unmarried couples raise their children every bit as successfully as married parents. But marriage is still the surest foundation for raising children and remains the choice of the majority of people in Britain.
>
> (*Supporting Families*, 1998: unpaginated)

Arguably the Labour Government is sending out mixed messages. While the government is intent on supporting 'families' it appears that the reduction of, rather than support of certain forms of, families is given priority. Thus, the *Supporting Families* document does recognise the diversity of family forms; however, this recognition is limited. Associated policy (for example in relation to teenage pregnancy and young parenthood – see below in Families: difference and diversity) could arguably, further isolate and exclude those that do not fit the idealised 'norm' [Hotlink → Political Science (Chapter 8); Hotlink → Social Policy (Chapter 5)].

Mavis Maclean and Jacek Kurczewski (1994) argue that the family is a 'political battleground' in both east and west Europe. In the west the political focus is on individual and family freedom from interference from the state leading to a 'privatisation' of the family. Whereas in the east there is a concern to retain welfare provision and, at the same time, an increased emphasis on fundamental religious values supporting gender differences and roles. Such values also deplore access to abortion and divorce which are seen as threats to the 'traditional' family.

Political rhetoric is persuasive and idealised images can affect the way in which we present our families to others (see A Closer Look 11.1).

Photographs record the significant events in the life course which allow people to make sense of their own lives and the lives of others. Wedding photographs 'hold' the moment and indicate change both in the lives of the couple whose marriage is recorded and their parents. Usually only images of the 'ideal' family are recorded in photographs. As Val Williams (1991) points out, the images in family 'snaps' are usually the result of a selection process, employed by the photographer, which emphasises domestic contentment and harmonious family relationships. No hint is given of power relationships between men and women and adults and children or the conflicts between family members to which these relationships give rise. Indeed, families use photography to reinforce and to obscure. A wedding photograph or one of a graduation where parents and children pose together in celebration of the event, tells us nothing about family problems and uneven power relations within the family. Thus, the Family Album is a political document (Cotterill and Letherby, 1993).

Stop and think 11.2

Look at your own collection of photographs and those of others you consider to be members of your family. What's missing?

Theories and experiences of family life

So how has the family been considered and constructed by social scientists? Traditionally the family was of little interest to researchers and theorists and when studied the focus was the traditional western nuclear unit. As this was the case this is the 'family' referred to in this section despite it not being the only form. Taking sociology as an example historically the interest was in public sphere and not in the private and personal lives of individuals. The state, work, politics – were considered to be the important things to study. When family and personal relationships were considered it was their relationship to the public sphere that was of concern (Bentilsson, 1991). Historically the sociology of the family was dominated by structural functionalism [Hotlink → Gendered Perspectives – Theoretical Issues (Chapter 1)]. One of the most notable theorists being Talcott Parsons (who wrote in the 1940s, 1950s and early 1960s). Parsons was concerned specifically with the modern isolated nuclear family as particularly well suited to modern industrial society. For

A closer look 11.1

The family album

In describing a personal collection of photographs Holland (1991: 3) argues that: 'the most private collection is also thoroughly public. Its meanings are social as well as personal – and the social influences the personal. Family photographs are shaped by the public conventions of the image and rely on a public technology which is widely available. They depend on a shared understanding.'

This 'shared understanding' starts with a definition of the 'normal, natural and inevitable' family form.

Parsons and other functionalist thinkers the family had several functions:

➤ It facilitates labour mobility (e.g. social mobility in a meritocratic society [**Hotlink → Education (Chapter 13)**] and geographical mobility).

➤ It socialises children (and prepares them for their place in the 'outside world').

➤ It provides a source of emotional support for adults in an otherwise competitive rootless and impersonal society (particularly for men, the bread-winners, by women, the nurturers).

Parsons (1954) compared the post-Second World War family to the pre-industrial society which were large-scale kinship units which performed religious, political, educational and economic 'functions' – i.e. places where work took place. As societies developed, he argued, some of the functions originally performed by the family began to be fulfilled elsewhere (the modern family does not engage in economic production, is not a significant force in political power systems etc.) so a once multi-functional unit (an institution serving many social needs) became functionally specific. Thus, from this perspective the nuclear family serves the needs of modern industrial families and the relationships within families – i.e. those between husband and wife and parents (especially mothers) and children – intensified (Parsons, 1954; Parsons and Bales, 1956). Stevi Jackson, on the other hand, highlights some of the negative consequences for women linked to these changes (see A Closer Look 11.2).

For Functionalists there are (and should be) distinct gender roles within the family with men – who are naturally instrumental (in their view) – being the obvious breadwinners in society and women – who are naturally expressive – assigned the role of carer of children and husbands. Modern society is rootless, competitive, impersonal and bureaucratised and the family meets the basic human needs for love and intimacy and is 'a haven in a heartless world' – see A Closer Look 11.3 for an alternative view. In 1957 David Young and Peter Willmott published the findings of their empirical study of family and community life in Bethnal Green in east London. Supporting the work of Parsons they argued that traditional extended family kin networks

A closer look 11.2

The development of the nuclear family

'Until the industrial phase of capitalism, most production, whether agricultural, craft or domestic industry, was centred on households. Everyone – men, women and children – contributed to the household economy. There was, however, a distinct sexual division of labour, and generally men controlled productive resources, including the labour of their wives (Middleton, 1983, 1988; Seccombe, 1992). With industrialization the removal of commodity production from households reduced most of the population to wage labour, and separated family life from paid work. Among the bourgeoisie in the early nineteenth century these changes were associated with a new 'domestic ideology' which defined the home as women's 'natural' sphere (Davidoff and Hall, 1987; Hall, 1992). This ideology was subsequently adopted by sections of the working class. Male-dominated labour organizations sought to exclude women from many forms of paid work and to establish the principle of the male breadwinner earning a 'family wage'. (Jackson, 1997: 327–8)

A closer look 11.3

Haven or hell?

'Coal is Our Life . . .' was a mid-twentieth-century empirical study of a mining community in Wales. The researchers observed a distinct sexual division of labour with husbands' role in the family ended when they had handed over their wage/part of their wage yet maintain authority and discipline whilst the management and care of the home was almost entirely the wife's responsibility. Adults had little expectation of companionship or emotional supportiveness from their partner and men looked for meaningful relationships with other men who they met at work or at leisure and women turned to other female kin for support, friendship and advice. The best that women hoped for was a man who was 'a good provider' and similarly men hoped to be married to a woman who 'kept a good, clean house'.

Dennis *et al.* (1956).

weakened as younger members of the family moved outside of the community on marriage.

It is possible to criticise the Functionalist view of the family on several accounts. Marxists, for example, suggest that the nuclear family is part of an oppressive structure in that it meets the needs of capitalism. Frederich Engels (1884) was the first to argue that the emergence of private property led to the need to establish paternity lines and therefore the emergence of the monogamous nuclear family. Whereas contemporary Marxist theorising argues that the family socialises children into the values and relations of capitalism and brings about the subordination of women to men by rendering them dependent on the husband's wage. Further, Marxists argue that the housewife role is a mechanism through which capitalism ensures the reproduction of the labour force at the lowest possible cost and has a 'reserve army' i.e. women are a source of cheap and flexible labour, available when the economy needs them [Hotlink → Work and Leisure (Chapter 14)].

In a later piece of work Young and Willmott (1973) argued that increased affluence and geographical mobility and the rising number of women working outside of the home led to a change in the family division of labour with men more involved in domestic labour and childcare and women more involved in making financial and other key decisions. Thus, they argued that the family was becoming more symmetrical and conjugal roles more equal. However, from the 1970s onwards feminist researchers and theorists began to challenge the view that the family was becoming more symmetrical. Rather they argue/d that the family is a site of inequality where women are subordinated and the sexual division of labour perpetuated and further the family also institutionalises heterosexuality and the view that only men can legitimate children. Following Willmott and Young (1973) Ann Oakley (1982) argued that even when conjugal roles were shared, men were often said to be 'helping' their wives, choosing the jobs that they wanted to help with. Thus, women remain responsible for the essential housework and childcare tasks even when they work outside of the home and whilst women made minor decisions the major decisions were still made by men.

These debates continue. In 1992 Anthony Giddens suggested that relationships in late modernity are characterised by equality in emotional give and take. And in 1995 Ullrich Beck and Elizabeth Beck-Gernsheim argued in relation to changes in gender, family and occupational roles that individuals seek out and negotiate relations that would previously have been part of the 'fate' of gender, of gendered expectations. However, despite the increasing numbers of women that are working outside of the home Coppock and colleagues noted in 1995 that in 75 per cent of families women still performed most unpaid, domestic work and household management. Housework and childcare, like no other job is intimately bound up with personal ties and women are responsible for the health of other family members [Hotlink → Health and Illness (Chapter 12)], there is no guaranteed time for leisure and no fixed job description, no agreed hours and conditions of work and no trade union or personnel department support [Hotlink → Work and Leisure (Chapter 14)]. On occasion though housework and childcare is performed by non-family members and this can have negative implications for those employed to do these tasks (see World in Focus 11.2).

Lynn Jamieson (1999) undertook empirical work on heterosexual couples and continued to find that men have more power than women in the partnerships; including for example having more choice concerning opting in and out of domestic work and childcare and exercising more control over money. Drawing on Arlie Hochschild's (1983) work Jean Duncombe and Dennis Marsden (1998: 211) add that it is mostly women who help to keep long-term marriages alive by doing 'emotion work' on themselves as well as on their husbands to sustain the image that 'we're ever so happy really'. So would women be better or worse off – financially at least – if they divorced their husbands?

In her study of marriage Hochschild (1990: 44–66) argues that women are forced to live the family myth which sometimes means they have to pretend to be content because of the continued gender imbalance of power in marital relationships and writes that whether women's emotion work is seen as 'a matter of denial . . . [or as] intuitive genius', it 'is often all that stands between . . . a wave of broken marriages'.

World in focus 11.2

Maid to order

In a society where 40 per cent of the wealth is owned by 1 per cent of households, while the bottom 20 per cent reports negative assets, the degradation of others is readily purchased . . . Housework . . . was supposed to be the great equalizer of women. Whatever women did – jobs, school, child care – we also did housework, and if there were some women who hired others to do it for them, they seemed too privileged and rare to include in the theoretical calculus. All women were workers, and home was their workplace: 'One thing you can say with certainty about the population of household workers is that they are disproportionately women of color . . . Of the 'private household cleaners and servants' it managed to locate in 1998, the Bureau of Labor Statistics [USA] reports that 36.8 per cent were Hispanic, 15.8 per cent black, and 2.7 per cent 'other'. Certainly the association between household cleaning and minority status is well established in the psyches of the white employing class . . . [an experience retold by Audre Lorde] 'I wheel my two-year-old daughter in a shopping cart through a supermarket . . . and a little white girl riding past in her mother's cart calls out excitedly, "Oh look Mommy, a baby maid".' (1984: 85–92)

And . . .

Whose mother am I?

Many of the women interviewed in a research project about domestic workers under apartheid in South Africa said that they had to look after two families and neglect their own in the process. Lack of educational opportunities and employment alternatives, coupled with the legislation restricting the movement of black workers, all combined to 'trap' black women in domestic service.

Source: Adapted from Ehrenreich (2002).

Controversy 11.1

Divorce 'makes men richer'

It makes financial sense for men to divorce or leave their partners, a study has found. Men who stay married invariably end up poorer than those who leave their live-in partners, according to social researcher Cecile Bourreau-Dubois.

Mrs Dubois found that the effect of divorce on a man's bank balance outweighed the financial benefits of either partner getting a better job. However, the reverse was true for women. Females starting a relationship were one-and-a-half-times more likely to improve their wealth than those who remained single.

Mrs Dubois based her findings on interviews with more than 75,000 adults in 11 different EU countries. Mark Stephens, a senior partner at law firm Finers Stephens Innocent, said the findings come as little surprise 'to those in the know'.

There was still a significant gender gap between men and women in the pay stakes. And women invariably retained custody of the children in a divorce, reducing their earning potential, he argued. The man's wage will often increase ahead of inflation, with maintenance payments quickly falling behind. Divorced men will also save on school fees, family holidays and other expenses.

Although this did not stop them complaining that they have got a raw deal.

And yet perhaps it is important to look beyond the figures:

wives often don't see themselves as having an equal right to husband's wage . . . [which] can result in hidden poverty in families . . . so previously married single mothers feel that they are as well off or better off financially than they were when with their partners . . . This is surprising given that nearly two out of three lone mothers live on state benefits and that households headed by lone mothers are three times as likely to be poor than are two-parent households.

(Jackson, 1997: 330)

However, recent studies suggest that there might be individual variations among men and women and how they do emotion work (see for example Duncombe and Marsden, 1998) and despite continuing inequalities in both the private and the public spheres it is now more acceptable for women and even expected (at least in the west) to maintain a public identity independent of home and family.

As women often earn less than men [**Hotlink →** **Work and Leisure (Chapter 14)**] when a couple do decide that one of them should stay home to care for their children or to care for dependent elderly relatives it is often the woman who leaves paid work outside of the home. This traps women into financial dependency and they may feel they have less right to spend the family income: women put their own needs last behind other members of the family and when money is short, women go without food, clothes and other necessities (Abbott et al., 2003). Even when women do work (full- or part-time) horizontal and vertical segregation within the labour market means that women usually earn less than their male partner [**Hotlink → Work and Leisure (Chapter 14)**]. Furthermore, the female partners of self-employed men from painters and decorators to lawyers, may provide free labour to businesses just as the wives and partners of heads of private schools and company directors are likely to have 'formal' duties associated with their partners' jobs. With this in mind Janet Finch (1983) argues that women, can in many ways, find themselves 'married to the job'.

In addition to the consequences of the normalised sexual division of labour in the home and financial inequalities Jackson (1997) notes that male violence, men's control over women's sexuality and reproduction [**Hotlink → Violence and Resistance (Chapter 16);** **Hotlink → Sex Sexuality (Chapter 15)**] and the state regulation of the family also lead to women's subordinated position within the family and within society.

However, as Jackson (1997) notes although it is important to draw attention to the persistent inequalities within the family it is important to challenge stereotypical views of family form (see A Critical Look 11.1) and structure when we do so as not to perpetuate the view of the white heterosexual middle-class nuclear family as the only way to organise family life. Black and anti-racist feminists have been critical of white feminists' concentration on the family as the basis of women's oppression. Slavery, colonialism, immigra-

tion and citizenship laws have significant effects on black and minority families worldwide and for some women the family may be a refuge from racism (e.g. bell hooks, 1982; Bhavani and Coulson, 1986) as well as a patriarchal institution. Many black and minority women do not seek to escape the nuclear family but sometimes struggle for the right to have one (Dua and Robertson, 1999). Yet, stereotypes persist:

> the Afro-Caribbean family is seen as being too fragmented and weak and the Asian family seems to be unhealthily strong, cohesive and controlling of its members . . . Afro-Caribbean women are stereotyped matriarchs, or seen as single mothers who expose their children to a stream of different men while Asian women are constructed as faithful and passive victims . . . identified as failures because of their lack of English and refusal to integrate.
>
> (Palmer, 1988: 199, cited by Jackson, 1997: 325)

Note the mother-blaming in both of these examples, an issue which we explore further below.

A critical look 11.1

By the numbers: Canadian families

In November 2004 the Vanier Institute of the Family released a new report based on national census and other data. Here are some extracts:

➤ 86 per cent – proportion of Canadians living in private households with relatives;

➤ 9.9 per cent – proportion of the population living alone;

➤ 3.1 – the number of people in the average Canadian family, down from 3.71 in 1971;

➤ 40 per cent – proportion of people in Quebec who are legally married (lowest in Canada);

➤ 27 per cent – proportion of Canadians who are single;

➤ 70,000 – number of same-sex couples in common-law relationships;

➤ 38 per cent – percentage of all marriages ending in divorce before 30th anniversary;

➤ Three out of ten – number of babies born to mothers who are not legally married, compared to two out of ten in 1991.

Source: CBC at http://www.cbc.ca/news/background.marriage/family.html (accessed September 2006).

Stop and think 11.3

Read A Critical Look 11.1: Canadian families. Now answer the following:

1. What is the lowest proportion of people who are legally married, and where?

2. What percentage of Canadians live in common-law partnerships?

3. How many same-sex couples are there in common-law relationships?

4. What percentage of Canadians are single?

5. Given that Toronto has the highest proportion of families – 51 per cent – which consist of a legally married couple with children, what does this say about the supposed stereotypical family?

Mothers and fathers

One stereotype of the family is that it needs to involve children. This means adults become parents, and these roles contain many gendered dimensions. Here we consider both mothers and motherhood, and fathers and fatherhood.

Mothers and motherhood

In her book *Of Woman Born: Motherhood as Institution and Experience*, Adrienne Rich (1976) distinguishes between the experience of mothering and the 'institution of motherhood'. By separating the biological act of mothering from the structures and ideology that surround it, Rich enables us to examine motherhood as a social construct. A useful explanation of why motherhood is seen to be so important for women is provided by Robert Connell (1987). He argues that although there are many different femininities and masculinities affected by ethnic, generational and class differences and so on, the global dominance of men over women gives rise to 'hegemonic masculinity'. This is constructed in relation to other subordinate masculininites and femininities and its public face helps to sustain male power. All femininities are therefore constructed in the context of the overall subordination of women to men. Connell identifies three types of femininity:

➤ compliant (or emphasised) femininity which is designed to accommodate the interests and desires of men;

➤ non-complaint femininity which is resistant, and

➤ a third option which is a combination of compliance and non-compliance.

Obviously, compliant/emphasised femininity is the most attractive to men and to society as the aim is to maintain support for male dominance and Connell argues that this option is supported by religious doctrine and practice, mass media content, wage structures, welfare and taxation policies and so forth. Similarly, Betsy Wearing (1984) argues that the ideology of motherhood serves capitalism as it acts to legitimate and perpetuate the relationship of dominance and subordination between classes and benefits males of all classes.

However, Mary Daly (1985) and Ann Oakley (1981) argue that children, for many women, represent their main possibility of achievement and power. Children are an achievement for women as a disadvantaged group and they can be viewed as a form of 'property' for women, a group who are otherwise placed by society in a propertyless condition. Many writers have suggested that motherhood is key to women's identity in a way that fatherhood is not to men's. It is more usual for women rather than men to be asked how many children they have and their experience/choices challenged if they say that they have none (Letherby, 1994; McAllister with Clarke, 1998; Gillespie, 2000). Further to this as Oakley and colleagues (1984) argue, 'choice' in this area for women is something of a misnomer given societal expectations. Thus:

> In Western Society, all women live their lives against a background of personal and cultural assumptions that all women are or want to be mothers and that for women motherhood is proof of adulthood and a natural consequence of marriage or a permanent relationship with a man.
>
> (Letherby, 1994: 525)

So, motherhood is something that all women are expected to do, but only in the 'right' social, economic and sexual circumstances. Thus, as Elena DiLapi (1989) argues there is a hierarchy of motherhood and teenage mothers along with lesbian mothers, older mothers, disabled mothers, non-biological mothers and so on are often defined as 'inappropriate'.

Furthermore, mothering is not something that women do without external comment and censure and women's mothering is defined as 'good' or 'bad'. As Deborah Chambers (2001) and Valerie Walkerdine and Helen Lucey (1989) note by the 1950s an ideology of 'bad' mothering was firmly associated with working-class and non-white families. So-called deviant and dysfunctional families – e.g. families with unemployed fathers, single parent families – were also thought to be at risk of 'low' standards of childcare. On the other hand 'intensive mothering', where the individual mother is primarily responsible for child-rearing is 'good mothering' (Hays, 1996).

Figure 11.2 Whose mother are you?

Source: WEA (1986) *Women and Health*, p. 208. Reproduced with thanks to Angela Martin.

Fathers and fatherhood

Unlike the identity of mother which is closely identified with caring and nurturing the identity of father is still primarily linked to the biological: the father is the provider of seed and his status is important in terms of genetic ties and family lines. Indeed, in a patriarchal society a child without a father is lesser, is illegitimate (e.g. Katz Rothman, 1988; Warner, 1985). Traditionally fatherhood has also been associated with power, authority and status and good fathers are good providers. Thus, the implication here is that the biological aspect of fatherhood is important for men and for masculine identity as is the status as patriarch, but other social and emotional elements of fathering such as caring and nurturing are less important.

Yet, research by Berit Brandth and Elin Kvande (1998) on fatherhood in Norway suggests that when men do value the social and emotional aspects of fatherhood, it is necessary for them to include childcare in their construction of masculinity. The men in this study felt that their own fathers' image as the distant breadwinner was negative. This image did not satisfy contemporary demands on fathers and they did not want to construct their fathering role in relation to mothering. They constructed their own role, and their own place in the family and the care they provided. Important elements of a father's way of providing care seemed to be becoming a friend with the child and to this end respondents spoke of being together and doing things together and teaching the child independence.

Stephen Whitehead (2002) focuses on the diversity of contemporary experience of fatherhood. While noting the growth in numbers of 'full-time' fathers in Britain, he warns against simple interpretation of this and other figures relating to the emergence of 'new fathers'. He comments that 'while there is some evidence of a shift in attitudes to family and domestic roles by some men, dominant discourses of masculinity [and of men's role within the family] do not sit easily with these practices' (Whitehead, 2002: 154). The continuing emphasis on father as provider (and patriarch) is clearly apparent in social policy in the UK. For example, the Child Support Act 1991 was designed to enforce maintenance payments after divorce or relationship break up from the absent parent (most often the father). It actively promotes the 'traditional' family and a father is expected to be economically responsible 'for life' for his 'first' family (Smart, 1997; Collier, 1999). Obligations in terms of contact with children or good fathering are much less clear. However, if we consider other aspects of social policy, e.g. the Family Law Act 1996 and the UK's recent reform of the divorce law there is support for the 'good father' who continues to be involved in parenting after divorce or separation. As Collier (1999) notes this is ironic because in Britain there has been little attempt to support joint parenting in marriage, not least because fathers in Britain work longer than in any other European country. The Family Law Act, again, supports traditional views of 'proper', 'real' and 'natural' families and supports traditional gender relations within the family (see McAllister and Letherby forthcoming for further discussion) [Hotlink → Social Policy (Chapter 5)].

Stop and think 11.4

Write a list of the characteristics that define a good mother and a good father. How can you account for the differences in the list? How different do you think your list would have been 50, 25, 10 years ago? Why?

'The family' and families: difference and diversity

Having considered some challenges to our view of the 'family' as always the same we now explore issues of difference and diversity further. In the UK between the 1970s and the 1990s, cohabitation became a popular choice for many as the number of first marriages in the UK fell by two-fifths, the number of divorces more than doubled and remarriages accounted for over one-third of all marriages. In the same period lone motherhood almost doubled and births outside marriage trebled. There has also been a significant increase in step-families and while there are no figures for non-heterosexual partnerships (as there is no category on the Census) there has been an increased awareness of and openness about their existence. On the other hand in the late 1990s, just under three-quarters of households were composed of a heterosexual couple, 40 per cent of people lived in a family comprising a couple with dependent children, with two-thirds of these couples being married and over three-quarters of dependent children in their mid-teens were living together with their biological parents (Ribbens et al., 2003). Statistics then could easily be used to argue for both the demise and the continuity of the 'nuclear family' – see A Critical Look 11.1 for comparable Canadian figures. Yet, as Jackson (1997) notes there is no simple, single entity that can be defined as 'the family' compared across cultures (see World in Focus 11.3).

World in focus 11.3

Female headed households

[A]n average of 35% of all households in the Caribbean and 21% in Latin America are headed by women. The proportions of female-headed households can reach as high as 44% in Barbados and 42% in Antigua and Barbuda.

At a minimum, one in six households in Latin America are headed by women. Furthermore, 54% of all separated or divorced women become female heads of households. In these households, an average of 3 to 5 children depend on the mother. Moreover, the proportion of female-headed households in Latin America and the Caribbean is rising. A recent study found that in Costa Rica, for example, the share of households headed by women increased by an estimated 150% between 1973 and 1992.

Source: Gender and Family – http://www.undp.org/rblac/gender/legislation/family.htm (undated accessed January 2006).

In addition, married 'couples' (as we call them in the west) do not always live together and children are not always raised by their biological parents. Marriage is sometimes monogamous, sometimes polygamous (see World in Focus 11.4) and it may be entered into (initially at least) for life after much consideration and negotiation or it may be a relatively informal arrangement. For some marriage is thought to be a confirmation of the love between two people, for others a contractual agreement. An example of such a contractual agreement is provided in World in Focus 11.5.

World in focus 11.4

Polygamy

Polygamy is having more than one spouse at the same time and there are two basic forms:

➤ polyandry – where a woman has more than one husband;

➤ polygyny – where a man has more than one wife.

The most common form both historically and today is polygyny. The term 'polygamy' is often used to mean polygyny.

Polygamy is most common in Middle Eastern and African nations. Cultural groups with a high incidence of polygamous marriage include the Kuwatis, Saudi Arabians, Bedouin Arabs, the Xhosa (South Africa), the Yononamo (Venezuela), Nigerians, Ghanians, the Kipogi and Datagal of East Africa, and the Yoraba of West Africa. There is also a history of polygamy in South and East Asia, including China, India , Bangladesh and Pakistan. Polygamy is not common but is practised in North America where it is illegal. Estimates of the number of people living in polygamous families in North America range from 30,000 to 210,000 and is most often associated with Fundamentalist Mormon groups. Gender issues are strong in these families; writing about the Mormons of North America Bala and colleagues conclude:

> There is the potential for competition and rivalry between wives, with some wives and their children favoured over others. Relationships between wives must be managed if familial harmony is to be maintained. Fundamentalist Mormon family structure is highly patriarchal, with the husband being viewed as the head of the household, and the one who will determine his wife's entry into heaven.
>
> (Bala *et al.*, 2005: 7)

World in focus 11.5

Cyber-chattels: buying brides and babies on the net

Those seeking a bride are offered a 'choice of women' 'broken down' into four categories – Asia, Latin, multi-ethnic and Soviet-based . . . Prospective buyers are warned of the extra financial outlay attached to women of certain nationalities: 'Whereas a Thai is unprepared for cold German winters – one has to buy her clothes – a Pole brings her own boots and fur coat. And she is as good in bed and as industrious in the kitchen'.

(Phizacklea, 1996, cited in Letherby and Marchbank, 2003)

The popular discourse surrounding men who buy brides is that they are pathetic and inadequate, unable to attract a woman by the more accepted routes of western courtship. However, Jedlicka's study* of American men seeking mail-order brides found that 94 per cent of the men where white and 50 per cent were college educated. Most were economically and professionally successful, with 64 per cent earning more than $20,000 a year and 42 per cent in professional or managerial positions (Jedlicka, 1988, cited in Glodava and Onizuka, 1994). So, stereotypically at least, it appears that these men were likely to be 'eligible' to women in their own communities and country . . . [Thus] it is possible to argue that the issue is not whether the men themselves are appropriate husband material but . . . that they themselves are rejected contemporary western marriage and partnerships.

Popular discourses surrounding women who offer themselves as brides are frequently judgemental and disapproving, often positioning the women as victims of their husbands and agencies. However, rather than viewing all women on mail-order Internet sites as victimised and exploited it is possible to argue that for some, seeking such a match may be an act of agency. Admittedly it may be interpreted as an act of limited agency, for truly free women would not need to seek such a marriage, but it may be the only kind of agency available to women who are entrapped in social and economic structures which limit their life opportunities. Evidence from the USA supports the conclusion that women are seeking improved life chances by offering themselves on 'bride' sites, for they 'for the most part come from places in which jobs and educational opportunities for women are scarce and wages low'.

*US Government Report on the Mail-Order Bride Industry, at **www.wtw.org/mob/mobappa.htm**)

Source: Adapted from Letherby and Marchbank (2003).

'Other' families: the 'pretend' family: gay and lesbian families

A local government shall not intentionally promote homosexuality . . . as a pretended family relationship.
(Section 2A of the Local Government Act, 1988)

In the 1990s, the then British Prime Minister, Margaret Thatcher, spoke of 'the right of a child to be brought up in a real family' (Reinhold 1994). A 'real' family is one based on a heterosexual relationship. This was made explicit in Section 2A of the 1988 Local Government Act which stipulated that local authorities should not 'promote the teaching in any maintained school of the acceptability of homosexuality as a pretended family relationship'. From this perspective lesbians and gay men could form only 'pretend', not 'real', families. In 2005 same-sex unions gained legal status in Britain with the passing of the Civil Partnership Act, though not full marriage rights – see World in Focus 11.6 for details of gay unions around the world.

It is important to make a distinction between full marriage rights and the more limited civil unions. Although many civil union laws provide similar protections as marriage they are not the same as marriage (see Controversy 11.2).

World in focus 11.6

Gay marriage and other legal unions around the world

➤ Denmark was the first country to grant same-sex partners the same rights as married couples in 1989, though church weddings are not allowed.

➤ Norway, Sweden and Iceland all enacted similar laws in 1996, as did Finland in 2002.

➤ The Netherlands was the first country to offer full civil marriage rights to gay couples in 2001.

➤ Gay marriage was allowed in Belgium in 2003.

➤ Spain legalised full marriage in 2005.

➤ Germany allows same-sex couples to register for 'life partnerships' since 2001; it is limited to inheritance and tenants' rights.

➤ France has a civil contract called the Pacs, introduced in 1999. It gives some rights to cohabiting couples regardless of sex. Luxembourg's 2004 law on civil partnerships is based upon this.

➤ British legislation, 2005, gives same-sex couples in registered relationships similar rights to married couples in areas such as pensions, property, social security and housing.

➤ Canada legalised full same-sex marriage in 2005.

➤ Argentina, the first Latin American country to recognise gay unions, provides rights similar to heterosexual couples, but excluding adoption and inheritance. The first civil union took place in 2003.

➤ New Zealand passed legislation recognising civil unions in 2004.

➤ In the USA several states have passed amendments defining marriage as being between a man and a woman and George W. Bush is pursuing federal legislation to confirm this nationally. Despite this some states, such as Vermont, Massachusetts, Oregon and California have issued marriage licenses to same-sex couples.

Source: Extracted from BBC News at http://news.bbc.co.uk/go/pr/fr/-/2/hi/americas/4081999.stm (accessed August 2006).

Controversy 11.2

Lesbians lose legal marriage bid

In August 2006 a lesbian couple, Celia Kitzinger and Sue Wilkinson lost their High Court case to have their legal Canadian marriage recognised as such in the UK. Here is how they explain their case.

We are a British same-sex couple who legally married in Canada in 2003. For the first two years of our marriage, it had no legal recognition at all in our home country. When the Civil Partnership Act became law (December 2005), we were told our marriage was now deemed a civil partnership. A different-sex couple married in Canada would automatically have had their marriage recognised as a marriage in the UK. We believe that to treat same-sex couples differently from heterosexual couples in this way is deeply discriminatory. (http://www.equalmarriagerights.org)

With the support of the human rights organisation Liberty, we sought a declaration of the validity of our marriage as a marriage in the UK. Our lawyers argued that any failure to recognise the validity of our marriage would constitute a breach of our rights under the European Convention on Human Rights. Our case was heard by the President of the Family Division of the High Court, Sir Mark Potter, on 6–8 June 2006. His judgment was handed down on 31 July. We lost.

The judge agreed that we are treated differently from a heterosexual couple, and that this constitutes discrimination. But he said that this discrimination is justified in order to protect the traditional definition of marriage as between a man and a woman, primarily to produce children. Drawing on British and European case law, he also ruled that a same-sex couple does not constitute 'a family'.

Denying our marriage does nothing to protect heterosexual marriage. It upholds discrimination and inequality. The judgment does not reflect the diversity of marriage and family life in Britain today. It will not stand the test of time.

(Kitzinger and Wilkinson, 2006)

Figure 11.3 Celia and Sue outside court after the judgment

Although lesbians and gay men enjoy some of the rights and legal responsibilities of heterosexuals, lesbians and gay men still have a greater risk of losing their children (i.e. in custody cases) and/or often have more difficulty in having children (i.e. in adoption and fostering and in obtaining infertility treatment) (Liazos, 2004; Arnup, 2005) and there is some suggestion that there are gender differences here, as Katherine Arnup writing about Canada notes:

Darryl Wishard claims, 'more courts have granted lesbian mothers the right to custody of their children than have granted custody to homosexual fathers' (Wishard, 1989). Perhaps the reason for this discrepancy lies in the fact that many gay men choose not to seek custody, either because they are afraid that they will be unsuccessful, or because they, like their heterosexual counterparts, do not wish to have primary care and custody of their children.

(Arnup, 2005: 188)

'Other' families: the 'abnormal' family: technologically assisted families

... the ideology of the family is not only demonstrated but also enhanced by efforts these couples are prepared to expend to become parents. The structure of the conventional form of 2-parents-plus-children is satisfied and the genetic composition begs no questions since the social, nurturing parents are also the genetic parents, so the resultant child is indubitably linked to her/his parents.

(Haimes, 1990: 164)

Infertility treatment involving the egg and sperm of a married or partnered heterosexual couple satisfies the definition and ideology of the 'normal' family. When a child is conceived or borne with the help of donation – of egg, sperm, womb – and is therefore no longer genetically/biologically linked to both parents and family identity is affected. Biological relatives, Strathern claims are not only those who share genes but they are the 'real' relatives. Real relatives, her argument adds, are likely to exercise choice and preference on one another's behalf.

Human kinship is regarded as a fact of society rooted in the facts of nature. Persons we recognize as kin divide into those related by blood or by marriage, that is the outcome of or in prospect of procreation. However, the process of procreation as such is seen as belonging not to the domain of society but to the domain of nature. *Kinship thus connects the two domains* (original emphasis).

(Strathern 1992: 16–17)

Thus, 'real' families are genetically related. However, at times it seems that stereotype builds on stereotype and stigma on stigma and so even though couples who strive for the heterosexual ideal through assisted conception are sometimes defined as 'undeserving':

In March 1991 the so-called 'Virgin Birth' issue was given copy in much of the UK media. The reports focused on the experience of three celibate women who attended a donor insemination clinic ... There is clearly a 'natural' and an 'unnatural' way to conceive ... There is no need to read between the lines to discover that for some commentators it is not the technological aspect of conception that is considered to be 'unnatural' but the sexuality of those concerned: 'the three would-be mothers (apparently for no medical reasons) are determined to maintain their virginity. They have a profound objection to sexual intercourse but a strong desire to enjoy the fruits of such congress ... is it likely that they will prove to be adequate mothers?'

(Leading article in *The Independent*, 12 March 1991: 18) (Letherby 2003: 53)

'Other' families: the 'irresponsible family': the young parent family

In his horrible way Hitler was pointing to a problem that is a constant and, in today's 'underclass', very serious. How do you stop single teenage mothers from breeding up tomorrow's football hooligans?

(Stone, 1989, cited by Phoenix, 1991: 2)

Although teenage pregnancy in the UK is not a recent phenomenon, politically it is an issue that is receiving more attention than ever before. Arguably this is due to the fact that teenage mothers are often reliant on the state for provision of money and housing rather than bringing up their children within the patriarchal family unit (Phoenix, 1991). Teenage pregnancy is regarded as 'often a cause and a consequence of social exclusion' (Social Exclusion Unit, 1999: 17). This notion has led to an abundance of research focusing on 'preventing teenage pregnancy and alleviating the direct negative health and social effects of teenage pregnancy' (NHS CRD, 1997: 2).

Political discourse then individualises the problems of teenage parenthood due to the focus on age rather than an examination of the structural factors that affect young people's lives (Phoenix, 1991). As Ann Phoenix (1991: 86) suggests: 'The negative focus is produced by people who are not, themselves, "young mothers" but rather outsiders. There is generally disjunction between "outsider" and "insider" perspectives.' With early motherhood (and fatherhood) constructed as a social problem these 'outsider' perspectives are ones that are given greater credence rather than the 'insider' perspectives of young mothers themselves.

Teenage pregnancy and parenthood are often associated with single women (Phoenix, 1991); see Controversy 11.3 for one approach to this 'problem'. Lone parenting, which is defined as problematic, is seen as inextricably linked with teenage pregnancy and parenthood. Furthermore, there is concern that because most pregnancies of unmarried teenagers are unplanned, this will have adverse social and health outcomes for both mother and child (Finlay, 1996). The stigmatisation of lone parents impacts on the position of mothers more significantly than fathers due to the fact that the heads of most lone-parent families are female (Robertson Elliot, 1994) and disproportionately affects teenage mothers as 'three-quarters of British women who become mothers in their teenage years do so while single' (Phoenix, 1991: 95). However, as Peckham (1992) notes unplanned does not necessarily mean unwanted and it is important to consider the complex experience of teenage parenthood:

> Some young parents spoke positively about parenting and its impact on their lives. It increased their self-esteem and enhanced their lives, providing a sense of security and stability in lives characterized by transience, detachment and low economic aspirations. However, expectations on them to work or study were seen as unrealistic. Services to help them achieve this – particularly childcare and support for young parents – were seen as poor quality and difficult to access; this undermined their ability to be good parents.
>
> (Teenage Pregnancy Unit, 2004: 3)

All of these 'other' families necessitate the need to consider the family album again (see A Closer Look 11.4).

Controversy 11.3

Marriage age and parenthood in the USA

In the USA all states set a minimum age for marriage without parental consent, this is usually 18 but in some cases 21. Marriage is permitted in many places at 16 with parental consent, however where a pregnancy is involved it can be as young as 14.

Who may marry in Virginia?

Age requirements and consent

> The minimum age for marriage in the Commonwealth of Virginia is 16 years for both bride and groom. If either party is under 18 years old, consent to the marriage must be given in person by the father, mother or legal guardian of the minor. The law permits marriage for a **Virginia resident** under the age of sixteen if the bride is pregnant when seeking a marriage license or has been pregnant within the nine months preceeding examination by a physician, and the parent or guardian of the underage party gives consent.
>
> (Whittle and Hogan, undated)

A closer look 11.4

The family album 2

Families which don't follow the 'expected' family life-course are likely to have unconventional family albums or indeed none at all. The adoptive parent may keep some photographs apart from the public collection to give to their child at a later date. The baby album of the child conceived following medical assistance may contain a picture of a fertilized egg. The couple that doesn't become a family in the accepted sense of what a family is, e.g. one without children, may record different things in different ways. Although stereotypical images of the childless couple dictate that they are more likely to have holiday albums recording scenic views rather than baby albums charting their child's development.

(Cotterill and Letherby, 1993)

Conclusion

The traditional view of the 'family' is simplistic and inaccurate. Family forms, structures and relationships have always been more complex than politicians and some social theorists have suggested. In addition, the so-called 'breakdown' of the traditional family is not the disaster that some would have us believe:

If this diagnosis [that the nuclear family is falling apart] is right, what will take over from the family, that haven of domestic bliss? The family, of course! Only different, more better: the negotiated family, the alternating family, the multiply family, new arrangements about divorce, remarriage, divorce again, new assortments form your, my, our children, our past and present families.

(Beck and Beck-Gernsheim, 1995: 2)

Thus, as David Morgan (1996) argues the family is not a thing, rather it is a fluid set of relationships which changes over time and differs across and within cultures.

Further reading

Jonathon Bradshaw, Christine Skinner, Carol Stimson and Julie Williams (1999), *Absent Fathers?*, London, Routledge. Drawing on data from the ESRC Programme n Population and Household Change this book explores debates around masculinities, men and fatherhood in the context of family breakdown.

Diana L. Gustafson (ed.) (2005), *Unbecoming Mothers, The Social Production of Maternal Absence*, The Haworth Press, New York. The chapters in this collection range across disciplines from Social Policy to Anthropology to Performing Arts to explore the dominant discourses of motherhood. The book explores the experiences of women living apart from their children either by choice or circumstance. The book gives voice to women's real experience, including Aboriginal women in both Canada and Australia; young mothers in care and African-American girls in kinship care.

Journal of LGBT Family Studies – the first journal to address issues of concern to LGBT (lesbian, gay, bisexual, transgender) families. It is an interdisciplinary, peer-reviewed journal and covers a wide range of issues: parent–child relationships; step families; sibling relationships; child development and more.

Websites

Polygamy Studies – a site by the Canadian Broadcasting Company providing access to academic and legal reports regarding polygamy. In addition the site links to other pages detailing the history of polygamy. It is available at **http://www.cbc.ca/fifth/bustupinbountiful/studies.html**

Intute (formerly SOSIG) – a free online service providing access to the very best Web resources for education and research, evaluated and selected by a network of subject specialists. Enter the site and type in *family gender* into the internal search engine and follow your interests. Available at **http://www.intute.ac.uk/socialsciences/**

End of chapter activity

Visit these two websites:

www.infoplease.com/spot/royal3.html

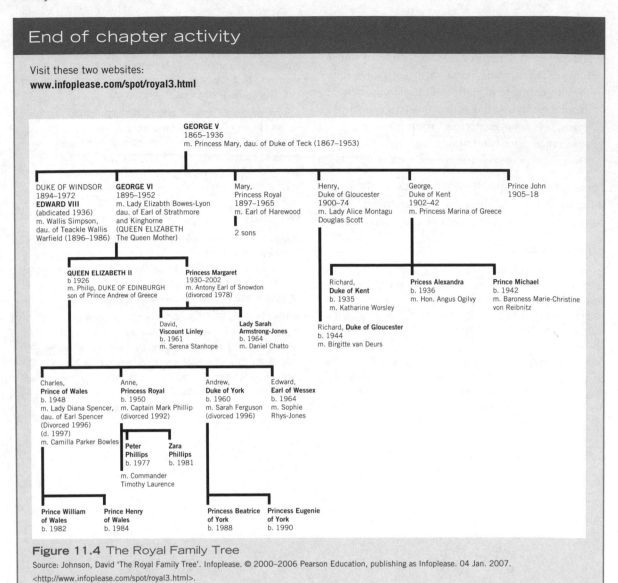

Figure 11.4 The Royal Family Tree

Source: Johnson, David 'The Royal Family Tree'. Infoplease. © 2000–2006 Pearson Education, publishing as Infoplease. 04 Jan. 2007.

<http://www.infoplease.com/spot/royal3.html>.

End of chapter activity continued

And:
www.poshandbecks.cwc.net/

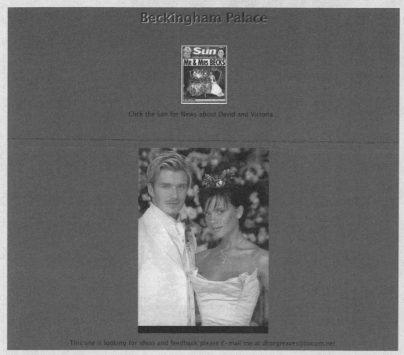

Figure 11.5
Source: www.poshandbecks.cwc.net

Click the Sun for News about David and Victoria . . .
This web site is currently under construction and will eventually aim to STOP the constant barrage of criticism David and Victoria suffer at the hands of the British public . . .

    What do you know about these families which suggest that they differ from the dominant ideal? Make a list of the ideologies that support the family (including ideologies of motherhood/fatherhood/heterosexuality etc.). In what ways are these ideologies gendered, in what ways do they work together, and in what ways are they contradictory?

Chapter 12

Health and Illness

Key issues in this chapter:

➤ Historical and contemporary 'measures' of health and illness in relation to gender.

➤ Mental, emotional, physical and reproductive gendered health issues.

➤ Lifestyles, life-chances, gender and health.

➤ The gendered experience of health care.

➤ The relationship between health, gender and other 'measures' of stratification.

At the end of this chapter you should be able to:

➤ Recognise the significance of different historical and current definitions and measures of health and illness.

➤ Explain the relationship between gender roles, masculinity and femininity, and health and illness.

➤ Understand the gendered aspects of health care.

➤ Recognise the need to take a gendered perspective, whilst acknowledging that other measures of stratification (e.g. class, ethnicity and age) are also important.

Introduction

The dawn of gender-specific drugs

By Vivienne Parry, presenter of *One Man's Medicine*

Some medicines that are safe for men are known to be lethal for women. But until recently, many medicines were not tested on women. Now that they are, more differences between the ways men and women respond to drugs are being discovered all the time. Could this be the beginning of gender prescribing?

Radio 4's *One Man's Medicine* takes a look at why men and women are so different when it comes to taking their medicine.

'What's not good science is to treat half the population with a drug you haven't tested on them' said Professor Lesley Doyal.

One Man's Medicine, a three-part series, was broadcast on Radio 4 between 6 and 20 August 2003.

Stop and think 12.1

With reference to the extract above why do you think it has taken so long for pharmaceutical industries to decide to test drugs on women as well as men. Also, can you identify any problems with the title of the programme on which this news was announced?

The relationship between gender and health began to be taken seriously in the 1970s. As A. Cribb (2000) notes it was then that gender began to be considered alongside other variables such as 'race' and ethnicity, socio-economic status, and geographical area when explaining patterns and experience of health and illness. It is no coincidence that at the same time there was also a growth in feminist research and in the activity of the women's movement, both of which contributed directly to the growth of the women's health movement. However, at this time researchers equated studies of gender, health and illness almost exclusively with women. It was the growth of interest in men's studies in the 1980s that led to consideration of the relationship between concepts of health, masculinity, men's lives and their experience of illness (Cribb, 1997).

However, despite the growing recognition of the importance of gender differences when explaining patterns of health and illness they are arguably still not taken seriously enough:

> masculine bodies can claim to 'represent' the interests of all other bodies. Male bodies can thus claim to literally incorporate other bodily interests within their own, including the interests of health, because they are the bodies which are seen to incarnate the desirable social order. Hence the health of the heterosexual male body can be made to stand for the health of the body politic in its entirety. Conversely, a threat to the health of this body can seem like a comprehensive threat to public health.
>
> (Walby, 1996: 342)

As we shall see this can have negative consequences for women and for men.

In this chapter we look at how gender differences have been present in health debates and practices, historically and contemporarily. Then we examine mental health, followed by a discussion on lifestyles and identities in relation to health issues. Reproductive issues are a very gendered area and these are presented next. We then turn to the issues of gendered health care and different differences.

'Measuring' gender differences in health: past, present and future

Historically we know that there are parallels in the way sexual difference and racial difference have been considered. In the development of eugenic policies from the middle ages through to the middle of the twentieth century analogies were drawn between women and non-European peoples in terms of physiological characteristics and psychological characteristics. Both women and colonised people were viewed as inherently primitive. For example, Darwin commented, 'some at least of those mental traits in which women may excel are traits characteristic of the lower race', and the craniologist F. Pruner argued, 'The Negro resembles the female in his love of children, his family and his cabin' (cited by Alsop *et al.*, 2002: 19–20).

Still thinking historically we know that the sixteenth and seventeenth centuries were particularly significant to our current understanding of the relationship between gender, health and illness in the western world. The scientific knowledge which emerged at the time insisted that women were not just different from but physically, psychologically and socially inferior to men (Doyal, 1995: 2). Women were thought to be 'sensitive, intuitive, incapable of objectivity and emotional detachment and immersed in the business of making and maintaining personal relationships' (Oakley, 1981: 38). Therefore they were considered naturally weak and easy to exploit and their psychological characteristics implied subordination, for example, submission, passivity, dependency and so on. If women adopted these characteristics they are considered well adjusted (Miller, 1976; Oakley, 1981), if deficit in relation to the male 'ideal'.

In the nineteenth century, middle-class women were thought to be particularly weak and susceptible to illness: menstruation was thought to be an 'indisposition' or illness which sapped women's energy, making it necessary for them to rest; childbirth was termed 'confinement' and a long period of bed rest was thought to be necessary after the birth of a baby; and the menopause was considered a disease which marked the beginning of senility (Webb, 1986). Working-class women though were not believed to be susceptible to the same problems: they were seen as physically stronger and emotionally less sensitive and well able to work 14 hours a day outside of the home and still be able to 'cook, clean and service their husbands, and bear children without such suffering' (Webb, 1986: 6). In addition, working-class women were seen as potentially polluting through their work in the kitchen, the nursery and the brothel (Abbott *et al.*, 2005). Historically then middle-class women were considered 'sickly' and working-class women 'sickening'. Our view of the ill/healthy man is of course also historically and socially constructed. Just as social definitions of femininity are key to an understanding of a healthy woman social definitions of masculinity are

key to definitions of a 'well-shaped man' (Buchbinder, 1998: 355).

There are of course legacies from historical 'measures' and explanations. Evidence from recent research suggests that women appear to feel less healthy than men and perceive themselves to be more ill than men making more use of health services (Annandale and Clark, 1996; Cribb, 2000). In addition when asked to think of someone they think of as healthy both men and women are likely to choose a man (Blaxter, cited by Miers, 2000). Furthermore, research suggests that psychologists and clinicians are more likely to define women's rather than men's health problems as psychological and definitions of mental health are often related to traditional, essentialist notions of masculinity and femininity: healthy men are thought to be independent, logical and adventurous and healthy women less aggressive, more emotional and easily hurt (Teri, 1982; Webb, 1986; Buchbinder, 1998; Miers, 2000). In addition it is argued that women's lives are more closely scrutinised by (patriarchal) medical science through the manufacture and mass-production of drugs designed to control the natural process of women's bodies from menstruation to menopause (Oudshoorn, 1994; Abbott *et al.*, 2005).

In A Closer Look 12.1 we provide evidence of differential perceptions of gendered health status.

This construction of women's health as poor has consequences for men too in that there is an implicit assumption that men's health is 'good' (Annandale

---

A closer look 12.1

Gender differences in health perceptions

The Oxford Regional Health Authority Lifestyle Survey of 13,000 randomly selected adults living in Berkshire, Buckinghamshire and Northamptonshire provides helpful data relating to exercise, smoking, alcohol consumption and dietary habits . . . More female than male respondents described their health status as poor, although they reported fewer examples of health-damaging behaviour.

(Cribb, 1997: 229)

and Clark, 1996; Watson, 2000). The result of this is that men's poor health remains invisible and this is problematic because 'it is important to look at the social context of men's health . . . [and] the assumption of absolute difference undermines our ability even to understand women's health (as different)' (Annandale and Clark, 1996: 32).

Stop and think 12.1

Describe a healthy person. Does your description fit the average male and/or the average woman?

Attention to twentieth-century mortality and morbidity rates show that the phrase 'women get sick and men die', does have some truth in it but is an over-simplification when studying the complex relationship between gender, health and illness (Annandale, 1998; Miers, 2000). Pamela Abbott and colleagues (2005) point out that a gendered health pattern is found in all societies with women on average living longer than men. However, there are social class differences between women within societies and the male–female gap in life expectancy varies significantly between countries. Russia has the largest male–female gap in life expectancy in the world of about fourteen years whereas in some countries in South East Asia, as well as parts of sub-Saharan and West Africa the gap is much smaller or even eliminated altogether, mainly, Abbott and colleagues add, due to the low value placed on female children:

A study conducted at a family health centre in Bangladesh . . . found that boys were seen more than twice as often by doctors as girls. In India and Latin America girls are often immunized later than boys or not at all. In some places, boys tend to be given more and better food than girls. Breastfeeding and weaning practices are also thought to favour boys in many developing countries. Hence, 'surveys of girls' and young women's health show that, globally speaking, childhood is a period of relative inequality.
(United Nations, 2003: 25, cited by Abbott et al., 2005: 121)

In societies where women do live longer it is inevitably the case that women make more use of health services as health service use increases with age. In addition when consultations related to menstruation, pregnancy, childbirth, post-natal care and menopause are taken into account it is not surprising that women visit the doctor more often. Furthermore, as Miers (2000) notes women appear to find it easier to discuss their own health and may find it more socially acceptable to do so and Watson (2000) suggests that also important are psychosocial factors such as how men and women evaluate symptoms.

Research suggests that men are reluctant to listen to health promotion messages and to go to the doctor for 'minor' complaints. Men's denial of illness is so strong that even the pain associated with a heart attack may be ignored so that the victim will not be seen as weak or effeminate (Cribb, 2000). Despite this a popular view among many women is that: '[t]o the average man, a bad cold has five-act potential and he will use it to extract every last drop of sympathy' (Watson, 2000: 17). On the other hand there is research that suggests that women are more likely than men to 'suffer in silence'. For example, Jocelyn Cornwell (1984), in her study in Bethnal Green found that women regarded themselves as 'not ill' if they could continue to 'carry on' caring for their home and family.

One response to socially constructed essentialist definitions and explanations of health and illness and sexism in health care (see below) has been the production of books that have been written with the aim of informing individuals about their own bodies and their own health. A Closer Look 12.2 provides some more detail on such publications.

A closer look 12.2

Self-help, books and gender specific services

A number of books providing health information by women for women hit bookstores in North America and the UK in the 1970s (perhaps the most well-known being *Our Bodies Our Selves*, first published by the Boston Women's Health Book Collective in 1973). Although these were written by women and were grounded in women's experiences as Hockey (1997) notes these early texts were relevant mostly for white middle-class audiences. It was not until the 1980s that books aimed at black, lesbian, working-class and older women began to appear. There are less books even today specifically concerned with men's health although, as Watson (2000) notes, during the 1990s men's health was an increasing concern within the media with reports on increasing stress and incidences of cancer and declining fertility and reluctance to visit the doctor. The mid-1990s saw the launch of two magazines dedicated to men and health and the first national conference in Britain on men's health (Cribb, 1997). One recent attempt in the UK to encourage men to pay more attention to their health has been the production of a men's health manual modelled on the car manuals produced by Haynes and the introduction of a Men's Health Helpline.

Mental health and psychological well-being

Statistics suggest that about twice as many women than men suffer from a mental disorder. Yet, it is important to note that there are distinctive gender patterns associated with different mental phenomena. For example, anorexia nervosa is a predominantly female condition and women report rates for anxiety, phobias and depression twice as often as men. On the other hand substance use disorders are more common among men than women and diagnoses of schizophrenia, paranoia or mania do not show a gender preference (Doyal, 1995; Busfield, 1996).

So how can we explain these differences? Joan Busfield (1996) argues that men and women respond differently to psychological problems and stressors on their lives. It appears that women are more likely to find supportive 'significant others' to discuss problems with or engage in self-harming behaviour whilst men are more likely to engage in excessive drinking, aggression or violence. This is not to say that women do not sometimes feel aggressive or violent; interestingly though this appears to be most 'newsworthy' when linked to women's hormones which are often portrayed as being unstable, as A Closer Look 12.3 demonstrates.

Violent tendencies

A survey of 400 women with moderate to severe PMS [premenstrual syndrome], carried out by the Natural Health Advisory Service, found that eight out of 10 women feel violent and aggressive for up to two weeks before their period, with 73 per cent claiming their sex drive takes a nose drive.

'PMS has caused great upset in my relationship' says 22-year-old Jemma. 'I have a wonderful, supportive partner, but when I'm premenstrual I don't want him anywhere near me. My perspective on how I feel about him changes completely, it's a horrible feeling.'

If 90 per cent of women suffer to some degree from PMS, then it's also safe to say that a number of families and partners must also feel the strain each month. A survey by website netdoctor.co.uk questioned 1,000 men, with two-thirds admitting they were subjected to irrational behaviour, heated arguments and floods of tears by their premenstrual partners.

Alarmingly, 13 per cent of 15- to 24-year-old men said they'd been physically assaulted by partners with PMS. 'I've seen men who have had to sleep in the car or garden shed because they cannot live with their wives and girlfriends when they are premenstrual' says Stewart.

Source: Christine Morgan 'Beat PMS for good', *Healthy*, March 2006, Issue 42: 11.

It is widely agreed that men in contemporary western societies find it difficult to express their emotions adequately. This failure to express emotions, in addition to the urge to be independent (which itself is encouraged by cultural definitions of masculinity) may significantly affect men's health-related behaviour and their ill/health status (Cribb, 2000). Cribb (2000) adds that part of men's resistance to acknowledging illness may be due to their fear of becoming dependent on women as carers because we know that contrary to the stereotypical view that women are dependent on men (Millett, 1969), it is actually girls and women who are brought up to care for children, husbands and other family members [**Hotlink → Family (Chapter 11)**].

With reference to formal mental health care in the UK for most of the twentieth century women made up most of the patient population in institution-based care. But in 1991 for the first time, men were in the majority in the population in mental health beds in England and Wales. Since then statistics suggest that women and men have become equal users of these services (Hayes and Prior, 2003). Although neglected in the past, the mental health care needs of men – particularly young men – need to be taken seriously by academics, by health planners and by men themselves (Hayes and Prior, 2003) as A Closer Look 12.4 suggests.

A closer look 12.4

Changing suicide rates

Over the past 15 years, suicide rates in the UK have declined in women yet risen steadily in men. This is particularly noticeable in young males aged 15–24, where the suicide rate has increased by 75 per cent since 1982 (DoH, 1992). Possible explanations for these changes include: the threat of unemployment, the greater independence of women, the reluctance of men to seek help, and men's often inadequate social networks (Cribb, 2000).

Public and private lifestyles and identities

Feminists argue that women's poorer health is explained by the fact that women are socially disadvantaged in terms of education, income and political influence: women have less money than men, less financial security, less desirable employment, and less political and social power (Annandale, 1998). In addition Sarah Payne (1991) adds that women's primary position in the home and secondary position in the labour market indicates both their economic dependence on men and their greater vulnerability to poverty and deprivation. This is important because socio-economic status, however it is measured, is a strong predictor of longevity and of health. As World in Focus 12.1 shows there are worldwide gender inequalities in health.

The main causes of death in women in the western world are breast cancer and cancers of the genito-urinary system whereas men suffer from higher rates of coronary heart disease, lung cancer and chronic obstructive airways disease, accidents, homicides, suicides and until recently AIDS (Hayes and Prior 2003;

World in focus 12.1

World Health Organisation

The Department of Gender, Women and Health (GWH) brings attention to the ways in which biological and social differences between women and men affect health and the steps needed to achieve health equity.

The main focus of GWH is to promote the inclusion of gender perspectives in the work of the WHO by collaborating with other departments and regional and country offices. It aims to increase knowledge of gender issues by conducting selected research, training and advocacy on how socio-cultural factors and discrimination affect health.

Whilst gender affects the health of both men and women, the department places special emphasis on the health consequences of discrimination against women that exist in nearly every culture. Powerful barriers including poverty, unequal power relationships between men and women, and lack of education prevent millions of women around the world from having access to health care and from attaining – and maintaining – the best possible health.

Source: **www.who.int/gender/en/**

Miers, 2000). As World in Focus 12.2 demonstrates the gendered experience of AIDS is changing.

Men are more likely to die of occupationally related illnesses, men engage in more physical risk-taking than women, and accidents and homicides have always been a feature of masculine rather than feminine behaviours. In addition, cigarette smoking has, hitherto, been a major cause of male death (although in the 1990s male and female smoking rates in the UK began to even out and recent reports suggest that more girls than boys are taking up smoking at the beginning of the twenty-first century), men drink more than women, and are more likely to die of alcohol related deaths (including those in motor vehicle accidents). However, men's higher level of exercise participation may counteract some of the health disadvantages apparently resulting from men's less healthy lifestyles (Miers, 2000).

One explanation for such differences, in both medical and lay discourse, is that poor men's health results from their trying to live up to a macho image and lifestyle which is itself dangerous to health. From this perspective much ill-health among men is a consequence of lifestyle. However, as Watson (2000) notes the challenge to change male behaviour and resist stereotypical masculinity is problematic because it presumes that masculinity is a unitary construct and that all men benefit equally from being male in a patriarchal society.

With reference to the relationship between gender, health and the home it seems that marriage is good for physical health and in the UK married people are much lower users than non-married people of health care services. But marriage appears to be more advantageous to the health of men than the health of women. Married men have lower death rates than those who have never married, and married men report better health than single men. Miles (1991) suggests that this may be due to the presence or absence of a significant female partner (carer) who encourages her male partner to seek medical help when they need it and sets the tone for a healthy life. However, being a 'good' wife and mother can actually make women sick. Evidence suggests that women prioritise the needs of other family members allocating them more resources and caring for them to the detriment of their own health, often because this is expected of them (Doyal, 1995; Abbott et al., 2005):

> They [women] are seen as responsible for bringing up healthy children and maintaining the health of their men for the nation. Health visitors, social workers and other professional state employees 'police' the family to ensure that women are carrying out their task adequately.
>
> (Abbott et al., 2005: 196)

Furthermore, the family home can be a dangerous place for many women and children who live in danger of ill-health, even death, as the result of men's emotional, psychological, sexual and physical violence [**Hotlink → Violence and Resistance (Chapter 16)**].

Despite enduring stereotypical views of women as weak and helpless worldwide they remain responsible for large amounts of physical and emotional labour – both unpaid and paid (Coppock et al., 1995; Evans, 1997; Frith and Kitzinger, 1998) [**Hotlink → Work and Leisure (Chapter 14); Hotlink → Family (Chapter 11)**]. However, even though women are now more evident within the workplace research and debate on the

---

World in focus 12.2

The global picture of aids

According to UNAIDS data, there were about 33.6 million people infected with the AIDS/HIV virus (UN Yearbook, 2000). In 1999 half of the AIDS mortality cases were women: about 12.7 million cases. Data now shows that women are the main victims of the AIDS crisis and the disease is spreading faster among women than men. Contrary to popular belief the majority of AIDS infection is 'through husbands/wives sexual contacts, heterosexual relations, homosexuality, prostitution, blood transfusion, mother to infants through placenta and breast feeding, and through contaminated blood and blood products'.

(Umerah-Udezula, 2001: 1–2)

Figure 12.1 What she needs is a prescription
Source: WEA (1986) *Women and Health*, p. 87. Reproduced with thanks to Angela Martin.

relationship between work and ill-health has focused on male-dominated occupations. It is widely believed that female jobs are neither physically hazardous nor stressful but recent research into nursing and clerical work demonstrates otherwise (Doyal, 1995). This sexist bias in occupational health research is further extended by traditional assumptions of women's weaknesses, reflected in the fact that although a significant amount of research has been conducted to determine whether or not menstruation interferes with women's capacity to work there has been much less interest in how women's work affects their experiences of menstruation (Doyal, 1995). A Critical Look 12.1 provides further examples of how work outside of the home can adversely affect women's health.

A critical look 12.1

Campaign to boost women workers' health

TUC General Secretary . . . said 'Women make up half the workforce. But health and safety standards are still set for the 'average man' and injury compensation is still paid mostly to men' . . . A 1995 report by the Health and Safety Executive suggests women are more likely than men to suffer from a range of injuries:

➤ They are more likely to suffer from work-related skin diseases than men and often suffer a double dose of exposure to chemicals due to their work in the home.

➤ Twice as many women suffer from eyestrain, mostly related to VDU work, than men.

➤ Women are a third more likely to report that they have been physically attacked by a member of the public in their work than men.

Part of the reason for the discrepancies is that women tend to be concentrated in professions that cause certain types of health hazards. For example, hairdressers have a high level of skin problems because of the chemicals involved. Women are also more likely to be working in the caring professions, such as nursing, which bring them into close contact with the public and which are associated with a high level of physical violence.

And they tend to be more exposed than men to repetitive and monotonous work which increase the danger of repetitive strain injury.

The Health and Safety Executive (HSE) says it has concentrated on risks related to specific jobs, rather than gender issues. It adds that men are more likely to suffer some health problems than women. For example, they are more than seven times more likely to suffer from deafness, three times more prone to work-related asthma and bronchitis and more likely to suffer from stress.

Source: BBC News 25 August 1999.

Reproduction and reproductive health

It is commonly assumed that the issue of reproductive health is 'women's business' and arguably for some women this assumption has been instrumental in their control over reproduction. It has also been the cornerstone of many feminist campaigns, which have demanded the right for women to 'control their own bodies' (Petchesky, 1986; Himmelweit, 1988; Kitzinger, 1992). However, the majority of women do not make reproductive choices in isolation from men (Earle and Letherby, 2003) and men both as medics and as partners have significant influence. For example:

. . . medical dominance in these areas of women's lives means that women are controlled to a large extent by medical men, and they rely on doctors for advice and information. For example, pregnant women are treated 'as if' something is going to go wrong – women are required to make regular ante-natal visits and are virtually forced to have their babies in hospital, where doctors control the management of labour and childbirth . . .

The key point is not that medical intervention has played no role in making pregnancy and childbirth safer, but that doctors have taken over total control of the management of pregnant women, so that women are unable to make informed decisions about their lives . . .

Doctors control the most effective means of birth control – the pill, the coil, the cap, and sterilisation. Women have to seek medical advice to be able to use these methods of controlling their fertility. The 1968 Abortion Reform law made abortion on medical grounds legal and more frequently available, but the decision as to whether a woman can have an abortion is made by doctors. Doctors also control the new reproductive technologies.

(Abbott *et al.*, 2005; 184)

. . . [a] recent example in the UK is the case of Stephen Hone who went to the High Court to stop his pregnant ex-girlfriend having an abortion (*Birmingham Evening Post*, 2001). Relevant also are cases of men instructing medics to maintain life support for their pregnant partners until the baby/ies were capable of surviving outside of the womb (Hartouni, 1997).

(Earle and Letherby, 2003: 4)

In addition, the labelling of an illness or a condition as 'women's business' has serious medical, social and emotional consequences for women as Frank van Balen and Inhorn's (2002: 7–8) comment on infertility (a condition that is often viewed to have its routes in psychological 'disorders' and therefore to be women's rather than men's business) demonstrates:

women worldwide appear to bear the major burden of infertility, in terms of blame for the reproductive failing; personal anxiety, frustration, grief, and fear; marital duress, dissolution, and abandonment; social stigma and community ostracism; and, in some cases, life-threatening medical interventions.

Research clearly highlights that infertility is an emotional as well as a medical experience and the inability to have children when one wants can have serious consequences to a woman's sense of self. For example:

'People can tell by looking at me that I'm handicapped. A failure to womankind . . . I'm like half a woman.' (Tracey)

'There are times when I don't feel like a real woman. I wonder how am I ever going to feel that whole.' (Gloria) (respondents from a research project conducted by Letherby, 1999: 363)

Yet it is important to acknowledge that men's self-esteem is likewise affected:

'I was worried then and now about other people finding out about my infertility. I feel I just couldn't cope with people knowing. I was in the pub once with some friends and there was talk about a male friend getting his wife pregnant and having proved himself. That remark still haunts me. I thought, what are they going to think about me if they find out I have no sperm? What will they say behind my back? I'm not a macho man but I work in an all-male environment where there are lots of crude jokes about sex and related things and I don't want to be the butt of those jokes about a seedless Jaffa*. I don't know what I would have done if someone had said that about me because social reaction bothers me though I know it shouldn't. I'm a married man, but we couldn't have a family because of something I couldn't do and that hurts. I have had to keep quiet about my infertility to protect my self-respect.'

(Matthew, respondent from a study by Mason, 1993: 91–2)

*A Jaffa is a seedless orange

Note how these individuals' concern is linked to conceptions of themselves as adequate women or men.

Stop and think 12.3

Research suggests that women who are unable to have children when they want them are subject to pity from others. Infertile men on the other hand often experience hostile humour from other men (see the account from Matthew above). Why do you think this is?

Whereas in the western world feminists are concerned with women's control over their own reproductive bodies worldwide concerns are sometimes more about maternal and child morbidity and mortality. World in Focus 12.3 demonstrates why.

The inescapable fact is that 20 million women submit to unsafe abortion every year. In some countries, it is the most common cause of maternal death (Figure 12.2).

Figure 12.2 When abortion isn't an option – some women have a stab at it anyway

Source: Agency: McCanns Manchester. Copywriter: Neil Lancaster. Art Director: Dave Price. Reprinted with permission of Marie Stopes International.

Gendered health care

There is evidence that women have always practised medicine and been involved in healing the sick (e.g. Verslusyen, 1981; Webb, 1986). The 'housewife' role in pre-industrial society encompassed a much wider remit than it does today and was synonymous with healing. Women knew about painkillers, digestive aids and anti-inflammatory agents. The care of infants and women in childbirth was also part of their role. Women healers possessed knowledge not available to men and were highly respected within their communities (Webb, 1986). Between 1300 and 1700, 'medicine' emerged as a male profession and female healers were suppressed although there are different views on why this happened with some writers linking the suppression of female healing to changes associated with the industrial revolution whilst others blame the witch-hunts (for a further discussion see Letherby, 2003b). What is clear is that the development of medicine as a science and a profession is also an example of how the making of knowledge, culture and ideology was an integral part of the development of capitalism (e.g. Smith, 1988). Medical science became 'masculine' science. The establishment of qualified medical guilds was instrumental in the displacement of women healers as was the development of hospitals and when women did become (re)involved in medicine it was as nurses under the regulation of doctors (Garmarnikow, 1978; Hearn, 1982; Hockey, 1993). The medical man-

World in focus 12.3

Maternal and child mortality

➤ Every day 1,600 women die in pregnancy and childbirth.

➤ Each year over 60 million women suffer acute complications from pregnancy.

➤ Around 20 million women sustain debilitating lifelong injuries or infections.

➤ Complications of pregnancy and delivery are the leading cause of death among reproductive-age women in developing countries.

➤ Every year, 1.4 million infants are stillborn and 1.5–2.5 million infants die in the first week of life from complications related to their mothers' pregnancy or experienced during delivery.

➤ 1 million or more children are left motherless each year by women who die from pregnancy-related causes.

➤ Motherless children are 2 to 10 times more likely to die within two years than children who live with both parents.

Source: Unicef – printed in 'Birth Matters: a special supplement of reproductive health in the developing world', *Guardian* 2004: 5

agement of childbirth, childcare, dying and death changed 'from a structure of control located in a community of untrained women, to one based on a profession of formally trained men' (Oakley, 1979: 18). Although of course we have women doctors now men still predominate, especially in specialisms considered to be high-skill and heroic and nursing remains a female dominated profession that is subservient to the medical profession.

Stop and think 12.4

Mind puzzle: A young boy is involved in a car accident and is taken to the local Accident and Emergency Department. His father travels with him in the ambulance. Once in the hospital the doctor assigned to treat the child approaches his bed, gasps and says 'I cannot treat him'. Why?

Of course it's because the doctor is the child's mother and medics are not supposed to treat family members but because we (often) assume that doctors are male (we often put the word lady or woman to denote a female doctor or indeed a female artist, writer, lecturer and so on) it often takes people a long time to work this puzzle out. Can you explain this?

It has long been argued that diseases and illnesses that proportionately affect men in greater numbers receive more resources than those that affect women more often. Writers now argue that it is not just that 'men's diseases' are taken more seriously but that male patients are too. Doyal (1998) argues that the continuing failure to include women in sufficient numbers either in epidemiological research or in clinical trials has made it difficult to investigate gender differences or to asses the overall significance of gender in the delivery of effective care.

Although men sometimes appear to find it difficult to communicate with health professionals women seem to find it even harder, both because of their socialisation and the stereotypical views that others have of them (Doyal, 1998). One example of sexist treatment is women's experience of breast cancer. Wilkinson and Kitzinger (1994) argue that the cultural

emphasis on breasts as objects of male sexual interest and male sexual pleasure is relevant within treatment. They suggest that 'Page 3' mentality [**Hotlink** → **see Culture and Mass Media (Chapter 18)**] is reproduced in the medical and psychological literature, as well as in the material produced by major cancer charities. Thus, the implicit assumption throughout is that women's breasts are there for men's sexual pleasure with the woman who has a mastectomy described as mutilated or disfigured.

Obviously, it is not only women who are disempowered by the health service. Male members of economically and ethnically marginalised or disadvantaged groups are likely to find it hard too. However, because of their reluctance to access services, white heterosexual middle-aged men – the so-called privileged group – are visible in public health literature but relatively invisible in practice (Watson, 2000). Sexist assumptions then affect the treatment and care available both for women and for men. However, it is important not to assume that individuals are completely passive in health-care encounters as women and men resist and challenge treatment and behaviour that they experience as inappropriate (Coyle, 1999).

It is possible to argue that sexist care reflects sexist policy. As Hayes and Prior (2003) note two of the most important developments in health policy in the UK in the early twentieth century were highly gendered in their impact. The first was a public health programme aimed at improving the health of children which highlighted poor mothering as the cause of children's poor health and the second, the introduction of National Health Insurance for employed people, which excluded most women and all children from the scheme. The National Health Service introduced in 1948, led to a rapid expansion in all areas of health service delivery, including a steady increase in the number of in-patient beds. As previously noted, this expansion had more of an impact on women than on men in that childbirth became medicalised. The 1970s saw the introduction of community care policies, which led to the discharge from hospital of thousands of people with a mental illness or learning disability. This in turn, led to an increasing burden on family carers, most of whom were women which takes us full-circle in our identification of women as the main carers within society.

Different differences

Of course differences of age, class, sexuality, ethnicity and so on are also relevant to our experience of health, illness and health care and all of these intersect with gender. Educational status, car ownership and housing tenure are also significant.

Taking ethnicity as an example, we know that 'race' adversely affects black women's and men's experiences in relation to health (and indeed all other areas of social life). Yet, 'race' is not a coherent category and the lives of those usually classified together under the label 'black' can be very different. Thus, culture, class, religion, nationality, sexuality, age and so on in addition to gender, can all have an impact on women's and men's lives and it is necessary to challenge the homogeneity of experience previously ascribed to women by virtue of being 'black'. For example, as Douglas (1998) notes the health status of black and minority ethnic women in the UK reflects the interaction between their experiences of 'race', gender, class and culture. So, health and well-being are determined in these groups of women by a complex mixture of social and psychological influences and biological and genetic factors. Black women are not an homogeneous group with uniform needs:

> They may be South Asian, Asian, Chinese, Vietnamese, African or African-Caribbean. They may have been born in the UK, may have migrated recently and may be refugees. They may have disabilities, be older, be lesbian. In attempting to examine the need for appropriate health services for black and minority ethnic women the similarities and differences in needs for black women must always be paramount.
>
> (Douglas 1998: 70)

Further as Maynard (1994a) points out individuals do not have to be black to experience racism as attention to the historical and contemporary experience of Jewish and Irish people demonstrates.

In the above example we see the intersection of ethnicity and gender. Now let us consider the intersections of class, occupation, education and gender. Social class continues to be a major factor determining the health of working age men and women but it is important to also acknowledge that whether or not a person is in paid employment is significant in terms of health status. For example a middle-aged man who loses his job is twice as likely to die in the next five years as a man who remains employed. In addition educational qualifications increasingly differentiate health in the working age group, especially among women (Arber and Cooper, 2000). World in Focus 12.4 provides an example of how morbidity rates reflect differential status in Australia.

For our final example focusing on the significance of different differences we return again to AIDS, this time focusing on black gay men's experience of AIDS. As Susan D. Cochran and Vickie M. Mays (2004, originally 1998), argue, focusing specifically on research in the United States of America, prior to the appearance of AIDS in the USA studies on the sexual preferences and behaviours of gay men usually ignored the specific experience of black men. Cochran and Mays (2004) add that following AIDS little has changed. Thus, whilst researchers usually recognise the importance of cultural differences, their approach has been to assume that black gay men would be more like white gay men than black heterosexuals. However, given the differences that have been observed in family structure and sexual patterns between black and white heterosexuals there is no empirical basis upon which to

World in focus 12.4

Health in Australia

Indigenous people, particularly those who have been colonised by members of dominant and powerful western cultures, experience very poor health. Although mortality statistics do not necessarily reflect the whole experience of women's health, the difference in life expectancy for indigenous and non-indigenous women in Australia – 63.8 and 79.9 years respectively – is so large that it cannot be ignored.

Source: Australian Bureau of Statistics (1995), Lee (1998: 10).

assume that black gay men's experience of homosexuality would perfectly mimic that of white gay men. This lack of attention to the differential experience of black and white men may have serious consequences:

> In the absence of a set of questions or framework incorporating important cultural, ethnic and economic realities of Black gay men, interpretations emanating from a White gay male standard may be misleading . . . There may be a reluctance among Black gay and bisexual men to engage in risk reduction behaviours because of the perception by some members of the Black community that AIDS is a 'gay white disease', or a disease of intravenous drug users (Mays and Cochran, 1987). In addition many risk reduction programmes are located within outreach programmes of primarily White gay organizations. These organizations often fail to attract extensive participations by Black gay men . . . Relative risk refers to the importance of AIDS in context with other social realities. For example, poverty, with its own attendant survival risks may outweigh the fear of AIDS in a teenager's decision to engage in male prostitution. Economic privilege, more common in the White gay community, assists in permitting White gay men to focus their energies and concerns on the AIDS epidemic. For Black gay men of lesser economic privilege other pressing realities of life may, to some extent, diffuse such concerns.
>
> (Cochran and Mays, 2004: 541–2)

Conclusion

Overall although there are differences between male and female bodies and male and female patterns of health and illness these patterns are more complicated than biology alone (Doyal, 1995). Whilst we need to acknowledge the significance of biology we need also to look for social explanations of health and illness. It is important then not to rely on sexist stereotypes of 'male' and 'female' patterns of health and illness and to challenge these stereotypes when they permeate routines and experiences and consequences of health care.

Further reading

Ellen Annandale and Kate Hunt (eds) (1999), *Gender Inequalities in Health*, Buckingham, Open University. This book starts with a broad discussion of developments in gender research and moves on to examine 'established wisdom' about gender and health, for example that women are more often sick and men die quicker. The chapters offer a critical examination of gender inequalities in health covering three decades. Mainly about Britain but there are also discussions of the USA and Eastern Europe.

Bernadette C. Hayes and Pauline M. Prior (2003), *Gender and Health Care in the United Kingdom: Exploring the Stereotypes*, Houndsmills: Palgrave Macmillan. This UK book provides a detailed examination of gender differences in the health needs. Key debates explored include the interrelation of age and gender and health; does marital status affect health? amongst others. Full of empirical information.

The Journal of Men's Health and Gender – contents listing available online at **http://www.jmhg.org/**. This journal is international in focus and aims to integrate both professional and lay perspectives and knowledge. A vast number of issues are covered, including genetics, gerontology, mental health, sports medicine and family and primary care amongst others.

Journal of Gender, Culture and Health – this journal covers biobehavioural, developmental, and psychosocial aspects of gender that relate to the health of men and women. It contains both theoretical and experimental articles. Abstracts are available online at:
http://www.ingentaconnect.com/content/klu/joog

Websites

World Health Organisation – **http://www.who.org**. The WHO is the United Nations' specialised agency for health, established in 1948. The website is an excellent international resource of information and research issues. Type 'gender' into the internal search engine and follow links that interest you.

Department of Health – the UK government site. The link here is for the publications pages, again type 'gender' in the internal search engine and follow the links:
http://www.dh.gov.uk/PublicationsAndStatistics/fs/

End of chapter activity

1. Re-read Stop and think 12.1. Having read this chapter what arguments can you make for health research that considers gender differences and similarities?

2. Go to the newsagents and look for magazines that focus on health and healthy living. Are the messages for men different from those for women?

Education

At the end of this chapter you should be able to:

➤ Discuss and explain differential rates of access to, and achievement in, education globally.

➤ Differentiate between formal and hidden curricula, outlining examples of both.

➤ Understand standard measures such as the Gender Parity Index and Percentage Performance measure.

➤ Describe and understand trends, patterns and debates regarding the gender gap in educational achievement.

➤ Relate your own educational biography to the material and issues in this chapter.

Introduction

Figure 13.1 Two school entrances

Source: Morton Primary, built 1909, picture 2005 © J. Marchbank.

Stop and think 13.1

Look at the pictures in Figure 13.1. They are of a state school built in 1909 that is still in operation today, though the children no longer use these doors as entrances. What gender messages do these pictures convey to you? What statements regarding gender would have been conveyed to a child in 1909, even 1969?

Gender and education

Why is gender of interest regarding education? Well, it is of interest for many reasons, not least because educational opportunities and experiences greatly influence a person's life chances beyond school, in relation to their position in the labour market, to the health of themselves and their family. Christine Skelton (1993) points out that there is a multiplicity of ways gender exists in all aspects of schooling, and she contends that these create inequalities between girls and boys. In this chapter we examine gendered patterns in school attendance worldwide, including the issues and reasons for non-attendance. Many gender patterns exist, and they are not the same at all levels of education. The next focus is on gender issues within educational systems. In this we will examine the curricula, resources, classroom interactions amongst other topics. Finally, we will analyse the key issue of the discourse of 'failing boys' which has relevance for many societies both industrial and developing.

So, we begin our exploration of gender and education by understanding who goes to school. It is the case that not all countries are able to provide comprehensive school cover and even in those countries where primary education is mostly free, such as India, not all children make it into school.

School participation

In most developed countries all children are required to, and do, attend school. In developing countries this is not always the case; even when schooling is available it is often difficult to get to and expensive to participate. Sarmistha Pal (2003) conducted a review of educational research literature focused on developing countries which, she concludes, indicates that boys are more likely than girls to be in school. Even where schooling is free girls attend less due to other factors – even if schooling is free there may be a cost from the loss of the child's labour in the fields, home or workplace. Other factors mitigate against the inclusion of girls in education in developing countries, especially for families with limited or no resources. School fees exist in many countries, over 100 according to UNESCO, and these deter parents from sending children, especially daughters, to school. In some cases, where a family can afford to send some children to school pure son preference within the culture means that boys have a greater chance of education than their sisters. Pal (2003) acknowledges that this was the case for some families in the study in which she participated in the Punjab, yet there are other reasons why girls are educated less than boys – some of these are outlined in Table 13.1.

Table 13.1 Reasons for boy preference in education in developing countries

1. Gender bias when money limited, expresses itself as son preference

2. Girls are needed at home to free mother to engage in paid work, this is gender specific as boys would not be expected to take on domestic roles to free the mother to work in many societies.

3. Lesser returns for the family on investment of girls' education as: girls leave home on marriage and educated girls earn less than educated boys [**Hotlink → Work & Leisure (Chapter 14)**].

4. Safety and cultural concerns regarding female children travelling to school, both in terms of their safety and propriety within certain cultures.

Source: Derived from: Baden and Milward (1997).

Variations exist regarding participation of girls within states and even regions. In an attempt to understand the reasons for these Pal (2003) analysed a number of factors involved in decisions around the attendance of children in primary schools in rural West Bengal, India. Her conclusions indicate that there are also several factors which can increase the likelihood of a girl receiving education; summarised these are:

1. Girls are more likely to be in school in areas and villages where there exists a tradition of educating women and girls.

2. In areas where men's wages are high there is an incentive for boys not to study but to work, therefore gender participation rates are more equal.

3. The influence of the mother – that is, there is a distinct correlation between the education of the mother and the education of her daughter/s; educated women send their daughters to school.

According to a report commissioned by UNESCO, as part of the campaign Education for All, the number of girls in primary schools worldwide has been increasing, and at a greater rate than the rate for boys. However, gender equality in participation is still a far off target in many states and of the estimated 104 million children of primary school age who are *not* in education over 57 per cent are girls (*EFA Global Monitoring Report*, 2003, cited in *id21 Research Highlight, 2004*) and in one region, sub-Saharan Africa, the enrolment of girls in primary schools is three-quarters that of boys. One measure of participation by gender is the Gender Parity Index; this shows the ratio of girls in school compared with boys in the same country – a figure of 1 means equal participation, less than 1 indicates girls' lesser participation and more than 1 girls' greater participation. So, for example the GPI in India for primary education at 0.83, clearly indicates that fewer girls are in school than boys. This index also allows us to see patterns within overall trends, one of which is the fact that many boys across the world do not go on to complete secondary level education, meaning that of the children who do make it to secondary level girls outnumber boys in a range of countries. This is the situation in countries along the development continuum (see Table 13.2).

So, the picture is not simply one of boys' greater access worldwide to education – there are many nuances within this picture. It is informative to look at examples from across the world, some snapshots, which go some way to illustrate the complexities

---

Table 13.2 Secondary education GPI by gender, selected countries

Developing	Bangladesh	1.05
Middle Income	Colombia	1.10
Developed	United Kingdom	1.17

Source: Derived from: *EFA Global Monitoring Report, 2003*.

within the overarching statement regarding boys' greater participation in education than girls'.

School 'drop outs'

As shown in Table 13.2, the rates of completion of secondary education by gender do not always favour boys and, in addition boys and girls may drop out of education for different reasons. In a study of Ghana and Botswana (Dunne *et al.*, 2005) it was found that more girls than boys drop out of school before completing their education due in the main to pregnancy and early marriage. The factors driving boys out of school in these countries was found to be that boys feared corporal punishment, which is often much more severe for boys than girls, and were also eager to start earning money. In addition, boys displayed poorer punctuality and greater truancy rates than girls. A USA study (Mid-Atlantic Equity Consortium, Inc. and The NETWORK, Inc., 1993) also found that early motherhood was a cause of girls dropping out of high school, with 44 per cent of girls in their study citing pregnancy or marriage as a major reason for their withdrawal from study (note, in certain US states the marriage age can be as low as 14 where a pregnancy is involved). Of the remaining 56 per cent of girls in the study who had dropped out other features were of note, these being that the girls were often from families which displayed very 'traditional' attitudes towards gender roles and as such did not greatly value the education of girls as they were expected to become housewives and mothers rather than breadwinners. In the USA girls drop out of education at lesser rates than boys, but when they do boys are more likely to return to education later, and this is also differentiated by ethnicity. The same USA report showed that of 'drop outs' 42 per cent of boys did later return compared with only 25 per cent of girls who had dropped out, whilst amongst 'drop outs' from African-American and Hispanic youth, boys return at a rate 10 per cent higher than girls from these groups (Mid-Atlantic Equity Consortium, Inc. and The NETWORK, Inc., 1993).

Gendered experiences outside of school have also been found to cause girls to drop out, in particular gender based violence, both in the community and within schools, along with the prevalence of sexually transmitted diseases all mitigate against girls finishing their education. The *EFA Global Monitoring Report 2003*, found that in two regions, the Caribbean and Southern Africa, girls between 15 and 19 are infected by HIV/AIDS at rates from four to seven times higher than boys.

Tertiary education

For those who do manage to complete secondary education there is the possibility of tertiary, or higher, education. There have been a number of changes to gender participation rates across the globe in higher education, as shown by the extract below:

> In the US there are two million more women than men in college and the National Centre for Educational Statistics estimates that within five years 61% of those entering college will be female. There have been reports that some ivy league universities are managing their admissions to avoid overloading their student bodies with women – much as the 11-plus had a higher pass mark for girls, or the grammar schools would have been swamped with them. At the University of Saskatchewan in Canada only 11 of the 71 students due to graduate in veterinary science in 2007 will be men. Sixty per cent of University of Ottawa students are women and they are the majority in nine out of 10 faculties. During the 1990s women accounted for 100% of enrolment growth at German universities and more than 60% in France and Australia. In Trinidad, unofficial figures suggest up to 75% of the student body is female.
>
> (Berliner, 2004)

These examples are illustrative rather than representative; however, they do indicate a specific trend, also identified by the Organisation for Economic Co-operation and Development (OECD) in their survey of 27 member countries (OECD, 2004). Not only does the OECD note that 'Low educational attainment concerns more young males than females in 19 of the 27 countries ... And particularly in Greece, Iceland, Ireland, Italy, Portugal and Spain' (OECD, 2004) but, in addition:

Younger women today are far more likely to have completed a tertiary qualification than women 30 years ago: in 19 of the 30 OECD countries, more than twice as many women aged 25 to 34 have completed tertiary education than women aged 55 to 64 do. In 21 of 27 OECD countries with comparable data, the number of women graduating from university-level programmes is equal to or exceeds that of men.

(OECD, 2004)

What is evident here is that young women are now catching up with the participation rates of young men in a number of countries, and in some cases, overtaking them. This is not due to the number of men decreasing but, in most cases, due to the rate of uptake of higher educational opportunities by women growing. In the UK, the Higher Education Statistics Agency (HESA) monitors tertiary education trends, and their figures show that of the increase in uptake of higher education in the UK in the past decade over 70 per cent of it has been created by women (HESA, 2004). This trend does not only apply to developed countries but is also found in other areas, for example Jamaica (see World in Focus 13.1).

What we see from World in Focus 13.1 is that changes to the gender participation rates in higher education derive not simply from stagnation, or even a decrease, in male enrolments but from greater increases in female involvement. This supports the

World in focus 13.1

University participation in the West Indies – where have all the young men gone?

In 1948 the student body of the University of the West Indies (UWI) was predominately male: with 70 per cent of students being men and only 30 per cent women. Now that figure has been reversed and men comprise the minority 30 per cent figure. Still, however, over 90 per cent of the professors are men and males retain a dominance in technical and vocational areas such as engineering. One explanation of the gender balance reversal is that girls have entered into those fields which were traditionally male bastions, such as medicine. The reverse cannot be said about boys entering female areas. Mark Figueroa (2000) has been trying to make sense of it all with his research based at UWI. His findings lead him to argue that the lower participation rates of men in higher education is not the result of any

forces of marginalisation but are actually due to historical patterns of privileging men. He argues that this historical privileging has resulted in forms of masculinity that create barriers for boys and reduce their educational aspirations. These can be summarised as follows:

1. Although a minority of boys can and do promote their masculine identity through academic success for the majority the early socialisation of boys, and society's expectations regarding appropriate male behaviour, hold them back in school. Figueroa notes that the hard male Caribbean image, strongest in Jamaica, causes boys to resist school as 'girlish'.

2. Part of this hard image is the connection it has to Creole languages in preference to English, as instruction in schools is in English boys are disadvantaged.

3. Whereas it is now acceptable for girls to have ambitions to enter

into male fields and professions, the same is not the case for boys wishing to enter female areas [**Hotlink → Work and Leisure (Chapter 14)**]. As such, girls have made inroads into traditionally male areas whilst boys have not done the reverse.

From these findings Figueroa concludes that a policy shift is required if boys are to be able to keep up with girls. It is not that boys need to be protected from the competition girls are putting up, but rather that there is a need for social intervention (we will return to the idea of failing boys later in the chapter). His recommendations are the development of policies which challenge societal notions of male privilege; raise the status of education; encourage boys to enter into areas currently defined as female; provide support for language development in English and for this all to be implemented at a national level with consistent monitoring.

findings of the OECD study, amongst others. So why are women and girls responding in manner differently from men? One explanation for the British experience is given in Controversy 13.1.

Controversy 13.1

Do we need more graduates?

The UK government has a target of 50 per cent of 18–30-year-olds experiencing higher education and recent years have seen a great deal of growth towards this target, with Scotland having already attained it (Macleod, 2002). Phillip Brown and Anthony Hesketh are sceptical about the needs of the economy for increasing numbers of graduates citing the fact that 40 per cent of graduates are actually in jobs which do not require graduate level skills (Brown and Hesketh, 2004). As the extract below shows this is having a differential effect on girls and boys from the working class.

> Brown is co-author of a controversial book out next month which argues that the need for graduate workers is not as great as the government predicts and that too many employers are asking for graduate skills they don't need. He believes middle-class boys are as interested in going to university as they ever were, but that working-class boys continue to be as uninterested as ever. The shift is occurring as a result of working-class girls and women seeking higher qualifications, because more jobs need credentials, thereby increasing the gender gap.
>
> He is not alone in this view. Diane Reay, professor of sociology of education at the Institute for Policy Studies in Education at London Metropolitan University, argues that the market for middle-class higher education students is now saturated. Even middle-class men and women who 10 years ago would not have considered themselves academic enough are going to university, which leaves any rise in university entry to come from the working classes. This is where the different approaches to education between the sexes, shown by her research, come into play. How girls and women work and respond to opportunities is the key to the rising gender gap in the higher education student body.
>
> 'Right from the start of school, girls assume different attitudes to learning,' says Reay. 'They have a willingness to play by the rules of the educational game and an engagement with learning. Even if they find things tedious, they get on with it, rather than get out.

'As we move from an elite to a mass higher education system, working-class girls are buying into it, while working-class boys are opting out. Nothing is going to pull these young working-class men in. They are disenchanted with education before the sixth form.'

Source: Extracted from Berliner (2004).

Although women are now taking greater advantage of higher education it remains the case that the subjects dominated by women are most probably related to gender inequality in earnings and occupational segregation (Loury, 1997) [**Hotlink → Work and Leisure (Chapter 14)**]. Table 13.3 illustrates this with figures from the USA.

Table 13.3 Percentage of women in majors* in one US college

Major subject	Women as a percentage of all students registered
English	70.6
History	39.5
Economics	29.8
Political Science	46.0
Psychology	77.7
Sociology	61.8
Biology	64.3
Chemistry	53.5
Physics	24.0
Geology	14.2
Mathematics	41.6
Business	44.6
Computers	14.4
Engineering	16.1
Education	76.8
Social Work	94.3

* A Major is the main subject studied.

Source: Derived from: Bettinger and Long (2004), Table 1. Original source Ohio Board of Regents HEI System.

Having now ascertained the main trends in educational participation it is time to focus on the ways that gender exists within education.

Gender issues within educational systems

In this section we will cover a number of issues from gendered curricula to the organisation of schools and learning. In doing so the main focus will be on education in England and Wales, though not exclusively, as many of the issues found elsewhere also exist, or existed, within the English and Welsh education system.

Compulsory schooling for boys and girls

In England and Wales prior to the first Education Act (known as the Forster Act) in 1870 education was voluntary though there had been a long tradition of educating boys from the middle and upper classes. Feminists in the nineteenth century campaigned for many causes, including the inclusion of girls in education. Most objections to educating girls were based on perceived 'natural' differences between the sexes, frequently citing the frailness of the female body as a reason for not educating girls (Spender, 1987). Likewise, arguments for educating girls reflected a gendered life role; just as it was hoped that compulsory education would socialise the working-class masses, so too it was hoped that the inclusion of girls would ensure better sanitation within working-class homes and improve infant mortality. From the outset the purpose of education for boys and girls was to be different: girls were to be educated to the domestic and motherhood role whilst boys to enter the labour market as useful employees.

There was also a social class element to education for what was deemed suitable for working-class girls was not the aim for middle-class girls. Working-class girls were to achieve practical skills in housekeeping and mothering, whilst a middle-class girl was charged with developing her abilities to organise her household (mostly through the employment of working-class women servants). However, as it was expected that the middle classes would make their own arrangement for the education of their children the main focus of the 1870 Act was on an appropriate education for working-class girls and boys. So, lessons such as needlework and cookery became compulsory subjects (as they remained for many girls until the late 1970s and beyond). Skelton (1993) notes that as much as a fifth of the curriculum for girls in the 1870s was spent on needlework. She goes on to explain how girls' education became very subscribed and limited:

> The 1876 Code stipulated that every girl entered for examination in the higher standards of elementary education had to take domestic economy as one of her subjects. As most schools only entered children for *one* subject, the vast majority of girls had no choice as to what they would be examined on.
>
> (Skelton, 1993: 327, emphasis in the original)

Social and economic change in the first half of the twentieth century should have advanced women's education. However the pushing of women out of the workplace and back into the domestic sphere which occurred at the end of both world wars, diminished the attempts within the 1944 Education Act to address issues of equality of opportunity, the first Act in fact to do so. Although equality of opportunity was included in the Act it achieved little. The Act held that all were entitled to a free secondary education and that the education system would be based on meritocracy, not on sex, age, ethnicity or class background of students. Two matters restricted girls' education. The first was the requirement that children be offered education suitable to their age, abilities and aptitudes. The second was the structure of secondary education. With regards to the first point: it was assumed that girls would have a domestic role and boys one in the world of work, so suitable curricula developed, again preparing each for a different role in adult life. The notion of meritocracy was enacted through the development of grammar schools to be attended by the students who scored best in an examination at 11 (referred to as the 11 Plus). Yet this was a managed meritocracy. Although girls consistently achieved higher scores than boys in this examination, they did not receive the majority of the places. It was not viewed as desirable to have girls win more of the prestigious educational places so the examinations scores were weighted differently based on gender. In other words, boys achieved a grammar school place for a lower score than did a girl (Deem, 1981).

Despite a number of educational reports little changed in the educational opportunities available to girls and boys. A major milestone came in 1975 with the Sex Discrimination Act. There was initial opposition to the inclusion of education in this Act and once it was eventually included it was in a very limited way (for further details see Arnot and Weiner, 1987; Skelton, 1993). Nonetheless, it opened the door for teachers, researchers and policy makers within education authorities to develop equality strategies within education, these dealt with both the official and the hidden curriculum (see A Closer Look 13.1).

Gender and curricula

As noted immediately above, writings on education refer to two forms of curricula, and an explanation of these is given below.

A closer look 13.1

Official and hidden curricula – definitions

Within an educational setting the Official Curriculum includes what is taught, basically the timetable of classes offered. For example, a requirement of girls to undertake domestic science and for boys to learn woodwork skills. It also is used to refer to activities organised by teachers be they part of the teaching programme or clubs and sports. The hidden curriculum is a term used as shorthand for things that are learned in schools through informal means, or simply unintentional messages absorbed from such things as the way learning and teaching are organised, for instance, the simple division of a class into groups based on gender which reinforces differences in children's minds about boys and girls. Other examples of the hidden curriculum that have been identified include teaching materials; school organisation (such as separate play areas for girls and boys) and administration, such as school registers divided into two lists, of girls and boys. In addition, teacher attitudes and approaches have been identified as adding to the hidden curriculum.

It is worthwhile to examine some of the gender issues in both the curricula, not just to illustrate the ways in which gender has been created and sustained within education but also because schooling is a very strong socialisation force. For many of you reading this much of this will not relate to your experience within schools as with greater awareness many practices and materials were replaced in the latter quarter of the twentieth century. Nonetheless, some aspects may be familiar.

Stop and think 13.2

Whilst reading this next section keep in mind your own educational experience to date. Note down where you have experienced the things described below; likewise, note down your experience of a non-gendered curricula where appropriate. You may find it useful to conduct a short interview with someone older regarding these issues in their educational experience.

School organisation

Look at the photographs at the beginning of this chapter – they are a perfect example of administrative devices employed by schools. The existence of separate entrances for girls and boys predates the Victorian education acts and in some cases continued to be used gender-exclusively into the 1970s (see A Closer Look 13.2, A schooling autobiography). Although in Britain single-sex schooling in the state system diminished greatly in the latter twentieth century this did not mean that sex segregation was removed. Gender remained an integral part of school organisation with some examples being the organisation of school registers being divided by gender and the lining up of children to enter class also being in two sex-divided groupings. It was a routine aspect of education until the 1980s (and beyond) to categorise and organise children and their activities based on gender, to send boys to play football whilst girls played netball for example. Education researchers have shown how such practices reinforce gender messages, in particular differences between genders, for example Skelton (1993) remembers how in her school teachers allowed children to leave the school assembly on the basis of 'quietness'. As she reports, the girls always won, sending a message that this was what was expected of girls whilst boys were expected to be noisy.

Teaching and learning resources

It may be difficult to perceive today but there is a great deal of evidence that shows that many of the resources employed by teachers in the past in the UK (which may still be being used elsewhere today) were heavily gendered. One such focus has been on reading schemes which employed stories such as *Janet and John, Peter and Jane* to introduce children to literacy for the first time. In these reading schemes very traditional roles were represented, in addition, the characters all appeared white and middle class. In *Janet and John* books children began their reading careers learning that Janet helped Mummy to wash dishes whilst John watched as Daddy put oil in the car. There is little need today to point out the sex stereotypes evident here. In addition, such reading schemes presented men and women in a restricted set of roles: women were predominately in domestic roles, or sex stereotyped occupations in the workplace. Likewise, men were virtually absent from domestic activities. In the past 30 years such schemes have fallen away, yet they shaped the socialisation experiences of many children for a number of decades.

Gender and social relations in the classroom

Dale Spender is an educationalist and author who has written extensively about various issues, especially regarding the education of girls and women. You would expect then that she would feel comfortable in teaching classes of both women and men, for with her awareness she would be able to ameliorate any gender differences in the treatment of pupils and students. Yet, for many years she required the men in her mixed groups to be silent or only speak in equitably allotted time. This is because she was aware that in class men continued to dominate communication. Such self-awareness is not always present. Spender's experiences tell us a great deal about interaction in the classroom. It appears that even if one is aware gender differences are not necessarily avoided in the treatment of pupils and steps, such as those Spender took, are required. Of course, some men protested that they felt excluded, which was just the experience that women had all along (Spender, 2006).

Research shows that there is a difference between the interactions between teacher and boy and teacher and girl. It is expected that boys will demand more of the teacher's time, be it only to discipline them, and research has shown that boys do receive a greater number of reprimands in class than do girls (see World in Focus 13.2). As such, teachers may attempt to engage boys more in the lesson and select material that interests them (Skelton, 1989). The greater verbalisation of boys has been observed in a number of contexts, leading teachers to ask them more difficult questions and to assess their abilities as greater than those of comparable girls (Mid-Atlantic Equity Consortium, Inc. and The NETWORK, Inc., 1993). Studies from the UK and the USA show that, in the 1980s at least, boys received more time from teachers, were assigned to higher groups of ability, received harsher punishments and were asked harder questions than girls (Goddard-Spear, 1989; Lee, 1990; Mid-Atlantic Equity Consortium, Inc. and The NETWORK, Inc., 1993).

World in focus 13.2

Gender and classroom behaviour

UK

Becky Francis (2000) has written about how the laddish behaviour of some boys affects their educational performance and that of others. This laddish behaviour includes a focus on activities deemed by the boys to be masculine: an interest in football; the sexual objectification of females; an attitude that rejects authority and general 'mucking about'. As Francis points out this can only diminish educational achievement as schooling requires both diligence and obedience. Of course, not all boys behave in this way but even some of those who do not still feel the peer pressure not to study and pretend to work less than they actually do.

Australia

A study undertaken for the Department of Employment, Education, Training and Youth Affairs, involving over 400 schools from across Australia noted that gender played a role in the disruption of the learning process, as reported by school students:

through 'mucking around', through ridiculing answers given by others in class, through deriding those who want to work . . . [each were] . . . reported by most students as happening in their school. 'Mucking around' was reported as something boys did often by around 60 per cent of students . . . Boys were reported two to three

times as often as girls as the perpetrators of all three of these disruptive behaviours.

(Collins *et al.*, 2002:4)

Jamaica

Refer back to World in Focus 13.1; Figueroa's points also include a rejection by boys of schools as 'girlish'.

Stop and think 13.3

Look at World in Focus 13.2. Why do you think this pattern of laddish behaviour is visible across the globe? Is it that boys are simply naughty? Is it that they bore more easily? Or is it, as some commentators argue, due to a particular form of masculinity being expressed? After reading the rest of the chapter come back to this question. Has your thinking changed?

Gender and the official curriculum

All of the issues discussed immediately above relate to aspects of the hidden curriculum. We have also seen how the development of education in England and Wales included a gendered official curriculum. In 1988 another Act came into effect, the Education Reform Act. A major aspect of this Act was the introduction of a National Curriculum. This National Curriculum requires that all pupils study a range of subjects and it has been responsible for a major change in the segregation of subjects studied at lower levels of high school resulting in a 'reduced sex segregation of subject choice up to the age of sixteen' (Arnot *et al.*, 1999: 20). This has also been influenced by a number of national projects encouraging girls into 'masculine' subjects, for example GIST – Girls into Science and Technology.

It has been claimed that prior to this girls' 'education lacked the breadth and depth normally associated with "good" schooling, and also precluded access to further and higher education' (Arnot *et al.*, 1999: 113). Yet, 'once subject choice was reintroduced [post 16] young men and women again chose sex-typed subjects and courses' (Arnot *et al.*, 1999: 21), (see Table 13.3).

Before looking at who studies what it is necessary to note that gender interplays with 'race', sexuality and social class in the decisions taken about education (see A Critical Look 13.1).

A critical look 13.1

Gender not the only issue

It is important to note that gender is not the only variable at play here: African-Caribbean girls in the UK display more gender freedom in subject choice than do white girls and working-class African-Caribbean girls also performed better academically in the 1990s than working-class African-Caribbean boys, though not better than boys from higher social class groups (Arnot *et al.*, 1999). It has been argued that this may be due to black girls adopting an instrumental approach which views learning as a means of avoiding experiencing a lack of control in their lives and to overcome sexism and racism. However, Heidi Mizra (1992) has pointed out that even when black girls did study non-stereotyped subjects they still ended up in stereotypical jobs and experienced discrimination in the job market.

Instrumentalism can also be seen in the education choices made by a group of non-heterosexual women studied by Gillian Dunne (1997). Dunne found that those women who knew early in their adulthood that marriage was not an option for them made decisions regarding education that permitted them to live independently. Whereas women who anticipated marriage, although later identifying as non-heterosexual, had been much more likely to abandon their studies, for example to support a partner in his studies.

Despite a reduction on sex stereotyping of subjects studied in school, it appears that when students once more have the opportunity of choice gender differences emerge. Table 13.4 indicates these differences at A Level and Scottish Highers.

Table 13.4 Gender differences in subject choice post 16, as percentage of entries for examination in GCE A Level and SCE Higher grade		
	Girls	Boys
English literature*	70	30
Social Studies*	70	30
Biological sciences	63	38
History	52	48
Chemistry	51	49
Business Studies	46	54
Mathematics	40	60
Physics	24	76

* England and Wales only.
Source: Derived from: Department for Education and Skills (2004), *Education and Training Statistics for the UK*, cited in EOC (2005: 4).

The continued gender differentiation indicates the influence of other social factors, though aspects of the hidden curriculum in the early teaching of subjects also add to the image of a subject as masculine or feminine; this could be as simple as the gender of the teachers leading the class in particular areas. The importance of role models has been raised frequently in the UK as an explanation as to why boys may 'switch off' from education in primary schools as they see few, if any, men in the classrooms and come to think that education is not, therefore, something that men do. It is interesting to note that the EFA Global Monitoring Team (EFA, 2003) has concluded that India's low primary level GPI of 0.83 is due to the absence of women teachers able to serve as role models for girls (many schools have only one teacher, around 20 per cent of Indian schools, and of these almost 90 per cent have a male teacher) [**Hotlink → Sex and Sexuality → Controversy 15.2 (Chapter 15)**].

A closer look 13.2

A schooling autobiography

I began school in 1969, and at that time I didn't perceive any major differences between boys and girls. However, by year 3 gender difference was really clear – when the bell went we all had to line up outside the doors. Except that there were two doors, one marked 'boys' and one marked 'girls' (these are the doors in Figure 13.1). Everyday we entered school in single-sex lines through the respective doors. Then my family moved and my brother and I went to a new school a few miles away. It was built in 1723 by a Glasgow Tobacco Lord's legacy. It was a beautiful building, still is, and it too had a 'boys' door and a 'girls' door. It also had playground areas associated with each entrance – it was taboo for the 'wrong' sex to be found playing in the 'wrong' playground. We did have a shared area too, but the interesting thing is that all of us, up to the age of 12, were fearful of ever entering, let alone being found, in the 'others' playground.

In all my Primary education I was never taught by a man, yet the Head of my first school was a classic patriarch – a kind, yet authoritarian man. Despite my next Head being female, so too were all the staff she managed, except for the janitor.

Actually, there was another signifier of gender evident from day one. Scottish state education usually requires school uniform. When I began school girls were only allowed to wear skirts and boys shorts or trousers. I stand today outside the same school with my child and watch the children enter, girls in trousers, older boys in long shorts. It is an interesting expression of uniform. In High School uniform was a little more relaxed, but not much: it was the late 1970s and early 1980s, it was a rural school with many of us getting there by bus. Remember too this was Scotland, in winter it was pretty cold. So, as girls we campaigned to be allowed to wear trousers, as it was far too cold to stand waiting for a bus in a skirt. We were allowed to wear trousers on the buses, but we had to change on entry – picture it, lots of teenage girls changing quickly into skirts in the toilets before class. Mind you, the jeans and cords worn by many of the boys (often due to their farming background) were banned from the bodies of us girls – in one explanation it was implied that such clothing might arouse the male teachers too much! We were not the only ones subject to a dress code – so too were the teachers. Teachers were held to account by the Head (called a Rector in Scotland) regarding their apparel.

As is normal within schools, nothing was secret, not even the fight between women teachers and the Rector regarding women wearing trousers in their professional capacity.

On reflection I can see other issues regarding gender, not so much 'hidden curriculum' issues but of the actual curriculum and how teaching was administered. In Primary girls were taught in one year knitting and in the next crochet, whilst boys were released into the playground to supervise themselves playing football. To me this was a failure of both of us. Why should boys be assumed to need no guidance in their activity? Why should the class be divided by sex at such a young age?

Moving onto Secondary (High) school boys and girls were divided into Houses, not based on sex, we initially attended classes together based on Houses until we were 'streamed' based on ability. Yet we were also subdivided by other criteria – that being sex. This occurred in two ways: the first was in the teaching of the same subjects – we all did science but we did it in small groups (good teaching) divided by sex. The second was in the subjects offered – woodwork and metalwork were mandatory for boys in the first two years of Secondary education whilst two classes of Domestic Economy were compulsory in the same years for girls. Even when we got to choose our options an element of gender difference was built in; for those of us permitted to take an extra subject (that is in addition to the Scottish standard of 7) the choice was Biology versus Engineering Drawing. Whereas boys had had two years of Biology before this choice had to be made, the girls had had no Engineering or technical education. It is not surprising that most academically strong boys went into one class and academically strong girls into the other.

Source: Jen Marchbank

Stop and think 13.4

After reading the autobiography in A Closer Look 13.2 analyse the text for examples of gender differentiation in terms of official and hidden curricula. Compare this with the autobiography and/or education history interview you were asked to do above. Are there any points of commonality or difference? How might these be explained?

Initially much that was written on gender and education focused on discrimination facing girls. More recently another key issue has come to the fore in many countries, and it is to this that we now turn.

Key issue – failing boys' discourse

We have already seen that the numbers of young men entering higher (tertiary) education is falling as a ratio across the majority of OECD countries and, in World in Focus 13.1, had presented an explanation for declining achievement amongst many boys in Jamaica. One explanation for this change has been an argument that whilst schools have challenged girls to take up educational opportunities the same cannot be said for boys, and this is related to societal change generally that has provided new roles for women in the labour market [**Hotlink → Work and Leisure (Chapter 14)**] and challenged notions of the male breadwinner [**Hotlink → Social Policy (Chapter 5)**] and traditional views of masculinity (Arnot *et al.*, 1999; Figueroa, 2000; EOC, 2001; Connolly, 2004). There has been considerable discussion of the impact of a 'crisis in masculinity' upon boys' views of future roles and the importance of education. Christine Skelton (1998) warns that a danger of such discourses is that it positions men and boys as victims of masculinity whilst at the same time ignoring women and girls, a situation that does nothing to resolve the perceived problem. So, what is the extent of the gender difference in achievement? A Closer Look 13.3 lists the facts for 2004.

Blame for the decline in boys' educational achievements has also been targeted at a perceived 'feminisation' of schools (see Connolly, 2004 for a discussion of this point). This discourse argues that curriculum content no longer favours boys; that the introduction of continual assessment and project work (as in GCSEs) favours the diligence of girls and suits their learning patterns better and that the absence of male teachers, especially in early years' education, all militate to feminise education and disadvantage boys compared to girls. The result of such approaches has been the proliferation of texts on how to 're-masculinise' the curriculum (e.g. Noble and

A closer look 13.3

Key trends in gender performance, England, 2004

In England school children are tested at a number of points, these are referred to as Key Stages (at ages 7, 11, 14) and can be charted to show progress to GCSE at 16.

➤ In English girls on average progress more than boys on average at every stage.

➤ At Key Stage 1 there is a difference of 8 percentage points between boys and girls in English (that is 8 per cent more girls achieve the required level of ability).

➤ At Key Stage 2 the gap for English increases to 11 percentage points and by Key Stage 3 it is 13 percentage points.

➤ At GCSE girls continue to do better, with a gap of 14 percentage points.

➤ 59 per cent of girls and 48 per cent of boys gained five or more GCSEs grades A*–C or equivalent.*

➤ 43 per cent of girls and 34 per cent of boys gained two or more A levels or equivalent.*

* cited in EOC (2005:1)

Source: Department for Education and Skills (2005).

Bradford, 2000, in the UK; Fletcher, 1997, in Australia) by introducing tests, shorter classes, more fact based material, less reflection and more learning based on activities; as Paul Connelly has observed, the 'result is a plethora of advice and guidance that tends to unashamedly pander to boys' immediate needs and interests' (Connolly, 2004: 43). In the USA, Canada and Australia some school authorities are experimenting with single-sex schooling (Phillips, 2003) based on such arguments regarding differential learning styles.

Gender and learning styles

[Hotlink → Pedagogy (Chapter 9)]
Although most educationalists agree that there are differences amongst children and their learning modes, not all support the argument that gender makes such a difference that schools have to provide differing learning experiences for girls and boys. However, as Susan Phillips summarises some research makes the opposite case:

What are some of the possible reasons for these gender differences in achievement and attitudes? Researchers suggest they include possible physiological reasons such as differences in brain wiring; preferences in learning style active versus verbal; types of materials chosen; teacher style; and perhaps even the volume and the tone of a teacher's voice.

Males and females report being less self-conscious and more focused on learning in single-sex classrooms. Teachers can adapt the teaching style, classroom layout, how to elicit responses, teacher voice level, manner of communicating, and materials chosen to maximize learning. Male academic success seems to improve when: boys are seated at tables to allow freedom of movement; teachers are more aggressive at eliciting responses; there are more 'teacher-led' activities with clear guidelines and activities; communication is 'side-by-side' rather than 'face-to-face'; kinaesthetic activities occur: and the material studies contains elements oriented to male interests. Most boys appear to prefer more hands-on, competitive instruction with smaller groups when group work is required. Females seem to thrive when: the classroom contains individual desks; the classroom is quieter and more controlled; the material is suited to their interests; and socially oriented cooperative larger group activities are used.

(Phillips, 2003: 1–2)

Likewise, an extensive review of research evidence conducted by Arnot and colleagues (1998) concluded that there are differences between girls and boys, they found that overall there is evidence that:

➤ Girls are more attentive in class and more willing to learn.

➤ Girls do better than boys on sustained tasks that are open-ended, require thought and are related to real-world situations.

➤ Boys prefer more traditional learning modes such as memorising abstract and unambiguous rules and facts.

➤ Boys are more likely to seek to achieve correct answers quickly than to gain a deeper understanding through sustained effort.

Stop and think 13.5

Do you agree with the notion that boys and girls have different learning styles? Can this explain why girls are now doing better in comparison with boys than before? Is your preferred learning style included above; does it fit with the 'right' gender demarcation?

Analysing the gender gap

There is no doubt that across the globe there is a change in education; the change has less to do with the achievement levels of boys and more to do with boys' achievement in comparison with girls. There is also little doubt that this has become a key issue for educationalists and policy makers from Australia to Canada to the Caribbean to Greece to the UK and beyond. It is true that girls are now out-performing boys in many areas of education yet, as shown earlier this was always the case in the UK (and required the 'fixing' of 11 plus results to ensure girls were not over-represented in grammar schools). A number of explanations for this have been given, from differential learning styles to biology to female ambition to a crisis of masculinity.

There is a problem with this focus on gender, that is, although it is true that there is evidence that girls are performing better, on the whole, than boys this is not true for all boys and in fact, as the British statistics show both boys and girls have been improving their results at GCSE, whilst, as already noted, there has always been a gender gap between boys' and girls' performance: as shown by the need to adjust the results of the 11 plus and that even in the 1970s more girls than boys achieved five or more O Levels (precursor of the GCSE) (Arnot *et al.*, 1999). There is a distinct pattern visible in the gender gap in England and Wales. Arnot and colleagues (1999) detail it in three periods:

1975–87   a period of stability with virtual parity in gender achievement;

1987–90   a period of rapid change in gender and achievement;

1990–95   a period of stability once more, but with a disparity in gender and achievement.

In other words, prior to 1987 the gender gap was small and unchanging but this went through rapid change; however, by 1990 that change had stopped though a gender gap pertained.

Rhetoric and reality

It is certainly true that since the mid-1970s an increasing gap has emerged between the performance of girls and boys, the most common measure used in England and Wales is performance at GCSE. This increasing gap is shown in Figure 13.2.

What is clear here is that there have been two trends: firstly, both boys and girls as groups have greatly increased their academic achievements; secondly, that there is an increasing difference between the genders in terms of achievement – this latter is the percentage point gap referred to earlier. This is a simple way to illustrate the percentage point gap, but what it does not show is the relative increase of boys' and girls' performance over the years. It also matters how many boys and girls achieved these grades, as Paul Connolly explains:

> there is, quite simply a need to keep these differences in proportion. For example, if only 5 per cent of boys and 10 per cent of girls passed a particular GCSE examination the percentage point difference (i.e. 10 − 5 = 5 percentage points) would be the same as if 90 per cent of boys and 95 per cent of girls had passed that exam (i.e. 95 − 90 = 5 percentage points). However, we would generally be more concerned about the differences evident in the former case than in the latter. To understand why we need to look at it proportionately. Thus, in the first instance girls are twice as likely to pass the examination than boys (i.e. 10/5 = 2) whereas, in the second instance, girls are only marginally (1.06 times) more likely to pass the examination than boys (i.e. 95/90 = 1.06). In this way, 'keeping a sense of proportion' requires us to calculate the relative chances of boys and girls achieving the required examination passes.
>
> (Connolly, 2004: 12–13)

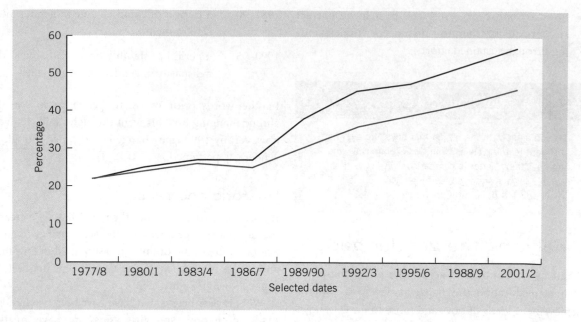

Figure 13.2 Percentage of Girls and Boys Achieving 5 (or more) GCSEs (A–C), England and Wales
Source: Derived from Connolly, 2004

Connolly has analysed the statistics in just this way providing the following findings:

| 1991/2 | 0.799 |
| 2001/3 | 0.813 |

In other words, for every 100 girls passing five or more GCSEs at A*–C, the number of boys also doing so in 1991/2 was 79.9 and 81.3 in 2001/3. What this analysis shows is that although a gender gap remains in this ten-year period boys had a greater *rate* of increase in achievement compared with girls. Connolly (2004) argues that this is a more valid way to examine trends over time and he concludes that:

> Rather than boys continuing to lag further behind girls in relation to GCSE performance as the rhetoric so strongly suggests . . . the actual reality is that while there is a difference between the achievements of boys and girls it has actually been stable over the last decade and, if anything, boys are now showing some limited signs of beginning to catch up with girls.
>
> (Connolly, 2004: 14)

Disaggregating the data – which boys and which girls?

As some boys do well and some girls do poorly educationally it is necessary to look at exactly what boys are failing and at patterns within the gender gap. As previously noted, gender is not the only factor at play in educational achievement or otherwise and we will discuss gender here in relation to these. Social class and ethnicity strongly influence the educational attainment of children (Epstein *et al.*, 1998), and comparing different groups of school students to the national average shows that there are some very high achieving boys in certain groups and some who do less well. Table 13.5 illustrates this.

It is clear from the table that not all girls are outperforming all boys, in fact, boys from the Higher Profession group out-perform all girls in all social classes except their own. Girls out-perform boys within each of the social classes and in all ethnic groups, yet black girls do less well than boys from Chinese, Indian and white families but better than boys with Bangladeshi, Pakistani and black ethnicities. Within social class groupings boys do best, relative to girls, in the Higher Professional class and worst in Routine class. Within ethnic groups Chinese boys do

Table 13.5 Proportions of boys and girls in England and Wales achieving five or more GCSE grades A* to C in 2000/1, by social class and ethnicity

	Total	Boys	Girls	No. of boys per 100 girls
Social Class				
Higher professional	77.1	72.1	82.6	87.3
Lower professional	64.5	58.9	70.1	84.0
Intermediate	51.8	46.7	56.6	82.5
Lower supervisory	34.9	29.5	40.8	72.3
Routine	31.8	26.1	37.4	69.8
Ethnicity				
Chinese	68.9	67.4	70.5	95.6
Indian	59.6	51.3	67.8	75.7
White	51.6	46.6	56.7	82.2
Bangladeshi	41.5	33.9	50.0	67.8
Pakistani	40.2	35.7	45.1	79.2
Black	36.3	32.0	40.2	79.6
TOTAL	51.1	46.1	56.2	82.0

Source: Connolly (2004), Table 1.3, he derived the figures from the Youth Cohort Study, 2002.

best, relative to girls, whilst Bangladeshi boys do worst compared to girls from their background.

Connolly (2004) has analysed educational performance data based on the three variables of gender, ethnicity and social class to calculate the relative odds of a young person achieving the benchmark of five GCSEs A*–C. As we already have seen the relative odds for boys achieving such a standard is around 0.813 (or 81 boys for every 100 girls). His analysis shows that, controlling for gender and either social class or ethnicity where relevant:

➤ Chinese young people are nearly seven times more likely to achieve the standard than black young people.

➤ Indian young people are over three times more likely to achieve the standard than black young people.

➤ Those from the Higher Professional class are nearly eight times more likely than those from the Routine class to achieve the standard.

➤ A young person's gender affects their chances of gaining the standard by a factor of 1.6 whilst their social class can affect their chances by a factor of 7.7 and their ethnic background by a factor of 6.8.

What this analysis shows is that it is not simply a case that boys are doing less well than girls, rather that young people's experiences of education and their personal achievements are influenced greatly by their social class and their ethnicity.

Gender and social change

There are many explanations in existence as to why boys and girls respond differently to education; these range from biological differences to 'feminine' schools to a lack of role models. One explanation that is coming to the fore is related to social change. Schools, from the UK to the Caribbean, have and are challenging girls to change to fit modern society, to take up new jobs and professions and to look beyond a role of housewife and mother. It appears that no similar challenge has been made to boys to rethink and adapt traditional notions of masculinity (Arnot *et al.*, 1999; Figueroa, 2000; Dunne *et al.*, 2005). Boys still display more traditional notions of household and family care than girls and even academically able boys seek masculine identity away from the classroom and books, finding it in sport or rebellious activities (Arnot *et al.*, 1999). However, not all boys have resisted changes in masculinity, as shown by the responses to attitudes to certain non-traditional occupations in a British survey of 11- to 16-year-olds (NOP Family, 2001). Nonetheless, the survey also showed that despite some intellectual changes boys still performed domestic tasks less frequently than girls, indicating that certain vestiges of gender stereotyping remain.

Conclusion

In this chapter we have covered a great deal of material regarding issues of gender and education. However, these are not the only ones. There is a great richness of work available on issues of gendered experiences of working in education, mostly women's gendered experience (see the Women's Higher Education Network series). Closely related to issues of gender are those of sexuality, both what is taught and what is experienced within educational systems by teachers and students alike (Lees, 1986, 1993; Epstein *et al.*, 2003). We hope that the insight you have gained from this chapter will aid your work on these other key issues.

Further reading

Debbie Epstein, Sarah O'Flynn and David Telford (2003), *Silenced Sexualities in Schools and Universities*, Stoke on Trent, Trentham Books. The first book to address issues of sexuality in all stages of formal education, from primary to tertiary. Easy to read, it combines literature reviews with research conducted by the authors to argue that educational institutions shape and manufacture sexualities.

Louise Morley and Val Walsh (eds) (1996), *Breaking Boundaries: Women in Higher Education*, London, Taylor & Francis. A wide ranging collection of chapters covering issues from the dilemmas of academic motherhood to sexuality to gender and age. Part of the WHEN series.

Diane Reay (2004), 'Cultural Capitalists and Academic Habitus: Classed and Gendered Labour in UK Higher Education', *Women's Studies International Forum*, 27(1): 31–9. In this article Reay clearly shows how advantages and disadvantages of class and gender interplay in the experiences of workers in higher education.

Pam Cotterill and Gayle Letherby (eds) (2005), 'Women in Higher Education: Issues and Challenges', Special issues of *Women's Studies International Forum*, 28 (2 & 3): 109–258. British and international articles that cover class, lesbian identity, inequality, leadership, resistance to feminism, 'mommy tracking' and the experiences of graduate study.

Gender and Education – an international, multidisciplinary journal publishing articles on educational research and ideas that focus on gender as a category of analysis. All levels of education are included, as are the experiences of girls, boys, women and men both as learners and teachers.

Websites

Intute – a free online service providing access to the very best Web resources for education and research, evaluated and selected by a network of subject specialists. Enter the site and type in *education gender* into the internal search engine and follow your interests. Available at **http://www.intute.ac.uk/socialsciences/**

Oxfam – Oxfam are a leading British charity working across the globe. This site is their portal to their pages on education internationally. Available at **http://www.oxfam.org.uk/ what_we_do/issues/education/index.htm**

End of chapter activity

1. What explanations exist for son preference in sending children to school in developing countries?

2. What factors increase the likelihood of a girl receiving an education in a developing country?

3. List the different ways masculinity is said to hinder the educational attainment of boys.

End of chapter activity continued

4. Social scientists need to be able to interpret data from graphs, tables and other sources, so using the data in Table 13.5 determine the following:

   (a) how many boys per 100 girls from the Lower Supervisory group achieved the benchmark of 5 or more GCSEs A*–C?

   (b) although black boys were the least well performing group they did better than boys in some other ethnic groups in what way?

   (c) which category performed best overall?

   Check your answers with the text.

Answers

4 (a) 72.3

   (b) In relation to girls from the same ethnic group, i.e. black boys per 100 black girls = 79.6, which is greater than Indian, Pakistani and Bangladeshi boys compared to girls from these ethnic groups.

   (c) Higher professional girls with 82.6% achieving 5A* to C passes.

Chapter 14

Work and Leisure

Key issues in this chapter:

➤ Work involves activities that are both paid and unpaid. Globally, men and women perform both, but more women than men perform the latter.

➤ There are gender differences in both economic activity rates and earnings globally.

➤ Labour markets are segregated, and gender plays a role in segregation both horizontally and vertically.

➤ A range of theoretical positions exist which attempt to explain differences in paid work and leisure, in relation to gender, ethnicity, age and social class.

➤ Generally, women's leisure is more constrained than men's, due to restrictions of time, space and finance and also due to social constraints.

➤ Work and leisure are not distinct activities.

At the end of this chapter you should be able to:

➤ Discuss the interrelationships between work, both paid and unpaid, and leisure.

➤ Debate the relative strengths of the various theoretical positions in relation to work and leisure.

➤ Recognise that men's experiences of work and leisure are not homogeneous, nor are women's, but do reveal certain patterns.

➤ Describe global patterns in work, both paid and unpaid.

Introduction

Figure 14.1
Source: © Jackie Fleming

Stop and think 14.1

Look at the cartoon in Figure 14.1. What does it tell you about gender differences in career expectations? What is it that makes this cartoon funny?

Why have we put these two topics – work and leisure – together? It is very simple. It is usually assumed that when you are not in work you are enjoying leisure time.

But this all depends on how we define work and an analysis of what happens to create leisure. The first distinction to make is the difference between work and employment. Employment is work for financial reward, but this is not the only kind of work. There is work involved in unpaid labour too, such as caring, household duties and community involvement [**Hotlink →** **Social Policy (Chapter 5); Hotlink → Geography (Chapter 10)**]. In addition, work 'may be embedded in non-work activities, and the identical activity may constitute "work" in some situations but not others' (Glucksmann, 2000: 18–19). Across the world women, men and children perform unpaid labour, a large amount of which is domestic labour, though this is not equally distributed (see World in Focus 14.1).

Given World in Focus 14.1, it appears that the major responsibility for such work remains with women. This relates directly to leisure in several ways: as it limits women's access to either paid employment or free time it means that women either lack the time or the finances (and often both) to pursue their own leisure. However, this is an assumption that leisure is a form of activity when it is much more complex than that:

> Some occupations, or tasks within an occupation, are perceived – and, sometimes experienced – as more like leisure than work (e.g. artists, actors, writers, tour guides or gardeners). Furthermore,

World in focus 14.1

Household labour and gender

In the following two pieces of information it is shown that housework is an important topic for consideration in regard to work and leisure. They are not direct comparisons but do indicate a general trend in two countries.

Britain

In the early 1970s Ann Oakley interviewed 40 housewives in London. She found that they spent an average of 77 hours each week on housework. She found that they experienced this work as monotonous, dissatisfying, of low status and that they were isolated.

USA

Romero (1992) argues that although feminists campaigned for men in family units to accept equal responsibility for household chores this has not happened. Although American women do less housework than before (17.5 hours per week in 1995 rather than 30 hours per week in 1965), this appears to be due to a lowering of standards and/or increase in technology rather than a redistribution of tasks, as women still perform two-thirds of whatever housework gets done (Ehrenreich, 2002: 89). When it comes to the least popular tasks, such as actual physical cleaning, there is less change. Between 1965 and 1995, men increased the time they spent cleaning floors and toilets by 240 per cent – a real figure of 1.7 hours a week – while women only decreased their cleaning time by 7 per cent, a real figure of 6.7 hours a week (Ehrenreich, 2002: 89).

discussions concerning work may take place during leisure activities (e.g. during a game of golf, or during an evening social event) and leisure sometimes takes place during the working day (e.g. 'popping out', surfing the net, playing computer games or doing the crossword).

(Letherby and Reynolds, 2005: 138)

Gendered labour

In this section we will look at both paid and unpaid labour, followed by a discussion of divisions in labour markets, 'private' responsibilities' influence on economic activity opportunities, pay levels and end with a review of various theoretical attempts to explain gender segregation in the labour market. Paid work is considered to be part of the 'public' world and separate from the 'private' world of family and household, yet feminists and others have challenged this notion of two separate spheres pointing out that gender relations in the labour market are related to gender relations in the 'private' sphere, for example it has been argued that women's greater contribution to domestic tasks is a crucial element in permitting men to compete freely in the labour market (Garmarnikov *et al.*, 1983). Both feminists and writers of critical studies of masculinity (CSM), have pointed out that this division has played a major role in defining femininities and masculinities: in that women have been either excluded from, or disadvantaged in, paid employment; and that men have been restricted by definitions of masculinity related only to the world of work. David Morgan (1991) argues that paid work is a key issue for understanding men as it has been a source of status.

Unpaid work

In a household with adults of different sexes (the majority situation) it is the case that gender relations interact with and shape paid work and leisure opportunities. Unpaid work occurs across the globe and is performed by women, men and children – see A Closer Look 14.2 for an example of how a woman's work is hidden. This is real work and can be tiring in

ways that other work is not, for example emotionally when caring for a dying elder (Graham, 1988). Paid work too involves emotion, in gendered ways (see A Closer Look 14.1).

A closer look 14.1

Emotion at work

Two books, over 20 years apart show the emotional labour required of certain workers. In her research on flight attendants Arlie Hochschild (1983) notes that they are required not only to always appear calm and polite, i.e. managing their own emotions, but also to deal with the behaviour of passengers, some of whom may be drunk or expressing air rage. She argues that this emotional labour is gendered in that it appears more in female-dominated occupations than in male. Gayle Letherby and Gillian Reynolds (2005), in their study of work and politics on trains show that there are jobs dominated by men that also involve emotional management by the employee of both self and clients.

Unpaid work is also gendered in who does what tasks: Jane Weelock (1990) found in a study of British families that although when unemployed men did take on a greater amount of household labour, there remained a gendering of domestic jobs with some being gender-neutral and some gender-segregated. This is supported by Judy Wajcman's (1983) study of employed women.

Stop and think 14.2

What jobs do you think are gender-neutral and which are segregated? Reflect on your own engendered domestic experience.

When gender is not an issue, such as in same-sex households, there is less evidence of task divisions, even when both partners are engaged in paid employment. Gillian Dunne's (1998) examination of lesbian couples found that the responsibilities for domestic tasks were much more flexible than in heterosexual couples.

A closer look 14.2

Labour of love

'Have you many children?' the doctor asked.

'God has not been good to me. Of fifteen born, only nine live', he answered

'Does your wife work?'

'No, she stays at home.'

'I see. How does she spend her day?'

'Well, she gets up at four in the morning, fetches water and wood, makes the fires and cooks breakfast. Then she goes to the river and washes clothes. After that she goes to town to get corn ground and buys what we need in the market. Then she cooks the midday meal.'

'You come home at midday?'

'No, no, she brings the meal to me in the fields – about three kilometres from home.'

'And after that?'

'Well, she takes care of the hens and pigs and of course she looks after the children all day . . . then she prepares the supper so it is ready when I come home.'

'Does she go to bed after supper?'

'No, I do. She has things to do around the house until about 9 o'clock.'

'But of course you say your wife doesn't work?'

'Of course she doesn't work. I told you, she stays at home.'

Source: International Labour Organisation (1977) cited in Mitter (1985).

Stop and think 14.3

What does the conversation in A Closer Look 14.2 tell you about how the farmer views 'work'? Would you consider what the wife performs each day as 'work'? Why do you think this?

A major area of domestic work involves caring for others, for details see [**Hotlink → Social Policy → World in Focus 2 (Chapter 5)**]. Across Europe the share of informal care is heavily skewed towards women (Grammenos, July 2003).

Paid labour

In western societies there has been change in the sexual division of labour since the end of the Second World War, and in Britain, since the mid-1970s women's position in the labour market has undergone considerable change. In fact, currently 69 per cent of women and 79 per cent of men of working age are in paid employment, which shows that there has been a decrease in the economic participation gender gap from 14 per cent in 1991 to 10 per cent in 2001 (Labour Force Survey, 2001).

A closer look 14.3

The difference between 'economically active' and 'employed'

Economically active means the whole labour market, that is both those currently in jobs and those who are of working age and who are available for work, although currently unemployed.

Employed means the actual number of persons in paid work, usually referred to as the employment rate.

Some of this can be attributed to developing gender equality but economic issues have also played their part: on the whole there has been a decline in manufacturing jobs and an increase in service jobs; as men tend to dominate the former and women the latter this too has decreased the economic activity gender gap. Despite these changes, feminists argue that women are still disadvantaged compared with men in paid employment. There remain persistent inequalities which are associated with the fact that men and women, as already noted, tend to be concentrated in different areas of work – this is known as a segregated labour market (see World in Focus 14.2). A gender gap in economic activity is not unique to the UK, as Figure 14.2 shows this exists across the globe.

Men and women not only predominately work in different sectors they also work in different ways (see World in Focus 14.2), in that, despite economic shifts and restructuring men still work full time whilst a sizeable minority of women work part time, in fact

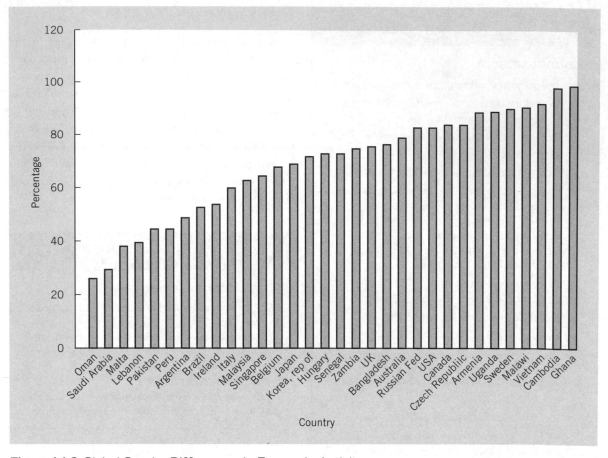

Figure 14.2 Global Gender Differences in Economic Activity

Source: Derived from ILO & UN statistics at Human Development Reports, http://cfapp2.undp.org/statistics/data/rc_report.cfm, by author Aug 2004.

World in focus 14.2

Women's work, men's work

In the UK women are concentrated in a limited range of work. Of all working women:

24% secretarial and administrative

14% personal services

12% sales and customer services

These three sectors account for over half of all women's employment yet make up only 12 per cent of men's employment.

Likewise in the USA, the equivalent categories for working women are:

33.2% managerial, professional

39.5% technical/sales and administrative support

17.6% service

For men, these sectors combined represented 58.8 per cent of all employments, compared with 90.3 per cent of women's jobs.
[**Hotlink → Geography (Chapter 10)**].

Source: Cited by UK Twomey 2002. USA Caiazza *et al.* (2004: 14).

although 43 per cent of employed women in Britain work part time only 8 per cent of men do (Twomey, 2002). Nonetheless some governments have recog- nised that labour market shifts might make for changes (see World in Focus 14.3). In relation to women's part-time work, see A Closer Look 14.4.

World in focus 14.3

The Dutch 'combination' model

This model was launched in 1995 after a government commission (translated as) Future Scenarios on the Redistribution of Unpaid Work. This model is a balanced combination of paid and unpaid work, the core concept being that both are equally valued. Men and women are able to 'choose a personal mix of paid labour in long part-time (or short full-time) jobs, part-time household production of care and part-time outsourcing of care' (Commissie Toekomstscenarios, 1995, cited in Plantenga, 2002: 54).

Part-time employment is also a core element of the combination model; flexible, non-full-time working hours for both men and women are deemed indispensable to reach gender equality. It is exactly this element which distinguishes the combination model from other ideal types like the Caregiver Parity model or the Universal Breadwinner Model.
(Plantenga, 2002: 55)

[Hotlink → Social Policy (Chapter 5)].

Although aimed at increasing gender equality in the workforce this has had its limits: part-time jobs have now an increased status and are no longer only available in marginal jobs. However, although women's economic participation rates increased from 34.7 per cent in 1987 to 51 per cent in 1999 this was not due to huge changes in work patterns. In fact, women took up opportunities for part-time work, from 48.5 per cent of the female labour force in 1987 to 60.5 per cent in 1999, yet the rate for men working part-time barely rose from the 1987 figure of 10.3 per cent of the male workforce, being only 11.4 per cent in 1999.

Equality has been increased as women have had some barriers to economic participation removed, but men have barely changed their patterns of work.

A closer look 14.4

Gender, parenting and economic activity

A major explanation for women's increased involvement in part-time work is parenting. Although men are also parents the majority of those whose work pattern is determined by parenthood are women (Marchbank, 2000). Women with young children are more prevalent in part-time work and this diminishes as the age of the youngest child increases. In the UK, of working mothers of children under 5, 67 per cent work part time but this falls to 45 per cent for those whose youngest is over 16 (Twomey, 2002). As only 32 per cent of women without children work part time it is obvious that motherhood is a major factor in women choosing part-time employment. Fatherhood does not appear to be a factor in men deciding to work part time. White women are also more likely than ethnic minority women to work part time, so although ethnic minority women have lower employment rates they are, when in work, more likely to work full time (Hibbett, 2002).

Of course, parenting, especially motherhood, also affects leisure choices – see later.

The segregated labour market

We have already met one form of segregation, *horizontal* segregation: the tendency for men and women to occupy different sections of the labour market. As shown above, even in the twenty-first century women remain concentrated in a narrower range of jobs than men (Twomey, 2002; Caiazza *et al.*, 2004) and also are over-represented in the ranks of part-time workers. *Vertical* segregation exists when men and women work together in an occupation yet occupy different strata within that occupation with men higher up in the better paid posts. Although women have broken into many previously 'male' jobs they are not equal and are not as senior. This is referred to as the 'glass ceiling', when women are entering high status professions but not making it to the top even though they may be as

Stop and think 14.4

Think about a professional job familiar to you. At what grades do men predominate? At what grades do women? Be careful, also consider what percentage of the workforce men and women each constitute. Are either over represented in the lower grades? Which? Are either over represented in the higher grades? Which?

talented as the men who do – it means that women can see through to where they want to be but are prevented by a ceiling – a glass one (see A Closer Look 14.5).

A closer look 14.5

Masculinised structure of work

It is argued that the very structure of work is a barrier to women's advancement as it is very 'masculinised'. That is it is organised around the notion of a male breadwinner who is free to participate in full-time employment as his other responsibilities are taken care of by a female partner. Even when governments attempt to change this through providing flexibility of working time such notions as male breadwinner are difficult to overcome:

UK flexible work time schemes

27 per cent of women and 18 per cent of men [are] employed in jobs which allow flexibility (*Labour Force Survey*, 2003).

Nordic parenting leave

Countries such as Denmark, Iceland, Finland, Sweden and Norway have had parenting leave rights longer than others, such as the European Union [**Hotlink →** **Social Policy (Chapter 5)**]. Yet a study in 1991 found that parenting leave was used very little by fathers as they were fearful of being thought of as not serious about their job (Kaul, 1991). However, by 2004 nearly all Icelandic fathers used their entitlement to three months off work on 80 per cent of their salary and in Denmark 46,000 men took paternity leave though Danish fathers spent an average of 3.6 weeks off work with their babies, compared with the mothers' average of 42.3 weeks, so it appears that some changes are being made.

Source: BBC, 2005 **http://news.bbc.co.uk/go/em/fr/-/2/hi/ europe/4629631.stm**

Gender is not the only segregation in the workforce. Annie Phizacklea and Carol Wolkowitz (1995) have pointed out that labour markets across Europe are not just gendered but racialised. Both men and women from ethnic minorities are less likely than whites to be in work. In the UK, this is most stark in relation to Pakistani and Bangladeshi women: in 2003, 72 per cent of white women worked whilst only 22 per cent of Pakistani and Bangladeshi women were recorded as in employment (Hibbett and Meager, 2003). However, once employed both ethnic minority men and women are no less likely than their white counterparts to be working in professional or managerial roles (Hibbett, 2002).

Pay

Across the world a gender pay gap is visible, in some cases it is an extensive gap, such as in Saudi Arabia where it is 79 per cent (i.e. women earn 21 per cent of men's wages) and the smallest gap exists in Sweden, where women earn 83 per cent of men's wages (see Figure 14.3).

In the UK, the gender pay gap is 40 per cent, that is women earned 60 per cent of men's earnings (see Figure 14.3). As more women than men work part time this explains part of this gap. However, even when we consider only those in full-time work a gap remains for, in 2001, women still earned only 81 per cent of men's average gross hourly earnings (an improvement from less than 78 per cent in 1991) (Twomey, 2002). The gender pay gap remains due to the differentiated labour forces, that is the areas in which women work are paid at a lesser rate than those which are male dominated.

Many countries now have legislation to equalize pay, yet differences persist. In the UK the Equal Pay Act was passed in 1970 and came into effect in 1975. It had little effect in its original form as there was evidence that employers deliberately segregated jobs that had previously been mixed to avoid giving women workers the same pay as men; this was due to the stipulation in the law that people had to be paid the same for the same job. An amendment in 1984 introduced the requirement to pay people the same for work of *equal value*. This was meant to allow for comparisons to be made and to bring into protection women working in areas with no men for the first time. Some women brought legal cases to argue their work, for example, school dinner cook is equivalent to a house painter, was of equal value and won, but as each of these only related to the individual occupations in the actual legal case the Act remained limited in scope. Many other women were reluctant to bring forward cases for fear of victimisation. The main reason for the

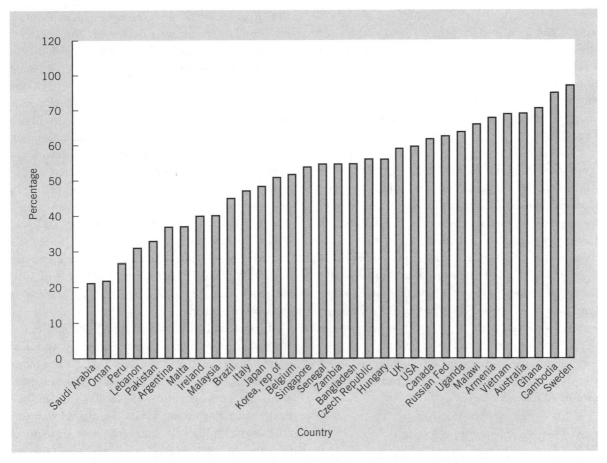

Figure 14.3 Gender Pay Gap Globally

Source: Derived from ILO & UN statistics at Human Development Reports, http://cfapp2.undp.org/statistics/data/rc_report.cfm, by author Aug 2004.

continuing gender pay gap, not just in the UK, is that differential pay is related to the structure of the labour market and such legislation has had little impact on this structure.

Why is the labour market gender segregated?

Many attempts have been made to explain the universal nature of gender segregated labour and gender pay gaps. Here we shall review a few of the main areas, including: economic arguments, in particular Human Capital theory; Marxist Feminist and combination of capitalism and patriarchy.

Human capital

Neoclassical economic theories attribute pay differences to productivity – simply put someone who is valuable to a company will receive a greater reward than another who contributes less to the firm's profits. Human capital theory (Becker, 1993) tries to explain wage differentials based on the education and experience of the individual. It is argued that women earn less than men as they have less human capital; that is they have lower levels of skills and work experience than men. These differences result from freely made decisions of individual women regarding the time they choose to allocate to work rather than domestic responsibilities. This theory also explains horizontal segregation and low pay as a result of choice; that is women choose jobs which penalise them least for non-standard work patterns and also provide maximum return for limited skills. There is an inherent assumption in this theory that all women will consider that they will spend less time in the labour force than men and, subsequently, may not invest in acquiring expensive skills.

This theory is weak in a number of ways. Firstly, it ignores sex discrimination for it does not explain why women who have equal human capital to men in terms of abilities and experience face the limitations of the 'glass ceiling' and do not get promoted posts at the same rates as equivalent men. Secondly, it determines 'skill' as something objective rather than subjective. In other words, why is it that being able to drive an HGV (heavy goods vehicle) lorry is viewed as more valuable (and paid more) than a nursery nurse? As Economist Steven Pressman (2002: 31) concludes in his investigation of gender poverty gaps 'the striking result . . . is that educational levels matter very little' and that deficiencies in women's education cannot explain earnings differences effectively.

Marxist feminist theory

Classical Marxist descriptions of the relationships between men selling their labour to capitalists who then exploit the surplus value of that labour by selling the proceeds at a profit did not include consideration of women in the labour market, except to note that capital required the existence of a reserve army of labour to weaken workers' bargaining powers in times of labour shortages. It became clear that women constituted such a reserve which was also able to be tapped in times of political crisis such as war. In both World Wars women were encouraged, and some were conscripted, into occupations which had been male bastions. At the end of the 'emergency' governments employed ideologies of domesticity to return women to the home to make sure that there would be 'jobs for heroes'.

Developments in Marxian thought recognise that women's labour is exploited and that to understand it we need to look at the structure of the labour market and the way that employers/capitalists ensure the segmentation of work to control the workforce by employing already existing social cleavages based on ethnicity, gender or age. Concepts such as Primary and Secondary Sectors were developed. Primary sector jobs are characterised as skilled, secure, with decent pay and conditions and the possibility of advancement through training and promotion. Conversely, the Secondary sector consists of work deemed unskilled, is insecure, with low wages, poor terms and conditions and which has very few prospects for advancement. We have already looked at the concentration of women and men in certain aspects of the labour force (horizontal segregation) and it is hardly surprising to note that women are in jobs which fit the description of Secondary sector at a higher rate than are men. Marxist feminist thought explains this due to the fact that women are more likely to leave work and are under-represented in the ranks of the trade unions, both of which make it easier for employers to dispense with women workers.

Of course, this explanation does not consider the role that men, as a group, play in the exclusion of women from work and the fact that trade unions themselves have been guilty of sustaining a segmented labour market (Cockburn, 1991). For example the Amalgamated Engineering Union negotiated a post-war settlement with the British government as a requirement for their acceptance of women into factories during the First World War. The result of these negotiations was the Restoration of Pre War Practices Act, 1919 which not only ensured that women were sacked from jobs previously held by men but also from some jobs that had never been the sole terrain of men at the end of the war. Another weakness of this approach is that it does not take into account the fact that there are women in the primary sector and men in the secondary sector, nor is it able to explain the differential experiences amongst women, for example the fact that ethnicity is related also to pay rates (see Figure 14.4).

A fundamental criticism of this approach is that it focuses too simply on the needs of capitalism without considering gender relations.

Putting patriarchy into the picture

Heidi Hartmann (1980) argues that the issues of gender segregation of the labour market and subsequent low pay for women is only explicable if the forces of capitalism are examined alongside those of

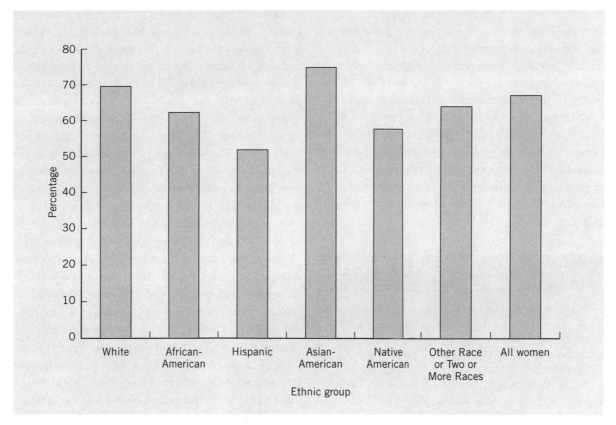

Figure 14.4 Ratio of Women's to White Men's Median Annual Earnings in the United States, by Race and Ethnicity, 1999.

Source: Caiazza *et al.* (2004:7)

Notes: 1. for full time, year round workers, 2. for women 16 plus

patriarchy, a system she labelled patriarchal capitalism. She argues that men have social and economic power as they control women's labour in both the domestic sphere and in the labour market. These two are linked in that, as men secured higher status, better paid jobs, women's presence in the domestic realm was reinforced. Likewise, men were then able to argue that their wages need to be sufficient to support a household, a family wage. Like others Hartmann argues that trade unions organised to exclude women from certain areas of work (however, it should not be forgotten that trade unions have also organised to keep certain groups of men out of certain trades in attempts to reserve jobs for their members and their male relatives). This has benefited both men as individuals, who acquire women in the home providing social reproduction [**Hotlink → Gendered Perspectives –**

Theoretical Issues (Chapter 1)] and employers who gain from the cheaper labour of women.

This seemingly harmonious relationship between patriarchy and capitalism has been modified. Sylvia Walby (1986) has also written about such a dual-system. She contends that the two are separate systems which interact together but not always smoothly. This is due to her observation that capitalism and patriarchy have conflicting interests when it comes to women's labour. Employers are keen to exploit all labour including women, so the male dominance of the labour force creates certain tensions. The increased entry of women into paid work, on increasingly equal terms in western societies, may be encouraged by capital but has the potential to undermine patriarchy. Walby provides an example of patriarchy's response in the way women were excluded from British factory work in the nineteenth century through the passing of a series of Factory Acts. She argues that patriarchy was under threat as increasing numbers of women entered factories, so under the auspices of protecting women's, and children's, health male workers were also able to ensure the dominance of men in these factories.

A critique of this dual-systems approach is that it does not consider gender enough, especially in relation to the way that gender segregation of the labour market reflects gender-specific roles, not just in who does what job but in how that job is expected to be done (Adkins, 1995) [**Hotlink → Sex and Sexuality (Chapter 15)**].

Stop and think 14.5

Each of these explanations has some credence. Reflect upon your own knowledge and experience of the world of work, both paid and unpaid, and draw links between that experience and the main aspects of each explanation. Which of them answers your questions about the differential experiences of men and women?

Theorising the link between work and leisure

When social scientists first started to theorise leisure it was seen as the activities undertaken when all other obligations, especially paid work, were attended to. Stanley Parker (1976) categorised leisure in three groups, in relation to how the participant viewed their paid employment:

➤ As an extension of work – for those whose main focus in life is job fulfilment, leisure is seen as an extension of work as it provides rest and recuperation to enable the worker to perform more effectively in the workplace.

➤ A neutral approach – in this participants view family and social life as central to their person and so leisure not viewed as facilitating better work performance.

➤ In opposition – here leisure, rather than family or work is the main focus of the person.

Parker's theory has been criticised for a number of reasons, primarily for a lack of consideration of how factors other than paid employment affect leisure, for example, children's and retired people's leisure follow different patterns than that of working adults. He was also criticised for not considering that certain activities appear across all of his groups – such as the prevalence of watching television as a leisure activity and for not noting the cultural specificity of his work. The main critique however, is that this theory is deterministic and leaves no space for the choice of individuals and therefore is limited in its explanatory abilities.

A couple of years later Ken Roberts (1978) developed an argument that leisure involves freedom of choice of individuals. He acknowledges that paid work does influence leisure, but adds factors such as life cycle and personal preference. He defines leisure differently from Parker taking it to be, not just time outside of paid work, but only time spent on activities (and non-activities) outside of other obligations too. As such, Roberts argues that only activities that are self-determined equate to leisure, therefore gardening can be leisure for one but an obligation for another. Roberts also looked across different kinds of people. He concluded that higher levels of education meant that more leisure time was spent socialising with friends and less in front of the television. He also concluded that women had more leisure time than men.

Conversly, Oriel Sullivan (1996) concluded that men did have a little more leisure time than women but that it was not significant. Her analysis of time diaries kept by 380 heterosexual couples in the UK showed that men spent a little more time than women sleeping, relaxing, socialising and eating and paid work. By contrast women spend more time on housework and childcare, this extra time being virtually equal to the additional time men spend in paid employment. The result being virtually equal leisure time, and this is supported by a cross-Europe study (*Eurostat Pocketbooks*, 2004) which found that women have between 4 and 5 hours free each day, whilst men have greater than 5 hours – a difference, but not a great one. However, this European study did also find that of this free time men participate more in sports and hobbies than women do – see A Closer Look 14.6 for international information.

So, we have one account which states that men have less leisure (in the UK) than women, and another that found that there were virtually no differences in the time available for leisure between the genders and cross-European support for this latter position – though it has to be noted that perhaps the differences are about time, that is the time that these studies were conducted. None of these definitions though really addresses the true interaction of leisure and work as outlined by Letherby and Reynolds (2005) above. As we will see views such as these have been heavily critiqued by feminists. However, before turning to gender it is necessary to scope out other differences in the experience of leisure, for gender is not the only social variable involved.

Differential experiences of leisure

The experience of leisure is not homogeneous, not just due to gender differences but other social differences such as age, ethnicity and employment status amongst others. As we have seen, much of the theorising around gender has focused on the relationship between paid employment and leisure. But what of the unemployed? How different is their experience?

Leisure and unemployment

As we would expect the leisure experiences of the unemployed are different from those in paid work – but not that great. The main points to note are that unemployment does mean more time is available for leisure pursuits but that these tend to be limited to activities such as watching the television: unemployed men spend 2 hours more per day than employed men, whilst unemployed women spend $1\frac{1}{2}$ hours more on activities such as television, listening to the radio, reading and sitting around (Gallie *et al.*, 1994). Despite fewer obligations on time such as paid work, unemployment does not mean a great increase in leisure for restricted finances mean that expensive pursuits, such as cinema, gym clubs, football matches are just not possible (Gallie *et al.*, 1994).

Other factors affecting leisure

Other factors influence the experience of leisure; Les Haywood and colleagues (1995) examine the ways in which the methodologies of leisure studies have shaped responses which can mask these differences. They consider how age, both youth and elderly, affects the ability to participate and the leisure choices made. They also examine how ethnicity, social class, gender and disability all affect leisure choices and can constrain the range of these choices. They conclude that certain choices come from the restrictions of money, space (as in free time) and individual capacities, but also are limited by individual social capital (Bourdieu,

1985). In a similar vein Peggy Warner-Smith and Peter Brown (2002) consider how gender and geography interact to create certain restrictions. Both social class, and the social capital it comes with, affect leisure choices, even within similar arenas: for example, two different people may choose a short holiday break, one whose social capital may include foreign languages or even just previous experiences of foreign travel, may select a Tuscan villa whilst another, whose social capital is more vested in working-class activities may decide to go to a holiday camp instead. Of course, there are also financial restrictions here, but often both such holidays can be found for similar costs. There is no judgement here as to what might be a 'better' holiday, just to note that different forms of social capital can help explain different choices. Other restrictions also apply; Warner-Smith and Brown note that the mid-aged women of their study in New South Wales, Australia, undertake leisure:

> within a framework of constraints which are both explicit, such as time in paid/unpaid work, restricted discretionary income and access to facilities and programs, and implicit, such as cultural expectations of appropriate behaviour for one's age and gender. Physically and metaphorically they inhabit an ageing, conservative social space.
>
> (2002: 53)

Other factors also come into play regarding leisure – see A Closer Look 14.7 for details of age, whilst A Closer Look 14.8 provides some information on health status and ethnicity.

A further influence on choice of leisure are activities which are deemed to be appropriate for an individual to undertake. Haywood and collegues report that:

> Britain has the lowest proportion of women taking part in sport in any country of similar economic status except for Italy. Spatio-temporal restrictions offer a partial explanation, but more crucially is the perception of sports by women themselves.
>
> (1995: 132)

A closer look 14.7

The leisure of the elderly

Many old people are faced with considerable constraints upon their leisure activity. These can be summarized as:

'decreasing economic, social and physical resources

increasing isolation from family and community

increasingly burdensome domestic chores and personal care concerns . . .

much communal leisure activity of older people sustains cultural activity of a by-gone age. Step into these spaces and time seems to have stood still. The elderly rely on community support networks (churches, local societies, village institutes) for out-of-home leisure. In these locations are found residues of self-organised community activity which were dominant in the past, and which stand in sharp contrast to the consumer-orientated technology-based leisure pursuits of contemporary society. Activities such as whist-drives, community singing, poetry reading, talks by local experts . . . Organized by local groups such as Townswomen Guilds, Mothers' Unions, Women's Institutes, Darby and Joan Clubs. Here, people consume the leisure they produce in self-organized collectives.'

(Haywood *et al.*, 1995: 143)

They go on to argue that both women and men choose their sporting activities based on perceptions of gender appropriate behaviour. This may be because, as John Clarke and Chas Critcher (1985) note, sport is one area where 'femininity' and 'masculinity' are 'celebrated'. This is supported and created by the fact that '[i]mages of appropriate activity are inculcated through early child-rearing practices, different movement experiences in physical education, and media portrayals of femininity' (Haywood *et al.*, 1995: 132). It would appear, from an examination of Table 14.1, that such images translate into lesser activity for women than men [**Hotlink → Geography (Chapter 10)**].

Table 14.1 Participation in sports in the UK

	1993	1996	2002
At least one activity			
Men	72%	71%	65%
Women	57%	58%	53%
At least one activity, excluding walking			
Men	57%	54%	51%
Women	39%	38%	36%

Source. Dreived from General Household Survey (1996: 219) and Fox and Rickards (2004: 7)

A closer look 14.8

Variations in sports and leisure (UK)

Some variations indicated from the 2002 General Household Survey:

Health status – 23 per cent of adults reporting a limiting longstanding illness or disability reported participation in a specialised arts activity (compared with 28 per cent of adults who have no illness or disability); 40 per cent of those with a longstanding illness or disability had participated in at least one activity (including walking) compared with 65 per cent of other adults.

Ethnicity – Pakistani/Bangladeshi, Other Asian Background and Indian people were less likely than expected, after controlling for age, to have participated in at least one of the arts; likewise, Pakistani/Bangladeshi, Indian, Black Caribbean and Black African people were less likely than expected, after controlling for age, to have participated in at least one sports activity, whilst White people were more likely.

Source: Derived from Fox and Rickards (2004: 10, 13–14).

Gender and leisure

We have already looked at a number of issues regarding gender and leisure differences. However, there are arguments than larger differences exist in leisure time than those indicated above.

Defining leisure from a feminist perspective

Many feminists have critiqued the very basis of what is considered leisure. Eileen Green, Sandra Hebron and Diana Woodward (1990) studied 707 women in Sheffield interviewing many and their husbands. They found that the definitions used by male sociologists were not useful in their study, being based on men with full-time jobs. In fact, many of their women had difficulty differentiating leisure from other aspects of their lives and referred to leisure less as an activity and more of a state of mind. That is, these women saw leisure as doing things they enjoyed or pleasing themselves, as such, certain jobs, even obligatory ones, such as ironing wcrc considered by some as enjoyable and therefore leisure.

Like other feminists they argue that there are important differences between men and women's leisure: firstly that women and men tend to do different things and that women have less access to leisure opportunities than men:

> The leisure activities which women do most frequently and on which they spend the majority of their free time are those that can be done at home; that can be done in the bits of time left over from doing other things, or that can be easily interrupted if necessary.
>
> (Green *et al.*, 1990: 84)

In addition, they found that it was harder for women to set aside work and embrace leisure due to having greater domestic responsibilities which are open ended, especially childcare. Indeed, some women viewed their part-time jobs (such as bar work) as leisure as they permitted them to escape from domestic chores and social isolation.

Green and colleagues (1990) admit that they were writing a socialist feminist study, and as such they included patriarchy as an essential consideration in their work. There is an emphasis on the constraints on women's leisure in their findings. Given women's lower earnings than men, women have less money than men to spend on leisure. In their study they found that wives were often financially dependent on husbands, which resulted in limitations on the range of activities available. Also, as women as a group have less access to private transport (Haywood *et al.*, 1996:

132) then the degree of freedom of choice between men and women about their leisure is marked.

Green and colleagues (1990) also found that men's attitudes act as a barrier to women, often including a view that women are supposed to choose their leisure from a range of things related to the home and family, i.e. socially acceptable, for example, family picnics, and so on. These limits derive, they claim, from the features of a capitalist patriarchal society. There exist systems of social control to limit women's access to leisure compared with men. So, apart from time, space and money what might these be?

Social constraints on women's leisure

Jalna Hanmer (1978) has written about how women are socially controlled not just by violence but by the fear of violence [**Hotlink → Violence and Resistance (Chapter 16); Hotlink → Geography (Chapter 10)**]. This fear can keep women at home, fearful of using public transport or being out after dark. Some husbands and fathers use this as a reason, in a protective manner, resulting in daughters being more limited in their movements than sons, for example. Both the fear within women, and the fear of their male relatives makes it more difficult for women and girls to pursue regular leisure activities than their male counterparts. In their Sheffield study, Green and colleagues (1990) found that husbands who did not wish their wives to go out used tactics from mild disapproval to physical violence to stop them. Restrictions were also based on the nature of the activity. Haywood and colleagues (1995) argue that gender stereotypes affect the leisure choices of women and men but it is more than that: the opinion of important others can also affect the range of choices. That is, certain activities are seen as more respectable: in the Sheffield study participating in yoga, keep fit and night school were seen by men as more acceptable things for their women (i.e. wives, partners, daughters) to do than to go clubbing or visit a pub. This experience is also differentiated by ethnicity, for women of ethnic minorities fear racial harassment as well as sexual and, in addition, face other cultural limitations to leisure. Green and colleagues (1990) cite a study by the Greater London Council (GLC) showing that Asian men discouraged women from going out, especially at night and that 95 per cent of Asian women surveyed said they would not go out at night alone [**Hotlink → Geography (Chapter 10)**]. Afro-Caribbean women were not so culturally restricted but remained limited by factors of gender and ethnicity (fear of attack), lack of childcare and demands of work.

Related to the restrictions above is the very nature of certain leisure venues, many of which are very masculinised spaces and therefore uncomfortable for women. Further, if women do dare enter it is as if they then have no further need of respect. See for example the case of women who sell beer in Korean bars (World in Focus 14.4).

Stop and think 14.6

Think about different leisure spaces. Think about one place where you feel you belong and another that makes you uncomfortable (perhaps even to the point of avoiding it). Now consider yourself to be a different sex, then a different ethnicity. Would you feel the same way about both places?

World in focus 14.4

Women beer vendors in Korea

Women working in a masculinised leisure space can face sexual harassment. Reports from Korea show that women who work in bars are constantly assumed to be selling more than beer and are frequently approached by the men in the bar for prostitution services. It would appear that simply by transgressing the gender boundaries of the bar – that is, by being there at all, even when working – women are assumed to be sexually available.

Source: *This Morning*, Radio 4, BBC, 16 June 2005.

So, feminists argue that women's leisure is constrained and controlled by finance, hostility and ideology. Indeed it is recognised that women often monitor their own and other females' behaviour as they accept patriarchal ideology about what is appropriate, for example mothers of young children can be criticised for going out socialising more so than the fathers of these children.

However, just as men's leisure is not homogeneous, neither is women's. Briefly summarised these can be listed as:

➤ Social class – the higher the class, the more time women have for leisure, wealthier women are involved in more sport and activities than other women.

➤ Marital status – single, young employed women have most freedom, as they have more money, less domestic responsibilities, and no husbands to pass judgement on them. In fact, in the Sheffield study it was found that getting married reduced sport participation more than having children. After marriage/partnership women's recreation often blurs into family recreation.

➤ Women are also *agents*, as they make opportunities for leisure, make friends at work or the school gate. Women are more involved than men in voluntary organisations; nonetheless, it has to be remembered that although these are 'safe' and do not challenge gender stereotypes at the same time they can increase independence (Green *et al.*, 1990).

Conclusion

We have looked at a wide range of issues in this chapter: from the structure of work to its implications for leisure. Fundamental however, is to remember that work has been structured in a capitalist society, and in many others, in masculinised manners. As such, men are advantaged over women (as a whole) in such systems. Remember also that although leisure is very much shaped by paid work, time away from paid work and finances (again related to paid work), these are not the only factors influencing the leisure of the population. In addition, for women social control factors also enter the equation.

Further reading

Les Haywood, Francis Kew, Peter Bramham, Jon Spink, John Capenhurst and Ian Henry (eds) (1995), *Understanding Leisure*, Cheltenham, Stanley Thorne Publishers. This is a comprehensive review of the literature, a sensible critique of existing leisure methodology and an accessible discussion of pertinent issues, including differences in people's leisure experiences and opportunities.

Cara Carmichael Aitchison (2003), *Gender and Leisure: Social and Cultural Perspectives*, London, Routledge. Drawing on a wide range of theoretical perspectives, as well as extensive empirical research, this book goes forward to offer a contemporary socio-cultural analysis of gender relations in leisure practice and leisure policy

Critical Social Policy: A Journal of Theory and Practice in Social Welfare, 2002, 22(1) – this special issue of the journal is entitled 'New Divisions for Labour: Alternatives for Caring and Working'. It contains seven articles covering a range of national situations.

Labour Market Trends – a government published journal which describes and discusses issues, patterns and changes in the UK labour market. Available online at **www.statistics.gov.uk** (follow links to articles)

Websites

Institute for Women's Policy Research – an independent research institute, based in Washington, DC. The IWPR collates vast amounts of data on the economic position of women in the USA, most of which is downloadable from their website: **www.iwpr.org**

European Industrial Relations Observatory Online – a repository of an amazing number of articles related to labour matters in Europe, at **www.eiro.eurofound.ie**

United Nations – the UN site has a great deal of information regarding Human Development and International Labour Organisation figures, tables, graphs etc. covering the whole world. Start at **www.un.org**

Higher Education Academy – This site is a guide to key texts and other sources concerned with leisure practice and its social, economic, political and cultural contexts. It includes a number of advanced and sometimes older texts that may be helpful. The emphasis of the guide is on leisure as it has been historically conceptualised and practised in the UK, however it does include some non-British texts where these contribute to a better understanding of the social and cultural aspects of leisure. Accessible at **http://www.hlst.heacademy.ac.uk /resources/guides/leisure_society.html**

End of chapter activity

1 Go back to the cartoon at the beginning of the chapter. Investigate the gender balance in the two careers of train driving and brain surgery. Reflect on what you have found.

2 Go to a local leisure centre. Observe which adults have children with them? Is it men or women, perhaps both? Of the different activities available who is involved in those focused on children rather than themselves?

3 Read the list of activities below. Which of these are generally perceived to be appropriate for men, which for women? For both? Why?

Snooker	Rugby	Knitting	Horse Racing
Yoga	Boxing	Surfing	Polo
Badminton	Ballet	Amateur Dramatics	Golf
Motor racing	Orienteering	Swimming	Opera
Cricket	Mountain Climbing	Rowing	Aerobics
Dog walking	Dog Racing	Hunting	Computers

Think about those that you have done/would like to do? Are you prevented from doing any?
What's the reason: cost, social class, ethnicity, age, ability, gender, sexuality?

Answer to stop and think 14.2

➤ Gender Neutral = washing up, tidying up, vacuuming making beds.

➤ Gender Segregated Female = cooking main meal, thorough cleaning, washing and ironing of clothes, anything managerial such as household budget or shopping. Usually the routine.

➤ Gender Segregated Male = gardening, cutting grass, repairs, taking out the rubbish. Usually non-routine, at intervals and outside. (Wajcman, 1983; Weellock, 1990).

Sex and sexuality

Key issues in this chapter:

➤ Sex and sexuality as biological destiny or social construction.
➤ Dominant – including medical, lay, religious, media, political – discourses of sex and sexuality.
➤ The gendered double standard.
➤ Sex and sexuality at work.
➤ The relationship between sex, sexuality, gender and other forms of difference.

At the end of this chapter you should be able to:

➤ Describe biological and social constructionist explanations of sex and sexuality.
➤ Identify and challenge dominant discourses surrounding sex and sexuality.
➤ Identify and challenge the gendered double standard of sexuality.
➤ Reflect on the relationship between sex and sexuality and work.
➤ Explain the relationship between sex, sexuality, gender and other forms of difference.

Introduction

Pearl, a respondent in Helen M. Lawson's book on American women carsales workers said: 'So they invited me to a sales meeting . . . first time ever. And I felt like I had really made it. I go to the back of the room and all the guys are sitting around laughing. The local prostitute is up on the table doing a strip, shaking her ass and they're looking at me for my reaction.' (2000: 2)

Stop and think 15.1

This quote is interesting as it tells us a lot about Pearl, about the men she works with and about the relationship between sex, sexuality and working relationships. Why do you think the men invited Pearl to the meeting? How was the way the men treated Pearl similar and different to their relationship with the woman they had hired to strip for them?

Everyone – from comedians to politicians, from the man and woman in the street to royalty and pop celebrity – is interested in sex and sexuality. Images of sex and sexuality are all around us. We are all encouraged to measure our sexual identity and sexual behaviour against a politically and popularly supported ideal and images of this ideal predominate in cultural representation. Sex is also used to sell us everything from cars to chocolate, from newspapers to insurance policies. On the other hand, sex and sexuality is a very personal thing and our personal relationship to it may give us pleasure, make us anxious or cause us pain. It may do all of these things. Despite the attention it receives in the media, on billboards, and over coffee break discussions some aspects of sex and sexuality are still taboo. Heterosexuality and heterosexual relationships are still sanctioned in law and social policy in a way that homosexuality and homosexual relationships are not and this is supported by lay understandings of heterosexuality as normal and natural and conversely homosexuality as abnormal and unnatural. These definitions are based on statistical (what most people do), religious (what one's religion permits or prohibits) and cultural (what one's culture encourages or discourages) norms (Holmes, 1991). Heterosexuality is also subject to sanction and censure. Particularly significant here is the gendered double standard and again the cultural significance afforded to sexuality is relevant in that it reflects and encourages the appropriation of women's bodies by men (Jackson and Scott, 1996; Abbott *et al.*, 2005). In other words the sexual subordination of women is culturally defined as normal and natural.

Social scientists, including gay and lesbian theorists have argued that sex is a political phenomenon characterised by power relations. Speaking of the dominant perceptions of normal and natural behaviours and practices in relation to sex and sexuality Julia Hirst notes that:

Such views become hegemonic because they are reinforced both by the institutionalized ideology of the day and by lay perceptions in providing explanations for subjective feelings and prejudices by giving them a clear and unavoidable cause.

(2004: 69)

In this chapter we explore these issues further. The remainder of the chapter is divided into five sections. In 'Sex and sexuality: explanations and theories' we consider essentialist and social constructionist explanations of sex and sexuality. This is followed by a consideration of double standards in relation to sex and sexuality in terms of gay and lesbian experience and heterosexual men and women. Following our focus on sex and sexuality within intimate relationships we move on to consider sex and sexuality at work before concluding.

Sex and sexuality: explanations and theories

Despite the large amount of attention to and interest in sex and sexuality there has been limited large-scale social research on sexual activity, as A Closer Look 15.1 demonstrates.

A closer look 15.1

Surveying sex

Considering the public interest, there is limited large-scale social research on sexual activity. Until the publication of *Sexual Behaviour in Britain* (Wellings *et al.*, 1994) anyone who wanted information about human sexual behaviour based on large-scale research had to look to the work of Kinsey and colleagues (1948, 1953) or Masters and Johnson (1966, 1970). The 1994 study was more extensive and more characteristic of the general population than the Kinsey study. The sample of 18,876 people interviewed was representative of the British population in terms of social class, education, ethnic background, age and region. The survey produced a vast amount of descriptive information about reported sexual behaviour. It also raised a whole range of methodological issues concerning the study of sexual behaviour. For example, the survey found that six in every hundred men said they had had some homosexual experience in their lives. Some gay activists have stressed that these numbers may be an underestimation because respondents questioned about 'partners' may have counted only long-term relationships. They also said that the home interviews used by the researchers would have led to an underestimation, as 'Closeted Gays are unlikely to admit their homosexuality to a total stranger who turns up on their door and asks them personal questions about the intimate details of their private life' (Peter Tatchell, quoted in I. Katz, 'Rights Group scorn one in 90 gay survey', The *Guardian*, 22.1.1994).

(Cited in Marsh, 2006: 277–8)

Stop and think 15.2

Here are the some dictionary definitions for the words normal, natural, abnormal and unnatural:

➤ Normal – right, not differentiating from the standard.

➤ Natural – constituted by nature – based on innate moral feelings of mankind (*sic*).

➤ Abnormal – deviating from the type, contrary to rule or system.

➤ Unnatural – not in accordance with the usual course of nature – monstrous.

Why do you think that some sexual behaviours and identities are defined as appropriate and others as sexually deviant? What are the consequences of a sexually deviant label?

Biological destiny or social construction?

Sexuality is often defined as a natural instinct or drive which demands fulfilment through sexual activity. This view of sexuality as a natural biological entity is referred to as *essentialism*. Much essential thinking links sex as a natural instinct to reproductive activity. As Hirst (2004) states essentialist perspectives on sexuality have a long history and in the eighteenth and nineteenth centuries medical and psychiatric identification of some sexual behaviours and identities as perverse and abnormally pathological replaced previous religious convictions on sinful sexual activity. As Jeffrey Weeks (1986) points out within essentialist approaches to sex and sexuality there is a clear link between biological sex and sexuality:

> Modern culture has assumed an intimate connection between the fact of being biologically male or female (that is having appropriate sex organs and reproductive potentialities) and the correct form of erotic behaviour (usually genital intercourse between men and women).
>
> (Weeks 1986: 13)

The view here then is that human sexuality is rooted in biology, and a normal sex drive is a heterosexual drive intended for the production of children and the perpetuation of the species. Deviation is considered to be pathological. Thus, any sexual activity that is not intended for procreation – including homosexual activity and prostitution – is defined as deviant, unnatural and perverse. Heterosexuality is the norm in this model for both women and men, and sex is properly expressed in stable, monogamous, ideally marital relationships. World in Focus 15.1 provides one example of how the so-called development of natural heterosexual masculinity is imposed on and reflected in popular culture.

World in focus 15.1

Fantasy islands

Gregory Woods' (1995) analysis of several films featuring remote islands included *Lord of the Flies, The Blue Lagoon, Return to the Blue Lagoon, Our Girl Friday, South Pacific* and *Castaway*. He argues that since the eighteenth century western culture has imposed its values on tropical 'desert islands'. Several main types of island narrative have emerged. For example, there is the scenario of marooned children of both sexes growing up through adolescent rites of passage into a 'natural' heterosexuality and division of gender roles. In another popular scenario isolated males form a relationship to each other, and renegotiate their masculine identity with each other before returning to heterosexual civilisation. Woods suggests that most twentieth-century island stories involve the testing of standards of masculinity and endorse the standards of 'natural' masculine behaviour which their central characters strain to live up to.

One challenge to this essentialist position was provided by Michel Foucault who argued that various *discourses* supported a particular view of the body and its pleasures. Foucault (1980, 1984) suggests that discourses are historically variable ways of specifying knowledge and truth and that through discourses we are encouraged to see what is and what is not 'the truth': 'Discourses are not merely linguistic phenomena, but are always shot through with power and are institutionalized as practices' (Foucault, cited by Ransom, 1993: 134). For Foucault then it is powerful discourses which shape our sexual values and beliefs and meanings attached to the body. Sex is not some biological entity governed by natural laws but an idea specific to certain cultures and historical periods. Sex and how we make sense of it is created through defini-tion. In World in Focus 15.2 the focus is on differential definitions of sex and sexuality across cultures.

A more recent critique of the essentialist position is provided by Jeffrey Weeks. Weeks (1986, 2000), like Foucault, stresses that sexual identities are historically and socially shaped. He rejects the idea that there is a true essence of sex, a 'uninformed pattern' which is 'ordained by nature itself' (Weeks, 1986: 15) and insists that it is simplistic to reduce a complex pattern of sexual relations and identities to biological factors. He stresses that it is important to study the history of sexuality in order to understand the range of possible identities, based on class, ethnicity, gender and sexual preference. Such a historical perspective also helps us to understand the interrelationship between gender and other differences. For example as Stuart Hall

World in focus 15.2

Defining sex and sexuality

Margaret Mead . . . sought to demonstrate that the traits which were deemed to be masculine or feminine – including the ways in which men and women express their sexuality – varied from one society to another. She studied three New Guinea societies and concluded that each of them had very different ideas about femininity, masculinity and sexuality . . . Anthropologists have since begun to raise more fundamental questions about Western conceptualisations of gender and sexuality, suggesting that not all cultures regard gender as a set of binary opposites permanently embodied in men and women. Nor do other cultures necessarily see gender and sexuality as parts of our inner being. Where early anthropologists catalogued an enormous array of diverse sexual practices, existing in human societies, more recent work has suggested that there is no reliable way of deciding in advance what constitutes a sexual act. What counts as sexual depends on the meanings of specific acts in both their wider cultural and immediate interpersonal contexts.

(Jackson and Scott, 1996: 8)

[Hotlink → Gendered Perspectives – Theoretical Issues (Chapter 1); Hotlink → Anthropology (Chapter 6)]

(1997) notes the hegemony of the white race was rein-forced against a backdrop of sexualised racist metaphors for Asian and African people with 'black' bodies defined as corruptive, promiscuous and animal-istic. Hirst (2004) reflects on the legacies of these views arguing that white people often perceive black men and women as naturally and pathologically more sexually voracious and uncontrolled than white people which 'legitimates ideas of black men as dangerous to white women, of black women as sources of illicit sex for white men, and of sexual relationships that cross racial boundaries as degrading and unacceptable' (2004: 69).

All this suggests that we learn how to be sexual beings. Our sexual feelings, activities, the ways in which we think about sexuality and our sexual identities are all the product of social and historical forces. Sexuality is shaped by the culture in which we live and religious teachings, laws, psychological theory, medical defini-tions, social policies and the media all inform us of its meaning. Thus, our socialisation affects our sexuality (Plummer, 1975, 1995; Hirst, 2004). Our sexuality is also influenced by our ethnicity, class position, our age and whether we are disabled or able-bodied. Does this mean then that the body has no influence? Of course not; biology places limits on our experience but the body and its anatomical structure and physiology does not directly determine what we do or the meaning this may have and anatomical differences are themselves more varied than often popularly believed. In 1993 Anne Fausto-Sterling wrote a piece entitled 'The Five Sexes' in which she argued that the two-sex system is not adequate to encompass the full spectrum of human sexuality [**Hotlink → Gendered Perspectives – Theoretical Issues (Chapter 1)**]. In its place, she sug-gested a five-sex system. In addition to males and females, she included 'herms' (named after true hermaphrodites, people born with both a testis and an ovary); 'merms' (male pseudohermaphrodites, who are born with testes and some aspect of female genetalia); and 'ferms' (female pseudohermaphrodites, who have ovaries combined with some aspect of male genitalia). In response to this Suzanne J. Kessler (1998) wrote:

> The limitation with Fausto-Sterling's proposal is that . . . [it] still gives genitals . . . primary signifying status and ignores the fact that in the everyday world gender attributions are made without access

to genital inspection . . . What has primacy in everyday life is the gender that is performed, regardless of the flesh's configuration under the clothes.

Fausto-Sterling's (2000) response was to agree that it would be better for intersexuals and their supporters to turn everyone's focus away from genitals. Not least because the intersexual or transgender person who pro-jects a social gender (what Kessler (date) calls 'cultural genitals') that conflicts with his or her physical genitals still suffers prejudice and discrimination for the trans-gression. For Fausto-Sterling one way to protect people whose cultural and physical genitals do not match would be to eliminate the category of gender from offi-cial documents, such as driver's licences and passports.

Stop and think 15.3

How many times in the last month have you been asked whether you are male or female? Was this question always necessary?

Feminists argue that rather than being a biological given, sexuality is embedded in power relations shaped by gender relations and by other aspects of identity such as social class, race and ethnicity, age, disability and global power relations (Abbott *et al.*, 2005). Catharine MacKinnon (1982), for example, argues that just as the exploitation of labour is at the heart of class relations, sexual exploitation is central to the, as she calls it, 'sex class system'. Following on from this Sheila Jeffreys (1990) argues that the co-option of women into heterosexuality is a clear manifestation of patriarchal power, just as the social assumptions sur-rounding 'having sex' are defined in heterosexual patriarchal terms. One aspect of the sexual exploita-tion of women is the objectification of women's bodies. As John Berger suggests:

> Men act and women appear. Men look at women. Women watch themselves being looked at. This determines not only most relations between men and women but also the relation of women to themselves. The survey of woman herself is male: the surveyed

female. Thus she turns herself into an object – and most particularly an object of vision: a sight.

(1972: 47)

One extreme version of this objectification is pornography. McKinnon (1987) argues that pornography is the foundation of male dominance as through its dehumanising portrayal of some women it shapes how men see all women. Such images also determine cultural norms of sexual attractiveness. Yet again though 'acceptable' body shape and body presentation reflects hierarchies of class and 'race' and ethnicity as well as gender prompting, for example, an increase in skin whitening alongside an increase in breast reconstruction (Alsop *et al.*, 2002) [**Hotlink → Culture and Mass Media (Chapter 18)**]. The example in A Closer Look 15.2 gives an example of how sexual pleasure for men can lead to bodily disfigurement for women.

A closer look 15.2

Women's feet and men's foot fetishisms

Foot and shoe fetishists (who are usually men) choose a part of a woman or an article of apparel as the focus of their sexual excitement rather than a whole woman.

Sheila Jeffreys (2005: 128) notes that 'The wearing of high heels causes pain, disability and, often permanent deformity for women'. She adds that although the majority of western women are probably unaware of the connections, high heels arch the feet at a similar angle to that achieved permanently in footbinding. A British Broadcasting Company (BBC1) study found that one in ten women would wear uncomfortable shoes to look good and that over 80 per cent would not change the type of shoes they wore solely to alleviate a foot problem. With specific reference to footbinding:

In Imperial China footbinding was gradually adopted by upper-class women from the eleventh century onwards until, by the nineteenth century when a protest movement arose to campaign against it, it had reached most areas of society. Binding was initiated at 6 or 7 years old and carried out by the girls' mothers. Strips of cloth were used to bind all toes except the big toe back onto the sole and to bend the arch of the foot down to such a sharp angle that the ball of the foot and the heel were pushed together . . . Locomotion was difficult thereafter and women could be reduced to getting about a room on their knees, using strategically placed stools. Women of higher classes would have their feet bound until they were only 3 inches long, whereas women of lower classes, who needed to get about to some extent would bind to 5 inches.

(Jeffreys, 2005: 130–1)

One explanation for this practice is the need to create a clear difference between men and women. Another was the sexual satisfaction it gave men who 'gained sexual pleasure from playing with the disabled foot, kissing it, sucking it and placing it in their mouths or around their penis' (Jeffreys, 2005: 131). This can be compared to the satisfaction contemporary foot fetishists gain from the serious health problems that result from the wearing of high heels, such as bunions, hammer toes and so on.

Although many feminists see footbinding as reflecting and perpetuating the subordinate position of women (e.g. Dworkin, 1974) others argue that women involved in footbinding may not have felt it to be oppressive but rather as a bonding exercise (e.g. Ko, 1997; Pong, 2000). Yet, as Jeffreys notes: 'Bonding to swap survival tips under domination, though it may be necessary, constitutes accommodation to oppression rather than an example of women's agency and creativity that is worth celebrating.'

(2005: 227)

Source: Adapted from Jeffreys (2005).

Figure 15.1

Source: Hugh Sitton/Photographer's Choice/Getty Images

Gay and lesbian experience

As the above section has highlighted both heterosexuality and homosexuality are social constructions. As some writers have pointed out there is no essential homosexual experience and the experience of being homosexual varies. The use of the term 'homosexual' to describe a certain type of person is a relatively recent phenomenon (Weeks, 1990, 1991, 2000); and as lesbianism has never been fully recognised under, for example, British law, in many historical periods a woman who had sex with another woman would not think of herself or be regarded as lesbian. As Hirst notes:

> A homosexual identity . . . is mediated not solely through same sex activity *per se* but through the individual's willingness or ability to deal with being labelled as homosexual. Whether one is 'out' as a homosexual or in the 'closet' (maintaining heterosexual identity but with desire and/or sexual involvement with the same sex) depends not so much on biological drives but on the individual, social and political circumstances that will or will not support the chosen identity.
>
> (2004: 79)

In Britain following the Wolfenden Committee's (HO 1957) recommendations homosexual activity amongst consenting adult males over 21 in private was decriminalised in 1967. Jeffrey Weeks (1986) argues that this change in the law did not really signify an acceptance of homosexuality but a change in its official definition. Homosexual activity was accepted, or perhaps tolerated, as long as it took place in private but the law led to a tripling of convictions for homosexual behaviour in public places.

According to opinion surveys, there was a continuing liberalisation in attitudes towards homosexuality from the late 1960s into the early 1980s, then a huge setback at least in part due to the labelling of AIDS as a 'gay plague'. So while in 1983, 62 per cent censured homosexual relationships, by 1987, this had risen to 74 per cent (Weeks, 2000).

In order to understand attitudes towards lesbianism it is necessary to consider female sexuality in general. Historically, and arguably to date, women are expected to be passive, receptive and dependent on the male. Forms of sexuality outside this model have been portrayed as deviant, dangerous and/or sick. In a classic piece of writing 'Compulsory heterosexuality and lesbian existence' Adrienne Rich (1980) argued that heterosexuality rather than a 'natural' choice was in fact imposed upon women. Thus, she posited the existence of a lesbian continuum on which all women could be placed. Some writers felt that this notion of a continuum denied the specificity of lesbian sexuality and lesbians' oppression as lesbians, others thought that Rich did not go far enough, that she focused too much on women's coercion into heterosexuality rather than on the oppressive nature of the institution itself (Jackson and Scott, 1996: 14).

As Stevi Jackson and Sue Scott (1996) note, in Britain and the USA the gay and feminist movements emerged more or less simultaneously at the end of the 1960s, and the more radical elements of both movements saw themselves as facing a common enemy: the patriarchal establishment. A more recent development has been the development of Queer theory and Queer politics, the aim of which is to demonstrate that gender and sexual categories are not given but constructed. Queer theory is not just relevant to gay men and lesbians but to bisexuality as well. In addition 'it can encompass heterosexual activity between lesbians and gay men and even between heterosexuals if their practices are sufficiently disruptive of straight sexual conventions (Jackson and Scott, 1996: 16).

The New Right political concern (in both the UK and America) with social authoritarianism and moral issues led to setbacks for a more humane and tolerant order in terms of the rights of individuals to sexual freedom. But the 1990s and 2000s have seen 'a recognition of the importance of the freedom of individuals to choose their own ways of being' influenced not least by the lesbian and gay politics of the past 35 years (Weeks, 2000: 239). Greater acceptance of gay and lesbian lifestyles, the equalising of the age of consent, civil partnership [**Hotlink → Family (Chapter 11)**], Gay Pride and so on have, given centuries of ingrained prejudice against homosexuality, been achievements made quickly and with relatively little struggle (Weeks, 2000). Yet, despite shifts in attitudes towards gay men, lesbians and bisexuals 'sexual citizenship' is still not equally experienced by all (Bell and Binnie, 2000). We can see an example of this in A Closer Look 15.3.

A closer look 15.3

Violence – sexuality – space

Beverley Skeggs, Leslie Moran, Paul Tyler, Karen Corteen and Lewis Turner (2000) carried out research in Manchester and Lancaster, concerned to explore issues of safety and danger for gay men and lesbians in public spaces.

Research background: Victim surveys have documented homophobic violence as an everyday feature of the lives of lesbians and gay men and promoted awareness of this as a social problem. We wanted to explore how people manage their safety in response to this violence and to examine the difference space makes in generating safety for different groups of people.

Research sites: There were two research locations – Manchester's gay village which is an established, durable, public visible gay space in the heart of Manchester. Lancaster which is a small provincial city offers only one public space identified as 'gay friendly' within which there was a series of irregular lesbian and gay events.

Some key findings

Safety and danger: The Manchester data suggests that 'heterosexuals' have emerged as a distinct category of 'danger'. This is not the case in Lancaster. Paradoxically, invisibility in Lancaster feeds perceptions of safety whereas in Manchester the visibility of the gay village marks gayness more directly, and hence makes one more likely to be recognised. The most frequent users of sustainable gay space report the lowest perceptions of safety. Gay men in the gay village worry about safety more than any other group, even lesbians. In Manchester lesbians in the gay village are much more likely to worry about their safety than heterosexual women. In Lancaster heterosexual men worry much more about safety than Lancaster lesbians and gay men. Yet in Manchester almost all heterosexuals feel safe in the village.

Responsible citizenship: Our data suggests that lesbians and gay men have always taken major responsibility for their own safety and security . . . Policies of 'safe-keeping' forces lesbians and gay men to act as if invisible . . . This reinforces experiences of social injustice.

Source: Adapted from Skeggs *et al.* (2000) p. 1–4.

Heterosexual men and women

Arguably the social construction of sex and sexuality and the way in which sexual relations have been institutionalised through heterosexuality have served to control and oppress not only lesbian, gay and bisexual men and women but all women (e.g. Rich, 1980; Jeffreys, 1990). For some women, heterosexuality and the social relations that accompany it (such as romance and marriage) have been crucial to the persistence of male dominance.

Historically, and to date, men have been/are defined as having a stronger sex drive than women and a natural tendency to promiscuity. Many theorists have argued that men's sexual identity is in some way shaped by masculine ideology and genital sex has been a way of confirming masculinity. On the other hand heterosexuality has always been risky for women, whether in terms of the double standard of respectability and in terms of fear of pregnancy, disease, violence and coercion.

Loss of reputation is a concern for girls as well as women. Sue Lees (1986, 1993) in her interviews with young adolescent girls found evidence of the double standard in the 1980s and 1990s. Young girls who got a reputation for 'sleeping' with men would be labelled 'slags', whereas girls who got a reputation for not engaging in sexual relations were labelled 'tight', 'drags' or 'lessies'. Lees argues that this verbal abuse not only demonstrates the sexual double standard but also serves as one way of controlling female sexuality. This is supported by Karin A. Martin's (2002) US based research on why adolescent girls have sex as demonstrated in World in Focus 15.3.

Wendy Hollway (1998) provides some explanations for differential gendered behaviour in this area arguing that the differences arise from the ways males and females position ourselves within particular discourses related to sex. The 'male sex drive' discourse assumes that men have a 'natural' need for regular sexual gratification and it is women's role to satisfy this need, and the 'have/hold' or 'romantic' discourse assumes that females' aim is to secure a male partner (within marriage) for protection and procreation. According to

World in focus 15.3

Keeping boys happy

Karin A. Martin (2002: 149–51) found that the teenage girls in her study often experienced sexual intercourse as shaming and frightening and many had sex before they wanted to in order to keep their boyfriends:

I thought it was digusting! Until eighth grade. And I was appalled, and I thought it was the grossest thing. Umm, hearing friends talk about it, I did have friends who had sexual intercourse in the middle school, and they would tell everyone about it or whatever and I thought it was like disgusting!

'Cause you're afraid that they're gonna leave you.

'Cause they're afraid the boy won't like them anymore or something would happen, you know, he'd get mad.

---

these discourses 'women who openly exhibit an interest in sex are considered to be inferior and amenable to exploitation, as loose women who deserve all they get' (Moore and Rosenthal, 1993: 87).

Not surprisingly feminist scholars have attacked this double standard and the view that sexuality is bad for women and that only 'bad' women are sexual. There have been demands for women to define their own sexuality and to see themselves as sexually active rather than passive objects of male desire and as A Closer Look 15.4 shows these demands are not new.

It is depressing then that although some recent research suggests that women are taking more control in heterosexual relationships and making greater demands, established power relations remain, as research with young women in England (Holland *et al.*, 1998), America (Karin, 2002; see World in Focus 15.3) and New Zealand (Jackson and Cram, 2003) demonstrates.

There is, however, some evidence of women naming and reclaiming their own sexual 'space'. In Controversy 15.1 we reflect on one particular word and the different sexual and other meanings attached to it to provide an example of this.

A closer look 15.4

Women should enjoy sex!

Marie Stopes (1918) emphasised the need for a woman to be aroused as a preliminary to sex, and for satisfactory orgasm for both parties. The female doctor Isabel Hutton (1923) also wrote of the importance of female orgasm. Another doctor Helena Wright (1930) placed supreme importance on women's right to sexual arousal and satisfaction. Wright and others were keen to challenge the view that sex was merely a woman's duty to her husband and advocated women familiarising themselves with their genitalia and exploring ways of stimulating themselves (Abbott *et al.*, 2005).

Controversy 15.1

The ultimate insult or positive sexual self-definiton?

Always a swear word? In the fourteenth century cunt was Standard English for the female pudendum (which derives from the Latin pudere, meaning to be ashamed). Since the nineteenth century the word has also been used to denote a woman regarded as a sex object, a dysphemism for sexual intercourse, and to describe a particularly unpleasant, stupid or disliked person of either sex.

As a term of abuse cunt has been applied to people and things considered worse than either excrement (shit-face is considered less abusive than cunt-face) or the penis which, as prick, was a term of endearment in the sixteenth and seventeenth centuries. As Germaine Greer wrote in *The Female Eunuch* (1971), 'the worst name any one can be called is a cunt'. *The Slangusage of Sex* suggests that as a term of abuse it 'reflects the deep fear and hatred of the female by the male in our culture. It is far a nastier and more violent insult than "prick" which tends to mean foolish rather than evil. This violent usage is a constant and disturbing reminder to

Controversy 15.1 continued

women of the hatred associated with female sexuality and leaves women with few positive words to name their own organs: (1985)' (Mills, 1991: 59–60).

Sometimes not; here is Eve Ensler talking about how she came to write *The Vagina Monologues*:

'I don't really remember how it began: a conversation with an older woman about her vagina her saying contemptuous things that shocked me and got me thinking about what other women thought about their vaginas. I remember asking friends who surprised me with the openness and willingness to talk . . .

Women talked to me about hair, smells, longings, smear tests, female genital mutilation and child abuse, infections and fantasies. I asked questions: if your vagina could talk, what would it say? If your vagina got dressed, what would it wear?

Since that first one-woman show at an off-Broadway theatre in 1996, the piece has been performed and published in over 25 countries . . .

. . . People ask me if I worry that *The Vagina Monologues* will titillate or turn audiences on. Because women are the subjects of the play and not the objects, it is my hope that people will find material within the pieces that is sexy and alive . . . Glenn Close gets 18,000 people to stand and chant the word 'cunt' at Madison Square Avenue.'
(The Vagina Monologues Scottish Tour Spring 2006, Eve Ensler unpaginated)

Whereas the reputation of girls and women still depends on sexual modesty, the reputation and identity of boys and men relies on sexual prowess. As Victor Seidler (1989) suggests, if a man has not had sex with a woman there is a great deal of pressure on him to pretend that he has had sex to prove his masculinity. Thus, that sex and masculinity are inextricably linked is reflected in the fact that infertile men are often assumed to be impotent and subject to much hostile humour (Exley and Letherby, 2001) [**Hotlink → Health and Illness (Chapter 12)**]. There is also the view that for men sex is related to maintaining control, power and conquest. This coupled with the fact that in many cultures women are sexually objectified as sexual objects for the pleasure of men (Stolenberg, 1990) leads to the legitimation of violence

against women by men and leads to violence against men by women being seen as a joke, a slur on the masculine identity of the man involved [**Hotlink → Violence and Resistance (Chapter 16)**].

Stop and think 15.4

Which of the following sexual relationships is criminal and/or deviant in Britain?

A 30-year-old man and an 8-year-old girl

A 30-year-old man and a 15-year-old girl

A 17-year-old boy and a 15-year-old girl

A 30-year-old woman and a 15-year-old boy

Two 15-year-old boys

A 30-year-old man and a 15-year-old boy

The answer of course is all of them but do we view some as more deviant that others? Why?

Before ending this section it is important to note that some theorists have challenged the view of women as necessarily disempowered sexual victims and men as inevitably sexually exploitative (Segal, 1994; Roiphe, 1995). If we view men as always sexually powerful and women as always sexually passive we reinforce traditional discourses of men's sexuality as naturally aggressive and women's sexual being as asexual (Jackson and Scott, 1996). Others argue that to stress sexuality as a form of social control has meant a neglect of the pleasures that many men and women get from sex (Vance, 1992).

Sex and sexuality at work

Sexual exploitation at work

Social Scientists argue that the labour market is not just a site of segregation but a place in which meanings about gender and sexuality are reinforced and created. Several studies of various industries have confirmed that not only are certain jobs done by women and others by men but that work is often gendered and sexualised (e.g. Cavendish, 1982; Adkins, 1995; Ramsay and Letherby, 2006). Adkins (1995) examined job specifications for various posts in the tourist industry and discovered that stereotypical 'male' and 'female' attributes were written into them, for example for one job done predominately by women a requirement was 'attractiveness', but this attribute was absent from the job specifications for 'male' jobs. Adkins also found that women were expected to present themselves in sexually attractive ways and to appear 'feminine'. There are also reports of similar expectations of women who work on the railways:

> Railman (*sic*) was an Equal Opportunities Commission report, published in 1986, that stands as a damning indictment of sex discrimination with BR. Researcher Diana Robbins noted that, of a total staff of 170,000 there were 11,000 women on BR (6.5%) . . . One manager thought 'lady guards' would be 'quite nice'; 'I would be looking for air-hostess type, I would capitalise on their femininity'. Another said that most men like to see a woman around, 'even if it's nothing more than to google at'.
>
> (Wojtczak, 2005: 301)

However, this is not to say that men are completely free from sexual exploitation at work as the example in Controversy 15.2 demonstrates.

Controversy 15.2

Sexual harassment of men

It is usually assumed that sexual harassment is done to women by men, and many studies have shown this is the majority case. Lisa Adkins (1995) argues that relations of sexuality are fundamental to the construction of women and men as certain kinds of workers. Consider the following report from *The Mail on Sunday* (12 June 2005) in relation to the way that men may feel excluded from employment due to being the minority in a female dominated work place.

Male teachers fear sexual harassment in the staffroom, by Caroline Churchill

> Male teachers are being sexually harassed and bullied by their female colleagues, education experts have warned.

> In some Scottish schools, staffrooms have become no-go areas for men because they fear being picked on by their female counterparts.
>
> Evidence of harassment and bullying was discovered during a study examining the large gender imbalance in the Scottish teaching profession.
>
> David Thomson, director of undergraduate studies at Moray House teacher training college in Edinburgh said: 'The attitude at the moment, with the atmosphere approaching a frenzy about paedophiles, doesn't help. The risk of complaints against male teachers is a real deterrent for men. . .'
>
> The number of men in the teaching profession has slumped to an all-time low. Only 6 per cent of primary school teachers are male.
>
> Martin Christison, one of only three men who will graduate from Edinburgh University this summer with a degree in primary school teaching, said: 'I know of one teacher who never goes into the staffroom because he just feels too awkward. I have already had comments from female teachers to the effect that I couldn't hack it in a secondary school so I choose primary. What's that all about? I chose to study primary teaching when I was still at school.'
>
> He added that some men who go into primary teaching are branded gay.
>
> A Scottish Executive spokesman said: 'We are aware of the gender imbalance. We will then look at the issues to see if we need to take any action.'

Selling sex

Given the view that men have sexual needs that must be met, it follows that if they do not have access to a regular partner then their 'needs' must be met elsewhere. If we add to this the objectification of women and women's bodies [**Hotlink → Culture and Mass Media (Chapter 18)**] it is not surprising that the buyers of prostitution (including male prostitution) are predominantly men (Jackson and Scott, 1996). This of course denies the personhood of the prostitute:

> Prostitute women may be socially constructed as Others and fantasized as nothing more than objectified sexuality, but in reality, of course, they are human beings. It is only if the prostitute is imagined as stripped of everything bar her sexuality that she can be completely controlled by the client's

money/powers. But if she were dehumanized to this extent, she would cease to exist as a person . . . Most clients appear to pursue a contradiction, namely to control as an object that which cannot be objectified.

(O'Connell Davidson, 1998: 161)

It appears though – as demonstrated in World in Focus 15.4 – that some men need to 'justify' the 'otherhood' of the prostitute before considering buying sex. [Hotlink → Anthropology → A Closer Look 6.1 (Chapter 5)].

Prostitution (and other sex work) provides employment for women and as such not only raises questions about the social construction of male and female sexuality and the sexual exploitation of women but also raises general questions about the exploitation of women in the labour market. Women's involvement in sex work is directly related to their lack of economic opportunities elsewhere (Jackson and, Scott, 1996; Scambler and Scambler; 1997, O'Connell Davidson and Sanchez Taylor, 2004). Additionally, it is necessary to consider the specific working conditions in which this particular group of women work. As Sharp and Earle (2003: 41) note 'Empirical Studies of women sex workers portray images of both power *and* powerlessness, and of choice *and* control, as well as exclusion *and* exploitation' (original emphasis). Thus, as within intimate heterosexual relationships, it is important not to view female prostitutes as inevitable victims with no agency. Just imagine how differently we might view prostitution if it was considered a job like any other.

Female prostitution has received a great deal of attention. Everyone from criminologists, sociologists, medical professionals, social control agencies, amongst others, have had something to say. Historically and arguably to date prostitution was seen as pathological – a deviation from normal femininity, a classic double deviant and the concern has always been with keeping the prostitute off the streets and out of the public eye [Hotlink → Crime and Deviance (Chapter 17)]. Thus, the prostitute and not prostitution is seen to be the problem and the risks associated with this work have been of less concern, sometimes with horrendous consequences, as A Closer Look 15.5 exemplifies.

World in focus 15.4

Exotic sex

Julia O'Connell Davidson and Jacqueline Sanchez Taylor (2004: 354) write:

> . . . one thing that stands out but stands unexplained is that a large percentage of sex customers seek (or sought) sex workers whose racial, national or class identities are (or were) different from their own (Shrange 1999: 142) . . . the demand for African, Asian and Latin American prostitutes by white Western men may 'be explained in part by culturally produced racial fantasies regarding the sexuality of these women' and that these families may be related to 'socially formed perceptions regarding the sexual and moral purity of white women' (ibid 48–50). So as Kempadoo (1995: 75–76) notes . . . [the] sex industry today depend[s] upon the exoticization of the ethnic and cultural Others suggest we are witnessing a contemporary form of eroticism which sustains postcolonial and post cold war relations of power and dominance . . .

To this they add:

> [As] sex tourists spend time in resorts and barrios where tourist related prostitution is widespread . . . so constantly encounter hedonistic scenes . . . [this provides] empirical vindication of Western assumptions of 'non-Western peoples living in idyllic pleasure, splendid innocence or Paradise-like conditions – as purely sensual, natural, simple and uncorrupted beings' (Kempadoo 1995: 76). Western sex tourists . . . say that sex is more 'natural' in Third World countries, that prostitution is not really prostitution but a 'way of life', that 'They' are 'at it' all the time.

> This explains how men who are not and would not dream of becoming prostitute users back home can happily practice sex tourism (the 'girls' are not really like prostitutes and so they themselves are not really like clients) the prostitute contract is not like the Western prostitution contract and so does not really count as prostitution'.

(2004: 457).

CURRICULUM VITAE 3

PERSONAL DETAILS
Name   Sandra
Born   1961
Ethnic Origin   White British
Current Position   Prostitute (street)
Job Alias   Sex therapist

EDUCATION/QUALIFICATIONS
I left school in my early teens and went straight to working on the streets.
Adult Education College – Access course in Psychology (Did not finish)

PREVIOUS EMPLOYMENT
Hoffman presser, Factory worker – ice cream packer, Factory worker – production line worker, making thermostats for fridges (three weeks), Media interviews on TV and radio, Prostitute

INTERESTS/ACTIVITIES
TV/Films, Shopping, Home decorating, Being a mother

CURRENT JOB
I currently work as a prostitute in Plymouth, on the street . . . I work full time mostly, every day from 5–11pm, sometimes later, sometimes not at all . . . I don't do any of that kinky stuff . . . Sometimes, punters come to my house too . . . When I worked as a Hoffman presser in Neal's, I used to start at 7, finish at 5, go home and have my tea, have a bath, get ready, go out on the street, earn my money, go into castaway's nightclub and work as a bar maid till two or three in the morning, go home, get a couple of hours' kip and go back to work. But I fell asleep and pressed my arm in the Hoffman presser, so I stopped and just went out on the street. I stopped signing on, because it was only £10 then a fortnight, and carried on working as a prostitute . . . Years later, I worked in Ranco calibrating for thermostats. I lasted three weeks there, and then I was packing ice cream, and that was a start at 5 in the morning until 5 at night, so I stopped. I'd rather just earn my money out on the street.

THOUGHTS ABOUT RETIREMENT
Well by rights really I should have retired by now. As you get older you're classed as an old face and the young ones are coming up behind you, so as the young ones are coming up you're losing more and more business. A life span of a prostitute I would say from, if she starts on the street at 18 maybe she's got til 30, if she's lucky, and I'm 37 and I'm still down there . . . I'll be on it when I'm old and grey.

HOPES/AMBITIONS
I never make plans long-term because you get disappointed if they don't turn out. I've got plans for doing the house up and everything and I will do that, you know, but as socially, love life or anything like that? No. I could be dead tomorrow, so live it while you're here. Live for the day. Tomorrow may never come, or else, 'Oh there's always tomorrow,' I just shrug my shoulders . . . I think it will get a lot easier for me, I've given myself a plan now where I'm going to buy all brand new furniture so I've started this year, I've done all the bedrooms out in pine . . . In the next six years I want to be . . . money in the bank, all the house done then I can go out when I want to. If I want to stay in for a whole week I can stay in for a whole week, just do it part-time, well I'm classed as a part-timer really now anyway so . . . no I'll decorate. You know, if I've got to do five nights, I'll take two nights off. I couldn't stand it out there seven nights a week any more. I'm too old for that, way too old. For the future, I'm still going to be doing what I'm doing, but at least I can relate to the girls down there.

FINANCIAL PLANS
If I'd used my head when I was 14 and up 'til like I was 26, 30, I could've been retired, had my own property and everything. But once it's in your hand you think, 'Oh yes,' it burns a hole in your pocket . . .

GETTING OLDER
When I think, 'Oh God I've got a bill,' and I've really got to go out and I think, 'Oh I wish I was like the normal person where they do the tea, do the dishes and they can sit down and watch what they want'.

FANTASY FUTURE
I'd buy a big country house and I'd have it for women who want to get away from their old man, like a battered wives thing, and maybe a holiday home for kids that's never seen the countryside or anything like that. Buy a house for myself. I'd give some money to charity. Just make sure that my family were alright . . . and maybe fight the prostitution cause . . . 'City Prostitute Wins Lottery,' – that would be good, wouldn't it? That'd show 'em. You need the money if you want the clout.

Figure 15.2 Sandra's Curriculum Vitae (Feminist Review 1994)

Source: Rickard, W. 'Been there, seen it, done it, I've got the T-shirt' in *Feminist Review*, Vol. 67, Issue 2, 2001, Palgrave Macmillan, Fig. 3, p. 119. Reproduced with permission of Palgrave Macmillan.

A closer look 15.5

Innocent girls

In October 1979, a senior West Yorkshire detective, Jim Hobson, made this appeal to Peter Sutcliffe, a serial killer known as the 'Yorkshire Ripper', at a press conference:

> He has made it clear that he hates prostitutes. Many people do. We, as a police force, will continue to arrest prostitutes. But the Ripper is now killing innocent girls. That indicates your mental state and that you are in urgent need of medical attention. You have made your point. Give yourself up before another innocent girl dies.
>
> (Smith, 1989: 127–8)

As Joan Smith comments: 'The thrust of Hobson's widely reported remarks is clear – the Ripper's madness manifested itself only when he turned to innocent girls . . . Even when Sutcliffe had been caught, and the full extent of his crimes was clear, some policemen persisted in speaking of the prostitute victims with as much distaste as they did the killer' (Smith, 1989: 127–8).

Of course men who pay for sex face risks also. From their analysis of 'Punternet', an Internet site which contains thousands of 'reviews' of British prostitutes by their clients (plus links to other sites which directly advertise the services of prostitutes, or which contain discussion boards aimed at prostitutes, clients or both) Keith Sharp and Sarah Earle (2003) have been able to access the motivations and experiences of a previously under-researched group: the prostitute's client. The risks of buying sex that Sharp and Earle identify for the client also explains the reluctance of this group to be involved in research:

> The considerable stigma attached to paying for sex has traditionally meant that men who do so are reluctant to reveal their activities to even their closest friends. The risks of being discredited as a man who pays for sex are considerable and multifaceted. First there is the obvious risk to a core feature of heterosexual masculine identity – namely, that one is sexually attractive to women and capable of attracting women as sexual partners.

An obvious implication of paying for sex is precisely that one is incapable of attracting women as sexual partners. Secondly, it appears that many men who pay for sex are married or engaged in long-term co-habiting relationships . . . Thirdly, and related to this, are commonly held beliefs about the risks of contracting sexually transmitted diseases from sexual encounters with prostitutes

(Sharp and Earle, 2003: 38–9)

The emergence of the Internet, however, makes it possible for prostitutes' clients (and others engaged in discredited/deviant activities) to 'meet' and to exchange information and experiences about these activities anonymously whilst continuing to conceal their activities from those around them. From Sharp and Earle's (2003) research it appears that whilst clients are also unaware or unconcerned of the risks for the prostitute they are aware and concerned of additional risks – such as disease, the risk of being seen, and the risk of damage to their cars in 'rough' areas – to themselves.

Conclusion

As this chapter has suggested, challenging biological determinism involves us in taking into account the social structures and cultural practices which constrain our sexuality. Jackson and Scott (1996) add that it is also necessary to consider the ways in which individuals actively construct their own understanding of sexuality and negotiate sexual activities within these constraints. Without an understanding of the interrelationship between the structures individuals inhabit and the agency of individuals, 'there can be no conceptualization of strategies for change' (Jackson and Scott, 1996: 6).

Returning briefly to Foucault's views on discourse, he argues:

> We must not imagine a world of discourse divided between accepted discourse and excluded discourse or between the dominant discourse and the dominated one; but as a multiplicity of discursive elements that can come into play in various strategies. Discourse transmits and produces power:

it reinforces it, but also undermines and exposes it, renders it feasible and makes it possible to thwart it.

(1984: 100)

So, where there is power there is resistance and resistance to power comes through new discourses. These produce new truths – 'counter discourses' – which oppose dominant truths. With this in mind it is important to remember that our understanding of the relationship between gender and sex and sexuality is ever changing.

Further reading

Susanne Thorbuck and Bandana Paltanaik (eds) (2006), *Transnational Prostitution: Changing Patterns in a Global Context*, London, Zed. This collection, written by activists and scholars, details the changes in patterns of prostitution across national boundaries in the modern world. It includes personal testimonies from prostitutes and clients, men and women. This volume also provides details of innovative policies in Sweden and the Netherlands.

Stephen Whittle (ed.) (2002), *Respect and Equality: Transsexual and Transgender Rights*, London, Routledge. This book argues for respect and legal equality to be accorded to transsexual and transgendered persons. It includes theoretical discussions of sex, sexuality, gender and the law drawing on extensive primary and secondary sources.

Journal of the History of Sexuality – This cross-cultural and cross-disciplinary journal traces 'the history of sexuality in all its expressions, recognizing various differences of class, culture, gender, race, and sexual orientation'. Articles come from historians, social scientists, and humanities scholars worldwide. The website below provides a list of publications that abstract or index the journal, and subscription information. It is edited in the USA. **http://www.utexas.edu/utpress/journals/jhs.html**

Journal of Psychology and Human Sexuality – Issues are addressed from a psychological perspective and include educational, counselling and clinical research on the study of human sexuality and sexual behaviour.

Sexualities. Studies in Culture and Society – *Sexualities* is an international journal providing a forum for debate and discussion on the changing nature of the social organisation of human sexual experience in the late modern world.

Websites

Intute (formerly SOSIG) – a free online service providing access to the very best Web resources for education and research, evaluated and selected by a network of subject specialists. Enter the site and type in *sexuality* into the internal search engine and follow your interests. Available at **http://www.intute.ac.uk/socialsciences/**

The Internet Public Library – available at **http://www.ipl.org/div/subject/browse/soc50.00.00/**. A searchable portal providing annotated links to relevant websites covering issues of gender and sexuality, especially in relation to society and culture.

Sexuality, Gender, and the Law: National and International – at **http://www.lib.uchicago.edu/~/lou/sexlaw.htm**. A site from the University of Chicago which provides a multitude of links to worldwide sites covering conferences, websites, activisms and legal information.

End of chapter activity

Lonely Hearts

MODEST, ATTRACTIVE male, 26, seeks similar lady, 18–30, for wining and dining. If you don't usually read these, I don't usually advertise, so why not reply?

LIVACIOUS DIVORCEE, 47, no ties, vital, intelligent, caring, seeks compatible man 40–55 for friendship. Wide interests. London and Home Counties. Details please.

Typically it is something to keep quiet about, except perhaps to one or two close friends. In the public mind . . . there is a stigma attached actually to advertising oneself. It is seen as a declaration of failure, a public acknowledgement of one's lonely status and inability to procure or retain a mate through the normal channels. As I hope to show in the pages that follow, these are attitudes that have to be changed in the light of social trends.

(Cockburn, 1988: Front cover and p. 3)

What do you think the changes John Cockburn identifies might be?

Cockburn's book was published in the late 1980s what social and technological changes since have impacted on the 'Lonely Hearts' experience?

End of chapter activity continued

Look at the 'Would Like to Meet' section of a local newspaper, national newspaper, or other publication. How is what people write related to the social construction of male and female sexuality? Do any of the biographical accounts challenge current dominant expectations?

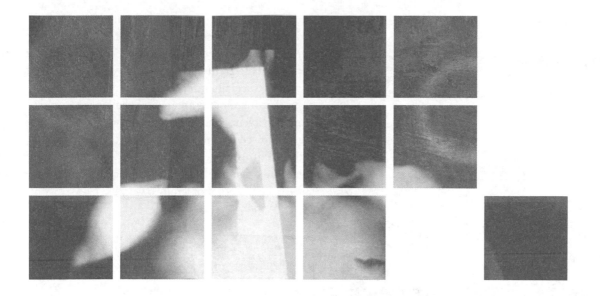

Violence and resistance

Key issues in this chapter:

➤ Violence is a highly gendered issue, deeply connected to the gender order of society.

➤ Women are much more likely than men to be victims of interpersonal violence, and men are predominant as the perpetrators of interpersonal violence.

➤ Violence between people of the same sex has only recently been addressed and has been a difficult issue for feminists.

➤ Feminists have played a major role in redefining violence, in activism to resist violence and in the lobbying for legislative change nationally and internationally.

➤ Resistance can be passive, active or aggressive and involves both women and men.

➤ War and conflict target the enemy in gendered and sexualised ways and post-conflict societies face disruptions to the gender order.

At the end of this chapter you should be able to:

➤ Summarise feminist theorising on violence and feminist critiques of other approaches.

➤ Discuss a range of strategies of resistance to violence.

➤ Evaluate the gender implications of interpersonal violence.

➤ Debate the role of women in resisting and sustaining conflict.

➤ Explain how conflict and violence both derive from and construct gender identities for both women and men.

Introduction

Figure 16.1 She lives with a respectable business man . . . last week he hospitalised her

Source: The Zero Tolerance Prevelance Campaign

This is one of a series of posters developed by Edinburgh District Council to challenge the way local people thought about domestic violence. Launched in 1992 it was the first public education campaign in Europe to tackle the issue of male violence against women and children by using the mass media. It was a deliberate act of resistance to the acceptance of domestic violence in Scottish society.

One response to the campaign was discomfort; many men felt uncomfortable being faced with domestic abuse being named as gender violence with men being clearly cited as the perpetrators and women and children as victims (later posters covered the issue of child sex abuse). Such naming is an example of the feminist project to have male violence defined in terms of gendered power relations, rather than in psychopathological or structural terms. Look at A Closer Look 16.1 – you will see that there have been a number of different social scientific explanations for violence, especially interpersonal violence. However, given that the most fundamental challenge to understanding violence has come from the work of feminists (and followed by those writing critically about masculinity) it is necessary to start our discussions regarding a gendered approach to violence and resistance from the point of feminist work.

A closer look 16.1

Perspectives on violence

Psychopathological

The presumption that violence and sexual abuse are exceptional and pathological acts, conducted by defective personalities. Such a position views men who beat women as holding rigid views of gender roles, as insecure in their masculine identity and as using violence to gain/regain power, control, authority.

Sociological

Violence linked to social and economic deprivation, such as poverty, bad housing etc. The argument is that men who have little power and control in other areas of their lives get it through abuse of power in the family. It is also argued that such behaviour is learned and passed from generation to generation in certain subcultures as the norm.

Structural

This view argues that pathological subcultures are not sufficient to understand interpersonal violence and focuses upon societal structure. Child abuse is not due to generational normalising within subcultures but due to the barriers poverty and deprivation impose which ensure that stress and frustration exist and that abuse is simply one element in child maltreatment. That is, child abuse is explicable in terms of class inequalities which control resources and which create deprived groups within which abuse can occur, get locked in.

Source: Derived from Elliot (1996).

After a review of feminist theorising on violence we will explore the gendered nature of violence and the way in which violence is able to reinforce gender, or in some cases (such as post-conflict Uganda – see later) has disrupted traditional gender roles. We look at violence at different levels: primarily interpersonal violence both in public and private spaces, then within communities and between nations. Although the majority of the situations covered here involve actual, physical acts it is important to remember that conflict and abuse can and do exist in situations where physical assault is not present, indeed 'the absence of war does not mean peace' (Gaulteng, 1969, cited in Jacobs *et al.*, 2000: 1). In the following we will examine men and women's experiences and actions both as victims and agents of violence, and of resistance to violence and conflict.

A note on resistance is necessary. A common sense understanding of resistance is of acting in opposition. However, in the context of gender and violence, resistance includes the 'potential for subversion and contestation . . . of the established order' (Kandiyoti, 1998: 141). As such it reflects acts of survival as well as political actions for policies and provision.

Violence is very much a gender issue. As Robert Connell (2001) argues violence is deeply connected to the gender order of society for the dynamics of a patriarchal society permit men to:

> gain a dividend . . . in terms of honour, prestige and the right to command . . . also a material dividend . . . [resulting in a] . . . structure of inequality . . . involving massive dispossession of social resources, [that] is hard to imagine without violence. It is, overwhelmingly, the dominant gender who hold and use the means of violence. Men are armed far more often than women. Indeed under many gender regimes women have been forbidden to bear or use arms . . . Patriarchal definitions of femininity (dependence, fearfulness) amount to a cultural disarmament that may be quite as effective as the physical kind. Domestic violence cases often find abused women, physically able to look after themselves, who have accepted the abusers' definitions of themselves as incompetent and helpless.
>
> (Connell, 2001: 43–4)

Connell goes on to argue that two forms of violence evolve from this: the first being the use of violence by dominant groups to maintain their privilege – the examples he provides range from wolf-whistling to rape to murder. His second point is that violence also becomes important in gender politics among men, citing the fact that most major violent acts (including war, murder, armed assault) occur between men. He is not alone in arguing that violence becomes a way of exerting masculinity, illustrated by homophobic attacks on gay men for example as well as upon women. In this he has followed earlier feminist work on rape and sexual assault. Writing about these issues Susan Brownmiller (1975) challenged the view that rape is a result of a biological urge, rather, that it is due to the social construction of a masculinity which favours and rewards aggression. That is, rape is the result of differential social power between the sexes. In addition, Brownmiller asserts, given that all women fear rape, the rape of some women by some men creates a climate in which all men benefit from the social control of women. The root of the problem for Brownmiller and other radical feminists, is the social construction of masculinity.

Feminism on violence

The Women's Liberation Movement (WLM) of the late 1960s and 1970s in western societies drew attention to violence. Beginning with an examination of the abuse of women, often by women analysing their own personal experiences, activists began not just to campaign against gendered violence but also to develop other means of resistance – such as the provision of services such as rape helplines and women's refuges. These services are based on the premise of self-help and voluntarism and have a history as long as the WLM – the first women's refuge opened in the UK in 1971 with the first rape crisis line opening in the USA in 1972 (Charles, 2000: 136–7). Feminists also devised new theoretical positions on violence and created alternative ways to raise awareness of the issue. Some of these ways included Reclaim the Night marches, when women marched together to claim the streets back for women, the aim being to draw attention to how restricted women's lives are when violence is feared.

Feminists did not view these actions and provisions as an end in themselves, rather they were intended to raise awareness, provide a place of safety and support, offer a means of escape from a violent situation and as places where women could develop an understanding of their situation. That understanding was based on a shared knowledge, that it was not something that individual women somehow cause in their own lives but actions which have developed from the social construction of masculinity and the gendered power relations within society.

A significant amount of, though not all, feminist thinking in this area has been developed by radical feminists who attempt to link together the different forms and ways in which violence is expressed and experienced, summed up in the 'continuum of violence' coined by Liz Kelly (1988). By this Kelly means that all violence is interconnected, all coming from the same social root – that of gender inequality and the subsequent sexualisation of women's bodies. It would be wrong however, to view this as a particularly modern insight. Taking the UK as an example; Victorian feminists had a sophisticated understanding of such issues resulting in campaigns for divorce based upon the violence of the husband. In addition, the growth of the temperance (anti-alcohol) movement amongst Victorian women was due to an understanding of the relationship between excessive alcohol use and wife beating (Rendall, 1985). Women such as Frances Power Cobbe, author of *Wife Torture in England*, did not believe that violence against women, for example wife beating, was a source of humour (as it was often treated) but indicated how society devalued wives. The view of Victorian feminists was not that violence was the result of the pathological behaviour of a few 'sick' men but that it results from, and was encouraged by, the social system. A social system of practices and laws which sanctioned men's rights and allowed men to view women as their property, under their control. As Mary Maynard (1993:100) states '[I]n many ways, first wave feminists' analyses of incest and wife beating are very reminiscent of feminist writing on male violence today.' The great contribution of Second Wave feminism was the placing of violence on the agenda through activism. Violence has not necessarily increased but feminist activism has increased the public focus on violence and forced consideration of gendered violence into the public domain, resulting in action (see World in Focus 16.1). However, it should also be noted that feminists have also struggled with how to name violence when discussing it in the public domain (see Controversy 16.1).

World in focus 16.1

Global action against violence against women

The Declaration on the Elimination of Violence against Women is the first international human rights instrument to exclusively and explicitly address the issue of violence against women and how it resricts women's human rights (United Nations, 1996). In 1994 the UN Commission on Human Rights appointed a Special Rapporteur on Violence Against Women whose role it is to research and compile information.

In recent years some countries have taken significant steps towards improving laws relating to violence against women. For example:

➤ 1991 – Mexico revised its rape law in several important ways. A provision was eliminated that allowed a man who rapes a minor to avoid prosecution if he agrees to marry her.

➤ 1994 – the Organisation of American States adopted the Inter-American Convention to Prevent, Punish and Eradicate Violence against Women (also called Convention of Belém do Parà), a new international instrument that recognises all gender-based violence as an abuse of human rights. This Convention provides an individual right of petition and a right for non-governmental organisations to lodge complaints with the Inter-American Commission of Human Rights.

➤ In Australia, a National Committee on Violence against Women was established to coordinate the development of policy, legislation and law enforcement at the national level as well as community education on violence against women.

➤ 1991 – the Government of Canada announced a four-year Family Violence Initiative intended to mobilise community action, strengthen Canada's legal framework, establish services on First Nation reserves and in Inuit communities, develop resources to help victims and stop offenders, and provide housing for abused women and children.

➤ In Burkina Faso, a strong advertising campaign by the Government as well as television and radio programmes on the unhealthy practice of genital mutilation were launched to educate and raise public awareness about the dangerous consequences of such an 'operation'. A National Anti-Excision Committee was established in 1990. The practice of genital mutilation has been eliminated in some villages and in others, there has been an huge

decrease in the number of girls excised: only 10 per cent of the girls are excised compared to 100 per cent 10 years ago.

➤ Some countries have introduced police units specially trained for dealing with spousal assault. In Brazil, specific police stations have been designated to deal with women's issues, including domestic violence. These police stations are staffed entirely by women.

Source: Derived from United Nations (1996) and Crawley (2000).

Controversy 16.1

Struggling with terminology

Feminists have argued that naming violence is vitally important in identifying it, bringing it into the public domain and for challenging and resisting. Yet there remains controversy as to the terminology to be employed to discuss women's involvement with violence when it is not in overt opposition. As Jacobs and colleagues (2000: 14) point out, this is a fraught issue:

What then are the terms available? Talking of women's 'involvement' with violence is very imprecise and 'co-responsibility' can indicate that women and men stand in a precisely equal relationship. 'Complicity' carries overtones of guilt, but is in use. These linguistic dilemmas raise profound questions of analysis and practice which require serious attention.

Yet the struggle continues as there is little agreement as to an appropriate term.

Redefining violence

In A Closer Look 16.1 a range of explanations for violence are summarised. Likewise there exists a range of definitions of violence; from legalistic to professional to feminist definitions based on the experiences of women (see A Closer Look 16.2).

A closer look 16.2

Legal and professional definitions of violence

Legal definitions

Legal definitions are usually the narrowest ones and they tend to carry a certain authority, since they determine whether agencies such as the police, social services and courts of law are able to intervene or prosecute in particular circumstances. Sylvia Walby (1990) points out that legal definitions tend to omit acts which many women would regard as violent. For example, in England until 1991, the law did not recognise that a woman could be raped by her husband, as she was deemed to have consented to sexual intercourse upon marriage. Further, the legal definition of rape in most countries is unlawful sexual intercourse, which means that the penis must penetrate the vagina. This excludes forcible penetration by other objects; and other forms of sex, such as anal sex (the inclusion of anal sex as rape did not occur in English law until 1996).

These kinds of legalistic problems have led feminist researchers to document how the law's definition of violence routinely takes precedence over women's definitions. This is because, by discounting the views and definitions of women, the law is giving legitimacy to those of their male assailants. In failing to challenge the latter, the right of all men to abuse women is upheld.

Professional/expert

Professional or expert definitions can be problematic because they usually involve the imposition of a particular set of meanings upon individuals who may interpret what has happened, been said to them, or what they are seeing, in a different way. For instance, feminist researchers have found that 'flashing' or the constant telling of 'dirty' jokes can be experienced as abusive, even though they are commonly held to be rather trivial activities. Women's definitions of violence and what is regarded as serious assault often differ from those held both by the law and by professionals.

Until the 1970s social scientists, especially psychologists, were particularly concerned with identifying the kind of personalities responsible for violent behaviour. However, others began to adopt feminist understandings in their studies, insisting that violence had to be examined on a social level. An example of this approach is the work of Russell and Rebecca Dobash (1980, 2005). The Dobashes, initially working on Scottish data, argue that violence has to be seen in its social context, not just in the way that masculinity and femininity are constructed but a social context which takes into account patriarchal marriage and the condonment of a patriarchal state. This means examining the way both the community and institutions react to gendered violence, or as they put it, a need to look at the ways in which institutions and processes continue to support patriarchal domination, especially in the use of violence. They focused on domestic violence and the treatment of cases by police, medical professionals and even priests. They conclude that the whole structure of society, being patriarchal, fails to challenge gendered violence and that, communities, neighbours and professionals by inaction permit male violence against their wives/partners to continue:

> [Everyone] . . . is responsible for the continued assaults on women and in some cases their deaths: the friends and neighbours who ignore or excuse violence, the physician who does not go beyond the mending of bones and the stitching of wounds, the social worker who defines wife beating as a failure

of communication, and the police or court officials who refuse to intervene. The violence is meted out by one man but the responsibility for that violence goes far beyond him.

(Dobash and Dobash, 1980: 222)

Therefore, although many feminists would agree that male violence is a mechanism through which men as a group, as well as individual men, can control women and maintain their dominance the Dobashes add in a consideration of the lack of challenge within communities to dismantle that mechanism. Feminist action has taken the form, not only of creating and providing services, but of challenging the mechanism, for feminists view violence not just as a product of women's subordination but as actively adding to that subordination – in other words, women can never have equality until gendered violence has ended. The major feminist theoretical positions on violence are summarised in A Closer Look 16.3.

Main aspects of feminist theory on violence

In the early 1970s women's groups began to discuss violence by men against women, redefining it in terms of gendered power. Feminists aimed to change how people thought about violence against women, to make it unacceptable and to have sexual crimes seen as violent. Through theorising and action, Second Wave feminism put violence on the agenda. Although original activism was based around different forms of violence, for example domestic and sexual harassment, feminists now see these as part of the same phenomenon and Liz Kelly (1988) devised the term 'continuum of violence' to express the interconnectedness of various forms of violence, including fear of violence (Hanmer, 1978). Feminists argue that men gain from the existence of a culture of violence as it leaves women in a state of constant fear, either through the experience of regular beatings or harassment or a more general concern regarding the possibility of rape and sexual attack. Women adapt their behaviour in ways in which they think (hope) might reduce the risk of attack. It is not that all men are abusers, it is just the case that as ordinary men do commit sexual assaults it is impossible for women to know who is a potential rapist (Brownmiller, 1976) – in other words, when walking down a dark road women do not know if the man coming towards them is dangerous or not and so fear him.

Feminists also redefined sexual violence as a term to indicate that such acts are experienced due to the sexualisation of women's bodies, recognising the construction of women as sexual. Sexual violence therefore is defined as 'any physical, visual or sexual act that is experienced by the woman or girl, at the time or later, as a threat, invasion or assault, that has the effect of hurting her or degrading her and/or takes away her ability to control intimate contact (Kelly, 1988: 41). This includes situations where overtly sexual acts are absent, in this sense it involves: 'violence involving racism, homophobia, xenophobia and other prejudices; violence on international and global levels, including trafficking in women and women's experiences of war violence' (Corrin, 1996: 1).

Radical feminists see male violence as both cause and effect of male dominance whilst Socialist and Marxist feminists, such as Michele Barrett (1980) argue that violence cannot be separated from other ways in which society controls women, for example unequal treatment in the workplace, position within the family and the way the media objectifies women.

Stop and think 16.1

Look at Kelly's definition of violence – does it apply only to females? Could the same apply for male victims, transgendered victims?

Having now reviewed the main aspects of feminist theory on violence and some acts of resistance we now turn to specific aspects of violence, remembering that they are interconnected (Kelly, 1988).

Interpersonal violence

Interpersonal violence has a strong gender profile, whilst women and children are the majority of victims of violence within the domestic sphere, men, especially younger men, are overwhelmingly the victims of inter-

personal violence on the streets and in other public places [**Hotlink → Geography (Chapter 10)**]. However, that is not to say that men are not assaulted in the home, nor that women are not attacked in the street, pub or workplace. For all, the home is the most dangerous place: in statistical terms, a person of any age or of any gender is far more likely to be subject to physical attack in the home than on the street at night.

Domestic violence

The House of Commons Home Affairs Committee on Domestic Violence (1993) defines domestic violence as:

Any form of physical, sexual or emotional abuse which takes place within the context of a close relationship. In most cases, the relationship will be between partners (married, cohabiting, or otherwise) or ex-partners.

Domestic violence accounts for about 25 per cent of all violent crime in the UK (Mirlees-Black, 1999) and even though it is experienced by both women and men the majority of domestic violence tends to be by men against a female partner or ex-partner. Estimations of figures differ from between 67 per cent of reported incidents (Mirlees-Black, 1999) to 90 to 97 per cent (Shaw, 2003) being by men upon women. In 1999, 37 per cent of women homicide victims were killed by present or former partners, compared with 6 per cent of men, a total of 92 women, or 2 women per week in England and Wales alone (Criminal Statistics England and Wales, 1999).

Examination of homicide figures (Daly and Wilson, 1988; Kelly, 1988) reveals men's use of violence to control female partners across industrial and non-industrial societies. Although, killing of women is relatively rare, the widespread use of violence is not. While men's violence to women is usually characterised as 'losing control', both battered women and the men who batter them tell the same story: that men's behaviour is used as a means of control.

Effects of domestic violence

The experience of living in a violent relationship clearly affects a person's, most frequently a woman's, psychological state. Battered women have tended to have a high frequency of psychosexual dysfunction, major depression, post-traumatic stress disorder, generalised anxiety disorder, and obsessive compulsive disorder (Cascardi *et al.*, 1995). Male victims too suffer psychological distress (see A Closer Look 16.4).

A closer look 16.4

Male victims of domestic violence

Figures on male victims vary considerably so it's difficult to state with any accuracy the true extent. However, the 2001/02 British Crime Survey (BCS) found 19 per cent of domestic violence incidents were reported to be male victims with just under half of these being committed by a female abuser.

Are there differences in how men and women experience domestic violence?

There are both similarities and differences. Some of the responses to violence from a partner are the same. Whoever you are, being hurt by someone you love and trust can be devastating. You may feel bewildered and confused. You may wonder if it's your fault. You may feel too ashamed or embarrassed to tell anyone. If you do tell, you may find that you are not believed or that your abuse is trivialised . . .

There are also important differences that can often be lost when we assume that what we know about women experiencing domestic violence automatically applies to male victims too. For example, many abused men may feel that they aren't 'real men' if they admit to having experienced abuse.

Source: Extracted from BBC – **http//www.bbc.co.uk/health/hh/men.shtm/#only**.

Interpersonal abuse occurs in heterosexual and homosexual relationships; to women in the majority but also to men; to elders and to children; to the physically capable and the disabled. In the latter case abuse may extend to withholding care or medical attention. In fact, it appears that disabled women are more likely than non-disabled women to suffer domestic abuse: one survey revealed that 12 per cent of disabled

women aged 16 to 29 years reported domestic violence compared with 8.2 per cent of non-disabled women of the same age (Mirless-Black, 1999). Whatever form it takes, and whoever is the victim, violence and abuse is a misuse of power.

Rape

The extent of rape is very difficult to assess as very few are reported to police. An average of 6,000 cases of rape and 17,500 instances of indecent assault are reported annually in the UK. However, a Home Office study estimates the true number of rapes and sexual assaults in Britain somewhere between 118,000 and 295,000 per year (The *Guardian*, 18 February 2000).

It is estimated that approximately 43 per cent of sexual assaults are committed by people known to the victim, i.e. relatives, friends, former partners or recent acquaintances. See World in Focus 16.2 for statistics from the USA.

Male rape

Male rape is still regarded as taboo, and largely gets ignored by society. Until 1994 rape of men was not recognised in Britain. Legislative changes now recognise that a man commits rape if he has sexual intercourse with a person (whether vaginal or anal) who does not consent, or if he is reckless as to whether the person consents, and since 1994 there have been several prosecutions for rape of men – 5 to 10 per cent of reported cases of rape or sexual abuse each year involve male victims (Scarce, 1997).

Stephanie Chester (1998) found in her study of men who had been raped that one of the most shocking revelations was the response of many wives and partners. Her findings suggest that in some cases heterosexual men do not receive support when they confide in their spouses – instead they find themselves being accused of experimenting with homosexuality. Other women simply choose not to continue a relationship with a man they felt was 'emotionally vulnerable'. Therefore, according to Chester, men find it difficult to admit they have been raped and many try to forget it ever happened (with psychological consequences such as self harm or aggression). [**Hotlink →** **Sex and Sexuality (Chapter 15)**].

World in focus 16.2

Snapshots of gender violence in the USA

Murder

Four women a day die in the USA as a result of domestic violence, approximately 1,400 women a year, according to the FBI (Federal Bureau of Investigation). The number of women who have been murdered by their intimate partners is greater than the number of soldiers killed in the Vietnam War.

Battering

Although only 572,000 reports of assault by intimates are officially reported to federal officials each year, the most conservative estimates indicate two to four million women of all 'races' and classes are battered each year. At least 170,000 are serious enough to require medical care.

Sexual assault

Annually, approximately 132,000 women report that they have been victims of rape or attempted rape, and more than half of them knew their attackers. It's estimated that two to six times that many women are raped, but do not report it. Every year 1.2 million women are forcibly raped by their current or former male partners, some more than once.

Who are the victims?

Women are 10 times more likely than men to be victimised by an intimate. Young women, women who are separated, divorced or single, low-income women and African-American women are disproportionately victims of assault and rape. Domestic violence rates are five times higher among families living below the poverty line, and severe spouse abuse is twice as likely to be committed by unemployed men as by those working full time. Violent attacks on lesbians and gay men have become two to three times more common than they were prior to 1988.

Source: Derived from **http://www.themodern religion.com/women/w_violence.htm**

Gender and conflict – beyond the individual

Conflict is visible across the world both between nations, commonly referred to as war, and within nations, either defined as civil war or community conflict. The 'classic' form of war appears to be becoming supplanted by an increase in armed conflicts within states. In addition, the nature of warfare has changed:

> . . . involving a widescale retreat from even a qualified observance of those historic rules of war which had offered protection to non-combatants. Instead, protagonists deliberately target civilians, including children, using the increasingly available technologies of rocket-propelled grenades, mortars, land mines and small arms.
>
> (Jacobs *et al.*, 2000: 4)

(See World in Focus 16.3)

There has also been an increasing awareness of the use of sexual assault and rape as weapons of war. However, it would be wrong to ignore the fact that women's bodies have 'historically been included in the privilege of the conqueror' (Jacobs *et al.*, 2000: 4) and we will return to

World in focus 16.3

Civilian casualties of war

Oxfam report that there has been a massive increase in the number of civilians killed in wars in the twentieth century.

First World War (1914–18)	14 per cent of casualties were civilians
Second World War (1939–45)	67 per cent casualties were civilians
1989	90 per cent of casualties of conflict were civilians

this later. War, whether it be between or within states, is never experienced in a uni-dimensional manner, nor has resistance been in one direction. In some cases resistance has taken the form of pacifist organisation whilst in others, in countries as diverse as Indonesia, Nicaragua and Eritrea, both women and men have joined national liberation movements. In addition, the nature of armed and security forces are changing. In the west women are increasingly joining such bodies as the police and the military and in some contexts, as Francine D'Amico

(2000) points out, women are actively seeking, and have received, a role in front line combat.

Feminists have found it difficult to confront the violence of women, be it at a theoretical or activism level, as Parita Mukta (2000) argues in her study of women and Hindu nationalism. Indeed, some feminists have asserted that there is an essential link between women, motherhood and peace/non-violence. This Maternalist position (Ruddick, 1992) argues that as women are engaged in 'mothering work' (be it as actual mothers or not) they have obvious motives for rejecting war, presumably that men do not have. In addition, this 'mothering' experience is taken to also imply that women have inherent abilities for peaceful conflict resolution. Yet it is difficult for others to accept this, not just because of the essentialism inherent within this theory, but due to evidence that women are involved in conflict, perhaps not as protagonists but certainly, as shown by Mukta (2000), as supporters and sustainers of that violence (see World In Focus 16.4). A further problem with Maternalist views is that not all mothers view it as their duty to reduce conflict, as Jan Jindy Pettman (1996: 12) reminds us: 'Some mothers understand their . . . Responsibilities as requiring either the sacrifice of their sons for the state or nation, or the use of violence against other women's sons – and daughters.'

Despite critiques of Maternalist views on peace and gender there have been significant acts of resistance which support this, for example, the anti-nuclear protesters at Greenham Common (England) in the 1980s quickly became a women-only protest. Many of these women articulated their aims as attempting to save the planet for their children and grandchildren, though others explained their pacifism in relation to religious faith. Conflicts with male protesters, over issues of personal insecurity experienced by some women, and the equation of their presence with a perceived male responsibility for war forced political debates resulting in men leaving the camp (Roseneil, 1995).

In recent years some feminists have begun to examine the complexities involved in a consideration of gender and violent conflict, especially in relation to women. Ronit Lentin (1997) argues that viewing women as victims only and never as actors does not allow us to understand the reasons for some women's involvement with violent conflict. However, she does not take this further. Despite books on women and wartime (Turshen and Twagiramariya, 1998), women in international relations (Pettman, 1996) and others (Jeffreys and Basu, 1998), there has been a lesser focus amongst feminists on issues of women's agency in relation to violence than on women's victimhood or agency in resistance, and even less by CMS on this issue. Susie Jacobs, Ruth Jacobson and Jen Marchbank (2000) raise this issue in their international collection on gender and resistance, yet they remain wary of tendencies of

World in focus 16.4

Hindu women and nationalism

Since 1984 Hindu nationalism in India has mobilised against the minority religious communities. Women of the Hindu right have been involved in public upsurges including the violent demolition of a mosque at Ayodhya (6 December 1992). Women as well as men have provided support for paramilitary organisations such as the Shiv Sena in Bombay. Mukta (2000) details three ways in which militant Hindu women have been involved in the communal movement, 'indelibly marking the violence endemic in this movement both as gendered and actively sanctioned by a vocal female community' (Mukta, 2000: 171):

1. Female (obstensibly) religious figures have acted to reconstitute Hindu identity in a violent manner, taunting Hindu men to rise up and be masculine, that is violent.

2. Through the organisation of women's wings of extra-constitutional bodies such as the Vishwa Hindu Parishad which have provided 'storm troopers' for Hinduism.

3. Through the involvement of women publicly in the demolition of the Ayodhya mosque and by their sanctioning of violence against both men and women of the Muslim community, including the rape of Muslim women.

However, it has to be remembered that other women, faced by the results of torchings, killings and rapes offered solidarity and shelter, often at considerable danger to themselves.

labelling women as 'just as bad as the boys' and recognise that in some contexts resistance, protest or even non-compliance could result in death, as in Rwanda where any attempts to refrain from involvement in the killing of Tutsis and moderate Hutus meant death.

Gender and conflict does not only relate to women. Men, who predominate in the military and other combatant forces, are also profoundly affected by the gender order. In the next section we will focus on three areas, each concerned with the construction and deconstruction of gender in a particular way.

Gender, conflict and the construction of gender

Here we will examine the role of the military in the construction of masculinity; the use of rape as a weapon of war, which can both sustain the masculinity of the aggressor whilst taunting the men of the victimised community, and changes to gender roles in post-conflict societies.

Militarised masculinity

This is my rifle
This is my gun
One is for killing
One is for fun

(quoted in Morgan, 1975: 154)

Stop and think 16.2

The above is a chant from the US military. 'My gun' is a euphemism; replace 'my gun' with 'my penis', for that is what is meant. Now read the chant again. Given this is what some soldiers have chanted whilst marching what messages does it send about who are soldiers? Think also about the consequence of the equation of killing with sex. What might this tell us about how militarised masculinity is constructed?

As we have seen in Chapter 1, masculinity is not some kind of genetic product but rather the result of social practices and discourses. Masculinity gains its mean-

ing in opposition to other categories such as femininity (Kimmel, 1994). A particular form of masculinity is created by the military, transcending beyond soldiers to civilian constructs of appropriate masculinity (Enloe, 1987). The relationship between gender and militarisation, which exists irrespective of the presence or otherwise of war, has become a significant area of feminist study and research. Cynthia Enloe (1987) argues that state bodies such as the military and security services have been dependent upon maleness and that this is the case historically and cross-culturally. Frank Barrett (2001: 97) agrees, going further to point out that: '[t]he military is a gendered institution. Its structure, practices, values, rites and rituals reflect accepted notions of masculinity and femininity. But it is also a gendering institution. It helps to create gendered identities.' The masculinity that the military constructs is one based on physical toughness, the ability to suffer hardship silently, is aggressive, unemotional, logical and heterosexual. This is achieved through training programmes that separate off recruits from the world to deliberately and systematically socialise them into becoming obedient, conforming violent professionals. One means of securing appropriate masculinity is to situate anything outside of accepted behaviour as the 'other', often through the invoking of femininity (Enloe, 1990). In many armies it is traditional to insult the enemy by calling them women (as we will see later, war rape is also used as a form of emasculation) and in US basic training drill instructors sometimes refer to marine recruits as 'faggots' to insinuate that they lack the appropriate level of aggression (Barrett, 2001). Barrett's own study of the US Navy revealed that recruits that did not 'keep up' were the targets of gendered insults: 'called girls, pussies, weenies, and wimps by the instructors' (Barrett, 2001: 82).

Stop and think 16.3

Look at the names some Navy recruits were called. Think about the times you have heard men insulted by calling them something female, often derogatory. What gender messages are conveyed when a boy is called 'a big Jessie' or a 'big girl's blouse'?

The entry of women into the military challenges masculinity: if the harsh training is meant to sort the men from the boys, there is a problem for masculinity when women succeed, as womanhood is associated with weakness. To deal with this, discourses of women as 'having it easy' develop: every officer interviewed by Barrett had a tale to tell about women and weakness, including how women were excused certain physical tasks. In addition, certain parts of the military have been reserved for men: in the US laws banning women from sea and air combat were rescinded in 1993 yet each branch of the military has exceptions to this rule – areas where women are not permitted, including army and Marine ground combat, submarines and all special forces (D'Amico, 2001). Women in the military are viewed differently from men by general society (see World in Focus 16.5).

Rape, war and gender

Rape as a weapon of war is not a new phenomenon (Brownmiller, 1975); it has been used as genocide, by impregnating the enemy with the sperm of the victor and to subjugate whole communities by indicating to them their inability to protect their women as in Bangladesh during the war for independence (Grech, 1993). Forcing people to sexually violate their own family members has also been used to destroy communities by forcing people to transgress social and moral taboos. As Helen Liebling's (2004) work on Uganda shows, in this way the social and cultural capital of societies are destroyed.

Some of the most shocking crimes that happened during the war in Bosnia-Herzegovina were those of extreme sexual violence and systematic rape, including a policy of 'genocidal rape' followed by the military and paramilitary units of the Serb and Bosnian Serb nationalist forces (Hague, 1997). This policy presented very particular relationships of power, subordination and masculinity. Connections between violence, gender and nationalisms formed the foundations of the policy.

All rape is an experience of power, domination, degradation and humiliation. The rapist takes a position of power, no matter if the victim is male or female, adult or child. The rapist takes the power-holding position which Euan Hague (1997) shows to be masculine, allowing the rapist to torture, attack and

---

World in focus 16.5

Canadian woman 16th soldier killed in Afghanistan

The death of a Canadian woman in combat with the Taliban created a national news event in Canada, unlike the coverage supplied for the previous 15 soldier deaths. Newspapers referred to her as a 'female soldier', showing that women in the front line are still seen as unusual.

A female soldier from Canada was killed while fighting Taliban insurgents in Afghanistan . . .

Capt. Nichola Goddard, 26, had been serving in Afghanistan with the Princess Patricia's Canadian Light Infantry . . .

She is the first Canadian woman to be killed in action since the Second World War, and the first female combat soldier killed on the front lines.

Source: CBC News, 17 May 2006. **http://www.cbc.ca/story/world/national/2006hanistan-cda.html**

Figure 16.2 Capt. Nichola Goddard

Source: © Captain Nichola Kathleen Sarah Goddard. Photo from Canadian Forces Image Gallery, http://www.combatcamera.forces.gc.ca. Department of National Defence. Reproduced with the permission of the Minister of Public Works and Government Services Canada, 2007.

brutalise the victims whom the rapist, or the policy deems as inferior. So in Bosnia-Herzegovina men and boys were also raped to show them they were inferior, that is feminine. By humiliating non-Serb persons through the practice of a systematic programme of raping women and girls, and by raping women, girls and boys as torture in prison camps, Bosnian Serbs not only bolstered their own masculinities and identities as 'Serbs' but eroded the identities of non-Serbs by the extreme humiliation associated with the rapes. The subjugation of the enemy as 'feminine' is central to a masculinity the perpetrator conceives as superior.

So rape embodies cultural meanings. In cultures where honour is a core value, the meaning of rape for each individual woman, and her family, is filtered through this discourse. In former Yugoslavia many believed that following rape a woman's honour, and that of her family, could only be regained through suicide. Countless women across the world face the choice of silence or stigma, and life choices are restricted when such women are known to have been raped (see A Closer Look 16.5 and World in Focus 16.6).

Feminist-informed analysis of gender violence during war refuses to see it as different from gender violence in other contexts – simply that sexual violence in the context of armed conflict intensifies already existing attitudes and behaviours.

After the conflict

Post-conflict societies face many challenges, including disruptions to the gender order. Demographic deficits,

A closer look 16.5

Prosecuting war rape

Rape has only been prosecuted as a war crime, by the International War Crimes Tribunal, since 1998. However, evidence of rape by soldiers was introduced in the Nuremberg War Crime trials after the Second World War. A United Nations medical team investigating rape in the former Yugoslavia in 1993 found evidence of rape on a massive scale, leading the UN Commission on Human Rights to pass a resolution placing rape clearly within the framework of war crimes. The International War Crimes Tribunal began prosecutions for mass rape in 2001.

Source: Andrew Osborn, The *Guardian*, 23 February 2001.

The Rome statute of the International Criminal Courts (in force 1 July 2002) also explicitly includes prohibitions against war rape.

that is the absence of men (either through death or continued absence after fighting), exist. In Rwanda, 70 per cent of the post-conflict population is female (El-Bushra, 2000). This creates changes in marriage patterns, in some cases the introduction of polygamy in previously monogamous communities. In others, suspicion of other clans who were on opposing sides prevents traditions in which women married outside of their own clans (see El-Bushra, 2000). In Uganda, a series of brutal civil wars from the 1960s to 1980s not only changed communities but the gender order within these: some have increased women's status

World in focus 16.6

The scale of rape during war

Korea – reports estimate that in the Second World War, Japanese soldiers abducted between 100,000 and 200,000 Asian women, mostly Korean, and sent them to the front lines where they were forced into sexual slavery; they were called 'comfort women'.

Bangladesh – estimates of the number of women raped during the country's 9-month war for independence in 1971 range from 250,000 to 400,000. These rapes led to an estimated 25,000 pregnancies according to International Planned Parenthood (Brownmiller, 1975).

Uganda – approximately 70 per cent of the women in the Luwero triangle district were raped by soldiers in the early 1980s. Many of the survivors were assaulted by as many as 10 soldiers in a single episode of gang rape.

Source: Giller *et al.* (1991).

whilst others have placed greater responsibility upon women. In addition, men have found it difficult to adjust, resulting in some ignoring their family responsibilities (see A Closer Look 16.6).

A closer look 16.6

Uganda

Until the 1970s gender relations among many Ugandan communities were characterised by a clear sexual division of labour: men were responsible for livestock and growing cash crops, meaning they had financial control and responsibility for expenses such as tax, school fees, clothes and basic household requirements. Women assisted their husbands in the family fields, doing lighter tasks than men. Women also kept fields, growing food for the family. Men had no access to these fields, women worked them alone and determined how produce was consumed. These fields were never sold.

Marriage practices supported this division of labour. Men had authority and control, including women's productive and reproductive labour, including all children. Women had certain rights, supported by the clan. Divorce was only possible if the husband repaid the bridewealth he received from the wife's family. Some areas also practised the inheritance of widows by brothers.

Social change post-conflict

➤ Violence and rape – the end of war and the disbanding of army camps has reduced the risk of violence from soldiers. However, women who have been raped, especially if they have become pregnant, may not be able to count on the support of their families.

➤ Domestic violence – previously, bad behaviour was controlled by the community. Due to the disruption of the community, violent husbands are no longer held up to community criticism. A positive result has been the reduction of brutal punishments meted out to unmarried pregnant girls (and the boy if identified).

➤ Family division of labour – this has become blurred. In men's absence, women had to farm and perform other, previously male, agricultural tasks. In addition, the loss of land and oxen during the war has placed a greater emphasis on growing cash crops. As such, women have tended to lose access to their own subsistence land due to a need to concentrate on crops for sale.

➤ Changes in responsibilities – payment of school fees and purchasing of household needs, previously a man's responsibility, has now transferred to women. This has created a greater burden of labour on women whilst their husbands enjoy leisure time. Loss of role for some men has resulted in alternative ways of expressing masculinity, such as using family money to buy beer, beating their wives or using family money to afford additional wives. However, others have taken the position of sharing domestic work with their wives.

➤ Marriage – these changes in the sexual division of responsibility are factors in the increased rate of marriage failure and unhappy marriages. Another factor causing marriage fragility is the damage caused by rape and assault.

➤ HIV/AIDS – an obvious result of sexual violence, marriage fragility and the presence of army camps is increased exposure to HIV. Women, in particular, are affected not only through their own sexual relations, but as mothers and grandmothers of AIDS sufferers.

➤ Community affairs – a positive outcome is a growing and widespread acceptance of women's role in community affairs. Women are involved in local government and women's groups.

Source: Derived from Oxfam (1994), *The Oxfam Gender Training Manual*.

Conclusion

No consideration of violence and conflict is complete without an examination of the ways in which acts of violence and resistance are the products of, and reinforce, constructs of femininity and masculinity. This is only gradually becoming accepted in the arena of International Relations (Jacobs *et al.*, 2000). In addition, the experience of conflict can substantially disrupt and change the established gender order, providing many losses but the occasional gain for women.

Further reading

Sasha Roseneil (1995), *Disarming Patriarchy: Feminism and Political Action at Greenham*, Buckingham, Open University Press. In this book the author analyses and describes the resistance to nuclear weapons by the women's peace camp at Greenham Common.

Jill Radford, Melissa Friedberg and Lynne Harne (eds) (2000), *Women, Violence and Strategies for Action: Feminist Research, Policy and Practice*, Buckingham, Open University Press. A collection of 12 papers covering violence and resistance including pornography, prostitution, stalking, child abuse and paedophilia. Most articles relate to the UK but also included are China, India and international violence via the Internet. Several chapters address activism and resistance.

Susie Jacobs, Ruth Jacobson and Jen Marchbank (eds) (2000), *States of Conflict: Gender, Violence and Resistance*, London, Zed. An international collection addressing women and men's agency in conflict and resistance in a variety of geographical contexts: such as Brazil, India, Northern Ireland, China, South Africa, Rwanda, Somalia, Uganda, the USA and international issues such as global security and refugees.

Websites

Zero Tolerance – **www.zerotolerance.org** – the site of the UK charity Zero Tolerance, includes current and past campaigns both UK and internationally based.

WAFE – **www.wafe.org** – Women's Aid Federation of England. An incredibly informative site providing details of statistics, legislation, policy, strategies of resistance and how to get assistance.

Mankind UK – **www.mankinduk.co.uk** – a service for men who have been sexually abused, sexually assaulted or raped.

Victim Support – **www.victimsupport.org** – Victim Support offer information and support for victims of crime whether or not they have been reported to the police.

The Sunflower Centre – **www.sunflower-centre.org** – this organisation offers a multi-agency service and support for victims of domestic abuse, both women and men.

End of chapter activity

1. Read the Uganda case study in A Closer Look 16.6. In what ways has conflict affected the sexual division of labour? What differences has war made to family organisation? What have been the effects on men and masculinity?

2. Using your local phone book (or the Internet addresses below) identify local sources of assistance for victims of violence. Do these serve both women and men? Do they serve transgendered people? If not, why do you think this might be so? Please *do not* phone these agencies as you may block the call of someone needing help.

Chapter 17

Crime and deviance

Key issues in this chapter:

➤ Gendered explanations of deviant and criminal behaviour.
➤ Gender bias within the criminal justice system.
➤ The relationship between gender and punishment.
➤ Women and men as victims of crime.
➤ Criminology as a multi-disciplinary area of study and its contributions to our gendered understandings of crime and deviance.

At the end of this chapter you should be able to:

➤ Critique crime statistics.
➤ Debate the issue of gender bias in the Criminal Justice System.
➤ Demonstrate how criminology has focused on men but not on masculinity.
➤ Discuss women's and men's experiences in prisons.
➤ Detail gendered experiences of being crime victims.

Introduction

Post-war developments in British criminology heavily profiled the 'delinquent' behaviour of young men and the construction of 'criminal areas'. These developments were noted in several decades of American work, particularly the Chicago School . . . While it was recognized that American theories could not be simply transposed on to British society . . . the emphasis remained the same: 'subcultures', 'delinquency' and 'gangs' were the sole province of men. The lives of young women did not feature. (Scraton, 1990: 18)

Stop and think 17.1

As Phil Scraton (1990) suggests the study of criminal and deviant behaviour by social scientists has historically ignored girls and women. Before you read the rest of this chapter write down (a) why you think this is the case, (b) the implications of this omission for a full understanding of women's criminal and deviant behaviour, and (c) the implications of this omission for a full understanding of men's criminal and deviant behaviour. When you have finished reading the chapter answer the questions again and note how your answers have changed.

Before we begin to consider the gendered aspects of deviance and crime we need to start with some definitions. Deviance describes any behaviour that differs from that that is considered to be the norm in society and behaving deviantly means breaking these (sometimes unwritten) norms or 'laws'. So deviant behaviour could be praised – as in extreme bravery – or deplored – for example when laws are broken or moral norms ignored. Crime on the other hand can be defined as an act that breaks the criminal law and if discovered will likely be followed by criminal proceedings and formal punishment. Although deviance is not necessarily criminal, crime is always (at least legally) deviant, although not paying the full fare when travelling or using work stationery or technology for personal use is often not viewed by many as 'real' crime. Behaviour defined as deviant and/or criminal is relative in that the written and unwritten laws that govern us differ over time and place. Even within one society different groups may have their own norms. Social reaction is important when determining whether a behaviour is criminal or deviant. No action is criminal or deviant in itself and only becomes so if society defines it as such (Marsh, 2006). Particularly significant for a gendered understanding of crime and deviance is the fact that what is seen as normal behaviour for men may be seen as deviant for women (and vice versa) and stereotypical views of male and female behaviour have influenced academic writing and the response of the criminal justice system to the crimes of men and women.

In the remainder of this chapter we focus mostly on behaviour that is defined as criminal, although of course this will involve us in a consideration of behaviour that is also considered to be deviant. A focus on the gendered aspects of criminal and deviant behaviour is of course not new, although several writers have suggested that Criminology – the area of work which studies criminal and deviant behaviour and which draws on various disciplines including sociology, psychology, history and law – was slow in its consideration of gender. Traditionally Criminology at best marginalised and at worst ignored gender. For an example here we can consider the *Oxford Handbook of Criminology* (edited by Mike Maguire, Rod Morgan, Robert Reiner in 1997); the handbook is 1,259 pages long and in their introduction the editors accept the importance of a consideration of gender differences and crime and agree that this was an area previously neglected by male criminologists. Given this they ask 'should gender (and race) be addressed in every chapter? Or should they be assigned to chapters for 'specialist coverage?' Their decision is to go for the 'specialist coverage' option and with reference to gender the result is Chapter 21: 'Gender and Crime' (by Frances Heidensohn). The consequence of course is that the rest of the book is sexless: a book about men without a gendered identity. Men remain the proper subject of criminology but the gendered nature of their crimes and experiences is not considered. Feminist writers argue that this continuing lack of a gender-integrated approach within Criminology remains problematic as A Critical Look 17.1 shows.

A critical look 17.1

Less than half a picture

Gender blindness is not a trivial oversight: it carries social and political significance. Moreover, theories which do not address gender are not merely incomplete; they are misleading.

(Gelsthorpe and Morris, 1988: 98, cited by Collier, 1988)

The costs to criminology of its failure to deal with feminist scholarship are perhaps more severe than they would be in any other discipline. The reason is that the most consistent and prominent fact about crime is the sex of the offender.

(Naffine, 1997: 5)

As you can see, arguments for the inclusion of a consideration of gender in regard to crime have been around for quite some time.

The offenders of crime are indeed more often than not men. In 2000, for example, 81 per cent of known offenders were male (Home Office, 2001, cited by Walklate, 2003: 74). A gendered analysis of criminal and deviant behaviour needs to consider why men commit crime, why women do not, whether men and women are treated differently by the criminal justice system when receiving punishment for their crimes, and are men or women more likely to be the victims of crime and why?

We attempt to answer these questions in the rest of this chapter within three main sections. In 'Males and females doing crime and deviance' we provide an overview of the types of crimes that men and women commit and consider historical and contemporary explanations for gender differences in criminal and deviant behaviour. In 'Gender bias within the criminal justice system' we give instances of and explanations for the differential treatment of males and females by the police and the courts and focus on the gendered punitive responses to criminal behaviour paying particular attention to imprisonment. Then having focused so far on gender differences in terms of the perpetration of crime in the final main section of this chapter – 'Men and women as victims of crime' – we briefly consider how gender also influences the types of crimes people fall victim to. We end the chapter with some brief conclusions.

Males and females doing crime and deviance

Facts and figures

Over 80 per cent of those convicted of serious offences in England and Wales are males; in 2001 around 380,000 male offenders and 86,000 female offenders were convicted (*Social Trends*, 2003, cited by Marsh, 2006). Women are convicted of all categories of crime but men commit far higher numbers of crimes in all categories. The two categories of crime, 'Theft and handling stolen goods' and 'Fraud and forgery' are the ones which women are most likely to be convicted of, with 'Theft and handling of stolen goods' accounting for 53 per cent of all females convicted and only 35 per cent of all men convicted. Even here though 79 per cent of all the people convicted in this category were men. In addition evidence shows that women are mainly convicted of shoplifting in this category and although shoplifting is considered to be the stereotypical female crime even here more men than women are convicted. In all other categories – other than 'Theft and handling stolen goods' and 'Fraud and forgery' – more than 85 per cent of those convicted are men (Crime Statistics for England and Wales, 2002, Home Office, 2003, cited by Abbott *et al.*, 2005). In addition, Sandra Walklate (2003) argues that if we also take account of the often hidden crimes of sexual and physical violence, which are disproportionately committed by men, then the maleness of lawbreaking behaviour is heightened.

However, there does appear to have been a recent change in women's deviant and criminal behaviour, or at least a change in the number of women convicted of criminal offences. Between 1977 and 1986 the number of women found guilty of crime in England and Wales increased steadily from 207,000 in 1977 to 277,000 in 1986 but declined to about 251,000 in 1993 and has remained reasonably stable since then (Walklate, 2004). However, one problem with official statistics on convictions is that they tell us only the numbers arrested and convicted for crimes and we know nothing about who commits the large number of unsolved crimes. Thus, as Pamela Abbott and colleagues (2005) note it is impossible to tell whether crime statistics represent a 'real' difference in the lawbreaking of men and women or reflect the fact that women are better at hiding their crimes and/or are less likely to be suspected of crimes because they do not fit the stereotype of 'the criminal'.

Stop and think 17.2

Without re-reading the above, list the problems that exist with statistics on crime and the sex of the offender.

Figure 17.1 Typical criminals? The Kray Brothers
Source: Evening Standard/Hulton Archive/Getty Images

Arguably, one of the reasons that more attention has been given to men and crime than women and crime is because (as noted above) it is overwhelmingly men who commit crime. When women commit crime this is seen as exceptional and unusual and women who are convicted of crime are seen as 'doubly deviant' in that they have not only broken the law but have also broken the unwritten norms of femininity. Male deviance and criminal behaviour is often associated with what it means to be 'a man' – using force, being aggressive and so on – whereas female deviance and criminal behaviour is associated with everything that is considered unfeminine. With this in mind we now explore the meanings and explanations of men's and women's criminal and deviant behaviour in more detail.

Gendered explanations of crime and deviance

Early explanations

At the end of the nineteenth century an Italian Criminologist Cesare Lombroso developed a biological theory of criminality. He believed in the potential for humans to evolve negatively into a criminal class, arguing that the criminal was a throwback to previous generations, this is known as degeneration theory – see A Closer Look 17.1 for more detail.

A closer look 17.1

Lombroso's theory

Lombroso concluded that skull and facial features were clues to genetic criminality – these features could be measured with craniometers and calipers with the results developed into quantitative research. Lombroso assumed that whites were superior to non-whites by heredity, and Africans were the first human beings that evolved upwards and positively to yellow then white. Racial development was signified by social progress from primitive to modern: 'only we white people have reached the ultimate symmetry of bodily form' Lombroso stated in 1871.

Lombroso's studies of female criminality began with measurements of females' skulls and photographs in his search for atavism. Lombroso concluded female criminals were rare and showed few

---

A closer look continued

signs of degeneration because they had 'evolved less than men due to the inactive nature of their lives'. Lombroso argued it was females' natural passivity that stopped them breaking the law, as women lacked the intelligence and initiative to become criminal.

Source: Wikipedia, **http://en.wikipedia.org/wiki/Cesare_ Lombroso**

While Lombrosian theories of crime are no longer given wide credence, biological theories continued to have some influence into the twentieth century in explanations of criminal behaviour and, to this day, influence lay perceptions and the workings of the criminal justice system (CJS). We consider this legacy for the CJS later in the chapter, but for now we concentrate on explanations of crime. Eighty years after Lombroso Otto Pollack (1950) argued that women are no less criminal than men just better at hiding their actions and that men are socialised into treating women in a protective manner. Women became good at hiding due to having a natural secrecy to enable the hiding of menstruation. Pollack also argued that women are essentially more deceitful than men due to their passive role which they have to assume during sexual intercourse. Menstruation has also been implicated by Katarina Dalton (1961) who suggested that some female crime can be explained by hormonal changes during the menstrual cycle. She argued that pre-menstrual tension leads to criminal behaviour.

Others have attempted to explain what appears to be totally incomprehensible behaviour by labelling the perpetrator as mentally sick and suggesting that he or she is mad and therefore not responsible for his or her actions, for instance Pollack (1950) thought women were especially vulnerable to certain mental illnesses such as kleptomania and nymphomania. In addition some criminal theorists have suggested that criminal behaviour is caused by serious mental pathology or at least is the result of some emotional disturbance. These types of explanation have been especially prevalent in explaining female criminality.

The social environment has also been raised in explanation for criminal behaviour. The most common versions of social conditions are:

1. those that locate criminal behaviour in the socialisation processes experienced by individuals and their families; and

2. those that see the immediate 'bad' environment as the cause.

A common example of the first case is spousal abuse which has frequently been explained by childhood experiences of offenders who grew up in homes where such abuse occurred. Likewise, child abuse is sometimes similarly explained. However, by the 1960s some sociologists began to challenge the idea that it was possible to establish the causes of social behaviour in the same way that it was possible to establish causes in the natural sciences [**Hotlink → Methods, Methodology and Epistemology (Chapter 2)**]. They pointed out that by paying attention to violations of law, Criminology had ignored the legal system and devalued the place of human consciousness and the meaning that criminal activities had for those engaged in them. Yet current research still focuses on environmental issues as A Closer Look 17.2 demonstrates.

Like Lombroso others have sought to find out if those who behave criminally differ in some way from those who do not and to establish what these differences may be. It has been suggested by Labelling theorists that if criminals do differ from non-criminals, then these very characteristics are used by society to label some people as criminal and ignore others. Maureen Cain (1973) and Steven Box (1971) both suggest that the police are more likely to suspect and arrest a working-class man than a middle-class one. A good example of how, when taking a gendered perspective, we need also to consider the relevance of other aspects of difference and diversity.

Another explanation of criminal behaviour is Strain Theory. In this theory offenders are considered to commit crimes when they meet with restraints and barriers to opportunity, such as decent jobs and education. Strain Theory has been critiqued by feminists for seeing the commission of crimes by men as somehow a normal, understandable response to meeting such barriers whereas when women commit crime Strain Theory refers to such acts as aspects of women's weakness (Naffine, 1987).

A closer look 17.2

Marriage saves men from a life of crime

A 70-year study of juvenile offenders born in the 1920s has found that those who married were far more likely to go straight in later life than those who remained single. The findings challenge much of contemporary thinking on social and criminal justice policy, which focuses heavily on the importance of childhood behaviour and background as a key predictor of criminality in adulthood. [The research was based on data from] 500 criminals from Boston, Massachusetts who were sent to reform school in the 1930s and 1940s . . . married men were 36 per cent less likely to reoffend than those who had not married . . .

The married men did not set out to distance themselves from their formal criminal activities, nor did marriage appear to have changed their moral outlook . . . Instead, marriage altered their daily routines and physically removed them from the scene of their past deviant behaviour. It was almost as if they dissociated themselves from crime by default.

Source: Alexandra Frean, *The Times* 14 January 2004, p. 20.

In critique of all of this it is suggested that the only way that criminals differ from non-criminals is that the former have been involved in the criminal justice system (CJS). Supporters of this argument are concerned to identify the key mechanisms by which crime is socially constructed through law creation, law enforcement and societal reaction. This approach is sometimes called New Criminology or Critical Criminology (Walklate, 1998). More recently the Left Realist position argues that New Criminology is idealistic and romanticises the criminal. Left realists point out that those who suffer most from criminal acts are working-class people. New Criminology is also criticised for neglecting women and crime and this failure to include women in their analysis means that biological and pathological explanations are left unchallenged.

Social Psychology has sought to explain criminal and deviant behaviour through the concept of role (Walklate, 2003). This concept acts as a means by which we can understand the ways that actions and behaviours reflect stereotypical assumptions and expectations, including assumptions related to social class, ethnicity and sex. Early sex role theory [**Hotlink → Gendered Perspectives – Theoretical Issues (Chapter 1)**] based on biological differences delineated distinct roles for males and females and this was also applied to criminal and deviant behaviour. The pervasiveness of sex role theory and biological influences can be seen in the fact that even those who foreground socialisation influences implicitly accepted the importance of biology. For example, Edwin Sutherland (1947, cited in Walklate, 2003) developed the notion of 'differential association' to explain boys' greater delinquency than girls'. The main elements of this view are that criminal behaviour was a learned behaviour just like any other and that those exposed to certain behaviours may favour deviant rather than rule-abiding behaviours. Sutherland explained boys' greater propensity towards delinquency as follows:

1. Boys are less strictly controlled by society and enjoy greater freedoms to socialise therefore may be exposed to delinquent elements more so than girls.

2. The socialisation process for boys encourages behaviours such as toughness, aggression and risk taking, all the right characteristics for delinquent and criminal actions.

Despite the focus here on social learning [**Hotlink → Gendered Perspectives – Theoretical Issues (Chapter 1)**] it is clear that boys were assumed to be naturally aggressive and tough whilst girls were equally naturally passive and gentle [**Hotlink → Family (Chapter 11)**]. The following quote regarding boys and street gangs in the 1950s clearly shows that Sutherland was not the only one to observe such masculine traits:

Here [in the street gangs] the assertion of power through physical prowess rather than negotiation, the taking of risks rather than keeping safe, and the thrill and excitement of breaking the rules rather than accepting them all provide not only the avenues and the motivation for delinquent behaviour but also an expression of themselves as young men.

(Cohen, 1955, cited in Walklate, 2003: 54)

Stop and think 17.3

Consider the time in which Sutherland was writing. Do you believe the social learning process remains the same today? How might it differ? Are boys still encouraged into the characteristics listed above? Are girls still socially monitored in the ways they were in the late 1940s? How relevant then is this theory to explaining gender differences in delinquency today?

The attractiveness of sex role theory lay, according to Robert Connell (1987), in the fact that it does move away from biological explanations and considers the role of social structures. In addition, it also offers the possibility of social and political change, as learned behaviours can be unlearned or adapted. Yet, problems remain here as the very categories used within sex role theory, 'male role', 'female role' remain firmly rooted in biology and, as such, limit the ways in which masculinity and femininity can be understood [Hotlink → Chapter 1].

Critiques and reworkings

From the late 1960s feminists began to challenge what they saw as gender distortions and stereotyping in traditional Criminology. This was not just a challenge to Criminology to pay more attention to women but also a concern to consider how sex and gender interplay with other social variables. Groundbreaking work was undertaken by Carol Smart (1977) and continued by others (Leonard, 1982; Heidensohn, 1985; Morris, 1987; Naffine, 1987). Smart (1977) argues that most discussions on crime from the nineteenth century onwards virtually ignore women and when women are present they are grouped alongside the mentally ill and juvenile delinquents. She goes on to point out that the study of Criminology is predominately conducted with reference to men – examining men's motivations, their alienation and even men's crime upon other men. As such, she argues that it has been assumed that women need not be considered as the male experience is extrapolatable to women. In addition, Smart argues that studies of women criminals are full of sexism and that unexamined ideas regarding women's nature (as passive) encouraged a focus on behaviours, such as

prostitution as sexually deviant [Hotlink → Sex and Sexuality (Chapter 15)]. Likewise, Claire Valier (2002) points out that huge numbers of studies seem to have ignored the presence of women offenders and have assumed that the male experience included and explained the female. Smart (1997) argues that Lombrosian notions on female criminality have endured and have been reinforced by policies based upon the view that criminal women are more 'mad than bad'.

Feminist critiques from the late 1970s and 1980s display some common foci:

1. they aimed to raise the visibility of women within criminological knowledge;

2. they sought to address women's relationships with crime not only as offenders but also as victims; and

3. they attempted to understand crime as a male-dominated activity produced not as a result of sex differences but as a product of gender differences.

However, many of these texts tended to treat the 'woman and crime problem' as if it were a separate and separable issue within Criminology (see the case of the *Oxford Handbook of Criminology* mentioned at the beginning of this chapter). This created its own problems as the more the question of women and crime was treated in this way, the more mainstream (read malestream) Criminology was left unchallenged (Brown, 1986). There are great dangers in this approach, not least of which is the presumption that when gender is mentioned it only refers to women and not to men. Further, as Smart's (1977) thesis suggests, the development of a subfield within Criminology called 'women and crime' has the potential to merely continue the marginalisation of gender-related questions whilst simultaneously guiding policy-makers to issues not necessarily in women's interests.

Lorraine Gelsthorpe and Alison Morris (1990) argue that the most fundamental question regarding women and crime is not just about representation nor inclusion, rather it is the issue of the whole relationship between feminism and Criminology. They argue that 'Criminology has for many feminist writers and researchers been a constraining rather than a constructive and creative influence. Indeed, in a sense our task . . . is to fracture its boundaries' (Gelsthorpe and Morris, 1990: 2). So what are these feminists' perspectives of which Gelsthorpe and Morris speak; how have they influenced Criminology, if at all, and how might they differently gender Criminology? We will explore the main aspects here.

One area of feminist critique was to challenge the positivism inherent in the New Criminology (Taylor *et al.*, 1973) showing how the positivist model allowed the world 'as it is' to remain unchallenged and encouraged a determinist view of human nature that legitimised interventionism. Smart argues that such a deterministic view is always oriented towards control over behaviour that deviates from norms, yet we need to ask who sets these norms? Such an approach diagnoses those whose acts do not fit with predefined normative standards as pathological and in need of 'treatment' to produce conformity to societal norms. Yet, as Smart outlines, this approach ignores the potential political significance of deviant behaviour:

> deviant individuals are not considered to be social critics, rebels or even members of a counter culture, rather they are treated as biological anomalies or as psychologically 'sick' individuals. Their actions are not interpreted as having particular social significance, as being possibly rational responses.
>
> (Smart, 1977, cited in Valier, 2002: 29)

Some feminist critics have asked the question 'can we add women to existing theories?' Eileen Leonard (1982) argues that this would be inadequate and called for the construction of new methods and theories for non-sexist ways of describing social reality. Such arguments were based on an observation that some feminist empiricism tended to accept men as the norm, unwittingly setting them up as the human standard. For instance, engagements with the chivalry thesis (see below) questioned whether women were treated the same as, or different from men. In other words, men were accepted as the norm to which women might be compared. In addition, this norm was predominately that of the white male and as Marcia Rice (1990) has shown ethnicity is also at play and black female offenders have been constructed as 'the other dark figure in crime'. In such ways, it has been argued that traditional Criminology has con-

structed racist as well as sexist ideologies of femininity and that in addition to a feminist perspective it is also necessary to add a black feminist perspective on crime and deviance. See A Closer Look 17.3 for further details of feminist responses.

A closer look 17.3

Feminists, women and crime

Feminists have suggested that to understand the issues surrounding women and crime two key questions need to be considered:

1. why do so few women commit crimes; and

2. why women who do commit crimes do so?

Abbott and colleagues (2005) suggest that malestream theories have either failed to tackle these questions or provided inadequate answers, for example psycho-positivistic (biological/psychological) theories of female criminality have stereotyped women and do not provide an adequate explanation yet maintain a position of dominance in explanations of female crime long after they have been seriously challenged. Examples of this are that women are more likely to be viewed as suffering from psychological problems, women more likely to be found insane or of diminished responsibility and, if convicted, more likely to be given psychiatric treatment in place of a penal sentence. One such example is the use of PMS (premenstrual syndrome) as a means of defence. On the other hand, sociological theories have with few exceptions ignored women. They have not seen gender as an important explanatory variable and have assumed that theories based on male samples and a male view of the world can be generalised to women. In some cases they have implicitly or explicitly accepted biological theories, as for example Emile Durkheim (1897) did in his study of suicide, when he agreed that women were less likely to commit suicide than men because they were biologically at a lower stage of development than men and therefore less influenced by the social forces.

Source: Abbott *et al.* (2005).

Feminists argue that to truly understand why some women transgress the law requires a paradigm shift. This shift needs to consider how gender interplays with class and ethnicity and must include a consideration of patriarchal relationships, contemporaneous ideologies of appropriate femininity and the role that women play within the family and community. As was noted by Sutherland, the ideology of femininity constructs girls and women in particular ways with the 'natural' role being seen as that of wife and mother, with the consequent conclusion that girls and women are seen as needing protection and care. Related to this view young girls tend to be controlled more than their brothers and given less freedom. While young men who come before the courts and are handled in the juvenile justice system have generally committed criminal offences, girls are more likely to come before the courts for being in need of care and protection, including from their own promiscuity – what are referred to as 'status offences', coming within the ambit of the law only because of the age of the 'offender'. This seems to remain true even when the girls have in fact committed criminal offences (Lloyd, 1995; Abbott *et al.*, 2005).

Arguing for the need to develop theories that are adequate for explaining and understanding the law-breaking of both men and women, does not mean that feminists are looking for a universal theory that will explain all criminal behaviour in all circumstances. There is no reason to assume that all criminal behaviour can be explained in the same way. What is necessary are theories of crime that take account of gender, ethnic and class division and studies that are situated in the wider moral, political, economic and sexual spheres which influence women's and men's status and position in society (see A Critical Look 17.2.)

Stop and think 17.4

Make a bullet list of the ways in which feminists have critiqued 'malestream' criminology.

Not all theorists have failed to examine masculinity in relation to criminal behaviour. James Messerschmidt (1993, cited in Walklate, 2003) has suggested that there are three social structures involved in the way masculinity is expressed across a range of criminal behaviour (from street violence to white-collar crime). These are:

A critical look 17.2

Criminology and men

It is not the case that men have been absent from studies of crime, deviance and delinquency. However, what is true is that it has been maleness, rather than masculinity that has been researched, examined and theorised.

> Men certainly have not been absent from criminological thinking. Indeed, the activities of young, urban males have preoccupied criminologists since the delinquency studies of the 1940s and 1950s. What criminologists have paid little attention to, however, are the potentially different ways in which the behaviour of young, urban males might be informed by their understanding of themselves as men; or indeed, how criminological analyses might be better understood as a reflection of male understandings about crime . . . Tolson (1997) explored the different ways in which dominant forms of thinking about masculinity constrained different men in different ways. In some ways, Tolson's work constituted a central moment in setting the further development of the exploration of masculinity. His work posed two key questions for that debate. Is there one overarching form of masculinity, or are there many diverse masculinities? Is masculinity best understood as a product of sex role development or gender relations?
>
> (Walklate, 2003: 81)

1. the gender division of labour [**Hotlink → Work and Leisure (Chapter 14)**];

2. the gender relations of power and sexuality [**Hotlink → Sex and Sexuality (Chapter 15)**], and

3. the objectification of women in the media [**Hotlink → Sex and Sexuality (Chapter 15); Culture and Mass Media (Chapter 18)**].

Accordingly, 'men construct masculinities in accord with their position in social structures and therefore their access to power and resources' (Messerschmidt, 1993: 119). Messerschmidt considers various sites of crime from the workplace to the home and to the street, examining the ways in which masculinity is expressed. Whether the site be the pimp on the streets or the executive in the office, Messerschmidt argues that each offer an opportunity for men to display their manliness to others and to themselves. He concludes that whereas the office offers the executive the opportunity for sexual harassment of female employees this differs little from the control a pimp has over prostitutes on the street. For Messerschmidt crime is merely one way in which masculinity can be expressed when other opportunities and resources are unavailable (Valier, 2002: 146).

It would appear then that there has been a tendency to accept that masculinity is related to crime whilst at the same time a fear of the female criminal has pertained. A Critical Look 17.3 shows how female crime seems to threaten not just the social order but the moral order of society.

A critical look 17.3

Girls go bad?

Consider the following taken from an article by Susan Batchelor (originally 2001) reproduced in Jewkes and Letherby, 2002a: 249). It comes from the tabloid the *Daily Record*, Scotland's biggest selling newspaper.

One newspaper claimed that 'One girl said she was too scared to leave the house for fear of being attacked. Another described how a girl gang member had held a knife to the throat of her best friend' . . . Another 'angle' adopted by the press involved misquoting the research to back up the girl gang story ('Deadly as the males – Experts probe explosion of violence by girl gangs' . . . 'The shocking extent of violence among teenage girls in Scotland was revealed yesterday. A study found girl gangs taking part in unprovoked attacks is now commonplace'. The article went on to allege that 'The number of violent crimes committed by girl thugs in Scotland had almost doubled in the last decade.'

Yet this is hardly new: Geoffrey Pearson (originally 1983), reproduced in Jewkes and Letherby 2002a: 15) writes:

A brawl among three women . . . resulted in one of them 'scoring her face with a door key' because

the other women 'tore her hair and beat her with a poker'. . . three girls aged 15 and 16 years were brought to court for robbing a woman of 9s 2½d after they had hustled her. Described by the police as a well-known gang of 'expert pick-pockets', the news headlines identified them as 'Girl Hooligans'. There were other mentions of 'Hooligan Girls' and 'Female Hooligans' and their 'hooliganesque' behaviour. Young women, for example, who were 'arm-in-arm' right across the pavement, and kept pushing people off, or another court report which described how 'a respectably-dressed young girl was set upon by four factory girls and unmercifully beaten'. She said that she had 'accidentally brushed against one of the four girls who were standing on the pavement', whereupon 'all four caught hold of her, and beat her in a most savage manner, using fearful language', and left her on the ground bleeding profusely from the nose and mouth (all reports from various English newspapers produced in August 1898).

Source: Jewkes and Letherby (2002a).

Despite the increasing number of articles focusing on 'girl gangs' the everyday experience of girls presents a very different picture (Batchelor, 2001). For example, in the article above the reporter did not cite the source of the data used and when we look at the data for the eleven years from 1987 to 1997 the number of women convicted of violent offending in Scotland had increased, but by 15 per cent (38 additional cases), not by close to 100 per cent as suggested by the *Daily Record*. For contrast it is interesting to note that in the same time period violent crime by men increased by 26 per cent (818 additional cases). It is also worth noting that because the number of such crimes committed by women is so low a very small rise can make a considerable difference in terms of percentage rises. The misrepresentation of available data in this way has serious consequences. This media stimulation of the 'myths' of girl gangs can contribute to unrealistic public attitudes and misdirected public policy (Batchelor, 2001). Further, the demonisation of young women by the media deflects attention away from the genuine problems that young women might have.

Gender bias within the criminal justice system

Chivalry or just desserts?

Recently Criminologists have engaged in a debate regarding the treatment of women offenders in the criminal justice system (CJS). There are basically two perspectives: the chivalry (or paternalism) view and the 'evil women' position.

1. Chivalry – this view basically argues that women are treated with greater leniency than men within the male-dominated justice system due to feelings of chivalry which lead men to seek to act protectively towards weak women. Of course, this simply reiterates and reinforces the perception of female offenders as victims and passive.

2. Evil Women – this view is that women who offend receive harsher treatment than men for women who commit crime are seen as doubly deviant. Women who commit crimes are viewed as offending against the law and also against social norms regarding gender roles (Nagel and Hagan, 1983).

Associated with the 'evil women' thesis is the view that female offending tends to be sexualised whereas male offending is not, with female offenders assumed to be sexually deviant. As such women's crime produces more punitive attitudes. Frances Heidensohn (1985) points out that whether this view is overt or covert (usually presenting as a concern for the welfare of the women offenders) it can lead to a situation whereby female deviance can once more be presented as a 'sickness' which may result in sentences which include treatment plans, resulting in a punishment which could be more intrusive than that issued to a male convicted of a similar offence.

Some empirical evidence was produced in the 1980s which found that women did receive less severe sentences than men (Farrington and Morris, 1983) but it should be remembered that women are more likely than men to be first offenders and to have committed a less serious form of the particular crime (for example, in the offence of theft they may have stolen goods of lesser value on average than men convicted of

theft). An examination of the different stages of contact with the CJS provides the following summary (derived from Cavadino and Dignan, 2002):

➤ Police stop and search men more often than women (almost twice as frequently);

➤ Delinquent boys are more likely to be stopped by police than delinquent girls, and

➤ Girls are more likely to be stopped if their lifestyles and behaviour were deemed to be 'unfeminine', for example, being in mixed sex groups, involved with alcohol etc.

So, it would appear that the police do not treat girls worse than boys but the above list does add credence to feminist claims that males and females experience differences in their treatment by arms of the CJS, with girls and women having their femininity policed as much as their offending.

Femininity can also be seen as working to the advantage of women and there is a 'tendency not to arrest females as often as males if they behaved in expected stereotypical ways' (Cavadino and Dignan, 2003: 182), such as displaying concern for their children or implying that they had been led astray. Support for this view comes from the observation that those females who presented themselves as hostile and aggressive are more frequently arrested than those who exhibit stereotypical female behaviour (Cavadino and Dignan, 2002).

> Judges tell me all the time that they never send women to prison. The truth is that the woman in the neat white blouse who is sorry and depressed is acceptable, but the girl in the leather jacket with the Mohican haircut and the drug problem is treated very badly.
>
> (Chris Tchaikovsky, Women In Prison, The *Guardian*, 9 February 1994)

Evidence also shows that female offenders receive cautions rather than sentences at a higher rate than men. In 1999, 48 per cent of females found guilty of, or cautioned for, an indictable offence received a caution, compared with 30 per cent of males (Abbott *et al.*, 2005). This may be seen as evidence of chivalry operating in women's favour. However, it is necessary to take into account the type of offences involved and the offenders' previous records in deciding whether any bias goes into the creation of the statistical difference between the sexes. In addition, other social variables such as class and ethnicity also influence sentencing as shown in World in Focus 17.1.

It may be that the Aboriginal women in Canadian prisons (detailed in World in Focus 17.1) are subject to bias against both sex and ethnicity. A Scottish study conducted by Pat Carlan (1983) concludes that sexist bias enters into the sentencing decision to the disadvantage of women who offend against the norms of femininity. From her interviews with sheriffs (Scottish judges) Carlan found that they expressed chivalrous views (such as saying they hated sending women to prison) and she concludes that they frequently include in their sentencing deliberations considerations such as their assessment of the woman's mothering role (being more likely to send a woman to prison if her children where in care). Despite this chivalry many also confessed that they sometimes imprisoned women in circumstances when they would have fined a man, because women were normally financially

dependent on men and often could not afford to pay a fine appropriate to the offence.

It appears that a disproprortionate number of women in prisons have 'unconventional' family backgrounds. Carlan's Scottish sample consisted of 20 women, of which only one was married at the time of the research. Likewise, Farrington and Morris (1983: 244–5) found that women who were divorced or separated or were deemed to have a 'deviant family background' were more likely to receive a relatively severe sentence, but these factors made no difference to the kind of sentences which male offenders received. However, this suggests that sexist bias may be functioning in two directions for women who are married and looking after their children may be the beneficiaries of chivalry and receive a lighter sentence than a man.

When all the research evidence is weighed it suggests that women who offend are not on the whole sentenced more severely than comparable males, and that they sometimes receive more lenient sentences, including escaping custody where a male would not. What is not known, however, is to what extent this

World in focus 17.1

Aboriginals in the Canadian prison system

Federal prisons discriminate against aboriginals, says ombudsman

The Canadian prison system is practising 'systemic discrimination' against aboriginal offenders, says the federal ombudsman for inmates – a finding that his political masters in the Conservative government refuse to accept. Howard Sapers, in his annual report Monday [16 October, 2006], said the Correctional Service of Canada too often overestimates the risk posed by native prisoners and sends them to

maximum-security institutions when less rigorous treatment would do. Aboriginals are also more likely than non-aboriginals to be sent to solitary confinement, and to be overlooked for early parole and thus end up serving too much time behind bars, said Sapers.

'The general picture is one of institutionalized discrimination,' he told a news conference. 'That is, aboriginal people are routinely disadvantaged once they are placed into the custody of the correctional service.'

. . .

Sapers pointed to statistics that show the total number of people

incarcerated in federal institutions went down by 12 per cent between 1996 and 2004. But the number of native inmates increased 21 per cent in the same period.

The figures were even more dramatic for native women, whose numbers rose by a startling 74 per cent.

Just as troubling, said Sapers, is the fact that four in 10 natives behind bars are aged 25 or under, reflecting the frequency with which young aboriginals run afoul of the law.

Source: Jim Brown, Canadian Press, **http://www.cbc.ca/cp/national/061016/n1016104.html**.

could be accounted for by arguably relevant differences in the situations of male and female offenders, such as childcare responsibilities.

A closer look 17.4

Sex, murder and sentencing

Joseph McGrail killed his drunken, abusive common-law wife by repeatedly kicking her in the stomach as she lay in an alcoholic stupor. He had finally snapped after 10 years of torment during which Marion Kennedy went on massive drinking binges and became addicted to sleeping pills 'to enhance the mental effects of the alcohol'. She had repeatedly sworn at him and forced him to feed her vodka habit during the years they lived together in Kinstanding, Birmingham.

. . .

McGrail was found guilty of manslaughter and walked free from Birmingham Crown Court with a two-year suspended prison sentence. The judge, Mr Justice Popplewell, said the woman he had killed 'would have tried the patience of a saint'.

Two days earlier, Sara Thornton's appeal to have her murder conviction for killing her husband Malcolm changed to manslaughter was heard. She had stabbed him in the stomach as he lay, like Marion Kenndy, in alcoholic stupor . . . Mrs Thornton had been repeatedly battered by her husband during their 10-month marriage. He had once knocked her unconscious and threatened to kill both her and her 12-year-old daughter. On other occasions, he had punched her on the eye and on the back of the head, broken a glass over her hand, threatened to throw her through a plate-glass window and smashed furniture when he was drunk. The court was heard that only two days before she stabbed him Mrs Thrornton told a friend: 'I'm going to kill him'.

Her appeal was rejected and she returned to Bullwood Hall prison in Essex to continue her life sentence for murder.

Source: Lloyd (1995: 72–3).

Stop and think 17.5

Do you think women and men are treated differently by the CJS? If so, how? If not, why not?

Imprisonment

For many men and women in prison, the feeling of stigmatisation and of being part of an underclass, with all its connotations of sub-humanness and subterranean invisibility, is the foremost aspect of their identity, and similarly 'washes away' all other facets of their personalities and histories. However, there are gender differences within the prison walls. As Joe Sim argued in 1994, despite focusing on men as the 'primary subject matter' (Sim, 1994: 100) many earlier prison studies failed to consider gendered aspects of male prisoners' experience: prisoners like criminals were sexless. Research focusing on masculinity and imprisonment suggests that for men prison life is characterised by fear, violence and represents a celebration of masculinity.

According to Erving Goffman (cited in Hester and Eglin, 1992) the initial experience of incarceration is often an emasculating one for men who are no longer able to fulfil their traditional masculine roles within their families. Perhaps as such then, one survival mechanism is to become hyper masculine. This may be manifest in physical demeanour or by demanding authority and control over other prisoners. This masculinity includes the exaggeration of heterosexuality, the expressing of homophobia, bragging about love letters from loyal women, outright sexism through to the rape of other men deemed to be less masculine both to feminise them and reinforce dominance of the rapist.

Incarceration is associated within some subcultures with masculinity, as almost a badge of honour or the entry into manhood. As Stanley 'Tookie' Williams (convicted of, and executed, for) murder describes below, prison was presented to him as a place to be a man.

I was eleven years old when Rock was released from the penitentiary where he had been imprisoned for murdering his father, who used to beat up his mother. I remember sitting wide-eyed on a porch with other kids my age, listening to Rock tell stories about the years he spent in different prisons, like Soledad, Folsom, and San Quentin . . . He said prisons were places where a man could prove his toughness to other men who were equally tough . . . Rock was a good storyteller. Now I see that he was good. His stories made prison sound like a fun place to hang out with your homeboys. Rock had most of us wanting to go to prison when we were old enough.

(Williams, 2001: 13–14)

One means of displaying masculinity within prisons is in the development of physical prowess through body building (see A Closer Look 17.5).

A closer look 17.5

Doing time, doing masculinity, doing sport

In the quotes below Don Sabo (2005, originally 2001) describes the role sport plays in constructing and preserving masculinity within prisons.

. . . many men in prison deploy sports and fitness activities as resources to do masculinity – that is, to spin masculine identities, to build reputations, to achieve or dissolve status. For the men in prison, as elsewhere, masculine identity is earned, enacted, rehearsed, refined, and relived through each day's activities and choices.

(Sabo, 2005: 110)

. . . the most striking aspect of prison sports is their visibility. The yard is often a hub of athletic activity. Weight lifters huddle in small groups around barbells and bench press racks. Runners circle the periphery, while hoopsters spin and shoot on the basketball courts . . . Depending on the facility and time of year, there may be football practices or games, replete with equipment and fans along the sidelines. Some prisons maintain softball leagues and facilities.

(Sabo, 2005: 109)

There is no doubt that prison, with its all male inhabitants and a guard regime which follows a military hierarchical form, exudes masculinity. As Don Sabo (2005), a teacher in prisons in the USA notes, this masculinity influences even workers in the prison system:

The prison environment triggers a masculine awareness in me . . . The masculinity that surfaces in the prison is more an attitude, a hazy cluster of concerns and expectations that get translated into emotion and physical movement in ways that never

quite become clear. Though there are a few women around (for example, an occasional female guard, some women teachers), I see and smell the prison as an all-male domain . . . I have been told not to trust anybody – prisoners, guard or bureaucrats. Nobody. It sounds crazy, but the tinges of distrust and paranoia almost feel good. Indeed, there are parts of me . . . that embrace the distrust and welcome the presumed danger and potential for danger.

(Sabo, 2005: 109–10)

This distrust and presumed danger can also be experienced as fear. Fear within prisons is justifiable, after all some of the inmates are serving sentences for violent crimes. The culture of masculinity in prison equates personal power with physical domination. Of course, this also reflects the outside world but inside the dominance can be total as there is nowhere to hide from the bullying of other prisoners. Prisoners' violence is often part of the symbol, ritual and reality of a hostile, male environment. It would appear then that the culture of prisons encourages a particular form of hegemonic masculinity [**Hotlink → Gendered Perspectives – Theoretical Issues (Chapter 1)**], one which values physical strength and violence yet, of course, such hegemonic masculinities also exist within other institutions.

Just as male prisons emphasise masculinity, female prisons emphasise femininity. For women the so-called 'chivalry factor' assumes that women who are sentenced to a custodial sentence are 'failed' women and so need to be 'retrained' into femininity and 'women's work'. So the work that women do in prison is still dominated by domestic-type tasks such as cleaning, sewing and cooking and these feature significantly in the training provided for female prisoners, along with training for traditionally female jobs [**Hotlink → Work and Leisure (Chapter 14)**] such as typing, catering and hairdressing (Lloyd, 1995; Cavadino and Dignan, 2002). In addition, the 'mad not bad' stereotype of female offenders has had a particular influence on prison regimes for women in that female prisoners are more likely to be prescribed psychotrophic medications than male prisoners, though, of course, this could also be the result of the stresses women prisoners face (Cavadino and Dignan, 2002).

Cavadino and Dignan (2002) note that on the one hand it appears that women in prison are treated better as women's prisons are, on the whole, less unpleasant places than those for males. As imprisoned women are disproportionately (in comparison with the general population) more likely to have experienced interpersonal violence, ironically prison may be a safer place than their previous home environments (Lloyd, 1995; Bradley and Davino, 2002).

As women are a relatively small proportion of the prison population it has been argued that they are often 'easily forgotten in a criminal justice system which is run, very largely by men, to deal with male offenders' (NACRO, 1991: 3). Cavadino and Dignan (2002) have pointed out that although, on the whole, it may appear that women in prison are treated better than men this is not necessarily the case. As women do make up such a small number of the overall population they are often incarcerated in prisons far from their homes and family support networks. The remote locations of such prisons often make visiting and, therefore, maintaining family ties, all the more difficult. Evidence of this is visible in both the UK and abroad. For example, in Scotland there is only one women's prison – Corton Vale – which although it is situated in central Scotland means that women from the north and south are imprisoned far outside of their own communities. Likewise in Canada, until 2000, all women convicted of a federal crime requiring a sentence of two years or more, were sent to the Prison 4 Women in Kingston, Ontario which for many women was thousands of miles away from home.

Recently women prisoners seem to have suffered at least as much as male inmates from the 'security first' regime despite the fact that they generally pose much less of a threat to security. One manifestation of this was a policy introduced in the UK in April 1995 stating that women prisoners, including those in advanced stages of pregnancy, should be handcuffed or chained when being treated in hospitals outside of the prison. See Figure 17.2.

There is evidence that both motherhood and fatherhood adds to the pain of incarceration as World in Focus 17.2 suggests.

It has been suggested (Heidensohn, 1985), that women find the experience of prison more traumatic

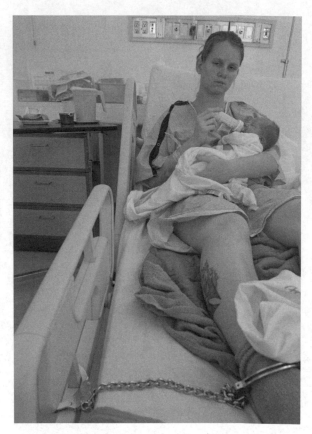

Figure 17.2 Birthing woman in chains
Source: Mark Allen Johnson/Relentlessphoto.com

than men resulting in a greater incidence of self harm within women's prisons from cutting to eating disorders. Yet it is important to recognise that men in prison feel distress too. A focus on aspects of their identity (such as fatherhood, see World in Focus 17.2) highlights the fact that imprisonment does not completely wash away all other aspects of a convict's identity. Similarly, Cohen and Taylor (2002) report on research undertaken in the 1940s in an American prison which describes the problems of outside relationships in terms of the amount of suffering that the presence of such relationships produces. The researchers found that those who had few contacts with the outside through letters and visits did not suffer much, those who had medium contact suffered a great deal, while those who had high contact were again found to be low in suffering. In order to reduce their suffering there was evidence of prisoners who cut off all contact in order to reduce suffering. One said: 'I

World in focus 17.2

Mothers, fathers and imprisonment

Mothers in prison in the UK

In the UK approximately half the women in prison are mothers and there is evidence to suggest that their family responsibilities continue:

> There's a lot of women still running the home from inside prison. All men care about is their baccy, their meals and whether they're top dog in the prison. But the women are still running the home and I've seen women in here (an open prison) write shopping lists every week to give their fellas when they come so they get the right food and things for the kids.
> (Senior Officer, quoted in Devlin, 1998: 54)

On the other hand of course imprisonment conflicts with and threatens the ideals of motherhood and some women in prison voluntarily stop seeing their children telling them they are in hospital or on holiday and others lose contact with their children. The threat of 'no visits' is also used to keep order in women's prisons.

(Adapted from Jewkes and Letherby, 2002b)

Fathers in prison in the US (and elsewhere)

Charles S. Lanier (2003), who himself was once an imprisoned father, points out that there are more men in prison than women and there are many more fathers than mothers yet there has been little research on fatherhood and imprisonment. Reflecting on one of the expected roles of fathers he argues that fathers on the 'inside' feel particularly distressed because they cannot provide for their children economically.

Source: Adapted from Lanier (2003).

do hard time. It's much easier if you get the outside off your mind and forget about your family, your folks and your wife' (Cohen and Taylor, 2002: 342).

One small group of prisoners who face great distress are those whose gender identity does not match their sex. For such transgendered prisoners the experience of being imprisoned in institutions which are incongruent with their sense of gender is both humili-ating and physically dangerous. As Richard Edney (2004) shows the experience of a transgendered person in prison is frequently a terrifying one as she or he is extremely vulnerable to sexual violence from other prisoners. Added to this is that they may not receive adequate medical care. As such, they are exposed to risks not faced by other prisoners (see World in Focus 17.3).

World in focus 17.3

Transgendered persons and prisons

In both Canada and Australia the prison experience of transgendered persons is beginning to be addressed.

CSC loses appeal in transsexual human rights case

> Canada's federal prisons will be forced to allow sex-change surgery for transsexual inmates as a result of a court ruling that concluded a blanket ban is discriminatory.

. . .

> Corrections Canada will revise its policy because of the decision, spokeswoman Michele Pilon-Santilli said. But she warned that sex-change operations will not be available for all transsexual inmates. The decision upholds a 2001 decision from the Canadian Human Rights Tribunal in the case of Synthia Kavanagh. The tribunal said that it was discriminatory for prisons to have a blanket ban on sex-change

operations but not on 'non-essential' services such as the removal of tattoos.

> The Corrections and Conditional Release Act requires prisons to provide essential health care to inmates. Kavanagh, a 41-year-old transsexual, alleged discrimination based on sex and disability after prison officials refused to allow her to undergo a sex-change operation that had been pre-approved before she was imprisoned. Kavanagh began

World in focus continued

hormone therapy and lived as a woman as a teenager. When she was convicted, she had been conditionally approved for sex reassignment surgery. She ended up paying the $14,000 for her operation because of the prison's ban. After spending more than a decade in various men's prisons, she was transferred more than two years ago to Joliette Institution, a medium-security women's prison north of Montreal.

The ruling is expected to affect less than a dozen transsexuals in Canadian prisons. In 2000, the most recent year for which statistics are available, 10 of the 2,500 inmates in federal penitentiaries were 'pre-operative' transsexuals, but not all of them wanted surgery. Sex-change surgery is considered an essential service that is covered by medicare in most provinces when a patient has been diagnosed with gender dysphoria, the medical term for people who believe they are the wrong sex. It should be no different in Canadian prisons, said Justice Layden-Stevenson.

Source: National Post, Janice Tibbetts, 7 February 2003, **www.nationalpost.com**

Stop and think 17.6

1. Is imprisonment a less appropriate punishment for women than men? Why?

2. Comment on what do you think of the irony that the home is less safe for some women than the prison, whereas it seems that men need the love of a 'good woman' to stay away from a life of crime?

3. In what ways does prison life exaggerate 'normal' hegemonic masculinity and emphasised femininity?

4. How do women and men resist emphasised/hegemonic gender roles in prison?

5. What particular dangers may be faced by transgendered prisoners?

Men and women as workers in the CJS

One contributing factor to gender bias in the CJS is the lack of women as workers – as police officers, prison officers, judges, lawyers and so on. Occupations that remain male dominated are more likely to reflect masculine values. Taking policing as an example Robert Reiner (2002) argues that police work is characterised by old-fashioned machismo. Sexism in police culture, he adds, is reinforced by discrimination in recruitment and promotion. In the 1970s women police officers took on full policing duties in both the UK and the US. In 1989, the UK Home Office issued a Circular about equal opportunities in the police service which set out objectives and guidelines for implementation. By March 1992 all forces in England had written equal opportunity policies. Despite this, research continues to suggest that women officers feel discriminated and discouraged and that a major problem for them is sexual harassment from male colleagues (Heidensohn, 1994, 2002; Reiner, 2002). In addition, it appears that for male police officers sexual opportunity is part of the job. As Reiner points out:

> Routinized 'sexual boasting and horseplay' [is] often at the expense of women colleagues (Policy Studies Insitute 1983, iv: 91–7). Policemen are not notorious for their aversion to illicit heterosexual activities. There's always a bit of spare around the corner because of the glamour of the job.
>
> (Reiner, 2002: 282)

Andrew Billen's (1992) newspaper article on the British judiciary highlights the fact that the judiciary is drawn from a narrow band of society. Not only are judges more likely to be male but they have mostly attended fee-paying schools and have Oxbridge backgrounds. As Billen (1992) cites, only one of the 1989–91 intake was a woman and, not surprisingly given the stereotype that women are more interested in family affairs than men, she was appointed to the High Court Family Division in 1990. Clearly then the judiciary is not representative of society in general which can have negative consequences for many of the people – who are not male, white and upper-class – who come before them. From Billen's (1992: 316) article it certainly appears that judges are 'out of touch with ordinary people and ordinary life'.

Men and women as victims of crime

As Abbott and colleagues (2005: 288) note women are likely to be victims of all forms of crime, but they are especially vulnerable to violent attacks by men, both sexual and physical. In addition, it is not just that women are the victims of crime but that fear of crime is a powerful control over women's lives. Worldwide, it is estimated that 130 million women and girls have undergone clitoridectomy (a form of female circumcision), a trade estimated to be worth $76 million annually. Between 700,000 and 4 million women are trafficked for commercial sex work and in the Rwandan genocide of 1994, women and children were raped, often by men who knew they were HIV positive. In India and China sex selection and the killing of baby girls occurs because of preference for boy children and in India women are killed by their husbands because their families of origin are unable to meet demands for dowries. In 48 surveys from around the world between 10 and 69 per cent of women reported being physically assaulted by male partners at some point in their lives (**www.who.org**) (Therborn 2004, Abbott *et al.*, 2005)

Tim Newburn and Elizabeth A. Stanko (2002[1994]: 257) point out that there have been relatively few studies of male victims of crime. The bulk of early victimology literature focused on victims as a group largely undifferentiated by gender and, more recently, attention has been directed at uncovering and detailing the impact of violence by men against women. Thus, little is known about men's experience of victimisation. Until recently it has been assumed that men would be unwilling to disclose their experience of crime which has perpetuated and justified the lack of attention to men as victims.

We do know though that although men are less likely to be victimised in the home when they are they are likely to meet with disbelief and disregard. Outside of the home especially where 'public' violence is concerned, men – particularly young men – are most likely to seek police or medical assistance for personal crime, and report such incidents to crime researchers.

Conclusion

It would appear then that the study of crime and deviance, housed within the interdisciplinary field of Criminology, is both peopled and dominated by men. Feminist theory has begun to dismantle the established and pervasive dichotomy of the daring and devilish male offender and the unappealing, inert and passive female offender. However, despite the fact that both the criminal and criminal activity are gendered, criminology has not yet truly become so.

Further reading

Rudy Wiebe and Yvonne Johnson (1998), *A Stolen Life: The Journey of a Cree Woman*, Canada, Vintage. This tells the tragic life story of Yvonne Johnson, a woman of Cree/White parentage. Yvonne suffered repeated physical and sexual abuse and was imprisoned for life for the murder of a man she and her friends suspected was a child abuser. This true story details the experiences of a native woman within the Canadian penal system.

Jake Blight (2000), 'Transgender Inmates', *trends and issues*, Australian Institute of Criminology, no. 168 at **http://www.aic.gov.au**. In this article Blight argues that people who transgress the traditional boundaries of sex and gender present a challenge for correctional systems. Blight argues that the small number of these inmates require particular policies to avoid self harm.

Yvonne Jewkes and Gayle Letherby (eds) (2002b), *Criminology: A Reader*, London, Sage. This edited collection covers a wide range of issues and topics, including men as victims, histories of the study of crime, crime mythologies, the CJS and crime and social stratification.

trends and issues, Australian Institute of Criminology, at **http://www.aic.gov.au**. This refereed journal, available online, is an excellent source of concise and informative articles relating to crime, deviance and criminology both in Australia and elsewhere.

Journal of Research in Crime and Delinquency – this journal explores the social, political and economic contexts of criminal justice and examine victims, criminals, courts and sanctions. It also covers theory, new research and statistical analyses.

Websites

In addition to those listed in end of chapter activity also see:

The Pelican Bay Prison Project – **http://www.pelicanbayprisonproject.org/history.htm**. This is a site written by prisoners in the supermax prison of Pelican Bay (California Department of Corrections). In particular read the writings of Donny Johnson, a lifer serving his sentence in solitary confinement.

End of chapter activity

Visit the following websites:

➤ Canadian Association of Elizabeth Fry Societies – **http://www.elizabethfry.ca**

➤ Women in Prison UK – **http://womeninprison.org.uk**

➤ Nacro – **http://www.nacro.org.uk**

Read about their work, their mission and their aims. Draw comparisons among them regarding their campaigns, their interests, their methods etc.

Culture and mass media

Key issues in this chapter:

➤ Culture as an important agent of gender socialisation and the mass media's role in the representation of culture
➤ The relationship between the mass media, gender stereotypes and gendered expectations.
➤ Beautiful bodies as defined and supported by media representation.
➤ Challenges to the view of the mass media as all pervasive and powerful in determining and perpetuating gender images and expectations.

At the end of this chapter you should be able to:

➤ Reflect on the relationship between culture, the mass media and gender socialisation.
➤ Explain the use and significance of stereotypes in the mass media.
➤ Detail the relationship between so-called ideal bodies and mass media representation.
➤ Outline challenges to the power of the mass media as determining and perpetuating gender images and expectations.

Perfectly pampered

Everyone loves a top-to-toe pampering session whether it's a facial, manicure or pedicure . . . Re-creating your own private health spa couldn't be easier. Argos has an extensive range of electric beauty products, which are perfect for an indulgent pampering session. Plus they'll make fantastic Christmas presents for your mum, sister or friends – or anyone in need of a mini spa of their own!

(Closer Promotion, *Closer*, October 2006: 62)

Stop and think 18.1

What does this advertisement tell us about the relationship between gender differences and expectations and the mass media?

Find some more examples of adverts aimed specifically at men and specifically at women. How easy would it be for the promoters to leave out the specific references to gender in the adverts?

Introduction

In the eighteenth century the term culture came to be used to refer to 'a way of life' – the values, attitudes, needs and expectations that bind people together regionally, nationally, internationally. By the beginning of the twentieth century, culture began to be used to describe the cultural forms used to express such characteristics – in language, printed texts, music and visual images. In contemporary society these cultural forms are primarily mass-produced by the culture industries for large, wide, undifferentiated audiences and so are best described as 'mass culture'. The control of the production and presentation of this mass culture by global corporations has left less room for cultural forms that make less money, yet 'folk' and/or 'art culture' does exist as an alternative to mass produced culture (Macionis and Plummer, 2002: 109). For Val Williams (1991: 18) culture is 'the signifying system through which . . . a social order is communicated, reproduced, experienced and explored'. This suggests that culture is important in shaping gender relations and reproducing gender inequalities and the

mass media is an important agent of gender socialisation throughout our lives (Woodward, 2003). For some the media dictates gender identity and reflects patriarchal power. For example:

From primary school reading schemes to Hollywood films, from advertising to opera, from game shows to art galleries, women are depicted in ways that define what it means to be a woman . . . what women are like (naturally), what they ought to be like, what they are capable of, and incapable of, what roles they play in society, and how they differ from men.

(Marchment, 1993: 124)

We are immersed from cradle to grave in a media and consumer society . . . The media are forms of pedagogy that teach us how to be men and women; how to dress, look and consume; how to react to members of different social groups; how to be popular and successful and avoid failure; and how to conform to the dominant system of norms, values, practices and institutions.

(Kellner, 1995: 5)

For others this approach is both overly deterministic and overly simplistic in that it:

➤ reduces all power relations to gender which neglects and denies other aspects of power such as class, dis/ability, race and ethnicity and sexuality;

➤ denies the pleasures that women (and men) derive from the media as active readers and consumers; and also denies the fact that the media offers us a variety of images and provides us with contradictory images in that it provides challenges to patriarchy as well as supporting it (Stacey 1994).

In this chapter we consider whether the mass culture is all pervasive and powerful in determining and perpetuating gendered images and gendered expectations. The rest of the chapter is divided into three main sections. In 'The mass media and gendered stereotypes' we reflect on the relationship between gendered stereotypes and mass media representation which we follow by specific reference to the mass media as a key agent in determining and perpetuating ideal bodily images in 'Media, culture and the gendered body beautiful'. In 'Ambivalent messages' we provide some challenges to more deterministic views of the mass medias' influence.

The mass media and gendered stereotypes

Coping with stereotypical gender images

Writers suggest that within the mass media stereotypes about gender, gendered ideologies and gender inequalities are reinforced. Stereotypes are useful because they are simple, easy to recognise and imply an assumed consensus of opinion. Their strength lies in the fact that they are actually a combination of validity and distortion, and can thus be a powerful means of socialisation (Condy and Condy, 1976). As Anne Cranny-Francis and colleagues (2003) note, when applied to the person stereotypes are frequently done so on the basis of appearance, thus stereotypes reduce groups of people to a few characteristics by which they can be easily identified. This is clearly demonstrated by the example in A Closer Look 18.1.

A closer look 18.1

Ladies and gents

The reasons the icons on the front of toilet doors (a woman in a skirt and a man in trousers) work is because they assume a visible and identifiable difference between men and women. The skirt is standing in for the breasts and female sex organs and the trousers for a penis and testes, usually invoked as the obvious indicators of difference between men and women. These visual differences are then yoked to a few simple easily identifiable characteristics (Cranny-Francis, 2003).

Stop and think 18.2

Can you think of any other examples of the use of visual gender stereotypes in everyday life?

With specific reference to women many writers suggest that women are represented in a restrictive and stereotypical range of ways, as sex objects or in a peripheral or supporting way. Thus, women are represented in ways that suit men's interest and pleasures. Feminists are concerned that the cultural representations of women as weaker and less capable than men not only create barriers for women in many spheres of society but also justify and contribute to inequality. Vicki Coppock and colleagues (1995: 111) argue that 'knowledge about women' portrayed in the media is always produced from something believed to be 'already known', acting as its seal of approval, endowing it with truth. When media messages coincide with and reinforce existing ideas and values widely held in society, the effect is cumulative and powerful. Thus, 'images of glamorous women or perfect mothers may not correspond to the experience of most women, but they do define femininity in ways which are perceived as actually existing' (Betterton, 1987: 22).

Similarly, Robert Connell (1987) argues that the mass media help maintain a large measure of consent for the current power relationships by their positive portrayal of emphasised femininity. As Perkins (1979: 147) notes:

> most stereotypes define women in terms of their relationship to men. They are ideological in that in general, what is good for men (for maintaining a system of gender inequality) is presented as laudatory and what is inconvenient or conflict producing is presented as objectionable.

Although there are many negative stereotypes about women (because as a subordinate group they are a problem, i.e. a possible threat) there are also some positive ones. Connell (1987) identifies two important ones: the 'sexually receptive' young woman and the older 'good mother'. They both fit the compliance option for they both involve availability of services to men (Itzin, 1986). Itzin adds that not only do these stereotypes help maintain the system of patriarchy, but they also serve the interests of capitalism. Detailed content analysis of the media reveals the dominance and usefulness (to patriarchy and capitalism) of these two stereotypes and some of the conflicts.

Coppock *et al.* (1995: 110) argue that the media denies women strong, powerful, independent images.

Adding that any 'aspect of womanhood which does not correspond to the traditional, male-defined image is ignored and marginalised'. Thus, as Janice Winship (1983) suggests, much media output helps to create a 'culture of femininity'. It shows women (and men) the 'ideal' and implies that every woman can and should be like this.

The presentation of these images has very real consequences. They are a distortion of reality for many women who find themselves isolated at home and dependent on men. Feminists such as Angela McRobbie (1982), Winship (1983) and Marjorie Ferguson (1985) argue that girls' and women's magazines in particular define and shape women's lives and expectations at every stage of their lives from childhood onwards. Winship (1983) suggests that women's magazines locate and exploit the fragmented position of women in the family and at work, both of which are required for the maintenance of capitalism. She adds that the emphasis of women's role in the family helps keep women out of the running for economic and political power. Thus, in defining appropriate sexuality and ascribing certain roles to them on the basis of sexuality, media images can help control the behaviour of women.

Marjorie Ferguson (1985) argues that magazines perpetuate the 'cult of femininity'; describing them as the high priestesses of this cult. The 'cult of femininity' defines what it is to be a good and a real woman and the magazines lay out rituals, rites, sacrifices and obligations – in relation to beautification, interpersonal relationships and housework – which women must maintain. Ferguson examined women's magazines from the 1940s to the 1980s and claimed that although the rituals change slightly, the cult of femininity remains fundamentally unchanged. She suggests that until the late 1970s the dominant themes were 'getting and keeping your man', 'the happy family', 'self-help', 'be more beautiful' and the 'working wife is a bad wife'. At this time 'ideal' femininity and womanhood was represented as the self-reliant, resourceful, domesticated wife and mother who kept herself looking good for her man. In the late 1970s and 1980s many of these themes endured but at this time the image of 'new woman' also began to emerge. Here, the focus is on the working wife as a good wife. Thus, economic activity was now com-

patible with femininity. As Ferguson (1985) notes even though it appears that the range of messages and the roles and expectations widened beyond the earlier emphasis on romance and marriage it was still necessary to get a man and be successful at marriage and motherhood in order to fulfil feminine expectations. In the late 1970s and 1980s then women's magazines contained two conflicting messages: be proud of who you are but at the same time ensure you are a good wife and mother. These conflicting messages, Ferguson (1985) argues, are the product of socio-economic changes, such as women's increasing role in the labour market and changing attitudes to sex and marriage. Women's magazines do not just reinforce and teach women traditional and emergent beliefs about the place of women in society; the covert message of the cult is that there is a feminine way of being that all women share and that women are fundamentally different from men (Ferguson, 1985; see also Marsh, 2006). Kath Woodward's (2003) focus is on motherhood in the media and she argues that a new figure of motherhood emerged in the 1990s and that this 'independent' mother was an amalgam of previous figures of caring and working mothers. In addition 'independent' motherhood adds sexuality to motherhood. See A Closer Look 18.2, which shows how women as mothers are defined as good or bad in the media.

A closer look 18.2

Mothers: the good and the bad

As Kath Woodward (2003) notes, media reports often focus on mothers as good or bad, with examples of bad mothers including those who abandon their children, leaving them at home while they go on holiday, or who selfishly put the interest of their own careers before the care of their children. Woodward adds that fathers are rarely subjected to the same kind of scrutiny or classification as 'bad' parents in similar cases.

As Woodward continues:

A variety of supermodels such as Kate Moss, pop singers such as Victoria Beckham (Posh Spice) and Jordan, actors, the merely famous, and several women whose pregnancies and births (predominantly by Caesarean section) are of interest because they are rich and occupy public media space are included . . . Magazines often run mother and daughter fashion features at Christmas time . . . The upmarket fashion magazines also feature famous women such as Jerry Hall who clearly demonstrate that it is possible to retain the body of a supermodel after having four (glamorous, attractive) children . . . What is new is that the women are not otherwise very different from their non-pregnant or non-maternal selves in what they wear and in looking sexually attractive. Successful motherhood is encoded as 'well-off' and sexually attractive.

(Woodward, 2003: 23–30)

Due to the particular presentation of images by the media, women may also feel guilt and anxiety. For example, as Winship (1983) argues the non-political nature of women's magazines encourages personal solutions to women's problems rather than collective and/or state supported ones. Women are therefore likely to feel personally inadequate when things go wrong in their lives. This is particularly ironic as magazines ostensibly offer friendship and support. Although the media presentation implies that emphasised femininity comes naturally to all women, at the same time it implies that they need help, for example, buy this product and you will become a more attractive woman or a better mother.

It is clear then that the 'positive' stereotypical images of women presented to us by the media have serious consequences for women. These consequences are likely to continue as the media is able to adapt to changes in society. Ann Kaplan's (1992) work on the representation of motherhood in popular culture and melodrama supports this and she argues that the late twentieth-century reification of motherhood as a source of self-fulfilment rather than as duty is something new.

Since the 1980s the construction of masculinity in the media has received attention. Although men may have a greater presence in the media, some theorists have been critical of the narrow definition of masculinity in popular cultural forms. As well as being produced through social practices and relations, masculinity 'is produced through cultural and ideological struggles over meaning' (Jackson, 1990: 223).

Just as the media is argued to help construct femininity it is also thought to construct masculinity. For example Anthony Easthope (1986) argues that 'the masculine myth' saturates media and popular culture in that the overwhelming image presented is of a masculine identity based on strength, competitiveness, aggression and violence. He argues that men internalise these features and a key source of the conscious and unconscious process of learning masculinity is in popular culture. Within films, advertising, comics and popular music lyrics, men are presented as masterful, in control of both nature and women, physically strong and heterosexual. The action heroes of the late twentieth-century and early twenty-first century seem to live out this myth.

Gender analyses of men's magazines, apart from pornography, are less developed than women's magazines; indeed it was only in the late 1980s that a modern group of general interest, glossy 'men's magazines' emerged containing articles on health, sport, fashion and personal care, relationships with women and children, sex and employment (Collier, 1992). This leads John Beynon (2004) to suggest that this new breed of men's magazines objectifies the male body in the same way that women's magazines objectify the female body. Certainly these publications presented men with contradictory images; sometimes focusing on stereotypical masculine characteristics and sometimes presenting a more challenging, progressive masculinity as something to aspire to. But whereas the men's magazines of the 1980s did at some level attempt to challenge traditional male (and female) images and expectations those launched in the 1990s reintroduced a strong heterosexual script which includes soft-porn shots of women and focus on the 'new lad' rather than the 'new man' through articles on partying, sport and heroes to aspire to. As Beynon (2004: 211) notes the message of these publications is that 'Real men get "loaded", "shag" women and watch football'.

So, it would seem that old-established images are hard to challenge. This is further reflected in the fact that publications intended to focus on work rather than leisure and to be of relevance to women as well as men still sometimes rely on images and text that objectify women for men's pleasure and present women as lesser than men. A Closer Look 18.3 focuses on one such example.

A closer look 18.3

Rail(men's) news

From its inception in 1969 until the middle of the 1980s, *Railnews* portrayed railwaywomen in a manner that undermined their struggle for equality and respect and encouraged their male colleagues to regard them in ways that were detrimental to women's career prospects.

All adult female staff were called 'girls', even those with 30 years' service or more. For example, under the title 'Girl in the Box' readers were invited to 'Meet one of the prettiest outdoor-job railgirls on BR', a crossing keeper who was married with two children. No man of any age would have been called a 'railboy'. Worse than this was the seemingly never-ending array of gratuitous 'glamour' photographs included in every issue. Women (often semi-naked) were photographed alongside fully-dressed railwaymen as though such juxtaposition required no explanation. In some cases the women were railway workers. One front page carried a photograph of a Rail-Air Hostess meeting some primary-school children from a train. *Railnews* did not explain why the children were wearing cardigans and sweaters while the hostess wore a bikini . . .

. . . *Railnews* featured female staff for no other reason than as decorative or sexual objects. It even set them up in competition with each other to be voted the prettiest, in a 'Dolly of the Month' contest. There was even one for the 'Dolliest Dolly'. Despite the abundance of voyeuristic imagery, when one railwayman was asked in 1972 for his opinion of *Railnews*, he replied that he wanted 'more girlie pictures'. The paper did not dispute his terminology, and subsequent editions show that his wish was granted.

Railnews trivialised many of the pioneers who entered traditionally-male railway occupations. The first woman chief steward was described as 'providing a spot of glamour' . . . the first woman appointed to BR Regional Board . . . was described as 'adding a touch of femininity'. The first woman physician to be appointed chief of a Railway Medical Centre was described as 'incredibly attractive, with the sort of figure that would add glamour to a pair of baggy dungarees'. The angle of the accompanying photograph leads the reader to peer up her skirt (Wojtczak, 2005: 271–2).

Stop and think 18.3

Compare a 'women's' magazine, a magazine aimed at men and a 'gender-neutral' publication. What similar and different gender stereotypes are presented in each publication?

Stereotypes and advertising

Globalisation has affected the process and production of advertisements. The advertisements in foreign countries are often created by the branch offices of American agencies and western styles are more often than not used when creating ad campaigns. It is not surprising then that some of the main criticisms of women's image in advertising in developing countries are similar to those of the developed world:

1. that women are depicted as less intelligent and competent than men;

2. women are shown as being servants to men;

3. women are shown as objects of sexual pleasure (Consumer Association of Penang, 1990).

Thus, worldwide stereotypical images of women are used to sell products to women and to men.

However, the advertising industry also uses images of 'ideal' masculinity to sell goods and services to men. As Jackson Katz (1995: 135) argues:

Advertising, in a commodity-driven consumer culture, is an omnipresent and rich source of gender ideology. Contemporary ads are filled with images of 'dangerous'-looking men. Men's magazines and mainstream newsweeklies are rife with ads featuring violent male icons, such as uniformed football players, big-fisted boxers and leather-clad bikers. Sports magazines aimed at men, and televised sporting events, carry millions of dollars worth of military ads. In the past decade, there have been hundreds of ads for products designed to help men develop muscular physiques, such as weight training machines and nutritional supplements.

Figure 18.1 Lynx TV advert
Source: © Advertising Archives

World in Focus 18.1 highlights both how adverts rely on stereotypes and in turn powerfully reinforce them.

Clearly adverts aimed solely at women and girls reinforce masculine as well as feminine stereotypes and vice versa. As Lance Strate (2004[1992]) notes, beer commercials present traditional, stereotypical images of men, and thus uphold the myths of masculinity and femininity and in promoting beer, advertisers also promote and perpetuate these images and myths. Strate (2004[1992]) adds that although aimed at an adult audience, beer commercials are highly accessible to children with American children possibly seeing as many as

100,000 of these ads between the ages of 2 to 18. The humour and excitement of these adverts is appealing to children and likely supports their already stereotypical views of gender and adulthood.

Challenging stereotypical gender images

Ellen Seiter (1986) suggests that because real people can identify with the reality within stereotypes, the image becomes very powerful. Everyone is likely to reject simple negative stereotypes such as 'the dumb blonde', but complex stereotypes which contain elements of reality are much more persuasive. However, a strength of stereotypes is that they can be changed or adapted, and that one of the ways in which the media operates to support the ruling ideology is by redefinition. A Critical Look 18.1 highlights the changing stereotypes associated with good (and bad) mothering and fathering.

However, in discussing media images of women and their consequences for women, it is important, as Susan Condor (1986: 112) notes, not to end up giving a derogatory image of women as 'passive victims of social forces'. She argues that women may possess a 'double consciousness': 'sharing a distinctive world view whilst simultaneously recognising the world as presented to them by the dominant male culture'

World in focus 18.1

Men and beer

Jacks, rock stars, and pick-up artists; cowboys, construction workers, and comedians; these are some of the major 'social types' found in contemporary American beer commercials. The characters may vary in occupation, race, and age, but they all exemplify traditional conceptions of the masculine role. Clearly, the beer industry relies on stereotypes of the man's

man to appeal to a mainstream, predominantly male target audience. That is why alternative social types, such as sensitive men, gay men, and househusbands, scholars, poets, and political activists, are noticeably absent from beer advertising . . . collectively the commercials provide a clear and consistent image of the masculine role; in a sense, they constitute a guide for becoming a man, a rulebook for appropriate

male behaviour, in short, a manual on masculinity. Of course, they are not the only source of knowledge on this subject, but nowhere is so much information presented in so concentrated a form as in television's 30-second spots, and no other industry's commercials focus so exclusively and so exhaustively on images of the man's man.

(Strate, 2004[1992]: 533)

A critical look 18.1

Positive images of mums and dads

Increasingly there are examples of lone mothers who have made the decision to have a baby without the support of a man . . . however these women are united by affluence and success and this affords them a large amount of control in the construction of their own maternal identities yet there is a fine line between the image of the successful independent mother and the selfish mother who puts her child before her career.

(adapted from Woodward 2003)

'Why every man should have one' (*Sunday Times*, 28 May 2000), pictures the footballers David Beckham and Dennis Wise holding their babies like trophies alongside a strikingly intimate photograph of the British prime minister, Tony Blair, lying beside his newborn son. Such open displays of paternal affection are now commonplace, with newspapers and magazines presenting a myriad of visual and textual images of pop stars, actors, sportsmen and politicians proudly parading their offspring and making enthusiastic pronouncements on the virtues of fatherhood.

(Freeman, 2003: 44)

(Condor, 1986: 110). Similarly, Easthope suggests that men do not swallow the ideal masculine image whole-sale, but, he argues, it is difficult for them to escape some influence on their gender identity:

> Clearly men do not passively live out the masculine myth imposed by the stories and images of the dominant culture. But neither can they live completely outside the myth since it pervades the culture. Its coercive power is everywhere – not just on screens, hoardings and paper but inside our own heads.
>
> (Easthope, 1986: 167)

It has also been acknowledged that people will read and make sense of media texts in varying ways. Writers suggest that the media are not simply vehicles for patriarchal ideologies but that there is space for women and men to express their viewpoints and experiences and hence resist restrictive stereotypes and present alternative images (e.g. Gamman and Marshment, 1988;

Ussher, 1997). We return to this argument in 'Ambivalent messages'.

Media, culture and the gendered body beautiful

As may be already evident, a recurring theme in the work on the representation of women in the media is that women's bodies are represented in a particularly limited way. With reference to the body in films, television programmes and magazines, women's bodies are presented as 'glamorous', 'beautiful', 'sexy' and often as 'thin'. Until recently social scientists paid little attention to the body; now though there is concern to explore how the body is taken up in culture and how culture constructs the body so it is understood as a biological given (Lupton, 2003; Fraser and Greco, 2005).

The feminine bodily ideal is presented to us in all aspects of the mass media and many feminists are concerned that this undermines women's autonomy and works against the development of unity between women encouraging as it does competition and hierarchy (Chapkis, 1986; Wolf, 1991; Ussher, 1997). The 'ideal' is impossible to achieve because the images and icons of the beauty industry are themselves fabricated and also because the ideal is constantly being redefined with a waif-like thin body being in fashion one year and a buxom look with big bottom the next. Beauty and fashion culture have been seen as closely intertwined with capitalist relations: 'Feminists in the second wave originally explained the fashion culture in terms of patriarchy in league with capitalism. Femininity in this analysis is false consciousness' (Gaines, 1990: 4).

The fashion, beauty, diet (and increasingly healthy eating) industries are big business within capitalism and also serve to reinforce differences between women and men and amongst women and undermine, control and restrict women. Naomi Wolf (1991) argues that the beauty myth has taken over other ideologies in undermining women's confidence. The beauty myth involves ideal standards of feminine beauty and body shape to which all women are expected to aspire. For Wendy Chapkis (1986), this ideal is white, youthful and able-bodied. Patricia Hill-

Collins (1990) points out that not only are eternally defined standards of beauty 'white', which can create anxieties for black women, who cannot live up to the white-skinned, blue-eyed, straight-haired ideal, but also this white ideal exists only in opposition to the black 'other'.

Wolf (1991) adds that the beauty myth is an insidious ideology which girls and women individually and collectively buy into. At work and at leisure women can never fully be themselves and focus their energies as they must always be concerned about how they present themselves, anxious about whether they match up to the 'beauty myth'. The pressures to aspire to the 'beauty myth' reduce women's confidence and sap their energies. So the diet industry and cosmetic surgery thrive on exploiting women's anxieties and insecurities. A Closer Look 18.4 gives an example of how lay and medical definitions of the ideal body is affected by culturally produced values.

As cosmetic surgery gradually becomes normalised, women who do not seek cosmetic surgery may be at risk of being labelled as abnormal, as deviant (Morgan, 1991).

In addition, cosmetic surgery is a gendered practice as surgeons are almost exclusively male and patients largely female (Davis, 2003). Although an increasing number of men are opting for cosmetic surgery (possibly a consequence of increasing attention to men's bodies in the media – see above). Kathy Davis argues that men will never seek surgery to the same extent as

women (except for hair transplants) because men's bodies are constituted as bodies that 'do' rather than bodies that are 'done to'. World in Focus 18.2 and the images that support it suggests perhaps that the view that women's bodies should be 'done to' is becoming more the norm than the exception.

As cosmetic surgery gradually becomes normalised, women who do not seek cosmetic surgery may be at risk of being labelled as abnormal, as deviant (Morgan, 1991).

A closer look 18.4

Which size breast is best

Peter Conrad and Heather T. Jacobson (2003) argue that body enhancements are a reflection of what is socially valued in a given society at a given time and the history of breast augmentation mirrors societies' view of the meanings and values of breasts with particular reference to the so-called ideal size, shape and function. This analysis shows how social values are often reflected in medical practice in that at different times 'small' and 'large' breasts have both been defined as a medical problem. With specific reference to the USA, Conrad and Jacobson consider what influences women and men to undergo cosmetic surgery on their breasts and elsewhere. These influences include family and friends, the medical profession and the media.

World in focus 18.2

Contradictory messages?

In 2005 the magazine *Marie Claire* included an article on 'The Miss Plastic Surgery' contest in China where women (and girls as young as 16) compete in the first pageant for 'artificial beauties' (p. 114).:

   at the height of the cultural revolution in the Sixties and

Seventies, Maoist officials condemned any form of grooming or beautification as 'unrevolutionary' and regularly beat women for owning a hairbrush, wearing blusher or painting their nails.

   In the past 30 years, the pursuit of beauty has made a comeback. Good looks are now a vital currency, especially for

women in search of well-paid jobs or rich husbands . . . Cosmetic surgery is now a £1.3 billion industry in China, growing at a rate of 20 per cent a year. More than 3.5 million surgical operations were performed between 2002 and 2003 (p. 115) . . .

   Dr Fushun Ma, a cosmetic surgeon at a large private clinic in

▶

World in focus continued

Bejing . . . [is quoted as saying] 'Rounder eyes and a higher nose are basic necessities, like food or water, for beauty-conscious young females . . . They don't deliberately want to copy the West, they just believe these features look prettier.'

Marie Claire question the celebratory stories of the contestants in the context noting the many cases of botched surgery that sometimes result in irreversible damage. They also argue that the increasing demand for 'artificial' beauty adds to the objectification and distress of all

women in China. Interesting then that at the end of the magazine there are no less than eight pages of adverts offering cosmetic surgery solutions to the readers of the magazine.

Source: Haworth (2005), *Marie Claire*.

Figure 18.2 Women's Magazine Advert
Source: © Advertising Archives

Figure 18.3 And the winner of Miss Plastic Surgery Is...
Source: © Jack Picone 2005

Ambivalent messages

The male gaze

The stereotypical portrayal of women as available to men in an image that men determine can be explained by the male gaze. Laura Mulvay (1975, cited by Abbott *et al.*, 2005: 320) suggests that the male gaze operates in three ways:

1. the gaze of the camera on the female (often sexualised) body, which is often from the male point of view;

2. male characters and identities, that gaze upon the female bodies in the narrative; and

3. male spectators who gaze at female bodies on the screen.

Thus, for Mulvay (1975) the male gaze can be characterised by voyeurism, fetishism and sadism [**Hotlink → Sex and Sexuality (Chapter 15)**]. Similarly Sandra Lee Bartky (1990: 72) argues that patriarchal culture provides the 'pan-optical [all seeing] male connoisseur' opportunities to both gaze and judge the women presented before him. From this perspective then the male spectator derives enjoyment from looking at women displayed for his enjoyment as well as deriving pleasure from identifying with men in films, texts, adverts and so on. In World in Focus 18.3 we provide an example of how women's looks and presumed sexual lifestyles are often the focus even when not of central concern to the issue:

The introduction and continuing popularity of 'The Page Three Girl' could be seen as an example of the male gaze in action [**Hotlink → Health and Illness (Chapter 12)**]. Rupert Murdoch bought the British newspaper the *Sun* in 1969 and announced that its selling points should now be 'sex, sport and contests'. Page Three Girls (topless models on page three of the paper) were introduced a year later. Patricia Holland (2004) notes that the *Sun*'s predecessor, the trade-union backed *Daily Herald* aimed to create a sense of tough working-class community among its readers between the First and Second World Wars. She adds that from the 1970s the *Sun* had a different aim emphasising new working-class prosperity, challenging deference and focusing on pleasure. The *Sun*'s intention was not to produce pornographic images of women but 'tastefully posed, ordinary young women,

World in focus 18.3

Sex in the dock

Saraswati Sunindyo (2004: 86) draws our attention to three cases of wife and mistress murder in Indonesia in the 1990s and argues that the media, professional and lay discussion of these cases engaged representations of sexuality with the victims being 'sexualised' and the aggressors 'desexualised'. One example is the attempted murder of Mrs Supadmi, mistress of a married army officer (hit on the head, shot and left for dead). Media reports included:

After the third day of the trial, the young and 'sexy' divorcee (the mistress) no longer covered her face as when she first entered the courtroom.

Many of the policemen's wives who attended the trial said, 'She knows how to dress herself up and be sexy'.

. . . the people (mostly young men) who went to the trial . . . remarks addressed . . . included 'Sister! Come on out and let's get acquainted'

. . . the defence lawyer started to challenge her as a 'responsible witness' and depicted her as primarily a sexual being, and a vengeful person who did not value love and devotion.

smiling at the reader and revealing their breasts' (Holland, 2004: 73). Ironically then, as Holland (2004) continues, the message was twofold, intended for women as well as men in that: 'Its message to men was age-old but its message to women was that women are now free to be sexual. Generations of Page Three "girls" encouraged women readers to join them, to be proud of their bodies and to have fun.' However, as we can see from A Critical Look 18.2 it seems that this irony is not always understood.

A critical look 18.2

Look but do not touch

'SEXY SAM MAULED BY CAVAN "CAVEMEN"' was the lead story in the *Sunday World*, an Irish tabloid . . .

Topless model Samantha Fox had to cut short a dancehall date . . . last week – after dozens of lusty Cavanmen invaded the stage . . .The . . . page-three girl had to flee to her dressing room after a series of very determined advances by male fans who took the title of her hit song 'Touch Me' just a bit too literally . . . A near-riot erupted when the crowd at the late-licensed disco became so excited that they burst through the protective ring of bodyguards and bouncers and on to the slightly raised stage where Sam was making her fully-clothed, non-singing public appearance . . . When the fans began grabbing Sam's arm, kissing her hand and trying to clutch at her clothing, the organisers decided enough was enough.

(Smith, 1989: 10–12)

Joan Smith (1989) follows her account of the media coverage of Samantha Fox's experience (see A Critical Look 18.2) by arguing that the existence of 'Page 3' puts pressure on all women [**Hotlink → Health and Illness (Chapter 12)**]. Recognition of this has led to demands that they should be banned which in turn leads to accusations of envy and prudery against those who call for the ban, particularly if they happen to be women.

Many feminists are critical of all pornography – from the 'softer' versions such as 'Page 3' to more sexually and violent explicit versions in both text and on

film; the central concern being that it is a specific example of male control over women's bodies. Robert Jensen (2004: 247) summarises the feminist critique of pornography as:

➤ the harm to women in the production of pornography;

➤ the harm to women who have pornography forced upon them;

➤ the harm to women who are sexually assaulted by men who use pornography; and

➤ the harm to all women living in a culture in which pornography reinforces and sexualises women's subordinate status (Dworkin, 1988; Itzin, 1992; Russell, 1993; Jensen, 2004).

With specific reference to the above some theorists claim that there is a direct causal link between pornography and sexual violence but others focus on pornography as a significant aspect of sexual abuse and misogyny more generally.

Before leaving this section focusing on the male gaze, it is important to note that not all men have equal access to this voyeurism. Thus, as Cranny-Francis and colleagues (2003: 163) note, black men do not have the same freedom to look, to gaze and 'up to the early or even mid-twentieth century a black man in the southern states of the United States who was perceived by a white man to be looking at – deriving pleasure from – a white woman was in danger of excessive racist violence'.

The female gaze

In the 1980s and 1990s feminists began to ask the questions:

➤ Can the male gaze be reversed?

➤ What about the female gaze? (Kaplan, 1984; Cranny-Francis *et al.*, 2003).

So, as Cranny-Francis *et al.* (2003) note, one feminist response to the objectification of women was to attempt to objectify men and to argue that heterosexual women can gain pleasure from looking at representations of the male body. The argument here is that if each sex objectifies the other then the situation is no longer one of inequality. But as Cranny-Francis and colleagues (2003) suggest, even if women could gain the same pleasure from the act of looking as men do (despite the fact that they are socialised to be looked at rather than to look) objectifying men, rather than freeing women from objectivity does not solve the problem.

There are representations of strong women in the media. Some of the most notable ones in recent years include Ripley in the *Alien* films, Buffy the Vampire Slayer in the television series of the same name and Scully in the *X Files* (Wilcox and Williams, 1996; Russell and Tyler, 2002; Abbott *et al.*, 2005). Scully, for example, 'represents the rationalistic world view usually associated with men, while Mulder [her male colleague] advocates supernatural explanations and a reliance on intuition usually associated with women' (Wilcox and Williams, 1996: 99). Furthermore, there is evidence of the media challenging and subverting dominant gendered racial ideologies in film and music (Abbott *et al.*, 2005).

Despite this though we know that the dominance of men as directors, cinematographers and so on leads Cranny-Francis and colleagues (2003: 163) to ask:

Can there be a female gaze as long as the very machinery which makes films (the camera) is coded as a masculine technology ([with] the process of filming often seen as intrusive, penetrative and voyeuristic in and of itself)?

In addition just as gender is not the only signifier of the male gaze, women's media use is likely to be structured by other differences. Not only have black feminists such as bell hooks (1992) been critical of the ways in which the mass media has reproduced racist stereotypes originating in slavery and in colonial societies but they have also been critical of white women media 'stars' like Madonna for their appropriation of black culture.

Stop and think 18.5

What do you understand by the terms male gaze and female gaze? Why do men look and why are women looked at?

Challenging gendered norms in the media

Although the mass media presents us with dominant stereotypical images of women and men it is interesting to note that male transvestism has a long history in the theatre. In the west it can be traced to Elizabethan times when women were not permitted (by the state) to act on stage and so male actors played female as well as male roles. In addition the pantomime is well known for its use of transvestite characters, with men playing women (e.g. Widow Twanky and Cinderella's stepsisters) and women playing men (e.g. Peter Pan and Puss in Boots) (Cranny-Francis *et al.*, 2003). Although this play with gender is presented as part of the joke it could also be read as subversive.

Cranny-Francis and colleagues (2003) suggest that in the place of both the male gaze and oppositional challenges to this (e.g. when advertisers play with the male gaze in role-reversal images or the attempts of feminist film makers to displace male voyeurism), the 'queer gaze' identifies moments in the text or the image that unsettle gendered and sexed images. Cranny-Francis *et al.* (2003) provide some famous examples, one of which is presented in A Closer Look 18.5

The value of the queering gaze, Cranny-Francis and colleagues (2003) suggest that it destabilises gender roles based on binaristic thinking; the thinking that constructs male and female, masculine and feminine and heterosexual and homosexual as oppositions. Queering the gaze suggests that gender is not a natural given but a perfomative process.

A closer look 18.5

It's gender Jim but not as we know it

Analyses of the original television series *Star Trek* shows that the relationship between Captain Kirk of the starship *Enterprise* and his First Officer Mr Spock was and has been consistently read as non-heteronormative; which is not to say that both characters did not also engage in relationships with women. However, the relationship that sustained them was seen (literally) as their mutual love for each other . . . (Cranny-Francis *et al.*, 2003, p. 175)

The media, pleasure and influence

It is important to note that is it not the main aim of the media to perpetuate stereotypes. The media is primarily a profit making business: what Chibnall (1977) calls 'the offspring of monopoly capitalism'. Thus, it is business considerations that dictate the politics at every stage of the game, not the perpetuation of gendered (and other) stereotypes.

The mass media is extremely successful. Many of us enjoy various types of media every day. Furthermore several theorists have acknowledged the pleasures of such consumption. For example women's magazines can act as both vehicles for dominant ideology and bearers of pleasures (Hermes, 1995; Ussher, 1997). Many women's magazines are popular because they do contain contradictory messages and these resonate with the contradictions of women's lives. A magazine may contain an article on sexual harassment at work and pieces which reinforce ideologies of domesticity and romance. In addition, Jane M. Ussher (1997) suggests that women can be critical of the 'beauty myth' and still get pleasure from 'doing femininity'. As Ussher herself adds: '[I]n a post feminist world, where women are supposed to reject traditional models of femininity and be independent and strong this is transgression (and therefore pleasurable) indeed' (1997: 68).

Conclusion

As Holland (2004: 84) notes women continue to have only minimal roles in the shaping of our popular media, so it is likely that the cultural forms it produces is more likely to reflect the interests, concerns and expectations of men. However, although the mass media does present us with many gendered stereotypes these are often complicated and contradictory and represent challenge to as well as acceptance of dominant gendered ideologies. Modleski (1982) suggests that we should not condemn the mass media or other cultural forms themselves or the men and women who engage with them but rather we should condemn the conditions that have made the mass media – in its current form – possible and necessary.

Further reading

Cynthia Carter and Linda Steiner (eds) (2004), *Critical Readings: Media and Gender*, Maidenhead, Open University Press. This is an edited multi-disciplinary book. Topics covered include: gender, identity and television talk shows; historical portrayals of women in advertising; the sexualisation of the popular press; pornography and masculine power; the cult of femininity in women's magazines; sexual violence in the media.

Another interesting and useful reader this time focusing on gender and other issues of difference is G. Dines and J. M. Humez (eds) *Gender, Race and Class in the Media: A Text reader*, Thousand Oaks: CA Sage.

For interesting reading in the area of the gendered body beautiful see for example Wendy Chapkis (1986) *Beauty Secrets*, London, Women's Press; Jane M. Ussher (1997), *Fantasies of Femininity: Reframing the Boundaries of Sex*, London, Penguin; and Naomi Wolf (1991), *The Beauty Myth*, London, Vintage.

Anne Cranny-Francis, Wendy Waring, Pam Stavropoulos and Joan Kirkby (2003), *Gender Studies, Terms and Debates*, Basingstoke, Palgrave Macmillan. This is an incredibly useful quick reference to detailed debates across a whole range of gender issues. It is particularly useful in its discussion of the male and female gaze.

Media, Culture & Society – this interdisciplinary, international journal provides a forum for the presentation of research and discussion concerning the media, including the newer information and communication technologies, within their political, economic, cultural and historical contexts.

Cultural Studies – an international journal which explores the relation between cultural practices, everyday life, material, economic, political, geographical and historical contexts. Special issues focus on specific topics, often not traditionally associated with cultural studies, and occasional issues present a body of work from a particular national, ethnic or special tradition.

Websites

Gender, Race, Ethnicity in Media – an amazing portal based at the Univesity of Iowa. It links to other sites, news stories and media broadcasts internationally. Available at: **http://www.uiowa.edu/%7Ecommstudy/resources/GenderMedia**

Washington State University – provides a site linking to a large number of online articles on issues of gender and popular culture. Available at: **http://www.wsu.edu/~amerstu/pop/gender.html**

End of chapter activity

Spend a day examining different media output.

Watch a breakfast television show, a lunchtime news programme, a teatime news programme and a mid/late evening news programme. In addition buy a selection of newspapers for the same day. Make some notes on the way in which gender is explaining and employed in the news stories you are reading and listening to and consider the relevance of gender to the story. Consider if and how the focus on gender affects your reaction to the story.

Also make some notes on the advertisements you come across on the television and in the newspapers. Detail the different ways that images of women and men are used to sell goods and services to women and men. Finally, compare the use of gendered stereotypes in news stories to the use of gendered stereotypes in advertisements. How are they similar and different?

Glossary

Agency   In social science terms a force, an acting subject, capable of transforming society.

Agents of socialisation   Institutions that contribute to the development of social norms within individuals, including family, peers, school, media, government.

Androgynous   A person who is neither masculine nor feminine but has a balance of masculine and feminine qualities.

Autonomy   The ability to act in a self-directed manner, to think, choose and act without guidance from another person or group.

Behaviouralism   An approach to political science that emphasises the study of observable and quantifiable political attitudes and actions of individuals and the scientific search for the 'laws' of politics. Dominant in the USA from the 1960s.

Biological   The branch of psychology that focuses on the role of organic elements such as anatomy, hormones, chromosomes, etc. in determining behaviour.

Brain studies   Focuses on understanding the role of the central nervous system in determining behaviour.

Budget Speech   The speech when the Finance Minister of the Government sets out details of taxes and benefits, and estimates economic growth.

Bureaucracy   An organisation defined by hierarchy and written rules, including a clear division of labour.

Canon   An authoratative and accepted list of works viewed to represent the most important, valid and fundamental ideas of an academic area.

Capitalism   An economic system organised on the basis of private ownership of the means of production and the employment of workers for wages. The capitalist sells the goods for more than the cost of production, thus profiting from the surplus value of the labour of the workers.

Chromosomal sex   The sex of an individual as determined by their chromosomes. Ordinarily this might be XY (male) or XX (female) although other possibilities exist and are defined in relation to intersexuality.

Citizenship   Membership of a nation-state, comes with rights and obligations. Liberal democracies have three important elements in citizenship: liberty, equality and solidarity.

Cognition   Mental action or process that involves thought.

Cognitive   The perspective within psychology that focuses on how we think.

Cognitive developmental theory   A developmental theory that focuses on the role of language and cognition in the process of learning about self and others.

Community   A group of individuals who either self-identify, or are viewed by others, as having common interests or attributes.

Conscientisation   Term coined by Paulo Friere (1970) to describe the process in which students, as empowered subjects, gain awareness of how their lives are affected and shaped by social forces and come to realise their own abilities to create social change.

Cultural capital   From Pierre Bourdieu, who argues that success in the educational system is determined by the extent to which students have internalised and conform to the dominant culture, have acquired the appropriate cultural capital.

Culture   A shared way of life, transmitted socially.

Decommodification   Term employed by Gösta Esping Andersen that refers to the ability to survive in society without resorting to selling one's labour, the extent to which a social welfare system supports individuals without requiring that they take paid employment.

Defamilialisation   Term employed by, mostly feminist, social policists to explain the extent of an individual's ability to survive economically without reliance on the family and the extent to which a social welfare system supports the individual directly, rather than through family relationships.

Descriptive   An analytical skill of applying appropriate conceptual labels to things, people, events and ideas that are observed.

Discourse   Following Foucault discourse is the means by which different understandings of truth and reality are contained and find meaning. Through naming things and their description via language (either written or spoken) both people and the world are shaped and given meaning.

Discrimination   To make social, and thereby potentially economic and political, distinctions between people based on perceived membership of a group, rather than on individual merit. Discrimination can be based on religion, ethnicity, sexual orientation, disability, sex, gender, class, etc.

Division of labour   The separation of work into distinct parts, each of which is conducted by an individual or a group, for reasons of increasing productivity, efficiency and specialisation of expertise.

Elite   Any select group with privileged status, often united by common ties, interests, aims and objectives.

Enfranchisement   The extension of the right to vote to certain groups/categories previously excluded.

Epistemology   A philosophical concern with issues of knowledge, such as its definition, what counts as knowledge, how it is acquired and the relationship between the knower and the known.

Essentialism   The view that due to natural/biological attributes all members of a group share certain core attitudes, experiences and behaviours.

Ethnography   A method and a process. As a method it concerns the study of a phenomenon in a specific cultural context in which a range of methods are used such as participant observation, formal and informal interviews, document analysis. The researcher is present for an extended period of time in the culture. As a product, an ethnography is the finished product developed from the research. It attempts to answer theoretical and empirical questions through supplying detail and description.

Evolutionary psychology   The application of evolutionary principles in order to explain behaviour.

Experimental method   A research design that involves isolating and controlling particular variables in order to determine their effect on other factors.

Feminine   Not only the fact of being biologically female but also it describes attributes associated with the female gender role.

Femininity   The culturally determined attributes associated with the female sex. These can vary across societies and historical periods.

Gender blind   The practice of ignoring gender so as to treat all without discrimination based on gender. Some prefer the term gender blinkered as it has less of a disabilist overtone.

Gender constancy   According to Kohlberg (1996) the stage at which a child becomes aware that gender is a consistent element and not open to change.

Gender knowledge   According to Kohlberg the stage at which a child has an accurate assessment of the characteristics of male and female gender.

Gender labelling   According to Kohlberg the stage at which a child is able to accurately distinguish between people as male and female and label them as so.

Gender schema theory   Sandra Bem's account of how children gain an understanding of gender through cognitive and social processes.

Gender stereotype   A set of beliefs held in a gender schema about the appropriate traits and behaviours of either men or women.

Hegemony   Term devised by Antonio Gramsci to explain and describe how one social group can use political power and ideology, rather than force, to achieve dominance over other groups. Now used more widely to explain ideological dominance generally.

Heterogeneous   The term used to describe something, an object, group, system, which encompasses a range of differences within it, e.g. a heterogeneous society is one which contains diverse peoples.

Historiography   The history of history and how it has been conducted, that is the methods of research and analysis. Also used to describe the study of historical writing.

Homogeneous Refers to the state of being the same throughout, e.g. a homogeneous group means one made up of similar members.

Ideology Framework of thought that is used in society to give order and meaning to the social world.

Industrial revolution Period of productive change, beginning in Britain in the mid-eighteenth century. Development of machinery, steam power and factories to manufacture goods.

Intersexuality Refers to a set of conditions where a person is born with the characteristics of both sexes, generally ascertained through chromosomal, homormonal or reproductive anomalies.

Longitudinal study Research design where a group of people are studied over an extended period.

Masculine Not only the fact of being biologically male but it also describes attributes associated with the male gender role.

Masculinity The culturally determined attributes associated with the male sex. These can vary across societies and historical periods.

Materialism The philosophical view that nothing exists except matter, that is those things which can be perceived via the senses, things that can be measured and known.

Meta-analysis Combines the results on a large number of studies that have investigated similar questions.

Methodology Refers to the philosophical assumptions inherent in a study which determines the choice of methods employed.

Methods The range of techniques used to investigate phenomena in the search for new knowledge and understanding, e.g. social survey, interview, experiment.

Monogamy The practice of having only one partner at a time, applies to both married and unmarried couples.

Müllerian system A structure within the embryo that gives it the capacity to develop a female reproductive system.

Multi-sited ethnography A form of ethnographic method which has been developed in the last decade and reflects the new directions of, especially, anthropological enquiry. Subjects such as globalisation and transnational-ism demand that the researcher becomes mobile moving between countries (as in the case of studies on migration) or between research locations, whether this be urban/rural, head office/subcontracting unit, etc.

Oedipus complex Drawing on the Greek myth where Oedipus married his mother and killed his father, Freud used this to describe the phallic stage in a boy's psychosexual development.

Operant conditioning A key form of learning within a behaviourist approach.

Oppression The negative result of the use of power upon a person or groups of people. How a particular group or individual can be denied opportunities or resources by unjust uses of power, e.g. authority, force or societal norms.

Patriarchy Originally the rule of the father over wife and children. Modern usage relates to the structuring of social systems and institutions in ways that preserve the dominance and privileges of men in relation to women.

Phallocentric A male-centred viewpoint. Used in particular as a critique of psychoanalytic approaches that tend to see power as represented by the phallus.

Pluralism Existence of diverse social forces, for example different political parties, labour unions, social and religious groups, who are all able and permitted to compete openly for political influence.

Polygamy Marriage to more than one spouse at a time. Polygyny is when a man has more than one wife. Polyandry is when a woman has more than one husband.

Polyvocality A term which developed out of the post modern turn in anthropology. It refers to the recognition that ethnography is not only constructed through the anthropologist's authority but in co-construction with the research subjects. The ethnography, therefore must give voice to the different voices involved in the research.

Postmodernism A perspective that argues that reality is not given but created via ideas, texts and discourses. Postmodernism challenges Enlightenment views of a search for the truth as it argues that it is possible for several different 'truths' to exist at the same time.

Power The capacity of individuals, groups and political bodies to ensure their decisions are enacted and realised.

Praxis   The process of putting theoretical knowledge into practice.

Progressive Education   Reformist educational principles from the early twentieth century that emphasise child-centred approaches, individual instruction, use of group discussions and laboratories as instructional techniques.

Proletariat   The term employed by Karl Marx for the social class that needs to sell its labour as it does not own the means of production.

Pronatalism   A policy or position that encourages child-bearing, often a deliberate policy of a government to raise fertility levels within their population.

Psychometric tests   The study and measurement of psychological traits and characteristics through the use of questionnaires.

Psychosexual stages   Freud's theory of development.

Qualitative research methods   A methodological approach that focuses on interpreting meanings and experiences. It tends to use texts and interviews rather than measurement scales. Findings provide in-depth understanding of particular cases rather than generalised laws of behaviour.

Quantatitive research methods   Methods which deal with anything that can be counted or measured. In the social sciences supporters of these methods advocate that only by using them can social science become truly scientific.

Reductionist   The assumption that complex behaviour can be explained at a simpler or more fundamental level e.g. that sexual behaviour could be explained in terms of biological processes such as hormone levels.

Reflexivity   A continual process throughout the different phases of research, concerning the researcher's ability to reflect on the choices that he or she makes, during the preparation (research proposal), research process (field-work), analysis and writing up. For a researcher to be reflexive, he or she must be willing to expose their biases or assumptions, be critical of the research relations, analyse the errors which occur in the field, and be conscious of the choices made during the writing up process. Being reflexive is one of the ways to guarantee that the research carried out is credible and realistically represents the actual culture or situation being studied.

Schema   A mental framework that organises information, beliefs and expectations and is then used as a guide to behaviour.

Schemata   The plural of schema.

Second Wave Feminism   The period of feminist activity, writing and theorising from the early 1960s to 1980s.

Sex hormones   Hormones that effect sexual development as well as sexual response.

Sexual division of labour   Division of tasks based on sex, sometimes legally enforced (viewed as protecting paid work for men), sometimes culturally created and maintained.

Social capital   From Pierre Bourdieu, social capital is acquired through education and skill acquisition and is required to intergrate successfully and fully into society.

Social learning theory   A theory about learning that is underpinned by behaviourist assumptions of reward and punishment.

Social stratification   A sociological term describing the hierarchical divisions of society into social classes or castes.

Social structure   This refers to groups, e.g. ethnic, gender, class, and how they relate to each other, and to the enduring patterns of that relationship.

Suffrage   The right of citizens to participate in the electoral process of a political system through the use of a vote.

Theory   A coherent interpretation of an event, phenomena, practice, observation and so on, that orders and makes sense of the world.

Unconscious   Freud theorises that this element is not usually accessible to conscious thought but often drives impulses and behaviours.

Welfare state   Nation-states with government insurance systems providing public assistance, education, health and housing programmes to improve and protect economic and social welfare of citizens.

Wolffian system   A structure within the embryo that gives it the capacity to develop a male reproductive system.

Bibliography

Abbott, Pamela, Wallace, Claire and Tyler, Melissa (2005) *An Introduction to Sociology: Feminist Perspectives* London, Routledge (third edition)

Adkins, Lisa (1995) *Gendered Work: Sexuality, Family and the Labour Market* Buckingham, Open University Press

Adler, Freda (1975) *Sisters in Crime: The Rise of the New Female Criminal* New York, McGraw Hill

Allen, Judith (1990), 'Does Feminism Need a Theory of the State?' in Sophie Watson (ed), *Playing the State, Australian Feminist Interventions* London, Verso

Almond, Gabriel and Verba, Sidney (1963) *The Civic Culture: Political Attitudes and Democracy in Five Nations* Princeton, Princeton University Press

Alsop, Rachel, Fitzsimons, Annette and Lennon, Kathleen (2002) *Theorizing Gender* Cambridge, Polity

American Psychological Association (2000) *Women in academe: Two steps forward, one step back.* Washington, DC: APA. Available from http://www.apa.org/pi/wpo/academe/toc.html accessed May 2005

Andersen, Kristi and Cook, Elizabeth (1985) 'Women, work and political attitudes' *American Journal of Political Science,* 29 (3), pp 606–625

Anderson, Pauline and Williams, Jenny (eds) (2001) *Identity and Difference in Higher Education 'Outsiders Within'* Aldershot, Ashgate

Annandale, Ellen (1998) *The Sociology of Health and Medicine: a critical introduction* Cambridge, Polity

Annandale, Ellen and Clark, Judith (1996) 'What is Gender? Feminist theory and the sociology of human reproduction' *Sociology of Health and Illness,* 18(1), pp 17–44

Arber, Sara and Cooper Helen (2000) 'Gender and inequalities in health across the lifecourse' in Ellen Annandale and Kate Hunt (eds) *Gender Inequalities in Health* Buckingham, Open University

Arnot, M., Gray, J., James, M., Ruddock, J with Duveen, G (1999) *Recent Research on Gender and Educational Performance* London, OFSTED (Office for Standards in Education)

Arnot, Madeleine and Weiner, Gaby (1987) *Gender and the Politics of Schooling* Hutchinson, London

Arnup, Katherine (2004) 'Lesbian and Gay Parenting.' in Nancy Mandell and Ann Duffy (eds) *Canadian Families: Diversity, Conflict, and Change* Toronto, Harcourt

Assiter, Alison (1996) *Enlightened Women: modernist feminism in a postmodern age* London, Routledge

Bacchi, Carole Lee (2000) *Women, Policy and Politics: the Construction of Policy Problems* London, Sage

Bala, Nicholas, Duvall-Antonacopoulous, Katherine, MacRae, Leslie and Paetsch, Joanne (2005) 'An International Review of Polgamy: Legal and Policy Implications for Canada' in Angela Campbell, Nicholas Bala, Katherine Duvall-Antonacopoulous, Leslie MacRae and Joanne Paetsch, Martha Bailey, Beverley Baines, Bita Amani and Amy Kaufman (eds) *Polygamy in Canada: Legal and Social Implication for Women and Children. A Collection of Policy Research Reports* The Alberta Civil Liberties Research Centre for Status of Women, Canada at http://www.swc-cfc.gc.ca/pubs/pubspr.html accessed September 2006.

Bandura, Albert (1986) *Social Foundations of Thought and Action: A Social Cognitive Theory* Englewood Cliffs, NJ, Prentice-Hall

Barker, Diane L. and Allen, Sheila (eds) (1976a) *Sexual Divisions and Society: Process and change* London, Longman

Barker, Diane L. and Allen, Sheila (eds) (1976b) *Dependence and Exploitation in Work and Marriage* London, Longman

Barrett, Frank J (2001) 'The Organized Construction of Hegemonic Masculinity; The Case of the US Navy' Harry

Brod and Michael Kaufman (eds) (1994) *Theorizing Masculinities* Thousand Oaks, CA, Sage

Barrett, Michele (1980) *Women's Oppression Today: Problems in Marxist Feminist Analysis* London, Verso

Bartky, Sandra Lee (1990) *Femininity and Domination* London, Routledge

Basu, Amrita (ed) (1995) *The Challenge of Local Feminisms: Women's Movements in Global Perspectives* Boulder, Colorado, Westview Press

Batchelor, Susan (2002) "The Myth of Girl Gangs" in Yvonne Jewkes and Gayle Letherby (eds) *Criminology: a reader* London, Sage

Bauman, Zygmunt (1990) *Thinking Sociologically* Oxford, Blackwell

Baxter, Sandra and Lansing, Marjorie (1983) *Women and Politics: The Visible Majority* Ann Arbor, Michigan, University of Michigan Press

BBC (2006) *Domestic Violence – Men as Victims*, http://www.bbc.co.uk/relationships/domestic_violence/menhh_index.html accessed July 2006

Beck, Ullrich and Beck-Gernsheim, Elizabeth (1995) *The Normal Chaos of Love* Cambridge, Polity

Becker, Gary (1993) *Human Capital* Chicago, University of Chicago Press

Beckwith, Karen (2005) 'A Common Language of Gender?' *Politics and Gender*, 1 (1), pp 128–137

Beddoe, Deirdre (1983) *Discovering Women's History: A practical manual* London, Pandora Press

Behar, Ruth and Gorden, Deborah (1995) "Introduction: Out of Exile" in Ruth Behar and Deborah Gorden (eds) *Women Writing Culture* Berkley, University of California Press

bell hooks (1982) *Ain't I a Woman: black women and feminism* London, Pluto

bell hooks (1998, originally 1984) 'Black Women and Feminist Theory' in Marsh, I. with Campbell, R. and Keating, M. (eds) *Classic and Contemporary Readings in Sociology* Essex, Addison Wesley Longman

bell hooks (1984) *Feminist theory from margin to center* Boston, South End Press

Bell, Colin and Newby, Howard (eds) (1977) *Doing Sociological Research* London, Allen and Unwin

Bell, David (2000) 'Farm boys and wild men: rurality, masculinity and homosexuality' *Rural Sociology*, 65, pp 547–561

Bell, David, Binnie, Jon, Cream, Julia and Valentine, Gill (1994) 'All hyped up and no place to go' *Gender, Place and Culture*, 1, pp 31–47

Bell, David and Binnie, Jon (2000) *The Sexual Citizen: queer politics and beyond* Cambridge, Polity

Bell, Elizabeth and Golombisky, Kim (2004) 'Voices and silences in our classrooms: strategies for mapping trails among sex/gender, race, and class' *Women's Studies in Communication*, 27 (3), pp 294–329

Beller, Michal and Gafni, Naomi (2000) 'Can item format (multiple choice vs. open-ended) account for gender differences in mathematics achievement?' *Sex Roles*, 42, pp 1–21

Bem, Sandra (1974) "The measurement of psychological androgyny" *Journal of Consulting and Clinical Psychology*, 42 pp 155–62

Bem, Sandra (1981) "Gender schema theory: A cognitive account of sex typing" *Psychological Review*, 88 pp 354–64

Bem, Sandra (1985) '"Androgyny and Gender" Schema theory: A conceptual and empirical integration' in T. B. Sonderegger (ed), *Nebraska Symposium on Motivation, 1984: Psychology and gender* pp 179–226 Lincoln, NE University of Nebraska Press

Bem, Sandra (1987) "Gender Schema theory and its implications for child development: Raising gender-aschematic children in a gender schematic society" in M. Roth Walsh (ed) *The psychology of women: Ongoing debates* pp 226–245, New Haven, CT, Yale University Press

Bem, Sandra (1993) *The lenses of gender* New Haven, CT: Yale University Press

Bentilsson, M.(1991) 'Love's Labour Lost?: a sociological views' in Mike Featherstone, Mike Hepworth, and Brian S. Turner (ed) *The Body: social process and cultural theory* London: Sage

Benyon, John (2004) "The Commercialization of Masculinities: From the 'New Man' to the 'New Lad'" in C. Carter and L. Steiner (eds) *Critical Readings: Media and Gender* Maidenhead, Open University Press

Berg, Lawrence D. (1998) 'Reading (post)colonial history: masculinity, 'race' and rebellious natives in Waikato, New Zealand – 1863' *Historical Geography*, 26, pp 101–127

Berg, Lawrence D. and Longhurst, Robyn (2003) 'Placing masculinities and geography' *Gender, Place and Culture*, 10:4, pp 351–360

Berger, John (1972) *Ways of Seeing* BBC and Penguin, London

Berger, P. (1967) *Invitation to Sociology: a humanistic perspective* Harmondsworth, Penguin

Berliner, Wendy (2004) 'Where have all the young men gone?' *The Guardian*, May 18th

Bettinger, Eric P and Long, Bridget Terr (2004) *Do Faculty Serve as Role Models? The Impact of Instructor Gender on Female Students* http://www.aeaweb.org/annual_mtg_papers/2005/0109_1015_0601.pdf accessed June 2006

Bhavani, Kum Kum and Coulson, Margaret (1986) "Transforming Socialist Feminism: the challenge of racism" *Feminist Review* 23

Bhavnani, Reena (1991) *Black Women in the Labour Market: a research review* Manchester, EOC

Billen, Andrew (2002) "The Injudiciary" in Yvonne Jewkes and Gayle Letherby (eds) *Criminology: a reader* London, Sage

Birke, Lindi (1992) 'In Pursuit of Difference! Science Studies of Men and Women' in Gill Kirkup and Laurie Smith Keller (eds) *Inventing Women: Science, Technology and Gender* Cambridge, Open University Press

Blom, Ida (2004) 'Global gender history – a new research area?' *North South. Gendered Views from Norway, Special Edition of Kvinnesforskning* (Journal of Gender Research in Norway) January 30th

Blomley, Nicholas K. (1996) 'I'd like to dress her all over: masculinity, power and retail space' in Neil Wrigley and Michelle Lowe (eds) *Retailing, Consumption and Capital: Towards the New Economic Geography of Retailing* London, Longman

Blunt, Alison and Varley, Ann (2004) 'Introduction: Geographies of the home' *Cultural Geographies*, 11, pp 3–6

Blunt, Alison and Wills, Jane (2000) *Dissident Geographies: An Introduction to Radical Ideas and Practice* Harlow, Pearson

Bly, John (1990) *Iron John. A Book About Men* Reading, MA, Addison-Wesley Publishing Company Inc

Boal, Augusto (1979) *The Theatre of the Oppressed* New York, Urizen Books

Bochel, Catherine and Briggs, Jacqui (2000) 'Do women make a difference?' *Politics*, 20 (2), pp 63–68

Bondi, Liz and Rose, Damaris (2003) 'Constructing Gender, Constructing The Urban: a review of Anglo-American feminist urban geography' *Gender, Place and Culture*, 10:3, pp 229–245

Bondi, Liz, Avis, Hannah, Bankey, Ruth, Bingley, Amanada, Davidson, Joyce, Duffy Rosaleen, Einagel, Victoria Ingrid, Green, Anja-Maaike, Johnston, Lynda, Lilley, Susan, Listerborn, Carina, Marshy, Mona, McEwan, Shonagh, O'Connor, Niamh, Rose, Gillian, Vivat, Bella and Wood Nichola (2002) *Subjectivities, Knowledges and Feminist Geographies: The Subjects and Ethics of Social Research* Lanham, MD, Rowman and Littlefield

Bondi, Liz, Davidson, Joyce and Smith, Mick (2005) 'Introduction: geography's 'emotional turn'' in Joyce Davidson, Liz Bondi and Mick Smith (eds) *Emotional Geographies* Aldershot, Ashgate

Boris, Eileen (1995) 'The Racialized Gendered State; Constructions of Citizenship in the United States' *Social Politics*, 2 (2), pp 160–180

Bornstein, Kate (1994) *Gender Outlaw, On Men, Women and the Rest of Us* New York, Routledge

Boston Women's Health Book Collective (1988) *Our Bodies Ourselves* (25th Anniversary Edition) New York, Touchstone

Bourdieu, Pierre (1985) *Distinction; a social critique of the judgement of taste* London, Routledge and Kegan Paul

Bourque, Susan and Grossholtz, Jean (1974) 'Politics an Unnatural Practice; Political Science looks at Female Participation' *Politics and Society*, Winter, pp 225–266

Bowlby, Sophie, Foord, Jo, McDowell, Linda and Momsen, Janet (1982) 'Environment planning and feminist theory: a British perspective' *Environment and Planning A*, 14, pp 711–716

Bowles, Gloria and Klein, Renate Duelli (eds) (1983) *Theories of Women's Studies* London, Routledge and Kegan Paul

Box, Steven (1971) *Deviance, Reality and Society* London, Holt, Reinhart and Winston

Boys, Jos (1998) 'Beyond maps and metaphors? Rethinking the relationship between architecture and gender' in Rosa Ainley (ed) *New Frontiers of Space, Bodies and Gender* London, Routledge

Bradley, Rebekah and Davino, Katrina (2002) "Women's Perceptions of the Prison Environment: when prison is 'the safest place I've ever been'" *Psychology of Women Quarterly* 26

Brandth, Berit and Kvande, Elin (1998) Masculinity and child care: the reconstruction of fathering *Sociological Review* 46(2)

Brannon, Linda (2005) *Gender: Psychological Perspectives* Boston, Pearson Education Inc

Breedlove, S. Marc (1994) "Sexual differentiation of the human nervous system" *Annual Review of Psychology*, 45, pp 389–418

Bridge (2002) *In Brief*, http://www.bridge.ids.ac.uk/dgbg10.html accessed September 2002

Brod, Harry and Kaufman, Michael (eds) (1994) *Theorizing Masculinities* Thousand Oaks, CA, Sage

Brodie, Janine (ed) (2002) *Critical concepts, an introduction to politics* Toronto, Pearson

Brown, Alice, Mackay, Fiona and Myers, Fiona (2002) *Women and the Scottish Parliament: Making a Difference?* ESRC End of Award report, R000223281

Brown, Beverly (1986) 'Women and Crime: the dark figure of criminology' *Economy and Society* 15(3) pp 355–402

Brown, Phillip and Hesketh, Anthony (2004) *The Mismanagement of Talent – Employability and Jobs in the Knowledge Economy* Milton Keynes, Open University Press

Brownmiller, Susan (1975) *Against Our Will: Men, Women and Rape* Harmondsworth, Penguin

Buchbinder, David (1998) *Performance Anxieties: re-producing masculinities* Sydney, Allen and Unwin

Burawoy, Michael (2005) "For Public Sociology" *American Sociological Review* 70 pp 4–28

Butler, Judith (1990) *Gender Trouble: Feminism and the Subversion of Identity* London, Routledge

Burman, Erica, Alldred, Pam, Bewley, Catherine, Goldberg, Brenda, Heenan, Colleen, Marks, Deborah, Marshall, Jane, Taylor, Karen, Ullah, Robina and Warner, Sam (1996) *Challenging Women: Psychology's Exclusions, Feminist Possibilities* Buckingham, Open University Press

Burr, Vivien (1998) *Gender and Social Psychology* London, Routledge

Burr, Vivien (2001) *Social Constructionism* London, Routledge

Busfield, Joan (1996) *Men, Women and Madness: understanding gender and mental disorder* Basingstoke, Macmillan

Buss, David (1994) *The Evolution of Desire: Strategies of Human Mating* London, Harper Collins

Butler, Judith (1990) *Gender Trouble: Feminism and the Subversion of Identity* New York, Routledge

Butler, Judith (1993) *Bodies that Matter: On the Discursive Limits of 'Sex'* London, Routledge

Caiazza, Amy, Shaw, April and Werschkul, Misha (2004) *Women's Economic Status in the States: Disparities by Race, Ethnicity, and Region* Washington, DC, Institute for Women's Policy Research, available at www.iwpr.org

Cain, Maureen (1973) *Society and the Policeman's Role* London, Routledge and Kegan Paul

Caplan, Pat (ed) (1987) *The Cultural Construction of Sexuality* London, Tavistock Publications

Carby, Hazel (1982) 'White women listen. Black feminism and the boundaries of sisterhood' in Centre for Contemporary Cultural Studies, *The Empire Strikes Back* London, Routledge

Carlen, Pat (1983) *Women's Imprisonment* A Study in Social Control, London, Routledge and Kegan Paul

Carrigan, Tim, Connell, Bob and Lee, John (1987) 'Toward a new sociology of masculinity' in Harry Brod (ed) *The Making of Masculinities: The New Men's Studies* Boston, Allen and Unwin

Cascardi, Michele, O'Leary, K. Daniel and Lawrence, Erikat (1995) 'Characteristics of women physically abused by their spouses and who seek treatment regarding marital conflict' *Journal of consulting and Clinical Psychology*, 63(4): 616–623

Casey, Catherine (1995) *Work, Self and Society: After Industrialisation* London, Routledge

Caulfield, Sueann (2001) 'The History of Gender in the Historiography of Latin America' *Hispanic American Historical Review*, 81 (3–4), pp 449–490

Cavadino, Michael and Dignan, James (2002) "The Penal System: an introduction" in Yvonne Jewkes and Gayle Letherby (eds) *Criminology: a reader* London, Sage

Cavendish, Ruth (1982) *Women on the Line* London, Routledge and Kegan Paul

CAWP (Center for American Women and Politics), (2000) *Gender Differences in Voter Turnout 2000 Battleground States*, www.cawp.rutgers.edu/Facts5./ Elections/Battleground2000.pdf accessed July 2006.

CAWP, (2004) *Gender Gap Persists in the 2004 Election*, www.cawp.rutgers.edu/Facts5./Elections/GG2004Facts.pdf accessed July 2006.

Chambers, Deborah (2001) *Representing the Family* London, Sage

Chapkis, Wendy (1986) *Beauty Secrets* London, Women's Press

Chapman, Jenny (1993) *Politics, Feminism and the Reformation of Gender* London, Routledge

Chappell, Louise (2000) 'Interacting with the State; Strategies and Political Opportunities' *International Feminist Journal of Politics*, 2 (2), pp 244–275

Charles, Nickie (2000) *Feminism, the State and Social Policy* Basingstoke, Macmillan

Charles, Nickie (2002) *Gender in Modern Britain* Oxford, Oxford University Press

Chester, Stephanie (1998) 'The hidden shame of male rape' *The Oxford Times*, Oct 15

Chibnall, Steven (1977) *Law and Order News: An Anaylsis of Crime Reporting in the British Press*, London, Tavistock

Childs, Sarah (2001a) 'Attitudinally feminist'? The New Labour Women MPs and the Substantive Representation of Women' *Politics*, 21 (3), pp 178–185

Childs, Sarah (2001b) 'In her own words: New Labour women and the substantive representation of women' *British Journal of Politics and International Relations*, 3 (2), pp 173–190

Childs, Sarah (2004) 'A British Gender Gap? Gender and Political Participation' *The Political Quarterly*, 75 (4), pp 422–424

Chodorow, Nancy (1978) *The Reproduction of Mothering, Psychoanalysis and the Sociology of Gender* Berkeley, CA, University of California Press

Crandall, Christian S., Tsang, Jo-Ann, Goldman, Susan, and Pennington, John T. (1999) 'Newsworthy moral dilemmas: Justice, caring and gender' *Sex Roles*, 40(3/4) pp 187–210

Chrisler, Joan C. (1996) 'Politics and Women's Weight' in Wilkinson, Sue and Kitzinger, Celia (eds) *Representing the Other: a feminism and psychology reader* London, Sage

Christy, Carole (1987) *Sex Differences in Political Participation: Processes of Change in Fourteen Countries* New York, Praeger

Clark, Ann and Millard, Elaine (1998) *Gender in the Secondary Curriculum Balancing the Books* London, Routledge

Clarke, John and Critcher, Chas (1985) *Devil Makes Work*, Basingstoke, Macmillan

Clifford, James and Marcus, George, E (eds)(1986) *Writing Culture. The Poetics and Politics of Ethnography* Berkeley, University of California Press

Closer Promotion (2006) *Closer*, October, p 62

CNN *The Million Man March* http://www-cgi.cnn.com/ US/9510/megamarch/march.html accessed November 2005

Coate-Bignell, Kelly (1996) 'Building Feminist Praxis out of Feminist Pedagogy: the importance of students' perspectives' *Women's Studies International Forum*, 19 (3), pp 315–325

Cockburn, Cynthia (1991) *In the Way of Women; Men's Resistance to Sex Equality in Organizations* London, Macmillan

Cockburn, John (1988) *Lonely Hearts: love among the small ads* London, Futura

Cohen, Stanley and Taylor, Laurie (2002[1972]) 'Psychological Survival: the experience of long-term imprisonment' in Yvonne Jewkes and Gayle Letherby (eds) *Criminology: a reader* London, Sage

Collier, Richard (1999) 'Men, heterosexuality and the changing family: (re)constructing fatherhood in law and social policy' in G. Jagger and C. Wright (eds) *Changing Family Values* London, Routledge

Collier, R. (2002) "The new man: fact or fad" *ArchillesHeel* 14

Collins, Cherry, Batten, Margaret, Ainley, John and Getty, Corinne (2002) *Gender and School Education* Tasmania, Dept of Employment, Education, Training and Youth Affairs, http://www.education.tas.gov.au/equitystandards/ gender/policies/acer.htm accessed November 2005

Collins, Peter (1998) 'Negotiated Selves: reflections on 'unstructured' interviewing' *Sociological Research Online* 3(3) www.socresonline.org.uk/socresonline/3/3/2.html

Coltrane, Scott (1994) 'Theorizing Masculinities in Contemporary Social Science' in Harry Brod and Michael Kaufman (eds) (1994) *Theorizing Masculinities* Thousand Oaks, CA, Sage

Condor, Susan (1986) "Sex Role Beliefs and Traditional Women – Feminist and Intergroup Perspectives" in Sue Wilkinson (ed) *Feminist Social Psychology: developing theory and practice* Milton Keynes, Open University Press

Condry, J. C., and Condry, S. (1976) 'Sex differences: A study in the eye of the beholder' *Child Development*, 47, 812-819

Connell, Robert W. (1983) *Which Way is Up? Essays on Sex, Class and Culture* Sydney Allen & Unwin

Connell, Robert W. (1985) 'Theorising Gender' *Sociology*, 19, pp 260–272

Connell, Robert W. (1987) *Gender and Power: Society, the Person and Sexual Politics* Cambridge, Polity Press

Connell, Robert W. (ed) (1993) 'Special Issue: Masculinities' *Theory and Society*, 22 (5)

Connell, Robert W. (1994) 'Psychoanalysis on Masculinity' in Harry Brod and Michael Kaufman (eds) (1994) *Theorizing Masculinities* Thousand Oaks, CA, Sage

Connell, Robert W. (1995) *Masculinities* Cambridge, Polity Press

Connell, Robert W. (2000) *The Men and the Boys* Cambridge, Polity

Connell, Robert W. (2001) 'The Social Organization of Masculinity' in Stephen M Whitehead and Frank J Barrett (eds) *The Masculinities Reader* Cambridge, Polity

Connolly, Paul (2004) *Boys and Schooling in the Early Years* London, Routledge Falmer

Conrad, Peter and Jacobson, Heather T. (2003) 'Enhancing Biology, cosmetic surgery and breast augmentation' in Simon J. Williams, Lindi Birke and Gillian Bendelow (eds) *Debating Biology: Sociological Reflections on Health, Medicine and Society* London, Routledge

Conway, M. Margaret (2000) 'Gender and Political participation' in Sue Tolleson-Rinehart and Jyl J Josephson (eds) *Gender and American Politics. Women, Men, and the Political Process* Armonk NY, ME Sharpe

Cook, Judith and Fonow, Mary Margaret (1990) 'Knowledge and Women's Interests: issues of epistemology and methodology in feminist sociological research' in McCarl Nielsen, Joyce (ed) *Feminist Research Methods: exemplary readings in the social sciences* Boulder, CO: Westview

Coontz, Stephanie and Henderson, Peta (eds) (1986) *Women's Work, Men's Property: The Origins of Gender and Class* London, Verso

Coppock, Vicki, Haydon, Deena, Richter, Ingrid (1995) *Illusions of 'Post-Feminism': new women, old myths* London, Taylor and Francis

Cornwall, Andrea and Lindisfarne, Nancy (1994) "Dislocating masculinity. Gender, power and anthropology" in Andrea Cornwall and Nancy Lindisfarne (eds) *Dislocating Masculinity. Comparative Ethnographies* London, Routledge

Cornwell, Jocelyn (1984) *Hard Earned Lives* London, Tavistock

Corrin, Chris (1996) 'Introduction' in Chris Corrin (ed) *Women in a Violent World: Feminist Analyses and Resistance Across 'Europe'* Edinburgh, Edinburgh University Press

Cotterill, Pamela (1992) 'Interviewing Women: issues of friendship, vulnerability and power' *Women's Studies International Forum* 15, 5/6 pp 593–606

Cotterill, Pamela and Letherby, Gayle (1993) 'Reviewing the Family Album: hidden lives and empty spaces' BSA Family Studies Group, Staffordshire (unpublished conference paper)

Cotterill, Pamela and Letherby, Gayle (1994) 'The Person in the Researcher' in Burgess, R. (ed) *Studies in Qualitative Methodology Volume 4* London, JAI Press

Cox, Pamela (1999) 'Futures for Feminists Histories' *Gender and History*, 11 (1), pp 164–168

Coyle, Joanne (1999) 'Exploring the Meaning of "Dissatisfaction" with health care: the importance of "Personal Identity Threat"' *Sociology of Health and Illness*, 18:1, 17-44

Crabtree, Louise (2006) 'Disintegrated houses: exploring ecofeminist housing and urban design options' *Antipode*, 38:4, pp 711–734

Cranny-Francis, Anne, Waring, Wendy, Stavropoulos, Pam and Kirkby, Joan (2003) *Gender Studies terms and debates* Basingstoke, PalgraveMacmillan

Crawley, Heaven (2000) 'Engendering the State in Refugee Women' Claim for Asylum' in Susie Jacobs, Ruth Jacobson and Jen Marchbank (eds) *States of Conflict: Gender, Violence and Resistance* Zed Books, London, pp 87–104

Cream, Julia (1995) 'Re-solving: riddles: the sexed body' in David Bell and Gill Valentine (eds) *Mapping Desire: Geographies of Sexualities* London, Routledge

Cresswell, Tim (1992) 'The crucial "where of graffiti": a geographical analysis of reactions to graffiti in New York' *Environment and Planning D: Society and Space*, 10, pp 329–344

Cribb, Ian (2000) 'Men's Health' in Jeanne Katz, Alyson Peberdy, and Jenny Douglas (eds) *Promoting Health* Buckingham, Open University

CSWPS (Committee on the Status of Women in Political Science) (2001) 'The Status of Women in Political Science: Female Participation in the Professoriate and the Study of Women and Politics in the Discipline' *PS: Political Science and Politics*, 34 (2) pp 319–26

D'Amico, Francine (2000) 'Citizen-Soldier? Class, Race, Gender, Sexuality and the US Military' in Susie Jacobs, Ruth Jacobson and Jennifer Marchbank (eds) *States of Conflict: Gender, Violence and Resistance* London, Zed, pp 105–122

Dahlerup, Drude (1984) 'Overcoming the barriers: An app roach to how women's issues are kept from the political agenda' in Judith H Stiehm (ed) *Women's Views of the Political World of Men* New York, Transnational Publishers

Dahlerup, Drude (ed) (1986) *The New Women's Movement: Feminism and Political Power in Europe and the USA* London, Sage

Dahlerup, Drude (1988) 'From a small to a large minority: Women in Scandinavian Politics' *Scandinavian Political Studies*, 11 (4), pp 275–298

Dalley, Gillian (1988) *Ideologies of Caring – Rethinking Community and Collectivism* Basingstoke, Macmillan

Dalley, Gillian (1997) 'Women's Welfare' *New Society*, August 28

Daly, Mary (1985) *Beyond God the Father: Toward a Philosophy of Women's Liberation* Boston, Beacon

Daly, Martin and Wilson, Mary (1988) *Homicide* New York, Aldine deGruyte

Darder, Antonio, Baltodano, Marta and Torres, Rodolfo D (eds) (2003) *The Critical Pedagogy Reader* New York, RoutledgeFalmer

Darder, Antonio, Baltodano, Marta and Torres, Rodolfo D (2003) 'Critical Pedagogy; An Introduction' in Antonio Darder, Marta Baltodano and Rodolfo D Torres (eds) *The Critical Pedagogy Reader* New York, RoutledgeFalmer

Darwin, Charles (1986) *The Descent of Man and Selection in Relation to Sex* New York, Appleton

David, Miriam (2003) *Personal and Political: Feminisms, sociology and family lives* Stoke-on-Trent, Trentham Book

Davidoff, Leonore and Hall, Catherine (1987) *Family Fortunes: Men and Women of the English Middle Class* Chicago, University of Chicago Press

Davidoff, Leonare, McClelland, Keith and Varikas, Eleni (1989) 'Why Gender and History?' *Gender and History*, 1 (1)

Davidoff, Leonore, McClelland, Keith and Varikas, Eleni (1999) 'Introduction: Gender and History – Retrospect and Prospect' *Gender and History*, 11 (3), pp 415–418

Davids, Tine and van Driel, Francien (eds) (2005) *The Gender Question in Globalization. Changing Perspectives and Practices* England, Ashgate Publishing

Davidson, Joyce, Bondi, Liz and Smith, Mick (eds) (2005) *Emotional Geographies* Aldershot, Ashgate

Davidson, Julia O'Connell and Taylor, Jacqueline Sanchez (2004 [originally 1999]) "Fantasy Islands: Exploring the Demand for Sex Tourism" from Kempadoo, Kamala (1999) Sun, Sex and Gold: Tourism and Sex Work in the Caribbean Lanham, MD: Rowman and Littlefield in Kimmel, M. S. and Messner, M. A. (eds) *Men's Lives* (sixth edition) Boston, New York and San Francisco, Pearson

Davis, Charlotte Aull (1999) *Reflexive Ethnography. A guide to researching selves and others* London, Routledge

Davis, Kathy (2003) *Dubious Equalities: cultural studies on cosmetic surgery* Oxford, Rowman and Littlefield

Dawkins, Richard (1976) *The selfish gene* New York and Oxford, Oxford University Press.

Dawson, Graham (1994) *Soldier Heroes: British Adventure, Empire and the Imaging of Masculinitie* London, Routledge

Daly, Martin and Wilson, Margo (1988) *Homocide* New York, Aldinede Gruyter

Day, Kristen (2006) 'Being feared: masculinity and race in public space' *Environment and Planning A*, 28, pp 569–586

De Beauvoir, Simone (1949) *Le Deuxieme Sexe* reprinted as (1972) *The Second Sex* Harmondsworth, Penguin

Deem, Rosemary (1981) 'State Policy and Ideology in the Education of Women 1944–1980' *British Journal of Sociology of Education*, 2 (2), pp 131–143

Deem, Rosemary (1986) *All Work and No Play?* Milton Keynes, Open University Press

Delamont, Sara (2003) *Feminist Sociology* London, Sage

Delli Carpini, Michael X and Keeter, Scott (2000) 'Gender and Political Knowledge' in Sue Tolleson-Rinehart and Jyl J Josephson (eds) *Gender and American Politics. Women, Men, and the Political Process* Armonk, NY, ME Sharpe

Delph-Janiurek, Tom (1999) 'Sounding gender(ed): vocal performances in English university teaching spaces' *Gender, Place and Culture*, 6, pp 137–154

Delphy, Christine (1984) *Close to Home: A Materialist Analysis of Women's Oppression* London, Hutchinson

Delphy, Christine and Leonard, Diane (1992) *Familiar Exploitation: A New Analysis of Marriage in Contemporary Western Societies* London, Polity

Dennis, Norman, Henriques, Fernando and Slaughter, Clifford (1956) *Coal is Our Life* London, Eyre and Spottiswoode

Department for Education and Skills (2002) *Education and Training Statistics for the United Kingdom* available at http://www.statistics.gov.uk/CCI/nugget.asp?ID=434 accessed Jan 2006

Department for Education and Skills (2004) *Gender and Achievement* The Standards Site http://www.standards .dfes.gov.uk/gender&achievement accessed November 2005

Dever, Maryanne (1999) 'Notes on Feminist Pedagogy in the Brave New (Corporate) World' *The European Journal of Women's Studies*, 6 (2), pp 219–225

Devlin, Angela (1998) *Invisible Women What's wrong with Women's prisons?* Waterside Press

DiLapi, Elaine M. (1989) 'Lesbian Mothers and the Motherhood Hierarchy' *Journal of Homosexuality* 18 (1-2)

Di-Stephano, Christine (1990) 'Dilemmas of Difference: feminism, modernity and postmodernism' in Linda Nicholson (ed) *Feminism/Postmodernism* London, Routledge

Dobash, Rebecca and Dobash, Russell (2005) 'Wives: The 'appropriate' victims of domestic violence' in Clare Renzetti, Raqel K Bergen and Jeffrey L Edleson (eds) *Classic Papers on Domestic Violence* New York Allyn and Bacon

Dobash, Russell and Dobash, Rebecca (1980) *Violence Against Wives* London, Open Books

Douglas, Jenny (1998) 'Meeting the Health Needs of Women from Black and Minority Ethnic Communities' in Lesley Doyal (ed) *Women and Health Care Services* Buckingham, Open University

Doyal, Lesley (1995) *What Makes Women Sick?: gender and the political economy of health* Basingstoke, Macmillan

Doyal, Lesley (1998) *Women and Health Services: an agenda for change* Buckingham, Open University Press

Dua, Enakshi and Robertson, Angela (1999) *Scratching the. Surface: Canadian Anti-Racist Feminist Thought* Toronto, Women's Press

Dudink, Stefan and Hagemann, Karen (2004) 'Masculinity in politics and war in the age of democratic revolutions 1750–1850' in Stefan Dudnick, Karen Hagemann and John Tosh (eds) *Masculinities in Politics and War Gendering Modern History* Manchester, Manchester University Press

Duncombe, Jean and Marsden, Dennis (1998) '"Stepford wives" and "hollow men"?: Doing emotion work, doing gender and "authenticity" in intimate heterosexual relationships' in Gillian Bendelow and Simon, J. Williams (eds) *Emotions and Social Life: critical themes and contemporary Issues* London, Routledge

Dunne, Gillian (1997) *Lesbian Lifestyles: Women's Work and the Politics of Sexuality* Basingstoke, Macmillan

Dunne, Gillian (1998) *Living "Difference": Lesbian Perspectives on Work and Family Life* New York, Haworth

Dunne, Mairead, Leach, Fiona, Chilisa, Bagele, Kutor, Nick, Asamoah, Alex, Dzama, Forde, Linda, Maundeni, Tapalogo and Tabulawa, Richard (2005) 'Making the difference; how schools influence gender identity' *id21 Research Highlight* http://www.id21.org, accessed October 2005

Dworkin, Andrea (1988) *Letters from a War Zone* London, Secker and Warburg

Earle, Sarah and Letherby, Gayle (2003) 'Introducing Gender, Identity and Reproduction' in Sarah Earle and Gayle Letherby (eds) *Gender, Identity and Reproduction: social perspectives* London, Palgrave

Earle, Sarah and Sharp, Keith (2007) *Sex in Cyberspace: men who pay for sex* Aldershot, Ashgate

Easthope, Anthony (1986) *What's a Man Gotta Do: the masculine myth in popular culture* London, Paladin

Easton, David and Dennis, Jack (1969) *Children in the Political System* New York, McGraw Hill

Eccles, Jacquelynne S. (1989) 'Bringing young women to math and science' in Mary Crawford and Margaret Gentry (eds) *Gender and thought: Psychological perspectives* pp 36–58. NY: Springer-Verlag

Edley, Nigel and Wetherell, Margaret (1995) *Men in perspective: practice, power and identity* London, Prentice Hall

Edney, Richard (2004) 'To Keep Me Safe from Harm? Transgender Prisoners and the Experience of Imprisonment' *Deakin Law Review*, 17, http://www.austlii.edu.au/au/journals/DeakinLRev/2004/17.html

Education for All Monitoring Report Team (2003) *EFA Global Monitoring Report 2003* UNESCO

Ehrenreich, Barbara (2002) 'Maid to Order' in Barbara Ehrenreich and Arlie Russell Ehrenreich (eds) (2002) *Global Women: Nannies, Maids and Sex Workers in the New Economy* New York, Henry Holt & Co

Eichler, Magrit (1988) *Non-Sexist Research Methods* London, Allen and Unwin

Eisenstein, Hester (1984) *Contemporary Feminist Thought* London, Unwin

Eisenstein, Hester (1990) 'Femocrats, Official Feminism and the Uses of Power' in Sophie Watson (ed) *Playing the State, Australian Feminist Interventions* London, Verso

Eisenstein, Zillah (1981) *The Radical Future of Liberal Feminism* New York, Longman

El-Bushra, Judy (2000) 'Transforming Conflict: Some Thoughts on a Gendered Understanding of Conflict Processes' in Susie Jacobs, Ruth Jacobson and Jen Marchbank (eds) *States of Conflict: Gender, Violence and Resistance* London, Zed Books, pp 87–104

Elder, Laurel (2004) 'Why Women Don't Run: Explaining Women's Underrepresentation in America's Political Institutions' *Women and Politics*, 26 (2), pp 27–56

Elliot, Faith Robertson (1994) *The Family: change or continuity?* London, Macmillan

Elliot, Faith Robertson (1996) *Gender, Family and Society* Basingstoke, Palgrave Macmillan

Elson, Diane and Pearson, Ruth (1981) "The Subordination of Women and the Internationalisation of Factory Production" in Kate Young, Carol Wolkowitz and Roslyn McCullagh (eds) *Of Marriage and the Market. Women's subordination in international perspective* London, CSE Books, pp 144–166

Engels, Frederick (1884) *The Origin of the Family, Private Property and the State* London, Lawrence and Sishart

England, Kim (1991) 'Gender relations and the spatial structure of the city' *Geoforum*, 22, pp 135–147

Enloe, Cynthia (1987) 'Feminist Thinking about War, Militarism and Peace' in Beth Hess and Myra Marx Ferree (eds) *Analysing Gender: A Handbook of Social Science Research* Newbury Park, Sage

Enloe, Cynthia (1990) *Bananas, Beaches and Bases: Making feminist sense of international politics* Berkeley, University of California Press

Ensler, Eve (2006) *The Vagina Monologues Scottish Tour* (Spring)

EOC (Equal Opportunities Commission) (1980) *The Experience of Caring for Elderly and Handicapp ed Dependants: A Survey Report* Manchester, EOC

EOC (1984) *Carers and Services: A Comparison of Men and Women Caring for Dependent Elderly People* Manchester, EOC

EOC (2001) *Young People and Sex Stereotyping* Manchester, EOC

EOC (2005) *Facts about Women and Men in Great Britain* Manchester, EOC

Epstein, Debbie, Elwood, Jannette, Hey, Valerie and Maw, Janet (1998) 'Schoolboy frictions: feminism and "failing boys"' in Debbie Epstein, Jannette Elwood, Valerie Hey and Janet Maw (eds) *Failing Boys? Issues in Gender and Achievement* Buckingham, Open University Press

Epstein, Debbie, O'Flynn, Sarah and Telford, David (2003) *Silenced Sexualities in Schools and Universities* Stoke on Trent, Trentham Books

Esping – Andersen, Gôsta (1990) *The Three Worlds of Welfare Capitalism* Cambridge, Polity Press

Esping – Andersen, Gôsta (1996) *Welfare States in Transition: National Adaptations in Global Economies* London, Sage

ESRC (Economic and Social Research Council) (2005) Gender, Participation, Citizenship, ESRC Seminar Series http://www.uwe.ac.uk/hlss/politics/esrc/furinfo.shtml accessed July 2006

Ettore, E.M. (1978) 'Women, Urban Social Movements and the lesbian ghetto' *International Journal of Urban and Regional Research*, 2, pp 499–520

European Opinion Research Group (2004) 'European's attitudes to parental leave' *Eurobarometer 189* Luxemburg, European Commission

Eurostate Pocketbooks (2004) *How Europeans spend their time: everyday lives of women and men, data 1998–2002* Luxembourg, European Commission

Evans, Mary (1997) *Introducing Contemporary Feminist Thought* Cambridge, Polity

Exley, Catherine and Letherby, Gayle (2001) 'Managing a Disrupted Lifecourse: issues of identity and emotion work' *Health* 5:1

Farrington, David, P. and Morris, Allison, M. (eds) 'Sex, Sentencing and Reconviction' *British Journal of Criminology*, 23 (3), pp 229–248

Fausto-Sterling, Anne (1993) "The five sexes: Why male and female are not enough" *The Sciences* (March-April): 20–24

Fausto-Sterling, Anne (2000) *Sexing the Body: Gender Politics and the Construction of Sexuality* New York, Basic Books

Ferguson, Kathy (1984) *The Feminist Case Against Bureaucracy* Philadelphia, Temple University Press

Ferguson, Marjorie (1985) *Forever Feminine: Women's Magazines and the Cult. of Femininity* Brookfield, VT: Gower, Foss

Figueroa, Mark (forthcoming) 'Male Privilege and Male Academic Underperformance in Jamaica' in Rhoda Reddock, (ed) *The Construction of Caribbean Masculinity* Kingston, Jamaica, The Press, UWI

Figueroa, Mark (2000) 'Making sense of male experience: the case of academic underachievement in the English-speaking Caribbean' *IDS Bulletin*, 31 (2) Brighton, University of Sussex

Finch, Janet (1983) *Married to the job: wives' incorporation in men's work* London, Allen and Unwin

Finch, Janet (1984) "It's Great to Have Someone to Talk to: the ethics and politics of interviewing women" in Colin Bell and Helen Roberts (eds) *Social Researching: politics, problems, practice* London, Routledge and Kegan Paul

Finch, Janet (1984) 'Community Care: Developing Non-Sexist Alternatives' *Critical Social Policy*, 9

Finch, Janet and Groves Dulcie (1980) 'Community care and the Family: A Case for Equal Opportunities' *Journal of Social Policy*, 9 (4), pp 487–511

Finch, Janet and Groves Dulcie (1983) (eds) *A Labour of Love: Women, Work and Caring*, London, Routledge and Kegan Paul

Finlay, Andrew (1996) 'Teenage Pregnancy, Romantic Love and Social Science: an uneasy relationship' in Veronica James and Jon Gabe *Health and the Sociology of Emotion* Oxford, Blackwell

Firestone, Shulamith (1971) *The Dialectic of Sex, the Case for Feminist Revolution* New York, Jonathan Cape

Flax, Jane (1987) "Postmodernism and gender relation in feminist theory" *Signs: Journal of Women in Culture and Society* 12 pp 334–51

Fletcher, Richard (1997) *Improving Boys' Education: a manual for schools* Newcastle, Australia, University of Newcastle

Ford, Maureen. R. and Lowery, Carol. R. (1986) '"Gender Differences in Moral Reasoning": A Comparison of the Use of Justice and Care Orientations' *Journal of Personality and Social Psychology*, 50 (4) pp 777–783

Foucault, Michel (1980) 'Truth and Power' in Colin Gorden (ed) *Power/Knowledge: Selected Interviews and Other Writings, 1972–1977* New York, Pantheon

Foucault, Michel (1984[1981][1976]) *The History of Sexuality Vol 1: An Introduction* Harmondsworth, Penguin

Fox, Kate and Rickards, Leicha (2004) *Sport and leisure: Results from the sport and leisure module of the 2002 General Household Survey* London, Office of National Statistics

Frampton, Caelie, Kinsman, Gary, Thompson, Andrew and Tilleczek, Kate (2006) *Sociology for Changing the World: Social Movements/Social Research* Nova Scotia Canada, Fernwood Publishing

Francis, Becky (2000) *Boys, Girls and Achievement* London, RoutledgeFalmer

Fraser, Marian and Greco, Marcia (eds) (2005) *The Body: a reader* London, Routledge

Fraser, Nancy (1989) *Unruly Practices: Power, Discourse and Gender in Contemporary Social Theory* Minneapolis, University of Minnesota Press

Fraser, Nancy (1997) 'After the Family Wage: A Post Industrial Thought experiment' in Nancy Fraser (ed) *Justice Interupp tus: Critical Reflections on the 'Postsocialist' Condition* London, Routledge

Freeman, Carla (2000) *High Tech and High Heels in the Global Economy* Durnham, NC, Duke University Press

Freeman, T. (2003) 'Loving Fathers or "Deadbeat Dads: the crisis of fatherhood in popular culture' in Sarah Earle and Gayle Letherby (eds) *Gender, Identity and Reproduction: social perspectives* Basingstoke, Palgrave Macillan

Freire, Paulo (1970) *The Pedagogy of the Oppressed* Harmondsworth, Penguin

Freud, Sigmund (1905/1991) " Three Essays on the Theory of Sexuality" reprinted in *On Sexuality: Three Essays on the Theory of Sexuality and Other Works* The Penguin Freud Library, Vol. 7 pp 33–169. London, Penguin

Freud, Sigmund (1925/1991) "Some Psychical Consequences of the Anatomical Distinction Between the Sexes" reprinted in *On Sexuality: Three Essays on the Theory of Sexuality and Other Works* The Penguin Freud Library, Vol. 7 pp 323–343). London, Penguin

Freud, Sigmund (1931/1991) "Female Sexuality" reprinted in *On Sexuality: Three Essays on the Theory of Sexuality and Other Works* The Penguin Freud Library, Vol. 7 pp 367–392. London, Penguin

Friedan, Betty (1963) *The Feminine Mystique* New York, W.W. Norton and Company Inc.

Frissen, Valerie (1995) 'Gender is Calling: some reflections on past, present and future uses of the telephone' in Grint,

Keith and Gill, Rosalind (eds) *The Gender-Technology Relation: contemporary theory and research* London, Taylor and Francis

Frith, Hannah and Kitzinger, Celia (1998) 'Emotion Work as a Participant Resource: a feminist analysis of young women's talk-in-interaction' *Sociology* 32(2) 299–320

Frith, Katherine Toland and Mueller, Barbara (2000) *Advertising and Society: global issues* New York, Peter Lang

Frosh, Stephen (1991) *Identity Crisis: modernity, psychoanalysis and the self* Basingstoke, MacMillan Education

Frosh, Stephen, Phoenix, Ann and Pattman, Rob (2002) *Young Masculinities: understanding boys in contemporary society* Basingstoke, Palgrave

Fuller, Mary (1980) 'Black girls in a London comprehensive school' in Rosemary Deem (ed) *Schooling for Women's Work* London, Routledge and Kegan Paul

Fuss, Diana (1990) *Essentially Speaking: Feminism, Nature and Difference* London, Routledge

Gaines, Jane and Herzog, Charlotte (1990) 'Introduction: fabricating the female body' in Jane Gaines and Charlotte Herzog (eds) *Fabrications: costume and the female body* London, Rougledge

Gallie, Duncan, Gershuny, Johnathon and Vogler, Carolyn (1994) 'Unemployment, the household and social networks' in Duncan Gallie, Catherine Marsh and Carolyn Vogler (eds) *Social Change and the Experience of Unemployment* Oxford, Oxford University Press

Gamarnikov, Eva, Morgan, David, Purvis, June and Taylorson, Daphne (1983) *The Public and the Private* London, Heinemann

Gamman, L. and Marshment, M. (1988) *The Female Gaze* London, Women's Press

Gathorne-Hardy, Flora (1999) 'Accommodating difference: social justice, disability and the design of affordable housing' in Ruth Butler and Hester Parr (eds) *Mind and Body Spaces: Geographies of Illness, Impairment and Disability* London, Routledge

Gavanas, Anna (2004) 'Domesticating Masculinity and Masculinizing Domesticity in Contemporary US Fatherhood Politics' *Social Politics*, 11 (2), pp 247–266

Gavey, Nicola (2005) *Just sex? The Cultural Scaffolding of Rape* London, Routledge

Gelb, Joyce and Palley, Marian Lief (1982) *Women and Public Policies* Princeton, Princeton University Press

Gelsthorpe, Lorraine and Morris, Alison (1990) *Feminist Perspectives in Criminology* Buckingham, Open University Press

Gergen, Mary (2001) *Feminist Reconstructions of Psychology: Narrative, Gender and Performance* London, Sage

Gergen, Mary and Davis, Sara (eds) (1997) *Toward a new psychology of gender* New York, Routledge

Ghorashi, Halleh (2005) "Layered Meanings of Community: Experiences of Iranian Women Exiles in 'Irangeles'" in Tine Davids and Francien van Driel (eds) *The Gender Question in Globalization. Changing Perspectives and Practices* Hants England, Ashgate Publishing, pp 197–213

Giddens, Anthony (1992) *The Transformation of Intimacy: sexuality, love and eroticism in modern societies* Cambridge, Polity

Giller, Joan, Bracken, Patrick and Kabaganda (1991) 'Uganda: War, women and rape' *Lancet*, 337, p604

Gillespie, Rosemary (2000) 'When No Means No: disbelief, disregard and deviance as discourses of voluntary childlessness' *Women's Studies International Forum* 23(2)

Gilligan, Carol (1982) *In a Different Voice: Psychological Theory and Women's Development* Cambridge, MA: Harvard University Press

Gilmore, David (1993) *Manhood in the Making. Cultural Concepts of Masculinity* New Haven, CT, Yale University Press

Githens, Marianne and Prestage, Jewel (1977) *A Portrait of Marginality: The Political Behavior of the American Woman* London, Longman

Glucksmann, Miriam (2000) *Cotton and Casuals: the Gendered Organization of Labour in Time and Space* Durham, Sociology Press

Goddard, Victoria (1987) "Honour and Shame: the control of women's sexuality and group identity in Naples" in Pat Caplan (ed) *The Cultural Construction of Sexuality* London: Tavistock Publications, pp 166–192

Goddard-Spear, Margaret (1989) 'Differences between the Written Work of Boys and Girls' *British Educational Research Journal*, 15 (3), pp 271–277

Goffman, Erving ([1976] 1979) *Gender Advertisements* New York, Harper & Row

Goldscheider, Frances K., Kaufman, Gayle (1996) 'Fertility and Commitment: Bringing Men Back In' *Population and Development Review*, Vol. 22, Supplement: Fertility in the United States: New Patterns, New Theories

Goot, Murray and Reid, Elizabeth (1974) 'Women and Voting Studies: Mindless Matrons or Sexist Scientism?' *Sage Professional Papers in Contemporary Political Sociology*, vol 1, London, Sage

Gordon, Linda (1990) 'The new feminist scholarship on the welfare state' in Linda Gordon (ed) *Women, the State and Welfare* Madison, University of Wisconsin Press

Gore, Jennifer (2003) 'What We Can Do For You! What Can "We" Do for "you"? Struggling Over Empowerment in Critical and Feminist Pedagogies' in Antonio Darder; Marta Baltodano and Rodolfo D Torres (eds) *The Critical Pedagogy Reader* New York, RoutledgeFalmer

Gough, Brendan (1998) 'Men and the discursive reproduction of sexism: repertoires of difference and equality' *Feminism & Psychology*, 8(1) pp 25–50

Graham, Hilary (1984) *Women, Health and the Family* Brighton, Wheatsheaf

Graham, Hilary (1988) 'Caring: a Labour of Love' in Janet Finch and Dulcie Groves (eds) *A Labour of Love* London, Routledge and Kegan Paul

Grammenos, Stefanos (2003) *Feasibility Study – Comparable Statistics in the Care of Dependent Adults in the European Union* Luxembourg, Office for Official Publications of the European Communities

Gramsci, Antonio (1998) *Selections from the Prison Notebooks* edited and translated by Quintin Hoare and Geoffrey Nowell Smith, London, Lawrence and Wishart

Gray, John (1993) *Men are from Mars, Women are from Venus: A practical guide for Improving Communications and Getting What you Want in your Relationships* London, Thorson

Grech, Joyoti (1993) 'Resisting War Rape in Bangladesh' *Trouble and Strife*, 26 pp 17–21

Green, Eileen, Hebron, Sandra and Woodward, Diana (1990) *Women's Leisure, What Leisure?* Basingstoke, Macmillan

Greer, Germaine (1971) *The female eunuch* St. Albans, Paladin

Greil. Arthur L. (1999) 'Infertility and Psychological Distress: A Critical Review of the Literature' *Social Science and Medicine* 45

Griffin, Christine (1989) 'I'm Not a Women's Libber but . . . : feminism, consciousness and identity' in Shevington, S. and Baker, D. (eds) *The Social Identity of Women* London, Sage

Griffin, Christine (1985) *Typical Girls? Young women from school to the job market* London, Routledge and Kegan Paul

Griffin, Susan (1979) *Rape: The Power of Consciousness* New York, Harper and Row

Griffin, Susan (1983) 'Introduction' in Léonie Caldecott and Stephanie Leland (eds) *Reclaim the Earth Women speak Out for Life on Earth* London, The Women's Press

Grimshaw, Patricia, Lake, Marilyn, McGrath, Ann and Quartly, Marian (1994) *Creating a Nation: A Dramatic New History That Challenges the Conventional View of Australia's Past as a Creation of White Men of British Descent* Ringwood, Victoria, Penguin

Grosz, Elizabeth (1994) *Volatile Bodies: Towards a Corporeal Feminism* Bloomington and Indianapolis, Indiana University Press

Gutmann Matthew (1997a) 'Trafficking in Men: The Anthropology of Masculinity' *Annual Review of Anthropology*, Vol 26: 385–409.

Gutmann Matthew (1997b) 'The meanings of Macho. Changing Mexican Male "Idenities"' in Louise Lamphere, Helena Ragoné and Patricia Zavella (eds) *Situated Lives. Gender and Culture in Everyday Life* New York, Routledge, pp 223–234

Guy, James John (2001) *People, Politics and Government. A Canadian Perspective* Toronto, Prentice Hall

Hague, Euan (1997) 'Rape, Power and Masculinity; The Construction of Gender and National Identities in the War in Bosnia-Herzegovina' in Ronit Lentin (ed) *Gender and Catastrophe* London, Zed

Haimes, Erica (1990) 'Recreating the Family?: policy considerations relating to the New Reproductive Technologies' in Maureen V. I. McNeil and Steven Yearley (eds) *The New Reproductive Technologies* Hampshire and London, Macmillan

Halford, Susan and Savage, Mike (1998) 'Rethinking restructuring: embodiment, agency and identity in organisational change' in Roger Lee and Jane Wills (eds) *Geographies of Economies* London, Arnold

Hall Carpenter Archives/Lesbian History Project (1989) *Inventing Ourselves: Lesbian Life Stories* London, Routledge

Hall, Stuart (1997) 'The spectacle of the "Other"' in Hall, S. (ed) *Representation: cultural representations and signifying practices* London, Sage

Hanmer, Jalna (1978) 'Violence and the Social Control of Women' in Gary Littlejohn *et al* (eds) *Power and the State* London, Croom Helm

Hannam, June (1993) 'Women, History and Protest' in Diane Richardson and Victoria Robinson *Introduction to Women's Studies* Basingstoke, Macmillan

Haraway, Donna (1991) *Simians, Cyborgs and Women. The Reinvention of Nature* New York City, Routledge

Harding, Sandra (1987) *Feminism and Methodology* Milton Keynes, Open University Press

Harding, Sandra (1993) 'Rethinking standpoint epistemology: what is strong objectivity?' in Linda Alcoff and Elizabeth Porter (eds) *Feminist Epistemologies* New York, Routledge

Hare-Mustin, Rachel. T. and Marecek, Jeannie (eds) (1990) *Making a difference: Psychology and the Construction of Gender* New Haven and London, Yale University Press

Hartmann, Heidi (1980) 'Capitalism, Patriarchy, and Job Segregation by Sex' in Elizabeth Abel and Emily K. Abel (eds) *The Signs Reader: Women, Gender and Scholarship* Chicago, University of Chicago Press

Hawkesworth, Mary (1997) 'Confounding gender' *Signs: Journal of Women in Culture and Society*, 22 (3), pp 649–84

Hawkesworth, Mary (2005) 'Engendering Political Science: An Immodest Proposal' *Politics and Gender*, 1 (1), pp 141–157

Haworth, Abigail (2005) 'And the Winner of Miss Plastic Surgery Is . . .' *Marie Claire*, November

Hayek, Frederik (1976) (originally 1944) *Road to Serfdom* London, Routledge and Kegan Paul

Hayes, Bernadette C. and Prior, Pauline M. (2003) *Gender and Health Care in the UK: exploring the stereotypes* Houndsmills, Palgrave

Hays, Sharon (1996) *The Cultural Contradictions of Motherhood* Yale, Yale University Press

Haywood, Les, Kew, Francis, Bramham, Peter, Spink, John, Capenhurst, John and Henry, Ian (1995) (eds) *Understanding Leisure* Cheltenham, Stanley Thorne Publishers

Hearn, Jeff (1982) 'Notes on Patriarchy, Professionalism and the Semi-Professionals' *Sociology* 26

Hearn, Jeff (1996) 'Is masculinity dead? A critique of the concept of masculinity/masculinities' in Mairtin Mac An Ghaill (ed) *Understanding Masculinities* Buckingham, Open University Press

Hearn, Jeff (1987a) 'Changing Men's Studies' *AchillesHeel*, 8, http://www.achillesheel.freeuk.com/article08_11.html accessed June 2006

Hearn, Jeff (1987b) *The Gender of Oppression. Men, Masculinities and the Critique of Marxism* Brighton, Harverster Wheatsheaf

Hearn, Jeff (1998) *The Violences of Men: How Men Talk About and How Agencies Respond to Men's Violence to Women* London, Sage

Hearn, Jeff (2001) 'Critical Studies on Men in four parts of the World' *NIKK magasin*, 3, pp 12–15

Hearn, Jeff (2004) 'From hegemonic masculinity to the hegemony of men' *Feminist Theory*, 5 (1), pp 49–72

Hearn, Jeff (2006) 'From masculinities back to men: tracing diverse psychological, social and political threads' *The Psychology of Women Section Review*, Vol. 8(1) pp 38–52

Hearn, J. Pringle, K., Muller, U., Oleksay, E., Lattu, E., Chernova, J., Ferguson, H., Gullvag Holter, O., Kolga, V., Novikova, I., Ventimiglia, C., Olsvik, E., and Tallberg, T. (2002) 'Critical Studies on men in ten European Countries' *Men and Masculinity* 4:4, pp 308–408

Hearn, Jeff, Sheppard, Deborah L., Tancred-Sheriff, Peta and Burrell, Gibson (1989) *The Sexuality of Organization* London, Sage

Heidensohn, Frances (1985) *Women and Crime* London, Macmillan

Heidensohn, Frances (1994) 'Fairer Cops?: questions about women in policing' in *Criminal Justice Matters*, 17, Autumn

Heidensohn, Frances (2000) *Sexual Politics and Social Control* Buckingham, Open University Press

Hekman, Susan (1990) *Gender and Knowledge: elements of a postmodern feminism* Cambridge, Polity

Henn, Matt, Weinstein, Mark and Forrest, Sarah (2005) 'Uninterested Youth? Young People's Attitudes towards party Politics in Britain' *Political Studies*, 53, pp 556–578

Herek, Gregory M. and Berrill, Kevin T. (1992) *Hate Crimes: Confronting Violence against Lesbians and Gay Men* London, Sage

Hermes, Joke (1995) *Reading Women's Magazines* London, Routledge

Hernes, Helga Maria (1984) 'Women and the welfare state: the transition from private to public dependence' in Harriet Holter (ed) *Patriarchy in a Welfare Society* Oslo, Universitetsforlag

Hernes, Helga Maria (1987) *Welfare State and Woman Power* Oslo, Norwegian University Press

Hester, Stephen and Eglin, Peter (1992) *A Sociology of Crime* London, Ontario, Routledge

Hibbett, Angelika (2002) *Ethnic Minority Women in the UK* London Women and Equality Unit, http://www.womenandequalityunit.gov.uk accessed July 2004

Hibbett, Angelika and Meager, Nigel (2003) 'Key indicators of women's position in Britain' *Labour Market Trends*, 111 (10), pp 503–512, available at www.statistics.gov.uk

Higher Education Statistics Agency (HESA) (2004) *Higher Education Statistics* http://www.hesa.ac.uk/products/pubs/home.htm, accessed September 2006

Hill-Collins, Patricia (1989) 'Black Feminist Thought' *Signs: Journal of Women in Culture and Society* 14, 4 pp 745–73

Hill Collins, Patricia (1990) *Black Feminist Thought: knowledge consciousness and the politics of empowerment* Unwin Hyman, Boston

Himmelweit, Susan (1988) 'More Than a Woman's Right to Choose?' *Feminist Review* 29, Spring

Hirst, John (1995) 'A Critique of 'Creating a Nation'' *Quadrant*, 34

Hirst, Julia (2004) 'Sexuality' in Taylor, Gary and Spencer, Steve (eds) *Social Identities: multidisciplinary approaches* London, Routledge

Hobsbawm, Eric (1971) 'From Social History to a History of Society' *Daedalus*, 100 (1)

Hochschild, Arlie (1983) *The Managed Heart: Commercialisation of Human Feeling* Berkley, University of California Press

Hochschild, Arlie R. (1990) *The Second Shift* London, Piakus

Hockey, Jenny (1993) 'Women and Health' in Diane Richardson and Victoria Robinson (eds) *Introducing Women's Studies: feminist theory and practice* London, Macmillan

Hodgson, Dorothy L (2001) "Introduction. Of Modernity/Modernities, Gender and Ethnography" in Dorothy Hodgson (ed) *Gendered Modernities. Ethnographic Perspectives* New York, Palgrave, pp 1–23

Holcomb, Briavel (1986) 'Geography and Urban Women' *Urban Geography*, 7, pp 448–456

Holland, Patricia (1991) 'Introduction: history, memory and the family album' in Spence, J. and Holland, P. (eds) *Family Snaps: the meanings of domestic photography* London, Virago

Holland, Janet, Ramazanoglu, Caroline, Sharpe, Sue and Thomson, Rachel (1998) *The male in the head: young people, heterosexuality and power* London, The Tufnell Press

Holland, Patricia (2004) 'The Politics of the Smile: 'soft news' and the sexualisation of the popular press' in Cynthia Carter and Linda Steiner (eds) *Critical Readings in the Media* Maidenhead, Open University Press

Hollway, Wendy (1989) *Subjectivity and method in psychology* London, Sage

Holter, Øystein Gullvåg (1995) 'Theory Reconsidered' in Tordis Borchgrevink and Øystein Gullvåg Holter (eds) *Labour of Love: Beyond the Self-Evidence of Everyday Life* Aldershot, Avebury

Home Office (HO) (1957) *The Wolfenden Committee's Report on Homosexual Offences and Prostitution* London, HMSO

Home Office (HO) (1998) *Supporting Families* London, Home Office

Home Office (1999) *Criminal Statistics* London, HMSO

Horne, John (2004) 'Masculinity in politics and war in the age of nation-states and world wars, 1850–1950' in Stefan Dudnick, Karen Hagemann and John Tosh (eds) *Masculinities in Politics and War Gendering Modern History* Manchester, Manchester University Press

Hoskyns, Catherine (1996) *Integrating Gender: Women, Law and Politics in the European Union* London, Verso

Hostettler, Eve, Davin, Anna and Alexander, Sally (1979) 'Labouring Women, A Reply to Eric Hobsbawn' *History Workshop Journal*

House of Commons (1993) Home Affairs Committee on Domestic Violence, London, HMSO

Humm, Maggie (1995) *The Dictionary of Feminist Theory* Hemel Hempstead, Prentice Hall/Harvester Wheatsheaf

Hunt, Catherine (2004) 'Alice Arnold of Coventry: Trade Unionism and Municipal Politics' unpublished PhD thesis, Coventry, University of Coventry

Hyde, Janet S. (1981) 'How large are cognitive gender differences? A meta-analysis using $w2$ and d' *American Psychologist*, 36, pp 892–901

Hyde, Janet S. and Linn, Marcia C. (eds) (1986) *The psychology of gender: Advances through meta-analysis* Baltimore, John Hopkins

Hyde, Janet S. and Linn, Marcia C. (1988) 'Gender differences in verbal ability: A meta-analysis' *Psychological Bulletin*, 104, pp 53–69

Hyde, Janet S., Fennema, Elizabeth and Lamon, Susan J. (1990) 'Gender differences in mathematics performance: A meta-analysis' *Psychological Bulletin*, 107, pp 139–155

id21 Research Highlight (2004) 'Far from the front line: how likely is universal primary completion by 2015?' http://www.id21.org/education/e1bb1g1.html accessed November 2006

Imrie, Rob (1996) *Disability and the City: International Perspectives* London, Paul Chapman

Imrie, Rob (2004) 'Disability, embodiment and the meaning of the home' *Housing Studies*, 19, pp 685–690

Inglehart, Ronald and Norris, Pippa (2000) 'The Developmental Theory of the Gender Gap: Women and Men's Voting Behavior in Global Perspective' *International Political Science Review Special Issue: Women and Representation*, 21 (4), pp 441–462

Itzin, Catherine (1986) 'Media Images of Women: the social construction of ageism and sexism' in Sue Wilkinson (ed) *Feminist Social Psychology: developing theory and practice* Milton Keynes, Open University Press

Itzin, Catherine (1992) *Pornography: women, violence and civil liberties* Oxford, Oxford University Press

Jackson, D. (1990) *Unmasking Masculinity: a critical autobiography* London, Routledge

Jackson, Peter (1989) *Maps of Meaning* London, Unwin Hyman

Jackson, Peter (1991) 'The cultural politics of masculinity: towards a social geography' *Transactions of the Institute of British Geographers*, 16, pp 199–213

Jackson, Peter, Stevenson, Nick and Brooks, Kate (1999) 'Making sense of men's lifestyle magazines' *Environment and Planning D: Society and Space*, 17, pp 353–368

Jackson, Peter, Stevenson, Nick and Brooks, Kate (2001) *Making Sense of Men's Magazines* Cambridge, Polity Press

Jackson, Stevi (1992) 'The Amazing Deconstructing Woman' *Trouble and Strife* 25 pp 25–31

Jackson, Stevi (1993) 'Women and the Family' in Diane Richardson and Victoria Robinson (eds) *Introducing Women's Studies* Houndsworth, Macmillan

Jackson, Stevi (1997) 'Women, Marriage and Family Relationships' in Victoria Robinson and Diane Richardson (eds) *Introducing Women's Studies* Houndsmills, Macmillan

Jackson, Stevi (1999) 'Feminist Sociology and Sociological Feminism' *Sociological Research Online* www.socresonline.org.uk/4/3/jackson.html

Jackson, Stevi and Scott, Sue (eds) (1996) *Feminism and Sexuality: a reader* Edinburgh, Edinburgh University Press

Jackson, Stevi and Scott, Sue (eds) (2002) *Gender: A Sociological Reader* London, Routledge

Jackson, S. and Cram, F. (2003) 'Disrupting the sexual double standard: young women's talk about heterosexuality' *British Journal of Social Psychology* 42(1)

Jackson, Sue (2004) 'Crossing Boundaries' *Journal of International Women's Studies*, 5 (3), pp 1–5

Jacobs, Susie Jacobson, Ruth and Marchbank, Jennifer (eds) (2000) *States of Conflict: Gender, Violence and Resistance* London, Zed

James, Nicky (1989) 'Emotional Labour: skills and work in the social regulation of feelings' *Sociological Review* 37(1): 5–52

Jamieson, Lynn (1999) 'Intimacy transformed?: a critical look at the "Pure Relationship"' *Sociology* 33: 3

Jayaratne, Toby Epstein (1983) 'The Value of Quantitative Methodology for Feminist Research' in Gloria Bowles and Renate Duelli Klein (eds) *Theories of Women's Studies* Boston MA, Routledge and Kegan Paul

Jayaratne, Toby Epstein and Stewart, Abigail J. (1991) 'Quantitative and Qualitative Methods in the Social Sciences: current feminist issues and practical strategies' in

Margaret M. Fonow and Judith A. Cook (eds) *Beyond Methodology: feminist scholarship as lived experience* Bloomington, IN, Indiana University

Jeffreys, Patricia and Basu, Amrita (1998) *Appropriating Gender: Women's Activism and Politicized Religion in South Asia* New York, Routledge

Jeffreys, Sheila (1990) *Anticlimax: A feminist perspective on the sexual revolution* London, The Women's Press

Jeffries, Sheila (2005) *Beauty and Misogyny: harmful cultural practices in the West* London, Routledge

Jelen, Ted G., Thomas, Sue and Wilcox, Clyde (1994) 'The Gender Gap in Comparative Perspective' *European Journal of Political Research*, 25, pp 171–186

Jensen, Robert (2004) 'Knowing Pornography' in Cynthia Carter and Linda Steiner (eds) *Critical Readings in the Media* Maidenhead, Open University Press

Jewkes, Yvonne and Letherby, Gayle (2002a) (eds) *Criminology: a reader* London, Sage

Jewkes, Yvonne and Letherby, Gayle (2002b) 'Mothering and Non-Mothering, Identities for Women in Prison' *The Prison Service Journal* 139

Johnson, Katherine (2007) 'Transsexualism: Diagnostic Dilemmas, Transgender Politics and the Future of Transgender Care' in Victoria Clarke and Elizabeth Peel (eds) *Out in Psychology: lesbian, gay, bisexual, trans and queer perspectives* London, Wiley

Johnson, Louise (1989) 'Embodying geography – some implications of considering the sexed body in space' *Proceedings of the 15th New Zealand Geographer's Conference* Dunedin

Johnson-Bailey, Juanita (2001) 'The Power of Race and Gender, Black Women's Struggle and Survival in Higher Education' in Ronald M. Cervero and Arthur L. Wilson and Associates (eds) *Power in Practice: Adult education and the Struggle for Knowledge and Power* San Francisco, Jossey-Bass

Jones, Kathleen B. and Jonasdittir, Anna G. (eds) (1998) *The Political Interests of Gender: Developing Research with a Feminist Face* London, Sage

Jones, M. (1991) 'Gender stereotyping in advertisements' *Teaching of Psychology* 18, 231–233

Jordanova, Ludmilla (1989) *Sexual Visions: Images of Gender in Science and Medicine between the Eighteenth and Twentieth Centuries* New York, Harvestor Wheatsheaf

Josephson, Jyl J. and Tolleson-Rinehart, Sue (2000) 'Introduction. Gender, Sex and American Political Life' in Sue Tolleson-Rinehart and Jyl J. Josephson (eds) *Gender and American Politics. Women, Men, and the Political Process* Armonk, NY, ME Sharpe

Kandiyoti, Deniz (1998) 'Gender, Power and Contestation: Rethinking Bargaining with Patriarchy' in Cecile Jackson and Ruth Pearson (eds) *Feminist Visions of Development* London, Routledge

Kann, Mark E. (1999) *The Gendering of American Politics. Founding Mothers, Founding Fathers and Political Patriarchy* Westport, CT, Praeger

Kaplan, Ann E. (1984) 'Is the Gaze Male?' in Ann Snitow, Christine Stansell and Sharon Thompson (eds) *Desire: the politics of sexuality* London, Virago

Kaplan, Ann E. (1992) *Motherhood and Representation: the mother in popular culture and melodrama* London, Routledge

Katz, Jackson (1995) 'Advertising and the Construction of Violent White Masculinity' in G. Dines and J. M. Humez (eds) *Gender, Race and Class in the Media: a text reader* Thousand Oaks, CA Sage

Katz Rothman, Barbara (1988) *The Tentative Pregnancy: prenatal diagnosis and the future of motherhood* London, Pandora

Kaufman, Michael (1994) 'Men, Feminism and Men's Contradicttory Expereinces of Power' in Harry Brod and Michael Kaufman (eds) *Theorizing Masculinities* Thousand Oaks, CA, Sage

Kaul, Hjordis (1991) 'Who Cares? Gender Inequality and Care Leave in the Nordic Countries' *Acta Sociologica*, 34, pp 115–125

Keddie, Amanda (2005) 'A Framework for "Best Practice" in Boys' Education: key requisite knowledges and productive pedagogies' *Pedagogy, Culture and Society*, 13 (1), pp 59–74

Keith, Michael (1995) 'Making the street visible: placing racial violence in context' *New Community* 21, pp 551–565

Kellner, David (1995) *Media Culture* London, Routledge

Kelly, Liz (1988) *Surviving Sexual Violence* Cambridge, Polity Press

Kelly, Liz, Burton, Sheila and Regan, Linda (1994) 'Researching Women's Lives or Studying Women's Oppression? Reflections on What Constitutes Feminist Research' in Mary Maynard and June Purvis (eds) *Researching Women's Lives From a Feminist Perspective* London, Taylor and Francis

Kempadoo, Kamala (1994) 'Prostitution, Marginality and Empowerment: Caribbean women in the trade' *Beyond Law* 5(14)

Kessler, Esther (2002, originally 1998) 'Defining and Producing Genitals' from *Lessons from the Intersexed* in Jackson, Sue and Scott, Sue (eds) *Gender: a sociological reader* London, Routledge

Kessler, Suzanne and McKenna, Wendy (1985) *Gender: An ethnomethodological approach* Chicago, USA: University of Chicago Press

Kimmel, Michael (1994) 'Masculinity as homophobia: fear, shame, and silence in the construction of gender identity' in Harry Brod and Michael Kaufman (eds) *Theorizing Masculinities* Thousand Oaks, CA, Sage

Kimmel, Michael (1995) (ed) *The Politics of Manhood. Profeminist Men Respond to the Mythopoetic Movement (and the Mythopoetic Leaders Respond)* Philadelphia, Temple University Press

Kirby, Kathleen M. (1995) *Indifferent Boundaries: Spatial Concepts of Human Subjectivity* London, Guilford Press

Kirby, Kathleen M. (1996) 'Cartographic vision and the limits of politics' in Nancy Duncan (ed) *BodySpace: Destabilising Geographies of Gender and Sexuality* London, Routledge

Kirby, Vicki (1992) *Addressing Essentialism Differently… Some Thoughts on the Corpo-real*, Occasional Paper Series, No. 4, University of Waikato, Department of Women's Studies

Kitzinger, Celia and Wilkinson, Sue (2006) 'Equal Marriage' at http://equalmarriagerights.org/maindefault. html, accessed August 2006

Kitzinger, Celia (1992) 'Birth and violence against women: generating hypothesis from women's accounts of unhappiness after childbirth' in Helen Roberts (ed) *Women's Health Matters* London, Routledge

Kohlberg, Lawrence (1958) *The Development of Modes of Moral Thinking and Choice in the Years 10 to 16* Chicago, University of Chicago

Kohlberg, Lawrence (1966) 'A cognitive-developmental analysis of children's sex-role concepts and attitudes' in E. E. Maccoby (ed) *The Development of Sex Differences* Stanford, CA: Stanford University Press

Kondo, Dorinne K. (1990) *Crafting Selves. Power, Gender and Discourses of Identity in a Japanese Workplace* Chicago, University of Chicago Press

Korpi, Walter and Palme, Joakim (1998) 'The paradox of redistribution and strategies of equality: Welfare state institutions, inequality and poverty in western countries' *American Sociological Review*, 63 (5), pp 661–687

Koskela, Hille (1997) 'Bold walk and breakings: women's spatial confidence versus fear of violence' *Gender, Place and Culture*, 4:3, pp 301–319

Koskela, Hille and Pain, Rachel (2000) 'Revisiting fear and place: women's fear of attack and the built environment' *Geoforum*, 31, pp 269–280

Krenske, Leigh and McKay, Jim (2000) 'Hard and heavy: gender and power in heavy metal music subculture' *Gender, Place and Culture*, 7:3, pp 287–304

Kulick, Don (1998) *The gender of Brazilian Transgendered Prostitutes* Chicago, Chicago University Press

Kulick, Don and Wilson, Margaret (1995) (eds) *Taboo: Sex, Identity and Erotique Subjectivity in anthropological fieldwork* London, Routledge

Lamphere, Louise, Ragoné, Helena and Zavella, Patricia (1997) 'Introduction' *Situated Lives. Gender and Culture in Everyday Life* New York: Routledge, pp 1–22

Land, Hilary (1978) 'Who cares for the family?' *Journal of Social Policy*, 7 (3), pp 257–284

Lanier, Charles C. (2003) '"Who's Doing the Time Here, Me or My Children?" Addressing the issues implicated by mounting numbers of fathers in prison' in Jeffrey I. Ross and Stephen C. Richards (eds) *Convict Criminology* Belmont USA: Thomson Wadsworth

Lash, Scott and Urry, John (1994) *Economies of Signs and Spaces* London, Sage

Laurie, Nina, Dwyer, Claire, Holloway, Sarah and Smith Fiona (1999) *Geographies of New Femininities* Harlow, Longman

Laws, Sophie (1990) *Issues of Blood: the politics of menstruation* Basingstoke, Macmillan

Lawson, Helen M. (2000) *Ladies on the Lot: women, car sales and the pursuit of the American Dream* Maryland, Rowman and Littlefield Publishers Inc.

Layika, F. (1996) 'War crimes against women in Rwanda' in Niamh Reilly (ed) *Without Reservation: The Beijing Tribunal on Accountability for Women's Human Rights* New Jersey, center for Women's Global Leadership

Leach, Edmund (1967) *A Runaway World?* London, BBC Publications

Leacock, Eleanor and Safa, Helen (eds) *Women's Work* Mass., Bergin and Garvey Publishers

Lee, Dorothy (1990) 'Chatterboxes' *Child Education*, 67 (7), pp 26–27

Lees, Sue (1986) *Losing Out: Sexuality and adolescent girls* London, Hutchinson

Lees, Sue (1993) *Sugar and Spice: Sexuality and Adolescent Girls* London, Penguin

Lee-Treweek, Geraldine and Linkogle, Stephanie (eds) (2000) *Danger in the Field: risk and ethics in social research* London, Routledge

Leibowitz, Lila (1986) 'In the Beginning … The Origins of the Sexual Division of Labour and the Development of the First Human Societies' in Stephanie Coontz and Peta Henderson (eds) *Women's Work, Men's Property: The Origins of Gender and Class* London, Verso

Office for National Statistics (2001) *Labour Force Survey* http://www.statistics.gov.uk accessed July 2005

Leidner, Robin (1991) 'Serving hamburgers and selling insurance' *Gender and Society*, 5, pp 154–177

Leidner, Robin (1993) *Fast Food: Fast Talk: The Routinisation of Everyday Life* Berkeley, CA, University of California Press

Lentin, Ronit (1997) (ed) *Gender and Catastrophe* London, Zed

Leonard, Eileen (1982) *A Critique of Criminology Theory: women, crime and society* London, Longman

Lerner, Gerda (1981) *The Majority Finds Its Past* Oxford, Oxford University Press

Lesbian History Group (1989) *Not a Passing Phase, Reclaiming Lesbians in History 1840–1985* London, Virago

Letherby, Gayle (1994) 'Mother or Not, Mother or What?: problems of definition and identity' *Women's Studies International* Forum 17:5

Letherby, Gayle (1999) 'Other than Mother and Mothers as Others: the experience of motherhood and non-motherhood in relation to 'infertility' and 'involuntary childlessness' *Women's Studies International* Forum 22:3

Letherby, Gayle and Marchbank, Jen (1999) '"I don't want to be empowered, just give me a reading pack!" Student Responses and Resistance to Different Forms of Teaching and Assessment' in Martyn Pearl and Pritnam Singh (eds) *Equal Opportunities in the Curriculum* Oxford, The Oxford Centre for Staff and Learning Development

Letherby, Gayle and Marchbank, Jen (2001) 'Why Do Women's Studies? A Cross England Profile' *Women's Studies International Forum*, 24, pp 587–603

Letherby, Gayle (2003b) '"I didn't think much of this bedside manner but he was very skilled at his job': medical encounters in relation to infertility" in Sarah Earle and Gayle Letherby *Gender Identity and Reproduction: social perspectives* London, Palgrave

Letherby, Gayle and Marchbank, Jen (2003) 'Cyber-chattels: buying brides and babies on the net' in Yvonne, Jewkes, (ed) *Dot.cons: crime, deviance and identity on the internet* Devon, Willan

Letherby, Gayle and Reynolds, Gillian (2005) *Train Tracks, Work, Play and Politics on the Railways* Oxford, Berg

Letherby, Gayle and Shiels, John (2001) '"Isn't He Good but can We Take Her Seriously?" Gendered Expectations in Higher Education' in Pauline Anderson and Jenny Williams (eds) *Identity and Difference in Higher Education 'Outsiders Within'* Aldershot, Ashgate

Lewis, Clare and Pile, Steve (1996) 'Woman, body and space: Rio carnival and the politics of performance' *Gender, Place and Culture*, 3, pp 23–41

Lewis, Jane (1992) 'Gender and the development of welfare regimes' *Journal of European Social Policy*, 2 (3), pp 159–173

Ley, David and Cybriwsky, Roman (1974) 'Urban graffiti as territorial markers' *Annals of the Association of American Geographers*, 64, pp 491–505

Liazos, Alex (2004) *Families: joys, conflicts and changes* London, Paradigm Publishers

Liddington, Jill and Norris, Jill (2000) *One Hand Tied Behind Us: The Rise of the Women's Suffrage Movement* London, Rivers Oram Press/Pandora

Liebling, Helen (2004) 'A Gendered Analysis of the experiences of Ugandan Women War Survivors' unpublished PhD, Warwick, University of Warwick

Liepins, Ruth (2000) 'Making men: the construction and representation of agriculture-based masculinities in Australia and New Zealand' *Rural Sociology*, 65, pp 605–620

Lipton, Richard A. (2005) *Gender, Nature and Nurture* (2nd Edition) Mahwah, New Jersey

Lister, Ruth (1994) 'Dilemmas in engendering citizenship' paper to Crossing Borders Conference, Stockholm, 27–29 May

Lister, Ruth (1997) *Citizenship, Feminist Perspectives* New York, New York University Press

Little, Jo (2002) *Gender and Rural Geography* London, Pearson

Lloyd, Ann (1995) *Doubly Deviant, Doubly Damned: society's treatment of violent women* London, Penguin

Lloyd, Justine and Johnson, Lesley (2004) 'Dream stuff: the postwar home and the Australian Housewife, 1940–60' *Environment and Planning D: Society and Space*, 22, pp 251–272

Longhurst, Robyn (1995) 'The body and geography' *Gender, Place and Culture*, 2:1, pp 97–105

Longhurst, Robyn (1997) '(Dis)embodied geographies' *Progress in Human Geography*, 21, pp 486–501

Longhurst, Robyn (2001) *Bodies: Exploring Fluid Boundaries* London, Routledge

Lorde, Audre (1984) *Sisters, Outsiders: essays and speeches* New York, Crossing Press

Loury, Linda Datcher (1997) 'The Gender Earnings Gap among College-Educated Workers' *Industrial and Labor Relations Review*, 50 (4), pp 580–593

Lovenduski, Joni (1981) 'Toward the Emasculation of Political Science: The Impact of Feminism' in Dale Spender (ed) *Men's Studies Modified: The Impact of Feminism on the Academic Disciplines* Oxford, Pergamon Press

Lovenduski, Joni (1998) 'Gendering research in political science' *Annual Review of Political Science*, 1, pp 333–356

Lovenduski, Joni (2001) 'Women and Politics: Minority Representation or Critical mass?' in Pippa Norris (ed) *Britain Votes 2001*, Oxford, Oxford University Press

Lovenduski, Joni and Randall, Vicky (1993) *Contemporary Feminist Politics: Women and Power in Britain* Oxford, Oxford University Press

Lubelska, Cathy (1991) 'Teaching Methods in Women's Studies: challenging the mainstream' in Jane Aaron and Sylvia Walby (eds) *Out of the Margins: Women's Studies in the Nineties* London, Falmer

Lupton, Deborah (2003) *Medicine as Culture: illness, disease and the body in Western Culture* London, Sage

Lysaght, Karen (2002) 'Dangerous friends and deadly foes – performances of masculinity in the divided city' *Irish Geography*, 35:1, pp 51–62

Macan Ghaill, Máirtín (ed) (1996) *Understanding Masculinities* Buckingham, Open University Press

Macionis, John and Plummer, Ken (2002) *Sociology: a global introduction* (2nd edition) London, Prentice Hall

MacKenzie, Suzanne (1984) 'Editorial introduction' *Antipode*, 16, pp 3–10

MacKinnon, Catherine (1988) 'Feminism, Marxism, method and the state: An agenda for theory' *Signs* 7

MacKinnon, Catherine (1987) *Feminism Unmodified: discourses on life and law* Cambridge MA, Harvard University Press

Mackintosh, James M. (1952) *Housing and Family Life* London, Cassell & Co

MacLean, Mavis and Kurczewski, Jacek (eds) (1994) *Families, Politics and the Law: Perspectives for East and West Europe* Oxford, Clarendon Press

Macleod, Donald (2002) 'Scotland hits participation target' *Education Guardian*, http://education.guardian.co.uk/universityaccess/story/o,,740778,00.html, accessed November 2006

Maguire, Mike, Morgan, Rod and Reiner, Robert (eds) (1997) *The Oxford Handbook of Criminology* (2nd edition) Oxford, Clarendon

Malinowski, Bronislaw (1967 [1914]) *A diary in the strict sense of the term* London, Routledge and Kegan Paul

Mandell, Nancy and Ann Duffy (eds) (2005) *Canadian Families: diversity, conflict and change* Toronto, Nelson, Thomson Canada Ltd

Marchbank, Jennifer (1996) 'The political mobilisation of women's interest issues: The failure of childcare' *Politics*, 16 (1), pp 9–15

Marchbank, Jennifer (2000) *Women, Power and Policy: Comparative Studies of Childcare* London Routledge

Marchbank, Jen and Letherby, Gayle with Lander, Kay, Walker, Angela and Wild, Andrea (2003) 'Empowering and Enabling or Patronising and Pressurising? Opening dialogues between staff and students' *Gender and Education*, 15 (1), pp 75–90

Marchbank, Jen and Letherby, Gayle (2002) 'Offensive and Defensive: Student Support and Higher Education Evaluation' in Gillian Howie and Ashley Tauchert (eds) *Gender, Teaching and Research in Higher Education: Challenges for the 21st Century* Hampshire, Ashgate

Marchbank, Jen and Letherby, Gayle (2006) 'Views and perspectives of Women's Studies: a survey of women and men students' *Gender and Education*, 18 (2), pp 157–182

Marchment, Margaret (1993) 'The Picture is Political: representations of women in contemporary popular culture' in Diane Richardson and Victoria Robinson (eds) *Introducing Women's Studies* London, Macmillan

Marcus, George (1995) "Ethnography In/Of the World System: the Emergence of Multi-Sited Ethnography" *Annual Review of Anthropology*, Vol. 24 pp 95–117

Marsh, Ian, Campbell, Rosie and Keating, Mike (eds) (1998[1984]) *Classic and Contemporary Readings in Sociology* Prentice Hall

Marsh, Ian and Keating, Mike (eds) (2006) *Sociology: making sense of society* Essex, Pearson Education Ltd (third edition)

Marshall, TH. (1950) *Citizenship and Social Class and Other Essays* Cambridge, Cambridge University Press

Mason, Mary-Claire (1993) *Male Infertility: men talking* London, Routledge

Martin, Karin A. (2002[originally 1996 and 2000]) '"I couldn't ever picture myself having sex . . . ": Gender Differences in Sex and Sexual Subjectivity' from 'Puberty, Sexuality and the Self, Girls and Boys at Adolescence' in C. L. Williams. and A. Stein (eds) (2002) *Sexuality and Gender: Blackwell Readers in Sociology* Massachusetts and Oxford, Blackwell

Massey, Doreen (1984) *Spatial Divisions of Labour* London, Macmillan

Matrix (1984) *Making Space: Women and the Man-Made Environment* London, Pluto Press

Maudsley, Henry (1874) 'Sex in mind and in education' *Fortnightly Review*, 15 pp 466–83

Mayall, Berry (2002) *Towards a Sociology of Childhood: thinking from children's lives* Buckingham, Open University Press

Maynard, Mary (1993) 'Violence Towards Women' in Diane Richardson and Victoria Robinson (eds) *Introducing Women's Studies* Basingstoke, Macmillan

Maynard, Mary (1994a) "'Race', gender and the concept of 'difference' in feminist thought" in Haleh, Afshar and Mary Maynard (eds) T*he Dynamics of 'Race' and Gender: some feminist interventions* London, Taylor and Francis

Maynard, Mary (1994b) 'Methods, Practice and Epistemology: the debate about feminism and research' in Mary Maynard and Jane Purvis (eds) *Researching Women's Lives from a Feminist Perspective* London, Taylor and Francis

Maynard, Mary and Purvis, Jane (eds) (1994) *Researching Women's Lives from a Feminist Perspective* London, Taylor and Francis

McAllister, Fiona with Clarke, Lynda (1998) '*A study of childlessness in Britain*' Family Policy Studies Center, Joseph Rowntree Foundation, London

McAllister, Fiona and Letherby, Gayle (forthcoming) 'Invisible Men?: fertility, fatherhood and nonfatherhood' *Sociological Review*

McBride Stetson, Dorothy and Mazur, Amy (eds) (1995) *Comparative State Feminism* London, Sage

McDonald, Lynn (1995) *The Early Origins of the Social Sciences* Montreal, McGill

McDowell, Linda (1983) 'Towards an understanding of the gender division of urban space' *Environment and Planning D: Society and Space*, 1, pp 59–72

McDowell, Linda (1995) 'Body work: heterosexual gender performances in City workplaces' in David Bell and Gill Valentine (eds) *Mapping Desire: Geographies of Sexualities* London, Routledge

McDowell, Linda (1997) *Capital Culture: Gender at Work in the City* Oxford, Blackwell

McDowell, Linda (1999) *Gender, Identity & Place: Understanding Feminist Geographies* Cambridge, Polity Press

McDowell, Linda (2002) 'Transitions to work: masculine identities, youth inequality and labour market change' *Gender, Place and Culture*, 9, 39–59

McDowell, Linda and Court, Gill (1994) 'Performing work: bodily representations in merchant banks' *Environment and Planning D: Society and Space*, 12, pp 727–750

McIntosh, Mary (1981) 'Feminism and Social Policy' *Critical Social Policy*, 1

McKay, Fiona (2004) 'Gender and Political Representation in the UK: The State of the Discipline' *British Journal of Politics and International Relations*, 6 pp 99–120

McKay, Fiona, Myers, Fiona and Brown, Alice (2003) 'Towards a new politics? Women and constitutional change in Scotland' in Alexandra Dobrowolsky and Vivien Hart (eds) *Women Making Constitutions: New Politics and Comparative Perspectives* Basingstoke, Palgrave

McMahon, Anthony (1993) 'Male readings of feminist theory: the psychologisation of sexual politics in the masculinity literature' *Theory and Society*, 22 (5), pp 675–696

McRobbie, Angela (1978) 'Working class girls and the culture of femininity' in Women's Studies Group, Centre for Contemporary Cultural Studies (ed) *Women Take Issue: aspects of women's subordination* London, Hutchinson

McRobbie, Angela (1982) 'The politics of feminist research: between talk, text, and action' *Feminist Review 12*

Mead, Margaret (1928) *The Coming of Age in Samoa : A study of sex in primitive society* New York, Morrow

Mead, Margaret (1930) *Growing up in New Guinea: A comparative study of primitive education* New York City, Blue Ribbon Books

Mead, Margaret (1935) *Sex and Temperament in Three Primitive Societies* Morrow, New York

Mead, Margaret (1962, originally 1949) *Male and Female: A Study of the Sexes in a Changing World* Harmondsworth, Penguin

Mee, Kathleen and Dowling, Robyn (2000) 'Working-class masculinity, suburbia and resistance: David Caesar's Idiot Box' in John Stephens (ed) *Proceedings of the Habitus Conference* Perth, Curtin University of Technology

Mehta, Anna and Bondi, Liz (1999) 'Embodied discourse: on gender and fear of violence' *Gender, Place and Culture*, 6, pp 67–84

Meigs, Anna (1990) 'Multiple Gender Ideologies and Statuses' in Peggy Sanday Reeves and Ruth Gallagher Goodenough (eds) *Beyond the Second Sex, New directions in the Anthropology of Gender* Philadelphia, University of Pennsylvania Press

Merchant, Carolyn (1990) *The Death of Nature: Women, Ecology and the Scientific Revolution* San Fransisco, CA, Harper & Row

Merrit, Sharyne (1977) 'Winners and losers: Sex differences in municipal elections' *American Journal of Political Science*, 21 (4), pp 731–743

Messner, Michael A. (1997) *Politics of Masculinities, Men in Movements* Thousand Oaks, CA, Sage

Michielsens, Magda (2003) 'Feminist Pedagogy' in Sara Goodman, Gill Kirkup and Magda Michielsens (eds) *ICTs in Teaching and Learning Women's Studies* Lund, Sweden, Athena

Miers, Margaret (2000) *Gender Issues and Nursing Practices* Houndsmills, Macmillan Press

Milbrath, Lester W. (1965) *Political Participation* Chicago, Rand McNally

Miles, Agnes (1991) *Women, Health and Medicine* Milton Keynes, Open University Press

Millen, Diane (1997) 'Some methodological and epistemological issues raised by doing feminist research on non-feminist women' *Sociological Research Online* 2, 3: www.socresonline.org.uk/socresonline/2/3/3.html

Miller, Jean Baker (1976) *Towards a New Psychology of Women* Boston, Beacon Press

Millett, Kate (1969) *Sexual Politics St Albans* Hertfordshire, Granada Publishing

Millet, Kate (1971) *Sexual Politics* London, Granta

Mills, C. Wright (1970[1959]) *The Sociological Imagination* Harmondsworth, Penguin

Mills, Jane (1991) *Womanwords: a vocabulary of culture and patriarchal society* London, Virago

Mirlees-Black, C (1999) *Domestic violence: BCS Self-Completion Questionnaire* British Crime Survey, London, Home Office

Mitchell, Juliet (1974) *Psychoanalysis and Women* Harmondsworth, Penguin

Mitchell, Juliet (1984 originally 1966) *Women: The Longest Revolution, Essays in Literature and Psychoanalysis* London, Virago

Mitter, Swasti (1985) *Common Fate, Common Bond* London, Pluto Press

Mizra, Heidi (1992) *Young, Female and Black* London, Routledge

Modleski, Tania (1982) *Loving with a Vengence: mass produced fantasies for women* Hamden CT, Archon Books

Mohanty, Chandra (1988) 'Under Western Eyes: Feminist Scholarship and Colonial Discourses' *Feminist Review*, No.30 Autumn pp 61–88

Moller Oken, Susan (1980) *Women in Western Political Thought* London, Virago

Monk, Janice and Hanson, Susan (1982) 'On not excluding half of the human in human geography' in *Professional Geographer*, 34:1, pp 11–23

Moore, Henrietta (1988) *Feminism and Anthropology* Oxford, Polity Press

Moore, S. and Rosenthal, D. (1993) *Sexuality in Adolescence* London, Routledge

Morgan, David (1992) *Discovering Men* London, Routledge

Morgan, David (1981) 'Men, Masculinity and the Process of Sociological Inquiry' in Roberts, Helen (ed) *Doing Feminist Research* London, Routledge and Kegan Paul

Morgan, David (1993) 'You Too Can Have Body Like Mine' in S. Scott and D. Morgan (eds) *Body Matters: Essays on the Sociology of the Body* London, Falmer

Morgan, David, H. J. (1996) *Family Connections: an introduction to family studies* Cambridge, Polity

Morgan, Robin (1989) *The Demon Lover: On the Sexuality of Terrorism* London, Methuen

Morley, Louise (1995) 'Measuring the Muse: Creativity, Writing and Career Development in Higher Education' in L. Morley and V. Walsh (eds) *Feminist Academics: Creative Agents for Change* London, Taylor and Francis

Morley, Louise (1996) 'Interrogating Patriarchy: the challenges of feminist research' in Louise Morley and Val Walsh (eds) *Breaking Boundaries: women in higher education* London, Taylor and Francis

Morley, Louise (2001) 'Mass Higher Education: Feminist Pedagogy in the Learning Society' in Pauline Anderson and Jenny Williams (eds) *Identity and Difference in Higher Education 'Outsiders Within'* Aldershot, Ashgate

Morris, Alison (1987) *Women, Crime and Criminal Justice* Oxford, Basil Blackwell

Morris, Jenny (1991) *Pride Against Prejudice: transforming attitudes to disability* Philadelphia, New Society

Mosse, George L. (1996) *The Image of Man: The Creation of Modern Masculinity* New York, Oxford University Press

Mukta, Parita (2000) 'Gender, Community, Nation: The Myth of Innocence' in Susie Jacobs, Ruth Jacobson and Jennifer Marchbank (eds) *States of Conflict: Gender, Violence and Resistance* London, Zed

Mulvay, Laura (1975) 'Visual Pleasure and Narrative Cinema' *Screen* 16(3)

Myers, Garth Andrew (2002) 'Colonial geography and masculinity in Eric Dutton's Kenya Mountain' *Gender, Place and Culture*, 9, pp 23–38

Mykhalovskiy, Eric (1996) 'Reconsidering Table Talk: critical thoughts on the relationship between sociology, autobiography and self-indulgence' *Qualitative Sociology* 19(1)

Naffine, Nadine (1987) *Female Crime* Sydney, Allen and Unwin

Naffine, Nadine (1997) *Feminism and Criminology* Cambridge, Polity

Naffine, Ngaire (1987) *Female Crime: The Construction of Women in Criminology* Boston, Allen and Unwin

Nanda, Serena and Warms, Richard L. (2002) *Cultural Anthropology*, 7th Edition, Belmont CA: Thomas Learning Inc.

Nash, June and Safa, Helen (eds) (1985) *Women and Change in Latin America* Mass., Bergin and Garvey Publishers

National Statistics Office (2002) *Carers 2000* London, HMSO

National Statistics Office (2003) *Labour Force Survey* available at http://www.nso.gov.uk

Nayak, Anoop (1999) '"Pale warriors": skinhead culture and the embodiment of white masculinities' in Avtar Brah, Mary J. Hickman and Máirtín Macan Ghaill (eds) *Thinking Identities: Ethnicity, Racism and Culture* Basingstoke, Macmillan

Nelson, Lise (1999) 'Bodies (and spaces) do matter: the limits of performativity' *Gender, Place and Culture*, 6, pp 331–54

Nelson, Lise and Seager, Joni (2005) (eds) *A Companion to Feminist Geography* Oxford, Blackwell

Nencel, Lorraine (1996) "Pacharacas, Putas and Chicas de su casa: Labelling, Femininity and Men's Sexual Selves in Lima, Peru" in Marit Melhuus and Kristi Anne StØlen (eds) *Machos, Mistresses, Madonnas. Contesting the Power of Latin American Gender Imagery* London, Verso

Nencel, Lorraine (2001) *Ethnography and Prostitution in Peru* London, Pluto Press

Nencel, Lorriane (2005) "Heterosexuality"in Philomena Essed, David T. Goldberg and Audrey Kobayashi (eds) *A companion to Gender Studies* Oxford, Blackwell

Newburn, Tim and Stanko, Elizabeth A. (1994) 'When Men are Victims: the failure of victimology' in Tim Newburn and Elizabeth A. Stanko (eds) *Just Boys Doing Business? Men, masculinities and crime* London, Routledge

NHS Centre for Reviews and Dissemination (1997) 'Preventing and reducing the adverse effects of unintended teenage pregnancies' *Effective Health Care* 3:1

Nieva, Veronica F. and Gutek, Barbara A. (1981) *Women and Work: A Psychological Perspective* New York, Praeger

Noble, Colin and Bradford, Wendy (2000) *Getting it Right for Boys … and Girls* London, Routledge

NOP Family (2001) *Young people and sex stereotyping* Manchester, EOC, available at http://www.eoc.org.uk

Norris, Pippa (1986) 'Conservative attitudes in recent British elections: and emerging gender gap?' *Political Studies*, 34 (1), pp 120–128.

Norris, Pippa (1999) 'Gender: A Gender-Generation Gap?' in Pippa Norris and Geoffrey Evans (eds) *Critical Elections: British Politics and Voters in Long-Term Perspective* London, Sage

Norris, Pippa (2001a) 'Gender and Contemporary British Politics' in Colin Hay (ed) *British Politics Today* Cambridge, Polity

Norris, Pippa (2001b) 'Women's Power at the Ballot Box' in International IDEA, *Voter Turnout from 1945 to 2000: A Global Report on Political Participation* Stockholm, International IDEA

Norris, Pippa and Lovenduski, Joni (2001) *Blair's Babes: Critical Mass Theory, Gender and Legislative Life*, paper to John F Kennedy School of Government, Harvard University, Faculty Research Working Paper Series, RWP01-039

Norris, Pippa and Lovenduski, Joni (2003) 'Westminster Women: The Politics of Presence' *Political Studies*, 51 (1), pp 84–102

Norris, Pippa, Lovenduski, Joni and Campbell, Rosie (2004) *Gender and Political Participation*, Electoral Commission http://www.electoralcommission.org.uk, accessed July 2006.

O'Connell Davidson, Julia (1998) *Prostitution, power and freedom* Cambridge, Polity

O'Connor, Julia (1993) 'Gender, class and citizenship in the comparative analyis of welfare state regimes:

Theoretical and methodological issues' *British Journal of Sociology*, 44, pp 501–518

O'Connor, Julia, Orloff, Ann Shola and Shaver, Sheila (1999) *States, Markets, Families: Gender, Liberalism and Social Policy in Australia, Canada, Great Britain and the United States* Cambridge, Cambridge University Press

Oakley, Ann (1972) *Sex, Gender and Society* London, Maurice Temple Smith

Oakley, Ann (1974) *Sociology of Housework* London, Martin Robertson

Oakley, Ann (1976) *Housewife* London, Penguin

Oakley, Ann (1979) *From Here to Maternity: Becoming a Mother* Martin Robertson, Oxford

Oakley, Ann (1980) *Women Confined: towards a sociology of childbirth* Oxford, Martin Robertson and Co

Oakley, Ann (1981a) 'Interviewing women: a contradiction in terms?' in Helen Roberts (ed) *Doing Feminist Research* London, Routledge

Oakley, Ann (1981b) *Subject Women* London, Fontana

Oakley, Ann (1982) *Subject Women* London, Fontana

Oakley, Ann (1998) 'Gender, methodology and people's ways of knowing: some problems with feminism and the paradigm debate in social science' *Sociology* 32(4)

Oakley Ann McPherson, Ann, Roberts, Helen (1984) *Miscarriage* London, Fontana

Oakley, Ann, (1999) 'People's Ways of Knowing: gender and methodology' in Suzanne Hood, Berry Mayall and Sandy Oliver (eds) *Critical Issues in Social Research* Buckingham, Open University

Oakley, Ann (2000) *Experiments in Knowing: gender, and method in the social sciences* Cambridge, Polity

Oakley, Ann (2004) Response to 'Quoting and counting: an autobiographical response to Oakley' in *Sociology* 38, 1: 191–192

Obler, Regina (1986) 'For Better or Worse: anthropologists and husbands in the field' in Tony Whitehead and Mary Ellen Conaway (eds) *Self, Sex and Gender in Cross-Cultural Fieldwork* Urbana IL, University of Illinois

OECD (2004) 'Education Levels Rising in OECD Countries but Low Attainment Still Hampers Some' report on *Education at a Glance* http://www.oecd.org/ edu/eag2004

Okley, Judith (1992) 'Anthropology and Autobiography: participatory experience and embodied knowledge' in Judith Okley and Helen Callaway (eds) *Anthropology and Autobiography* London, Routledge

Olsen, Tillie (1980) *Silences*, London, Virago

Orloff, Ann Shola (1993) 'Gender and the social rights of citizenship: the comparative analysis of gender relations and welfare states' *American Sociological Review*, 58 (3), pp 303–328

Ortner, Sherry (1974) 'Is Female to Male as Nature is to Culture?' in Michelle Zimbalist Rosaldo and Louise Lamphere (eds) *Woman Culture & Society* California, Stanford University Press

Ortner, Sherry (1996) 'Making Gender. Toward a Feminist, Minority, Postcolonial, Subaltern, Etc., Theory of Practice' in Sherry Ortner *Making Gender. The politics and Erotics of Culture* Boston, Beacon Press

Oudshoorn, Nellie (1994) *Beyond the Natural Body: an archaeology of sex hormones* London, Routledge

Outshoorn, Joyce (1986) 'The feminist movement and abortion politics in the Netherlands' in Drude Dahlerup (ed) *The New Women's Movement: Feminism and Political Power in Europe and the USA* London, Sage

Oxfam (1994) *The Oxfam Gender Training Manual* Oxford, Oxfam

Oxfam, with Amnesty International (2003) *Shattered Lives, the case for tough international arms control*

Pahl, Jan (1980) 'Patterns of Money Management within Marriage' *Journal of Social Policy*, pp 313–335

Pahl, Jan, (1989) *Money and Marriage* Basingstoke, Macmillan

Pain, Rachel (1999) 'Women's experiences of violence over the life course' in Elizabeth Kenworthy Teather (ed) *Embodied Geographies: Spaces, Bodies and Rites of Passage* London, Routledge

Pal, Sarmistha (2003) *How Much of the Gender Difference in Child School Enrolment Can Be Explained? Evidence from Rural India* Economics Working Paper Archive at http://ideas.repec.org/p/wpa/wuwphe/0309004.html

Panelli, Ruth (2004) *Social Geographies: From Difference to Action* London, Sage

Parker, Richard R., Barbosa, Regina Maria and Aggleton, Peter (eds) (2000) *Framing the Sexual Subject* Berkley, University of California Press

Parker, Richard, Herdt, Gil and Carballo (1991) "Sexual Culture, HIV Transmission and AIDS Research" *The Journal of Sex Research* (special issue) 28: pp 77–98

Parker, Stanley (1976) 'Work and Leisure' in Eric Butterworth and David Weir (eds) *The Sociology of Leisure* London Allen and Unwin

Parsons, Talcott (1954) 'The Kinship System of the Contemporary United States' in T. Parsons *Essays in Sociological Theory* New York, Free Press

Parsons, Talcott and Bales, Robert (1956) *Family, Socialization and Interaction Process* London, Routledge and Kegan Paul

Pascall, Gillian (1986) *Social Policy: A Feminist Analysis* London, Tavistock

Pateman, Carole (1988a) 'The patriarchal welfare state' in Amy Gutmann (ed) *Democracy and the Welfare State* Princeton, Princeton University Press

Pateman, Carole (1988b) *The Sexual Contract* Cambridge, Polity Press

Payne, Sarah (1991) *Women, Health and Poverty: An Introduction* New York, Harvester Wheatsheaf

Pease, Allan and Pease, Barbara (1999) *Why men don't listen and women can't read maps* NSW, Pease Training International

Peckham, S. (1992) *Unplanned Pregnancy and Teenage Pregnancy: A Review* Wessex Research Consortium, Institute for Health Policy Studies, University of Southampton

Pels, Peter and Nencel, Lorraine (1991) 'Introduction: Critique and the Deconstruction of Anthropological Authority' in Lorraine Nencel and Peter Pels (eds) *Constructing Knowledge. Authority and Critique in Social Science* London, Sage

Pember Reeves, Maud (1913) *Round About a Pound a Week* London, G Bell and Sons

Perkins, T. E. (1979) 'Rethinking Stereotypes' in Michele Barrett, Philip Corrigan, Annette Kuhn and Janet Wolff (1979) *Ideology and Cultural Reproduction* Croom Helm Ltd.

Petchesky, Rosalind, P. (1987) 'Foetal Images: the power of visual culture in the politics of reproduction' in Michelle Stanworth (ed) *Reproductive Technologies* Cambridge, Polity

Peterson, V Spike and Sisson Runyan, Anne (1999) *Global Gender Issues* Boulder, Co, Westview Press

Pettman, Jan Jindy (1996) *Worlding Women: A Feminist International Politics* Sydney, Allen and Unwin

Phillips, Anne (1998) *Feminism and Politics* Oxford University Press, Oxford

Phillips, Ruth (1997) *Mapping Men and Empire: A Geography of Adventure* London, Routledge

Phillips, Susan (2003) *Tackling the Gender Gap* Society for the Advancement of Excellence in Education Canada http://www.saee.ca/policy/D_059_FFH_LON.php

Phizacklea, Annie and Wolkowitz, Carol (1995) *Homeworking Women: Gender Racism and Class at Work* London, Sage

Phoenix, Anne (1991) 'Mothers under twenty: outsider and insider views' in Ann Phoenix, Anne Woollett and Eva Lloyd (eds) *Motherhood: meanings, practices and ideology* London, Sage

Pink, Sarah (2004) *Home Truths: gender, domestic objects and everyday life* Oxford, Berg

Plantenga, Janneke (2002) 'Combining work and care in the polder model: an assessment of the Dutch part-time strategy' *Critical Social Policy*, 22 (1), pp 53–71

Platt, Jennifer (2003) *The British Sociological Association: a sociological history* Durham, Sociologypress

Pleck, Joseph (1987) 'The theory of male sex role identity: its rise and fall from 1936 to the present' in Brod, Harry (1987) (ed) *The making of masculinities: the new men's studies* Boston, Allen and Unwin pp 21–38

Plummer, Ken (1975) *Sexual Stigma: An interactionist account* London and Kegan Paul

Plummer, Ken (1995) *Telling Sexual Stories: power, change and social worlds* London, Routledge

Pollack, Otto (1950) *The Criminality of Women* Philadelphia, University of Pennsylvania Press

Pressman, Steven (2002) 'Explaining the Gender Poverty Gap in Developed and Transitional Economies' *Journal of Economic Issues*, XXXVI, (1)

Prieur, A. (1998) *Mema's House. On Transvestites, Queens, and Machos* Chicago, University of Chicago Press

Pringle, Keith (1995) *Men, Masculinities and Social Welfare* London, UCL Press

Pringle, Rosemary and Watson, Sophie (1992) 'Women's interests and the post-structuralist state' in Michelle Barrett and Sophie Watson (eds) *Destabilizing Theory: Contemporary Feminist Debates* Cambridge, Polity Press

Quicke, John (1998) 'Gender and Underachievement. Democratic educational reform through academic evaluation' in Ann Clark and Elaine Millard *Gender in the Secondary Curriculum Balancing the Books* London, Routledge

Rahji, M.A.Y. and Falusi, A.O. (2005) 'A gender analysis of farm households labour use and its impacts on household income in southwestern Nigeria' *Quarterly Journal of International Agriculture*, 44 (2), pp 155–166

Rai, Shirin and Lievesley, Geraldine (eds) (1996) *Women and the State, International Perspectives* London, Taylor and Francis

Ramazanoglu, Caroline (1989) 'On feminist methodology, male reason versus female empowerment' *Sociology* 26(2), pp 201–12

Ramon, Maria Dolors Garcia, Simonsen, Kirsten and Vaiou, Dina (2006) 'Guest editorial: does Anglophone hegemony permeate?' *Gender, Place and Culture*, 13:1, pp 1–5

Ramsay, Karen (1996) 'Emotional Labour and Organisational Research: how I learned not to laugh or cry in the field' in Stina E. Lyon and Joan Busfield (eds) *Methodological Imaginations* London, Macmillan

Ramsay, Karen and Letherby, Gayle (2006) 'The Experience of Academic Nonmothers in the Gendered University' *Gender, Work and Organisation* 13:1

Randall, Vicky (1982) *Women and Politics* Basingstoke, Macmillan

Randall, Vicky (2002) 'Feminisms' in David Marsh and Gerry Stoker (eds) *Theory and Methods in Political Science* Basingstoke, Macmillan

Ransom, Jane (1993) 'Feminism, difference and discourse: the limits of discursive analysis for feminism' in Caroline Ramazanoglu (ed) *Up Against Foucault: explorations of some tensions between Foucault and Feminism* London, Routledge

Randall, Vicky and Waylen, Georgina (eds) (1998) *Gender, Politics and the State* London, Routledge

Reiter, Rayna R. (ed) (1975) "Introduction", *Toward an Anthropology of Women* New York, Monthly Review Press, pp 11–19

Ravetz, Alison (1989) 'The home of women: a view from the interior' in Judy Attfield and Pat Kirkham (eds) *A View from the Interior: Feminism, Women and Design* London, Women's Press

Reavey, Paula and Warner, Sam (eds) (2003) *New feminist stories of child sexual abuse: sexual scripts and dangerous dialogues* London, Routledge

Reay, Diane (2004) 'Cultural capitalists and academic habitus: Classed and gendered labour in UK higher education' *Women's Studies International Forum*, 27, pp 31–39

Reinhold, Susan (1994) 'Through the Parliamentary Looking Glass: 'Real' and 'Pretend' Families in Contemporary British Politics' *Feminist Review*, No. 48, The New Politics of Sex and the State

Reiner, Robert (2002) *The Politics of the Police* (3rd edition) Oxford, Oxford University Press

Reiter, Rayna R. (ed) (1975) "Introduction" in Rayna Reiter (ed) *Toward an Anthropology of Women* New York, Monthly Review Press

Rendall, Jane (1985) *The Origins of Modern Feminism* London, Macmillan

Reynolds, Gillian (1993) 'And Gill Came Tumbling Down . . . : gender and a research dilemma' in Mary Kennedy, Cathy Lubelska and Val Walsh (eds) *Making Connections: women's studies, women's movements, women's lives* London, Taylor and Francis

Reysoo, Fenneke (2005) "Reproductive Rights Violations: A comparison of Export-Oriented Industires in Mexico and Morocco" in Tine Davids and Francien van Driel (eds) *The Gender Question in Globalization. Changing Perspectives and Practices* Hants England, Ashgate Publishing

Ribbens, Jane (1989) 'Interviewing Women: an unnatural situation' *Women's Studies International Forum* 12(6), pp 579–92

Ribbens McCarthy, Jane, Edwards, Ros and Gillies, Val (2003) *Making Families: moral tales of parenting and stepparenting* Durham, Sociology Press

Rice, Marcia (1990) 'Challenging Orthodoxies in Feminist Theories: a black feminist critique' in Lorraine Gelsthorpe and Alison Morris (eds) *Feminist Perspectives in Criminology* Milton Keynes, Open University Press

Rich, Adrienne (1976) *Of Woman Born: Motherhood as Experience and Institution* New York, Norton

Rich, Adrienne (1980) *On Lies, Secrets and Silence, Selected Prose 1966–78* London, Virago

Richman, Joel (1994) 'Male Sociologist in a Woman's World: aspects of a medical partnership' in Burgess, R. (ed) *Studies in Qualitative Methodology Volume 4* London, JAI Press

Riley, Denise (1983) *War in the Nursery: Theories of the Child and Mother* London, Virago

Riley, Denise (1988) *Am I That Name?: Feminism and the category 'Women' in History* Basingstoke, Macmillan

Riley, Sarah, Frith, Hannah, Archer, Louise and Veseley, Louise (2006) 'Institutional sexism in academia' *The Psychologist*, Vol. 19: 94–97

Roberts, Helen (1993) 'The Women and Class Debate' in David Morgan and Liz Stanley (eds) *Debates in Sociology* Manchester, Manchester University Press

Roberts, Helen (ed) (1981, 1990) *Doing Feminist Research* London, Routledge and Kegan Paul

Roberts, Helen (ed) (1992) *Women's Health Matters* London, Routledge

Roberts, Ken (1978) *Contemporary Society and the Growth of Leisure* New York, Longman

Roberts, Marion (1991) *Living in a Man-Made World: Gender Assumptions in Modern Housing Design* London, Routledge

Robinson, Victoria (1993) 'Introducing Women's Studies' in Diane Richardson and Victoria Robinson (eds) *Introducing Women's Studies, Feminist Theory and Practice* Basingstoke, Macmillan

Roiphe, K. (1993) *The Morning After: sex, fear and feminism* London, Hamish Hamilton

Romero, Mary (1992) *Maid in the USA* New York, Routledge

Rosaldo M. (1980) 'The Use and Abuse of Anthropology: reflections on Feminism and Cross-Cultural Understanding' *Signs*, 5(3) pp 389–417

Rosaldo, Michelle Zimbalist (1974) 'Women, Culture and Society; A Theoretical Overview' in Michelle Zimbalist Rosaldo and Louise Lamphere (1974) (eds) *Women, Culture and Society* California, Stanford University Press

Rose, Gillian (1993) *Feminism and Geography: The Limits of Geographical Knowledge* Cambridge, Polity Press

Rose, Gillian (1997) 'Situating knowledges: positionality, reflexivities and other tactics' *Progress in Human Geography*, 21, pp 305–320

Roseneil, Sasha (1995) *Disarming Patriarchy: Feminism and Political Action at Greenham* Milton Keynes, Open University Press

Rousseau, Jean Jacques (1911 orig 1762) *Emile* London, Dent

Rowbotham, Sheila (1973a) *Woman's Consciousness, Man's World* Harmondsworth, Penguin

Rowbotham, Sheila (1973b) *Hidden from History* London, Pluto

Rowbotham, Sheila (1983) 'The Trouble with Patriarchy' in Sheila Rowbotham (ed) *Dreams and Dilemmas: Collected Writings* London, Virago

Rowbotham, Sheila (1995) *Women in Movement, Feminism and Social Action* London, Routledge

Rubin, Gayle (1975) "The traffic in Women: Notes on the 'Political Economy' of Sex" in Rayna Rapp (ed) *Toward an Anthropology of Women* New York, Monthly Review Press

Rubin, Gayle (1985) "Thinking Sex: Notes for a Radical Theory of the Politics of Sexuality" in Carol Vance (ed) *Pleasure and Danger. Exploring Female Sexuality* Boston, Routledge and Kegan Paul

Ruddick, Sara (1990) *Maternal Thinking* London, The Women's Press

Ruddick, Sara (1992) *Maternal Thinking: Towards a Politics of Peace* Boston, Beacon Press

Russell, Diana E. H. (1993) *Making Violence Sexy: feminist views on pornography* New York, Teachers College Press

Russell, Rachel and Tyler, Melissa (2002) 'Thank Heaven for Little Girls: "Girl Heaven" and the commercialisation of feminine childhood' *Sociology* 36(3) pp 619–637

Sabo, Don (2005) 'Doing Time, Doing Masculinities: sports in prison' in D. Sabo, T. A. Kupers and W. London (eds) *Prison Masculinities* Temple University Press in M. B. Zinn, P. H.-Sotelo and M. A. Messner (eds) *Gender Through a Prism of Difference* (3rd edition) New York, Oxford University Press

Sainsbury, Diane (1996) *Gender, Equality and Welfare States* Cambridge, Cambridge University Press

Salmenniemi, Suvi (2005) 'Civic Activity – Feminine Activity? Gender, Civil Society and Citizenship in Post Soviet Russia' *Sociology*, 39 (4), pp 735–753

Salzinger, Leslie (2000) 'Manufacturing Sexual Subjects. Harassment, Desire and Discipline on a Maquiladora Shopfloor' *Ethnography* Vol.1, no.1: 67–92

Sapiro, Virginia (1984) *The Political Integration of Women, Roles, Socialization and Politics* Chicago, University of Illinois Press

Sapiro, Virginia (1990) 'The gender Basis of American Social Policy' in Linda Gordon (ed) *Women, the State, and Welfare* Madison, University of Wisconsin Press

Sapiro, Virginia, (1991) 'Gender politics, gendered politics: the state of the field' in William Crotty (ed) *Political Science: Looking to the Future. The Theory and Practice of Political Science* Evanston, Illinois, Northwestern University Press

Sapiro, Virginia (2004) 'Not Your Parents' Political Socialization: Introduction for a New Generation' *Annual Review of Political Science*, 7, pp 1–23

Sawer, Marion (1995) 'Femocrats in Glass Towers?: The Office of the Status of Women in Australia' in Dorothy McBride Stetson and Amy Mazur (eds) *Comparative State Feminisms* Thousand Oaks, CA, Sage

Sawer, Marion (2004) 'The Impact of Feminist Scholarship on Australian Political Science' *Australian Journal of Political Science*, 39 (3)

Scambler, Graham and Scambler, Annette (1997) *Rethinking Prostitution: purchasing sex in the 1990s* London, Routledge

Scranton, Paul, Sim, Joe and Skidmore, Paula (1991) *Prisons Under Protest* Milton Keynes, Open University Press

Scott, Joan Wallach (1988) *Gender and the Politics of History* New York, Columbia University Press

Scott, Joan Wallach (1996) 'Introduction' in Joan Wallach Scott (ed) *Feminism and History* Oxford, Oxford University Press

Scott, John (2005) 'Sociology and Its Others: Reflections on Disciplinary Specialisation and Fragmentation' in *Sociological Research Online* www.socresonline.org.uk/10/1/scott.html

Scourfield, Jonathan and Drakeford, Mark (2002) 'New Labour and the "problem of men"' *Critical Social Policy*, 22 (4), pp 619–640

Scraton, Phil (1990) 'Scientific knowledge or masculine discourses? Challenging patriarchy in criminology' in Lorraine Gelsthorpe and Alison Morris (eds) *Feminist Perspectives in Criminology* Buckingham, Open University Press

Segal, Lynne (1990) *Slow Motion: changing men, changing masculinities* London, Virago

Segal, Lynne (1994) 'Straight Sex' *The Politics of Pleasure* London, Virago

Segal, Lynne. (1999) *Why Feminism? Gender, Psychology, Politics* Cambridge, Polity

Seidler, Victor (1989) *Rediscovering Masculinity* London, Routledge

Seiter, Ellen (1986) 'Feminism and Ideology: the terms of women's stereotypes' *Feminist Review* 22

Sharp, Joanne P. (1996) 'Gendering nationhood: a feminist engagement with national identity' in Nancy Duncan (ed) *BodySpace: Destabilising Geographies of Gender and Sexuality* London, Routledge

Sharp, Keith and Earle, Sarah (2003) 'Cyberpunters and cyberwhores: prostitution on the internet' in Yvonne Jewkes (ed) *Dot.cons: crime, deviance and identity on the internet* Devon, Willan

Sharpe, Sue (1976) *Just Like a Girl: how girls learn to be women* Harmondsworth, Penguin

Shaver Hughes, Sarah and Hughes, Brady (1995) *Women in World History, volume 1 – Readings from Prehistory to 1500* Armonk, NY, ME Sharpe

Shilling, Chris (1993) *The Body and Social Theory* London, Sage

Shrange, Laurie (1994) *Moral Dilemmas of Feminism* London, Routledge

Sim, Joe (1994) 'Tougher than the Rest? Men in prison' in Tim Newburn and Elizabeth A. Stanko (eds) *Just Boys Doing Business: men, masculinities and crime* London, Routledge

Simien, Evelyn M. (2004) 'Black Feminist Theory: Charting a Course for Black Women's Studies in Political Science' *Women and Politics*, 26 (2), pp 81 – 93

Skeggs, Bev (1995) *Feminist Cultural Theory: process and production* Manchester, Manchester University Press

Skeggs, Bev (1997) *Formations of Class and Gender* London, Sage

Skeggs, Bev (2005) 'The Making of Class and Gender through Visualizing Moral Subject Formation' *Sociology* 39(5) pp 965–983

Skelton, Christine (ed) (1989) *Whatever Happens to Little Women?* Milton Keynes, Open University Press

Skelton, Christine (1993) 'Women and Education' in Diane Richardson and Victoria Robinson (eds) *Introducing Women's Studies, Feminist Theory and Practice* Basingstoke, Macmillan

Skelton, Christine (1998) 'Feminism and research into masculinities and schooling' *Gender and Education*, 10, pp 217–227

Skocpol, Theda (1992) *Protecting Soldiers and Mothers* Cambridge, MA, Harvard University Press

Smart, Carol (1977) *Women, Crime and Criminology* London, Routledge and Kegan Paul

Smart, Carol (1989) *Feminism and the Power of the Law* London, Routledge

Smart, Carol (1997) 'Wishful thinking and harmful tinkering? Sociological reflections on family policy?' *Journal of Social Policy* 26(3)

Smith, Catrin (2002) 'Punishment and pleasure: women, food and the imprisoned body' *The Sociological Review*

Smith, Dorothy (1988) *The Everyday World as Problematic: a feminist sociology* Milton Keynes, Open University Press

Smith, Joan (1989) *Misogynies* London, Faber

Smith, Susan J. (1984) 'Crime in the News' in *British Journal of Criminology*, 24, pp 289–295

Social Exclusion Report (SEU) (1999) *Report on Teenage Pregnancy* www.socialexclusionunit.gov.uk/publications/reports/pdfs/teen_preg.pdf

Soja, Edward W. (1985) 'The spatiality of social life: towards a transformative theory' in Derek Gregory and John Urry (eds) *Social Relations and Spatial Structures* London, Macmillan

Sommers, Jeff (1998) 'Men at the margin: masculinity and space in Downtown Vancouver, 1950–1986' *Urban Geography*, 19, pp 287–310

Spender, Dale (ed) (1981) *Men's Studies Modified: The Impact of Feminism on the Academic Disciplines* Oxford, Pergamon

Spender, Dale (ed) (1987) *The Education Papers: Women's Quest for Equality in Britain 1850–1912* London, Routledge and Kegan Paul

Spender, Dale (2006) Private Communication with Jen Marchbank, 6 June

Stacey, Jackie (1994) *Star Gazing: Hollywood cinema and female spectatorship* London, Routledge

Stacey, Judith (1988) "Can there be a Feminist Ethnography?" *Women's Studies International Forum*, 11(1). pp 21–27

Stacey, Judith (1991) 'Can there be a feminist ethnography?' in Sherna Gluck and Daphne Patai (eds) *Women's Words: The Feminist Practice of Oral History* New York, Routledge

Stacey, Margaret (1981) 'The Division of Labour Revisited or Overcoming the Two Adams' in Philip Abrams, Rosemary Deem, Janet Finch and Paul Rock (eds) *Practice and Progress: British Sociology 1950–1980* London, George Allen and Unwin

Stainton-Rogers, Wendy and Stainton-Rogers, Rex (2001) *The Psychology of Gender and Sexuality* Buckingham, Open University Press

Stake, Jayne (2006) 'Pedagogy and Student Change in the Women's and Gender Studies Classroom' *Gender and Education*, 18 (2), pp 199–212

Stanley, Liz (1990) *Feminist Praxis: Research, theory and epistemology in feminist sociology* London, Routledge

Stanley, Liz (2005) 'A Child of Its Time: Hybrid Perspectives on Othering' in *Sociological Research Online* 10, 3: www.socresonline.org.uk/10/3

Stanley, Liz (1984) 'Should 'sex' really be 'gender' or 'gender' really be 'sex'?' in Robert J. Anderson and W. W. Sharrock (eds) *Applied Sociological Perspectives* London, Allen and Unwin

Stanley, Liz and Wise, Sue (1990) 'Method, Methodology and Epistemology in Feminist Research Processes' in Liz Stanley (ed) *Feminist Praxis: research, theory and epistemology in feminist sociology* London, Routledge

Stanley, Liz and Wise, Sue (1993) *Breaking Out Again: Feminist Ontology and Epistemology* London, Routledge and Kegan Paul

Stevenson, Andrew (2001) *Studying Psychology* Basingstoke, Palgrave

Stewart, Ann (1996) 'Should women give up on the State? The African experience' in Shirin Rai and Geraldine Lievesley (eds) *Women and the State, International Perspectives* London, Taylor and Francis

Stolenberg, J. (1990) *Refusing to be a man* London, Fontana

Stone, Leonard A. (2002) 'How Was it For You? The Oligarchic Structure of International Relations and Feminist Theory' *Journal of International Women's Studies*, 4 (1) http://www.bridgew.edu/ SoAS/jiws

Strate, Lance (2004) 'Beer Commercials: a manual on masculinity' in M.S. Kimmell and M. A. Messner (eds) *Men's Lives* (6th edition) Boston, Pearson

Strathern, Marilyn (1992) 'After Nature: English Kinship in the Twentieth Century' Cambridge, Cambridge University Press

Strauss, Anselm and Corbin, Juliet (1990) *Basics of Qualitative Research: grounded theory procedures and techniques* London, Sage

Sullivan, Oriel (1996) 'Time co-ordination, the domestic division of labour and affective relations: time use and enjoyment of activities within couples' *Sociology*, 30 (1)

Sundberg, Juanita (2005) 'Looking for the critical geographer, or why bodies and geographies matter to the emergence of critical geographies of Latin America' *Geoforum*, 36, pp 17–28

Sunindyo, Saraswati (2004) 'Murder, Gender and the Media: sexualizing politics and violence' in Cynthia Carter and Linda Steiner (eds) *Critical Readings: media and gender* Maidenhead, Open University Press

Sweibel, Joke (1998) 'The gender of bureaucracy: Reflections on policy making for women' *Politics*, 8 (1) pp 14–19

Taylor, Ian, Walton, Paul and Young, Jock (1973) *The New Criminology* London, Routledge and Kegan Paul

Teenage Pregnancy Unit (TPU) (2004) Teenage pregnancy policy statement http://www.fpa.org.uk/ news/policy/PDFs/Teenagepregnancypolicystatement.pdf

Temple, B. (1997) ''Collegiate Accountability' and Bias: the solution to the problem?" *Sociological Research Online* 2(4) www.socresonline.org.uk/socresonline/2/4/8html

Teri, Linda (1982) 'Effects of Sex and Sex Role Style on Clinical Judgement' *Sex Roles* 8(6)

Tervo, Mervi (2001) 'Nationalism, sports and gender in Finnish sports journalism in the early twentieth century' *Gender, Place and Culture*, 8, pp 357–373

The Mid-Atlantic Equity Consortium, inc and The NET-WORK in (1993) *Beyond Title IX: Gender Equity Issues in Schools* Chevy Chase, MD, The Mid-Atlantic Equity Center http://www.maec.org/beyond.html accessed July 2006

Therborn, Gôran (2004) *Between Sex and Power: family in the world 1900–2000* London, Routledge

Thorne, Barrie (2002, originally 1993) 'Do Girls and Boys Have Different Cultures?' from *Gender Play* Buckingham, Open University in Stevi Jackson and Sue Scott (eds) *Gender: a sociological reader* London, Routledge

Thorne, John (2001) '"Comments" on a Specialised Theme – Masculinity as practice and representation' 19th International Congress of Historical Sciences, August, Oslo. http://www.oslo2000.uio.no/program/st11.htm, accessed July 2005

Thurner, Manuela (2003) 'Issues and Paradigms in American Women's History' in Mary Beth Norton and Ruth M. Alexandeer (eds) *Major Problems in American Women's History* Boston, Houghton Mifflin Corp

Tivers, Jacqueline (1985) *Women Attached: The Daily Lives of Women with Young Children* London, Croom Helm

Tobias, Sheila (1997) *Faces of Feminism: An Activist's Reflections on the Women's Movement* Boulder, Colorado, Westview Press

Tolleson-Rinehart, Sue and Josephson, Jyl J. (eds) (2000) *Gender and American Politics. Women, Men, and the Political Process* Armonk, NY, ME Sharpe

Tosh, John (1991) 'What should historians do with masculinity?' *History Workshop Journal*, 38, pp 184–187

Tosh, John (1999) *A Man's Place: Masculinity and the Middle-Class Home in Victorian England* New Haven, Connecticut, Yale University Press

Tosh, John (2004) 'Hegemonic masculinity and the history of gender' in Stefan Dudnick, Karen Hagemann and John Tosh (eds) *Masculinities in Politics and War Gendering Modern History* Manchester, Manchester University Press

Tosh, John (2005) *Manliness and Masculinities in Nineteenth-Century Britain. Essays on gender, family and empire* London, Pearson Longman

Trimble, Linda (2002) 'Gender and the Politics of Feminism' in Janine Brodie (ed) *Critical Concepts, an Introduction to Politics* Toronto, Prentice Hall/Pearsons

Turner, Bryan S. (1996) *The Body and Society* Oxford, Basil Blackwell

Turshen, Meredith and Twagiramariya, Clotilde (eds) (1998) *What Women Do in Wartime: Gender and Conflict in Africa* London, Zed Books

Twomey, Brenda (2002) 'Women in the labour market: results for the spring 2001 LFS' *Labour Market Studies*, 110 (3)

Umerah-Udezula, Ifeyinwa (2001) 'Resensitising African Health Care and Policy Practitioners: the gendered nature of AIDS epidemics in Africa' *Jenda: A Journal of Culture and African Women's Studies* 1:2

Unger, Ronda and Crawford, Mary (1992) *Women and Gender: A Feminist Psychology* London, McGraw-Hill

United Nations (1996) *Gender-based Abuse* United Nations Department of Public Information http://www.un.org/rights/dpi/772e.htm accessed June 2005

US Department of Justice, Federal Bureau of Investigation, *Crime in the United States 2004, Hate Crime* http://www.fbi.gov/ucr/cius_04/offenses_reported/hate_crime/

Ussher, Jane M. (1989) *The psychology of the female body* London, Routledge.

Ussher, Jane M. (1991) *Women's madness: misogyny or mental illness?* London, Harvester Wheatsheaf

Ussher, Jane M. (1997) *Fantasies of Femininity: Reframing the Boundaries of Sex* London, Penguin

Valentine, Gill (1989) 'The geography of women's fear' *Area*, 21, pp 385–390

Valentine, Gill (1992) 'Images of danger: women's sources of information about the spatial distribution of male violence' *Area*, 24, pp 22–29

Valentine, Gill (1993) '(Hetero)sexing space: lesbian perceptions and experiences of everyday spaces' *Environment and Planning D: Society and Space*, 11, pp 395–413

Valentine, Gill (1996a) '(Re)negotiating the heterosexual street' in Nancy Duncan (ed) *BodySpace: Destabilizing Geographies of Gender and Sexuality* London, Routledge

Valentine, Gill (1996b) 'Children should be seen and not heard? The role of children in public space' *Urban Geography*, 17, pp 205–220

Valier, Claire (2002) *Theories of Crime and Punishment* Essex, Pearson Education Ltd

Vallance, Elizabeth (1979) *Women in the House* London, Althone Press

van Balen, Frank and Inhorn, Marcia C. (2002) 'Introduction: Interpreting Infertility: a view from the social sciences' in M.C. Inhorn and F.van Balen (eds) *Infertility Around The Globe: new thinking on childlessness, gender and reproductive technologies* Berkeley and Los Angeles, California: University of California Press

van Eerdewijk, Anouka (2005) 'Being a Man:"Young Masculinities and Safe Sex in Dakar"' pp 59–73 in Tine Davids and Francien van Driel (eds) *The Gender Question in Globalization. Changing Perspectives and Practices* Hants England, Ashgate Publishing

van Hoven, Bettina and Hörschelmann, Kathrin (2005) 'Introduction: from geographies of men to geographies of women and back again?' in Bettina van Hoven and Kathrin Hörschelmann (eds) *Spaces of Masculinities* London, Routledge

Vance, C. (1992) *Pleasure and Danger: exploring female sexuality* London, Routledge

Verba, Sidney, Nie, Norman and Kim, Jae-On (1978) *Participation and Social Equality* Cambridge, Massachusetts, Harvard University Press

Verba, Sidney, Scholzman, Kay and Brady, Henry (1995) *Voice and Equality* Cambridge, Massachusetts, Harvard University Press

Verslusyen, M. C. (1981) 'Midwives, medical men and 'poor women labouring of child': lying-in hospitals in eighteenth-century London' in H. Roberts (ed) *Women, Health and Reproduction* London, Routledge and Kegan Paul

Wajcman, Judy (1983) *Women in Control: Dilemmas of a Workers' Co-operative* Basingstoke, Palgrave Macmillan

Wajcman, Judy (1991) *Feminism Confronts Technology* Cambridge, Polity

Walby, Sylvia (1986) *Patriarchy at Work: patriarchal and capitalist relations in employment* Cambridge, Polity Press

Walby, Sylvia (1994) 'Is Citizenship Gendered?' *Sociology*, 28 (2), pp 379–395

Waldby, C. (1996) *AIDS and the Body Politic: Biomedicine and Sexual Difference* London and New York, Routledge

Walker, Lisa (1995) 'More than just skin-deep: fem(me)ininity and the subversion of identity' *Gender, Place and Culture*, 2, pp 71–76

Walkerdine, Valerie and Lucey, Helen (1989) *Democracy in the Kitchen: regulating mothers and socialising daughters* London, Virago

Walkerdine, Valerie (1990) *Schoolgirl Fictions* London, Verso

Walklate, Sandra (2003) *Understanding Criminology: current theoretical debates* Buckingham, Open University Press

Warner, Marina (1985) *Alone of All Her Sex: The Myth and Cult of the Virgin Mary* Picador, London

Warner-Smith, Penny and Brown, Peter (2002) 'The town dictates what I do!: the leisure and well-being of women in a small Australian country town' *Leisure Studies*, 21, pp 39–56

Warren, Carol (1988) *Gender Issues in Field Research* Newbury Park, CA, Sage

Warren, Simon (2003) 'Good Boys Are Problems Too!' *Culture and Society*, 11 (2), pp 201–213

Warrington, Molly (2001) '"I must get out": the geographies of domestic violence' *Transactions of the Institute of British Geographers*, 26, pp 365–382

Watson, Jonathon (2000) *Male Bodies: Health, Culture, and Identity* Buckingham, Open University Press

Watson, Sophie (ed) (1990) *Playing the State, Australian Feminist Interventions* London Verso.

Watt, Paul (1998) 'Going out of town: youth, 'race', and place in the South East of England' *Environment and Planning D: Society and Space*, 16, pp 687–703

Watt, Paul and Stenson, Kevin (1998) '"It's a bit dodgy around here": safety, danger, ethnicity and young people's use of public space' in Tracey Skelton and Gill Valentine (eds) *Cool Places: Geographies of Youth Cultures* London, Routledge

Wearing, Betsy (1984) *The Ideology of Motherhood* London, Allen and Unwin

Webb, Christine (1986) *Feminist Practice in Women's Health Care* Chichester, John Wiley and Sons Ltd

Webster, Colin (1996) 'Local heroes: violent racism, localism and spacism among Asian and white young people' *Youth and Policy*, 53, pp 15–27

Weeks, Jeffrey (1986) *Sexuality: Key Ideas* New York, Kegan Paul

Weeks, Jeffrey (1990) *Coming Out* Aylesbury, Hazell

Weeks, Jeffrey (1991) *Against Nature: essays on history, sexuality and identity* London, Rivers Oram Press

Weeks, Jeffrey (2000) *Making Sexual History* Cambridge, Polity

Weiler, Kathleen (2003) 'Feminist Analyses of Gender and Schooling' in Antonio Darder, Marta Baltodano and Rodolfo D Torres (eds) *The Critical Pedagogy Reader* New York, RoutledgeFalmer

Weiler, Kathleen (2004) 'What can we learn from progressive education?' *Radical Teacher*, 69, March

Weisstein, Naomi (1968/1993) 'Psychology constructs the Female, or the Fantasy Life of the Male Psychologist (with some Attention to the Fantasies of his Friends, the Male Biologist and the Male Anthropologist)' *Feminism & Psychology*, 3(2): 195–210

Welch, Penny (2002) 'Feminist Pedagogy and Power in the Academy' in Gillian Howie and Ashley Tauchert (eds) *Gender, Teaching and Resistance in Higher Education. Challenges for the 21st Century* Aldershot, Ashgate

Wheelock, Jane (1990) *Husbands at Home – the Domestic Economy in a Post-Industrial Society* London, Routledge

Whitehead, Stephen (1999) 'Hegemonic Masculinity Revisited' *Gender, Work and Organisation*, 6, (1), pp 58–62

Whitehead, Stephen M. and Barrett, Frank J. (eds) (2001) *The Masculinities Reader* Cambridge, Polity

Whitehead, Stephen (2002) *Men and Masculinities: Key Themes and New Directions* London, Blackwell

Whitehead, Tony Larry and Conaway, Mary Ellen (eds) (1986) *Self, Sex, and Gender in Cross-cultural Fieldwork* Chicago, University of Illinois Press

Whittle, Stephen (2002) *Respect and Equality: Transsexual and Transgender Rights* London, Routledge

Whittle, Terry and Hogan, Rebecca, *Marriage License Information* http://www.win-/redclerk.com/marriage1.htm#WHO accessed September 2006

Wickman, Jan (2003) 'Masculinity and female bodies' *NORA Nordic Journal of Women's Studies*, 11, (1), pp 40–54

Wilcox, R. and Williams, J. P. (1996) 'What do you Think? The X Files, Legitimacy and gender pleasure' in David Lavery, Angela Hague and Marla Cartwright (eds) *Deny All Knowledge: reading the X Files* London, Faber and Faber

Wilkinson, Sue (ed) (1986) *Feminist Social Psychology: developing theory and practice* Buckingham, Open University

Wilkinson, Sue and Kitzinger, Celia (1994) 'Towards a Feminist Approach to Breast Cancer' in Sue Wilkinson and Celia Kitzinger (eds) *Women and Health: feminist perspectives* London, Taylor and Francis

Wilkinson, Sue (1997) 'Feminist Psychology' in Dennis Fox and Isaac Prilleltensky (eds) *Critical Psychology: An Introduction* London, Sage

Wilkinson, Sue (1999) 'Focus groups: A feminist method' *Psychology of Women Quarterly*, 23 (2), pp 221–244

Wilkinson, Sue and Kitzinger, Celia (eds) (1996) *Representing the Other* London, Sage

Williams, Fiona (1989) *Social Policy: A Critical Introduction, Issues of Race, Gender and Class* Cambridge, Polity Press

Williams, Stanley 'Tookie' (2001) *Life in Prison* San Francisco, SeaStar Books

Williams, Val (1991) 'Decades of Remembrance: war and the displacement of family photography' in Jo Spence and Patricia Holland (eds) *Family Snaps: the meanings of domestic photography* London, Virago

Willingham, Warren W. and Cole, Nancy S. (1997) *Gender and fair assessment* Mahwah, NJ, Erlbaum

Willis, Paul (1977) *Learning to Labour: how working class kids get working class jobs* Farnborough, Saxon House

Willott, Sara and Griffin, Christine. (1997) 'Wham bam, am I a man?: unemployed men talk about masculinities' *Feminism & Psychology*, 7(1): 107–28

Wilson, Elizabeth (1977) *Women and the Welfare State* London, Tavistock

Winship, Janice (1983) 'Femininity and Women's Magazines' *Unit 6 The Changing Experience of Women* Milton Keynes, The Open University

Wise, Sue and Stanley, Liz (1987) *Georgie Porgie: Sexual Harassment in Everyday Life* London, Pandora Press

Wise, Sue and Stanley, Liz (2003) 'Looking Back and Looking Forward: Some Recent Feminist Sociology Reviewed' *Sociological Research Online*, 8(3), www.socresonline.org.uk/8/3/wise.html

Wojtczak, Helena (2005) *Railway Women: exploitation, betrayal and triumph in the workplace* Hastings Press

Wolf, Diane (1996) "Situating Feminist Dilemmas in Fieldwork" in Diane Wolf (ed) *Feminist Dilemmas in Fieldwork* Colorado, Westview Press

Wolf, Naomi (1991) *The Beauty Myth* London, Vintage

Wollstonecraft, Mary (1792) *A Vindication of the Rights of Women* Boston, Peter Edes

Women and Geography Study Group (1984) *Geography and Gender* London, Hutchinson in association with The Explorations in Feminism Collective

Women and Geography Study Group (1997) *Feminist Geographies: Explorations in Diversity and Difference* Harlow, Longman

Woods, Gregory (1995) 'Fantasy Islands: popular topographies of marooned masculinities' in D. Bell and Gill, Valentine *Mapping Desire: geographies of sexualities* London, Routledge

Woodward, Kath (2003) 'Representations of Motherhood' in Sarah Earle and Gayle Letherby (eds) *Gender, Identity and Reproduction: social perspectives* Houndsmills, Palgrave Macmillan

Woolf, Virginia (1977, originally 1938) *Three Guineas* Harmondsworth, Penguin

World Health Organisation (WHO) (1997) *Violence Against Women: A Primary Health Priority Issues*, www.who.int/violence_injury_preventions/vaw/infopack.htm accessed July 2005

Yanagisako, Sylvia and Delany, Carol (eds) (1995) *Naturalizing Power. Essays in Feminist Cultural Analysis* New York City, Routledge

Yelvington, Kevin (1995) *Producing Power. Ethnicity, Gender and Class in a Caribbean Workplace* Philadelphia, Temple University Press

Yelvington, Kevin (1996) 'Flirting in the Factory' *Journal of the Royal Anthropological Institute*, Vol.2: 313–33

Young, E.H. and Lee, R. (1996) 'Fieldworker Feelings as Data: 'emotion work' and 'feeling rules' in first person accounts of sociological fieldwork' in Veronica James, and Jonathon Gabe (eds) *Health and the Sociology of Emotions* London, Blackwell

Young, Iris Marion (1990) *Throwing Like a Girl and Other Essays in Feminist Philosophy and Social Theory* Bloomington and Indianapolis, Indiana University Press

Young, Kate, Wolkowitz, Carol and McCullagh, Roslyn (eds) (1981) *Of Marriage and the Market. Women's subordination in international perspective* London, CSE Books

Young, Michael and Willmott, Peter (1973) *The Symmetrical Family* London, Routledge and Kegan

Ypeij, Annelou (2005) 'Gendered Travels: Single Mothers Experiences at the Global/Local Interface' pp 109–124, in Tine Davids and Francien van Driel (eds) *The Gender Question in Globalization. Changing Perspectives and Practices* Hants England, Ashgate Publishing

Zimbalist Rosaldo, Michelle and Lamphere, Louise (eds) (1974) *Woman Culture & Society* California, Stanford University Press

Zmroczek, Christine and Mahoney, Pat (eds) (1997) *Class Matters: Working class women's perspectives on social class* London, Taylor and Francis

Index